THE ANNALS
OF
AMERICA

THE ANNALS OF AMERICA

Volume 10

1866 - 1883

Reconstruction and Industrialization

ENCYCLOPÆDIA BRITANNICA, INC.

Chicago London New Delhi Paris Sydney Taipei Tokyo Seoul

The editors wish to express their gratitude for permission to reprint
material from the following sources:

The Arthur H. Clark Company for Selections 24, 46, 49, from *A Documentary History of American Industrial Society*, ed. by John R. Commons *et al.*

Columbia University Press for Selection 90, from *Negro Folk Music, U.S.A.*, by Harold Courlander.

Helen Hartness Flanders for Selection 57, from *Ballads Migrant in New England*, by Helen Hartness Flanders and Marguerite Olney, New York: Farrar, Straus & Young, 1953.

Harvard University Press for Selection 60, from *From Scotland to Silverado*, by Robert Louis Stevenson, ed. by James D. Hart, Cambridge, Mass.: The Belknap Press of Harvard University Press, Copyright 1966 by the President and Fellows of Harvard College. Also for Selection 95, from *This Was America*, ed. by Oscar Handlin, Cambridge, Mass.: Harvard University Press, Copyright 1949 by the President and Fellows of Harvard College.

Emily Davie Kornfeld for Selection 51, from *Profile of America: An Autobiography of the U.S.A.*, ed. by Emily Davie, New York: The Viking Press, Inc., 1954.

The University of Minnesota Press for Selections 16, 69, from *Land of Their Choice: The Immigrants Write Home*, ed. by Theodore C. Blegen, Minneapolis: The University of Minnesota Press, © Copyright 1955 by the University of Minnesota.

Yale University Press for Selection 39, from *Twenty Years on the Pacific Slope: Letters of Henry Eno from California and Nevada 1848-1871*, ed. by W. Turrentine Jackson, New Haven: Yale University Press, 1965.

CODED SOURCES IN THIS VOLUME

Allen   *Cowboy Lore.* Edited by Jules Verne Allen. San Antonio, 1933.

Blegen   *Land of Their Choice.* Edited by Theodore C. Blegen. Minneapolis, 1955.

Commons   *A Documentary History of American Industrial Society.* Edited by John R. Commons *et al.* In 10 vols. Cleveland, 1910-1911.

Globe   *Congressional Globe.* A record of the proceedings of Congress from 1833 to 1873, arranged by number of Congress and by session. In 46 vols. Washington, 1834-1873.

OSL   *Old South Leaflets.* Published by the Directors of the Old South Work, Old South Meeting House. In 8 vols. (Documents 1-200). Boston, n.d.

PRFA   [United States Department of State] *Papers Relating to Foreign Affairs.* Compiled annually since 1861 except for 1869 with supplements issued periodically. Title changed to *Papers Relating to Foreign Relations of the United States* in 1870 and to *Foreign Relations of the United States* in 1947. Washington, 1862 *et seq.*

Record   *Congressional Record.* A record of the proceedings of Congress from March 3, 1873, to date, arranged by number of Congress and by session. Washington, 1874 *et seq.*

Richardson   *A Compilation of the Messages and Papers of the Presidents 1789-1897.* Edited by James D. Richardson. In 10 vols. Washington, 1896-1899. New edition extended to 1908. Washington, 1909.

Statutes   *The Public Statutes at Large of the United States of America from the Organization of the Government in 1789, etc., etc.* In 79 vols. as of August 1966. 1845 *et seq.* Vol. 14, 17 edited by George P. Sanger, Boston, 1868, 1873. Vol. 22, Washington, 1883.

TWA   *This Was America.* Edited by Oscar Handlin. Cambridge, 1949.

94 U.S. 113   *United States Reports* [Supreme Court].
109 U.S. 3   Vol. 94, pp. 113ff.;
     Vol. 109, pp. 3ff.

4 Wallace 2   *Cases Argued and Adjudged in the Supreme Court of the United States.*
16 Wallace 36   Edited by John W. Wallace, Vol. 4, Washington, 1868, pp. 2ff.; Vol. 16, Washington, 1873, pp. 36ff.

Contents

RECONSTRUCTION
AND
INDUSTRIALIZATION
In Pictures

With the release of time, money, and energy granted by the ending
of war, the nation continued its interrupted path of development.
The trend toward urbanization became clearly a dominant force
in American life as the established cities articulated themselves
and attracted to themselves money and, less successfully, culture.

The political life of the nation following the Civil War was an
unhappy blend of vindictiveness toward the South, acrimony among
factions and leaders, and a general loss of moral vigor that was
epitomized by the corruption in Grant's cabinet.

The release from war brought with it also an increased interest
in leisure, recreation, and entertainment. Prompted both by the
understandable reaction to war and by the increased availability
of money, culture on every level became a major concern.

Growth and Consolidation 355-364

To deal with a continental nation, new industrial techniques and economic forms were equally necessary. The great expansion of the economy after the war was directed by a new kind of leader, the financier; that regulation, within industry or from government, lagged behind such developments was to become a major problem.

Growth and Recovery 423-437

The most advanced sections of the country were most affected by the great post-war expansion. In the South, undeveloped and devastated, economic progress was painfully slow; inertia and a severe shortage of capital combined to hold the Southern economy to its bare-subsistence level. The Midwest, with natural advantages in land and transportation, began to develop its potential slowly but confidently.

Growth and Expansion 519-530

The business of exploring and filling the West that had been interrupted by the Civil War was resumed with boundless energy. The first requirement, railroads, was soon met, and exploitation began in earnest. The fact that the West was occupied with no regard to its indigenous people, the Indians, was camouflaged under successive policies of treaty-making and paternalism.

1866

1.

WILLIAM F. G. SHANKS: The American Soldier

With the exception of a few West Point graduates, most Civil War officers were, like their men, citizen soldiers in an amateur army. Discipline was uneven, if it existed at all. Officers were appointed by state governors, or elected by their own troops. One compensating factor that favored both North and South was that those who went to war went because they wanted to, at least in the early stages of the war. That the characteristics of the American military represented something new and different in the annals of war is suggested in the following account, written by New York Herald *correspondent William Shanks in 1866.*

Source: *Personal Recollections of Distinguished Generals*, New York, 1866, pp. 322-327.

ONE OF THE MANY FALLACIES which have been dissipated by our late warlike experience is the idea which once prevailed that an uneducated man made as good, if not a better, soldier than the educated man. When the late war began, it was an assertion made as positively as frequently. It was believed, particularly by the regular officers, that the persons of the former class more readily and completely adapted themselves to the discipline of the camps — more readily became the pliant and obedient tools that regular soldiers are too often made. It is to the veteran volunteers of the late war for the Union that we are indebted for the explosion of this fallacy. The proofs of its falsity are not less interesting than conclusive.

Every reader familiar with the history of modern warfare in Europe must have noticed, in watching the events of the late rebellion in this country, the very great difference between the practice of war as carried on in Europe and by ourselves. The rules have been the same; the theory of war is too firmly and philosophically established to be changed. It cannot be said that we originated a single new rule, but our application of those long established has been unlike any other practice known to history. The extent of the field of operations, the peculiar configuration of the country, and the extended line of coast and inland frontier which each party to the contest had to guard, conspired to this end, and caused to be originated such peculiarities of warfare as long and arduous raids by entire armies, flank marches of an extent and boldness never before conceived, the construction of many leagues of fortified lines, and the execution of strategic marches of great originality and brilliancy, while there have been effected at the same time, owing to changes and improvements in the arms, several innovations in minor tactics not less curious than important.

The contending parties fought dozens of battles, each of which would have been decisive of a war between any two of the great powers of Europe. There, the limits of the field of operations are restricted by the presence of armed neutral powers on each frontier. Here, the line of frontier extended across a whole continent. No necessities exist there, as here, for large numbers of large armies. The most important and extensive modern European wars witnessed the prosecution of only one important operation at a time, while in this country we have carried on several campaigns simultaneously and fought pitched battles, whose tactical as well as strategic success depended on the result of operations 500 miles distant. Bragg won the victory of Chickamauga only by the aid of reenforcements sent him from Richmond; the besieged army of Rosecrans at Chattanooga was saved from dispersion only by the timely reenforcements sent him, under Hooker, from Washington; while Schofield, with 20,000 men, after fighting at Nashville, Tennessee, in the middle of winter, was operating in North Carolina, opening communications with Sherman, a fortnight subsequently. . . .

In Europe, cavalry plays an important part on every battlefield, while, in this country, its assistance has seldom been asked in actual battle, though a no less effective application has been made of it in destroying communications. Except in the battle of General Sheridan, and in some instances where accident has brought cavalry into battle, our troopers were never legitimately employed. The art of marching as practised in Europe was also varied here, and the European system of supplying an army is very different from our own. Their lines of march are decided by the necessities for providing cantonments in the numerous villages of the country, while, on this conti-

nent, marches are retarded, if not controlled, by the necessity of carrying tents for camps. The parallel which is here merely outlined might be pursued by one better fitted for the task to a highly suggestive and interesting conclusion.

In the same sense, and in still better defined contrast, the armies of America and of Europe have differed in their personnel. The armies of the principal powers of Europe are composed of men forced to arms by necessity in time of peace and conscriptions in time of war; not, like the people of our own country, volunteering when the crisis demanded, with a clear sense of the danger before them and for the stern purpose of vindicating the flag, and forcing obedience to the laws of the country. The European soldiers are conscripted for life, become confirmed in the habits of the camp, and are subjected to a system of discipline which tends to the ultimate purpose of rendering them mere pliant tools in the hands of a leader; while those of the United States, separated from the outer world only by the lax discipline necessary to the government of a camp, are open to every influence that books, that letters, and to a certain extent, that society can lend.

The highest aim of the European system is to sink individuality and to teach the recruit that he is but the fraction of a great machine, to the proper working of which his perfectness in drill and discipline is absolutely necessary. In the United States volunteer army, this same system was only partially enforced, and individuality was lost only on the battlefield, and then only so far as was necessary to *morale* did the man sink into the soldier. The private who in camp disagreed and disputed with his captain on questions of politics or science was not necessarily disobedient and demoralized on the battlefield.

No late opportunity for a comparison between the prowess of our own and any European army has been presented, though the reader will have very little difficulty in convincing himself that the discipline of our troops in the South was better than that of the English in the Crimea or the French in Italy; while the "outrages of the Northern soldiers," at which England murmured in her partiality for the Rebels, were not certainly as horrible as those committed by her own troops in India.

This same difference was visible in the personnel of our own and the Rebel armies, and it resulted from the same cause, and that cause was education. The Union Army was superior in prowess to that of the South because superior in discipline, and it was superior in discipline because superior in education. The Union Army was recruited from a people confirmed in habits of industry and inured to hard and severe manual and mental labor. That of the Rebels was recruited from among men reared in the comparative idleness of agricultural life and not habituated to severe toil; or conscripted from that hardier class of "poor whites" whose spirits had been broken by long existence in a state of ignorance and of slavery not less abject because indirectly enforced and unsuspectedly endured.

Neither fraction of the Rebel army, as a class, was the equal either in refinement, education, or habits of the men of the North, nor were both combined in an army organization equal in discipline, or the courage and effectiveness which results from it, to that which sprang to the nation's aid in 1861.

2.

ANDREW JOHNSON: Veto of Freedmen's Bureau Bill

The Freedmen's Bureau, created by Congress at the end of the Civil War, was intended to protect African Americans from any form of reenslavement and to improve their economic and material condition. When Congress enacted a new bill, February 19, 1866, extending the powers of the Bureau for an indefinite period and proposing enforcement of its provisions by the military, President Johnson objected, on several points of constitutionality, in a veto message of the same day. The conflict between the President and the Radical Republican Congress that had been brewing since Johnson's Amnesty Proclamation of May 1865 now came into the open. Congress passed a Freedmen's Bureau Bill over his veto in July. A portion of the veto message is reprinted below.

Source: Richardson, VI, pp. 398-405.

To the Senate of the United States:

I have examined with care the bill, which originated in the Senate and has been passed by the two houses of Congress, to amend an act entitled "An act to establish a bureau for the relief of freedmen and refugees," and for other purposes. Having with much regret come to the conclusion that it would not be consistent with the public welfare to give my approval to the measure, I return the bill to the Senate with my objections to its becoming a law.

I might call to mind in advance of these objections that there is no immediate necessity for the proposed measure. The act to establish a bureau for the relief of freedmen and refugees, which was approved in the month of March last, has not yet expired. It was thought stringent and extensive enough for the purpose in view in time of war. Before it ceases to have effect, further experience may assist to guide us to a wise conclusion as to the policy to be adopted in time of peace.

I share with Congress the strongest desire to secure to the freedmen the full enjoyment of their freedom and property and their entire independence and equality in making contracts for their labor, but the bill before me contains provisions which in my opinion are not warranted by the Constitution and are not well suited to accomplish the end in view.

The bill proposes to establish, by authority of Congress, military jurisdiction over all parts of the United States containing refugees and freedmen. It would by its very nature apply with most force to those parts of the United States in which the freedmen most abound, and it expressly extends the existing temporary jurisdiction of the Freedmen's Bureau, with greatly enlarged powers, over those states "in which the ordinary course of judicial proceedings has been interrupted by the rebellion."

The source from which this military jurisdiction is to emanate is none other than the President of the United States, acting through the War Department and the commissioner of the Freedmen's Bureau. The agents to carry out this military jurisdiction are to be selected either from the Army or from civil life; the country is to be divided into districts and subdistricts, and the number of salaried agents to be employed may be equal to the number of counties or parishes in all the United States where freedmen and refugees are to be found.

The subjects over which this military jurisdiction is to extend in every part of the United States include protection to "all employees, agents, and officers of this bureau in the exercise of the duties imposed" upon them by the bill. In eleven states it is further to extend over all cases affecting freedmen and refugees discriminated against "by local law, custom, or prejudice." In those eleven states the bill subjects any white person who may be charged with depriving a freedman of "any civil rights or immunities belonging to white persons" to imprisonment or fine, or both, without, however, defining the "civil rights and immunities" which are thus to be secured to the freedmen by military law. This military jurisdiction also extends to all questions that may arise respecting contracts.

The agent who is thus to exercise the office of a military judge may be a stranger, entirely ignorant of the laws of the place and exposed to the errors of judgment to which all men are liable. The exercise of power over which there is no legal supervision by so vast a number of agents as is contemplated by the bill must, by the very nature of man, be attended by acts of caprice, injustice, and passion.

The trials having their origin under this bill are to take place without the intervention of a jury and without any fixed rules of law or evidence. The rules on which offenses are to be "heard and determined" by the numerous agents are such rules and regulations as the President, through the War Department, shall prescribe. No previous presentment is required nor any indictment charging the commission of a crime against the laws; but the trial must proceed on charges and specifications. The punishment will be, not what the law declares, but such as a court-martial may think proper; and from these arbitrary tribunals there lies no appeal, no writ of error to any of the courts in which the Constitution of the United States vests exclusively the judicial power of the country.

While the territory and the classes of actions and offenses that are made subject to this measure are so extensive, the bill itself, should it become a law, will have no limitation in point of time, but will form a part of the permanent legislation of the country.

I cannot reconcile a system of military jurisdiction of this kind with the words of the Constitution which declare that "no person shall be held to answer for a capital or otherwise infamous crime unless on a presentment or indictment of a grand jury, except in cases arising in the land or naval forces, or in the militia, when in actual service in time of war or public danger," and that "in all criminal prosecutions the accused shall enjoy the right to a speedy and public trial by an impartial jury of the state and district wherein the crime shall have been committed."

The safeguards which the experience and wisdom of ages taught our fathers to establish as securities for the protection of the innocent, the punishment of the guilty, and the equal administration of justice are to be set aside; and for the sake of a more vigorous interposition in behalf of justice, we are to take the risks of the many acts of injustice that would necessarily follow from an almost countless number of agents established in every parish or county in nearly a third of the states of the Union, over whose decisions there is to be no supervision or control by the federal courts. The power that would be thus placed in the hands of the President is such as in time of peace certainly ought never to be entrusted to any one man.

If it be asked whether the creation of such a tribunal within a state is warranted as a measure of war, the question immediately presents itself whether we are still engaged in war. Let us not unnecessarily disturb the commerce and credit and industry of the country by declaring to the American people and to the world that the United States are still in a condition of civil war. At present there is no part of our country in which the authority of the United States is disputed. Offenses that may be committed by individuals should not work a forfeiture of the rights of whole communities. The country has returned, or is returning, to a state of peace and industry, and the

rebellion is in fact at an end. The measure, therefore, seems to be as inconsistent with the actual condition of the country as it is at variance with the Constitution of the United States. . . .

Undoubtedly the freedman should be protected, but he should be protected by the civil authorities, especially by the exercise of all the constitutional powers of the courts of the United States and of the states. His condition is not so exposed as may at first be imagined. He is in a portion of the country where his labor cannot well be spared. Competition for his services from planters, from those who are constructing or repairing railroads, and from capitalists in his vicinage or from other states will enable him to command almost his own terms. He also possesses a perfect right to change his place of abode, and if, therefore, he does not find in one community or state a mode of life suited to his desires or proper remuneration for his labor, he can move to another where that labor is more esteemed and better rewarded.

In truth, however, each state, induced by its own wants and interests, will do what is necessary and proper to retain within its borders all the labor that is needed for the development of its resources. The laws that regulate supply and demand will maintain their force, and the wages of the laborer will be regulated thereby. There is no danger that the exceedingly great demand for labor will not operate in favor of the laborer.

Neither is sufficient consideration given to the ability of the freedmen to protect and take care of themselves. It is no more than justice to them to believe that as they have received their freedom with moderation and forbearance, so they will distinguish themselves by their industry and thrift, and soon show the world that in a condition of freedom they are self-sustaining, capable of selecting their own employment and their own places of abode, of insisting for themselves on a proper remuneration, and of establishing and maintaining their own asylums and schools. It is earnestly hoped that instead of wasting away they will by their own efforts establish for themselves a condition of respectability and prosperity. It is certain that they can attain to that condition only through their own merits and exertions.

In this connection the query presents itself whether the system proposed by the bill will not, when put into complete operation, practically transfer the entire care, support, and control of 4 million emancipated slaves to agents, overseers, or taskmasters, who, appointed at Washington, are to be located in every county and parish throughout the United States containing freedmen and refugees. Such a system would inevitably tend to a concentration of power in the executive which would enable him, if so disposed, to control the action of this numerous class and use them for the attainment of his own political ends.

I cannot but add another very grave objection to this bill. The Constitution imperatively declares, in connection with taxation, that each state *shall* have at least one representative, and fixes the rule for the number to which, in future times, each state shall be entitled. It also provides that the Senate of the United States *shall* be composed of two senators from each state, and adds with peculiar force "that no state, without its consent, shall be deprived of its equal suffrage in the Senate." The original act was necessarily passed in the absence of the states chiefly to be affected, because their people were then contumaciously engaged in the rebellion. Now the case is changed, and some, at least, of those states are attending Congress by loyal representatives, soliciting the allowance of the constitutional right for representation.

At the time, however, of the consideration and the passing of this bill, there was no senator or representative in Congress from the eleven states which are to be mainly affected by its provisions. The very fact that reports were and are made against the good disposition of the people of that portion of the country is an additional reason why they need and should have representatives of their own in Congress to explain their condition, reply to accusations, and assist by their local knowledge in the perfecting of measures immediately affecting themselves. While the liberty of deliberation would then be free and Congress would have full power to decide according to its judgment, there could be no objection urged that the states most interested had not been permitted to be heard.

The principle is firmly fixed in the minds of the American people that there should be no taxation without representation. Great burdens have now to be borne by all the country, and we may best demand that they shall be borne without murmur when they are voted by a majority of the representatives of all the people. I would not interfere with the unquestionable right of Congress to judge, each house for itself, "of the elections, returns, and qualifications of its own members"; but that authority cannot be construed as including the right to shut out in time of peace any state from the representation to which it is entitled by the Constitution. At present all the people of eleven states are excluded — those who were most faithful during the war not less than others.

The state of Tennessee, for instance, whose authorities engaged in rebellion, was restored to all her constitutional relations to the Union by the patriotism and energy of her injured and betrayed people. Before the war was brought to a termination, they had placed themselves in relations with the general government, had established a state government of their own, and, as they were not included in the Emancipation Proclamation, they by their own act had amended their constitution so as to abolish slavery within the limits of their state. I know no reason why the state of Tennessee, for example, should not fully enjoy "all her constitutional relations to the United States."

The President of the United States stands toward the country in a somewhat different attitude from that of any member of Congress. Each member of Congress is chosen from a single district or state; the President is chosen by the people of all the states. As eleven states are not at this time represented in either branch of Congress, it would seem to be his duty on all proper occasions to present their just claims to Congress. There always will be differences of opinion in the community and individuals may be guilty of transgressions of the law, but these do not constitute valid objections against the right of a state to representation. I would in nowise interfere with the discretion of Congress with regard to the qualifications of members; but I hold it my duty to recommend to you, in the interests of peace and the interests of union, the admission of every state to its share in public legislation when, however insubordinate, insurgent, or rebellious its people may have been, it presents itself, not only in an attitude of loyalty and harmony but in the persons of representatives whose loyalty cannot be questioned under any existing constitutional or legal test.

It is plain that an indefinite or permanent exclusion of any part of the country from representation must be attended by a spirit of disquiet and complaint. It is unwise and dangerous to pursue a course of measures which will unite a very large section of the country against another section of the country, however much the latter may preponderate. The course of emigration, the development of industry and business, and natural causes will raise up at the South men as devoted to the Union as those of any other part of the land; but if they are all excluded from Congress, if in a permanent statute they are declared not to be in full constitutional relations to the country, they may

think they have cause to become a unit in feeling and sentiment against the government. Under the political education of the American people the idea is inherent and ineradicable that the consent of the majority of the whole people is necessary to secure a willing acquiescence in legislation.

The bill under consideration refers to certain of the states as though they had not "been fully restored in all their constitutional relations to the United States." If they have not, let us at once act together to secure that desirable end at the earliest possible moment. It is hardly necessary for me to inform Congress that in my own judgment most of those states, so far, at least, as depends upon their own action, have already been fully restored and are to be deemed as entitled to enjoy their constitutional rights as members of the Union. Reasoning from the Constitution itself and from the actual situation of the country, I feel not only entitled but bound to assume that with the federal courts restored and those of the several states in the full exercise of their functions the rights and interests of all classes of people will, with the aid of the military in cases of resistance to the laws, be essentially protected against unconstitutional infringement or violation.

Should this expectation unhappily fail, which I do not anticipate, then the executive is already fully armed with the powers conferred by the act of March 1865 establishing the Freedmen's Bureau, and hereafter, as heretofore, he can employ the land and naval forces of the country to suppress insurrection or to overcome obstructions to the laws.

In accordance with the Constitution, I return the bill to the Senate in the earnest hope that a measure involving questions and interests so important to the country will not become a law, unless upon deliberate consideration by the people it shall receive the sanction of an enlightened public judgment.

3.

ANDREW JOHNSON: Against the Radical Republicans

On the evening of February 22, 1866, President Johnson delivered an impromptu address to a crowd of citizens gathered on the White House lawn in celebration of Washington's Birthday. Johnson expressed annoyance at congressional criticism of his veto of the Freedmen's Bureau Bill three days before. As the President's advisers had warned, the speech was fully reported in the next day's newspapers and drew an outburst of angry public reaction.

Source: *New York Herald*, February 23, 1866.

I HAVE ALREADY REMARKED that there were two parties — one for destroying the government to preserve slavery, and the other to break up the government to destroy slavery. The objects to be accomplished were different, it is true, so far as slavery is concerned, but they agreed in one thing, and that was the breaking up of the government. They agreed in the destruction of the government, the precise thing which I have already stood up to oppose. Whether the disunionists come from the South or the North, I stand now where I did then, to vindicate the Union of these states and the Constitution of the country. . . .

Who, I ask, has suffered more for the Union than I have? I shall not now repeat the wrongs or suffering inflicted upon me; but it is not the way to deal with a whole people in the spirit of revenge. . . . There is no one who has labored harder than I have to have the principal conscious and intelligent traitors brought to justice; to have the law vindicated, and the great fact vindicated that treason is a crime. Yet, while conscious, intelligent traitors are to be punished, should whole states, communities, and people be made to submit to and bear

the penalty of death? I have, perhaps, as much hostility and as much resentment as a man ought to have; but we should conform our action and our conduct to the example of Him who founded our holy religion. . . .

But, gentlemen, I came into power under the Constitution of the country and by the approbation of the people. And what did I find? I found 8 million people who were, in fact, condemned under the law — and the penalty was death. Under the idea of revenge and resentment, they were to be annihilated and destroyed. . . .

Let them repent and let them acknowledge their allegiance. Let them become loyal and willing supporters and defenders of our glorious stripes and stars and the Constitution of our country. *Let their leaders, the conscious, intelligent traitors, suffer the penalty of the law;* but for the great mass who have been forced into this rebellion and misled by their leaders, I say *leniency, kindness, trust, and confidence.*

But, my countrymen, after having passed through the rebellion and given such evidence as I have — though men croak a great deal about it now — when I look back through the battlefields and see many of these brave men, in whose company I was in part of the rebellion where it was most difficult and doubtful to be found — before the smoke of battle has scarcely passed away; before the blood has scarcely congealed — what do we find? The rebellion is put down by the strong arm of the government in the field, *but is it the only way in which we can have rebellion?* They struggled for the breaking up of the government, but before they are scarcely out of the battlefield, and before our brave men have scarcely returned to their houses to renew the ties of affection and love, we find ourselves almost *in the midst of another rebellion.*

The war to suppress our rebellion was to prevent the separation of the states and thereby change the character of the government and weakening its power. Now, what is the change? There is an attempt to concentrate the power of the government in the hands of a few, and *thereby bring about consolidation which is equally dangerous and objectionable with separation.* We find that powers are assumed and attempted to be exercised of a most extraordinary character. What are they? We find that *governments can be revolutionized, can be changed without going into the battlefield.* . . .

Now, what are the attempts? What is being proposed? We find that, in fact, by an irresponsible central directory, nearly all the powers of government are assumed without even consulting the legislative or executive departments of the government. Yes, and by resolution, reported by a committee upon whom all the legislative power of the government has been conferred, that principle in the Constitution which authorizes and empowers each branch of the Legislative Department to be judges of the election and qualifications of its own members has been virtually taken away from those departments and conferred upon a committee, who must report before they can act under the Constitution and allow members duly elected to take their seats. By this rule they assume that there must be laws passed; that there must be recognition in respect to a state in the Union, with all its practical relations restored before the respective houses of Congress, under the Constitution, shall judge of the election and qualifications of its own members.

What position is that? You have been struggling for four years to put down the rebellion. You denied in the beginning of the struggle that any state had the right to go out. You said that they had neither the right nor the power. The issue has been made, and it has been settled that a state has neither the right nor the power to go out of the Union. And when you have settled that by the executive and military power of the government and by the public judgment, you *turn around and assume that they are out and shall not come in.*

I am free to say to you, as your Executive, that *I am not prepared to take any such position.* I said in the Senate, at the very inception of the rebellion, that states had no right to go out and that they had no power to go out. That question has been settled. And I cannot turn round now and give the direct lie to all I profess to have done in the last five years. I can do no such thing. I say that when these states comply with the Constitution, when they have given sufficient evidence of their loyalty and that they can be trusted, when they yield obedience to the law, I say, *extend to them the right hand of fellowship,* and let peace and union be restored.

I have fought traitors and treason in the South; I opposed the Davises and [the] Toombses, the Slidells, and a long list of others whose names I need not repeat; and now, when I turn around at the other end of the line, I find men — I care not by what name you call them — who still stand opposed to the restoration of the Union of these states; and I am free to say to you that I am still for the preservation of this compact; I am still for the restoration of this Union; I am still in favor of this great government of ours going on and following out its destiny.

A gentleman calls for their names. Well, suppose I should give them. I look upon them — I repeat it, as President or citizen — as being as much opposed to the fundamental principles of the government and believe they are as much laboring to prevent or destroy them as were the men who fought against us. *I say Thaddeus Stevens of Pennsylvania; I say Charles Sumner; I say Wendell Phillips and others of the same stripe are among them.* Some gentleman in the crowd says, "Give it to Forney." I have only just to say that *I do not waste my ammunition upon dead ducks.* I stand for my country, I stand for the Constitution, where I placed my feet from my entrance into public life. They may traduce me, they may slander me, they may vituperate; but let me say to you that it has no effect upon me. And let me say in addition that *I do not intend to be bullied by my enemies.*

I know, my countrymen, that it has been insinuated, and not only insinuated but said directly — the intimation has been given in high places — that if such a usurpation of power had been exercised 200 years ago in a particular reign, it would have cost a certain individual his head. What usurpation has Andrew Johnson been guilty of? The usurpation I have been guilty of has always been standing between the people and the encroachments of power. And because I dared to say in a conversation with a fellow citizen, and a senator too, that I thought amendments to the Constitution ought not to be so frequent; that their effect would be that it would lose all its dignity; that the old instrument would be lost sight of in a short time — because I happened to say that if it was amended such and such amendments should be adopted, it was a usurpation of power that would have cost a king his head at a certain time.

And in connection with this subject it was explained by the same gentleman that we were in the midst of an earthquake; that he trembled and could not yield. Yes, *there is an earthquake coming. There is a ground swell coming of popular judgment and indignation.* The American people will speak by their interests, and they will know who are their friends and who their enemies.

What positions have I held under this government? Beginning with an alderman and running through all branches of the legislature. Some gentleman says I have been a tailor. Now, that did not discomfit me in the least; for when I used to be a tailor I had the reputation of being a good one, and making close fits — always punctual with my customers and always did good work. . . . I was saying that I had held nearly all positions, from alderman, through both branches of Congress, to that which I now occupy, and who is there that will say Andrew Johnson ever made a pledge that he did not redeem or made a promise he did not fulfill? Who will say that he has ever acted otherwise than in fidelity to the great mass of the people?

They may talk about beheading and usurpation; but when I am beheaded I want the American people to witness. I do not want by innuendoes, by indirect remarks in high places, to see the man who has assassination brooding in his bosom exclaim, "This presidential obstacle must be gotten out of the way." I make use of a very strong expression when I say that I have no doubt the *intention was to incite assassination* and so get out of the way the obstacle from place and power.

Whether by assassination or not, there are individuals in this government, I doubt not, who want to destroy our institutions and change the character of the government. Are they not satisfied with the blood which has been shed? Does not the murder of Lincoln appease the vengeance and wrath of the opponents of this government? Are they still unslaked? Do they still want more blood? Have they not got honor and courage enough to attain their objects otherwise than by the hands of the assassin? If it is blood they want, let them have courage enough to strike like men. I know they are willing to wound, but they are afraid to strike.

If my blood is to be shed because I vindicate the Union and the preservation of this government in its original purity and character, let it be shed; let an altar to the Union be erected; and then, if it is necessary, take me and lay me upon it, and the blood that now warms and animates my existence shall be poured out as a fit libation to the Union of these states. But let the opponents of this government remember that when it is poured out, "the blood of the martyrs will be the seed of the church."

Gentlemen, this Union will grow — it will continue to increase in strength and power though it may be cemented and cleansed with blood.

4.

Debate on Civil and States' Rights

The Civil Rights and Freedmen's Bureau bills, designed to protect Southern African Americans from such discriminatory legislation as the Black Codes, passed Congress early in 1866 only to be vetoed by President Andrew Johnson on the grounds that they necessitated unconstitutional extension of federal power and that the states principally concerned were not represented in Congress. The prestigious Senator Lyman Trumbull of Illinois, a former lawyer and judge, attacked Johnson's veto of the Civil Rights Bill in a speech to the Senate, April 4, 1866. Trumbull brilliantly turned Johnson's own words against him by quoting an earlier Johnson address attacking a veto by President Buchanan. Largely because of Trumbull's objections and Johnson's declining popularity, Congress passed the Civil Rights Bill over the presidential veto on April 9, 1866. Johnson's veto message of March 27 and portions of Trumbull's reply follow.

Source: Richardson, VI, pp. 405-413.
       Globe, 39 Cong., 1 Sess., pp. 1755-1761.

I.

ANDREW JOHNSON:
Veto of Civil Rights Bill

To the Senate of the United States:

I regret that the bill, which has passed both houses of Congress, entitled "An act to protect all persons in the United States in their civil rights and furnish the means of their vindication" contains provisions which I cannot approve consistently with my sense of duty to the whole people and my obligations to the Constitution of the United States. I am therefore constrained to return it to the Senate, the house in which it originated, with my objections to its becoming a law.

By the 1st Section of the bill, all persons born in the United States and not subject to any foreign power, excluding Indians not taxed, are declared to be citizens of the United States. This provision comprehends the Chinese of the Pacific states, Indians subject to taxation, the people called gypsies, as well as the entire race designated as blacks, people of color, Negroes, mulattoes, and persons of African blood. Every individual of these races born in the United States is by the bill made a citizen of the United States.

It does not purport to declare or confer any other right of citizenship than federal citizenship. It does not purport to give these classes of persons any status as citizens of states except that which may result from their status as citizens of the United States. The power to confer the right of state citizenship is just as exclusively with the several states as the power to confer the right of federal citizenship is with Congress.

The right of federal citizenship thus to be conferred on the several excepted races before mentioned is now for the first time proposed to be given by law. If, as is claimed by many, all persons who are native-born already are, by virtue of the Constitution, citizens of the United States, the passage of the pending bill cannot be necessary to make them such. If, on the other hand, such persons are not citizens, as may be assumed from the proposed legislation to make them such, the grave question presents itself whether, when eleven of the thirty-six states are unrepresented in Congress at the present time, it is sound policy to make our entire colored population and all other excepted classes citizens of the United States.

Four million of them have just emerged from slavery into freedom. Can it be reasonably supposed that they possess the requisite qualifications to entitle them to all the privileges and immunities of citizens of the United States? Have the people of the several states expressed such a conviction? It may also be asked whether it is necessary that they should be declared citizens in order that they may be secured in the enjoyment of the civil rights proposed to be conferred by the bill.

Those rights are, by federal as well as state laws, secured to all domiciled aliens and foreigners, even before the completion of the process of naturalization; and it may safely be assumed that the same enactments are sufficient to give like protection and benefits to those for whom this bill provides special legislation. Besides, the policy of the government, from its origin to the present time, seems to have been that persons who are strangers to and unfamiliar with our institutions and our laws should pass through a certain probation, at the end of which, before attaining the coveted prize, they must give evidence of their fitness to receive and to exercise the rights of citizens as contemplated by the Constitution of the United States.

The bill in effect proposes a discrimination against large numbers of intelligent, worthy, and patriotic foreigners, and in favor of the Negro, to whom, after long years of bondage, the avenues to freedom and intelligence have just now been suddenly opened. He must, of necessity, from his previous unfortunate condition of servitude, be less informed as to the nature and character of our institutions than he who, coming from abroad, has to some extent at least, familiarized himself with the principles of a government to which he voluntarily entrusts "life, liberty, and the pursuit of happiness."

Yet it is now proposed, by a single legislative enactment, to confer the rights of citizens upon all persons of African descent, born within the extended limits of the United States, while persons of foreign birth who make our land their home must undergo a probation of five years and can only then become citizens upon proof that they are "of good moral character, attached to the principles of the Constitution of the United States, and well-disposed to the good order and happiness of the same."

The 1st Section of the bill also contains an enumeration of the rights to be enjoyed by these classes so made citizens "in every state and territory in the United States."

These rights are "to make and enforce contracts; to sue, be parties, and give evidence; to inherit, purchase, lease, sell, hold, and convey real and personal property," and to have "full and equal benefit of all laws and proceedings for the security of person and property as is enjoyed by white citizens." So, too, they are made subject to the same punishment, pains, and penalties, in common with white citizens and to none other.

Thus a perfect equality of the white and colored races is attempted to be fixed by federal law in every state of the Union over the vast field of state jurisdiction covered by these enumerated rights. In no one of these can any state ever exercise any power of discrimination between the different races. In the exercise of state policy over matters exclusively affecting the people of each state, it has frequently been thought expedient to discriminate between the two races.

By the statutes of some of the states, Northern as well as Southern, it is enacted, for instance, that no white person shall intermarry with a Negro or mulatto. Chancellor Kent says, speaking of the blacks, that:

> Marriages between them and the whites are forbidden in some of the states where slavery does not exist, and they are prohibited in all the slaveholding states; and when not absolutely contrary to law, they are revolting and regarded as an offense against public decorum.

I do not say that this bill repeals state laws on the subject of marriage between the two races, for as the whites are forbidden to intermarry with the blacks, the blacks can only make such contracts as the whites themselves are allowed to make, and therefore cannot under this bill enter into the marriage contract with the whites. I cite this discrimination, however, as an instance of the state policy as to discrimination and to inquire whether if Congress can abrogate all state laws of discrimination between the two races in the matter of real estate, of suits, and of contracts generally, Congress

may not also repeal the state laws as to the contract of marriage between the two races.

Hitherto every subject embraced in the enumeration of rights contained in this bill has been considered as exclusively belonging to the states. They all relate to the internal policy and economy of the respective states. They are matters which, in each state, concern the domestic condition of its people, varying in each according to its own peculiar circumstances and the safety and well-being of its own citizens. I do not mean to say that upon all these subjects there are not federal restraints — as, for instance, in the state power of legislation over contracts there is a federal limitation that no state shall pass a law impairing the obligations of contracts; and, as to crimes, that no state shall pass an *ex post facto* law; and, as to money, that no state shall make anything but gold and silver a legal tender.

But where can we find a federal prohibition against the power of any state to discriminate, as do most of them, between aliens and citizens, between artificial persons, called corporations, and natural persons, in the right to hold real estate? If it be granted that Congress can repeal all state laws discriminating between whites and blacks in the subjects covered by this bill, why, it may be asked, may not Congress repeal in the same way all state laws discriminating between the two races on the subjects of suffrage and office? If Congress can declare by law who shall hold lands, who shall testify, who shall have capacity to make a contract in a state, then Congress can by law also declare who, without regard to color or race, shall have the right to sit as a juror or as a judge, to hold any office, and, finally, to vote "in every state and territory of the United States."

As respects the territories, they come within the power of Congress, for as to them the lawmaking power is the federal power; but as to the states, no similar provision exists vesting in Congress the power "to make rules and regulations" for them.

The object of the 2nd Section of the bill is to afford discriminating protection to colored persons in the full enjoyment of all the rights secured to them by the preceding section. It declares:

That any person who, under color of any law, statute, ordinance, regulation, or custom, shall subject, or cause to be subjected, any inhabitant of any state or territory to the deprivation of any right secured or protected by this act, or to different punishment, pains, or penalties on account of such person having at any time been held in a condition of slavery or involuntary servitude, except as a punishment for crime whereof the party shall have been duly convicted, or by reason of his color or race, than is prescribed for the punishment of white persons, shall be deemed guilty of a misdemeanor, and on conviction shall be punished by fine not exceeding $1,000, or imprisonment not exceeding one year, or both, in the discretion of the court.

This section seems to be designed to apply to some existing or future law of a state or territory which may conflict with the provisions of the bill now under consideration. It provides for counteracting such forbidden legislation by imposing fine and imprisonment upon the legislators who may pass such conflicting laws or upon the officers or agents who shall put or attempt to put them into execution. It means an official offense, not a common crime committed against law upon the persons or property of the black race. Such an act may deprive the black man of his property but not of the *right* to hold property. It means a deprivation of the right itself, either by the state judiciary or the state legislature.

It is therefore assumed that under this section members of state legislatures who should vote for laws conflicting with the provisions of the bill, that judges of the state courts who should render judgments in antagonism with its terms, and that marshals and sheriffs who should, as ministerial officers, execute processes sanctioned by state laws and issued by state judges in execution of their judgments, could be brought before other tribunals and there subjected to fine and imprisonment for the performance of the duties which such state laws might impose.

The legislation thus proposed invades the judicial power of the state. It says to every state court or judge: If you decide that this act is unconstitutional; if you refuse, under the prohibition of a state law, to allow a Negro to testify; if you hold that over such a subject matter the state law is paramount, and "under color" of a state law refuse the exercise of the right to the Negro, your error of judgment, however conscientious, shall subject you to fine and imprisonment. I do not apprehend that the conflicting legislation which the bill seems to contemplate is so likely to occur as to render it necessary at this time to adopt a measure of such doubtful constitutionality.

In the next place, this provision of the bill seems to be unnecessary as adequate judicial remedies could be adopted to secure the desired end without invading the immunities of legislators, always important to be preserved in the interest of public liberty; without assailing the independence of the judiciary, always essential to the preservation of individual rights; and without impairing the efficiency of ministerial officers, always necessary for the maintenance of public peace and order. The remedy proposed by this section seems to be in this respect not only anomalous but unconstitutional; for the Constitution guarantees nothing with certainty if it does not insure to the several states the right of making and executing laws in regard to all matters arising within their jurisdiction, subject only to the restriction that in cases of conflict with the Constitution and constitutional laws of the United States the latter should be held to be the supreme law of the land.

The 3rd Section gives the district courts of the United States exclusive "cognizance of all crimes and offenses committed against the provisions of this act," and concurrent jurisdiction with the circuit courts of the United States of all civil and criminal cases "affecting persons who are denied or cannot enforce in the courts or judicial tribunals of the state or locality where they may be any of the rights secured to them by the first section." The construction which I have given to the second section is strengthened by this third section, for it makes clear what kind of denial or deprivation of the rights secured by the first section was in contemplation. It is a denial or deprivation of such rights "in the courts or judicial tribunals of the state."

It stands, therefore, clear of doubt, that the offense and the penalties provided in the second section are intended for the state judge who, in the clear exercise of his functions as a judge, not acting ministerially but judicially, shall decide contrary to this federal law. In other words, when a state judge, acting upon a question involving a conflict between a state law and a federal law and bound, according to his own judgment and responsibility, to give an impartial decision between the two, comes to the conclusion that the state law is valid and the federal law is invalid, he must not follow the dictates of his own judgment, at the peril of fine and imprisonment. The Legislative Department of the government of the United States thus takes from the Judicial Department of the states the sacred and exclusive duty of judicial decision and converts the state judge into a mere ministerial officer, bound to decide according to the will of Congress.

It is clear that in states which deny to persons whose rights are secured by the first section of the bill any one of those rights, all criminal and civil cases affecting them will, by the provisions of the third section, come under the exclusive cognizance of the federal tribunals. It follows that if, in any state which denies to a colored person any one of all those rights, that person should commit a crime against the laws of a state — murder, arson, rape, or any other crime

— all protection and punishment through the courts of the state are taken away, and he can only be tried and punished in the federal courts.

How is the criminal to be tried? If the offense is provided for and punished by federal law, that law, and not the state law, is to govern. It is only when the offense does not happen to be within the purview of federal law that the federal courts are to try and punish him under any other law. Then resort is to be had to "the common law, as modified and changed" by state legislation, "so far as the same is not inconsistent with the Constitution and laws of the United States." So that over this vast domain of criminal jurisprudence provided by each state for the protection of its own citizens and for the punishment of all persons who violate its criminal laws, federal law, whenever it can be made to apply, displaces state law.

The question here naturally arises, from what source Congress derives the power to transfer to federal tribunals certain classes of cases embraced in this section. The Constitution expressly declares that the judicial power of the United States "shall extend to all cases, in law and equity, arising under this Constitution, the laws of the United States, and treaties made or which shall be made under their authority; to all cases affecting ambassadors, other public ministers, and consuls; to all cases of admiralty and maritime jurisdiction; to controversies to which the United States shall be a party; to controversies between two or more states, between a state and citizens of another state, between citizens of different states, between citizens of the same state claiming lands under grants of different states, and between a state, or the citizens thereof, and foreign states, citizens, or subjects."

Here the judicial power of the United States is expressly set forth and defined; and the act of September 24, 1789, establishing the judicial courts of the United States, in conferring upon the federal courts jurisdiction over cases originating in state tribunals, is careful to confine them to the classes enumerated in the above-recited clause of the Constitution. This section of the bill undoubtedly comprehends cases and authorizes the exercise of powers that are not, by the Constitution, within the jurisdiction of the courts of the United States. To transfer them to those courts would be an exercise of authority well calculated to excite distrust and alarm on the part of all the states, for the bill applies alike to all of them, as well to those that have as to those that have not been engaged in rebellion.

It may be assumed that this authority is incident to the power granted to Congress by the Constitution, as recently amended, to enforce, by appropriate legislation, the article declaring that:

> Neither slavery nor involuntary servitude, except as a punishment for crime whereof the party shall have been duly convicted, shall exist within the United States or any place subject to their jurisdiction.

It cannot, however, be justly claimed that, with a view to the enforcement of this article of the Constitution, there is at present any necessity for the exercise of all the powers which this bill confers. Slavery has been abolished, and at present nowhere exists within the jurisdiction of the United States; nor has there been, nor is it likely there will be, any attempt to revive it by the people or the states. If, however, any such attempt shall be made, it will then become the duty of the general government to exercise any and all incidental powers necessary and proper to maintain inviolate this great constitutional law of freedom.

The 4th Section of the bill provides that officers and agents of the Freedmen's Bureau shall be empowered to make arrests and also that other officers may be specially commissioned for that purpose by the President of the United States. It also authorizes circuit courts of the United States and the superior courts of the territories to appoint, without limitation, commissioners, who are to be charged with the performance of quasi-judicial duties.

The 5th Section empowers the commissioners so to be selected by the courts to appoint in writing, under their hands, one or more suitable persons from time to time to execute warrants and other processes described by the bill. These numerous official agents are made to constitute a sort of police, in addition to the military, and are authorized to summon a *posse comitatus,* and even to call to their aid such portion of the land and naval forces of the United States, or of the militia, "as may be necessary to the performance of the duty with which they are charged." This extraordinary power is to be conferred upon agents irresponsible to the government and to the people, to whose number the discretion of the commissioners is the only limit and in whose hands such authority might be made a terrible engine of wrong, oppression, and fraud.

The general statutes regulating the land and naval forces of the United States, the militia, and the execution of the laws are believed to be adequate for every emergency which can occur in time of peace. If it should prove otherwise, Congress can at any time amend those laws in such manner as, while subserving the public welfare, not to jeopard the rights, interests, and liberties of the people.

The 7th Section provides that a fee of $10 shall be paid to each commissioner in every case brought before him, and a fee of $5 to his deputy or deputies "for each person he or they may arrest and take before any such commissioner," "with such other fees as may be deemed reasonable by such commissioner," "in general for performing such other duties as may be required in the premises." All these fees are to be "paid out of the Treasury of the United States," whether there is a conviction or not; but in case of conviction they are to be recoverable from the defendant. It seems to me that under the influence of such temptations bad men might convert any law, however beneficent, into an instrument of persecution and fraud.

By the 8th Section of the bill, the United States courts, which sit only in one place for white citizens, must migrate with the marshal and district attorney (and necessarily with the clerk, although he is not mentioned) to any part of the district upon the order of the President, and there hold a court, "for the purpose of the more speedy arrest and trial of persons charged with a violation of this act;" and there the judge and officers of the court must remain, upon the order of the President, "for the time therein designated."

The 9th Section authorizes the President, or such person as he may empower for that purpose, "to employ such part of the land or naval forces of the United States, or of the militia, as shall be necessary to prevent the violation and enforce the due execution of this act." This language seems to imply a permanent military force that is to be always at hand and whose only business is to be the enforcement of this measure over the vast region where it is intended to operate.

I do not propose to consider the policy of this bill. To me the details of the bill seem fraught with evil. The white race and the black race of the South have hitherto lived together under the relation of master and slave — capital owning labor. Now, suddenly, that relation is changed, and, as to ownership, capital and labor are divorced. They stand now each master of itself. In this new relation, one being necessary to the other, there will be a new adjustment, which both are deeply interested in making harmonious. Each has equal power in settling the terms, and, if left to the laws that regulate capital and labor, it is confidently believed that they will satisfactorily work out the problem. Capital, it is true, has more intelligence, but labor is never so ignorant as not to understand its own interests, not to know its own value, and not to see that capital must pay that value.

This bill frustrates this adjustment. It intervenes between capital and labor and attempts to settle questions of political economy through the agency of numerous officials whose interest it will be to foment discord between the two races; for, as the breach widens, their employment will continue, and when it is closed their occupation will terminate.

In all our history, in all our experience as a people living under federal and state law, no such system as that contemplated by the details of this bill has ever before been proposed or adopted. They establish for the security of the colored race safeguards which go infinitely beyond any that the general government has ever provided for the white race. In fact, the distinction of race and color is by the bill made to operate in favor of the colored and against the white race. They interfere with the municipal legislation of the states, with the relations existing exclusively between a state and its citizens, or between inhabitants of the same state — an absorption and assumption of power by the general government which, if acquiesced in, must sap and destroy our federative system of limited powers and break down the barriers which preserve the rights of the states.

It is another step, or rather stride, toward centralization and the concentration of all legislative powers in the national government. The tendency of the bill must be to resuscitate the spirit of rebellion and to arrest the progress of those influences which are more closely drawing around the states the bonds of union and peace.

My lamented predecessor, in his proclamation of the 1st of January, 1863, ordered and declared that all persons held as slaves within certain states and parts of states therein designated were and thenceforward should be free; and further, that the executive government of the United States, including the military and naval authorities thereof, would recognize and maintain the freedom of such persons. This guarantee has been rendered especially obligatory and sacred by the amendment of the Constitution abolishing slavery throughout the United States. I, therefore, fully recognize the obligation to protect and defend that class of our people whenever and wherever it shall become necessary, and to the full extent compatible with the Constitution of the United States.

Entertaining these sentiments, it only remains for me to say that I will cheerfully cooperate with Congress in any measure that may be necessary for the protection of the civil rights of the freedmen, as well as those of all other classes of persons throughout the United States, by judicial process, under equal and impartial laws, in conformity with the provisions of the federal Constitution.

I now return the bill to the Senate, and regret that in considering the bills and joint resolutions — forty-two in number — which have been thus far submitted for my approval, I am compelled to withhold my assent from a second measure that has received the sanction of both houses of Congress.

II.

LYMAN TRUMBULL:
Reply to Johnson

MR. PRESIDENT, I fully share with the President of the United States the regret expressed that he was unable to sign the bill "to protect all persons in the United States in their civil rights and secure the means of their vindication." I regret it on my own account because the just expectations raised when this bill was presented to the President before its introduction into the Senate have been disappointed. I regret it on the President's account because it is calculated to alienate him from those who elevated him to power and would gladly have rallied around his administration to sustain him in the principles upon which he was elected.

But above all, sir, I regret it for liberty's sake, to secure which to ourselves and our posterity this government was founded. Yet, if the bill is unconstitutional or unjust to the whole people, I would not have had the President approve it. . . .

Gladly would I refrain from speaking of the spirit of this message, of the dangerous doctrines it promulgates, of the inconsistencies and contradictions of its author, of his encroachments upon the constitutional rights of Congress, of his assumption of unwarranted powers, which, if persevered in and not checked by the people, must eventually lead to a subversion of the government and the destruction of liberty.

Congress, in the passage of the bill under consideration, sought no controversy with the President. So far from it, the bill was proposed with a view to carry out what were supposed to be the views of the President and was submitted to him before its introduction into the Senate. I am not about to relate private declarations of the President, but it is right that the American people should know that the controversy which exists between him and Congress in reference to this measure is of his own seeking. Soon after Congress met it became apparent that there was a difference of opinion between the President and some members of Congress in regard to the condition of the rebellious states and the rights to be secured to freedmen.

The President in his annual message had denied the constitutional power of the general government to extend the elective franchise to Negroes, but he was equally decided in the assertion of the right of every man to life, liberty, and the pursuit of happiness. This was his language:

> But while I have no doubt that now, after the close of the war, it is not competent for the general government to extend the elective franchise in the several states, it is equally clear that good faith requires the security of the freedmen in their liberty and their property.

Lyman Trumbull; photo by John Carbutt in 1868

There were some members of Congress who expressed the opinion that in the reorganization of the rebellious states the right of suffrage should be extended to the colored man, though this was not the prevailing sentiment of Congress. All were anxious for reorganization of the rebellious states and their admission to full participation in the federal government as soon as these relations could be restored with safety to all concerned. Feeling the importance of harmonious action between the different departments of the government and an anxious desire to sustain the President, for whom I had always entertained the highest respect, I had frequent interviews with him during the early part of the session.

Without mentioning anything said by him, I may with propriety state that, acting from the considerations I have stated and believing that the passage of a law by Congress, securing equality in civil rights when denied by state authorities to freedmen and all other inhabitants of the United States, would do much to relieve anxiety in the North, to induce the Southern states to secure these rights by their own action, and thereby remove many of the obstacles to an early reconstruction, I prepared the bill sub-

stantially as it is now returned with the President's objections. After the bill was introduced and printed, a copy was furnished him; and, at a subsequent period, when it was reported that he was hesitating about signing the Freedmen's Bureau Bill, he was informed of the condition of the Civil Rights Bill then pending in the House, and a hope expressed that if he had objections to any of its provisions he would make them known to its friends that they might be remedied, if not destructive of the measure; that there was believed to be no disposition on the part of Congress, and certainly none on my part, to have bills presented to him which he could not approve.

He never indicated to me, nor, so far as I know, to any of its friends, the least objection to any of the provisions of the bill till after its passage. And how could he, consistently with himself? The bill was framed, as was supposed, in entire harmony with his views, and certainly in harmony with what he was then and has since been doing in protecting freedmen in their civil rights all through the rebellious states. It was strictly limited to the protection of the civil rights belonging to every freeman, the birthright of every American citizen, and carefully avoided conferring or interfering with political rights or privileges of any kind.

The bill neither confers nor abridges the rights of anyone but simply declares that in civil rights there shall be an equality among all classes of citizens and that all alike shall be subject to the same punishment. Each state, so that it does not abridge the great fundamental rights belonging, under the Constitution, to all citizens, may grant or withhold such civil rights as it pleases; all that is required is that, in this respect, its laws shall be impartial.

And yet this is the bill now returned with the President's objections; and such objections! What are they? That:

> In all our history, in all our experience as a people, living under federal and state laws, no such system as that contemplat-

ed by the details of this bill has ever before been proposed or adopted. . . .

He says "the tendency of this bill must be to resuscitate the spirit of the rebellion." What assumption in one who denies the authority to punish those who violate United States laws under color of state authority — a doctrine from which the rebellion sprung and in entire harmony with the declaration of Mr. Buchanan, that there was no power to coerce a state. But, sir, out of the mouth of Senator Andrew Johnson I will prove that President Andrew Johnson has violated the spirit of the Constitution, if not its letter, in vetoing this bill. It will be remembered that the bill passed both houses of Congress by more than a two-thirds majority — the vote in the Senate being, yeas 33 to nays 12, and, in the House, yeas 111, nays 38. I will read from the remarks of Senator Andrew Johnson on the veto of the Homestead Bill by Mr. Buchanan:

> The President of the United States *presumes* — yes, sir, I say *presumes* — to dictate to the American people and to the two houses of Congress, in violation of the spirit, if not the letter, of the Constitution, that this measure shall not become a law. Why do I say this? I ask, is there any difference in the spirit of the Constitution whether a measure is sanctioned by a two-thirds vote before its passage or afterward? When a measure has been vetoed by the President, the Constitution requires that it shall be reconsidered and passed by a two-thirds vote in order to become a law. But here, in the teeth of the Executive, there was a two-thirds vote in favor of this bill. The vote was 36 to 2 in this body. The two houses have said that this bill is constitutional and right. In the other house, reflecting the popular sentiment of the nation, the vote was 112 to 51 — ten more than the two-thirds majority which the Constitution requires; and when there is a two-thirds vote for a measure, I say it is against the spirit of the Constitution for the Executive to say. "No, you shall not have this measure; I will take all the chances of vetoing it."

Apply this language to the facts connected with this bill and then say who has violated the spirit of the Constitution.

This bill in no manner interferes with the municipal regulations of any state which protects all alike in their rights of person and property. It could have no operation in Massachusetts, New York, Illinois, or most of the states of the Union. How preposterous, then, to charge that unless some state can have and exercise the right to punish somebody or to deny somebody a civil right on account of his color, its rights as a state will be destroyed. It is manifest that, unless this bill can be passed, nothing can be done to protect the freedmen in their liberty and their rights.

Whatever may have been the opinion of the President at one time as to "good faith requiring the security of the freedmen in their liberty and their property," it is now manifest from the character of his objections to this bill that he will approve no measure that will accomplish the object. That the second clause of the constitutional amendment gives this power, there can be no question. Some have contended that it gives the power even to confer the right of suffrage. I have not thought so, because I have never thought suffrage any more necessary to the liberty of a freedman than of a nonvoting white, whether child or female. But his liberty under the Constitution he is entitled to, and whatever is necessary to secure it to him he is entitled to have, be it the ballot or the bayonet. If the bill now before us, and which goes no further than to secure civil rights to the freedman, cannot be passed, then the constitutional amendment proclaiming freedom to all the inhabitants of the land is a cheat and a delusion.

I cannot better conclude what I have to say than in the language of Mr. Johnson on the occasion of the veto of the Homestead Bill, when, after stating that the fact that the President was inconsistent and changed his opinion with reference to a great measure and a great principle is no reason why a senator or representative who had acted understandingly should change his opinion, he said:

I hope the Senate and House of Representatives, who have sanctioned this bill by more than a two-thirds majority, will, according to the Constitution, exercise their privilege and power and let the bill become a law of the land, according to the high behest of the American people.

5.

Civil Rights Act

The Civil Rights Act of April 9, 1866, conferred citizenship on African Americans and was designed to supersede the Dred Scott decision and such discriminatory legislation as the Mississippi Black Codes. It was the first federal statute to define citizenship and to guarantee civil rights within states. Because there was some doubt in Congress as to the constitutionality of the Act, its more prominent features were later incorporated in the Fourteenth Amendment. President Andrew Johnson had vetoed the Act in March 1866, but his opponents in Congress gathered enough votes to pass the bill over his veto. The ability to override presidential vetoes made it clear that Congress was assuming full control of the Reconstruction program. Portions of the Act follow below.

Source: *Statutes*, XIV, pp. 27-29.

An Act to Protect all Persons in the United States in their Civil Rights, and Furnish the Means of their Vindication.

Be it enacted by the Senate and House of Representatives of the United States of America in Congress assembled, that all persons born in the United States and not subject to any foreign power, excluding Indians not taxed, are hereby declared to be citizens of the United States; and such citizens, of every race and color, without regard to any previous condition of slavery or involuntary servitude, except as a punishment for crime whereof the party shall have been duly convicted, shall have the same right, in every state and territory in the United States, to make and enforce contracts; to sue; be parties, and give evidence; to inherit, purchase, lease, sell, hold, and convey real and personal property; and to full and equal benefit of all laws and proceedings for the security of person and property as is enjoyed by white citizens, and shall be subject to like punishment, pains, and penalties, and to none other, any law, statute, ordinance, regulation, or custom to the contrary notwithstanding.

Section 2. *And be it further enacted,* that any person who, under color of any law, statute, ordinance, regulation, or custom, shall subject, or cause to be subjected, any inhabitant of any state or territory to the deprivation of any right secured or protected by this act, or to different punishment, pains, or penalties on account of such person having at any time been held in a condition of slavery or involuntary servitude, except as a punishment for crime whereof the party shall have been duly convicted, or by reason of his color or race, than is prescribed for the punishment of white persons, shall be deemed guilty of a misdemeanor, and, on conviction, shall be punished by fine not exceeding $1,000 or imprisonment not exceeding one year, or both, in the discretion of the court.

Section 3. *And be it further enacted*, that the district courts of the United States, within their respective districts, shall have, exclusively of the courts of the several states, cognizance of all crimes and offenses committed against the provisions of this act, and also, concurrently with the circuit courts of the United States, of all causes, civil and criminal, affecting persons who are denied or cannot enforce in the courts or judicial tribunals of the state or locality where they may be any of the rights secured to them by the 1st Section of this act; and if any suit or prosecution, civil or criminal, has been or shall be commenced in any state court, against any such person, for any cause whatsoever, or against any officer, civil or military, or other person, for any arrest or imprisonment, trespasses, or wrongs done or committed by virtue or under color of authority derived from this act or the act establishing a bureau for the relief of freedmen and refugees, and all acts amendatory thereof, or for refusing to do any act upon the ground that it would be inconsistent with this act, such defendant shall have the right to remove such cause for trial to the proper district or circuit court in the manner prescribed by the "Act relating to habeas corpus and regulating judicial proceedings in certain cases," approved March 3, 1863, and all acts amendatory thereof. . . .

Section 4. *And be it further enacted*, that the district attorneys, marshals, and deputy marshals of the United States, the commissioners appointed by the circuit and territorial courts of the United States, with powers of arresting, imprisoning, or bailing offenders against the laws of the United States, the officers and agents of the Freedmen's Bureau, and every other officer who may be specially empowered by the President of the United States, shall be, and they are hereby, specially authorized and required, at the expense of the United States, to institute proceedings against all and every person who shall violate the provisions of this act, and cause him or them to be arrested and imprisoned, or bailed, as the case may be, for trial before such court of the United States or territorial court as by this act has cognizance of the offense.

And with a view to affording reasonable protection to all persons in their constitutional rights of equality before the law, without distinction of race or color, or previous condition of slavery or involuntary servitude, except as a punishment for crime, whereof the party shall have been duly convicted, and to the prompt discharge of the duties of this act, it shall be the duty of the circuit courts of the United States and the superior courts of the territories of the United States, from time to time, to increase the number of commissioners so as to afford a speedy and convenient means for the arrest and examination of persons charged with a violation of this act; and such commissioners are hereby authorized and required to exercise and discharge all the powers and duties conferred on them by this act, and the same duties with regard to offenses created by this act, as they are authorized by law to exercise with regard to other offenses against the laws of the United States. . . .

Section 8. *And be it further enacted*, that whenever the President of the United States shall have reason to believe that offenses have been or are likely to be committed against the provisions of this act within any judicial district, it shall be lawful for him, in his discretion, to direct the judge, marshal, and district attorney of such district to attend at such place within the district, and for such time as he may designate, for the purpose of the more speedy arrest and trial of persons charged with a violation of this act; and it shall be the duty of every judge or other officer, when any such requisition shall be received by him, to attend at the place and for the time therein designated.

Section 9. *And be it further enacted*, that it shall be lawful for the President of the United States, or such person as he may empower for that purpose, to employ such part of the land or naval forces of the United States, or of the militia, as shall be necessary to prevent the violation and enforce the due execution of this act.

Section 10. *And be it further enacted*, that, upon all questions of law arising in any cause under the provisions of this act, a final appeal may be taken to the Supreme Court of the United States.

6.

ALEXANDER H. STEPHENS: For Immediate Restoration of the State Governments

The attempt by Radical Republicans to secure African American suffrage in the South after the Civil War was frought with complications. Most Northern blacks still were denied the vote by state law or by such devices as literacy tests and property qualifications. The right to vote, of course, had been from the beginning a right conferred by individual states. By making questions of suffrage preconditions of Southern restoration, Congress was, in fact, arguing on thin constitutional grounds. It was precisely for this reason that the Radical Republican Congress had to resort to the Fourteenth Amendment to enforce its program. At a Joint Congressional Committee on Reconstruction, Alexander Stephens, former vice-president of the Confederacy, was asked if Georgia would accept full African American suffrage as a condition for readmission to the Union. Portions of his testimony of April 11, 1866, couched in terms of "states' rights," are reprinted below.

Source: *Report of the Joint Committee on Reconstruction,* 39 Congress, 1 Session, Washington, 1866, Pt. 3, pp. 158-164.

Question: If the proposition were to extend [the] right of suffrage to those who could read and to those who had served in the Union armies, would that modification affect the action of the state?

Answer: I think the people of the state would be unwilling to do more than they have done for restoration. Restricted or limited suffrage would not be so objectionable as general or universal. But it is a matter that belongs to the state to regulate. The question of suffrage, whether universal or restricted, is one of state policy exclusively, as they believe. Individually, I should not be opposed to a proper system of restricted or limited suffrage to this class of our population. But, in my judgment, it is a matter that belongs of constitutional right to the states to regulate respectively each for itself. . . .

The only view in their opinion that could possibly justify the war which was carried on by the federal government against them was the idea of the indissolubleness of the Union; that those who held the administration for the time were bound to enforce the execution of the laws and the maintenance of the integrity of the country under the Constitution. And since that was accomplished, since those who had assumed the contrary principle — the right of secession and the reserved sovereignty of the states — had abandoned their cause, and the administration here was successful in maintaining the idea upon which war was proclaimed and waged, and the only view in which they supposed it could be justified at all — when that was accomplished, I say, the people of Georgia supposed their state was immediately entitled to all her rights under the Constitution. That is my opinion of the sentiment of the people of Georgia, and I do not think they would be willing to do anything further as a condition precedent to their being permitted to enjoy the full measure of their constitutional rights.

I only give my opinion of the sentiment of the people at this time. They expected as soon as the Confederate cause was abandoned that immediately the states would be brought back into their practical relations with the government as previously constituted. That is what they looked to. They expected that the states would immediately have their representatives in the Senate and in the House; and they expected, in good faith, as loyal men, as the term is frequently used — loyal to law, order, and the Constitution — to support the government under the Constitution. That was their feeling. They did what they did believing it was best for the protection of constitutional liberty.

Toward the Constitution of the United States the great mass of our people were always as much devoted in their feelings as any people ever were toward any laws or people. This is my opinion. As I remarked before, they resorted to secession with a view of more securely maintaining these principles. And when they found they were not successful in their object in perfect good faith, as far as I can judge from meeting with them and conversing with them, looking to the future development of their country in its material resources as well as its moral and intellectual progress, their earnest desire and expectation was to allow the past struggle, lamentable as it was in its results, to pass by and to cooperate with the true friends of the Constitution, with those of all sections who earnestly desire the preservation of constitutional liberty and the perpetuation of the government in its purity.

They have been a little disappointed in this, and are so now. They are patiently waiting, however, and believing that when the passions of the hour have passed away, this delay in representation will cease. They think they have done everything that was essential and proper, and my judgment is that they would not be willing to do anything further as a condition precedent. They would simply remain quiet and passive.

Question: Does your own judgment approve the view you have given as the opinion of the people of the state?

Answer: My own judgment is very decided that the question of suffrage is one that belongs, under the Constitution, and wisely so too, to the states, respectively and exclusively.

Question: Is it your opinion that neither of the alternatives suggested in the question ought to be accepted by the people of Georgia?

Answer: My own opinion is that these terms ought not to be offered as conditions precedent. In other words, my opinion is that it would be best for the peace, harmony, and prosperity of the whole country that there should be an immediate restoration, an immediate bringing back of the states into their original practical relations; and let all these questions then be discussed in common council. Then the representatives from the South could be heard, and you and all could judge much better of the tone and temper of the people than you could from the opinions given by any individuals.

You may take my opinion, or the opinions of any individual, but they will not enable you to judge of the condition of the state of Georgia so well as for her own representatives to be heard in your public councils on her own behalf. My judgment, therefore, is very decided that it would have been better, as soon as the lamentable conflict was over, when the people of the South abandoned their cause and agreed to accept the issue, desiring as they do to resume their places for the future of the Union, and to look to the arena of reason and justice for the protection of their rights of the Union — it would have been better to have allowed that result to take place, to follow under the policy adopted by the administration, than to delay it or hinder it by propositions to amend the Constitution in respect to suffrage or any other new matter.

I think the people of all the Southern states would in the halls of Congress discuss these questions calmly and deliberately, and if they did not show that the views they entertained were just and proper, such as to control the judgment of the people of the other sections and states, they would quietly, philosophically, and patriotically yield to whatever should be constitutionally determined in common council. But I think they feel very sensitively the offer to them of propositions to accept while they are denied all voice in the common council of the Union, under the Constitution, in the discussion of those propositions. I think they feel very sensitively that they are denied the right to be heard. And while, as I have said,

Library of Congress

Alexander H. Stephens; engraving from a daguerreotype

they might differ among themselves in many points in regard to suffrage, they would not differ upon the question of doing anything further as a condition precedent to restoration. And in respect to the alternate conditions to be so presented, I do not think they would accept the one or the other.

My individual general views as to the proper course to be pursued in respect to the colored people are expressed in a speech made before the Georgia legislature, referred to in my letter to Senator Stewart. This was the proper forum, as I conceive, to address them, and my utmost exertions shall be, if I live, to carry out those views. But I think a great deal depends in the advancement of civilization and progress, that these questions should be considered and kept before the proper forum.

Question: Suppose the states that are represented in Congress, and Congress itself, should be of the opinion that Georgia should not be permitted to take its place in the government of the country except upon its assent to one or the other of the two propositions suggested. Is it, then, your opinion that, under such circumstances, Georgia ought to decline?

Witness: You mean the states now represented, and those only?

Mr. Boutwell: Yes.

Witness: You mean by Congress, Congress as it is now constituted, with the other eleven states excluded?

Mr. Boutwell: I do.

Witness: And you mean the same alternative propositions to be applied to all the eleven states as conditions precedent to their restoration?

Mr. Boutwell: I do.

Answer: I think she ought to decline under the circumstances and for the reasons stated, and so ought the whole eleven. Should such an offer be made and declined, and those states, should they be kept out, a singular spectacle would be presented — a complete reversal of positions would be presented. In 1861 these states thought they could not remain safely in the Union without new guarantees; and now, when they agree to resume their former practical relations in the Union, under the Constitution, the other states turn upon them and say they cannot permit them to do so safely to their interests without new constitutional guarantees. The Southern states would thus present themselves as willing for immediate union, under the Constitution, while it would be the Northern states opposed to it. The former disunionists would thereby become the unionists, and the former unionists the practical disunionists.

7.

Report of the Joint Committee on Reconstruction

The Joint Committee on Reconstruction was created by Congress in December 1865 to investigate and make recommendations on all bills relating to Reconstruction. The Committee consisted of nine representatives and six senators; only three members were Democrats, the dominant Republican bloc being led by Thaddeus Stevens. The Committee's Report of June 20, 1866, on the status of the South reflected the Radical views of the majority of the members. An extract from the introduction to the Report is reprinted here.

Source: *Report of the Joint Committee on Reconstruction,* 39 Congress, 1 Session, Washington, 1866, Pt. 3, pp. vii-xxi.

WHEN CONGRESS ASSEMBLED in December last, the people of most of the states lately in rebellion had, under the advice of the President, organized local governments, and some of them had acceded to the terms proposed by him. In his annual message he stated, in general terms, what had been done, but he did not see fit to communicate the details for the information of Congress. While in this and in a subsequent message the President urged the speedy restoration of these states, and expressed the opinion that their condition was such as to justify their restoration, yet it is quite obvious that Congress must either have acted blindly on that opinion of the President, or proceeded to obtain the information requisite for intelligent action on the subject. The impropriety of proceeding wholly on the judgment of any one man, however exalted his station, in a matter involving the welfare of the republic in all future time, or of adopting any plan, coming from any source, without fully understanding all its bearings and comprehending its full effect, was apparent.

The first step, therefore, was to obtain the required information. A call was accordingly made on the President for the information in his possession as to what had been done, in order that Congress might judge for itself as to the grounds of the belief expressed by him in the fitness of states recently in rebellion to participate fully in the conduct of national affairs. This information was not immediately communicated. When the response was finally made, some six weeks after your committee had been in actual session, it was found that the evidence upon which the President seemed to have based his suggestions was incomplete and unsatisfactory. Authenticated copies of the new constitutions and ordinances adopted by the conventions in three of the states had been submitted, extracts from newspapers furnished scanty information as to the action of one other state, and nothing appears to have been communicated as to the remainder. There was no evidence of the loyalty of those who had participated in these conventions, and in one state alone was any proposition made to submit the action of the conventions to the final judgment of the people. . . .

The evidence of an intense hostility to the federal Union, and an equally intense love of the late Confederacy, nurtured by the war, is decisive. While it appears that nearly all are willing to submit, at least for the time being, to the federal authority, it is equally clear that the ruling motive is a desire to obtain the advantages which will be derived from a representation in Congress. Officers of the Union Army, on duty, and Northern men who go South to engage in business, are generally detested and proscribed. Southern men who adhered to the Union are bitterly hated and relentlessly persecuted. In some localities prosecutions have been instituted in state courts against Union officers for acts done in the line of official duty, and similar prosecutions are threatened elsewhere as soon as the United States troops are removed. All such demonstrations show a state of feeling against which it is unmistakably necessary to guard.

The testimony is conclusive that after the collapse of the Confederacy the feeling of the people of the rebellious states was that of abject submission. Having appealed to the tribunal of arms, they had no hope except that, by the magnanimity of their conquerors, their lives, and possibly their property, might be preserved. Unfortunately, the general issue of pardons to persons who had been prominent in the Rebellion, and the feeling of kindliness and conciliation manifested by the executive, and very generally indicated through the Northern press, had the effect to render whole communities forgetful of the crime they had committed, defiant toward the federal government, and regardless of their duties as citizens.

The conciliatory measures of the government do not seem to have been met even halfway. The bitterness and defiance exhibited toward the United States under such circumstances is without a parallel in the history of the world. In return for our leniency we receive only an insulting denial of our authority. In return for our kind desire for the resumption of fraternal relations we receive only an insolent assumption of rights and privileges long since forfeited. The crime we have punished is paraded as a virtue, and the principles of republican government which we have vindicated at so terrible a cost are denounced as unjust and oppressive.

If we add to this evidence the fact that, although peace has been declared by the President, he has not, to this day, deemed it safe to restore the writ of habeas corpus, to relieve the insurrectionary states of martial law, nor to withdraw the troops from many localities, and that the commanding general deems an increase of the army indispensable to the preservation of order and the protection of loyal and well-disposed people in the South, the proof of a condition of feeling hostile to the Union and dangerous to the government throughout the insurrectionary states would seem to be overwhelming.

With such evidence before them, it is the opinion of your committee:

1. That the states lately in rebellion were, at the close of the war, disorganized communities, without civil government, and without constitutions or other forms, by virtue of which political relations could legally exist between them and the federal government.

2. That Congress cannot be expected to recognize as valid the election of representatives from disorganized communities, which, from the very nature of the case, were unable to present their claim to representation under those established and recognized rules, the observance of which has been hitherto required.

3. That Congress would not be justified in admitting such communities to a participation in the government of the country without first providing such constitutional or other guarantees as will tend to secure the civil rights of all citizens of the republic; a just equality of representation; protection against claims founded in rebellion and crime; a temporary restoration of the right of suffrage to those who have not actively participated in the efforts to destroy the Union and overthrow the government, and the exclusion from positions of public trust of, at least, a portion of those whose crimes have proved them to be enemies to the Union and unworthy of public confidence.

Your committee will, perhaps, hardly be deemed excusable for extending this report further; but inasmuch as immediate and un-conditional representation of the states lately in rebellion is demanded as a matter of right, and delay and even hesitation is denounced as grossly oppressive and unjust, as well as unwise and impolitic, it may not be amiss again to call attention to a few undisputed and notorious facts, and the principles of public law applicable thereto, in order that the propriety of that claim may be fully considered and well understood.

The state of Tennessee occupies a position distinct from all the other insurrectionary states, and has been the subject of a separate report, which your committee have not thought it expedient to disturb. Whether Congress shall see fit to make that state the subject of separate action, or to include it in the same category with all others so far as concerns the imposition of preliminary conditions, it is not within the province of this committee either to determine or advise.

To ascertain whether any of the so-called Confederate States "are entitled to be represented in either house of Congress," the essential inquiry is, whether there is, in any one of them, a constituency qualified to be represented in Congress. The question how far persons claiming seats in either house possess the credentials necessary to enable them to represent a duly qualified constituency is one for the consideration of each house separately, after the preliminary question shall have been finally determined.

We now propose to restate, as briefly as possible, the general facts and principles applicable to all the states recently in rebellion:

First. The seats of the senators and representatives from the so-called Confederate States became vacant in the year 1861, during the second session of the Thirty-sixth Congress, by the voluntary withdrawal of their incumbents, with the sanction and by direction of the legislatures or conventions of their respective states. This was done as a hostile act against the Constitution and government of the United States, with a declared intent to overthrow the same by forming a Southern confederation. This act of declared hostility was speedily followed by an organization of the same states into a Confederacy, which levied and waged war, by sea and land, against the United States.

This war continued more than four years, within which period the Rebel armies besieged the national capital, invaded the loyal states, burned their towns and cities, robbed their citizens, destroyed more than 250,000 loyal soldiers, and imposed an increased national burden of not less than $3,500 million, of which $700 million or $800 million have already been met and paid. From the time these confederated states thus withdrew their representation in Congress and levied war against the United States, the great mass of their people became and were insurgents, rebels, traitors, and all of them assumed and occupied the political, legal, and practical relation of enemies of the United States. This position is established by acts of Congress and judicial decisions, and is recognized repeatedly by the President in public proclamations, documents, and speeches.

Second. The states thus confederated prosecuted their war against the United States to final arbitrament, and did not cease until all their armies were captured, their military power destroyed, their civil officers, state and confederate, taken prisoners or put to flight, every vestige of state and confederate government obliterated, their territory overrun and occupied by the federal armies, and their people reduced to the condition of enemies conquered in war, entitled only by public law to such rights, privileges, and conditions as might be vouchsafed by the conqueror. This position is also established by judicial decisions, and is recognized by the President in public proclamations, documents, and speeches.

Third. Having voluntarily deprived themselves of representation in Congress for the criminal purpose of destroying the Federal Union, and having reduced themselves, by the act of levying war, to the condition of public enemies, they have no right to complain of temporary exclusion from Congress; but, on the contrary, having voluntarily renounced the right to representation, and disqualified themselves by crime from participating in the government, the burden now rests upon them, before claiming to be reinstated in their former condition, to show that they are qualified to resume federal relations. In order to do this, they must prove that they have established, with the consent of the people, republican forms of government in harmony with the Constitution and laws of the United States, that all hostile purposes have ceased, and should give adequate guarantees against future treason and rebellion — guarantees which shall prove satisfactory to the government against which they rebelled, and by whose arms they were subdued.

Fourth. Having, by this treasonable withdrawal from Congress, and by flagrant rebellion and war, forfeited all civil and political rights and privileges under the Federal Constitution, they can only be restored thereto by the permission and authority of that constitutional power against which they rebelled and by which they were subdued.

Fifth. These rebellious enemies were conquered by the people of the United States, acting through all the coordinate branches of the government, and not by the Executive Department alone. The powers of conqueror are not so vested in the President that he can fix and regulate the terms of settlement and confer congressional representation on conquered rebels and traitors. Nor can he, in any way, qualify enemies of the government to exercise its lawmaking power. The authority to restore rebels to political power in the federal government can be exercised only with the concurrence of all the departments in which political power is vested; and hence the several proclamations of the President to the people of the Confederate States cannot be considered as extending beyond the purposes declared, and can only be regarded as provisional permission by the commander in chief of the army to do certain acts, the effect and validity whereof is to be determined by the constitutional government, and not solely by the executive power.

Sixth. The question before Congress is, then, whether conquered enemies have the right, and shall be permitted at their own pleasure and on their own terms, to participate in making laws for their conquerors; whether conquered Rebels may change their theater of operations from the battlefield, where they were defeated and overthrown, to the halls of Congress, and, through their representatives, seize upon the government which they fought to destroy; whether the national Treasury, the Army of the nation, its Navy, its forts and arsenals, its whole civil administration, its credit, its pensioners, the widows and orphans of those who perished in the war, the public honor, peace and safety, shall all be turned over to the keeping of its recent enemies without delay, and without imposing such conditions as, in the opinion of Congress, the security of the country and its institutions may demand.

Seventh. The history of mankind exhibits no example of such madness and folly. The instinct of self-preservation protests against it. The surrender by Grant to Lee, and by Sherman to Johnston, would have been disasters of less magnitude, for new armies could have been raised, new battles fought, and the government saved. The anticoercive policy, which, under pretext of avoiding bloodshed, allowed the rebellion to take form and gather force, would be surpassed in infamy by the matchless wickedness that would now surrender the halls of Congress to those so recently in rebellion until proper precautions shall have been taken to secure the national faith and the national safety.

Eighth. As has been shown in this report, and in the evidence submitted, no proof has been afforded to Congress of a constituency in any one of the so-called Confederate States, unless we except the state of Tennessee, qualified to elect senators and representatives in Congress. No state constitution, or amendment to a state constitution, has had the sanction of the people. All the so-called legislation of state conventions and legislatures has been had under military dictation. If the President may, at his will, and under his own authority, whether as military commander or chief executive, qualify persons to appoint senators and elect representatives, and empower others to appoint and elect them, he thereby practically controls the organization of the Legislative Department. The constitutional form of government is thereby practically destroyed, and its powers absorbed in the executive. And while your committee do not for a moment impute to the President any such design, but cheerfully concede to him the most patriotic motives, they cannot but look with alarm upon a precedent so fraught with danger to the republic.

Ninth. The necessity of providing adequate safeguards for the future, before restoring the insurrectionary states to a participation in the direction of public affairs, is apparent from the bitter hostility to the government and people of the United States yet existing throughout the conquered territory, as proved incontestably by the testimony of many witnesses and by undisputed facts.

Tenth. The conclusion of your committee, therefore, is that the so-called Confederate States are not, at present, entitled to representation in the Congress of the United States; that, before allowing such representation, adequate security for future peace and safety should be required; that this can only be found in such changes of the organic law as shall determine the civil rights and privileges of all citizens in all parts of the republic, shall place representation on an equitable basis, shall fix a stigma upon treason, and protect the loyal people against future claims for the expenses incurred in support of rebellion and for manumitted slaves, together with an express grant of power in Congress to enforce those provisions. To this end they offer a joint resolution for amending the Constitution of the United States, and the two several bills designed to carry the same into effect, before referred to.

Before closing this report, your committee beg leave to state that the specific recommendations submitted by them are the result of mutual concession, after a long and careful comparison of conflicting opinions. Upon a question of such magnitude, infinitely important as it is to the future of the republic, it was not to be expected that all should think alike. Sensible of the imperfections of the scheme, your committee submit it to Congress as the best they could agree upon, in the hope that its imperfections may be cured, and its deficiencies supplied, by legislative wisdom; and that, when finally adopted, it may tend to restore peace and harmony to the whole country, and to place our republican institutions on a more stable foundation.

8.

DAVID DAVIS: *Ex Parte Milligan*

As a wartime measure, Congress in March 1863 authorized President Lincoln to suspend the writ of habeas corpus in cases where officers held civilians for offenses against the military. Lambdin P. Milligan, a civilian, was arrested in 1864 for inciting insurrection, tried and found guilty by a military tribunal, and sentenced to be hanged. He petitioned the U.S. Circuit Court for the District of Indiana for a writ of habeas corpus. The case went to the U.S. Supreme Court in 1866. The Court's decision condemned military trials for civilians in areas where the civil courts were functioning. The decision became unpopular with Radical Republicans, who viewed it as casting doubt on the legality of their military occupation of the South. Portions of the opinion of the Court, given by Justice Davis, are reprinted below.

Source: 4 Wallace 20.

THE CONTROLLING QUESTION in the case is this: Upon the *facts* stated in Milligan's petition and the exhibits filed, had the military commission mentioned in it *jurisdiction*, legally, to try and sentence him? Milligan, not a resident of one of the rebellious states or a prisoner of war, but a citizen of Indiana for twenty years past, and never in the military or naval service, is, while at his home, arrested by the military power of the United States, imprisoned, and, on certain criminal charges preferred against him, tried, convicted, and sentenced to be hanged by a military commission, organized under the direction of the military commander of the military district of Indiana. Had this tribunal the *legal* power and authority to try and punish this man?

No graver question was ever considered by this Court, nor one which more nearly concerns the rights of the whole people; for it is the birthright of every American citizen when charged with crime to be tried and punished according to law. The power of punishment is alone through the means which the laws have provided for that purpose; and if they are ineffectual, there is an immunity from punishment, no matter how great an offender the individual may be or how much his crimes may have shocked the sense of justice of the country or endangered its safety. By the protection of the law, human rights are secured; withdraw that protection, and they are at the mercy of wicked rulers or the clamor of an excited people.

If there was law to justify this military trial, it is not our province to interfere; if there was not, it is our duty to declare the nullity of the whole proceedings. The decision of this question does not depend on argument or judicial precedents, numerous and highly illustrative as they are. These precedents inform us of the extent of the struggle to preserve liberty and to relieve those in civil life from military trials. The founders of our government were familiar with the history of that struggle; and secured in a written Constitution every right which the people had wrested from power during a contest of ages. By that Constitution and the laws authorized by it this question must be determined.

The provisions of that instrument on the administration of criminal justice are too plain and direct to leave room for misconstruction or doubt of their true meaning. Those applicable to this case are found in that clause of the original Constitution which says that "the trial of all crimes, except in case of impeachment, shall be by jury"; and in the 4th, 5th, and 6th articles of the amendments. The 4th proclaims the right to be secure in person and effects against unreasonable search and seizure; and directs that a judicial warrant shall not issue "without proof of probable cause supported by oath or affirmation." The 5th declares "that no person shall be held to answer for a capital or otherwise infamous crime unless on presentment by a grand jury, except in cases arising in the land or naval forces, or in the militia, when in actual service in time of war or public danger, nor be deprived of life, liberty, or property, without due process of law." And the 6th guarantees the right of trial by jury, in such manner and with such regulations that, with upright judges, impartial juries, and an able bar, the innocent will be saved and the guilty punished.

It is in these words: "In all criminal prosecutions the accused shall enjoy the right to a speedy and public trial by an impartial jury of the state and district wherein the crime shall have been committed, which district shall have been previously ascertained by law, and to be informed of the nature and cause of the accusation, to be confronted with the witnesses against him, to have compulsory process for obtaining witnesses in his favor, and to have the assistance of counsel for his defense." These securities for personal liberty thus embodied were such as wisdom and experience had demonstrated to be necessary for the protection of those accused of crime. And so strong was the sense of the country of their importance, and so jealous were the people that these rights, highly prized, might be denied them by implication, that when the original Constitution was proposed for adoption it encountered severe opposition; and, but for the belief that it would be so amended as to embrace them, it would never have been ratified. . . .

Have any of the rights guaranteed by the Constitution been violated in the case of Milligan? And, if so, what are they? . . .

This Court has judicial knowledge that in Indiana the federal authority was always unopposed and its courts always open to hear criminal accusations and redress grievances; and no usage of war could sanction a military trial there for any offense whatever of a citizen in civil life, in nowise connected with the military service. Congress could grant no such power; and to the honor of our national legislature be it said, it has never been provoked by the state of the country even to attempt its exercise. One of the plainest constitutional provisions was, therefore, infringed when Milligan was tried by a court not ordained and established by Congress, and not composed of judges appointed during good behavior.

Why was he not delivered to the Circuit Court of Indiana to be proceeded against according to law? No reason of necessity could be urged against it; because Congress had declared penalties against the offenses charged, provided for their punishment, and directed that court to hear and determine them. And soon after this military tribunal was ended, the Circuit Court met, peacefully transacted its business, and adjourned. It needed no bayonets to protect it and required no military aid to execute its judgments. It was held in a state eminently distinguished for patriotism, by judges commissioned during the rebellion, who were provided with juries, upright, intelligent, and selected by a marshal appointed by the President. The government had no right to conclude that Milligan, if guilty, would not receive, in that court, merited punishment; for its records disclose that it was constantly engaged in the trial of similar offenses and was never interrupted in its administration of criminal justice.

If it was dangerous, in the distracted condition of affairs, to leave Milligan unrestrained of his liberty because he "conspired against the government, afforded aid and comfort to rebels, and incited the people to insurrection," the *law* said arrest him, confine him closely, render him powerless to do further mischief; and then present his

case to the grand jury of the district, with proofs of his guilt, and, if indicted, try him according to the course of the common law. If this had been done, the Constitution would have been vindicated, the law of 1863 enforced, and the securities for personal liberty preserved and defended.

Another guarantee of freedom was broken when Milligan was denied a trial by jury. . . . *This right* — one of the most valuable in a free country — is preserved to everyone accused of crime who is not attached to the Army or Navy or militia in actual service. . . . *All other persons*, citizens of states where the courts are open, if charged with crime, are guaranteed the inestimable privilege of trial by jury. This privilege is a vital principle, underlying the whole administration of criminal justice; it is not held by sufferance and cannot be frittered away on any plea of state or political necessity.

When peace prevails and the authority of the government is undisputed, there is no difficulty of preserving the safeguards of liberty; for the ordinary modes of trial are never neglected, and no one wishes it otherwise; but if society is disturbed by civil commotion — if the passions of men are aroused and the restraints of law weakened, if not disregarded — these safeguards need, and should receive, the watchful care of those entrusted with the guardianship of the Constitution and laws. In no other way can we transmit to posterity unimpaired the blessings of liberty, consecrated by the sacrifices of the Revolution.

It is claimed that martial law covers with its broad mantle the proceedings of this military commission. The proposition is this — that in a time of war the commander of an armed force (if in his opinion the exigencies of the country demand it, and of which he is to judge) has the power, within the lines of his military district, to suspend all civil rights and their remedies and subject

David Davis; justice who offered the majority opinion in Milligan's case

citizens as well as soldiers to the rule of *his will,* and in the exercise of his lawful authority cannot be restrained, except by his superior officer or the President of the United States.

If this position is sound to the extent claimed, then, when war exists, foreign or domestic, and the country is subdivided into military departments for mere convenience, the commander of one of them can, if he chooses, within his limits, on the plea of necessity, with the approval of the Executive, substitute military force for and to the exclusion of the laws, and punish all persons as he thinks right and proper, without fixed or certain rules.

The statement of this proposition shows its importance; for, if true, republican government is a failure, and there is an end of liberty regulated by law. Martial law, established on such a basis, destroys every guarantee of the Constitution and effectually renders the "military independent of and superior to the civil power" — the attempt to do which by the king of Great Britain

was deemed by our fathers such an offense that they assigned it to the world as one of the causes which impelled them to declare their independence. Civil liberty and this kind of martial law cannot endure together; the antagonism is irreconcilable; and, in the conflict, one or the other must perish.

This nation, as experience has proved, cannot always remain at peace and has no right to expect that it will always have wise and humane rulers, sincerely attached to the principles of the Constitution. Wicked men, ambitious of power, with hatred of liberty and contempt of law, may fill the place once occupied by Washington and Lincoln; and if this right is conceded and the calamities of war again befall us, the dangers to human liberty are frightful to contemplate.

If our fathers had failed to provide for just such a contingency, they would have been false to the trust reposed in them. They knew — the history of the world told them — the nation they were founding, be its existence short or long, would be involved in war; how often or how long continued, human foresight could not tell; and that unlimited power, wherever lodged at such a time, was especially hazardous to freemen. For this, and other equally weighty reasons, they secured the inheritance they had fought to maintain by incorporating in a written Constitution the safeguards which *time* had proved were essential to its preservation. Not one of these safeguards can the President, or Congress, or the judiciary disturb, except the one concerning the writ of habeas corpus.

It is essential to the safety of every government that, in a great crisis like the one we have just passed through, there should be a power somewhere of suspending the writ of habeas corpus. In every war there are men of previously good character wicked enough to counsel their fellow citizens to resist the measures deemed necessary by a good government to sustain its just authority and overthrow its enemies; and their influence may lead to dangerous combinations. In the emergency of the times, an immediate public investigation according to law may not be possible; and, yet, the peril to the country may be too imminent to suffer such persons to go at large. Unquestionably, there is then an exigency which demands that the government, if it should see fit in the exercise of a proper discretion to make arrests, should not be required to produce the persons arrested in answer to a writ of habeas corpus.

The Constitution goes no further. It does not say after a writ of habeas corpus is denied a citizen that he shall be tried otherwise than by the course of the common law; if it had intended this result, it was easy by the use of direct words to have accomplished it. The illustrious men who framed that instrument were guarding the foundations of civil liberty against the abuses of unlimited power; they were full of wisdom, and the lessons of history informed them that a trial by an established court, assisted by an impartial jury, was the only sure way of protecting the citizen against oppression and wrong. Knowing this, they limited the suspension to one great right and left the rest to remain forever inviolable.

But it is insisted that the safety of the country in time of war demands that this broad claim for martial law shall be sustained. If this were true, it could be well said that a country, preserved at the sacrifice of all the cardinal principles of liberty, is not worth the cost of preservation. Happily, it is not so.

It will be borne in mind that this is not a question of the power to proclaim martial law when war exists in a community and the courts and civil authorities are overthrown. Nor is it a question what rule a military commander, at the head of his army, can impose on states in rebellion to cripple their resources and quell the insur-

rection. The jurisdiction claimed is much more extensive. The necessities of the service during the late rebellion required that the loyal states should be placed within the limits of certain military districts and commanders appointed in them; and it is urged that this, in a military sense, constituted them the theater of military operations; and, as in this case, Indiana had been and was again threatened with invasion by the enemy, the occasion was furnished to establish martial law.

The conclusion does not follow from the premises. If armies were collected in Indiana, they were to be employed in another locality where the laws were obstructed and the national authority disputed. On *her* soil there was no hostile foot; if once invaded, that invasion was at an end, and with it all pretext for martial law. Martial law cannot arise from a *threatened* invasion. The necessity must be actual and present; the invasion real, such as effectually closes the courts and deposes the civil administration.

It is difficult to see how the *safety* of the country required martial law in Indiana. If any of her citizens were plotting treason, the power of arrest could secure them until the government was prepared for their trial, when the courts were open and ready to try them. It was as easy to protect witnesses before a civil as a military tribunal; and as there could be no wish to convict, except on sufficient legal evidence, surely an ordained and established court was better able to judge of this than a military tribunal composed of gentlemen not trained to the profession of the law.

It follows, from what has been said on this subject, that there are occasions when martial rule can be properly applied. If, in foreign invasion or civil war, the courts are actually closed, and it is impossible to administer criminal justice according to law, *then*, on the theater of active military operations, where war really prevails, there is a necessity to furnish a substitute for the civil authority, thus overthrown, to preserve the safety of the army and society; and as no power is left but the military, it is allowed to govern by martial rule until the laws can have their free course. As necessity creates the rule, so it limits its duration; for, if this government is continued *after* the courts are reinstated, it is a gross usurpation of power. Martial rule can never exist where the courts are open, and in the proper and unobstructed exercise of their jurisdiction. It is also confined to the locality of actual war. Because, during the late rebellion it could have been enforced in Virginia, where the national authority was overturned and the courts driven out, it does not follow that it should obtain in Indiana, where that authority was never disputed, and justice was always administered. And so in the case of a foreign invasion, martial rule may become a necessity in one state, when, in another, it would be "mere lawless violence." . . .

If the military trial of Milligan was contrary to law, then he was entitled, on the facts stated in his petition, to be discharged from custody by the terms of the act of Congress of March 3, 1863. The provisions of this law having been considered in a previous part of this opinion, we will not restate the views there presented. Milligan avers he was a citizen of Indiana, not in the military or naval service, and was detained in close confinement, by order of the President, from the 5th day of October, 1864, until the 2nd day of January, 1865, when the Circuit Court for the District of Indiana, with a grand jury, convened in session at Indianapolis; and afterward, on the 27th day of the same month, adjourned without finding an indictment or presentment against him. If these averments were true (and their truth is conceded for the purposes of this case), the court was required to liberate him on taking certain oaths prescribed by the law, and entering into recognizance for his good behavior.

But it is insisted that Milligan was a prisoner of war, and, therefore, excluded from the privileges of the statute. It is not easy to see how he can be treated as a prisoner of war, when he lived in Indiana for the past twenty years, was arrested there, and had not been, during the late troubles, a resident of any of the states in rebellion. If in Indiana he conspired with bad men to assist the enemy, he is punishable for it in the courts of Indiana; but, when tried for the offense, he cannot plead the rights of war; for he was not engaged in legal acts of hostility against the government, and only such persons, when captured, are prisoners of war. If he cannot enjoy the immunities attaching to the character of a prisoner of war, how can he be subject to their pains and penalties?

I have come home to look after my fences.
JOHN SHERMAN, speech to his neighbors in Mansfield, Ohio, *c.* 1866, referring to the fences around his farm. Said to be the origin of the political phrase.

9.

Innes Randolph: "The Good Old Rebel"

"The Good Old Rebel" was reportedly written by Major Innes Randolph, a Virginian and an officer on the staff of General "Jeb" Stuart. It was sung to the tune of "Joe Bowers," a favorite camp song of the Forty-niners. The song was popular with unreconstructed Rebels, many of whom headed for Texas and Mexico in their stubborn effort to avoid any allegiance to the United States. Edward VII, who heard it at a reception in London, called it "that fine American song with the cuss words in it" — which is a fair enough description.

✺ THE GOOD OLD REBEL

Oh, I'm a good old Rebel,
Now that's just what I am,
For this "fair land of Freedom"
I do not care a damn.
I'm glad I fit against it —
I only wish we'd won;
And I don't want no pardon
For anything I've done.

I hates the Constitution,
This great Republic, too;
I hates the Freedmen's Bureau,
In uniforms of blue.
I hates the nasty eagle,
With all his brag and fuss;
But the lyin', thievin' Yankees,
I hates 'em wuss and wuss.

I hates the Yankee nation,
And everything they do;
I hates the Declaration
Of Independence, too;
I hates the glorious Union,
'Tis dripping with our blood;
And I hates the striped banner —
I fit it all I could.

I followed old Mars' Robert
For four year, near about,
Got wounded in three places,
And starved at Pint Lookout.
I cotch the roomatism
A-campin' in the snow,
But I killed a chance of Yankees —
And I'd like to kill some mo'.

Three hundred thousand Yankees
Is stiff in Southern dust;
We got three hundred thousand
Befo' they conquered us.
They died of Southern fever
And Southern steel and shot;
And I wish it was three millions
Instead of what we got.

I can't take up my musket
And fight 'em now no mo',
But I ain't a-goin' to love 'em,
Now this is sartin sho';
And I don't want no pardon
For what I was and am,
And I won't be reconstructed,
And I don't care a damn.

10.

Herman Melville: Consideration for Our Late Enemies

Herman Melville, an ardent opponent of both slavery and war, turned his attention from prose to poetry during the Civil War and published a collection of poems in 1866 under the title Battle-Pieces and Aspects of the War. *The collection was unique among the works of Northern authors for its magnanimous attitude toward both sides in the conflict. Sometime during the summer of 1866 Melville appended to* Battle-Pieces *the following essay, in which he pleaded for a humane policy of Reconstruction. There were several indications at the time that the nation might follow such a policy: The Fourteenth Amendment, guaranteeing civil rights for African Americans, had yet to be ratified, and the Radical members of Congress were withholding their more severe attacks on the South until after the fall elections.*

Source: *Battle-Pieces and Aspects of the War*, New York, 1866, Supplement.

WERE I FASTIDIOUSLY ANXIOUS for the symmetry of this book, it would close with the notes. But the times are such that patriotism — not free from solicitude — urges a claim overriding all literary scruples.

It is more than a year since the memorable surrender, but events have not yet rounded themselves into completion. Not justly can we complain of this. There has been an upheaval affecting the basis of things; to altered circumstances complicated adaptions are to be made; there are difficulties great and novel. But is reason still waiting for passion to spend itself? We have sung of the soldiers and sailors, but who shall hymn the politicians?

In view of the infinite desirableness of re-establishment, and considering that, so far as feeling is concerned, it depends not mainly on the temper in which the South regards the North but rather conversely; one who never was a blind adherent feels constrained to submit some thoughts, counting on the indulgence of his countrymen.

And, first, it may be said that, if among the feelings and opinions growing immediately out of a great civil convulsion, there are any which time shall modify or do away, they are presumably those of a less temperate and charitable cast.

There seems no reason why patriotism and narrowness should go together, or why intellectual impartiality should be confounded with political trimming, or why serviceable truth should keep cloistered because not partisan. Yet the work of reconstruction, if admitted to be feasible at all, demands little but common sense and Christian charity. Little but these? These are much.

Some of us are concerned because as yet the South shows no penitence. But what exactly do we mean by this? Since down to the close of the war she never confessed any for braving it, the only penitence now left her is that which springs solely from the sense of discomfiture; and since this evidently would be a contrition hypocritical, it would be unworthy in us to demand it. Certain it is that penitence, in the sense of voluntary humiliation, will never be displayed. Nor does this afford just ground for unreserved condemnation. It is enough, for all practical purposes, if the South have been taught by the terrors of civil war to feel that secession, like slavery, is against destiny; that both now lie buried in one grave; that her fate is linked with ours; and that together we comprise the nation.

The clouds of heroes who battled for the Union it is needless to eulogize here. But how of the soldiers on the other side? And when of a free community we name the soldiers, we thereby name the people. It was in subserviency to the slave interest that secession was plotted; but it was under the plea, plausibly urged, that certain inestimable rights guaranteed by the Constitution were directly menaced that the people of the South were cajoled into revolution. Through the arts of the conspirators and the perversity of fortune, the most sensitive love of liberty was entrapped into the support of a war whose implied end was the erecting in our advanced century of an Anglo-American empire based upon the systematic degradation of man.

Spite this clinging reproach, however, signal military virtues and achievements have conferred upon the Confederate arms historic fame, and upon certain of the commanders a renown extending beyond the sea — a renown which we of the North could not suppress, even if we would. In personal character, also, not a few of the military leaders of the South enforce forbearance; the memory of others the North refrains from disparaging; and some, with more or less of reluctance, she can respect. Posterity, sympathizing with our convictions, but removed from our passions, may perhaps go farther here. If George IV

could, out of the graceful instinct of a gentleman, raise an honorable monument in the great fane of Christendom over the remains of the enemy of his dynasty, Charles Edward, the invader of England and victor in the rout at Prestonpans — upon whose head the king's ancestor but one reign removed had set a price — is it probable that the grandchildren of General Grant will pursue with rancor, or slur by sour neglect, the memory of "Stonewall" Jackson?

But the South herself is not wanting in recent histories and biographies which record the deeds of her chieftains — writings freely published at the North by loyal houses, widely read here, and with a deep though saddened interest. By students of the war such works are hailed as welcome accessories and tending to the completeness of the record.

Supposing a happy issue out of present perplexities, then, in the generation next to come, Southerners there will be yielding allegiance to the Union, feeling all their interests bound up in it, and yet cherishing unrebuked that kind of feeling for the memory of the soldiers of the fallen Confederacy that Burns, Scott, and the Ettrick Shepherd felt for the memory of the gallant clansmen ruined through their fidelity to the Stuarts — a feeling whose passion was tempered by the poetry imbuing it, and which in nowise affected their loyalty to the Georges, and which, it may be added, indirectly contributed excellent things to literature. But, setting this view aside, dishonorable would it be in the South were she willing to abandon to shame the memory of brave men who, with signal personal disinterestedness, warred in her behalf, though from motives, as we believe, so deplorably astray.

Patriotism is not baseness, neither is it inhumanity. The mourners who this summer bear flowers to the mounds of the Virginian and Georgian dead are, in their domestic bereavement and proud affection, as sacred in the eye of heaven as are those who go with similar offerings of tender grief and love into the cemeteries of our Northern martyrs. And yet, in one aspect, how needless to point the contrast.

Cherishing such sentiments, it will hardly occasion surprise that, in looking over the battle pieces in the foregoing collection, I have been tempted to withdraw or modify some of them, fearful lest in presenting, though but dramatically and by way of a poetic record, the passions and epithets of civil war, I might be contributing to a bitterness which every sensible American must wish at an end. So, too, with the emotion of victory as reproduced on some pages, and particularly toward the close. It should not be construed into an exultation misapplied — an exultation as ungenerous as unwise, and made to minister, however indirectly, to that kind of censoriousness too apt to be produced in certain natures by success after trying reverses. Zeal is not of necessity religion, neither is it always of the same essence with poetry or patriotism.

There were excesses which marked the conflict, most of which are perhaps inseparable from a civil strife so intense and prolonged, and involving warfare in some border countries new and imperfectly civilized. Barbarities also there were, for which the Southern people collectively can hardly be held responsible, though perpetrated by ruffians in their name. But surely other qualities — exalted ones — courage and fortitude matchless, were likewise displayed, and largely; and justly may these be held the characteristic traits, and not the former.

In this view, what Northern writer, however patriotic, but must revolt from acting on paper a part anyway akin to that of the live dog to the dead lion; and yet it is right to rejoice for our triumph, so far as it may justly imply an advance for our whole country and for humanity.

Let it be held no reproach to anyone that he pleads for reasonable consideration for our late enemies, now stricken down and unavoidably debarred, for the time, from speaking through authorized agencies for themselves. Nothing has been urged here in the foolish hope of conciliating those men — few in number, we trust — who have resolved never to be reconciled to the Union. On such hearts everything is thrown away except it be religious commiseration, and the sincerest. Yet let them call to mind that unhappy secessionist [Edmund Ruffin], not a military man, who, with impious alacrity, fired the first shot of the Civil War at Sumter, and a little more than four years afterward fired the last one into his own heart at Richmond.

Noble was the gesture into which patriotic passion surprised the people in a utilitarian time and country; yet the glory of the war falls short of its pathos — a pathos which now at last ought to disarm all animosity.

How many and earnest thoughts still rise, and how hard to repress them. We feel what past years have been, and years, unretarded years, shall come. May we all have moderation; may we all show candor. Though, perhaps, nothing could ultimately have averted the strife and though to treat of human actions is to deal wholly with second causes, nevertheless, let us not cover up or try to extenuate what, humanly speaking, is the truth; namely, that those unfraternal denunciations, continued through years, and which at last inflamed to deeds that ended in bloodshed, were reciprocal; and that, had the preponderating strength and the prospect of its unlimited increase lain on the other side, on ours might have lain those actions which now in our late opponents we stigmatize under the name of Rebellion.

As frankly let us own — what it would be unbecoming to parade were foreigners concerned — that our triumph was won not more by skill and bravery than by superior resources and crushing numbers; that it was a triumph, too, over a people for years politically misled by designing men, and also by some honestly erring men, who, from their position, could not have been otherwise than broadly influential; a people who, though, indeed, they sought to perpetuate the curse of slavery, and even extend it, were not the authors of it but (less fortunate, not less righteous than we) were the fated inheritors; a people who, having a like origin with ourselves, share essentially in whatever worthy qualities we may possess. No one can add to the lasting reproach which hopeless defeat has now cast upon secession by withholding the recognition of these verities.

Surely we ought to take it to heart that the kind of pacification, based upon principles operating equally all over the land, which lovers of their country yearn for, and which our arms, though signally triumphant, did not bring about, and which lawmaking, however anxious or energetic or repressive, never by itself can achieve, may yet be largely aided by generosity of sentiment public and private. Some revisionary legislation and adaptive is indispensable; but with this should harmoniously work another kind of prudence, not unallied with entire magnanimity. Benevolence and policy — Christianity and Machiavelli — dissuade from penal severities toward the subdued. Abstinence here is as obligatory as considerate care for our unfortunate fellowmen late in bonds, and, if observed, would equally prove to be wise forecast. The great qualities of the South, those attested in the war, we can perilously alienate, or we may make them nationally available at need.

The blacks, in their infant pupilage to freedom, appeal to the sympathies of every humane mind. The paternal guardianship which, for the interval, government exercises over them was prompted equally by duty and benevolence. Yet such kindliness should not be allowed to exclude kindliness to communities who stand nearer to us in nature. For the future of the freed slaves we

Yale University Library
Herman Melville

may well be concerned; but the future of the whole country, involving the future of the blacks, urges a paramount claim upon our anxiety. Effective benignity, like the Nile, is not narrow in its bounty, and true policy is always broad.

To be sure, it is vain to seek to glide, with molded words, over the difficulties of the situation. And for them who are neither partisans, nor enthusiasts, nor theorists, nor cynics, there are some doubts not readily to be solved. And there are fears. Why is not the cessation of war now at length attended with the settled calm of peace? Wherefore in a clear sky do we still turn our eyes toward the South, as the Neapolitan, months after the eruption, turns his toward Vesuvius? Do we dread lest the repose may be deceptive? In the recent convulsion has the crater but shifted?

Let us revere that sacred uncertainty which forever impends over men and nations. Those of us who always abhorred slavery as an atheistical iniquity, gladly we join in the exulting chorus of humanity over its downfall. But we should remember that emancipation was accomplished not by deliberate legislation; only through agonized violence could so mighty a result be effected. In our natural solicitude to confirm the benefit of liberty to the blacks, let us forbear from measures of dubious constitutional rightfulness toward our white countrymen — measures of a nature to provoke, among other of the last evils, exterminating hatred of race toward race.

In imagination let us place ourselves in the unprecedented position of the Southerners — their position as regards the millions of ignorant manumitted slaves in their midst, for whom some of us now claim the suffrage. Let us be Christians toward our fellow whites, as well as philanthropists toward the blacks, our fellowmen. In all things and toward all, we are enjoined to do as we would be done by. Nor should we forget that benevolent desires, after passing a certain point, cannot undertake their own fulfillment without incurring the risk of evils beyond those sought to be remedied. Something may well be left to the graduated care of future legislation, and to heaven.

In one point of view the coexistence of the two races in the South — whether the Negro be bond or free — seems (even as it did to Abraham Lincoln) a grave evil. Emancipation has ridded the country of the reproach, but not wholly of the calamity. Especially in the present transition period for both races in the South, more or less of trouble may not unreasonably be anticipated; but let us not hereafter be too swift to charge the blame exclusively in any one quarter. With certain evils men must be more or less patient. Our institutions have a potent digestion, and may in time convert and assimilate to good all elements thrown in, however originally alien.

But, so far as immediate measures looking toward permanent reestablishment are concerned, no consideration should tempt us to pervert the national victory into oppression for the vanquished. Should plausible promise of eventual good, or a deceptive or spurious sense of duty, lead us to essay this, count we must on serious consequences, not the least of which would be divisions among the Northern adherents of the Union. Assuredly, if any honest Catos there be who thus far have gone with us, no longer will they do so, but oppose us, and as resolutely as hitherto they have supported. But this path of thought leads toward those waters of bitterness from which one can only turn aside and be silent.

But supposing reestablishment so far advanced that the southern seats in Congress are occupied, and by men qualified in accordance with those cardinal principles of representative government which hitherto have prevailed in the land — what then? Why, the congressmen elected by the people of the South will — represent the people of the South. This may seem a flat conclusion; but, in view of the last five years, may there not be latent significance in it? What will be the temper of those Southern members? And, confronted by them, what will be the mood of our own representatives? In private life, true reconciliation seldom follows a violent quarrel; but, if subsequent intercourse be unavoidable, nice observances . . . are indispensable to the prevention of a new rupture. Amity itself can only be maintained by reciprocal respect, and true friends are punctilious equals.

On the floor of Congress, North and South are to come together after a passionate duel in which the South, though proving her valor, has been made to bite the dust. Upon differences in debate shall acrimonious recriminations be exchanged? Shall censorious superiority assumed by one section provoke defiant self-assertion on the other? Shall Manassas and Chickamauga be retorted for Chattanooga and Richmond? Under the supposition that the full Congress will be composed of gentlemen, all this is impossible. Yet, if otherwise, it needs no prophet of Israel to foretell the end. The maintenance of congressional decency in the future will rest mainly with the North. Rightly will more forbearance be required from the North than the South, for the North is victor.

But some there are who may deem these latter thoughts inapplicable, and for this reason: Since the test-oath operatively excludes from Congress all who in any way participated in secession, therefore none but Southerners wholly in harmony with the North are eligible to seats. This is true for the time being. But the oath is alterable; and in the wonted fluctuations of parties not improbably it will undergo alteration, assuming such a form, perhaps, as not to bar the admission into the national legislature of men who represent the populations lately in revolt. Such a result would involve no violation of the principles of democratic government. Not readily can one perceive how the political existence of the millions of late secessionists can permanently be ignored by this republic. The years of the war tried our devotion to the Union; the time of peace may test the sincerity of our faith in democracy.

In no spirit of opposition, not by way of challenge, is anything here thrown out. These thoughts are sincere ones; they seem natural, inevitable. Here and there they must have suggested themselves to many thoughtful patriots. And, if they be just thoughts, ere long they must have that weight with the public which already they have had with individuals.

For that heroic band — those children of the furnace who, in regions like Texas and Tennessee, maintained their fidelity through terrible trials — we of the North felt for them, and profoundly we honor them. Yet passionate sympathy, with resentments so close as to be almost domestic in their bitterness, would hardly in the present juncture tend to discreet legislation. Were the unionists and secessionists but as Guelphs and Ghibellines? If not, then far be it from a great nation now to act in the spirit that animated a triumphant town faction in the Middle Ages.

But crowding thoughts must at last be checked; and, in times like the present, one who desires to be impartially just in the expression of his views moves as among sword points presented on every side.

Let us pray that the terrible historic tragedy of our time may not have been enacted without instructing our whole beloved country through terror and pity; and may fulfillment verify in the end those expectations which kindle the bards of progress and humanity.

I Repose in This Quiet and Secluded Spot
Not from Any Natural Preference for Solitude,
But Finding Other Cemeteries Limited as to Race,
By Charter Rules,
I Have Chosen This That I Might Illustrate
In My Death
The Principles Which I Advocated
Through a Long Life:
Equality of Man Before His Creator
THADDEUS STEVENS, epitaph on his grave at Schreiners Cemetery, Lancaster, Pennsylvania

11.

Walt Whitman: "When Lilacs Last in the Dooryard Bloomed"

"Of all the days of the war," Whitman wrote in Specimen Days, *"there are two especially I can never forget. Those were the day following the news, in New York and Brooklyn, of that first Bull Run defeat, and the day of Abraham Lincoln's death. I was home in Brooklyn on both occasions. The day of the murder we heard the news very early in the morning. Mother prepared breakfast — and other meals afterward — as usual; but not a mouthful was eaten all day by either of us. We each drank half a cup of coffee; that was all. Little was said. We got every newspaper morning and evening, and the frequent extras of that period, and passed them silently to each other."* Whitman went to work on *"When Lilacs Last in the Dooryard Bloomed,"* considered his greatest poem and one of the most beautiful elegies ever written, soon after the assassination. It was published in its final form in the 1881 edition of Leaves of Grass.

Source: *Leaves of Grass*, Boston, 1881.

WHEN LILACS LAST IN THE DOORYARD BLOOMED

1

When lilacs last in the dooryard bloomed,
And the great star early drooped in the western sky in the night,
I mourned, and yet shall mourn with ever-returning spring.

Ever-returning spring, trinity sure to me you bring,
Lilac blooming perennial and drooping star in the west,
And thought of him I love.

2

O powerful western fallen star!
O shades of night — O moody, tearful night!
O great star disappeared — O the black murk that hides the star!
O cruel hands that hold me powerless — O helpless soul of me!
O harsh surrounding cloud that will not free my soul.

3

In the dooryard fronting an old farmhouse near the white-washed palings,
Stands the lilac bush tall-growing with heart-shaped leaves of rich green,
With many a pointed blossom rising delicate, with the perfume strong I love,
With every leaf a miracle — and from this bush in the dooryard,
With delicate-colored blossoms and heart-shaped leaves of rich green,
A sprig with its flower I break.

4

In the swamp in secluded recesses,
A shy and hidden bird is warbling a song.

Solitary the thrush,
The hermit withdrawn to himself, avoiding the settlements,
Sings by himself a song.

Song of the bleeding throat,
Death's outlet song of life (for well dear brother I know,
If thou wast not granted to sing thou wouldst surely die).

5

Over the breast of the spring, the land, amid cities,
Amid lanes and through old woods, where lately the violets peeped from the
        ground, spotting the gray debris,
Amid the grass in the fields each side of the lanes, passing the endless grass,
Passing the yellow-speared wheat, every grain from its shroud in the
        dark-brown fields uprisen,
Passing the apple-tree blows of white and pink in the orchards,
Carrying a corpse to where it shall rest in the grave,
Night and day journeys a coffin.

6

Coffin that passes through lanes and streets,
Through day and night with the great cloud darkening the land,
With the pomp of the inlooped flags with the cities draped in black,
With the show of the states themselves as of crape-veiled women standing,
With processions long and winding and the flambeaus of the night,
With the countless torches lit, with the silent sea of faces and the unbared heads,
With the waiting depot, the arriving coffin, and the somber faces,
With dirges through the night, with the thousand voices rising strong and solemn,
With all the mournful voices of the dirges poured around the coffin,
The dim-lit churches and the shuddering organs — where amid these you journey,
With the tolling tolling bells' perpetual clang,
Here, coffin that slowly passes,
I give you my sprig of lilac.

7

(Nor for you, for one alone,
Blossoms and branches green to coffins all I bring,
For fresh as the morning, thus would I chant a song for you O
     sane and sacred death.

All over bouquets of roses,
O death, I cover you over with roses and early lilies,
But mostly and now the lilac that blooms the first,
Copious I break, I break the sprigs from the bushes,
With loaded arms I come, pouring for you,
For you and the coffins all of you O death.)

8

O western orb sailing the heaven,
Now I know what you must have meant as a month since I walked,
As I walked in silence the transparent shadowy night,
As I saw you had something to tell as you bent to me night after night,
As you drooped from the sky low down as if to my side (while the
     other stars all looked on),
As we wandered together the solemn night (for something I know not
     what kept me from sleep),
As the night advanced, and I saw on the rim of the west how full you were of woe,
As I stood on the rising ground in the breeze in the cool transparent night,
As I watched where you passed and was lost in the netherward
     black of the night,
As my soul in its trouble dissatisfied sank, as where you sad orb,
Concluded, dropped in the night, and was gone.

9

Sing on there in the swamp,
O singer bashful and tender, I hear your notes, I hear your call,
I hear, I come presently, I understand you,
But a moment I linger, for the lustrous star has detained me,
The star my departing comrade holds and detains me.

10

O how shall I warble myself for the dead one there I loved?
And how shall I deck my song for the large sweet soul that has gone?
And what shall my perfume be for the grave of him I love?

Sea winds blown from east and west,
Blown from the Eastern sea and blown from the Western sea,
     till there on the prairies meeting,
These and with these and the breath of my chant,
I'll perfume the grave of him I love.

11

O what shall I hang on the chamber walls?
And what shall the pictures be that I hang on the walls,
To adorn the burial house of him I love?

Pictures of growing spring and farms and homes,
With the Fourth-month eve at sundown, and the gray smoke lucid and bright,
With floods of the yellow gold of the gorgeous, indolent, sinking sun,
        burning, expanding the air,
With the fresh sweet herbage under foot, and the pale green
        leaves of the trees prolific,
In the distance the flowing glaze, the breast of the river, with a
        wind-dapple here and there,
With ranging hills on the banks, with many a line against the sky, and shadows,
And the city at hand with dwellings so dense, and stacks of chimneys,
And all the scenes of life and the workshops, and the workmen homeward returning.

12

Lo, body and soul — this land,
My own Manhattan with spires, and the sparkling and hurrying tides, and the ships,
The varied and ample land, the South and the North in the light,
        Ohio's shores and flashing Missouri,
And ever the far-spreading prairies covered with grass and corn.

Lo, the most excellent sun so calm and haughty,
The violet and purple morn with just-felt breezes,
The gentle soft-born measureless light,
The miracle spreading bathing all, the fulfilled noon,
The coming eve delicious, the welcome night and the stars,
Over my cities shining all, enveloping man and land.

13

Sing on, sing on you gray-brown bird,
Sing from the swamps, the recesses, pour your chant from the bushes,
Limitless out of the dusk, out of the cedars and pines.

Sing on dearest brother, warble your reedy song,
Loud human song, with voice of uttermost woe.

O liquid and free and tender!
O wild and loose to my soul — O wondrous singer!
You only I hear — yet the star holds me (but will soon depart),
Yet the lilac with mastering odor holds me.

14

Now while I sat in the day and looked forth,
In the close of the day with its light and the fields of spring, and
        the farmers preparing their crops,

In the large unconscious scenery of my land with its lakes and forests,
In the heavenly aerial beauty (after the perturbed winds and the storms),
Under the arching heavens of the afternoon swift passing, and the
    voices of children and women,
The many-moving sea tides, and I saw the ships how they sailed,
And the summer approaching with richness, and the fields all busy with labor,
And the infinite separate houses, how they all went on, each with its
    meals and minutia of daily usages,
And the streets how their throbbings throbbed, and the cities pent
    — lo, then and there,
Falling upon them all and among them all, enveloping me with the rest,
Appeared the cloud, appeared the long black trail,
And I knew death, its thought, and the sacred knowledge of death.

Then with the knowledge of death as walking one side of me,
And the thought of death close-walking the other side of me,
And I in the middle as with companions, and as holding the hands of companions,
I fled forth to the hiding receiving night that talks not,
Down to the shores of the water, the path by the swamp in the dimness,
To the solemn shadowy cedars and ghostly pines so still.

And the singer so shy to the rest received me,
The gray-brown bird I know received us comrades three,
And he sang the carol of death, and a verse for him I love.

From deep secluded recesses,
From the fragrant cedars and the ghostly pines so still,
Came the carol of the bird.

And the charm of the carol rapt me,
As I held as if by their hands my comrades in the night,
And the voice of my spirit tallied the song of the bird.

Come lovely and soothing death,
Undulate round the world, serenely arriving, arriving,
In the day, in the night, to all, to each,
Sooner or later delicate death.

Praised be the fathomless universe,
For life and joy, and for objects and knowledge curious,
And for love, sweet love — but praise! praise! praise!
For the sure-enwinding arms of cool-enfolding death.

Dark mother always gliding near with soft feet,
Have none chanted for thee a chant of fullest welcome?
Then I chant it for thee, I glorify thee above all,
I bring thee a song that when thou must indeed come, come unfalteringly.

Approach strong deliveress,
When it is so, when thou hast taken them I joyously sing the dead,
Lost in the loving floating ocean of thee,
Laved in the flood of thy bliss O death.

From me to thee glad serenades,
Dances for thee I propose saluting thee, adornments and feastings for thee,
And the sights of the open landscape and the high-spread sky are fitting,
And life and the fields, and the huge and thoughtful night.

The night in silence under many a star,
The ocean shore and the husky whispering wave whose voice I know,
And the soul turning to thee O vast and well-veiled death,
And the body gratefully nestling close to thee.

Over the tree tops I float thee a song,
Over the rising and sinking waves, over the myriad fields and the prairies wide,
Over the dense-packed cities all and the teeming wharves and ways,
I float this carol with joy, with joy to thee O death.

15

To the tally of my soul,
Loud and strong kept up the gray-brown bird,
With pure deliberate notes spreading filling the night.
Loud in the pines and cedars dim,
Clear in the freshness moist and swamp-perfume,
And I with my comrades there in the night.

While my sight that was bound in my eyes unclosed,
As to long panoramas of visions.

And I saw askant the armies,
I saw as in noiseless dreams hundreds of battle flags,
Borne through the smoke of the battles and pierced with missiles I saw them,
And carried hither and yon through the smoke, and torn and bloody,
And at last but a few shreds left on the staffs (and all in silence),
And the staffs all splintered and broken.

I saw battle corpses, myriads of them,
And the white skeletons of young men, I saw them,
I saw the debris and debris of all the slain soldiers of the war,
But I saw they were not as was thought,
They themselves were fully at rest, they suffered not,
The living remained and suffered, the mother suffered,
And the wife and the child and the musing comrade suffered,
And the armies that remained suffered.

16

Passing the visions, passing the night,
Passing, unloosing the hold of my comrades' hands,
Passing the song of the hermit bird and the tallying song of my soul,
Victorious song, death's outlet song, yet varying ever-altering song,
As low and wailing, yet clear the notes, rising and falling, flooding the night,
Sadly sinking and fainting, as warning and warning, and yet again bursting with joy,
Covering the earth and filling the spread of the heaven,
As that powerful psalm in the night I heard from recesses,
Passing, I leave thee lilac with heart-shaped leaves,
I leave thee there in the dooryard, blooming, returning with spring.

I cease from my song for thee,
From my gaze on thee in the west, fronting the west, communing with thee,
O comrade lustrous with silver face in the night.
Yet each to keep and all, retrievements out of the night,
The song, the wondrous chant of the gray-brown bird,
And the tallying chant, the echo aroused in my soul,
With the lustrous and drooping star with the countenance full of woe,
With the holders holding my hand nearing the call of the bird,
Comrades mine and I in the midst, and their memory ever to keep, for
　　　the dead I loved so well,
For the sweetest, wisest soul of all my days and lands — and this for his dear sake,
Lilac and star and bird twined with the chant of my soul,
There in the fragrant pines and the cedars dusk and dim.

A scene in Five Points, a tenement section of New York, during the 1880s

THE POSTWAR CITY

The city at the end of the Civil War was on the verge of becoming the dominant force in the country. But as yet, without the technology that would come in the next three decades, the word "city" was essentially a description of sheer size. The distinctive elements of an urban milieu were only beginning to appear: steam trolleys and elevated railroads replaced the horse-powered variety; culture, largely imported by the wealthy and often of dubious value, began to be associated with the larger cities; in 1857 Frederick Law Olmstead designed New York's revolutionary Central Park as an escape for urban dwellers into a well-planned wilderness. Also new, and destined unfortunately to be distinctive of the city, was the slum area which in this period began to take on a permanence and character which distinguished it from a construction site shanty town or a migrant settlement. Populated largely by immigrants, the several tenement districts of the cities developed into ethnic neighborhoods, often virtually ghettos, which were to prove a major urban problem in years to come. As the end of the war released capital for investment and development, the profits of industry began to concentrate, not just in the city, but in a small part of the city — Harlem, Back Bay, Chestnut Hill grew up, often within hailing distance of the slum.

(Above) **View of residences along Eighth Avenue, New York, c. 1875;** (below) street scene, Five Points, about 1870

(Left) Boiler makers, probably photographed along New York waterfront, about 1868; (center) public school built next door to a slaughter-pen in one of the New York wards, 1865; (bottom) girls play area at a Negro orphan asylum in New York, 1860s

(Top) View of New York's Central Park; lithograph by Geissler of a painting by Martel, 1864; (center) two women in Central Park, 1881; (right) carriage of the Ringold Hose Co., 1865

The William H. Vanderbilt family in 1873; painting by Seymour Guy

Photograph for a ''carte-de-visite'' by C. Silvy

Gilsey House Drug Store, a deluxe apothecary in New York City during the 19th century

(Above) "The 9:45 Accommodation, Stratford, Connecticut"; painting by Edward Lamson Henry, 1867

(Right) Steam-powered train on the elevated railroad, New York City, about 1876

(Below) Interior of Grand Central Depot, New York, about 1875

(Above) Canal locks at Lockport, New York, about 1870

(Left) Winter scene about 1865; possibly in Buffalo, New York

(Below) Lake steamers in docks at Buffalo, N.Y., about 1880

(Above) Aerial view of Boston and the harbor in 1870; drawn by F. Fuchs

(Right) Looking up Franklin Street in Boston, Mass.; photographed by John P. Soule

(Above) **Old State House in Boston;** from a stereograph by the Bierstadt brothers; (below) view of the Harvard campus

Three views of university students: (Top left) The Freshman; (top right) The Sophomore; both by J. N. Mead; (left) Harvard student

In postwar America, higher education remained for the most part the privilege of the wealthy — mainly the wealthy male. But new currents were stirring in this field, some of them sharply at odds with the tenor of the period. Despite the apparent celebration of vulgarity in the arts and the general disdain for aesthetic matters, Harvard in 1874 hired Charles Eliot Norton as its first lecturer in the fine arts.

Initiation ceremony for a Yale University secret society during the 1860s

(Above) Vassar Female College, near Poughkeepsie, N.Y., opened in 1864; lithograph by F. Mayer

(Left) Students at Howard University in Washington, D.C.; about 1885

(Below) View of the buildings and grounds of Northfield School for Girls, founded by Dwight Moody along the Connecticut River in Massachusetts

(Above) View of Broad Street in Philadelphia in the 1880s with City Hall in left background

In 1876 Philadelphia's position as one of America's cultural centers of gravity was reinforced by the construction in that city of the Centennial Exposition — a celebration of the country's progress since independence. It is an interesting comment on the prevailing cultural standards that one of the exhibits was a statue modeled in Arkansas butter and displayed in an iced tin frame.

(Left) Blue Anchor Inn, in existence since before the Revolution, during the 1880s; (below) horse car at Delaware River Wharf, 1880

American Museum of Photography

(Above) Members of the "Artists Saving Fund Society" in Fairmont Park, Philadelphia, 1879

(Left) Model kindergarten set up during the Philadelphia Exposition, 1876; (below) Merrick Street as seen from Filbert, about 1870, later torn down to make way for the Broad Street Station of the Pennsylvania Railroad

Library of Congress

American Museum of Photography

(Above) View down Pennsylvania Avenue with the U.S. Capitol in the background, 1880s; old Willard Hotel on the left; (below) Washington Depot of the B.&O. Railroad, 1872

As business and government drew close to partnership in the postwar period, the long-undeveloped city of Washington began to flourish. During the 1870s much of the Capitol was landscaped by Frederick Law Olmstead, the designer of Central Park in New York. However, it was also during this decade that a routine report announced the destruction of Capitol shrubbery by stray neighborhood cows.

(Above left) Madame Catacazy, wife of Russian ambassador and leader of Washington society, 1870s; (above right) scene in Washington, 1889, along the 14th Street bus line

(Below left) Lady clerks leaving the Treasury Department; sketch by Waud for "Harper's Weekly"; (below right) corridor in the U.S. Patent Office, 1870

12.

Amasa Walker: Wealth and the Division of Labor

Between 1860 and 1869, Amasa Walker, who maintained a lifelong interest in currency problems, was a lecturer on economics at Amherst College. He established his reputation as an expert on the monetary system during the financial Panic of 1857, when he warned the businessmen of Boston that maintaining specie payments would tighten credit and ruin many business firms. Walker's advice was ignored, only to be proved correct by the events of the next two weeks. The publicity attendant on this episode put Walker in demand as an economic adviser and contributed to the success of his 1866 work, The Science of Wealth. *The selection below is taken from the chapters on the division of labor.*

Source: *The Science of Wealth: A Manual of Political Economy,* Boston, 1866, pp. 33-52.

What is the significance of division of labor, as expressed in the fewest words? It is that each workman confine himself to a single operation. In this way, all great and successful manufactures are carried on.

Take, for illustration, that of boots. One person cuts the fronts; one crimps; one cuts in; one cuts out the backs, one the linings; one pastes together; one strips out the sole leather; one cuts the soles; one makes the heels; one stitches the backs; one sides up; one binds; one bottoms; one buffs; one trees; one packs, marks, etc. Here are sixteen persons employed in the production of a single boot. In many cases, a still further division of the parts is made with success. In passing, it may be remarked that, of those operations, seven are performed by the aid of machines, as distinguished in popular acceptation from tools, which latter are controlled by the hand and have all their motive power in the muscular force of man.

As long ago as Adam Smith wrote, it took sixteen persons to make a pin.

Such, in description, is division of labor. Let us consider its advantages . . . and disadvantages.

THE ADVANTAGES OF DIVISION OF LABOR

First, it gives increased dexterity. All common observation testifies how rapid and accurate our motions become, when confined to a single operation. . . .

Second, it allows the workman a better knowledge of his business. This is to the mental powers what the first is to the bodily. It gives intellectual dexterity. The man has a mastery of his special operation. He knows more about it than if he had two things to think of and care for. He becomes shrewd in every motion. He adapts his labor to the material; he discriminates between the qualities of that material. He meets the little difficulties of his work with more skill and less waste. These two advantages of the division of labor are shown in the different wages which skilled mechanics obtain as compared with unskilled, able seamen with landsmen.

Third, it saves time in passing from one work to another. In the making of a chair after the primitive fashion, we have supposed a great deal of time will be spent in passing from one part of it to another, from the place of one operation to that of another. And, even where we suppose a laborer to be engaged in two operations only, there is still a loss inflicted, just as often as he has occasion to leave one for another. It is not a loss alone of the time physically necessary in effecting the transition, but each operation will leave something to harass the mind in the other. During the first part, the attention will be distracted by what has just been left. During the last part, the attention will run on, anticipating what is to come. The shadow is cast both ways upon the mind.

Fourth, it facilitates the invention of tools and machines. If a treasure of gold or iron or oil is hid under the ground, the discoverer is more apt, other things being equal, to be the man who owns the land, and resides and works on it, than a casual visitor. So, if there is a possibility of adapting foreign forces to the production of values, the inventor will, on the same condition, more probably be the workman than anyone else; he is constantly engaged upon the operation; he desires, of course, to simplify it since it is a law of mind to do as little work as possible for a certain result; he knows the wants of the subject; he knows all the capabilities of his material; he thinks about it all the time and can try an experiment without changing his place.

Therefore, by the logic of nature, he invents. And, in fact, few of the great aids to industry have been discovered by disinterested science. They came from the laboring brain of the mechanic. Where the work was almost too delicate for human eyes, a thousand iron fingers go around to do it, never losing their nimbleness nor ever getting weary; where the work was too great for human strength, monster arms swing the hammer or toss the load in air.

The history of American manufactures expounds the phrase, "Necessity is the mother of invention." Even the slaves of the South have been directed to important mechanical discoveries in the way we have described.

One simple operation, constantly employing the attention, must, in time, lose all its secrets.

Fifth, it secures the better adaptation of physical and mental abilities. No consideration is more vital than this. The work which man finds to do, the efforts he has to make for satisfactions, however high his wants may rise, will be of the most various character and require the most diverse powers. There are operations which demand great strength; others, rapid motion; others, good judgment; others, a mechanical eye; others, fidelity and trust; others, high intelligence and education. Such qualities, even those purely physical, are not found equally in all; nay, by the compensations of nature, they are generally, though not necessarily, found apart. Therefore, unless work were divided according to the several qualities required, a deficiency in one would neutralize all the others and exclude the workman from employment, or compel him to work at great disadvantage.

The extensive applications of this principle will occur to every mind. Each man finds the sphere of his highest usefulness as he is endowed by nature. Those who are gifted with education and ingenuity devote all their time and energy to duties appropriate to such powers. They thus confer on others the advantage of their own gifts and are themselves spared from drudgery and uncongenial labor. The poorest in qualifications, also, find a place in which they can produce within the great partnership of society. Women are enabled to undertake business of the most delicate and important character, to which their strength is sufficient; while children of all ages take parts that would otherwise occupy men.

The power saved or gained by such an adaptation of talents to special branches of industry is incalculable. Without it, a great part of the human race would be helpless paupers, and the remainder would earn a scanty and miserable livelihood. Man working by himself is a poacher on the domain

Engraving of Amasa Walker, author of "The Science of Wealth"

of nature; men in industrial society found empires, build cities, and establish commerce.

And not merely do all find in a proper division of labor their full occupation and fair reward, but the work of each is just as truly productive as that of any other. The boy who watches crows does as much at that business as the bravest and greatest of earth. He takes the place of someone who goes away to do a larger work. In anthropology, this is only a boy; in political economy, he is a man. He and the other make together two men.

Sixth, it increases the power of capital in production, tends to concentrate manufactures in large establishments and reduce profits.

Supposing all men equally capable of carrying on independent business, which is not the case. If we compare seven men each with a capital of $1,000 and one man with a capital of $7,000, we shall find the economical advantage greatly in favor of the latter. The former must do business on a small scale and purchase materials in small quanti-

ties. The latter can buy at wholesale prices, can afford to go often to market, and to keep himself well informed, and will sell as well as buy to great advantage. In addition to this, the large manufacturer can afford to work for a smaller rate of profit.

A single hatter, for example, who makes only $2,000 worth of hats, must secure 25 percent in order to have a net income of $500; while the man who can make $20,000 worth of hats will, if he realize only 12½ percent, have an income of $2,500. A cotton manufacturer who makes 3,000 yards per day, or 900,000 per annum, if he gets but half a cent per yard profit has an income of $4,500; the man who makes but 300 yards per day, at one cent per yard, or double the profit, gets but $900.

We see from these illustrations why the great establishments drive smaller ones out of the market. A tendency to a reduction of profits is a natural consequence of this. Therefore, other things being equal, it is desirable that manufacturing establishments should be sufficiently large to secure all the advantages of concentrated capital and effect the complete division of labor.

Seventh, it shortens apprenticeship. Every art, trade, or profession must be preceded by an apprenticeship, more or less extended, according to what is necessary to be learned. A trade which, in order to be perfectly understood in all its parts, requires an apprenticeship of seven years, if it be subdivided into seven different operations, may, it is evident, be obtained with as great a degree of perfection by an average in each branch of one year's service. Some of the parts may require more than one year, others less. . . .

It will be observed that these are years of apprenticeship, not of labor. In considering what is the saving to the wealth of the country, we must estimate the amount of values created by these workmen during the apprenticeship under the first system supposed. *Per contra*, we must take into account the greater amount of material destroyed in teaching each man to do all the parts and the greater interruption of the employer or journeyman.

If we suppose these years saved from apprenticeship to have an average value of $200, we have a saving of $90 million *for each generation* of skilled workmen in Massachusetts. The principle under which this saving of time is made cannot be disputed.

Eighth, it gives opportunity for greater social development and increases the social power of labor. This is immediately of moral interest; but it has important economic bearings. The principle itself is indisputable. Not only is the workman brought near his fellows and, by such contact, stimulated to industry, to acquisition, to taste; not only does such association of purposes and means afford more of the instruments of intellectual advancement — schools, lectures, churches, journals; not only does the close neighborhood of mind quicken and brighten all the faculties, teaching by example and firing by controversy; but by such association workmen are brought nearer their employers, have a greater sympathy and cooperation, act intelligently and harmoniously as to their rights, and form a public opinion among themselves which has often been found a great power, economically and civilly. Such an association, moreover, brings the workman nearer the government and the public force; sometimes for evil, but often for good. A population thus concentrated is capable of prodigious impulses. All the artisans of the empire are not equal to the mob of the capital. Government knows and respects the power of this class, no matter how fully disfranchised it may be in the law.

THE DISADVANTAGES OF THE DIVISION OF LABOR

First, it tends to enervate the laborer because it does not, as a general fact, give full activity and development to all the functions of the body.

We shall proceed to show that this is true of those classes who perform what we have designated as material labor, while the very distinction of mental labor implies such a separation between the natural functions as seems not to consist with the best physical condition of those engaged. Common observation will affirm that this is strikingly true. It is not necessary, but the tendency exists.

In the material occupations it is found that confinement to a single operation is often highly injurious. There are forms of labor which sufficiently exercise the several parts of the body. The mere fact of uniformity of motion brings no objection to such as these. But there are those which require the constant fatiguing use of some member to the injury of the rest of the body; others require a cramping posture that oppresses and disorders the vital organs; others, still, require the workman to poison his blood with unwholesome gases. In the great centers of capital and labor — whether we regard the mill, or that larger mill, the city itself — it is notorious that distortion, paralysis, and organic feebleness are more common than where labor is diffused and the laborer changes his work and his place frequently.

That this will occur in the course of all manufacturing industry is probable. That it is inevitable does not so clearly appear. The sanitary arts keep even pace with the advance of machinery. The Civil War in America developed astonishingly the resources, which are at the command of government, to suppress malaria and reform the habitations of disease. The growth of manly sports and the cultivation of gymnastics for health's sake are likely to work a great change for the better in the sanitary conditions of our people. The intelligent precaution of operatives in every country, where their remuneration is anything less than robbery, can guard against all excessive derangement of the bodily functions.

It is perhaps significant to the question

whether the application of the bodily powers to a single, continuous action is really in practice injurious, that we find in the statistics of Massachusetts, ranging over sixteen years, the average life of "laborers having no special trades" to be less by two years than that of "active mechanics in shops."

Mechanical operations were formerly considered as disqualifying for military service; and even our modern philosophy has found in them a reason for the employment of mercenaries and the maintenance of standing armies. But the great Civil War just referred to exhibited the novel fact that, beyond all dispute, the troops raised in agricultural districts are not so hardy in the privations and exposures of camp and field as those coming from the towns. This does not, however, imply a better state of health at home. It may be that the latter class find, in the constant exercise and the outdoor employment, just that *change* of habit and condition which they needed. All that is different from their usual course of life is in the direction of more air and light and motion; while the agricultural laborers find no change except for the worse. They have been accustomed to active employment; but the harsh necessities of the service come to them fresh and strong.

It is perhaps the *direction* of influences more than the degree of them which determines these matters of health; or it may be that mechanical occupations, contrary to general opinion and in spite of some plain drawbacks, do tend to compact the frame and the sinew, and lend force and vitality to the organs. Whatever the explanation, we will rest with the fact that, in the severe trial of strength and endurance made by the war, the mechanical occupations have not been discredited.

Second, this system, in some of its applications and in certain degrees of extension, does not give that full employment and expansion to all the powers of the mind which its normal development requires. This is obvious. The mind, if intensely devoted for a whole life to a single effort, and that perhaps of the most simple kind, cannot but be unfavorably affected. Unless counteracting influences are resorted to, it will undoubtedly be contracted and enervated.

To this liability are opposed three compensations:

a. The great communicativeness observable in such circumstances, the eager discussions, the free inquiry, the school, and the lyceum.

b. The saving principle that the employment of one member is, to a certain extent, the employment of all. The human faculties, mental and physical, are a knot. They interpenetrate so completely that it is impossible to move one without affecting the rest. If we compare the mind to a reservoir, we may say that the individual powers and dispositions flow out of it as so many streams; but there is nothing to prevent them from flowing back if the level is sufficiently disturbed. The special use of one may develop it greatly — make it more strong and active than the others. But such a predominance is not distortion. Few minds are capable of even and temperate growth. In this principle resides the variety of human character.

It may be questioned whether any but the most gifted can be educated in any other way so thoroughly and efficiently as by interested application to some single matter. Generalization and broad philosophy rouse the full powers of but few intellects. In the majority of cases, it will remain true that intense, spirited, persistent labor directed to one point is better than the languid, nerveless, unspurred, rambling play of all the faculties. Mind, to be energetic, must not be republican. The powers must be centralized. Some must be despotic.

Indeed, the argument against division of labor on this score would be better expressed by saying that the constant repetition of single acts so far dispenses with thought, and even with consciousness, in the operation that it makes man, in some sense, a machine. This is, to a considerable extent, true; the compensation being that it affords a greater opportunity for discussion and reflection if the workman chooses to avail himself of the kind of mental leisure which is afforded by the monotony of his occupation. It is, therefore, not the excessive use but the disuse of the intellectual faculties that is to be feared in those arts to which labor has been carried to its fullest division.

c. The laborer is not all workman. While his special occupation provides for his subsistence and endows him with energy, industry, and concentrativeness of mind and character, he has other hours and other duties, ample, if reasonably used, to compensate for all the evil mental effects of his continuous toil.

It will be observed that it is only to the division of labor *beyond a certain point* that the objections we have discussed have any application. A more ill-developed society, with more ill-developed members, could not be conceived than where this principle was not applied at all. In fact, there could be neither members nor society; but here and there a savage would bask in the summer sun or hide himself in the storms of winter in hopeless, helpless barbarism.

However we may speculate, *a priori,* on the consequences of dividing minutely the parts of labor, we may perhaps get a stronger light and a better view by observing the mightiest experiment of industry ever known in the world — that of England today. Nowhere are the natural advantages of agriculture more apparent; nowhere has manufacturing been more elaborated. Yet no person can be cognizant of the condition of the English population without being assured that the manufacturing, laboring class is almost immeasurably above the agricultural in intelligence, in independence of character, and obedience to law. Probably the most conservative nobleman of the Realm would admit that the former class is far better qualifed for the franchise. . . .

Fourth, the division of labor lessens the number of those who do business on their own account. This is a natural consequence of what has been shown. We have said that capital has a tendency toward concentration; and if it be aggregated, labor must also be. The result of this in agriculture is to absorb the yeomanry into the class of those who labor by the day or month, with no interest in the land. The result in manufacturing is to subordinate hundreds of operatives to the control of a single will.

This has a threefold relation:

a. To the formation of character. Something of independence and self-respect is unquestionably lost, so far as these depend on external conditions. Position and responsibility do foster and strengthen manliness and self-mastery. By the division of labor, the independence of each is sacrificed to the good of all. It will not be doubted that on the whole it is desirable that it should be so; nor can it be denied that there are partial drawbacks, even in this plain tendency of civilization. It is the sacrifice man has to make in society, in industry, in government.

b. To the fairness of remuneration. A very few now participate in the profits. The great bulk of workmen receive only wages, and that on temporary engagements. This disproportion may be excessive and is likely to be where laws or institutions check enterprise and discourage individual effort. In such cases, laborers are practically a herd of cattle driven about from place to place, receiving bare subsistence, and unable to mend their condition. This is a lamentable state of things; an abuse of a good principle.

No one can deny, however, that the worst-treated operatives of the civilized world receive infinitely more than if the efforts of men were all individual and independent and each was left to satisfy his wants from the primitive resources of nature. But even if we come forward from the barbarous state to that in which the work of man has divided itself into numerous trades, each of these, however, yet remaining distinct, and compare this with the present state, in which trades have been repeatedly subdivided — capital aggregate and labor subordinate — we shall yet find that the share of the poorest laborer in the mighty product of our industry of today is greater than ever before. Augustus, says Arbuthnot, had neither glass to his windows nor a shirt to his back.

Thus much could be urged of the wretchedest operatives on the earth; but when we regard the condition of labor as it exists in nearly all the countries of the world, we shall quickly confess that, though the laborer has given up his share of profits, he receives back as wages far more objects of desire than he could have obtained in the old way.

c. To the steadiness of employment. By the attraction of labor to great centers, the fate of many laborers is made dependent on that of a few capitalists. This is a great fact, scientifically and historically. It must continue. It has issued, in the past, in the form of great industrial distresses, of a general suspension of *mechanical* labor from causes affecting only the *mercantile* credit of the employers, of frantic appeals for support, of laws in which government assumes the duty of providing work for its whole population, of riots and revolution. So far as this will occur in spite of prudence and careful management, it is the condition on which we have the advantages of division of labor. Men cannot cross the great ocean alone. They must go together, have help of each other, and embark their fortunes on a common bottom. More of them would perhaps be safe if each was on a ship of his own; but that cannot well be.

Even in regard to steadiness of employment, the aggregation of capital and consequent division of labor assist the workman *up to a certain point.* That point is the great catastrophe which no structure can withstand. Then, the greater the structure, the more completely it crushes the laborer.

Where capital is concentrated, it is stronger, protects itself better; and, of course, the workman shares in this power and immunity. Where the industry of thousands is controlled by the mind of one, it will be more intelligently and harmoniously administered, and with a larger view of the business. By such superiority of union in production (for that is synonymous with division of labor), the industry of a country is lifted clean over obstacles which individual enterprise could not pass, is preserved amid storms that would shatter the feeble fabric of single hands. Industry in masses, when it receives a shock, can hold on to the accumulations of the past and to the credit of the future, and so stands firm.

But when the blow becomes so heavy as to shatter even the great workshops of modern industry and they come down, then truly the fall is great. The ruin is more complete than if the storm had prostrated a village of huts. The reservoir of gathered power has burst; the springs have long since been broken down; the wells been filled up; and there is no supply for immediate wants. Such a loss is repaired slowly. The trampled grass raises itself and looks up again; but the oak lies as it falls.

Independence has been discouraged by collective industry; the shop has been abandoned for the mill; each workman has learned only the fraction of a trade; no one can buy, make, and sell; no one dares to undertake any business, foreseeing that the corporation must rise again. For a while, all is distress. It is only when the stately fabric of associated industry is reared again that plenty is known in the land.

We have discussed, somewhat at length, the relations which division of labor holds to the condition of the laborer by depriving him of the opportunity to do business on his own account. Until recently, it has been supposed that the advantages of the principle could not practically be obtained without this defect; that capital could not be concentrated and the trades perfected without diminishing the independence and self-reliance of labor. But recent developments seem to be anticipating the objection.

It is now a matter of common practice to admit the laborer to an interest in business, a share in profits. This is done by merchants to their salesmen, by master mechanics to their workmen, by shipowners to their hands. All stock companies, of whatever character, admit of this principle. Mutual industrial associations for trade, mining, and insurance furnish its most significant and hopeful applications. There is no reason why these should not be extended much further by a gradual growth as they are found convenient and profitable. Just so far as a sufficient spring of self-interest can be maintained in the effort, both of the employer, or manager, and of the operative, so far may mutuality of profits be applied to all departments with the most beneficial results.

13.

Efforts to Encourage Immigration to the South

The loss of slave labor created an acute disorganization of the labor force in the South after the Civil War. To achieve a stable labor force and to diversify its economic system the South attempted to attract immigrants from Europe. These efforts met with competition from Northern industrial centers and westward expansion, but several states pressed their efforts through creation of agricultural commissions charged with advertising the attractions of the state. One method employed was the distribution in the North and throughout several European countries of pamphlets encouraging emigration to the Southern states. The South Carolina legislation that follows is typical of the measures adopted.

Source: *The Statutes at Large of South Carolina*, Vol. XIII, Columbia, 1875, pp. 380-381.

An act for the encouragement and protection of European immigration, and for the appointment of a commissioner and agents, and for other purposes therein expressed

1. *Be it enacted* by the Senate and House of Representatives, now met and sitting in General Assembly, and by the authority of the same, that for the purpose of encouraging, promoting, and protecting European immigration to and in this state, the sum of $10,000 be appropriated from the contingent fund, to be expended under the direction of the government, for the purposes and in the manner hereinafter provided.

2. That the governor, by and with the advice and consent of the Senate, shall appoint a commissioner of immigration, who shall open an office in the fireproof building in Charleston, to perform such duties as may appertain to his office, and shall be paid for his services the salary of $1,500 per annum out of the fund aforesaid in quarterly payments.

3. That it shall be the duty of said commissioner of immigration to advertise in all the gazettes of the state for lands for sale; to cause such lands, after having been duly laid off, platted and described, at the expense of the owner or owners of said lands, to be appraised by three disinterested persons, and their titles to be examined by the

attorney general or solicitors of the state, and endorsed by them, as the case may be; to open a book or books for the registry of the same, together with the price demanded and the conditions of payment. And in case such lands be selected by any immigrant, to superintend the transfer of title and other necessary instruments and proceedings of conveyance.

4. That the said commissioner shall periodically publish, advertise, and cause to be distributed in the Northern and European ports and states, descriptive lists of such lands as have been registered and offered for sale, together with this act, and a statement of such advantages as this state offers in soil, climate, productions, social improvements, etc., to the industrious, orderly, and frugal European immigrant. . . .

6. That the said commissioner shall be specially charged with the protection of the immigrants in the proper selection of their lands; in the procurement of their transportation; in the guarding of them against fraud, chicanery, and peculation; in their temporary location in proper and reasonable places of board and lodging on their arrival; and in making all such regulations and provisions as may be in any manner necessary or conducive to their welfare. And all officers of the state are hereby required and commanded to aid and assist him in the objects aforesaid whenever requested.

7. That the commissioner shall keep a separate book wherein he shall register all applications from citizens, free of charge, for immigrant artisans, mechanics, farmers, or male or female help of any kind, together with the kind of service demanded and the compensation offered; and another book wherein he shall record the names, crafts, and qualifications of immigrants that are looking for employment; and he shall make memoranda of such contracts as shall be made in consequence hereof.

14.

George Nye Boardman: Government Aid to the Poor

The Protestant churches, by accepting the principles of laissez faire economics and rugged individualism, were singularly unable to cope with social problems in the years after the Civil War. Massive growth of industry and concentration of economic power put individual workingmen at a great disadvantage. One of the few clergymen who saw the need for collective action to help the laboring class was George Nye Boardman, a Presbyterian minister from Binghamton, New York. The following selection is taken from his article "Political Economy and the Christian Ministry," published in 1866.

Source: *The Bibliotheca Sacra*, Edwards A. Park and Samuel H. Taylor, eds., Vol. XXIII, Boston, 1866, pp. 100-104.

ANOTHER QUESTION ON WHICH THE CLERGY have a right to speak, and in the solution of which they occupy a vantage ground, relates to the aim of governments. Is the world governed too much? Are the intents of government essentially negative, having in view the protection of the people against evils, or do they propose also to promote interests by positive legislation? Is government to leave the poor to take care of themselves, leave feeble interests to take care of themselves, or is its office that of protection and support to the needy?

There can be no doubt that the main source of human wealth and comfort is in private enterprise and individual industry. Any philosophy that teaches the young that the government is not the chief almoner of blessings; that it has very little to do with the really positive enjoyments and attainments of mankind; that it plays but an insignificant part in human life is to be hailed as a friend and commissioned to its important work. Still we must not hold that governments are ordained simply to prevent wrongs; they have interests also to promote.

Could legislation prevent every possible wrong, that might answer its end; but the only practical means of effecting this is by making sure certain necessary interests of the people. Recent legislation in favor of homesteads, in favor of widows, in distribution of bounty lands indicates a recognition of the duty here referred to.

Without an attempt to decide the question — whose servant governments are — there is to us something repulsive in the thought that it should disregard the social relations which God has established, and should consider itself as simply the minister of cold justice. It may without injury rise to a higher level at once and stand as the protector of interests without which society cannot exist. We lose much in defining the province of governments by losing sight of the fact that there is a self-seeking which is also benevolence; that there are social interests which are identical with personal interests.

But political economy is attempting now to establish itself on the principle that self-seeking will secure the best result through checks upon itself, not by being identical with seeking the good of others. It holds that commercial war is the natural state of man, i.e., competition is the natural state of business. Political economy teaches, or is attempting to teach, that the world will be best provided for when every man provides for himself as best he can; that justice is best promoted by each man's making sure of his own rights.

But the question is: Are men able to fight each other in this way, and all with success; is there a victory for every man? Is it not true that there must be some superintending power, protecting the weak, repressing violence? Is infinite war the same as peace — every man's holding every other in place the same as everyone's leaving everyone untouched? Does infinite selfishness amount to the same thing as infinite benevolence? Morality and virtue are confessedly the highest or cheapest good if they can universally prevail; but inasmuch as they can only be imperfect in their influence, are we to enforce them by law, or are we to adopt infinite vice as the same thing as perfect virtue, and so set each man's injustice to act as a guard against any injustice toward himself?

Is all legislation a mere carrying out of this principle, so that the murderer is hung, not because righteousness requires it but because self-protection requires it? And, to carry the matter out perfectly, is a man to contend for the gratifications of self at the present moment in opposition to the self of any other time? Is he to say, of all times, *now* is the most important, only the pleasures of the present hour must not vitiate the pleasures of the present hour by giving occasion to fear for the future?

Perhaps the clergyman is in a better position to view this question than any other man, and the Word of God aids him to a reply to the question, though it be one of social economy. It is supposable, indeed, that the poor and needy should contend with the strong, and appeal from physical to moral means to carry on a contest; and the poor man might declare that he and his family would starve rather than degrade themselves and degrade labor by working for inadequate wages; and so the man in power, the possessor of wealth, might have his choice between starving his neighbors or paying them fairly for their work. But this is only a supposition. The world is not peopled by heroes; men do work for such wages as they can get and live uncomfortably if they cannot live comfortably.

There is thus always a large class of the population who depend for the comforts of life on the virtue, benevolence, or justice of their employers; and the clergyman will demand a somewhat higher grade of these qualities than the mere man of the world. He will remember that the family is the atom of society; that whatever crushes that pulverizes it, reduces it to individuality and to selfishness — is sin against God. He will remember that the church cannot exist without the family, that national existence even depends upon it, and therefore that its rights must be sacredly guarded. While therefore he will, with Chalmers, teach the parents providence, and throw around all the restraints of duty, he will also claim that there is a morality for the rich, for the employer, that they may not wantonly crush the instincts of the poorer classes, and doom to single life, aimless, dreary, ending in suicide perhaps, those who are dependent upon the daily wages they receive.

Nor will the clergyman be satisfied when those to whom he preaches are barely sustained in life; there are some moral qualities indispensable to the family which extreme poverty destroys. Not to speak of the wanton laceration of the family and the profaning of its sanctity which is seen in connection with slavery, there are families to be found in every land in which fathers and mothers are obliged to labor till their muscles are knotted and their bones misshapen, till weariness is ingrained in the very tissues, till the feeling of fatigue is general and continuous, till patience is gone, till complaint, sighing, faultfinding have settled down upon the family circle like a blight; and these are in reality families no longer.

When the children who are so unfortunate as to survive infancy are driven out by taskmasters while they should still be at play or at school; when they are obliged to *earn* the bread they *eat*, the house is a slave pen, the household has no ties that can characterize it as a family. When children show in their countenances an unnatural maturity, are wrinkled with age, and especially are prematurely old in sin, are unnaturally vicious because they can find no diversions but in crimes against nature, then they are not really members of a family, and, practically, there is not any way open for them into the kingdom of heaven, the family of God.

The minister of Christ looking upon men in such condition as this, asks himself: Is there no protection for this class of the human race; are they to be left to themselves and to the "tender mercies" of their employers? He will see that often there are men who with the utmost kindness furnish the poor with labor, who most benevolently care for them; but he will certainly sometimes see that the employer, driven by competition to afford his products at the lowest price and yet resolved to make his own profits the highest possible, heartlessly sets the poor man's wages at the smallest amount. Such a view will disclose a meaning which the inspiring Spirit intended, if the apostle did not, in the text: "The wages of sin is death."

A bare look at humanity shows that death is its doom if not reward. The race dies constantly, not from old age but dies out from the distemper of poverty and consequent crime. The less favored ones are living briefly in wretchedness and dying hopelessly; those extruded from the inner circle of privileges — the extremities of humanity, as it were — are falling constantly the victims of a wasting consumption that seems to be devouring the outskirts of the race; children are thrown into the arms of death at birth; man, hardened and debased, dies blaspheming his God; woman, wronged, crushed, in despair hurls herself unbidden to the bar of her Judge; and so death is the awful wages we receive for our work.

The human race hardly increases in numbers; does not at all improve in morals, except where the Savior of the world rescues a people for Himself. He who preaches the gospel to the poor will have no doubt, in view of such facts, that governments and all social institutions are to be based on positive virtue, on morality, not on selfishness, not on each man's ability to take care of himself. He will have no hesitation in deciding that legislation in favor of the poor, in the form of poor laws, or as the compulsory support of free schools, is only the legitimate increase of the wages paid by the employer; it is the wages due to the family over and above that due to the individual.

15.

Religious Schooling for Wayward Youths

At the close of the Civil War, Archbishop Martin J. Spalding received permission from Rome to convene a national council of the Catholic clergy at Baltimore in 1866. The reason for the council was "that at the close of the national crisis, which had acted as a dissolvent upon all sectarian ecclesiastical institutions, the Catholic Church might present to the country and the world a striking proof of the strong bond of unity with which her members are knit together." The council's Pastoral Letter of 1866 included statements of policy on many social and ecclesiastical issues, including the schooling of wayward youths.

Source: *The National Pastorals of the American Hierarchy (1792-1919),* Peter Guilday, ed., Westminster, Md., 1954, pp. 216-217.

CONNECTED with this subject of education is the establishment of protectories and industrial schools for the correction or proper training of youth, which has of late years attracted universal attention. It is a melancholy fact, and a very humiliating avowal for us to make, that a very large proportion of the idle and vicious youth of our principal cities are the children of Catholic parents. Whether from poverty or neglect, the ignorance in which so many parents are involved as to the true nature of education, and of their duties as Christian parents, or the associations which our youth so easily form with those who encourage them to disregard parental admonition; certain it is that a large number of Catholic parents either appear to have no idea of the sanctity of the Christian family and of the responsibility imposed on them of providing for the moral training of their offspring, or fulfill this duty in a very imperfect manner.

Day after day these unhappy children are caught in the commission of petty crimes, which render them amenable to the public authorities; and day after day are they transferred by hundreds from the sectarian reformatories in which they have been placed by the courts to distant localities, where they are brought up in ignorance of, and most commonly in hostility to, the religion in which they had been baptized. The only remedy for this great and daily augmenting evil is to provide Catholic protectories or industrial schools to which such children may be sent; and where, under the only influence that is known to have really reached the roots of vice, the youthful culprit may cease to do evil and learn to do good.

We rejoice that in some of our dioceses — would that we could say in all! — a beginning has been made in this good work; and we cannot too earnestly exhort our venerable brethren of the clergy to bring this matter before their respective flocks, to endeavor to impress on Christian parents the duty of guarding their children from the evils above referred to, and to invite them to make persevering and effectual efforts for the establishment of institutions wherein, under the influence of religious teachers, the waywardness of youth may be corrected, and good seed planted in the soil in which, while men slept, the enemy had sowed tares.

16.

Anonymous: A Norwegian in Minnesota

The unknown author of this letter addressed his comments and descriptions to friends in Norway. The letter, written from Faribault, Minnesota, was published in the Norwegian newspaper Aftenbladet, *September 28, 1866. The author came to America ahead of the great mass of Norwegian immigrants. During the latter half of the nineteenth century, more than 800,000 Norwegians immigrated, most of them settling in the Middle Western states. In the peak year, 1882, the Norwegian language was as much used in Minnesota as English.*

Source: Blegen, pp. 431-435.

AFTER FOUR DAYS' STAY in New York, I left by railroad for the West, through the states of New York, Pennsylvania, Ohio, Indiana, and Illinois, to Chicago. On my way, I went through a great many large cities and villages. In Norway I had read that the railroad tracks in America go right through the middle of the streets, and this had seemed most peculiar to me. But now I saw that it was quite true. Any possible danger is avoided by having the trains move very slowly through the cities and by the ringing of big, sonorous bells on the fronts of the locomotives.

Chicago is a large and splendid city. The degree of briskness and business activity here is not much less than in London or New York. As you know, Chicago is considered the most important grain market in the world. At the present time it has more than 200,000 inhabitants; in 1840 it had 4,470. But the location of the city is very unhealthful.

After a day's stay in Chicago, I bought a ticket for La Crosse, the destination of my journey for the time being. I came through another large city, Milwaukee, which has more than 100,000 inhabitants. La Crosse, like Milwaukee, is located in the state of Wisconsin. It is on the Mississippi River and is still a small town of not over 8,000 inhabitants, of whom more than a third seem to be Norwegians. Here I met four clerks, all of whom I knew from Christiania. They had no good news for me, for they said that it would be difficult to get a job just then, as I had arrived at a very inopportune season.

These clerks had not had easy going during the first period of their stay in America. For a long time they had had to earn their living by manual labor. One of them had been a painter, another a tanner, and the third had worked as a simple laborer on a raft on the Mississippi going down to St. Louis. They advised me to get a similar job until the times became more favorable, but for quite awhile I did not feel much like doing this. An older clerk from Christiania, who arrived in La Crosse a couple of days after me, took service as a waiter in a boarding house, as he could not get a position in trade either in Chicago or La Crosse. After a few more days in La Crosse, I decided to go farther west.

In St. Peter I became acquainted with a Swede, L., who was head clerk in a bank there. He advised me to go to Faribault to look for a job, and he was kind enough to give me a recommendation to an important man of his acquaintance there. Consequently, I went to Faribault and got a job.

Faribault, which was founded recently, is a beautiful small town of 5,000 inhabitants, six-and-a-half Norwegian miles east of St. Peter. Like all towns here it is growing rapidly. My bosses, partners in a firm called E.A.R. and Company, are both Americans. One of them, the "Major," as he is called, because he had the rank of a major during the war, is a full-blooded Yankee from New Hampshire. The other, Daniels, is from New York. I had always wanted to work with Yankees — I never put any stock in the *Times* characterization of the

Yankees nor in its other nonsense about American conditions; and I must say that I have every reason to be satisfied. My bosses are very kind and obliging people, and working conditions with them are as good as I might wish for.

Everything is terribly expensive here, with the exception of food. Last winter the farmers offered their wheat for sale — and Minnesota wheat is the best in the world — at 50 cents a bushel without getting buyers. A barrel of salt costs about $5, coffee, 35 or 40 cents a pound, and nearly all other groceries are more expensive than in Norway. Almost all kinds of dry goods are twice as expensive as they are in Norway, but the Americans are not satisfied to make such a poor profit as people do in Norway. There seems almost to be a silent agreement among all kinds of businessmen here that everybody is to make a good profit on what he has to sell.

It is also much more pleasant to wait on customers here than it is in Norway. All conversation and aggressive recommendation of merchandise, which was always so distasteful to me, is nonexistent here. We also have extensive barter with the farmers. They bring us wool, butter, and eggs and get in return the things they need. Butter and eggs we sell to the people of the town at a profit of 33 percent. In New York butter costs 60 cents a pound; in La Crosse, 15 cents; and here the price is 30 cents. But for that matter, the prices of these goods vary considerably.

Many Norwegians trade here. In Faribault proper there are not many Norwegians, but out in the country there are a great many Norwegian and Swedish settlements. More particularly, there is a sizable settlement two Norwegian miles east of the town. Considering the short time I have been here, I have associated quite a bit with the Norwegians both here and in Wisconsin. I must say that their circumstances and way of life have surprised me highly. As you know, it was the poorest of our countrymen who, oppressed by the hardships they endured in their native country, left Norway to seek a better home in America. And they have not sought in vain.

Minnesota, which is still a young state, can undoubtedly look ahead to a great future. By the end of this century it will probably be one of the richest and mightiest states in the whole Union. Its size is about 85,000 square miles. Its fertility is unmatched by that of any other country in the world. The climate is healthful and pleasant, though the summer is terribly hot. Although the winter is short, it is said to be almost as severe as in Norway. Miles of vast prairies alternate with extensive oak forests here (the Big Woods). Nowhere in all the vast areas of land I have traveled through have I seen as great an elevation as Egebergbakken in Norway. With regard to communications, Minnesota has been backward thus far; but this is due not to lack of enterprise on the part of the inhabitants but to the huge size of the country and the newness of everything.

In the meantime, construction of several important railroads is being carried forward with energy. I advise everybody in Norway who lives under unhappy and straitened circumstances to come to Minnesota. But there are many tribulations and privations to be faced in the beginning. This is not the fault of the country; it must simply be attributed to a deficient knowledge of the language and conditions here. I have talked to many who were dissatisfied in the beginning, but this dissatisfaction soon changed into a feeling of content.

As to the general character of the Americans, I must say that they are a very strong, enterprising, and energetic people with a practical approach to all kinds of problems. Even if it is only a matter of making an insignificant thing like a lamp chimney or a shoebrush, you note that they are more efficient than people in the Old Country. All

kinds of machines have been developed to a high degree of perfection. They use machines for the harvesting of grain and the mowing of hay. They have machines for taking up potatoes; these are designed in such a way that the potatoes are seized and thrown up into the barrel. They also have machines for milking and churning, for washing clothes and wringing them dry. Horses are used in the sawing of wood.

I like American customs and habits, opinions, and views very much, especially the fact that there is no class distinction here. The principle of equality has been universally accepted and adopted. The artisan, the farmer, and the laborer enjoy the same degree of respect as the merchant and the official. There is one class, however, which the Americans look askance at, that is the saloonkeepers, those who sell beer and liquor.

In this small town there are seven churches belonging to seven different congregations. Indeed, religious sects and nationalities are blended here in the most variegated manner; deep and sincere religious feeling is found side by side with the most uncompromising kind of rationalism.

With regard to political opinion, the parties are very sharply divided. The deep split between the President and the Congress, which was recently adjourned, you probably know about just as well as I do. Presumably you are also familiar with the murders in Memphis and New Orleans, with Wilkes Booth, John-copper-son, Arm in Arm or the Bread-and-Butter Convention in Philadelphia, as the Republican newspapers call it.

I now consider President Johnson a big ———, though I defended him when I was in Christiania. He has surrendered completely to "the Copperheads" and the Rebels in the South allied with them, and is furiously opposing the party that elevated him to power. Because of this, the Rebels have begun to stir once more. It has almost got to be so that a loyal man cannot travel, let alone stay, in most of the Southern states. During the absence of Sheridan — he has received military charge of Texas and Louisiana — the military in New Orleans was placed under the command of a former Rebel general by telegraphed order from the President. It is hard to imagine a greater insult either to the Army or the country.

But President Johnson is hardly furthering the cause of the South by behaving in this manner, as time will show very soon. The Republican press is breathing smoke and fire. Hundreds of newspapers which supported the President six months ago have changed their attitude completely. But the Republican Party is so strong that for a while yet it will have a majority both in the Senate and in Congress; and the South will not be allowed to send representatives until the North has received complete guarantees that the money and the blood expended on the defense of the Union were not sacrificed in vain.

The thunder and lightning here are quite dreadful. There is really something terrifying about the electric storms in this country. When they get really severe, it is as if the sky and everything you see were in flames, and the peals of thunder are so loud that they sound as if a thousand of the biggest Armstong guns were being fired at the same time. I have never been afraid at sea even during the most furious storms, and I believe that I am not chickenhearted; but I must confess that when the thunderstorms really break loose here, I do get scared.

17.

ANDREW JOHNSON: Representation for All Southern States

The political winds of 1866 did not favor President Johnson's program for restoration of the Rebel states. In spite of his summer speechmaking tour, Republican Radicals won a resounding victory in the fall elections. The Republicans had run on the qualified promise that the newly devised Fourteenth Amendment would provide the basis for Southern readmission to the Union. That the President had no intention of falling in line with the Republican policies is evident from the following portion of his second annual message to Congress, delivered on December 3, 1866.

Source: Richardson, VI, pp. 445-459.

IN MY MESSAGE of the 4th of December, 1865, Congress was informed of the measures which had been instituted by the executive with a view to the gradual restoration of the states in which the insurrection occurred to their relations with the general government. Provisional governors had been appointed, conventions called, governors elected, legislatures assembled, and senators and representatives chosen to the Congress of the United States. Courts had been opened for the enforcement of laws long in abeyance. The blockade had been removed, customhouses reestablished, and the internal-revenue laws put in force in order that the people might contribute to the national

Andrew Johnson; photo from the Brady-Handy Collection

income. Postal operations had been renewed, and efforts were being made to restore them to their former condition of efficiency. The states themselves had been asked to take part in the high function of amending the Constitution and of thus sanctioning the extinction of African slavery as one of the legitimate results of our internecine struggle.

Having progressed thus far, the Executive Department found that it had accomplished nearly all that was within the scope of its constitutional authority. One thing, however, yet remained to be done before the work of restoration could be completed, and that was the admission to Congress of loyal senators and representatives from the states whose people had rebelled against the lawful authority of the general government. This question devolved upon the respective houses, which by the Constitution are made the judges of the elections, returns, and qualifications of their own members; and its consideration at once engaged the attention of Congress.

In the meantime, the Executive Department — no other plan having been proposed by Congress — continued its efforts to perfect, as far as was practicable, the restoration of the proper relations between the citizens of the respective states, the states, and the federal government, extending from time to time, as the public interests seemed to require, the judicial, revenue, and postal systems of the country. With the advice and consent of the Senate, the necessary officers were appointed and appropriations made by Congress for the payment of their salaries.

The proposition to amend the federal Constitution so as to prevent the existence of slavery within the United States or any place subject to their jurisdiction was ratified by the requisite number of states; and, on the 18th day of December, 1865, it was officially declared to have become valid as a part of the Constitution of the United States. All of the states in which the insurrection had existed promptly amended their constitutions so as to make them conform to the great change thus effected in the organic law of the land; declared null and void all ordinances and laws of secession; repudiated all pretended debts and obligations created for the revolutionary purposes of the insurrection; and proceeded in good faith to the enactment of measures for the protection and amelioration of the condition of the colored race.

Congress, however, yet hesitated to admit any of these states to representation, and it was not until toward the close of the eighth month of the session that an exception was made in favor of Tennessee by the admission of her senators and representatives. I deem it a subject of profound regret that Congress has thus far failed to admit to seats loyal senators and representatives from the other states whose inhabitants, with those of Tennessee, had engaged in the rebellion.

Ten states — more than one-fourth of

the whole number — remain without representation; the seats of fifty members in the House of Representatives and of twenty members in the Senate are yet vacant, not by their own consent, not by a failure of election, but by the refusal of Congress to accept their credentials. Their admission, it is believed, would have accomplished much toward the renewal and strengthening of our relations as one people and removed serious cause for discontent on the part of the inhabitants of those states. It would have accorded with the great principle enunciated in the Declaration of American Independence that no people ought to bear the burden of taxation and yet be denied the right of representation. It would have been in consonance with the express provisions of the Constitution that "each state shall have at least one representative" and "that no state, without its consent, shall be deprived of its equal suffrage in the Senate."

These provisions were intended to secure to every state and to the people of every state the right of representation in each house of Congress; and so important was it deemed by the framers of the Constitution that the equality of the states in the Senate should be preserved that not even by an amendment of the Constitution can any state, without its consent, be denied a voice in that branch of the national legislature.

It is true it has been assumed that the existence of the states was terminated by the rebellious acts of their inhabitants, and that, the insurrection having been suppressed, they were thenceforward to be considered merely as conquered territories. The Legislative, Executive, and Judicial departments of the government have, however, with great distinctness and uniform consistency, refused to sanction an assumption so incompatible with the nature of our republican system and with the professed objects of the war. Throughout the recent legislation of Congress the undeniable fact makes itself apparent that these ten political communities are nothing less than states of this Union.

At the very commencement of the rebellion, each house declared, with a unanimity as remarkable as it was significant, that the war was not "waged upon our part in any spirit of oppression, nor for any purpose of conquest or subjugation, nor purpose of overthrowing or interfering with the rights or established institutions of those states, but to defend and maintain the supremacy of the Constitution and all laws made in pursuance thereof, and to preserve the Union, with all the dignity, equality, and rights of the several states unimpaired"; and that as soon as these objects were "accomplished the war ought to cease." In some instances, senators were permitted to continue their legislative functions; while, in other instances, representatives were elected and admitted to seats after their states had formally declared their right to withdraw from the Union and were endeavoring to maintain that right by force of arms.

All of the states whose people were in insurrection, as states, were included in the apportionment of the direct tax of $20 million annually laid upon the United States by the act approved August 5, 1861. Congress, by the act of March 4, 1862, and by the apportionment of representation thereunder also recognized their presence as states in the Union; and they have, for judicial purposes, been divided into districts, as states alone can be divided. The same recognition appears in the recent legislation in reference to Tennessee, which evidently rests upon the fact that the functions of the state were not destroyed by the rebellion but merely suspended; and that principle is of course applicable to those states which, like Tennessee, attempted to renounce their places in the Union.

The action of the Executive Department of the government upon this subject has been equally definite and uniform, and the purpose of the war was specifically stated in the proclamation issued by my predecessor on the 22nd day of September, 1862. It was then solemnly proclaimed and declared "that hereafter, as heretofore, the war will be prosecuted for the object of practically restoring the constitutional relation between the United States and each of the states and the people thereof in which states that relation is or may be suspended or disturbed."

The recognition of the states by the Judicial Department of the government has also been clear and conclusive in all proceedings affecting them as states had in the Supreme, Circuit, and District courts.

In the admission of senators and representatives from any and all of the states, there can be no just ground of apprehension that persons who are disloyal will be clothed with the powers of legislation, for this could not happen when the Constitution and the laws are enforced by a vigilant and faithful Congress. Each house is made the "judge of the elections, returns, and qualifications of its own members," and may, "with the concurrence of two-thirds, expel a member."

When a senator or representative presents his certificate of election, he may at once be admitted or rejected; or, should there be any question as to his eligibility, his credentials may be referred for investigation to the appropriate committee. If admitted to a seat, it must be upon evidence satisfactory to the house of which he thus becomes a member that he possesses the requisite constitutional and legal qualifications. If refused admission as a member for want of due allegiance to the government and returned to his constituents, they are admonished that none but persons loyal to the United States will be allowed a voice in the legislative councils of the nation, and the political power and moral influence of Congress are thus effectively exerted in the interests of loyalty to the government and fidelity to the Union.

Upon this question so vitally affecting the restoration of the Union and the permanency of our present form of government, my convictions, heretofore expressed, have undergone no change, but, on the contrary, their correctness has been confirmed by reflection and time. If the admission of loyal members to seats in the respective houses of Congress was wise and expedient a year ago, it is no less wise and expedient now. If this anomalous condition is right now — if in the exact condition of these states at the present time it is lawful to exclude them from representation — I do not see that the question will be changed by the efflux of time. Ten years hence, if these states remain as they are, the right of representation will be no stronger, the right of exclusion will be no weaker.

The Constitution of the United States makes it the duty of the President to recommend to the consideration of Congress "such measures as he shall judge necessary and expedient." I know of no measure more imperatively demanded by every consideration of national interest, sound policy, and equal justice than the admission of loyal members from the now unrepresented states. This would consummate the work of restoration and exert a most salutary influence in the reestablishment of peace, harmony, and fraternal feeling. It would tend greatly to renew the confidence of the American people in the vigor and stability of their institutions. It would bind us more closely together as a nation and enable us to show to the world the inherent and recuperative power of a government founded upon the will of the people and established upon the principles of liberty, justice, and intelligence.

Our increased strength and enhanced prosperity would irrefragably demonstrate the fallacy of the arguments against free institutions drawn from our recent national disorders by the enemies of republican government. The admission of loyal members from the states now excluded from Congress, by allaying doubt and apprehension, would turn capital now awaiting an opportunity for investment into the channels of trade and industry. It would alleviate the present troubled condition of those states, and, by inducing emigration, aid in the settlement of fertile regions now uncultivated and lead to an increased production of those staples which have added so greatly to the wealth of the nation and commerce of the world. New fields of enterprise would be opened to our progressive people, and soon the devastations of war would be repaired and all traces of our domestic differences effaced from the minds of our countrymen.

In our efforts to preserve "the unity of government which constitutes us one people" by restoring the states to the condition which they held prior to the rebellion, we should be cautious lest, having rescued our nation from perils of threatened disintegration, we resort to consolidation, and in the end absolute despotism, as a remedy for the recurrence of similar troubles. The war having terminated, and with it all occasion for the exercise of powers of doubtful constitutionality, we should hasten to bring legislation within the boundaries prescribed by the Constitution and to return to the ancient landmarks established by our fathers for the guidance of succeeding generations.

The constitution which at any time exists till changed by an explicit and authentic act of the whole people is sacredly obligatory upon all. . . . If in the opinion of the people the distribution or modification of the constitutional powers be in any particular wrong, let it be corrected by an amendment in the way which the Constitution designates; but let there be no change by usurpation, for . . . it is the customary weapon by which free governments are destroyed.

Washington spoke these words to his countrymen when, followed by their love and gratitude, he voluntarily retired from the cares of public life. "To keep in all things within the pale of our constitutional powers and cherish the federal Union as the only rock of safety" were prescribed by Jefferson as rules of action to endear to his "countrymen the true principles of their Constitution and promote a union of sentiment and action, equally auspicious to their happiness and safety." Jackson held that the action of the general government should always be strictly confined to the sphere of its appropriate duties, and justly and forcibly urged that our government is not to be maintained nor our Union preserved "by invasions of the rights and powers of the several states. In thus attempting to make our general government strong, we make it weak. Its true strength consists in leaving individuals and states as much as possible to themselves; in making itself felt, not in its power but in its beneficence; not in its control but in its protection; not in binding the states more closely to the center but leaving each to move unobstructed in its proper constitutional orbit."

These are the teachings of men whose deeds and services have made them illustrious, and who, long since withdrawn from the scenes of life, have left to their country the rich legacy of their example, their wisdom, and their patriotism. Drawing fresh inspiration from their lessons, let us emulate them in love of country and respect for the Constitution and the laws.

The principle [states' rights] for which we contended is bound to reassert itself, though it may be at another time and in another form.

JEFFERSON DAVIS, after the Civil War

1867

18.

Thomas J. Wood: Difficulties of Law Enforcement in Mississippi

Northerners watched the South closely in the months after the Civil War for signs of hostility and attitudes that might lead to a resurgence of rebellion. Every account of an injustice toward Union men or African Americans was fully reported in Northern newspapers. A committee in the House of Representatives collected such reports and launched an investigation in January 1867. Several Union military commanders whose assignments were in the South were called to testify. The testimony of Major General Thomas J. Wood, on January 28, about the situation in Mississippi is representative of what the committee heard.

Source: 39 Congress, 2 Session, House Report No. 23, pp. 29-31.

By the Chairman:

Q. You are in charge of a military department?

A. From November 1865 until the middle of August 1866, I was in command of the State of Mississippi, which was called the Department of Mississippi. From August 1866 until the middle of January 1867, it was called the District of Mississippi, but I exercised the same command for fourteen months as military commander; and for eight months, from the 1st of May, 1866, until the middle of January 1867, I was also assistant commissioner of the Freedmen's Bureau for that state, as well as military commander of the department and district.

Q. During your residence in the state I wish to inquire as to the frequency of criminal offenses against Union men, United States soldiers, and freedmen?

A. During the time I was in command in Mississippi the commission of such crimes as are described in the question have been frequent. It might be well to add that the commission of crime generally has been frequent, but more particularly against persons of Union proclivities and of Northern men who have emigrated to Mississippi since the termination of the troubles and against freed people. Murder was quite a frequent affair against freedmen everywhere in that community, and the commission of crimes of a lesser grade was still more frequent than the commission of murder, such as beating and assaults.

Q. Have you reported to General Howard all these offenses that have come to your knowledge?

A. Yes, sir; I made a report at the end of each month, so far as I could get any reliable evidence. At the time I left Mississippi I was engaged in collecting the reports of well-authenticated murders that had been committed. That report was not quite completed when I left Mississippi, but I presume my successor has completed and forwarded it.

Q. So far as you can judge, was the number of offenses of this description on the increase or decrease?

A. I could not say. There was a great deal of variation; some months more cases were reported and others less. My impression is that the number of cases of killing was on the increase; although, without a reference to my reports, I could not state that fact with certainty. As military commander I had troops stationed in the different parts of the state. The officers in charge of these troops were required to make reports of the state of public feeling, the occurrence of crime, and the administration of justice. As assistant commissioner of the bureau I had an officer stationed in each district whose business it was to give me a general account of the condition of affairs in this respect, not only as to offenses committed, but in respect to all the interests of the class subject to their charge as officers of the Freedmen's Bureau. I recollect that about September or October the number of cases so reported to me of offenses committed was greater than it had been any months previous. But that may have been merely one of those fluctuating periods when bad men gratified their revenge and did not indicate any regular increase of crime.

Q. You say the measures heretofore taken for the suppression of crime do not seem to have affected sensibly the diminution of crime?

A. No, sir; it seemed to me that the condition of things remained about the same.

Q. State as to the machinery for bringing those people to justice in the civil courts; whether they are adequate or inadequate.

A. The criminal laws of the state of Mississippi are, I think, very similar to the criminal laws of other states. The same grade of crimes is punishable by the statute in about the same way. The result of my observation was that great trouble grew out of the manner in which the executive and judicial officers performed their duties. They do not take proper means to bring criminals to justice. They do not use that vigilance as magistrates in investigating these cases, in issuing warrants of arrest, and in causing the constables and sheriffs to execute these warrants, that is essential to the proper administration of justice. When cases come into the higher courts, some of the better classes of judges are more disposed to do justice and to have the laws fairly executed; but my observation during the time I have held command in Mississippi has been that justice cannot be administered with the public sentiment of the people of the state such as it remains, against the black people and against Union men.

Q. Was that machinery so utterly defective as to the matter of protection of this class of people and the punishment of these offenses as to make the courts entirely unreliable?

A. Yes, sir; I should call it unreliable. That is a very good word. Not that in all cases these people are not protected in their rights. There are cases where black people and Union white people sue in the courts and recover judgment. The defect was not so much in the law as in the application of the law, though there are police laws in that state which are odious in their character.

Q. Do you know of any cases where citizens of Mississippi had been punished for high offenses against freedmen?

A. I have never heard of but one. That was, I think, in Madison County, where a white man was tried for killing a freedman and convicted of manslaughter and was sentenced to the penitentiary for one year. I am not positive that there have not been other cases, but that is the only one I ever heard of, and my information has been pretty good about the condition of affairs in that state as to the administration of justice.

Q. Without change in the administration of justice, what, in your judgment, is the prospect of affairs in that state in respect to the future?

A. Taking the whole code of laws of Mississippi, civil and criminal, including the police laws, which discriminate between the white men and black men, and taking the condition of public sentiment with the masses of the people, although there are some good people disposed to do justice, I do not think the administration of justice, as the laws are applied, is sufficient to secure the rights of liberty and property and the pursuits of peace to the freed people.

Q. Could you suggest any remedy for these difficulties?

A. Of course, it would be merely a matter of opinion, and perhaps not worth a great deal. The result of my observation in Mississippi led me to the conclusion that there should, by legislation of the government, be established some system by which, when the local courts fail to administer justice, some higher power could be brought into play to secure it. Of course, I do not go into details as to any particular plan. If a flagrant outrage is committed, and the local courts fail to take cognizance, or taking cognizance, their decision is flagrantly in viola-

tion of justice, there should be some revisory power, I do not say whether civil or military — that is for the legislature to decide — under which these offenders should be brought to justice.

Q. Would you say that, with the present condition of things, there is encouragement to believe they will be improved in the future?

A. In the present unsettled condition of a great portion of the Southern country — and I speak now particularly in reference to Mississippi — the want of a due administration of justice by the civil authorities, taken as a whole, in cases in which Union men or freedmen are concerned, taken in connection with the failure of the crops and the destitution that prevails, I do not think matters are likely to grow better; my observation in life having been that whenever crime goes unpunished, it becomes more instead of less frequent.

By Mr. Cooper:

Q. If the defect in the administration of justice is owing to the existence of the animosity you speak of, would not time have something to do with the removal of that feeling and the creation of a better public sentiment?

A. I suppose it is the history of troubles and animosities that they are ameliorated somewhat by time, but as a concomitant to that state of affairs, it seems to me that a fair administration of justice should go along with it, and as a part of the necessary amelioration of sentiment, I think that prosperity is important. I cannot see how, in any country, and especially an agricultural country, the people can prosper when the masses of the laboring people do not feel perfect and full security for all their rights.

Q. Within your department, for the last twelve months, have you known of any case of homicide committed upon a soldier, either white or colored, that has gone unpunished?

A. Yes, sir; there was one which happened during the last twelve months. It was the case of an officer of the Freedmen's Bureau, an officer also of the Army, who was assassinated at Grenada, Mississippi, and the criminal has never been apprehended or punished. In that case, however, it is proper to remark that, so far as I know, the civil authorities did exert themselves to have the man arrested; and, as a further proof that it was not their fault, I may say that I used due diligence with the military force at my command, and never succeeded in arresting the man, although I offered $1,000 for his apprehension. The difficulty is that the fellows who commit these crimes are screened by their confederates in crime. They are not known to the military, and they may be in our midst and still not be arrested because they are not known to us. One great difficulty is, as I have said, in the public sentiment. The better classes of the people, although they do not themselves commit crime, do not seem to feel a proper interest in bringing criminals to justice, nor is crime properly denounced in the press or through public meetings. In the case of this murder committed at Grenada, the murderer, whose name I believe was ascertained to be Wilson, I think he escaped to Texas. I was engaged in laying plans to secure his arrest before I left Mississippi.

By Mr. Farnsworth:

Q. In the present condition of popular feeling in Mississippi, can any adequate redress be obtained for crimes against freedmen, Union men, and United States soldiers through the civil courts?

A. In the present state of public feeling in Mississippi, taking the bulk of the people, I do not think there is a certain reliance that crime would be punished when committed against United States soldiers, Union men, or freedmen, or at least that a full measure of justice would be dealt out. I have known cases in which I think justice had been fairly administered, in civil cases, where a freedman or Union man was one of the litigants. But there is a want of assurance that justice will be fairly meted out, whether in civil or criminal cases, and that of itself tends to create a restless feeling on the part of emigrants there. It keeps away capital and prevents further immigration, of course. There are there, as everywhere, people who were willing to go there for the sake of money, and take the risk. I may repeat that it is not the better class of people who commit these crimes; they are committed by the rabble or by the lower order. The poorer classes, who still retain the malignant prejudices generated before and during the war, against Northern men and freedmen, they commit these crimes. But the complaint is made against the better classes of people that they are not diligent in bringing these men to justice; they are apathetic in their feelings and do not give the information which would enable the authorities to bring offenders to justice.

———————◆———————

If you shoot a Republican out of season, the fine will be ten dollars and costs.
                    Saying in Jackson, Mississippi, 1870s

19.

Andrew Johnson: Veto of Tenure of Office Act

The important off-year election of 1866 went heavily in favor of the Radical Republicans. By the time the 39th Congress convened in December it was apparent that the President's authority and prestige were much diminished. His vetoes were repeatedly ineffective against Congress. One more effort to detract from presidential power was the Tenure of Office Act, passed over a veto on March 2, 1867. The Act forbade the President to remove any officeholder, including Cabinet members, who had been appointed with Senate consent. It was the President's alleged violation of this Act by trying to remove Secretary of War Stanton that led to impeachment proceedings in 1868. Portions of the March 2 veto are reprinted below.

Source: Richardson, VI, pp. 492-498.

To the Senate of the United States:

I have carefully examined the bill "to regulate the tenure of certain civil offices." The material portion of the bill is contained in the 1st Section, and is of the effect following, namely:

That every person holding any civil office to which he has been appointed, by and with the advice and consent of the Senate, and every person who shall hereafter be appointed to any such office and shall become duly qualified to act therein, is and shall be entitled to hold such office until a successor shall have been appointed by the President, with the advice and consent of the Senate, and duly qualified; and that the secretaries of state, of the treasury, of war, of the Navy, and of the interior, the postmaster general, and the attorney general shall hold their offices respectively for and during the term of the President by whom they may have been appointed and for one month thereafter, subject to removal by and with the advice and consent of the Senate.

These provisions are qualified by a reservation in the 4th Section, "that nothing contained in the bill shall be construed to extend the term of any office the duration of which is limited by law." In effect, the bill provides that the President shall not remove from their places any of the civil officers whose terms of service are not limited by law without the advice and consent of the Senate of the United States. The bill in this respect conflicts, in my judgment, with the Constitution of the United States.

The question, as Congress is well aware, is by no means a new one. That the power of removal is constitutionally vested in the President of the United States is a principle which has been not more distinctly declared by judicial authority and judicial commentators than it has been uniformly practised upon by the Legislative and Executive departments of the government. The question arose in the House of Representatives so early as the 16th of June, 1789, on the bill for establishing an Executive Department, denominated "the Department of Foreign Affairs." The first clause of the bill, after recapitulating the functions of that officer and defining his duties, had these words: "To be removable from office by the President of the United States."

It was moved to strike out these words, and the motion was sustained with great ability and vigor. It was insisted that the President could not constitutionally exercise the power of removal exclusively of the Senate; that *The Federalist* so interpreted the Constitution when arguing for its adoption by the several states; that the Constitution had nowhere given the President power of removal, either expressly or by strong implication, but, on the contrary, had distinctly provided for removals from office by impeachment only. . . .

The nature of things, the great objects of society, the express objects of the Constitution itself require that this thing should be otherwise. To unite the Senate with the President in the exercise of the power, it was said, "would involve us in the most serious difficulty. Suppose a discovery of any of those events should take place when the Senate is not in session; how is the remedy to be applied? The evil could be avoided in no other way than by the Senate sitting always." In regard to the danger of the power being abused if exercised by one man, it was said "that the danger is as great with respect to the Senate, who are assembled from various parts of the continent, with different impressions and opinions"; "that such a body is more likely to misuse the power of removal than the man whom the united voice of America calls to the presidential chair. As the nature of government requires the power of removal," it was maintained, "that it should be exercised in this way by the hand capable of exerting itself with effect; and the power must be conferred on the President by the Constitu-

tion as the executive officer of the government." . . .

Under these circumstances, as a depositary of the executive authority of the nation, I do not feel at liberty to unite with Congress in reversing it by giving my approval to the bill. At the early day when this question was settled, and, indeed, at the several periods when it has subsequently been agitated, the success of the Constitution of the United States, as a new and peculiar system of free, representative government, was held doubtful in other countries and was even a subject of patriotic apprehension among the American people themselves. A trial of nearly eighty years, through the vicissitudes of foreign conflicts and of civil war, is confidently regarded as having extinguished all such doubts and apprehensions for the future.

During that eighty years, the people of the United States have enjoyed a measure of security, peace, prosperity, and happiness never surpassed by any nation. It cannot be doubted that the triumphant success of the Constitution is due to the wonderful wisdom with which the functions of government were distributed between the three principal departments — the Legislative, the Executive, and the Judicial — and to the fidelity with which each has confined itself or been confined by the general voice of the nation within its peculiar and proper sphere. While a just, proper, and watchful jealousy of executive power constantly prevails, as it ought ever to prevail, yet it is equally true that an efficient executive, capable, in the language of the oath prescribed to the President, of executing the laws and, within the sphere of executive action, of preserving, protecting, and defending the Constitution of the United States, is an indispensable security for tranquillity at home and peace, honor, and safety abroad.

Governments have been erected in many countries upon our model. If one or many of them have thus far failed in fully securing to their people the benefits which we have derived from our system, it may be confidently asserted that their misfortune has resulted from their unfortunate failure to maintain the integrity of each of the three great departments while preserving harmony among them all.

Having at an early period accepted the Constitution in regard to the executive office in the sense in which it was interpreted with the concurrence of its founders, I have found no sufficient grounds in the arguments now opposed to that construction or in any assumed necessity of the times for changing those opinions. For these reasons I return the bill to the Senate, in which house it originated, for the further consideration of Congress which the Constitution prescribes. Insomuch as the several parts of the bill which I have not considered are matters chiefly of detail and are based altogether upon the theory of the Constitution from which I am obliged to dissent, I have not thought it necessary to examine them with a view to make them an occasion of distinct and special objections.

20.

Congressional Interference with the Command of the Army

The attempt of Congress, under the Radical Republicans, to assert its supremacy over the states and the executive was perhaps the most significant attack on the separation of powers that the Constitution has ever faced. On March 2, 1867, Congress, by means of an amendment tacked on to the Army Appropriation Act, succeeded in circumventing the President's position as commander in chief of the Army. The amendment provided that the President channel all military orders through the general of the Army, who could not be removed or reassigned without the consent of the Senate. Johnson signed the bill in order to obtain the military appropriations but not without entering a protest against the provisions depriving him of his power. A portion of the Appropriation Act is reprinted here.

Source: *Statues*, XIV, pp. 485-487.

An Act making appropriations for the support of the Army for the year ending June 30, 1868, and for other purposes. . . .

Section 2. *And be it further enacted,* that the headquarters of the General of the Army of the United States shall be at the city of Washington, and all orders and instructions relating to military operations issued by the President or secretary of war shall be issued through the General of the Army, and, in case of his inability, through the next in rank. The General of the Army shall not be removed, suspended, or relieved from command, or assigned to duty elsewhere than at said headquarters, except at his own request, without the previous approval of the Senate; and any orders or instructions relating to military operations issued contrary to the requirements of this section shall be null and void; and any officer who shall issue orders or instructions contrary to the provisions of this section shall be deemed guilty of a misdemeanor in office; and any officer of the Army who shall transmit, convey, or obey any orders or instructions so issued contrary to the provisions of this section, knowing that such orders were so issued, shall be liable to imprisonment for not less than two nor more than twenty years, upon conviction thereof in any court of competent jurisdiction.

21.

The Struggle Between Congress and the President Over Reconstruction

The First Reconstruction Act became law March 2, 1867, after many months of disagreement in Congress. Thaddeus Stevens had proposed and the House finally approved a military-government bill that would have suspended Southern political life until further notice. The Senate, however, had insisted on the insertion of an amendment, proposed by James G. Blaine, that offered readmission to the Southern states after they had ratified the Fourteenth Amendment and guaranteed African American suffrage. On second hearing the House further modified the Senate bill by adding the Wilson and Shellabarger amendments, but imposed wide scale disfranchisement and defined the existing civil governments as temporary in character and subject to military control. President Andrew Johnson vetoed the bill on March 2, rejecting its basic assumption that there were no lawful governments in the seceded states. Congress repassed the bill the same day over Johnson's veto. One of the main provisions of the First Reconstruction Act soon failed in practice when it became clear that the Southern states would prefer military rule to civil government based partially on African American suffrage. Congress therefore passed a supplementary Reconstruction Act, March 23, 1867, authorizing military commanders to supervise elections and generally to provide the machinery for constituting new governments. President Johnson vetoed this Second Reconstruction Act also, on March 23, on the grounds that it interfered with the right of the American citizen to "be left to the free exercise of his own judgment . . . when he is engaged in the work of forming the fundamental law under which he is to live." Once again, Congress passed the act over Johnson's veto that very day. In the selection below, the First Reconstruction Act is complete, as is the second veto; the first veto is reprinted in part.

Source: *Statutes,* XIV, pp. 428-429.   Richardson, VI, pp. 498-511, 531-535.

I.

First Reconstruction Act

An act to provide for the more efficient government of the Rebel states.

Whereas no legal state governments or adequate protection for life or property now exists in the Rebel states of Virginia, North Carolina, South Carolina, Georgia, Mississippi, Alabama, Louisiana, Florida, Texas, and Arkansas; and *whereas* it is necessary that peace and good order should be enforced in said states until loyal and republican state governments can be legally established; therefore,

Be it enacted by the Senate and House of Representatives of the United States of America in Congress assembled, that said Rebel states shall be divided into military districts and made subject to the military authority of the United States as hereinafter prescribed, and for that purpose Virginia shall constitute the first district; North Carolina and South Carolina the second district; Georgia, Alabama, and Florida the third district; Mississippi and Arkansas the fourth district; and Louisiana and Texas the fifth district.

Section 2. *And be it further enacted,* that it shall be the duty of the President to assign to the command of each of said districts an officer of the Army, not below the rank of brigadier general, and to detail a sufficient military force to enable such officer to perform his duties and enforce his authority within the district to which he is assigned.

Section 3. *And be it further enacted,* that it shall be the duty of each officer assigned as aforesaid to protect all persons in their rights of person and property, to suppress insurrection, disorder, and violence, and to punish or cause to be punished all disturbers of the public peace and criminals; and to this end he may allow local civil tribunals to take jurisdiction of and to try offenders, or, when in his judgment it may be necessary for the trial of offenders, he shall have power to organize military commissions or tribunals for that purpose, and all interference under color of state authority with the exercise of military authority under this act shall be null and void.

Section 4. *And be it further enacted,* that all persons put under military arrest by virtue of this act shall be tried without unnecessary delay, and no cruel or unusual punishment shall be inflicted, and no sentence of any military commission or tribunal

hereby authorized affecting the life or liberty of any person shall be executed until it is approved by the officer in command of the district, and the laws and regulations for the government of the Army shall not be affected by this act, except insofar as they conflict with its provisions: *Provided,* that no sentence of death under the provisions of this act shall be carried into effect without the approval of the President.

Section 5. *And be it further enacted,* that when the people of any one of said Rebel states shall have formed a constitution of government in conformity with the Constitution of the United States in all respects, framed by a convention of delegates elected by the male citizens of said state, twenty-one years old and upward, of whatever race, color, or previous condition, who have been resident in said state for one year previous to the day of such election, except such as may be disfranchised for participation in the rebellion or for felony at common law, and when such constitution shall provide that the elective franchise shall be enjoyed by all such persons as have the qualifications herein stated for electors of delegates, and when such constitution shall be ratified by a majority of the persons voting on the question of ratification who are qualified as electors for delegates, and when such constitution shall have been submitted to Congress for examination and approval, and Congress shall have approved the same; and when said state, by a vote of its legislature elected under said constitution, shall have adopted the amendment to the Constitution of the United States, proposed by the Thirty-ninth Congress and known as Article Fourteen, and when said article shall have become a part of the Constitution of the United States, said state shall be declared entitled to representation in Congress, and senators and representatives shall be admitted therefrom on their taking the oath prescribed by law, and then and thereafter the preceding sections of this act shall be inoperative in said state: *Provided*, that no person excluded from the privilege of holding office by said proposed amendment to the Constitution of the United States shall be eligible to election as a member of the convention to frame a constitution for any of said Rebel states, nor shall any such person vote for members of such convention.

Section 6. *And be it further enacted*, that, until the people of said Rebel states shall be by law admitted to representation in the Congress of the United States, any civil governments which may exist therein shall be deemed provisional only, and in all respects subject to the paramount authority of the United States at any time to abolish, modify, control, or supersede the same; and in all elections to any office under such provisional governments all persons shall be entitled to vote, and none others, who are entitled to vote under the provisions of the 5th Section of this act; and no person shall be eligible to any office under any such provisional governments who would be disqualified from holding office under the provisions of the 3rd Article of said constitutional amendment.

II.

Andrew Johnson: First Reconstruction Veto

To the House of Representatives:

I have examined the bill "to provide for the more efficient government of the Rebel states" with the care and anxiety which its transcendent importance is calculated to awaken. I am unable to give it my assent for reasons so grave that I hope a statement of them may have some influence on the minds of the patriotic and enlightened men with whom the decision must ultimately rest. . . .

All the information I have on the subject convinces me that the masses of the Southern people and those who control their public acts, while they entertain diverse opinions on questions of federal policy, are completely united in the effort to reorganize their society on the basis of peace and to restore their mutual prosperity as rapidly and as completely as their circumstances will permit.

The bill, however, would seem to show upon its face that the establishment of peace and good order is not its real object. The 5th Section declares that the preceding sections shall cease to operate in any state where certain events shall have happened. These events are, first, the selection of delegates to a state convention by an election at which Negroes shall be allowed to vote; second, the formation of a state constitution by the convention so chosen; third, the insertion into the state constitution of a provision which will secure the right of voting at all elections to Negroes and to such white men as may not be disfranchised for rebellion or felony; fourth, the submission of the constitution for ratification to Negroes and white men not disfranchised, and its actual ratification by their vote; fifth, the submission of the state constitution to Congress for examination and approval, and the actual approval of it by that body; sixth, the adoption of a certain amendment to the federal Constitution by a vote of the legislature elected under the new constitution; seventh, the adoption of said amendment by a sufficient number of other states to make it a part of the Constitution of the United States.

All these conditions must be fulfilled before the people of any of these states can be relieved from the bondage of military domination; but when they are fulfilled, then immediately the pains and penalties of the bill are to cease, no matter whether there be peace and order or not, and without any reference to the security of life or property. The excuse given for the bill in the preamble is admitted by the bill itself not to be real. The military rule which it establishes is plainly to be used, not for any purpose of order or for the prevention of crime but solely as a means of coercing the people into the adoption of principles and measures to which it is known that they are opposed and upon which they have an undeniable right to exercise their own judgment.

I submit to Congress whether this measure is not in its whole character, scope, and object without precedent and without authority, in palpable conflict with the plainest provisions of the Constitution, and utterly destructive to those great principles of liberty and humanity for which our ancestors on both sides of the Atlantic have shed so much blood and expended so much treasure. . . .

It is plain that the authority here given to the military officer amounts to absolute despotism. But to make it still more unendurable, the bill provides that it may be delegated to as many subordinates as he chooses to appoint, for it declares that he shall "punish or cause to be punished." Such a power has not been wielded by any monarch in England for more than 500 years. In all that time no people who speak the English language have borne such servitude. It reduces the whole population of the ten states — all persons, of every color, sex, and condition, and every stranger within their limits — to the most abject and degrading slavery. No master ever had a control so absolute over the slaves as this bill gives to the military officers over both white and colored persons.

It may be answered to this that the officers of the Army are too magnanimous, just, and humane to oppress and trample upon a subjugated people. I do not doubt that Army officers are as well entitled to this kind of confidence as any other class of men. But the history of the world has been written in vain if it does not teach us that unrestrained authority can never be safely trusted in human hands. . . .

I come now to a question which is, if possible, still more important. Have we the power to establish and carry into execution a measure like this? I answer, certainly not, if we derive our authority from the Constitution and if we are bound by the limitations which it imposes.

This proposition is perfectly clear, that no branch of the federal government — executive, legislative, or judicial — can have any just powers except those which it derives through and exercises under the organic law of the Union. Outside of the Constitution we have no legal authority more than private citizens, and within it we have only so much as that instrument gives us. This broad principle limits all our functions and applies to all subjects. It protects not only the citizens of states which are within the Union but it shields every human being who comes or is brought under our jurisdiction. We have no right to do in one place more than in another that which the Constitution says we shall not do at all. If, therefore, the Southern states were in truth out of the Union, we could not treat their people in a way which the fundamental law forbids.

Some persons assume that the success of our arms in crushing the opposition, which was made in some of the states to the execution of the federal laws, reduced those states and all their people — the innocent as well as the guilty — to the condition of vassalage and gave us a power over them which the Constitution does not bestow or define or limit. No fallacy can be more transparent than this. Our victories subjected the insurgents to legal obedience, not to the yoke of an arbitrary despotism. When an absolute sovereign reduces his rebellious subjects, he may deal with them according to his pleasure, because he had that power before. But when a limited monarch puts down an insurrection, he must still govern according to law.

If an insurrection should take place in

one of our states against the authority of the state government and end in the overthrow of those who planned it, would that take away the rights of all the people of the counties where it was favored by a part or a majority of the population? Could they for such a reason be wholly outlawed and deprived of their representation in the legislature? I have always contended that the government of the United States was sovereign within its constitutional sphere; that it executed its laws, like the states themselves, by applying its coercive power directly to individuals, and that it could put down insurrection with the same effect as a state and no other. The opposite doctrine is the worst heresy of those who advocated secession and cannot be agreed to without admitting that heresy to be right.

Invasion, insurrection, rebellion, and domestic violence were anticipated when the government was framed, and the means of repelling and suppressing them were wisely provided for in the Constitution; but it was not thought necessary to declare that the states in which they might occur should be expelled from the Union. Rebellions, which were invariably suppressed, occurred prior to that out of which these questions grow; but the states continued to exist and the Union remained unbroken. In Massachusetts, in Pennsylvania, in Rhode Island, and in New York, at different periods in our history, violent and armed opposition to the United States was carried on; but the relations of those states with the federal government were not supposed to be interrupted or changed thereby after the rebellious portions of their population were defeated and put down.

It is true that in these earlier cases there was no formal expression of a determination to withdraw from the Union, but it is also true that in the Southern states the ordinances of secession were treated by all the friends of the Union as mere nullities and are now acknowledged to be so by the

states themselves. If we admit that they had any force or validity or that they did in fact take the states in which they were passed out of the Union, we sweep from under our feet all the grounds upon which we stand in justifying the use of federal force to maintain the integrity of the government. . . .

It will be observed that of the three kinds of military jurisdiction which can be exercised or created under our Constitution there is but one that can prevail in time of peace, and that is the code of laws enacted by Congress for the government of the national forces. That body of military law has no application to the citizen, nor even to the citizen soldier enrolled in the militia in time of peace. But this bill is not a part of that sort of military law, for that applies only to the soldier and not to the citizen, while, contrariwise, the military law provided by this bill applies only to the citizen and not to the soldier. . . .

This bill holds every person not a soldier answerable for all crimes and all charges without any presentment. The Constitution declares that "no person shall be deprived of life, liberty, or property without due process of law." This bill sets aside all process of law and makes the citizen answerable in his person and property to the will of one man, and as to his life, to the will of two. Finally, the Constitution declares that "the privilege of the writ of habeas corpus shall not be suspended unless when, in case of rebellion or invasion, the public safety may require it"; whereas this bill declares martial law (which of itself suspends this great writ) in time of peace, and authorizes the military to make the arrest, and gives to the prisoner only one privilege and that is a trial "without unnecessary delay." He has no hope of release from custody, except the hope, such as it is, of release by acquittal before a military commission.

The United States are bound to guarantee to each state a republican form of government. Can it be pretended that this obligation is not palpably broken if we carry out a measure like this, which wipes away every vestige of republican government in ten states and puts the life, property, liberty, and honor of all the people in each of them under the domination of a single person clothed with unlimited authority? . . .

The purpose and object of the bill — the general intent which pervades it from beginning to end — is to change the entire structure and character of the state governments and to compel them by force to the adoption of organic laws and regulations which they are unwilling to accept if left to themselves. The Negroes have not asked for the privilege of voting; the vast majority of them have no idea what it means. This bill not only thrusts it into their hands but compels them, as well as the whites, to use it in a particular way. If they do not form a constitution with prescribed articles in it and afterward elect a legislature which will act upon certain measures in a prescribed way, neither blacks nor whites can be relieved from the slavery which the bill imposes upon them.

Without pausing here to consider the policy or impolicy of Africanizing the southern part of our territory, I would simply ask the attention of Congress to that manifest, well-known, and universally acknowledged rule of constitutional law which declares that the federal government has no jurisdiction, authority, or power to regulate such subjects for any state. To force the right of suffrage out of the hands of the white people and into the hands of the Negroes is an arbitrary violation of this principle. . . .

The bill also denies the legality of the governments of ten of the states which participated in the ratification of the amendment to the federal Constitution abolishing slavery forever within the jurisdiction of the United States and practically excludes them from the Union. If this assumption of the bill be correct, their concurrence cannot be considered as having been legally given, and the important fact is made to appear that the consent of three-fourths of the states — the requisite number — has not been constitutionally obtained to the ratification of that amendment, thus leaving the question of slavery where it stood before the amendment was officially declared to have become a part of the Constitution.

That the measure proposed by this bill does violate the Constitution in the particulars mentioned and in many other ways which I forbear to enumerate is too clear to admit of the least doubt. . . .

While we are legislating upon subjects which are of great importance to the whole people, and which must affect all parts of the country, not only during the life of the present generation but for ages to come, we should remember that all men are entitled at least to a hearing in the councils which decide upon the destiny of themselves and their children. At present, ten states are denied representation, and when the Fortieth Congress assembles on the 4th day of the present month, sixteen states will be without a voice in the House of Representatives. This grave fact, with the important questions before us, should induce us to pause in a course of legislation which, looking solely to the attainment of political ends, fails to consider the rights it transgresses, the law which it violates, or the institutions which it imperils.

III.

ANDREW JOHNSON: Second Reconstruction Veto

To the House of Representatives:

I have considered the bill entitled "An act supplementary to an act entitled 'An act to provide for the more efficient government of the Rebel states,' passed March 2, 1867, and to facilitate restoration," and now return it to the House of Representatives with my objections.

This bill provides for elections in the ten states brought under the operation of the original act to which it is supplementary. Its details are principally directed to the elections for the formation of the state constitutions, but by the 6th Section of the bill, "all elections" in these states occurring while the original act remains in force are brought within its purview.

Referring to these details, it will be found that, first of all, there is to be a registration of the voters. No one whose name has not been admitted on the list is to be allowed to vote at any of these elections. To ascertain who is entitled to registration, reference is made necessary, by the express language of the supplement, to the original act and to the pending bill. The 5th Section of the original act provides, as to voters, that they shall be "male citizens of the state, twenty-one years old and upward, of whatever race, color, or previous condition, who have been residents of said state for one year." This is the general qualification, followed, however, by many exceptions.

No one can be registered, according to the original act, "who may be disfranchised for participation in the rebellion" — a provision which left undetermined the question as to what amounted to disfranchisement, and whether without a judicial sentence the act itself produced that effect. This supplemental bill superadds an oath, to be taken by every person before his name can be admitted upon the registration, that he has "not been disfranchised for participation in any rebellion or civil war against the United States." It thus imposes upon every person the necessity and responsibility of deciding for himself, under the peril of punishment by a military commission if he makes a mistake, what works disfranchisement by participation in rebellion and what amounts to such participation.

Almost every man — the Negro as well as the white — above twenty-one years of age who was resident in these ten states during the rebellion, voluntarily or involuntarily, at some time and in some way, did participate in resistance to the lawful authority of the general government. The question with the citizen to whom this oath is to be proposed must be a fearful one, for while the bill does not declare that perjury may be assigned for such false swearing nor fix any penalty for the offense, we must not forget that martial law prevails; that every person is answerable to a military commission, without previous presentment by a grand jury, for any charge that may be made against him, and that the supreme authority of the military commander determines the question as to what is an offense and what is to be the measure of punishment.

The 4th Section of the bill provides "that the commanding general of each district shall appoint as many boards of registration as may be necessary, consisting of three loyal officers or persons." The only qualification stated for these officers is that they must be "loyal." They may be persons in the military service or civilians, residents of the state or strangers. Yet these persons are to exercise most important duties and are vested with unlimited discretion. They are to decide what names shall be placed upon the register and from their decision there is to be no appeal. They are to superintend the elections and to decide all questions which may arise. They are to have the custody of the ballots and to make return of the persons elected. Whatever frauds or errors they may commit must pass without redress. All that is left for the commanding general is to receive the returns of the elections, open the same, and ascertain who are chosen "according to the returns of the officers who conducted said elections." By such means and with this sort of agency are the conventions of delegates to be constituted.

As the delegates are to speak for the people, common justice would seem to require that they should have authority from the people themselves. No convention so constituted will in any sense represent the wishes of the inhabitants of these states, for under the all-embracing exceptions of these laws, by a construction which the uncertainty of the clause as to disfranchisement leaves open to the board of officers, the great body of the people may be excluded from the polls and from all opportunity of expressing their own wishes or voting for delegates who will faithfully reflect their sentiments.

I do not deem it necessary further to investigate the details of this bill. No consideration could induce me to give my approval to such an election law for any purpose and especially for the great purpose of framing the constitution of a state. If ever the American citizen should be left to the free exercise of his own judgment, it is when he is engaged in the work of forming the fundamental law under which he is to live. That work is his work, and it cannot properly be taken out of his hands. All this legislation proceeds upon the contrary assumption that the people of each of these states shall have no constitution except such as may be arbitrarily dictated by Congress and formed under the restraint of military rule. A plain statement of facts makes this evident.

In all these states there are existing constitutions, framed in the accustomed way by the people. Congress, however, declares that these constitutions are not "loyal and republican," and requires the people to form them anew. What, then, in the opinion of Congress, is necessary to make the constitution of a state "loyal and republican"? The original act answers the question: It is universal Negro suffrage — a question which the federal Constitution leaves exclusively to the states themselves. All this legislative machinery of martial law, military coercion,

and political disfranchisement is avowedly for that purpose and none other. The existing constitutions of the ten states conform to the acknowledged standards of loyalty and republicanism. Indeed, if there are degrees in republican forms of government, their constitutions are more republican now than when these states, four of which were members of the original thirteen, first became members of the Union.

Congress does not now demand that a single provision of their constitutions be changed except such as confine suffrage to the white population. It is apparent, therefore, that these provisions do not conform to the standard of republicanism which Congress seeks to establish. That there may be no mistake, it is only necessary that reference should be made to the original act, which declares "such constitution shall provide that the elective franchise shall be enjoyed by all such persons as have the qualifications herein stated for electors of delegates." What class of persons is here meant clearly appears in the same section; that is to say, "the male citizens of said state twenty-one years old and upward, of whatever race, color, or previous condition, who have been resident in said state for one year previous to the day of such election."

Without these provisions no constitution which can be framed in any one of the ten states will be of any avail with Congress. This, then, is the test of what the constitution of a state of this Union must contain to make it republican. Measured by such a standard, how few of the states now composing the Union have republican constitutions! If in the exercise of the constitutional guaranty that Congress shall secure to every state a republican form of government, universal suffrage for blacks as well as whites is a *sine qua non*, the work of reconstruction may as well begin in Ohio as in Virginia, in Pennsylvania as in North Carolina.

When I contemplate the millions of our fellow citizens of the South with no alternative left but to impose upon themselves this fearful and untried experiment of complete Negro enfranchisement — and white disfranchisement, it may be, almost as complete — or submit indefinitely to the rigor of martial law, without a single attribute of freemen, deprived of all the sacred guaranties of our federal Constitution, and threatened with even worse wrongs, if any worse are possible, it seems to me their condition is the most deplorable to which any people can be reduced. It is true that they have been engaged in rebellion, and, that their object being a separation of the states and a dissolution of the Union, there was an obligation resting upon every loyal citizen to treat them as enemies and to wage war against their cause.

Inflexibly opposed to any movement imperiling the integrity of the government, I did not hesitate to urge the adoption of all measures necessary for the suppression of the insurrection. After a long and terrible struggle, the efforts of the government were triumphantly successful, and the people of the South, submitting to the stern arbitrament, yielded forever the issues of the contest. Hostilities terminated soon after it became my duty to assume the responsibilities of the chief executive officer of the republic, and I at once endeavored to repress and control the passions which our civil strife had engendered, and, no longer regarding these erring millions as enemies, again acknowledged them as our friends and our countrymen. The war had accomplished its objects. The nation was saved and that seminal principle of mischief which from the birth of the government had gradually but inevitably brought on the rebellion was totally eradicated.

Then, it seemed to me, was the auspicious time to commence the work of reconciliation; then, when these people sought once more our friendship and protection, I considered it our duty generously to meet them in the spirit of charity and forgiveness

and to conquer them even more effectually by the magnanimity of the nation than by the force of its arms. I yet believe that if the policy of reconciliation then inaugurated, and which contemplated an early restoration of these people to all their political rights, had received the support of Congress, every one of these ten states and all their people would at this moment be fast anchored in the Union and the great work which gave the war all its sanction and made it just and holy would have been accomplished. Then, over all the vast and fruitful regions of the South, peace and its blessings would have prevailed, while now millions are deprived of rights guaranteed by the Constitution to every citizen and after nearly two years of legislation find themselves placed under an absolute military despotism.

"A military republic, a government founded on mock elections and supported only by the sword," was nearly a quarter of a century since pronounced by Daniel Webster, when speaking of the South American states, as "a movement, indeed, but a retrograde and disastrous movement, from the regular and old-fashioned monarchical systems"; and he added:

If men would enjoy the blessings of republican government, they must govern themselves by reason, by mutual counsel and consultation, by a sense and feeling of general interest, and by the acquiescence of the minority in the will of the majority, properly expressed; and, above all, the military must be kept, according to the language of our Bill of Rights, in strict subordination to the civil authority. Wherever this lesson is not both learned and practised there can be no political freedom. Absurd, preposterous is it, a scoff and a satire on free forms of constitutional liberty, for frames of government to be prescribed by military leaders and the right of suffrage to be exercised at the point of the sword.

I confidently believe that a time will come when these states will again occupy their true positions in the Union. The barriers which now seem so obstinate must yield to the force of an enlightened and just public opinion, and sooner or later unconstitutional and oppressive legislation will be effaced from our statute books. When this shall have been consummated, I pray God that the errors of the past may be forgotten and that once more we shall be a happy, united, and prosperous people, and that at last, after the bitter and eventful experience through which the nation has passed, we shall all come to know that our only safety is in the preservation of our federal Constitution and in according to every American citizen and to every state the rights which that Constitution secures.

22.

Ferdinand V. Hayden: Trees for the Arid West

Ferdinand Hayden, a Civil War surgeon turned geologist, in 1866 undertook an expedition through the Great Plains for the Academy of Natural Sciences of Philadelphia. This vast plains area, known as the "Great American Desert," was the last section of the country to be settled; it was the domain of the Indian and the cattleman and would remain so until farmers could learn to cope with the low rainfall and absence of trees for housing and fencing. Hayden's 1866 expedition and a later one for the General Land Office convinced him to join other ecologists in advocating a program of tree planting. Out of his work came the establishment of the United States Geological Survey in 1879. It was not until the 1930s that President Franklin D. Roosevelt instituted a program of planting forest belts, as Hayden had recommended in the following letter to the commissioner of the General Land Office, dated July 1, 1867.

Source: 40 Congress, 2 Session, House Executive Document No. 1, pp. 152-205.

I WOULD . . . SPEAK of the great importance of planting trees in this country and the great ease with which these cultivated forests may be produced.

I do not believe that the prairies proper will ever become covered with timber except by artificial means. Since the surface of the country received its present geological configuration, no trees have grown there, but, during the Tertiary Period, when the lignite, or "brown coal," beds were deposited, all these treeless plains were covered with a luxuriant growth of forest trees like those of the Gulf states or South America. Here were palm trees, with leaves having a spread of twelve feet; gigantic sycamores — several species; maples, poplars, cedars, hickories, cinnamon, fig, and many varieties now found only in tropical or subtropical climates.

Large portions of the Upper Missouri country, especially along the Yellowstone River, are now covered with the silicified trunks of trees, sixty to seventy feet in length and two to four feet in diameter, exhibiting the annual rings of growth as perfectly as in our recent elms or maples. We are daily obtaining more and more evidence that these forests may be restored again to a certain extent, at least, and thus a belt or zone of country about 500 miles in width east of the base of the mountains be redeemed. It is believed, also, that the planting of ten or fifteen acres of forest trees on each quarter section will have a most important effect on the climate, equalizing and increasing the moisture and adding greatly to the fertility of the soil.

The settlement of the country and the increase of the timber has already changed for the better the climate of that portion of Nebraska lying along the Missouri, so that within the last twelve or fourteen years the rain has gradually increased in quantity and is more equally distributed through the year. I am confident this change will continue to extend across the dry belt to the foot of the Rocky Mountains as the settlements extend and the forest trees are planted in proper quantities. . . .

I propose to show that these ideas are not purely theoretical, and that the influence of trees on climate and humidity has been investigated by some of the ablest scientific men in this country and in Europe. . . .

The forest presenting a considerable surface for evaporation gives to its own soil and the adjacent ground an abundant and enlivening dew. Forests, in a word, exert in the interior of continents an influence like that of the sea on the climates of islands and of coasts; both water the soil and thereby insure its fertility. . . . I might cite many examples from the African deserts how the planting of palm trees is redeeming those barren sands.

Much might also be said in regard to the influence of woods in protecting the soil and promoting the increase in number and the flow of springs, but all I wish is to show the possibility of the power of man to restore to these now treeless and almost rainless prairies the primitive forests and the humidity which accompanies them.

The counties of Otoe, Nemaha, and Richardson contain more timberland than any other portion of the state, and the aggressive character of the patches of woodland can be seen everywhere. Hundreds of acres have been covered over with a fine healthy growth of hickory, walnut, oak, soft maple, coffee, bean, basswood, etc., within the past ten or twelve years, since the fires have been kept away and protection afforded the young trees by the settlements.

In the more southern counties, the success in planting trees and in raising fruits, especially the smaller kinds, is even more marked than north of the Platte. All kinds of garden vegetables grow better in Nebraska than in any region with which I am acquainted. The crops, when not injured by the grasshopper, are looking very fine at this time. The corn has escaped so far, and is pressing forward with great rapidity.

Up to the 1st of July, I did not see any grasshoppers, except within a radius of four or five miles around Nebraska City. There they were most abundant and destructive. July 2 and 3 they commenced their flight northward, filling the air as high as the eye could reach, looking much like flakes of snow. They have committed some depredation in south Nebraska, but more especially in Kansas. Whenever counties become more thickly settled and more densely wooded so that the annual amount of moisture is more equally distributed over the year, this pest, I believe, will entirely disappear.

23.

Proposal for an Agricultural Society

The National Grange of the Patrons of Husbandry was organized by Oliver H. Kelley, along with six associates, in December 1867 as a mutual improvement and assistance society for farmers. It laid the groundwork for the National Granger movement that flourished during the latter part of the nineteenth century. Kelley had toured the South as an employee of the Bureau of Agriculture; shocked by the inefficient agricultural methods employed there, he resolved to organize farmers for education and social reform. Kelley outlined his program in the following letter, of which only 300 copies were mailed in November 1867. As the movement grew to a membership of 800,000 by 1874, it became increasingly active politically, then partially collapsed in 1880. Later reorganization returned the group to Kelley's original principles of educational and social progress divorced from political action.

Source: Oliver H. Kelley, *Origin and Progress of the Order of the Patrons of Husbandry in the United States,* Philadelphia, 1875, pp. 38-40.

A NUMBER OF GENTLEMEN engaged in agriculture and its kindred branches in different states are now perfecting a ritual for an order, to be composed wholly of persons, male and female, directly interested in agricultural pursuits.

The order will secure to its members all the advantages of Masonry, but while that is speculative, this will be operative; its main object being to encourage and advance education in all branches of agriculture.

The order will have its lodges, known as "temples of industry," or similar appellation. The work in a temple will be divided into four degrees.

The ceremonies of passing from one degree to the other are made pleasing and instructive. Every tool used in agriculture has its appropriate lecture, the aim being to instruct practically and morally in every possible way, and also add an interest to the most noble of all occupations — the cultivation of the soil.

It is believed that by admitting the young folks of both sexes at fourteen or sixteen years of age, it will have a tendency to instill in their minds a fondness for rural life and prevent, in a great measure, so many of them flocking to the cities, where all occupations are now crowded, and at the same time depriving the country of that class of young men so much needed there.

The ceremonies in the degrees for the ladies are slightly different but of the same nature, and intended to lighten and render their household duties more pleasing.

The whole, it is believed, will do much toward elevating our occupation, as well as establishing a unity of sentiment among the farmers of the country, and materially increase the circulation of publications devoted to the interests of agriculture, and consequent increase of knowledge.

Politics and religion are *not* subjects of discussion. Private work of the order will occupy one evening each month. Public meetings for lectures and discussions are proposed to be held once a week.

Libraries and museums (the latter to contain among other things samples of each year's crop of all cereal productions) are considered necessary appendages to each temple.

It is designed to have at least one temple in each county, with one delegate from each to the state temple. These will send one delegate each to the national temple, which is to be the head of the order. Persons holding office under government cannot be delegates to either the state or national temple.

Should such an organization meet your approval, and you see fit to offer any suggestions to enable the originators to make any further improvements before it is introduced to the public, the same will be most cordially received and duly considered.

24.

Andrew C. Cameron: The Problems and Prospects of Labor

The National Labor Union tried to unify the labor movement in the face of the growing business expansion of the mid-nineteenth century. It campaigned for the eight-hour workday, producers' cooperatives, and political action by labor. At the first congress of the Union, held in Baltimore, Maryland, in August 1866, a committee was appointed to prepare an address to all the workingmen of the country. Andrew Cameron, who chaired the committee and wrote the following address, edited the Working Man's Advocate, *official organ of the Chicago Trades' Assembly and later of the National Labor Union. The address was prepared in time for the next meeting of the Union in August 1867 and published the same year.*

Source: *The Address of the National Labor Congress to the Workingmen of the United States,* Chicago, 1867 [Commons, IX, pp. 141-168].

THE QUESTION OF ALL OTHERS which at present engrosses the attention of the American workman, and, in fact, the American people, is the proposed reduction of the hours of daily labor and the substitution of the eight- for the ten-hour system, now recognized as the standard of a legal day's work. As might have been expected, the employing capitalists, aided by a venal press, have set up a howl of rage and protested against the adoption of such a monstrous innovation, though it is worthy of note that the chief opposition comes from those who confessedly have given the subject the least consideration.

The committee do not intend, in this address, to enter into any lengthened defense of the measure, but prefer to present its claims, justice, and necessity upon a few simple truths, which must commend themselves to the judgment of the public at large. In all the discussions by the partisan press — from the metropolitan journal to the village croaker — every moral consideration has been waived, every plea put forth by its advocates omitted, and every argument adduced has been based on a purely selfish, dollars-and-cents standpoint.

On the contrary, the producing classes assert that other and higher considerations than those heretofore advanced by its opponents should enter into the discussion of its merits or practicability. They insist it is a self-evident proposition that the success of our republican institutions must depend on the virtue, the intelligence, and the independence of the working classes; and that any system, social or political, which tends to keep the masses in ignorance, whether by unjust or oppressive laws, or by overmanual labor, is injurious alike to the interests of the state and the individual. But while standing on this principle they claim that even from a financial standpoint the benefits its adoption would confer can be demonstrated beyond a peradventure.

They realize that the present is emphatically an age of progress; that day by day the genius of man — the toiler — is developing some system, some theory, some invention to lessen human labor and increase the already enormous accumulations of capital. They find, also, that the examination of the records both of our own and the British Patent Office divulges the fact that three-fourths of the laborsaving machinery perfected during the past twenty-five years has been the creation of the workingman's own brain; further, that since the adoption of the ten-hour system, these inventions have increased over seventy-five percent, while their position remains virtually the same, proving conclusively that capital has reaped the advantages obtained by such discoveries. In view of these truths, they ask that the wealth-producer should share, if not equally, at least partially, the benefits derived — a demand the justice of which, we think, few will have the temerity to deny.

But there is still another phase of the question which entitles it to serious consideration. While the invention and application of laborsaving machinery has, in all cases, redounded to the interests of the employer, its operation has been, in many instances, injurious both to the physical and intellectual welfare of the workman; his duties frequently partaking of an automatic character, while it denies all opportunity for the healthy exercise of the mind. A workman who planned, gauged, and constructed employed his intellectual as well as his physical energies, while the man who merely performs the monotonous functions of a mere automaton, as thousands of our factory employees do from year to year, must eventually descend both in the intellectual and social scale.

It is certainly strange that even its most ardent friends, outside the labor ranks, speak of its success as problematical, ignoring the fact that in countries less favored than our own, where it has obtained a full and impartial trial, its staunchest advocates are the employers themselves; in a country, too, which is represented with credit in its legislative halls by men who earn their living by the sweat of their brows.

The plea urged that the laboring classes would not use the leisure time obtained to their own, and, consequently, to the benefit of the community, is one which is disproved by the experience of the past. Every similar reformation, although ushered in with equally ominous prediction, has not only tended to the development of the resources and material prosperity of the country inaugurating it but has been the means of improving the physical and intellectual condition of the laboring classes; and there is certainly no reason for supposing that the adoption of the eight-hour system would not have an equally beneficial result. The truth is that the wish is father to the thought, and it is because they know to the contrary that these reckless assertions are indulged in.

The charge that workingmen, as a class, are ignorant and illiterate, instead of being an argument against, is one of the strongest reasons which could be urged in favor of its adoption. They are ignorant because they are overworked; because they have been denied the privileges which others, more favored, have reaped. They have realized, by practical experience, that the relation between the physical and intellectual energies is such that injury to one means injury to both; and that the ignorance complained of is the result of that system that they are now determined to destroy. That so long as it exists, so long will they occupy their present menial position; to occupy another or more exalted one they must think more and work less; devote more time to their own advancement and less to the enrichment of the drones of society.

These truths and a thousand others equally applicable might be cited, but we forbear. What is needed is the cooperation of the workingmen of America to bring into operation this much desired reform. While some states have nobly led the van, others have stood idly by. Of its ultimate triumph we cannot, dare not, entertain a doubt. The repulse of the skirmish line should only nerve to more determined action and show the necessity of united effort. There is certainly no cause for despondency. The future is big with hope. From all quarters come words of encouragement and cheer. We believe, if a proper energy is manifested at the next session of our national legislature, an eight-hour law will be passed by an almost unanimous vote, which will doubtless impart the needed energy to those who have heretofore neglected their duty. All that is wanted, fellow citizens, then, is faith in the right, harmony, unity, and resolve; and eight hours will shortly become, by legal enactment, a day's work in every state in the American Union.

This question naturally leads us to the consideration of a subject which is intimately associated with its adoption, viz.: Cooperation. The question of cooperative stores and cooperative associations for trading and manufacturing purposes has the widest bearing and effect upon the condition of the workingmen; and although anything like a full discussion of the principles of cooperative industry is beyond the scope of an address of this character, the committee feel it their duty not to pass the subject by without a brief reference to its beneficial results. In England, where cooperative stores were first introduced, they have proved eminently successful, beyond even the hopes of their originators; and their diffusion over the Kingdom and their introduction into other countries are a sufficient attestation of their benefits. . . .

And there are special reasons and needs for the existence of cooperative efforts in this country, for here there is less disposition on the part of capital to combine and cooperate with labor than elsewhere, in consequence of the excessive accumulations of capital by the great rates of interest which prevail in this country. A false, vicious financial system endows capital with powers of increase largely in excess of the development of national wealth by natural productions.

Labor increases the wealth of the country yearly but little in advance of 3 percent, as the census statistics amply attest. The national wealth, as the product of the national labor, augments at this rate; whereas capital employed in banking and manufacturing enterprises, in railroad bonds or invested in mortgages, accumulated at a rate three or four times greater than the increase in wealth by the production of labor. Hence the proprietors of a house must receive by way of rent not only the interest which the money expended in the purchase of the lot and building of the house would yield, if invested in bank stock, railroad bonds, federal securities, or loaned out on mortgage, but also enough in addition to maintain repairs and pay insurance and taxes.

Unless capital invested in houses will do this, its owner has no object in employing it thus; hence the high rates which consume so much of the workingman's wages. Hence he is obliged to live in poor houses in the suburbs of our large cities, miles away from his shop or place of work. And the same thing is true of the manufacturer. His capital must yield him not only this profitable rate of interest but must also be enough above them to pay for the wear and breakage of machinery and the risks of trade. And in order to secure this excessive profit, he demands the protection of government by the machinery of tariff laws.

This extraordinary power of accumulation which the laws give to money in this country renders everything the workingman wears and the rent of the house which shelters his family very high; and as this accumulative power is many times in excess of the accumulation of wealth by labor, the prices of clothing and the cost of rent are largely out of proportion to the price of wages.

Let the workingman toil ever so hard and constantly, let his habits be ever so economical — at the end of the year he finds his inevitable expenses have consumed all his wages. He has no remedy against this but to combine his earnings with his brothers in labor, and build his own house, manufacture his own goods, and supply his and his family's needs with his own provisions.

The natural cooperation is between capital and labor, but the rapid increase of the former, through the agency of interest laws and banking systems, makes capital not only independent but oppressive of labor. The earnings of the latter go to the former with the directness and inevitableness of an inexorable law. And until capital and labor become organized into a system of mutual cooperation, the workingmen must protect themselves by means of cooperation with one another. But the advantages which they will derive from it will make them, to a much greater extent than now, masters of their own time. It will secure to them the means of study, which will enable them to comprehend the just relations between capital and labor, and the power of organizing these relations into law.

We confidently look forward to a period not remote when the cooperative principle will carry on the great works and improvements of the age. It will build all our cities, dig our ores, fill the land with the noise of loom and spindle. The workingman, as he is now in many instances his own purveyor through cooperative stores, will become contractor, builder, manufacturer, reaping the rewards of his own industry and the profits of his own labor.

Trades' Unions. There are, probably, no organizations upon the nature of which so much real ignorance exists, even among workingmen, or against which such a persistent and systematic opposition has been urged, as trades' unions. Their aims and objects have been grossly misrepresented, and public prejudice has been aroused by those who only know enough to pander to popular ignorance. In spite of this opposition, however, they are daily increasing in numbers and influence, and the committee trust that the day is not far distant when every competent and honorable workman will be embraced within their folds.

So far from encouraging the spirit of hostility to employers, all properly organized unions recognize an identity of interest between and confer as many benefits on the employer as the employed.

That their establishment has been beneficial to the community in general and the working classes in particular can best be demonstrated by reference to the reforms inaugurated through their agency, and the social and intellectual status of those mechanics who refuse to become connected with them. Just in proportion as they have increased in influence have pauperism and crime decreased, and the principles of cooperative industry proved successful. Trades' unions have a tendency to develop those principles of self-respect, justice, and independence which are characteristic only of a true manhood, and which must prove in the future, as they have in the past, the grand educational schools from which so many of our most worthy and influential mechanics have graduated.

Preposterous as the assertion may seem, we claim they have been the creation of necessity and that they are purely defensive in character. They insist, and justly so, that the employee shall have, at least, an equal voice with the employer in determining the value of the labor performed, and, knowing that isolation is weakness and combination strength, they prefer trusting to the power and justice of their united claims than in the magnanimity or generosity of capital.

It may seem inconsistent, but it is nevertheless true, that those who decry their arbitrary exactions have no conscientious scruples about receiving the standard of wages adopted through their exertions. The truth of the matter is, no mechanic who is not a moral coward or an incompetent workman can give a satisfactory reason why his name is not found on a union register.

We are well aware that a vindictive, arbitrary spirit — a spirit at variance with the principles inculcated — may, too often, be found in many of our local societies; but we cannot recognize the validity of this argument for nonmembership, as in too many instances we have reason to believe it is used as a mere subterfuge to escape that responsibility which rests on the head of everyone who refuses or neglects to comply with his imperative duty.

A too-common error, and one into which even workingmen are prone to fall, is the charge that they demand the same wages for an inferior as a superior workman. This is far from being the case. While it is true they establish a minimum rate of wages, they do not prevent, in any instance, a superior workman from receiving such extra compensation, over and above that schedule, as his services may entitle him to. The high standard of moral worth demanded by our labor organizations of their members also entitle them to public favor. Many,

who a few years ago were among the most thriftless and dissolute of men, upon whom reason and entreaty were alike thrown away, are today, through their influence, the peers in intelligence, faithfulness, and sobriety of any body of mechanics in the country.

The committee therefore feel it to be their duty to urge upon every nonunion man the necessity of at once allying himself with a trades' association. Infringing on the religious or political sentiments of no one; guarding alike the interests of employer and employee, guaranteeing a *quid pro quo* in all cases where their workings are unobstructed, they furnish most effective barriers against the aggressions of capital, without which all would be strife, anarchy, and confusion. . . .

Strikes. With regard to the question of strikes, the committee feel they cannot too strongly deprecate all appeals to such extreme measures, except as a *dernier* resort, believing that by the appointment, where practicable, of a conference committee, whose duty it would be to lay the nature of the grievance before the employer and ask redress for the same, many, if not all, of the difficulties complained of could be satisfactorily removed. "An ounce of prevention is worth a pound of cure," and as a large majority of the strikes end in failure and disaster, our unions have everything to gain and nothing to lose by the adoption of such a course.

Nor is this view the only one to be taken; failure, in many instances, exposes weaknesses which render them more liable than heretofore to fresh encroachments. These remarks, however, are intended only for general applications; there are emergencies when no other alternative but a strike is presented. On such occasions the duty of all honorable workmen is plain and unmistakable, and that is to make common cause, to unite as one man, to act in concert — a course, which if adopted and adhered to, would bring about very different results to those which generally attend such demonstrations. . . .

Political Action. If there is one fact more than another which has impressed itself upon the attention of workingmen during the past year, it is the absolute necessity of cutting aloof from the ties and trammels of party, manipulated in the interests of capital and using the advantages conferred by American citizenship — the ballot — to the furtherance of their own interests and welfare. It is not the possession but the proper use of this privilege which can avail aught in the struggle for the mastery. In fact, it may well be questioned whether, in many instances, it has not proven a curse rather than a blessing to its possessors. No matter by what name the various political elements have been divided, no matter upon what issues the line of demarcation has been drawn, the moment the interests of capital have been endangered the tocsin of alarm has been sounded, party ties have been obliterated, and our so-called legislators have stood shoulder to shoulder, as one man, in defense of a common interest. The legislation of the past has been the legislation of capital; the legitimate result of which is seen in the present menial, degraded position occupied by the very class whose welfare it was pledged to defend.

The interest of the consumer has always been the primary, the interest of the producer the secondary consideration in our state and national councils. Nor should this be a matter of surprise. Indeed, it would be strange were it otherwise. We had no right to expect a different result. That an antagonism between labor and capital should or must necessarily exist, we do not believe; that under our iniquitous monetary and financial system — the result of legislation — it does exist, is a self-evident proposition. No man will refuse to recognize the truth of this statement; neither can anyone who has had practical experience and has looked about him in the world fail to perceive that the one grand cause of all the evils to which we have alluded, and many others which will forever remain unspoken and unwritten, but which are silently gnawing at the hearts of thousands, is the robbery which capital perpetrates on labor through legislation.

Under these circumstances the aim of our lawmakers — taken almost exclusively from the ranks of capital — has been to foster, protect, and perpetuate these wrongs, a position to which the producing classes have been a party by their virtual acquiescence and endorsement. They have been satisfied with the husks, with the casket rather than the jewel; they have placed too much dependence on the opinion of others and too little on their own; the appeal of the demagogue has accomplished more than the words of earnest, practical common sense. While they have expended their commiseration on the downtrodden masses of the Old World — and thanked God that American institutions were not as other institutions — they seemed to ignore the fact that human nature was the same in the New as in the Old World, and that these same institutions were assimilating daily more and more to those to whom it seemed to be their pleasure and their duty to decry.

But, we are speaking of the past; we have brighter anticipations for the future. The signs of the times are propitious. The working classes are fast rousing from the lethargy in which they have been sunk. They are realizing that, as the evils which weigh with crushing effect upon society are legislative in character, that the remedy must therefore be legislative. They realize, also, that a new era has been ushered in, that the sectional issues of the past have been swept away; that the Civil War which has blighted our fair land has ceased; that our national authority has been reestablished over every rood of American soil, and the starry flag floats once more in undisputed triumph from the Kennebec to the Rio Grande; that with these results have come new duties and responsibilities; that during the period of transformation it becomes their duty to prepare themselves for the impending conflict.

They realize, as they have never realized before, their tremendous responsibility. They know that issues of a more permanent character than those which have heretofore engrossed the attention of the American people must now be presented; issues, doubtless, which time will change and modify, but which, nevertheless, will remain as monuments of their folly or discernment as they may determine to make their influence felt in this eventful crisis; issues, too, in which their interests are more indissolubly connected than any which have ever preceded them.

Fellow citizens, your duty, under these circumstances, is plain and unmistakable. It is to discard the claptrap issues of the past. Select your representatives in the state and national councils from the ranks of labor; from men who acknowledge allegiance to no ism or party; from those whose welfare is your welfare, and who, when the conflict comes, as come it must, will be found nobly battling for your rights and the recognition of human progress.

We have faith, fellow citizens, that you will be found equal to the task of assuring your own liberty. We believe the men who make nations great by their toil and who defend them with their bayonets will be able to maintain as well as institute a popular government; will be able to overcome the principles and efface the legislation which in creating monopolies create privileged classes incompatible with that equality of right which is the basis of a true democracy.

At the last session of the national Congress, the National Labor Party was ushered into existence; at its next meeting we hope its organization will be more thoroughly effected; and trust that by the fall of 1868 its ramifications may be found in every city, town, and village in the United States, and that by united exertion and perseverance, the highest official in the land, for the first time in the history of our country, may be elected by the voice of the people, on the broad platform of justice, equality, and fraternity.

Conclusion. Having somewhat briefly referred to a few of the more prominent topics which presented themselves to the committee, we trust you may find in the suggestions thrown out something worthy of your attention. We now extend a cordial invitation to all to participate in our deliberations. Come from the North and the South, from the East and the West; come from the anvil and the loom; from the workbench and the forge, every craft and every trade; come as the representatives of states' assemblies or trades' unions, singly or in delegations, all will be equally welcome; come with fraternal greetings, bearing the olive branch of peace; come prompted by a common interest and actuated by a common motive; come forgetting the past and its issues, ignoring alike the appeals and denunciations of partisanship; come realizing the importance of the crisis and the necessity of decided action; come as lovers of a common country, and help by your counsels and deliberations to hasten that glorious time,

> When man to man the world o'er
> Shall brothers be and a' that.

When worth, not wealth, shall rule mankind; when tyranny and oppression of every character shall be uprooted and destroyed; and when the laborers of America, intelligent, united, and disenthralled, shall occupy that proud position which God in His kind providence intended they should occupy — a position they never can aspire to until the evils complained of are redressed by and through their own exertions. Finally, brethren, come one and all and help to marshal those mighty forces of labor which, when disciplined, will march to certain victory.

25.

Child Labor and School Attendance

The child labor system began with the spinning schools established in the colonies. The growth of the textile industry after the Revolution greatly expanded the demand for child labor, and by 1870 the first child labor statistics showed that some 750,000 children between ten and fifteen years of age were employed. While public opinion in the eighteenth century generally approved of the system, by the mid-nineteenth century the public was concerned that long hours and unhygienic working conditions for children would impair their health and hinder their educational advancement. Popular agitation led to legislation in several Eastern states limiting work hours and establishing minimum standards for school attendance. A Massachusetts commission in 1867 issued a report recommending legislation to improve the conditions of child labor. Part of the report appears here.

Source: *Reports of Commissioners on the Hours of Labor,* Massachusetts House Document No. 44, 1867.

WHILE WE DO NOT RECOMMEND to Your Excellency that any law be passed interfering with the hours of adult laborers who can choose their own employments, we earnestly recommend that a law be enacted similar to that of Great Britain, that no person under eighteen years of age shall be employed more than ten hours each day or sixty hours per week. That such a law, the rightfulness of which we think no one can well dispute, would cause a general reduction in the hours of labor for *all* employed in factories, as well as minors, we have no doubt. Such was the effect in England, very fortunately, and such would unquestionably be the result here. . . .

In reply to our eighth inquiry, "How would a reduction of time to ten hours affect production?" we have generally received the answer, *"In the same ratio,"* or "one-eleventh."

That the adoption of ten instead of eleven hours would reduce the immediate production of goods we readily grant; not indeed to the precise extent of one-eleventh, as some manufacturers have assumed, but doubtless nearly to that extent. This at the present time would be an advantage rather than otherwise; but we do not admit that in the long run anything would be lost to production, for several decided benefits would be derived from this course.

1. The operatives would be more able to perform ten than eleven hours' labor, and would work more profitably to their employers.

2. There would be a great deal less of lost time. As it now is, these minors often get jaded out by their long hours of labor and are compelled of necessity to lay by for a few days, and, after awhile, to leave the business for months or years to recruit. This fact is well known to manufacturers.

3. By reducing the hours, employers are certain to get a higher grade of laborers, more able and intelligent hands. As *some* mills now are, there is an evident deterioration in the character of those employed. None can be had to work in them, except the most dependent families. If the time

was reduced as proposed, it would operate as a powerful inducement for many of a better class to work in the mill who now refuse to do so. The last hour of the eleven implies more hardship than two hours in the previous ten would do.

That all the best interests of operatives would be promoted by such a reduction is acknowledged by many of the largest and best manufacturers in the country.

In reply to question number ten, "Do the social and sanitary interests of operatives, especially minors, require a reduction of the time of labor to ten hours per day?" Hon. Amos A. Lawrence gives the following answer: "Yes. The physical, intellectual, moral, and religious interests of our people require a reduction. The present system of labor is debasing the native New England stock and forcing them to emigrate to the West, South, and foreign countries. The population which displaces ours is inferior in every respect." In a note accompanying the return, Mr. Lawrence adds: "On the main question of work within doors, and especially the employment of children, I have believed for thirty years that our practice was bad." . . .

From the Hamilton Company, at Lowell, we have the following: "In my judgment, the social and sanitary interests of all would be materially advanced by such a reduction."

Others, again, reply that the reduction would be desirable, provided the system were extended throughout New England.

In answer to this it may be said that if Massachusetts adopted the ten-hour rule, other states would doubtless feel compelled to follow. Such has been the case hitherto. Once the factories of Massachusetts ran for twelve or thirteen hours daily. As they have been gradually reduced to eleven, other communities have fallen into the same limit; and now, when it is proposed to establish ten hours, there seems to be the best of reasons for believing that such would become the general rule. . . .

It is very gratifying to be able to state at this point that several of the largest mills in some of our most important manufacturing cities have, since the organization of this Commission, voluntarily reduced their hours of labor to ten each day, or sixty hours per week.

In reply to our ninth question, "How would it operate to run your machinery with two sets of hands, eight hours each, provided sufficient laborers could be obtained?" we have received generally the answer we expected; viz., that it would be, in most cases, impracticable. Many kinds of manufactures are of such a character that the change could not be made, though in others there would be little difficulty. That a great object would be attained if capital or investments could be made to work sixteen hours, while human beings were obliged to labor but eight, will be admitted by all; and that such a consummation will be ultimately reached seems very possible; but at present the experiment is rather a matter of anticipation than anything to be practically attempted. . . .

The answers given have varied greatly. Many are directly and positively in the negative; others as directly in the affirmative; others, still, are conditional, that is, "provided the operatives would make a good use of their additional leisure," of which many express a strong doubt. In regard to this last point, we suppose that the answers given have been influenced by the social condition of the general population in which the establishment is situated. In those well-ordered communities where no places of demoralization are permitted, the reply would naturally be that the additional leisure hour would be an advantage because it would be well spent; while in those of an opposite character, the reply would come very emphatically in the negative.

That the *sanitary condition* of factory operatives would be greatly improved by a reduction of one hour each day, we think no reasonable man can deny; but this point has been so fully and ably discussed in the report of the previous Commission on the Hours of Labor, and in various documents before the public, that we deem it quite unnecessary to dwell upon it. . . .

The state very properly assumes the right to provide that all its children shall be furnished with the means of education; and for years has required that children of tender age shall not be employed in factories unless they have attended school a certain number of months in each year. The law enacted last year increased the number of months to six, which in some towns covers all the time in which schools are maintained. We have no means of knowing how well the law is enforced. We have reason to suppose, in some cases, when children are out of the factories for the purpose, they do not attend school.

26.

Walt Whitman: "One's-Self I Sing"

Whitman wrote a number of inscriptions, or epigraphs, for the various editions of Leaves of Grass *that he issued during his lifetime. "One's-Self I Sing" seems to have been his favorite, for after its first appearance in the edition of 1871, he always used it to introduce his volume, in every edition until his death. These few lines, indeed, express one of Whitman's most cherished ideas — that of democratic society as made up of individuals, but at the same time a passionate and free communion of the whole.*

Source: *Leaves of Grass*, Washington, 1871.

❦ ONE'S-SELF I SING

One's-self I sing, a simple separate person,
Yet utter the word Democratic, the word En-Masse.

Of physiology from top to toe I sing,
Not physiognomy alone nor brain alone
  is worthy for the Muse,
  I say the Form complete is
  worthier far,
The Female equally with the Male I sing.

Of Life immense in passion pulse, and power,
Cheerful, for freest action formed under the laws divine,
The Modern Man I sing.

1868

27.

Illinois Proposal for a Compulsory School Law

It was one thing for a state to offer free public education to all children; it was another matter entirely to get the children to the schools. One of the basic obstacles was the prevalence of child labor. Questions also arose concerning the constitutional right of the state to compel a child to attend school in the face of parental or other objections. The first compulsory school attendance law was passed in Massachusetts in 1852. Immediately following the Civil War the issue was being debated in Illinois, as attested by this portion of the Report of the Superintendent of Public Instruction for 1868.

Source: *Seventh Biennial Report of the Superintendent of Public Instruction of the State of Illinois, 1867-1868*, pp. 42-44.

THE QUESTION of compulsory attendance has been widely discussed in all parts of the country during the past two years. While there may be doubts as to whether that would be the best remedy for us, all things considered, those doubts do not, in my estimation, attach to the question of legal competency, but only to that of expediency.

Every state school system must of necessity rest down at some points upon the idea of compulsion — of the supreme authority of a commonwealth to do what is deemed needful for the well-being of the body politic. The primary maxim upon which every free-school law is grounded and defended, and which has become a part of the settled convictions of the American people — that a state has a just moral claim upon so much of the property of the people as may be required to educate its children and fit them for usefulness as good citizens — involves the idea of compulsion in the last resort.

The state two-mill tax, which is the legitimate fruitage of that maxim, is collected from all alike, whether willing or unwilling. Those who refuse to pay the tax are compelled to pay it; there is compulsory school-tax paying all over the state. And the power that justly demands and enforces, in virtue of its benevolent care and sovereignty, the payment of a tax for the noble purpose of educating and uplifting the people, may surely provide that the end sought shall not fail of attainment through the indifference or perverseness of others. The hand that forcibly takes the tax money from the pocket of an unwilling nonresident to support a school in a distant district in which he has no personal interest is at least as rough and arbitrary as would be the hand that forcibly leads the children to the doors of the schoolroom. If the former act is right, though the very essence of compulsion, how can the latter be wrong?

Indeed, all general laws, both state and national, involve and imply the right of compulsion, in the last resort, and could not be otherwise executed. So far, therefore, as the question of the constitutional right and competency of a state to pass a school law that shall be compulsory in regard to attendance is concerned, it seems to me there can be no doubt. If the fundamental principle is conceded, the rest is a logical sequence — if a state may enact a general free-school law, it may see that its supreme purpose is not defeated.

And what *is* that purpose but the education of all the children between the prescribed ages? And how can this be if they do not attend? Regarded from this standpoint, may not the more rational question be: Has the state a right to *stop short* of compulsory attendance; to leave it optional with the very persons to be benefited, whether, after all, the whole system shall be a success or a failure? Hence, the question of compulsory attendance is not one of jurisdiction or competency on the part of the state but of expediency only.

It may be that a general compulsory law would not work well in a country and people like ours. It will certainly be a grander success if we can make the schools so good, so attractive and pleasant that all will seek them and be drawn to them by a higher and nobler compulsion — the love of knowledge, of improvement, of culture, of country, and of God. But in whatever aspect it is considered, and whatsoever remedy may be the best, absenteeism is an evil of alarming magnitude and must continue to receive the earnest attention of the friends of public education, until attendance upon the public schools shall be universal and the system shall secure the maximum amount of good of which it is capable.

Now is the time for all good men to come to the aid of the party.

CHARLES E. WELLER, sentence used to test the first typewriter, constructed at Milwaukee by Christopher L. Sholes, 1867. The sentence was also used as a slogan in U. S. Grant's first presidential campaign, 1868.

28.

Knowledge, Mental Training, and Classical Study

As the study of science grew increasingly sophisticated during the nineteenth century, educational innovators demanded that a systematic science program be included in the college curriculum. To that end, Yale College established a new Department of Philosophy and the Arts in 1847, and in 1854 created the Sheffield Scientific School by merging the Schools of Engineering and Applied Chemistry. In reply to traditionalists who argued that college study should be limited to the classics, Yale commissioned the following report on the Scientific School's methods and curriculum. The report was probably written by Daniel Coit Gilman, an organizer of the new school and for many years its librarian, secretary, and professor of physical and political geography.

Source: *Third Annual Report of the Sheffield Scientific School of Yale College . . . 1867-8,* New Haven, 1868, pp. 10-17.

THE OBJECT OF ALL EDUCATION is to increase our capacity of happiness and usefulness to enable us the better to enjoy our own lives and help others to enjoy theirs. In calling forth and training the powers of the individual, it has this double end distinctly in view. Very few are so situated as not to be required to make their lives valuable to others that others may help them to live; and the few who are not thus compelled are led to it by an enlightened self-interest, since otherwise they miss what is the noblest and highest pleasure of all — that of doing good to those about them. Everyone has a part to play, a work to perform in the great task of human improvement; and he must be duly fitted for it.

That is a low idea of education which limits it to any particular period of life. Even in the humblest occupation, acquisition of skill and experience should be ever enabling a man to rise to higher station and to do more valuable work. He is either very unfortunate or else worthy of blame on account of wasted opportunity, whose life, even to its end, is not constantly becoming of greater worth, to himself and others, by growth of knowledge and of power to accomplish. Yet youth is eminently the season of acquisition and preparation. Everyone's energies must at some time begin to be mainly absorbed in applying what he has acquired, in exercising what he has prepared for.

The time comes sooner or later, according to circumstances. There are those who have to begin the hard work of life as soon as they have learned to walk and to talk; others are pressed into the ranks at every age. Nor must active service be begun too late lest the capacity for it be lost; a life of which too much is spent in preparation is apt to lead to nothing.

If education be taken in this narrow sense, of preparation for the active work of life and for what comes along with this, then that is evidently the best and most successful education which, in any given case, most thoroughly fits the man for his special work, and, at the same time, plants him upon the broadest and deepest foundation for improvement both within and without his own department; which least narrows his views and capacities; which makes him the ablest workman and, along with that, the fullest man. Some occupations, of course, are in their nature more narrowing than others, and that is the most noble and satisfying which demands the widest basis of preparation and calls into exercise the highest and most varied capacities.

But in our community, more than elsewhere, no one is expected to limit himself to preparation for his own craft, since our idea of equality is that each person be encouraged to rise as high above the station in which his birth and circumstances have placed him as his powers and opportunities allow. Nay, more; no one *may* thus limit himself, since each is also the citizen of a free state, having powers and responsibilities which he cannot properly sustain without education, and to fit him for which he cannot possibly have more than enough education.

Education is constantly changing its ground and methods by reason both of the increase of knowledge and of the multiplication of vocations. It must include within its scope every existing department of human knowledge and every valuable mode of its application. . . . No theory of education can possibly be sound which does not recognize the absolute worth of all human knowledge, or which contemns "facts" of any kind, philological, historical, or scientific.

Every branch must have its own followers, so trained that they shall be able to extend and perfect it, both in itself and in its relations to other branches. That man is a specialist whose training unfits him duly to appreciate any part of that which is known. But every one of us is and must be a spe-

cialist, for the field of knowledge has become much too vast to be occupied, or even to be overlooked and judged, by any individual. It was long since said that he only is wise who knows that he knows nothing — and the saying is becoming truer every day, not with reference only to what man would fain know but also to what he already knows. Each man has to turn his back deliberately on much that he would fain possess that he may prepare himself for what he has to do.

The various branches of knowledge have a comparative value, which varies with the ground and point of view occupied by each learner. There comes a time when we must cease laying a general foundation and build up our own building; and earlier or later, according to our different circumstances. A certain common substructure lies beneath all the forms of special training, and the broader this is made, in any class or country, the higher is the standard of education there.

Our mother tongue is the first thing we learn — a most important means both of training and enlightenment, and the indispensable preliminary to all that is to follow. Then come the alphabet, the multiplication table, and the writing book. No one questions the universal necessity of the "three R's," as they are familiarly styled ("reading, 'riting and 'rithmetic"). But from this point begins the difference of opinion and dispute as to what must be added, and in what proportion; the branches of desirable knowledge begin to jostle and crowd out one another.

Into the dispute we do not wish or need to enter here. Practically, it is irreconcilable; there will always be room to maintain that something which *I* know and value constitutes a more essential part of a true education than what another recommends for the same reason. It is, however, evident that the greater and more varied the mass of human knowledge and the modes of human activity, the earlier must the diversity of educational training begin. It is not possible to raise the standard of education at a rate corresponding to the growth of its means and its ends.

Formerly, only members of the "learned professions," and gentlemen who could afford to train themselves after their pattern, were regarded as needing to be "educated"; and a little of the old feeling remains, though put out-of-date by the different aspect of affairs in our time. Other occupations used to be mere trades, the preparation for which consisted in the acquisition of a certain amount of mental and manual dexterity, handed down in guilds and the like, and communicated by private instruction.

Now, nearly all the arts of life are raised to a vastly higher plane; the causes and modes of action which they involve are understood; underneath each lies a science whose comprehension is necessary to their highest and most successful pursuit; a science, too, whose establishment has perhaps required as much learning and insight, as much faithful labor in investigation and logical acuteness of deduction, as much accumulation of wisdom, as high gifts of intellect as any known branch of human knowledge; whose acquisition costs as thorough preparation, as long study, and as distinguished capacity; and which offers as keen satisfaction to the curious intellect, and has as wide and direct a bearing upon human happiness. All is here included that can give dignity to a calling and to the preparation for it.

The scientific man, as he is often called — for example, the engineer, the chemist, the naturalist — is by his occupation challenged to not less ability and disinterestedness and promised not less usefulness than the lawyer or physician; his due training is as real a part of the higher education, all that fits him for his work is as truly disciplinary as anything else in the whole scheme of study.

It is not well possible to lay too much stress upon discipline; but it is comparatively easy to misunderstand what is meant by that word. Anything is disciplinary which prepares the mind for the worthy exercise of its powers, which fits it to receive and utilize truth. There is a too-current disposition nowadays to divorce discipline from acquisition of knowledge, to contemn the useful as ignoble. This is a natural reaction against the opposite tendency, to regard no knowledge as worth acquiring of which the utility is not immediate and obvious. Either error is equally detrimental; and either, when nakedly presented, is sure to be rejected by any enlightened mind; but it is not so easy to avoid some admixture of the one or the other.

It might be difficult to say whether an education of bare discipline, always preparing for something to come and never reaching it, or an education of pure cram, thrusting in information that is immediately assimilable and nothing else, would turn out the most of a failure. The result would depend on the force of mind and natural disposition of the individuals subjected to the training; but it is quite as likely that the one scholar would be turned into a mere machine, with capacity and desire for knowledge extinguished, as that the other's powers of combining and reasoning would be destroyed by overloading. . . .

The idea of spending the season of "education" wholly or mainly in a sort of mental gymnastics, of laying out a scheme of preparation for the active work of life which does not include as an essential part the storing of the mind with a variety of useful information, is as erroneous as anything can be. It implies that the rest of life is to be devoted to the acquisition of knowledge, under the guidance of competent instructors who will see to it that the powers they have trained are directed to worthy objects. It tends directly to make and keep men specialists, turned out as they are with minds imperfectly and desultorily furnished, to give themselves up to work in one direction. He who is to know and love what lies aside from his own narrow track must have learned so much that he has tasted the pleasure of knowing in many departments; that he has a nucleus of acquisitions in more than one kind to which new acquisitions may attach themselves; that he can overlook to some extent the field of knowledge and see what part is more valuable than others, in itself or for him.

It would be, no doubt (to adopt a current comparison), a good thing in itself to have gained by steady and consistent drill such a power of concentration as to be able to keep the eye and the thought fixed for half an hour upon the point of a needle without flinching; but one might spend upon this accomplishment so much of the force of his education as to acquire a morbid taste for it, and to be ready to pass his life gazing at needlepoints, not knowing that there is anything else better worth doing. . . . The ends of education must not be lost sight of in the means; those ends are practical, and must be pursued by means likely to result in their attainment.

What is the best discipline for one is not the best for another, even though both may aim at an equal degree of general culture, if their disposition is different or if they are to follow different walks in life. Each method must be judged by the fruit it yields; that is wasted labor from which in the end no appreciable advantage is derived; the mental effort spent in it might better have been given to something else.

There are those who hold that classical studies are what we have called above "high disciplinary." This is, however, a wholly erroneous impression — although, perhaps, not illegitimately derived from the claims sometimes put forth in behalf of these studies. . . . Classical studies put us in communication with the best thought of both ancient and modern times; they give a kind and degree of mental culture which has been attainable by no other means, and which long custom, as well as its intrinsic character, leads the community to estimate at, to say the least, its full worth.

It is true that . . . the prominence of the classics as a means of education is upon the wane — not by their loss of absolute value but by the uprise of other means to the same end, possessing a not-less urgent and conspicuous importance; partly, also, by the transfusion of their valuable content into other and modern forms, so that their influence is obtainable indirectly. An immeasurable amount of enlightenment and inspiration is still to be drawn from them, as well as a vast deal of work to be done upon them for the benefit of the race; their knowledge will be the essential prerequisite to all original and profound investigation of the history of man and human culture; they will always form one of the most important branches of study and means of discipline; they will train the literary taste, the linguistic sense, the faculty of interpretation and criticism, the power to think oneself into the thoughts of other men and other times, the comprehension of humanity and its work.

They will demand not less attention in amount than they have hitherto won; although there will be large classes of students whose training may and must be gained without them by the aid of the abundant fruits of culture which have now been stored up outside of them, and, although, on the other hand, he who is versed in them alone can no longer make the same pretension to discipline as formerly. There was a time when to be merely a good Latin and Greek scholar was to be well educated; now, such a one is only a specialist, and may be a narrow-minded pedant, as really deficient in due discipline as if he knew nothing but mathematics, or chemistry, or zoology.

The objection is often brought against

classical study that those who devote to it so large a proportion of the time given to training never carry it, after all, beyond the stage of preliminary discipline, do not begin to derive fruit and enjoyment from it, and drop it abruptly when the work of life is begun, hardly if at all conscious of benefit obtained. Much more is apt to be made of this objection than it is really worth; for, on the one hand, no one is capable of measuring the good that a study does him in exercising the powers of his mind and increasing its range and capacity; and, on the other hand, the higher benefits of education are not within the reach of everyone. A host of minds are only limitedly receptive of general culture; are capable, perhaps, of becoming fair specialists in some line which engages all their energies; nothing more. All education is to this extent experimental and liable to failure. The liability does, however, constitute a powerful and valid argument against limiting education to one unvarying pattern, since many a mind which is repelled and stagnated by one set of studies may be incited to independent and healthy action by another.

We have entered into so much of detail respecting classical study because the scientific courses are mainly peculiar, and exposed to distrust on the part of many in the community, in virtue of the inferior place which they assign to such study and because they seem to some to deny hereby its value, and cast reproach upon it. This is not at all our intent. We hold that every scientist is the better for all the classical training he can get, even for vastly more than is given in the ordinary college course. Only we also hold that it does not outweigh in importance everything else, and constitute to everyone the *summum bonum* of mental training.

These, then, are the fundamental principles on which reposes our opinion of the value of the Scientific School, as a worthy and dignified portion of the general system of education, as a disciplinary institution as well as a professional — that all knowledge is valuable for discipline, each kind of knowledge giving its own kind of training and both abundance and variety of positive knowledge being indispensable to the acquirement of that sound judgment which makes the practical wisdom of life, as well as of that love of knowledge for its own sake which conducts to some of the highest and keenest enjoyment that life furnishes; that but a fragment of what is known lies within the reach of any person, and that each, in view of his own needs and opportunities, must choose the part which will be worth most to him; that a system of general education must aim to effect a due compromise, not neglecting the qualification of the pupil for his speciality but also seeing to it that his mind is expanded, made receptive of truth from every source, and prepared for its utilization; and that there is no other criterion of the comparative dignity and worth of different branches of study than their utility in one or both of these directions.

———◆———

The trouble with most folks isn't so much their ignorance, as knowing so many things that ain't so.

HENRY WHEELER SHAW ("JOSH BILLINGS")

29.

Samuel J. Tilden: Arraignment of the Republican Party

Samuel Tilden was a Northern Democrat who viewed with foreboding the unprecedented centralization of power in the federal government during the Civil War. His anxieties carried over into the postwar years as he saw the reins of authority being gathered into the hands of a Radical Republican Congress. This he saw as not only a violation of states' rights but a threat to the separation of powers in the federal structure. As head of the New York State Democratic Party, he delivered on March 11, 1868, the following speech condemning the Republican Congress for rejecting President Johnson's liberal Reconstruction policies.

Source: *The Writings and Speeches of Samuel J. Tilden,* John Bigelow, ed., New York, 1885, Vol. I, pp. 395-420.

A COMPLETE AND HARMONIOUS RESTORATION of the revolted states would have been effected if the Republican Party had not proved to be totally incapable of acting in the case with any large, wise, or firm statesmanship.

A magnanimous policy would not only have completed the pacification of the country but would have effected a reconciliation between the Republican Party and the white race in the South. Every circumstance favored such a result. The Republican Party possessed all the powers of the government, and held sway over every motive of gratitude, fear, or interest. The Southern people had become thoroughly weary of the contest; more than half of them had been originally opposed to entering into it, and had done so only when nothing was left to them but to choose on which side they would fight.

Few would ever have favored the measures which led to the conflict of arms if they had anticipated such a conflict; many had all the while felt a lingering regret in ceasing to belong to a great country which they had been accustomed to regard with proud ambition; and all remembered that they had been prosperous, contented, and happy as American citizens. The mass yearned to come back to what was left of their birthright. On the surrender of General Lee, every hostile sword fell, and the abolition of slavery was yielded as a peace offering with universal alacrity.

All that was necessary to heal the bleeding wounds of the country and to allow its languishing industries to revive, was that the Republican Party — which boasts its great moral ideas and its philanthropy — should rise to the moral elevation of an ordinary pugilist, and cease to strike its adversary after it was down.

This crisis was the trial of the Republican Party. The question was whether it could become a permanent party in the country, continuing to govern for the present, capable of being, from time to time, called to govern; or whether it must admit itself to be but a revolutionary faction, accepted by the people during the war, accepted for the venom, if not the vigor, with which it could strike, acting often "outside the Constitution," often converting the regular and lawful organs of the government into a French committee of public safety or a Jacobin club, and now incapable of adapting itself to the work of pacification when that has become the commanding public necessity; and, therefore, its mission being fulfilled, having nothing left to it but to die and be forever dismissed from our national history.

In this trial the Republican Party completely failed. . . .

The Republican Party recoiled for a while on the fatal brink of the policy on which it at last embarked. It had not the courage to conciliate by magnanimity, and to found its alliances and its hopes of success upon the better qualities of human nature. It totally abandoned all relations to the white race of the ten states. It resolved to make the black race the governing power in those states, and by means of them to bring into Congress twenty senators and fifty representatives — practically appointed by itself in Washington.

It is evident that the internal government of those states was not the main object of this desperate expedient. The state organizations had been comparatively neglected. It was only through new state organizations and new electoral bodies that the twenty senators and fifty representatives could be secured to the Republican Party after it refused to trust to pacification.

The effect of a gain to the Republican Party of twenty senators and fifty representatives is to strengthen its hold on the federal government against the people of the North. Nor is there the slightest doubt that the paramount object and motive of the Republican Party is by these means to secure itself against a reaction of opinion adverse to it in our great populous Northern commonwealths. The effect of its system and its own real purpose is to establish a domination over us of the Northern states.

When the Republican Party resolved to establish Negro supremacy in the ten states in order to gain to itself the representation of those states in Congress, it had to begin by governing the people of those states by the sword. The 4,500,000 whites composed the electoral bodies. If they were to be put under the supremacy of the 3 million Negroes, and twenty senators and fifty representatives were to be obtained through these 3 million Negroes, it was necessary to obliterate every vestige of local authority, whether it had existed before the Rebellion, or been instituted since by Mr. Lincoln or by the people. A bayonet had to be set to supervise and control every local organization. The military dictatorship had to be extended to the remotest ramifications of human society. That was the first necessity.

The next was the creation of new electoral bodies for those ten states, in which, by exclusions, by disfranchisements and proscriptions, by control over registration, by applying test oaths operating respectively and prospectively, by intimidation, and by every form of influence, 3 million Negroes are made to predominate over 4,500,000 whites. These 3 million Negroes — three-fourths of the adult male portion of whom are field hands who have been worked in gangs on the plantations, and are immeasurably inferior to the free blacks whom we know in the North, who have never had even the education which might be acquired in the support of themselves or in the conduct of any business, and who, of all their race, have made the least advance from the original barbarism of their ancestors — have been organized in compact masses to form the ruling power in these ten states. They have been disassociated from their natural relations to the intelligence, humanity, virtue, and piety of the white race, set up in complete antagonism to the whole white race, for the purpose of being put over the white race, and of being fitted to act with unity and become completely impervious to the influence of superior intellect and superior moral and social power in the communities of which they form a part.

Of course such a process has repelled, with inconsiderable exceptions, the entire white race in the ten states. It has repelled the moderate portion who had reluctantly yielded to secession. It has repelled those who had remained Unionists. The first fruit of the Republican policy is the complete separation of the two races, and to some extent their antagonism. . . .

If those 3 million Negroes elect twenty senators and fifty representatives, they will have ten times as much power in the Senate of the United States as the 4 million whites in the state of New York. On every question which concerns the commercial metropolis — every question of trade, of finance, of currency, of revenue, and of taxation — these 3 million liberated African slaves will count ten times as much in the Senate as 4 million New Yorkers. One freedman will counterbalance thirteen white citizens of the Empire State. These 3 million blacks will count ten times as much as 3 million white people in Pennsylvania; ten times as much as 2,500,000 in Ohio; ten times as much as 2,225,000 or 2,500,000 in Illinois; ten times as much as 1,500,000 in Indiana. These 3 million blacks will have twice the representation in the Senate which will be possessed by the five great commonwealths — New York, Pennsylvania, Ohio, Indiana, and Illinois — embracing 13,500,000 of our people.

Let me not be told that this enormous wrong is nothing more than an original defect of the Constitution. I answer that it derives most of its evil and its danger from the usurpations of the Republican Party.

We have now reached a period when everything valuable in the Constitution and in the government as formed by our fathers is brought into peril. Men's minds are unsettled by the civil strifes through which we have passed. The body of traditional ideas which limited the struggles of parties within narrow and fixed boundaries is broken up. A temporary party majority, having complete sway over the legislative bodies, discards all standards, whether embodied in laws, constitutions, or in elementary and organic principles of free government; acts its own pleasure as absolutely as if it were a revolutionary convention; and deems everything legitimate which can serve its party aims.

Changes are dared and attempted by it with a success which, I trust, is but temporary — changes which revolutionize the whole nature of our government.

1. If there be anything fundamental in government or in human society, it is the question, what elements shall compose the electoral bodies from which emanate all the governing powers. The Constitution left the states with exclusive power over the suffrage, and the states have always defined and protected the suffrage from change by their fundamental laws. Congress now usurps control over the whole subject in the ten states and creates Negro constituencies, and vests them with nearly a third of the whole representation in the Senate, and nearly a quarter of the whole representation in the House. The leaders of the Republican Party also claim the power by congressional act to regulate the suffrage in the loyal states, and, without the consent of the people of those states, to alter their constitutions and involve them in a political partnership with inferior races.

2. Congress, by the methods and means I have traced, usurps control over the representation in the two branches of the national legislature and packs those bodies with delegates, admitting or rejecting for party ends, and at length attempting to create a permanent majority by deputies from Negro constituencies formed for that purpose.

3. Congress has not only fettered the trade and industries of the country for the benefit of special interests and classes but it has absorbed many powers and functions of the state governments which are, in the words of Mr. Jefferson's celebrated inaugural, "the most competent administrations for our domestic concerns, the surest bulwark against anti-republican tendencies"; and it is rapidly centralizing all our political institutions.

4. Congress is systematically breaking

down all the divisions of power between the coordinate departments of the federal government which the Constitution established, and which have always been considered as essential to the very existence of constitutional representative government.

The conviction of all our revered statesmen and patriots is, in the language of Mr. Jefferson, that "the concentration of legislative, executive, and judicial powers in the same hands is precisely the definition of despotic government." "An elective despotism," said he, "was not the government we fought for, but one which should not only be founded on free principles but in which the powers of government should be so divided among several bodies of magistracy as that no one could transcend their legal limits without being effectually checked and restrained by the others."

In violation of these principles, Congress has stripped the President of his constitutional powers over his subordinates in the executive function, and even over his own confidential advisers, and vested these powers in the Senate. It is now exercising the power of removing from office the President elected by the people and appointing another in his place, under the form of a trial, but without the pretense of actual crime, or anything more than a mere difference of opinion.

It has menaced the judiciary, at one time proposing to create by law an incapacity in the Supreme Court to act by a majority in any case where it should disagree with Congress; at another time proposing to divest that tribunal of jurisdiction, exercised by it from the foundation of the government, to decide between an ordinary law and the Constitution, which is the fundamental and supreme law. There is reason to believe also that a plan has been matured to overthrow the court by the creation of new judges, to make a majority more subservient to Congress than the judges appointed by Mr. Lincoln are found to be.

These changes are organic. They would revolutionize the very nature of the government. They would alter every important part of its structure on which its authors relied to secure good laws and good administration, and to preserve civil liberty. They would convert it into an elective despotism. The change could not by possibility stop at that stage.

I avow the conviction, founded on all history and on the concurring judgment of all our great statesmen and patriots, that such a system, if continued, would pass into imperialism. I feel not less certain that the destruction of all local self-government in a country so extensive as ours, and embracing such elements of diversity in habits, manners, opinions, and interests, and the exercise by a single, centralized authority of all the powers of society over so vast a region and over such populations, would entail upon us an indefinite series of civil commotions and repeat here the worst crimes and worst calamities of history.

It is time for the people to stay these destructive tendencies, and to declare that the reaction from secession toward centralism shall not effect the ruin which secession could not directly accomplish. . . .

The masses of the Republicans do not understand the real nature of the system they are contributing to establish. They are misled by party association and party antagonism, by the animosities created by the war, and the unsettled ideas which grow out of the novelty of the situation. The leaders are full of party passion and party ambition, and will not easily surrender the power of a centralized government, or the patronage and profits which are incident to an official expenditure of $500 million a year. The grim Puritan of New England — whose only child, whose solitary daughter is already listening to the soft music of a Celtic wooer — stretches his hand down along the Atlantic coast to the receding and decaying African, and says: "Come, let us rule this continent together!" The twelve senators from New England, with twenty from the ten states, would require only a few from Missouri, Tennessee, West Virginia, and from new states to make a majority.

I do not forbid the banns; I simply point to the region which stretches from the Hudson to the Missouri. It is there that the democracy must display their standards in another, and I trust final, battle for constitutional government and civil liberty. I invited you to that theater last year; I come now to bid you Godspeed!

Every business, every industrial interest is paralyzed under excessive taxation, false systems of finance, extravagant cost of production, diminished ability to consume. You cannot obtain relief until you change your governmental policy. You cannot change that until you change the men who administer your government. The causes of the dangers in respect to our political institutions and civil liberty and the causes of your suffering in business are identical. For the safety of the one and for the relief of the other you must demand of the people a change of administration as now carried on by Congress.

30.

The Impeachment of Andrew Johnson

Andrew Johnson was the first President of the United States to be impeached. The idea had been in the minds of Radical Republicans since it had become apparent that the President would not go along with their Reconstruction policies. The specific issue on which it was finally possible to draw up a list of charges that Congress would accept was Johnson's violation of the Tenure of Office Act. On February 21, 1868, the President removed Secretary of War Edwin Stanton from office. Four days later eleven articles of impeachment were accepted by the House of Representatives. The trial, held in the Senate in March, was presided over by Chief Justice Salmon P. Chase. In two separate votes, taken in the latter half of May, the Senate acquitted the President by one vote. The trial of Andrew Johnson was the most serious threat to the separation of powers in the federal structure that the United States has faced. The following two speeches, reprinted in part, reflect opposing views of the impeachment proceedings. Senator Charles Sumner reveals the attitude of the Radical Republicans toward the President; Senator James Grimes of Iowa supports the President on legal and constitutional grounds. It was, incidentally, Grimes's vote, the last to be cast, that decided for acquittal.

Source: *Trial of Andrew Johnson, etc., etc.*, Benjamin P. Poore, ed., Washington, 1868, Vol. III, pp. 247-281, 328-340.

I.

CHARLES SUMNER: For Conviction

THIS IS ONE OF THE LAST great battles with slavery. Driven from these legislative chambers, driven from the field of war, this monstrous power has found a refuge in the executive mansion, where, in utter disregard of the Constitution and laws, it seeks to exercise its ancient, far-reaching sway. All this is very plain. Nobody can question it. Andrew Johnson is the impersonation of the tyrannical slave power. In him it lives again. He is the lineal successor of John C. Calhoun and Jefferson Davis; and he gathers about him the same supporters.

Original partisans of slavery, North and South; habitual compromisers of great principles; maligners of the Declaration of Independence; politicians without heart; lawyers for whom a technicality is everything, and a promiscuous company who at every stage of the battle have set their faces against equal rights; these are his allies. It is the old troop of slavery, with a few recruits, ready as of old for violence — cunning in device and heartless in quibble. With the President at their head, they are now entrenched in the executive mansion.

Not to dislodge them is to leave the country a prey to one of the most hateful tyrannies of history. Especially is it to surrender the Unionists of the Rebel states to violence and bloodshed. Not a month, not a week, not a day should be lost. *The safety of the republic requires action at once.* The lives of innocent men must be rescued from sacrifice.

I would not in this judgment depart from that moderation which belongs to the occasion; but God forbid that, when called to deal with so great an. offender, I should affect a coldness which I cannot feel. Slavery has been our worst enemy, assailing all, murdering our children, filling our homes with mourning, and darkening the land with tragedy; and now it rears its crest anew, with Andrew Johnson as its representative. Through him it assumes once more to rule the republic and to impose its cruel law.

The enormity of his conduct is aggravated by his barefaced treachery. He once declared himself the Moses of the colored race. Behold him now the Pharaoh. With such treachery in such a cause there can be no parley. Every sentiment, every conviction, every vow against slavery must now

be directed against him. Pharaoh is at the bar of the Senate for judgment.

The formal accusation is founded on certain recent transgressions, enumerated in articles of impeachment, but it is wrong to suppose that this is the whole case. It is very wrong to try this impeachment merely on these articles. It is unpardonable to higgle over words and phrases when, for more than two years, the tyrannical pretensions of this offender, now in evidence before the Senate . . . have been manifest in their terrible, heartrending consequences. . . .

This usurpation, with its brutalities and indecencies, became manifest as long ago as the winter of 1866, when, being President, and bound by his oath of office to preserve, protect, and defend the Constitution, and to take care that the laws are faithfully executed, he took to himself legislative powers in the reconstruction of the Rebel states; and, in carrying forward this usurpation, nullified an act of Congress, intended as the cornerstone of Reconstruction, by virtue of which Rebels are excluded from office under the government of the United States; and, thereafter, in vindication of this misconduct, uttered a scandalous speech in which he openly charged members of Congress with being assassins, and mentioned some by name. Plainly he should have been impeached and expelled at that early day. The case against him was complete. . . .

Meanwhile, the President proceeded in his transgressions. There is nothing of usurpation which he has not attempted. Beginning with an assumption of all power in the Rebel states, he has shrunk from nothing in the maintenance of this unparalleled assumption. This is a plain statement of fact. Timid at first, he grew bolder and bolder. He saw too well that his attempt to substitute himself for Congress in the work of reconstruction was sheer usurpation, and, therefore, by his secretary of state, did not hesitate to announce that "it must be distinctly understood that the restoration will be *subject to the decision of Congress.*" On

Charles Sumner, who favored conviction of Andrew Johnson

two separate occasions, in July and September 1865, he confessed the power of Congress over the subject; but when Congress came together in December, this confessor of congressional power found that he alone had this great prerogative. According to his newfangled theory, Congress had nothing to do but admit the states with the governments which had been instituted through his will alone. . . .

Had this assumption of power been incidental, for the exigency of the moment, as under the pressure of war, and especially to serve the cause of human rights, to which before his elevation the President had professed such vociferous devotion, it might have been pardoned. It would have passed into the chapter of unauthorized acts which a patriot people had condoned. But it was the opposite in every particular. Beginning and continuing in usurpation, it was hateful beyond pardon because it sacrificed the rights of Unionists, white and black, and was in the interest of the rebellion and of those very Rebels who had been in arms against their country.

More than one person was appointed provisional governor who could not take the oath of office required by act of Congress. Other persons in the same predicament were appointed in the revenue service. The effect of these appointments was disastrous. They were in the nature of notice to Rebels everywhere, that participation in the rebellion was no bar to office. If one of their number could be appointed governor, if another could be appointed to a confidential position in the Treasury Department, then there was nobody on the long list of blood who might not look for preferment. And thus all offices from governor to constable were handed over to a disloyal scramble.

Rebels crawled forth from their retreats. Men who had hardly ventured to expect their lives were now candidates for office, and the rebellion became strong again. The change was felt in all the gradations of government, whether in states, counties, towns, or villages. Rebels found themselves in places of trust, while the truehearted Unionists, who had watched for the coming of our flag and ought to have enjoyed its protecting power, were driven into hiding places. All this was under the auspices of Andrew Johnson. It was he who animated the wicked crew. He was at the head of the work. Loyalty everywhere was persecuted. White and black, whose only offense was that they had been true to their country, were insulted, abused, murdered. There was no safety for the loyal man except within the flash of our bayonets. The story is as authentic as hideous. . . .

The officers he had appointed in defiance of law were paid also in the same defiance. Millions of property were turned over without consideration to railroad companies whose special recommendation was their participation in the rebellion. The Freedman's Bureau, that sacred charity of the republic, was despoiled of its possessions for the sake of Rebels, to whom their forfeited estates were given back after they had been vested by law in the United States. The proceeds of captured and abandoned property, lodged under the law in the national Treasury, were ravished from their place of deposit and sacrificed. Rebels were allowed to fill the antechambers of the executive mansion and to enter into his counsels. The pardoning power was prostituted, and pardons were issued in lots to suit Rebels, thus grossly abusing that trust whose discreet exercise is so essential to the administration of justice.

The powers of the Senate over appointments were trifled with and disregarded by reappointing persons who had been already rejected, and by refusing to communicate the names of others appointed by him during the recess. The veto power conferred by the Constitution as a remedy for ill-considered legislation was turned by him into a weapon of offense against Congress and into an instrument to beat down the just opposition which his usurpation had aroused. The power of removal, which patriot Presidents had exercised so sparingly, was seized as an engine of tyranny and openly employed to maintain his wicked purposes by the sacrifice of good citizens who would not consent to be his tools.

Incompetent and dishonest creatures, whose only recommendation was that they echoed his voice, were appointed to office, especially in the collection of the internal revenue, through whom a new organization, known as the "Whisky Ring," has been able to prevail over the government and to rob the Treasury of millions at the cost of taxpaying citizens, whose burdens are thus increased. Laws enacted by Congress for the benefit of the colored race, including that great statute for the establishment of the Freedman's Bureau, and that other great statute for the establishment of civil rights, were first attacked by his veto; and, when finally passed by the requisite majority over his veto, were treated by him as little better

than dead letters, while he boldly attempted to prevent the adoption of a constitutional amendment by which the right of citizens and the national debt were placed under the guarantee of irrepealable law.

During these successive assumptions, usurpations, and tyrannies, utterly without precedent in our history, this deeply guilty man ventured upon public speeches, each an offense to good morals, where, lost to all shame, he appealed in coarse words to the coarse passions of the coarsest people, scattering firebrands of sedition, inflaming anew the rebel spirit, insulting good citizens, and, with regard to officeholders, announcing in his own characteristic phrase that he would "kick them out" — the whole succession of speeches being from their brutalities and indecencies in the nature of a "criminal exposure of his person," indictable at common law, for which no judgment can be too severe. But even this revolting transgression is aggravated when it is considered that through these utterances the cause of justice was imperiled and the accursed demon of civil feud was lashed again into vengeful fury.

All these things from beginning to end are plain facts, already recorded in history and known to all. And it is further recorded in history and known to all, that, through these enormities, any one of which is enough for condemnation, while all together present an aggregation of crime, untold calamities have been brought upon our country; disturbing business and finance; diminishing the national revenues; postponing specie payments; dishonoring the Declaration of Independence in its grandest truths; arresting the restoration of the Rebel states; reviving the dying rebellion, and instead of that peace and reconciliation so much longed for, sowing strife and wrong, whose natural fruit is violence and blood.

For all these, or any one of them, Andrew Johnson should have been impeached and expelled from office. The case required a statement only, not an argument. Unhappily this was not done. As a petty substitute for the judgment which should have been pronounced, and as a bridle on presidential tyranny in "kicking out of office," Congress enacted a law known as the Tenure of Office Act, passed March 2, 1867, over his veto by the vote of two-thirds of both houses. And in order to prepare the way for impeachment, by removing certain scruples of technicality, its violation was expressly declared to be a high misdemeanor.

The President began at once to chafe under its restraint. Recognizing the act and following its terms, he first suspended Mr. Stanton from office, and then, on his restoration by the Senate, made an attempt to win General Grant into a surrender of the department so as to oust Mr. Stanton and to render the restoration by the Senate ineffectual. Meanwhile, Sheridan in Louisiana, Pope in Alabama, and Sickles in South Carolina, who, as military commanders, were carrying into the pacification of these states all the energies which had been so brilliantly displayed in the war, were pursued by the same vindictive spirit.

They were removed by the President, and rebellion throughout that whole region clapped its hands. This was done in the exercise of his power as commander in chief. At last, in his unappeased rage, he openly violated the Tenure of Office Act so as to bring himself under its judgment by the defiant attempt to remove Mr. Stanton from the War Department, without the consent of the Senate, and the appointment of Lorenzo Thomas, adjutant general of the United States, as secretary of war *ad interim.*

The Grand Inquest of the nation, which had slept on so many enormities, was awakened by this open defiance. The gauntlet was flung into its very chamber, and there it lay on the floor. The President, who had already claimed everything for the executive with impunity, now rushed into conflict with Congress on the very ground selected in advance by the latter. The field was narrow, but sufficient. There was but one thing for the House of Representatives to do. Andrew Johnson must be impeached, or the Tenure of Office Act would become a dead letter, while his tyranny would receive a letter of license, and impeachment as a remedy for wrongdoing would be blotted from the Constitution.

II.

JAMES GRIMES: For Acquittal

THE PRESIDENT OF THE UNITED STATES stands at the bar of the Senate charged with the commission of high crimes and misdemeanors. The principal offense charged against him is embodied in various forms in the first eight articles of impeachment. This offense is alleged to consist in a violation of the provisions of the 1st Section of an act of Congress entitled "An act regulating the tenure of certain civil offices," approved March 2, 1867, in this, that on the 21st day of February, 1868, the President removed, or attempted to remove, Edwin M. Stanton from the office of secretary for the Department of War, and issued a letter of authority to General Lorenzo Thomas as secretary for the Department of War *ad interim.*

The House of Representatives charge in their three first articles that the President attempted to remove Mr. Stanton, and that he issued his letter of authority to General Thomas with an intent to violate the law of Congress, and with the further "intent to violate the Constitution of the United States." The President, by his answer, admits that he sought to substitute General Thomas for Mr. Stanton at the head of the Department of War; but insists that he had the right to make such substitution under the laws then and now in force, and denies that in anything that he has done or attempted to do he intended to violate the laws or the Constitution of the United States. . . .

Impeachment Commission: (standing, left to right) James F. Wilson, George S. Boutwell, John A. Logan; (seated, left to right) Ben Butler, Thaddeus Stevens, Thomas Williams, John Bingham

The first section of this act reads as follows:

That every person holding any civil office to which he has been appointed by and with the advice and consent of the Senate, and every person who shall hereafter be appointed to any such office and shall become duly qualified to act therein, is and shall be entitled to hold such office until a successor shall have been in a like manner appointed and duly qualified, except as herein otherwise provided.

Then comes what is "otherwise provided":

Provided, that the secretaries of state, of the treasury, of war, of the Navy, and of the interior, the postmaster general, and the attorney general shall hold their offices respectively for and during the term of the President by whom they may have been appointed, and for one month thereafter, subject to removal by and with the advice and consent of the Senate. . . .

It is clear to my mind that the proviso does not include, and was not intended to include, Mr. Stanton's case. It is not possible to apply to his case the language of the proviso unless we suppose it to have been intended to legislate him out of office; a conclusion, I consider, wholly inadmissible. He was appointed by President Lincoln during his first term of office. He cannot hereafter go out of office at the end of the

term of the President by whom he was appointed. That term was ended before the law was passed. The proviso, therefore, cannot have been intended to make a rule for his case; and it is shown that it was not intended.

This was plainly declared in debate by the conference committee, both in the Senate and in the House of Representatives, when the proviso was introduced and its effect explained. The meaning and effect of the proviso were then explained and understood to be that the only tenure of the secretaries provided for by this law was a tenure to end with the term of service of the President by whom they were appointed; and, as this new tenure could not include Mr. Stanton's case, it was here explicitly declared that it did not include it. . . .

Believing, as I do, that the orders of the President for the removal of Mr. Stanton and the designation of General Thomas to act *ad interim* were legal orders, it is manifestly impossible for me to attach to them any idea of criminal conspiracy. If those orders had not been, in my judgment, lawful, I should not have come to the conclusion, upon the evidence, that any actual intent to do an unlawful act was proved. . . .

I come now to the question of intent. Admitting that the President had no power under the law to issue the order to remove

Mr. Stanton and appoint General Thomas secretary for the Department of War *ad interim*, did he issue those orders with a manifest *intent* to violate the laws and "the Constitution of the United States" as charged in the articles, or did he issue them, as he says he did, with a view to have the constitutionality of the Tenure of Office Act judicially decided? It is apparent to my mind that the President thoroughly believed the Tenure of Office Act to be unconstitutional and void. He was so advised by every member of his Cabinet when the bill was presented to him for his approval in February 1867. . . .

I cannot believe it to be our duty to convict the President of an infraction of a law when, in our consciences, we believe the law itself to be invalid, and therefore having no binding effect. If the law is unconstitutional, it is null and void, and the President has committed no offense and done no act deserving of impeachment. . . .

It is not denied, I think, that the constitutional validity of this law could not be tested before the courts unless a case was made and presented to them. No such case could be made unless the President made a removal. That act of his would necessarily be the basis on which the case would rest. He is sworn to "preserve, protect, and defend the Constitution of the United States." He must *defend* it against all encroachments from whatever quarter.

A question arose between the Legislative and Executive departments as to their relative powers in the matter of removals and appointments to office. That question was — Does the Constitution confer on the President the power which the Tenure of Office Act seeks to take away? It was a question manifestly of construction and interpretation. The Constitution has provided a common arbiter in such cases of controversy — the Supreme Court of the United States. Before that tribunal can take jurisdiction a removal must be made. The President attempted to give the court jurisdiction in that way. For doing so he is impeached. . . .

This was a *punitive* statute. It was directed against the President alone. It interfered with the prerogatives of his department as recognized from the foundation of the government. It wrested from him powers which, according to the legislative and judicial construction of eighty years, had been bestowed upon him by the Constitution itself. In my opinion, it was not only proper but it was his duty to cause the disputed question to be determined in the manner and by the tribunal established for such purposes. This government can only be preserved and the liberty of the people maintained by preserving intact the coordinate branches of it — legislative, executive, judicial — alike. I am no convert to any doctrine of the omnipotence of Congress. . . .

Mr. Johnson's character as a statesman, his relations to political parties, his conduct as a citizen, his efforts at reconstruction, the exercise of his pardoning power, the character of his appointments, and the influences under which they were made are not before us on any charges and are not impugned by any testimony.

Nor can I suffer my judgment of the law governing this case to be influenced by political considerations. I cannot agree to destroy the harmonious working of the Constitution for the sake of getting rid of an unacceptable President. Whatever may be my opinion of the incumbent, I cannot consent to trifle with the high office he holds. I can do nothing which, by implication, may be construed into an approval of impeachments as a part of future political machinery.

However widely, therefore, I may and do differ with the President respecting his political views and measures, and however deeply I have regretted, and do regret, the differences between himself and the Congress of the United States, I am not able to record my vote that he is guilty of high crimes and misdemeanors by reason of those differences. I am acting in a judicial capacity, under conditions whose binding obligation can hardly be exceeded, and I must act according to the best of my ability and judgment, and as they require. If, according to their dictates, the President is guilty, I *must* say so; if, according to their dictates, the President is not guilty, I *must* say so.

In my opinion, the President has not been guilty of an impeachable offense by reason of anything alleged in either of the articles preferred against him at the bar of the Senate by the House of Representatives.

31.

Civil War Amendments to the Constitution

The so-called Civil War Amendments were intended, from a variety of motives, to settle the uncertain status of African Americans in the United States. The Thirteenth Amendment, ratified eight months after the surrender of the Confederate army at Appomattox, put a legal end to slavery, thus completing what the Emancipation Proclamation had failed to do. The Fourteenth and Fifteenth Amendments were devised by the Radical Republican members of Congress as part of their Reconstruction program. The Fourteenth, ratified in July 1868, conferred citizenship upon African Americans; ratification was a precondition of readmission to the Union for the Rebel states. The "due process" clause of this amendment came to have great significance in subsequent decades as the "persons" mentioned in Section 1 were understood by the courts to be business corporations as well as individuals. The purpose of the Fifteenth Amendment, ratified March 30, 1870, was to give African Americans the right to vote. Between 1890 and 1910 white Southerners labored to negate the effects of the amendment.

AMENDMENT XIII

Passed by Congress February 1, 1865. Ratified December 18, 1865.

Section 1. Neither slavery nor involuntary servitude, except as a punishment for crime whereof the party shall have been duly convicted, shall exist within the United States or any place subject to their jurisdiction.

Section 2. Congress shall have power to enforce this article by appropriate legislation.

AMENDMENT XIV

Passed by Congress June 16, 1866. Ratified July 28, 1868.

Section 1. All persons born or naturalized in the United States and subject to the jurisdiction thereof are citizens of the United States and of the state wherein they reside. No state shall make or enforce any law which shall abridge the privileges or immunities of citizens of the United States; nor shall any state deprive any person of life, liberty, or property without due process of law; nor deny to any person within its jurisdiction the equal protection of the laws.

Section 2. Representatives shall be apportioned among the several states according to their respective numbers, counting the whole number of persons in each state, excluding Indians not taxed. But when the right to vote at any election for the choice of electors for President and Vice-President of the United States, representatives in Congress, the executive and judicial officers of a state, or the members of the legislature thereof, is denied to any of the male inhabitants of such state, being twenty-one years of age, and citizens of the United States, or in any way abridged, except for participation in rebellion or other crime, the basis of representation therein shall be reduced in the proportion which the number of such male citizens shall bear to the whole number of male citizens twenty-one years of age in such state.

Section 3. No person shall be a senator or representative in Congress, or elector of President and Vice-President, or hold any office, civil or military, under the United States, or under any state, who, having previously taken an oath as a member of Congress, or as an officer of the United States, or as a member of any state legislature, or as an executive or judicial officer of any state to support the Constitution of the United States, shall have engaged in insurrection or rebellion against the same or given aid or comfort to the enemies thereof. But Congress may, by a vote of two-thirds of each house, remove such disability.

Section 4. The validity of the public debt of the United States, authorized by law, including debts incurred for payment of pensions and bounties for services in suppressing insurrection or rebellion, shall not be questioned. But neither the United States nor any state shall assume or pay any debt or obligation incurred in aid of insurrection or rebellion against the United States, or any claim for the loss or emancipation of any slave; but all such debts, obligations, and claims shall be held illegal and void.

Section 5. The Congress shall have power to enforce, by appropriate legislation, the provisions of this article.

AMENDMENT XV

Passed by Congress February 27, 1869. Ratified March 30, 1870.

Section 1. The right of citizens of the United States to vote shall not be denied or abridged by the United States or by any state on account of race, color, or previous condition of servitude.

Section 2. The Congress shall have power to enforce this article by appropriate legislation.

I am sick and tired of war. Its glory is all moonshine. It is only those who have never fired a shot nor heard the shrieks and groans of the wounded who cry aloud for blood, more vengeance, more desolation. War is hell.

GENERAL WILLIAM TECUMSEH SHERMAN

32.

The Ku Klux Klan

The threat of Radical Reconstruction, which aimed at elevating Southern blacks to political power in an effort to destroy the white power structure of the pre-Civil War period, led a group of six young Confederate veterans to organize the Ku Klux Klan in Pulaski, Tennessee, on Christmas Eve, 1865. It was originally formed as a social club to shield white people from humiliation by African Americans. As African Americans gained political power the Klan was transformed into a political group aimed at undermining black power and ultimately reasserting white supremacy. In May of 1867, an organizational plan was adopted and former Confederate general Nathan Bedford Forrest was elected Grand Wizard of the Order. Klansmen wore long white robes, masks, and high cardboard hats and operated at night to frighten African Americans and to conceal their identity from federal troops. Though the Klan proved effective in intimidating African Americans and weakening their alliance with the Republican Party, its growing use of terrorism and violence alienated many Southerners. In 1869, Forrest formally dissolved the Order, but local groups were active for many years after. We reprint the "Organization and Principles" (1868) of the Order.

Source: *Documentary History of Reconstruction,* Walter L. Fleming, ed., Vol. II, Cleveland, 1907, pp. 347-349.

Appellation

This organization shall be styled and denominated, the Order of the ———

Creed

We, the Order of the ———, reverentially acknowledge the majesty and supremacy of the Divine Being and recognize the goodness and providence of the same. And we recognize our relation to the United States government, the supremacy of the Constitution, the constitutional laws thereof, and the Union of states thereunder.

Character and Objects of the Order

This is an institution of chivalry, humanity, mercy, and patriotism; embodying in its genius and its principles all that is chivalric in conduct, noble in sentiment, generous in manhood, and patriotic in purpose; its peculiar objects being:

First, to protect the weak, the innocent, and the defenseless from the indignities, wrongs, and outrages of the lawless, the violent, and the brutal; to relieve the injured and oppressed; to succor the suffering and unfortunate, and especially the widows and orphans of Confederate soldiers.

Second, to protect and defend the Constitution of the United States, and all laws passed in conformity thereto, and to protect the states and the people thereof from all invasion from any source whatever.

Third, to aid and assist in the execution of all constitutional laws, and to protect the people from unlawful seizure and from trial, except by their peers in conformity to the laws of the land.

Titles

Section 1. The officers of this Order shall consist of a Grand Wizard of the Empire and his ten Genii; a Grand Dragon of the Realm and his eight Hydras; a Grand Titan of the Dominion and his six Furies; a Grand Giant of the Province and his four Goblins; a Grand Cyclops of the Den and his two Night Hawks; a Grand Magi, a Grand Monk, a Grand Scribe, a Grand Exchequer, a Grand Turk, and a Grand Sentinel.

Section 2. The body politic of this Order shall be known and designated as "Ghouls."

Territory and Its Divisions

Section 1. The territory embraced within the jurisdiction of this Order shall be coterminous with the states of Maryland, Virginia, North Carolina, South Carolina, Georgia, Florida, Alabama, Mississippi, Louisiana, Texas, Arkansas, Missouri, Kentucky, and Tennessee; all combined constituting the Empire.

Section 2. The Empire shall be divided into four departments, the first to be styled the Realm and coterminous with the boundaries of the several states; the second to be styled the Dominion and to be coterminous with such counties as the Grand Dragons of the several Realms may assign to the charge of the Grand Titan. The third to be styled the Province and to be coterminous with the several counties; *provided,* the Grand Titan may, when he deems it necessary, assign two Grand Giants to one Province, prescribing, at the same time, the jurisdiction of each. The fourth department to be styled the Den, and shall embrace such part of a Province as the Grand Giant shall assign to the charge of a Grand Cyclops.

Questions To Be Asked Candidates

1. Have you ever been rejected, upon application for membership in the ———, or have you ever been expelled from the same?

2. Are you now, or have you ever been, a member of the Radical Republican Party, or either of the organizations known as the "Loyal League" and the "Grand Army of the Republic"?

3. Are you opposed to the principles and policy of the Radical Party, and to the Loyal League, and the Grand Army of the Republic, so far as you are informed of the character and purposes of those organizations?

4. Did you belong to the Federal Army during the late war, and fight against the South during the existence of the same?

5. Are you opposed to Negro equality, both social and political?

6. Are you in favor of a white man's government in this country?

7. Are you in favor of constitutional liberty, and a government of equitable laws instead of a government of violence and oppression?

8. Are you in favor of maintaining the constitutional rights of the South?

9. Are you in favor of the reenfranchisement and emancipation of the white men of the South, and the restitution of the Southern people to all their rights, alike proprietary, civil, and political?

10. Do you believe in the inalienable right of self-preservation of the people against the exercise of arbitrary and unlicensed power?

The true Southern watermelon is a boon apart, and not to be mentioned with commoner things. It is chief of this world's luxuries, king by the grace of God over all the fruits of the earth. When one has tasted it, he knows what angels eat. It was not a Southern watermelon that Eve took; we know it because she repented.

SAMUEL L. CLEMENS ("MARK TWAIN")

33.

The Knights of the White Camelia

The Knights of the White Camelia, a secret society whose organizational structure closely paralleled that of the Ku Klux Klan, was founded in New Orleans in 1867. Like the Klan, the Knights' principle aim was to maintain white supremacy in the South despite the stringent measures of the Reconstruction program. The Knights employed Klan tactics of terrorism and social reprisal to fend off the African Americans' increasing political and economic power. The "Constitution and Ritual" of the Order, presented here, was adopted in 1868 at a meeting in New Orleans.

Source: *Documents Relating to Reconstruction,* Walter L. Fleming, ed., Morgantown, W. Va., 1904, No. 1.

PREAMBLE

Whereas, Radical legislation is subversive of the principles of the government of the United States as originally adopted by our fathers:

And whereas, our safety and our prosperity depend on the preservation of those grand principles and believing that they can be peacefully maintained; therefore, we adopt the following:

CONSTITUTION

Title I. Division of the Order

Article 1. This Order shall consist of a Supreme Council of the United States, and of Grand, Central, and Subordinate Councils.

Title II. Supreme Council

Article 2. The Supreme Council shall be organized as soon as five states shall have established each a Grand Council.

Article 3. This Council shall be composed of delegates from each state in which a Grand Council shall be established.

Article 4. Each state shall send to the Su-preme Council five delegates, whose appointment shall continue for one year and who shall be elected, from their own bodies, by the several Grand Councils of the Order.

Article 5. All past grand commanders in good standing shall be ex-officio members of the Grand Council and shall be entitled to all the rights and privileges of the members of that body.

Article 6. The Supreme Council shall hold its sessions in the city of New Orleans, state of Louisiana, but may, by a vote of two-thirds of its members, change its place of meeting to any other city in the United States.

Article 7. The Supreme Council shall be the head of the Order and the court of last appeal in all matters of disagreement, except in cases hereinafter specified. It shall make all laws for the general government of the Order; shall take cognizance of all acts; and shall be the arbiter of all disputes which may arise between the Grand and Central Councils of any state and Grand Councils and their grand commanders.

Article 8. The officers of the Supreme Council shall be as follows: (1) supreme commander; (2) supreme lieutenant commander; (3) supreme sentinel; (4) supreme corresponding secretary; (5) supreme treasurer.

QUESTIONS

1. Do you belong to the white race? *Answer.* — I do.

2. Did you ever marry any woman who did not, or does not, belong to the white race? *Ans.* — No.

3. Do you promise never to marry any woman but one who belongs to the white race? *Ans.* — I do.

4. Do you believe in the superiority of your race? *Ans.* — I do.

5. Will you promise never to vote for anyone for any office of honor, profit, or trust who does not belong to your race? *Ans.* — I do.

6. Will you take a solemn oath never to abstain from casting your vote at any election in which a candidate of the Negro race shall be opposed to a white man attached to your principles, unless or prevented by severe illness or any other physical disability? *Ans.* — I will.

7. Are you opposed to allowing the control of the political affairs of this country to go in whole or in part into the hands of the African race, and will you do everything in your power to prevent it? *Ans.* — Yes.

8. Will you devote your intelligence, energy, and influence to the furtherance and propagation of the principles of our Order? *Ans.* — I will.

9. Will you, under all circumstances, defend and protect persons of the white race in their lives, rights, and property against all encroachments or invasions from any inferior race, and especially the African? *Ans.* — Yes.

10. Are you willing to take an oath forever to cherish these grand principles and to unite yourself with others who, like you, believing in their truth, have firmly bound themselves to stand by and defend them against all? *Ans.* — I am.

The commander shall then say: If you consent to join our Association, raise your right hand and I will administer to you the oath which we have all taken:

OATH

I do solemnly swear, in the presence of these witnesses, never to reveal, without authority, the existence of this Order, its objects, its acts, and signs of recognition; never to reveal or publish, in any manner whatsoever, what I shall see or hear in this Council; never to divulge the names of the members of the Order or their acts done in connection therewith. I swear to maintain and defend the social and political superiority of the white race on this continent; always and in all places to observe a marked distinction between the white and African races; to vote for none but white men for any office of honor, profit, or trust; to devote my intelligence, energy, and influence to instill these principles in the minds and hearts of others; and to protect and defend persons of the white race in their lives, rights, and property against the encroachments and aggressions of an inferior race.

I swear, moreover, to unite myself in heart, soul, and body with those who compose this Order; to aid, protect, and defend them in all places; to obey the orders of those who, by our statutes, will have the right of giving those orders; to respond at the peril of my life to a call, sign, or cry coming from a fellow member whose rights are violated; and to do everything in my power to assist him through life. And to the faithful performance of this oath, I pledge my life and sacred honor. . . .

CHARGE

Brothers:

You have been initiated into one of the most important Orders which have ever been established on this continent; an Order, which, if its principles are faithfully observed and its objects diligently carried out, is destined to regenerate our unfortunate country and to relieve the white race from the humiliating condition to which it has lately been reduced in this republic. It is necessary, therefore, that before taking part in the labors of this Association, you should understand fully its principles and objects and the duties which devolve upon you as one of its members.

As you may have already gathered from the questions which were propounded to you, and which you have answered so satisfactorily, and from the clauses of the oath which you have taken, our main and fundamental object is the *maintenance of the supremacy of the white race* in this republic. History and physiology teach us that we belong to a race which nature has endowed with an evident superiority over all other races, and that the Maker, in thus elevating us above the common standard of human creation, has intended to give us over inferior races a dominion from which no human laws can permanently derogate. The experience of ages demonstrates that, from the origin of the world, this dominion has always remained in the hands of the Caucasian race, while all the other races have constantly occupied a subordinate and secondary position; a fact which triumphantly confirms this great law of nature.

Powerful nations have succeeded each other on the face of the world and have marked their passage by glorious and memorable deeds; and among those who have thus left on this globe indelible traces of their splendor and greatness, we find none but descended from the Caucasian stock. We see, on the contrary, that most of the countries inhabited by the other races have remained in a state of complete barbarity; while the small number of those who have advanced beyond this savage existence have, for centuries, stagnated in a semibarbarous condition, of which there can be no progress or improvement. And it is a remarkable fact that as a race of men is more remote from the Caucasian and approaches nearer to the black African, the more fatally

that stamp of inferiority is affixed to its sons and irrevocably dooms them to eternal imperfectibility and degradation.

Convinced that we are of these elements of natural ethics, we know, besides, that the government of our republic was established by white men, for white men alone, and that it never was in the contemplation of its founders that it should fall into the hands of an inferior and degraded race. We hold, therefore, that any attempt to wrest from the white race the management of its affairs in order to transfer it to control of the black population is an invasion of the sacred prerogatives vouchsafed to us by the Constitution, and a violation of the laws established by God Himself; that such encroachments are subversive of the established institutions of our republic; and that no individual of the white race can submit to them without humiliation and shame.

It, then, becomes our solemn duty, as white men, to resist strenuously and persistently those attempts against our natural and constitutional rights, and to do everything in our power in order to maintain, in this republic, the supremacy of the Caucasian race and restrain the black or African race to that condition of social and political inferiority for which God has destined it. This is the object for which our Order was instituted; and, in carrying it out, we intend to infringe no laws, to violate no rights, and to resort to no forcible means, except for purposes of legitimate and necessary defense.

As an essential condition of success, this Order proscribes absolutely all social equality between the races. If we were to admit persons of African race on the same level with ourselves, a state of personal relations would follow which would unavoidably lead to political equality; for it would be a virtual recognition of *status*, after which we could not consistently deny them an equal share in the administration of our public affairs. The man who is good enough to be our familiar companion is good enough also to participate in our political government; and if we were to grant the one, there could be no good reason for us not to concede the other of these two privileges.

There is another reason, brothers, for which we condemn this social equality. Its toleration would soon be a fruitful source of intermarriages between individuals of the two races; and the result of this miscegenation would be gradual amalgamation and the production of a degenerate and bastard offspring, which would soon populate these states with a degraded and ignoble population, incapable of moral and intellectual development, and unfitted to support a great and powerful country. We must maintain the purity of the white blood if we would preserve it for that natural superiority with which God has ennobled it.

To avoid these evils, therefore, we take the obligation *to observe a marked distinction between the two races,* not only in the relations of public affairs but also in the more intimate dealings and intercourse of private life which, by the frequency of their occurrence, are more apt to have an influence on the attainment of the purposes of the Order.

Now that I have laid before you the objects of this Association, let me charge you specially in relation to one of your most important duties as one of its members. Our statutes make us bound to respect sedulously the rights of the colored inhabitants of this republic and, in every instance, to give to them whatever lawfully belongs to them. It is an act of simple justice not to deny them any of the privileges to which they are legitimately entitled; and we cannot better show the inherent superiority of our race than by dealing with them in that spirit of firmness, liberality, and impartiality which characterizes all superior organizations. Besides, it would be ungenerous for us to undertake to restrict them to the narrowest limits as to the exercise of certain rights, without conceding to them, at the same time, the fullest measure of those which we recognize as theirs; and a fair construction of a white man's duty toward them would be not only to respect and observe their acknowledged rights but also to see that these are respected and observed by others.

From the brief explanation which I have just given you, you must have satisfied yourselves that our Association is not a political party and has no connection with any of the organized parties of the day. Nor will it lend itself to the personal advancement of individuals or listen to the cravings of any partisan spirit. It was organized in order to carry out certain great principles from which it must never swerve by favoring private ambitions and political aspirations. These, as well as all sentiments of private enmity, animosity, and other personal feelings, we must leave at the door before we enter this Council. You may meet here, congregated together, men who belong to all the political organizations which now divide, or may divide, this country; you see some whom embittered feuds and irreconcilable hatred have long and widely separated; they have all cast away these rankling feelings to unite cordially and zealously in the labors of our great undertaking. Let their example be to you a useful lesson of the disinterestedness and devotedness which should characterize our efforts for the success of our cause!

Brothers, I now consign you to the lieutenant commander of this Council, who will instruct you as to the signs and other means of recognition of this Association and other details of its organization and order.

The lieutenant commander will now instruct the new brothers as to the sign, grip, cry, dialogue, rap, password, etc., taking care to charge them particularly as to the circumstances and occasion of their use. He will also inform them of the mode of initiation and other details of order which they are required to know.

34.

Spirituals

"Most of the verses of the plantation songs had some reference to freedom," wrote
African American educator Booker T. Washington in Up from Slavery. *"True, they
had sung those same verses before, but they had been careful to explain that the
'freedom' in these songs referred to the next world, and had no connection with life in
this world. Now they gradually threw off the mask and were not afraid to let it be
known that the 'freedom' in their songs meant freedom of the body in this world."
Spirituals like the ones reprinted below became widely known and appreciated after the
Civil War. Many of them were published by Allen, Garrison, and Ware in 1867, and
others were popularized by the Fisk Jubilee Singers in the 1870s.*

Source: J. B. T. Marsh, *The Story of the Jubilee Singers; With Their Songs,*
Revised edition, Boston, 1880.

DIDN'T MY LORD DELIVER DANIEL?

Didn't my Lord deliver Daniel,
  Deliver Daniel,
  Deliver Daniel,
Didn't my Lord deliver Daniel,
And why not a every man?

He delivered Daniel from the lion's den,
Jonah from the belly of the whale,
And the Hebrew children from the
    fiery furnace,
And why not a every man?

Didn't my Lord deliver Daniel,
  Deliver Daniel,
  Deliver Daniel,
Didn't my Lord deliver Daniel,
Then why not a every man?

MARY AND MARTHA

Mary and Martha just gone along,
Mary and Martha just gone along,
Mary and Martha just gone along
To ring those charming bells.

Chorus:
Crying free grace and dying love,
Free grace and dying love,
Free grace and dying love,
To ring those charming bells.

The preacher and the elder's just
    gone along, etc.

My father and mother's just gone
    along, etc.

The Methodist and Baptist's just
    gone along, etc.

THE GOSPEL TRAIN

The gospel train is coming,
I hear it just at hand,
I hear the car wheels moving
And rumbling through the land.

Chorus:
Get on board, children,
Get on board, children,
Get on board, children,
For there's room for many a more.

I hear the bell and whistle,
The coming round the curve;
She's playing all her steam
And straining every nerve.

No signal for another train
To follow on the line;
O sinner, you're forever lost
If once you're left behind.

JOSHUA FIT THE BATTLE OF JERICHO

Joshua fit the battle of Jericho,
  Jericho,
  Jericho,
Joshua fit the battle of Jericho,
And the walls come a-tumbling down.

You may talk about your King of Gideon,
You may talk about your man of Saul,
There's none like good old Joshua
At the battle of Jericho.

Up to the walls of Jericho,
He marched with spear in hand,
"Go blow them ram horns," Joshua cried,
" 'Cause the battle am in my hand."

Then the lamb ram sheep-horns begin
    to blow:
Trumpets begin to sound,
Joshua commanded the children to shout,
And the walls come a-tumbling down.

That morning,
Joshua fit the battle of Jericho,
  Jericho,
  Jericho,
Joshua fit the battle of Jericho,
And the walls come a-tumbling down.

EZEKIEL SAW THE WHEEL

Ezekiel saw the wheel
  up in the middle of the air.
Ezekiel saw the wheel
  way up in the middle of the air.
Big wheel run by faith,
  little wheel run by the grace of God.
Wheel in a wheel,
  way up in the middle of the air.

Some go to church for to sing and shout
Before six months they're all turned out.

You never can tell what a hypocrite'll do:
He'll lie about me and he'll lie about you.

One of these days about twelve o'clock
This old world going to reel and rock.

Ezekiel saw the wheel
  up in the middle of the air.
Ezekiel saw the wheel
  way up in the middle of the air.
The big wheel run by faith,
    the little wheel run by the grace of God.
Wheel in a wheel
  way up in the middle of the air.

MY LORD, WHAT A MOURNING

My Lord, what a mourning.
My Lord, what a mourning.
My Lord, what a mourning,
When the stars begin to fall.

You'll hear the trumpet sound
To wake the nations underground,
Looking to my God's right hand,
When the stars begin to fall.

My Lord, what a mourning, etc.

You'll hear the sinner mourn,
To wake the nations underground,
Looking to my God's right hand,
When the stars begin to fall.

My Lord, what a mourning, etc.

You'll hear the Christian shout,
To wake the nations underground,
Looking to my God's right hand,
When the stars begin to fall.

My Lord, what a mourning, etc.

1869

35.

Congressional Debate on Haiti and Santo Domingo

The Civil War brought to the attention of the navy the need for island bases in the Caribbean. Secretary of State Seward took it upon himself to press the matter both during and after the war. The most likely spot seemed to be Santo Domingo, where continued political instability offered hope of annexation. Seward persuaded President Johnson to suggest to Congress, in December 1868, "the acquisition and incorporation into our federal Union of the several adjacent continental and insular communities." Congress would have none of it and, in January 1869, turned down a resolution proposing a protectorate over the island of Santo Domingo and Haiti. Following are portions of the debates on the resolution in the House of Representatives January 13, 1869.

Source: *Globe*, 40 Cong., 3 Sess., pp. 333-340.

Mr. Butler [Massachusetts]. I offer the following as a substitute for the joint resolution:

Resolved by the Senate and House of Representatives of the United States of America in Congress assembled, that the President of the United States be, and he hereby is, authorized to extend the protection of the United States over either of the islands of the Antilles to such extent as he may deem expedient and not inconsistent with the laws of nations whenever the government established in either of them or the people thereof shall desire such protection of the United States: *Provided,* that any action in this behalf on the part of the executive shall be forthwith reported to Congress: *And provided further,* that no payment or expenditure of money in carrying this resolution into effect shall be made or contracted for without previous authority of Congress.

Mr. Spalding [Ohio]. I desire to offer an amendment to the substitute.

Mr. Banks [Massachusetts]. I yield for that purpose.

Mr. Spalding. I move to insert after the word "Antilles" the words "or any other islands in the Atlantic or Pacific oceans which lie nearer to the coast of the United States than to that of any foreign government."

Mr. Banks. I will yield to my colleague who introduced the substitute to debate it if he pleases. I only desire to say that it stands on a different principle from that of the original resolution. While I do not object to it if the House chooses to extend it, I do not wish to be understood as approving the substitute.

Mr. Butler. Mr. Speaker, I desire the attention of the House for one moment to the amendment which I have proposed. The original proposition is that whenever the governments of Haiti and San Domingo desire the protection of the United States, the President of the United States shall be in a condition, by the authorization of Congress, to extend it, provided that it shall not involve the United States in any breach of treaty obligations or expenses. The amendment which I have offered extends this right of protection to all the islands of the Antilles; and the honorable member from Ohio proposes to extend the principle to every island adjacent to our territory on either shore, looking, I suppose, to the Sandwich Islands, if the time shall come or is ripe for most of these islands coming under our protection.

The amendment that I have offered proposes that wherever in the islands of the American seas any body of men associated together under the forms of government desire the protection of the United States, the President shall have a right, in his discretion, to extend that protection. I cannot help looking forward to the immediate future, and not a far-distant future, when the whole system of government in the islands of the Antilles — whether the governments of Denmark or of Spain, or the republican governments there — will crumble to pieces, and the islands will go out, by natural process, from under their former governments. And they belong to us so far by position and by the laws of nature that it is required for us to interpose our good offices to aid them to come to us and under our laws.

Let me say here that no question of feeling against the present executive or what the executive may do should influence any gentleman on this question, for this power is needed to meet a case that may arise when we are not in session. When we are in session we can at once advise or restrain movements in this direction as we choose. There is now a revolution going on in Cuba in which we can take no part until the people of that government have put themselves in a position to receive our protection by conquering their own independence, and then we should be in condition to assert our traditional doctrine, known as the Monroe Doctrine, that there must be no unwilling dependencies of a European government on the American continent. I call the attention of gentlemen who represent states that are interested in having the Mississippi River open to the navigation of the world to the fact that it is necessary to the full enjoyment of that navigation that we should have a right to extend our protection to our commerce in all the islands of the West Indies.

Let me say further that we have by our action put ourselves in a very anomalous position in regard to some of these islands. Our executive called upon Denmark and asked to have the people of St. Thomas vote whether they would belong to Denmark or to this country. That people voted that they preferred to belong to this country, and thereupon they seem to have shut themselves off from Denmark; while we are not yet ready or willing to ratify the treaty by which we agreed to pay money for that island. And let me say to this House that, by my proposition, I do not look in any degree toward paying any money for any island or other land on the American continent. As I opposed the purchase of Alaska, so I should oppose hereafter the purchase of any foot of soil.

But the question now is as to extending the protection of a republican government. Gentlemen may ask, "Do you propose armed intervention?" To that I answer that the resolution carefully and expressly guards itself by providing that the intervention or protection shall not be inconsistent with the laws of nations, violating no treaty stipulation and no national right. How such protection can be extended within the laws of nations is perfectly well settled by almost every textwriter that treats upon that subject. Therefore the simple question is this, to put it in plain, homely language: Shall we have our mouths open, ready to catch the plum which is now ripe and ready to fall, or shall we keep them shut and permit it to fall in the mouths of others?

And a word further; that, for one, I think the time has come for action upon this subject. This project cannot be met successfully by the assertion that there is no precedent for it. Sir, there is no precedent for our position in the history of the world. There is no precedent for our power. There is no precedent for our influence on this continent. But there is a precedent for us in every act of this government toward the young republics of South America; in every act extending a helping hand to every people desiring either a republican government or a stable government under republican forms. And I trust that we shall not throw cold water upon the effort for the emancipation of slavery in Cuba, whether white or black, upon the efforts toward good government in Dominica and Haiti, and upon the disposition of those islands, so valuable in a commercial point of view, to put themselves under our protection.

I have listened to the amendment of my very conservative friend from Ohio. I know that he only desires to add to this resolution so that possibly the Sandwich Islands, and perhaps some others in the Pacific Ocean, may be brought within its scope. Now, while I do not mean to antagonize the propositions submitted by the chairman of the Committee on Foreign Affairs, which I shall support if I cannot get my own adopted, still I desire that we shall make

this a general provision, putting in the hands of the executive the power to act, provided he shall pay no money for purchase, shall incur no expenditure, and do no act unless he immediately reports to Congress, and especially that he shall do no act contravening the law of nations. . . .

Mr. Spalding. As I have offered an amendment to the substitute moved by the gentleman from Massachusetts, I desire to say a few words. I think I have oftentimes said upon the floor of this House that I was impressed with the belief that it was the destiny of the American government to spread itself, not only over the whole continent of America; but over all the islands adjacent thereto. And I believe this: If there be anything decreed in the councils of infinite wisdom it is this very fact. It is merely a question of time.

Now, sir, I do not say that it is sound national policy at this time to adopt any resolution upon this subject. But if we adopt any resolution to any extent, then, I say, let us open it wide enough to embrace acquisitions from either ocean, the Atlantic or the Pacific. And the gentleman from Massachusetts does me no more than justice when he says I have reference to a cluster of islands in the Pacific Ocean in which the work of disintegration is now rapidly going on. The pear is nearly ripe enough to fall, and when it does fall it must fall into the American lap.

I ask, therefore, that the members of this House, and especially those who are interested in the prosperity of the Pacific Coast, vote for my proposition which is in accordance with the spirit engraved upon the substitute offered by the gentleman from Massachusetts. It strikes me, sir, that the proposition is sufficiently guarded. We incur no risk of expense; we incur no risk of a breach of a treaty of peace or of any neutrality laws. We guard against that by the provision inserted by the astute gentleman from Massachusetts in his substitute. The

President can only extend this protectorate when the application comes voluntarily from the people interested and without infringing any law of nations, any treaty, or any neutrality law. No money can be expended except upon application to Congress. No armed force can be employed but by the authority of Congress. The resolution being thus guarded, I, as a conservative man (the gentleman emphatically says I am "conservative," but upon this subject — perhaps it is the only one — he will find me more radical, I trust, than himself), will go "as far as he who goes the furthest." I shall vote for the amendment to the substitute; I shall then vote for the substitute as amended and for the original resolution. . . .

Mr. Shellabarger [Ohio]. Mr. Speaker, I have not sought the floor upon this extraordinary proposition because of any supposition that the views I may submit to the House will be either new or useful but simply to indicate why I cannot support either the original proposition of the chairman of the Committee on Foreign Affairs or any of the amendments that have been submitted to the House. It is conceded both by the chairman and by other gentlemen who have spoken that this proposition is extraordinary — not only extraordinary in the common sense of the term but so extraordinary that it is unprecedented in the history of this government. That a proposition thus unprecedented should be brought into the House at this time, unapproved as it is by any committee of this House, and sought to be disposed of as this one is sought to be, is to me rather a subject of surprise.

Let us for a moment or two examine what this proposition is. In its substance and effect I understand it to be a proposition by which the power, the force, the authority of the government of the United States shall be transferred by Congress to the executive of the United States, to be exercised under his unrestrained discretion in "protecting" — that is the operative and significant word of the resolution — in protecting the governments or the people of those islands indicated in the resolution. If it does not mean this, it means just nothing at all. The executive is to be authorized to protect these governments or these people.

Now, in the first place, I ask my fellow members to consider what that word "protect" involves and means. If there is to be protection extended, it must be a protection to be found in something, or else, as I have said, the resolution is meaningless. I shall assume, for the purpose of what I have to say, that it does mean something. That protection, Mr. Speaker, can be given by the exercise of the authority of this government in the only way in which that authority of the government can be exercised; that is, by the force which is found in the protection of the military and naval authority of your government. You have no other way of "protecting" them than this. That moral protection which is to be found in the mere adoption of resolutions, in declarations of sympathy, or of approval or disapproval, or which is to be found in the ordinary instrumentalities of diplomacy — such moral protection is clearly not the protection meant. Then, sir, it comes to this: a proposition that we shall now protect by the military and the naval authority of this government the peoples of these islands or their governments.

I know there are "salvos" in the latter part of the resolution requiring that the President shall submit to Congress his action in the matter, and also a proviso that it shall cost us nothing. But I submit that these provisions and salvos in the resolution of the chairman of the Committee on Foreign Affairs, if it were not introduced by a gentleman so honorable, so ingenuous, so frank and outspoken, might be denominated a "springe to catch woodcocks"; and it would, I think, be a very young woodcock in legislation that would be caught by that which is appended to this resolution. It is to cost us nothing, is it? We, by the resolution, solemnly decide that these governments and their people shall be protected, and then there is an authorization to the President to extend that protection. It is to be effectual; it is not to be meaningless, but it is to be protection, and the President is demanded by the high command of the two houses of Congress, speaking in the imperial voice of the law, to attain that high end — the protection of these peoples and governments. And then we admonish him that this execution of our high command shall cost us nothing!

First, the action is to go forward; the protection is to proceed; the befriended government is to be, by our commanding guardianship, made perpetual. This is the thing authorized by the resolution. When the protection of this republic goes to these new wards of the nation, it goes out under the sanction of Congress given in a joint resolution of the two houses of Congress. We command the President, in all the emphasis and meaning of that word "protect," but protect so that it shall not cost. That is what the resolution, it is averred, comes to. But, sir, the resolution means that there shall be an effective thing done under it, and that thing cannot be less than that this government shall protect; and by the resolution we agree that all the costs and consequences involved in giving that protection and in making it good and perpetual against all who may come to forbid come either from the people there or other nations.

Suppose that the President has done this thing — has protected; that our navy has been used for the purpose of this protection; that it has been sent there and done what amounts to protection, and it has involved expenditure — who would vote that that protection thus authorized, thus expensive, shall not be compensated? Bring it back to its original elements and I submit to the gentleman who introduced the proposition that it comes to this: That it is a declaration of war on the part of the government of the United States against some-body — nay, sir, against everybody who may come to forbid our protection.

I admit I do not know who we declare the war against. The resolution does not inform us whom it is we are to protect against. What that belligerent is that we are to fight is not indicated. But if it means something, as it does, it means that this government shall embark now, here, today, in that protection that can only be given by war in favor of somebody and against somebody, in favor of everybody whom the President — mark it — whom the President may deem it fit to make this government the ally of, and a war against everybody who may be the enemy of our, or rather the President's, ally and ward.

Now, Mr. Speaker, I know that it may be old-fashioned, perhaps "stale and unprofitable," so here to do; still I will venture to bring my own mind, and so far as my feeble effort may enable me to do so, to bring the minds of my fellow members back to those rules of national obligation, of wisdom, and of duty touching our foreign policies and affairs upon which your government was founded and upon which it has ever since so sublimely endured. Not long ago, within the memory of all of us, an old man fell stricken with death within the space now reached by the sound of my voice. That old man was young once, and when a boy he indicated and in letters gave to his country and mankind that which passed afterward into immortality in the "Farewell Address of the Father of his Country."

The great intellect of John Quincy Adams originated, matured, gathered into the forms and force of irresistible argument and precept the doctrines of that most approved, most cherished, and most loved part of the "Farewell Address of the Father of his Country" which admonished his countrymen against the intervention of this nation in the affairs of others and against all entangling alliances — that policy which was first announced by your government on the

25th of April, 1793, in the proclamation of George Washington, declaring the neutrality of this government as between the French government and the people of Europe. To the intervention in these affairs our people were then impelled by all the promptings of sympathy and of gratitude toward our recent ally, the people of France. The policy then and there inaugurated, I say, is one which I earnestly pray may be in our country perpetual and for which I feebly beg.

This government, sir, may be strong in itself, may be irresistible in itself, may, God grant, be perpetual. But, sir, that immortality is to be found in our being to ourselves and for ourselves a government of ourselves; not involving or embroiling ourselves in or interfering with the affairs of other governments. That policy thus inaugurated has continued from that day to this. We have by our moral forces, which are growing into omnipotence, given our cheer to the struggling everywhere. Let us give it today to these people, to any people, to all peoples struggling for their rights, for the right. It is in that sublime moral power of your government that you have found your controlling forces for good.

I beg, then, that the House shall pause. It is a feeble power, perhaps, against which our guns are now to be by this resolution pointed, or whom we may now challenge to the determinations of war. But, sir, it is not the feebleness of the power but the potency of the precedent that I now comment upon. To that I point; against that I implore my fellow members to be on their guard. Be warned! The first step is here — is today. The last is — where? In departing from the inculcations of the fathers of the republic, when they told us to let foreign wars alone, we embark on new seas — seas you and I have not explored. I pause; I fear; I refuse to go. . . .

Mr. Mullins [Tennessee]. I do not know that it is within my power to enlighten this House touching this question that is under consideration. I may be permitted to say that it is, of all the questions that have come up here since the assembling of this Congress for its last session, the most important that has addressed itself to my consideration. In the five minutes allowed me I cannot, of course, dwell upon the subject in detail. I must come up to the main features that present themselves to my mind.

We are not a city that is to be buried. We are a city set upon a hill, whose light should not be hid under a bushel but should shine forth that the nations of the earth that are living in darkness and bondage may see the light and look to us as their great lighthouse. And where do we hail from? We hail from an ancestry that God, in my opinion, has destined should spread its light over the whole earth and break the chains and fetters of empires, kingdoms, and dominions. And we will not only break those chains and fetters but we will ride in grandeur and triumph. We spread out our arms like seas to those who are in fetters and bondage, and say "Come to us, and we will give you protection."

We do not propose to fight their battles. That, I believe, is contrary to the fundamental principles, as has been indicated by the gentleman who has just preceded me. As was wisely declared by the gentleman from Massachusetts [Mr. Butler], we put a stopper on this thing of buying territory. We define this position to this people adjacent to our land, to the great people here in the United States; and I declare, as I have a right to do, that in my opinion this is the new Jerusalem that comes down to us, and it will be the gathering in of all nations, showing its light to all. It is a harbor for all the ships that are not only to crowd around the Old World but to come from there here.

Let us say to these little islands and to these people, "We sympathize with your republican governments as the fundamental principle of life that God has ordained when He established the Garden and covenanted with man, that man was a moral free agent, and no monarch, king, or despot is decreed of God to domineer over the world." Let man in his own consciousness of right speak to these islands in darkness and let them know that they have a friend here who sympathizes with them. And when the people, the fundamental strata upon which stands the republic of the United States, shall respond to the will of the people of these islands, then they come to us as ripe fruit, and I would not let them lay there after they are ripe and become sour and spoil.

I for one will say this: that rather than go into war with these lands and this people, I would let them alone; they will come to us themselves. Let us under the auspices of this resolution, that covenants nothing but friendship — no blood to be spilled, no gold to be paid — it is a mere expression of the will of the American people that we sympathize with them. They will feel it; they will get the knowledge almost as a spiritual thing; it will be received by them as a sympathetic cord that reaches across from them to us and will draw them here naturally when they are ripe. If there was a destiny of God in the formation of this government — and I declare that the governments and the nations of the Old World are held in check by it — then it is that we shall inhabit this land and all adjacent to it. This Saxon people are a burning meteor rushing on in space, and their empire is land and dominion upon earth. Five hundred years have given them empire over a portion, and 5,000 more will give them the whole world. . . .

Mr. Judd [Illinois]. Mr. Speaker, I recognize and subscribe to this doctrine of manifest destiny as connected with our surroundings as strongly perhaps as any gentleman upon this floor. I think the influence of our institutions is not to be limited simply to the territory that now belongs to us, but that in the process of time, if our government remains stable and perpetuated, it is to extend to other lands; and I have no doubt but that influence will, by its own momentum, peaceably and consistently with all our engagements with other nations, bring these islands as well as the territory adjoining us within the embrace of our institutions. But it is with me a question of what is the proper manner in which to make our influence felt and to spread that influence to these islands and to other portions of the earth.

I freely confess that I listened to the able remarks of the distinguished chairman of the Committee on Foreign Affairs [Mr. Banks] on yesterday for the purpose of getting, if possible, at some reason for immediate action and of obtaining information and facts, if there are any, that are in the possession of any department of this government showing the necessity for any action at the present time. The chairman of the committee replied that there was no information that could be given to the public. His mode of reply certainly left upon my mind the impression that there were some negotiations that for some reason could not be submitted to this House. It is due to the legislative branch of the government that it should be fully advised as to what is going on in the Executive Department when called upon to invest it with these extraordinary powers. With annexation, vast expenditures may follow in the train of the proposed action, and this House is called upon to invest all these in the Executive Department in advance.

It is not a year since these halls resounded with denunciation, in which, I think, my friend from Massachusetts [Mr. Butler] took part, taking exception to the secret diplomacy of the executive branch of the government, under which and without the knowledge and assent of Congress, territory was acquired, large liabilities incurred, which Congress must meet, and new populations introduced into our system. And all this by the executive branch of the government. I may add, Mr. Speaker, that the people of this country were struck with amazement at the pretense and claims of this branch of the government. Having apparently involved the honor of the nation, Congress was compelled under this cry to ratify such doings.

In objecting to these propositions I do not lose sight of the fact that such propositions, when properly presented to the Congress of the United States, who hold the purse of the nation and the power of war, by responsible parties who have an interest in a stable government, and ask for protection, will deserve the consideration and action of Congress. I freely confess, Mr. Speaker, that I have no such confidence in executive power as to be willing, under this resolution or any other, to delegate to it powers that properly and rightfully belong to the legislative branch of the government.

It has been truly said by the honorable gentleman from Ohio [Mr. Shellabarger] that we do not know where this thing may lead. We do not know what interests may operate with the chief of the State Department to involve this government, if not in a war, in an acquisition of territory which, if submitted to Congress before the making of this proposition, would not have been tolerated for one moment. My objection to this proposition at this time is that it contemplates the delegation to the Executive Department of a power which we cannot control and which, by and by, under action which may be taken either carelessly or by design, may involve this Congress and this nation in consequences such as have been described by the honorable gentleman from Ohio.

We ought not to delegate to the executive the power of recognizing governments in foreign countries, and especially in cases where there may be a dispute as to which is

the rightful government, and the additional power after such recognition to bring the power of this country to settle such contest. Such discretion ought not to be delegated to any one man in the nation. I am not so fond of extending executive power, and we have no information that any exigency exists calling for such action even by the legislative branch of the government. As the gentleman from Massachusetts said yesterday, we are to give our moral support to the government in the island of San Domingo. Who is to select the authority that is to be sustained when there is internal dissensions and revolution? According to the propositions in these resolutions, it is the Executive Department only that is to determine the question which is the rightful government.

Where there are two conflicting interests, where there is a government (established under revolution, if you please) based upon republican principles, who is to determine whether the whole power of the government shall be thrown into the one scale or the other? It is the Executive Department. I say, Mr. Speaker, that I dare not trust this power to the executive; I prefer that it should be retained in the hands of the legislative branch of the government. Let such questions be determined by Congress; and the executive, in carrying out the determination of Congress, will reflect the will of the people. . . .

Mr. Robinson [New York]. Mr. Speaker I intend before the vote is taken to offer an amendment to the amendment of the gentleman from Massachusetts. I propose to insert before the word "Haiti" the word "Ireland." . . .

The resolution with the amendment of the gentleman from Massachusetts and other amendments proposed will refer, in its phraseology, to "islands lying adjacent to the coast of the United States"; and as steam power and the telegraph, particularly the telegraph, have made Ireland the most adjacent country to us in that part of the world, I desire that Ireland shall be protected. Her claims to our protection are higher than those of any other country. The blood and the heart of Ireland are in this country. Her people are brothers of ours and aliens to the government which has usurped control over that country during seven centuries of oppression.

I have no doubt, Mr. Speaker, that the time will come when Ireland will be annexed to this country. I have no more doubt of that than I have that Cuba will be annexed to this country. Both of them will come to us by the natural laws of affinity, by their sympathy with us upon questions of politics and statesmanship. In the natural course of things, Ireland will become a part of the United States and will be represented upon this floor according to her population, and in the other end of the Capitol according to the number of the states of which she may be composed.

I have intended to take the floor upon some proper occasion to make a lengthy statement of my views on this subject. We want no war with England. We shall have no war with England. We shall obtain possession of Ireland peaceably. Her heart, as I have said, is here. She is a burden upon England — always has been and always will be. The heavings of revolutionary feeling under British rule will continue. England, so long as she attempts to hold Ireland in subjection, will have no peace; she ought to have no peace. The people of Ireland and the people of the world will give England no peace. God Almighty, who rules the universe, will give her no peace until she lets the people of Ireland go; and the natural affinity of Ireland is with the United States. . . .

Mr. Butler. Mr. Speaker, I desire to add but a word or two in answer to what has fallen from the gentleman from Ohio who so eloquently and urgently asked our attention to the words of the father of the country. I believe they are in the manuscript

writing of Alexander Hamilton, and I have not been so loyally his follower all the days of my life as to think that all intelligence and all progress in national affairs died when he did. I am inclined to think that we must adapt our legislation to the power and to the position and to the influence which we, as a nation, have now and not to the power, not to the position, not to the influence that as a nation among the nations of the world we had in 1798.

Sir, I have no fear of war. The 1,400,000 veteran soldiers that we disbanded when we ended the rebellion, on one side alone — and I doubt not that even the Confederate soldiers would rally around the old flag now against any foreign foe — I say that 1,400,000 settled the question of war between us and any other nation, so long as we are true to ourselves and our own honor; and this nation will never do anything not consistent with that honor. We are strong enough to do right; we can appreciate the right; and no nation will go to war with us unless we are ourselves in the wrong.

Again, sir, I desire gentlemen to think whether or not we shall wait in our action because we may not have special confidence in this man or that man who may be at the head of the Executive Department or of the State Department. I want gentlemen to arise above all that as legislators and as men having the guardianship of the great interests of this country, looking forward to what is to come in the future, knowing that we are able to restrain any action that is wrong on the part of the executive. Rising above all considerations, except that of statesmanship, I want gentlemen to see what is best for this country and what is best for republican institutions throughout the world.

And can any man say here in his heart that he doubts that within a short time, ay, a very short time in the history of nations, these islands must belong to us? Then, if this House answers that question in the affirmative, must we not further say that we ought to be ready to extend protection over them; and I do not by any means intend to belittle that word "protection." It is the protection which the strong can give to the weak without the former being involved in the affairs of the latter. It is the protection which the powerful always gives; the protection which only a united, prosperous country can give to a weak and divided one. And in answer to the gentleman from Illinois, allow me here to say that it is to give to the executive of this government some right to determine between these factions now destroying themselves and destroying American interests in these islands that I desire this protection. I say I fear not that we shall be involved in war thereby.

One word further. I had hoped that we might have been spared by the learned gentleman from New York a dissertation on Ireland at this time. No man can more deeply feel than I do the wrongs of Ireland and the necessity that something should be done to right those wrongs. But let me say to him, respectfully, that the way to get Ireland to have any protection from this government is not to drag before us in season and out of season, at any and every turn, an amendment as a rider to everybody's proposition. It simply trails her in the dust.

Mr. Robinson. I ask the gentleman from Ohio [Mr. Delano] to allow me a single word, simply to say that I have never dragged Ireland in as a rider on any measure. The gentleman, I know, does not mean to be unjust, but he is extremely so in saying what he does. Ireland is suffering, and our citizens want protection there, and I ought to drag her in oftener, but I have refrained, because I do not want to obtrude myself too frequently upon the attention of the House.

Mr. Delano [Ohio]. Mr. Speaker, the proposition now before the House in the resolution submitted by the honorable chairman of the Committee on Foreign Affairs is in itself so grave and so extraordinary that I desire as a part of my remarks the reading of the resolution, for the purposes of having the House distinctly understand and duly comprehend its import, its magnitude, its importance, its novelty. Will the clerk do me the favor to read the resolution?

The Clerk read the resolution, as follows:

Be it resolved by the Senate and House of Representatives of the United States of America in Congress assembled, that the President of the United States be, and hereby is, authorized to extend to the governments and people of the republics of Haiti and San Domingo the protection of the United States, for the purpose of assisting them to establish permanent republican institutions whenever those governments, or either of them, shall apply to the United States for its protection, or whenever the President shall be satisfied that the government and people of those republics desire or voluntarily consent to the protection of this government: *Provided,* that the President shall communicate to the two houses of Congress immediate information of any action which the government of the United States may take upon this subject: *And provided also* that no action which may call or require any appropriation of money from the Treasury of the United States shall be authorized or commenced under the authority of this resolution without the previous consent of Congress. . . .

Mr. Bingham [Ohio]. Mr. Speaker, believing as I do that the people of the United States have the power and the right for their own defense to intervene, under the authority of their own law and with their army and navy, in the affairs of any other people on this continent or adjacent thereto whenever it may be essential to their own safety so to do, and of the necessity of which intervention they are themselves the judges, responsible always for the exercise of that judgment to the nations of the world — because of this conviction,

Mr. Speaker, I felt it my duty to listen to the proposition for the protection of the people and governments of the Antilles as it came from the Committee on Foreign Affairs. I was desirous to know what the condition of things was that so affected the interests of the people of the United States as to require our intervention. I have listened, Mr. Speaker, but have listened in vain for any suggestion from any quarter intimating any condition of things in any of the islands of the Antilles that involves, to any considerable extent at least, the interests of the people of this country, much less their interest to such an extent as to require the intervention by the people of the United States, through the lawmaking authority, of the whole power of this nation in the internal affairs of that people.

Mr. Speaker, what I desire to say to the House here, and what I attempted to suggest to the chairman of the Committee on Foreign Affairs yesterday, when he was kind enough to allow me a moment to interrupt him, is that whatever the relations of things may be between the people of the United States and any other people upon this continent or adjacent thereto requiring intervention, it is all-important that that intervention be made in accordance with the requirement of the Constitution of this country.

I listened with much interest to what was said by my honorable colleague [Mr. Shellabarger] founded upon the early legislation of this government touching our neutrality laws, and upon the suggestion of that very profound and wonderful state paper, known as the "Farewell Address of the Father of our Country"; and I must say that I heard with something of surprise the remark of the honorable gentleman from Massachusetts [Mr. Butler] in reply thereto, almost partaking of the language of sneer, when he intimated that he was not willing to consent that political wisdom had died with the author of the Farewell Address of Washing-

ton. Sir, nobody claims that; but intelligent men in this land and in all lands know right well that the accredited author of that paper, Mr. Hamilton and the great man who accepted it and made it his own are entitled not only to the respectful consideration but to the profoundest gratitude of the living generations of men.

Passing, however, out of the text of the Farewell Address and into the text of the Constitution of the country, I come to the discussion of this measure. I say here, for myself, that, in my judgment, it is not within the compass of human wisdom to frame any bill of any kind or on any subject more directly in conflict with the express limitation of the Constitution of the country than this. That instrument is not to be disposed of by a sneer here or anywhere else. Through it and by it we came to be a people; through it and by it we must continue to be one people if we continue to be one people at all. The warmaking power of this country, which is involved in this resolution, is in my judgment, by the express terms of the Constitution, not by mere construction but by its express, solemn words, restricted to the Legislative Department of this government. Congress alone, by the terms of the instrument, is authorized "to declare war," and Congress cannot delegate that authority.

It is an old-time principle of the common law, known and accepted among intelligent men everywhere, all over the globe, that a delegated power never can be transferred by the agent without the consent of the principal. The people are the principal in this matter, and they delegated this great power, which involves the issue of life and death to all the people of this country, to the Legislative Department of this government, and to that Legislative Department alone. Congress cannot authorize the President of the United States, therefore, at his pleasure, and, in the language of the substitute offered by the gentleman from Massachusetts, when he may "deem it expedient," to make war either among the people of the Antilles or among the peoples allied to them upon continental Europe. . . .

Mr. Maynard [Tennessee]. Mr. Speaker, I cannot quite agree with the declaration of the chairman of the Committee on Foreign Affairs, made in reply to the question proposed to him, that we had no precedent for a proceeding like this. With deference, certainly, to his superior information, I think we have had more than one precedent, and that of no small importance. The Monroe Doctrine is the protectorate by this government over all the governments upon the American continent; and when my friend from Ohio stands upon the outposts of the Constitution and challenges the production of any authority under that instrument for the measure that is here proposed, I reply by the same authority which has authorized us to assert the Monroe Doctrine in every possible form except by force of arms and the expenditure of money to enforce it — by executive rescripts, by the action of our legislature, by the action of our national conventions, and, more than all, by the imperial authority of the ballot box more than once announced.

One example, sir, is Mexico, menaced as she was during our late War of the Rebellion. We established a protectorate over her which found its way into our legislation in the form of "the Republic of Mexico," and in the adoption of a resolution by this body, offered by my deceased friend, then a representative from Maryland, in which we declared that the empire of Maximilian should not be established in Mexico, such being the sense of this body, reflecting the judgment of the people. That was a protectorate of a higher kind than that of arms. It showed the high moral purpose which was in force in this world at the close of the nineteenth century, more powerful than the prowess of your arms. . . .

I am satisfied, Mr. Speaker, that the people of the United States have a mission upon this continent higher and broader and loftier than to sit down and make money to put into our pockets. God Almighty did not plant this nation here to live for itself and itself alone. Our mission is coextensive with the continent upon which we are placed. It has been our instinctive feeling, and our perhaps not always conscious action since our beginning; and in adopting this resolution we are doing nothing different in kind or character from what we have been doing in numberless instances in this House by acts of legislation and every other form of expression of our opinion.

Mr. Woodward. Mr. Speaker, ever since Christopher Columbus discovered this continent, these islands have been for some purposes considered as a part of it. Geographically, they ought, perhaps, to be considered as a part of this continent. I am told by those who know more about such subjects than I do that the commerce of this country needs one or more West India ports. I know that the relations existing between these islands and ourselves are from time to time subject to disturbance, I know that more than once in the history of this nation there have been propositions to purchase Cuba, and perhaps other islands in the West Indies.

Now, sir, speaking only for myself and according to the information I now possess, I regard these islands as a part of the American continent. I believe they naturally belong to us, and if I am in public position when any reasonable measure is brought forward for the acquisition and annexation of those islands I shall support it according to the best of my ability. I believe that we need them, and that we shall need them more in the future than we have in the past. I believe that the fathers of our country, who have been fortunately alluded to in this debate, considered them as part of our continent; and when they spoke of a Continental Congress and a Continental Army, and called their money Continental money, and when everything they said or thought of seemed to be Continental, I suppose they embraced these islands in their thoughts as possibly belonging in the future to our political system.

I have spent my life in endeavoring to carry out the ideas and principles of the fathers of this republic, and what remains of it, Mr. Speaker, shall be devoted to the same end. I believe they included these islands in their thoughts of a Continental government. I include them in my thought of a Continental government. But, sir, I would acquire them in a manner worthy of ourselves. I would either buy them by open and fair negotiations or I would conquer them by our military power. I would not steal them, sir, as this resolution proposes; and by just so much as I approve of the ultimate acquisition of these islands in a fair, honorable, manly mode I am opposed to the proposition reported by the gentleman from Massachusetts [Mr. Banks], from the Committee on Foreign Affairs, of acquiring them by indirection, which his resolution certainly contemplates. . . .

This proposition, sir, to engage the government in a military protectorate which is most likely to involve us in a general European war, seems to me to be ill-timed in all of its aspects, and especially while we have a national debt like that which is oppressing us at this moment. Why, sir, we have a war debt now which is far from being provided for. Gentlemen are not well agreed as to what should be done with it. Do they propose to increase it by bringing on another war, and that for the purpose of adjusting our relations with islands which will ultimately gravitate to us and become a part of this country? This is no time for such a policy, and the gentleman's resolution if

otherwise unobjectionable would be exceedingly objectionable in point of time.

I think the entire energies of this country ought to be directed to the paying of our national debt. I say the paying of it and not the funding of it. You may change the form of our public debt as much as you please, but still it will exist as a burden and incubus upon us until it is paid. I am not, therefore, for any measure which will withdraw the country from that great central point and destroy those energies and abilities which should be directed to the extinguishment of that debt.

Let me tell you, Mr. Speaker, that unless we get rid of the debt we will have no republic of our own in the future to maintain. I believe that every monarchy in the world has been built upon a national debt, and that a great debt hanging over any people is inconsistent with republican institutions. If we would maintain our republican institutions, therefore, we must put ourselves back upon the principles of the fathers of the country, avoid all entangling alliances with all foreign governments and concentrate all our energies toward a redemption of our own country from the great burden of a national debt. If there was any one principle of George Washington and the other founders of the republic better defined in their minds than another, it was that this should be a nation out of debt — a free and independent people, untaxed; and such a people we cannot be with such a debt as that which oppresses us at this time.

Now, Mr. Speaker, without going further into this debate, I will move that the resolution and the pending amendments be laid upon the table. . . .

The question was taken; and it was decided in the affirmative — yeas 126, nays 36, not voting 60.

36.

Charles W. Eliot: The Training Proper in Scientific Schools

Charles W. Eliot, American scholar and educational reformer, returned to the United States after two years of studying European educational systems and published, in 1869, an important article on "The New Education: Its Organization," from which the following excerpt is taken. Eliot's reputation as an educator led to his election as president of Harvard University in 1869. He retained this post until 1909 and brought about significant administrative and educational reforms. The college and the professional schools of law and medicine were completely reorganized and a program of graduate studies was added.

Source: *Atlantic Monthly*, February, March 1869.

THE SIMULTANEOUS CARRYING ON of what should be such different courses of instruction [classical and scientific] within the same walls, in the same community of students, and by one and the same corps of instructors is, we believe, very disadvantageous to both systems of training. Such a combination has been thoroughly tried in the *lycées* of France and has completely failed and been abandoned. In Germany it has seemed expedient to separate the two courses, even during the schoolboy period; and, for the higher instruction of both systems, entirely separate institutions have been found necessary.

The fact is that the whole tone and spirit of a good college ought to be different in kind from that of a good polytechnic or scientific school. In the college, the desire for the broadest culture, for the best formation and information of the mind, the enthusiastic study of subjects for the love of th n without any ulterior objects, the love of learning and research for their own sake should be the dominant ideas. In the poly-

technic school should be found a mental training inferior to none in breadth and vigor, a thirst for knowledge, a genuine enthusiasm in scientific research, and a true love of nature; but underneath all these things is a tempter or leading motive unlike that of a college.

The student in a polytechnic school has a practical end constantly in view; he is training his faculties with the express object of making himself a better manufacturer, engineer, or teacher; he is studying the processes of nature in order, afterwards, to turn them to human uses and his own profit. If he is eager to penetrate the mysteries of electricity, it is largely because he wants to understand telegraphs; if he learns French and German, it is chiefly because he would not have the best technical literature of his generation sealed for him; if he imbues his mind with the profound and exquisite conceptions of the calculus, it is in order the better to comprehend mechanics.

This practical end should never be lost sight of by student or teacher in a polytechnic school, and it should very seldom be thought of or alluded to in a college. Just as far as the spirit proper to a polytechnic school pervades a college, just so far that college falls below its true ideal. The practical spirit and the literary or scholastic spirit are both good, but they are incompatible. If commingled, they are both spoiled.

It is not to be imagined that the mental training afforded by a good polytechnic school is necessarily inferior in any respect to that of a good college, whether in breadth, vigor, or wholesomeness. Certain it is that an average graduate of the Zurich Polytechnicum or the Paris Ecole Centrale has a much better title to be called "learned" than most graduates of American colleges and professional schools. He has studied more, harder, and to better effect, though in a different spirit. But the two kinds of education cannot be carried on together, in the same schedules, by the same teachers.

The classical course will hurt the scientific, and the scientific, the classical. Neither will be at its best. The experience of the world and common sense are against such experiments as those of Brown, Union, and Michigan. Nevertheless, they may be good temporary expedients during a transition period or in crude communities where hasty culture is as natural as fast eating. They do good service in lack of better things.

The incompatibility of the practical spirit and the literary spirit . . . may appear to some to limit unduly the number of subjects proper to be taught in colleges. The tendency to the practical side of every subject which befits a good polytechnic school would be improper in a college; but the same subjects may to a very great extent be taught in both. One and the same subject may be studied in two very unlike frames of mind. We have only desired to urge the incompatibility of one temper with another temper, both being good in their separate places.

Another unjust inference might be drawn from what has been said of the impossibility of carrying on two long courses of instruction of different aim and essence within the same schedules of hours and terms and the same walls. It might be inferred that the applied sciences are necessarily unfit to be taught or studied in a university, taking that word in its best sense. It cannot be said too loudly or too often, that no subject of human inquiry can be out of place in the program of a real university. It is only necessary that every subject should be taught at the university on a higher plane than elsewhere.

Even scholars are apt to be intolerant of this subject or that in university schemes; one can see no sense in archaeology; another condemns natural history as being without practical applications, useless for training, and frightfully absorbent of money; a third finds pure science wholesome meat, but applied science, utilitarian chaff. It is impossible to be too catholic in this matter.

But the American university has not yet grown out of the soil, and we are rather meeting a theoretical than a practical objection. The incidental remark may be permitted that a university, in any worthy sense of the term, must grow from seed. It cannot be transplanted from England or Germany in full leaf and bearing. It cannot be run up, like a cotton mill, in six months, to meet a quick demand. Neither can it be created by an energetic use of the inspired editorial, the advertising circular, and the frequent telegram. Numbers do not constitute it, and no money can make it before its time.

There is more of the university about the eight or ten Yale graduates who are studying in the Yale Department of Philosophy and the Arts than in as many hundred raw youths who do not know more than a fair grammar school may teach. When the American university appears, it will not be a copy of foreign institutions, or hotbed plant, but the slow and natural outgrowth of

American social and political habits and an expression of the average aims and ambitions of the better educated classes. The American college is an institution without a parallel; the American university will be equally original.

Besides the scientific schools connected with colleges, and the scientific or English courses within colleges, there exist in the United States several independent schools in which mathematics, the exact sciences and their applications, the modern languages, and philosophy form the staple of instruction. Such are the Rensselaer Polytechnic Institute at Troy, and the school of the Massachusetts Institute of Technology at Boston. These two schools have a certain general resemblance; they are independent establishments; they have the same minimum age of admission, namely, sixteen years, although practically the average age of the students who enter these institutions is decidedly above this minimum; they do not require any Latin or Greek for admission and do not admit these languages to their courses of study; finally, in each the course of study lasts four years. In the comprehensiveness of their courses of instruction, in the number of teachers employed, and in their general scale of operations, these schools differ materially. . . .

The most ample course of instruction which has been thus far offered in this country to students who demand a liberal and practical education as well as a training specially adapted to make them ultimately good engineers, manufacturers, architects, chemists, merchants, teachers of science, or directors of mines and industrial works, is that organized by the Massachusetts Institute of Technology at Boston. The course extends through four years. The studies of the first and second years, and certain general studies in the third and fourth years, are required of all regular students. At the beginning of the third year, each student selects one of six courses, which he follows during his third and fourth years at the school. These six courses are: 1. mechanical engineering; 2. civil engineering; 3. chemistry; 4. geology and mining; 5. building and architecture; 6. general science and literature. . . .

Two points deserve special mention: first, the unusual development given to instruction in the modern languages; and, second, the stress laid upon drawing in all the courses. The position of architectural design in the scheme is also worth noting. Here is a course of liberal training which includes as one of its elements a subject usually confined to amateurs and professional men, and yet a subject which is a valuable part of aesthetic culture. People who complain that, as a general rule, even the education called liberal does not recognize the artistic side of human nature will find here a unique provision. . . .

People who think vaguely about the difference between a good college and a good polytechnic school are apt to say that the aim of the college course is to make a rounded man, with all his faculties impartially developed, while it is the express object of a technical course to make a one-sided man — a mere engineer, chemist, or architect. Two truths are suppressed in this form of statement.

First, faculties are not given by God impartially — to each round soul a little of each power, as if the soul were a pill, which must contain its due proportion of many various ingredients. To reason about the average human mind as if it were a globe, to be expanded symmetrically from a center outward, is to be betrayed by a metaphor. A cutting tool, a drill, or auger would be a juster symbol of the mind. The natural bent and peculiar quality of every boy's mind should be sacredly regarded in his education; the division of mental labor, which is essential in civilized communities in order that knowledge may grow and society improve, demands this regard to the peculiar constitution of each mind, as much as does the happiness of the individual most nearly concerned.

Second, to make a good engineer, chemist, or architect, the only sure way is to make first, or at least simultaneously, an observant, reflecting, and sensible man, whose mind is not only well stored but well trained also to see, compare, reason, and decide. The vigorous training of the mental powers is therefore the primary object of every well-organized technical school. At the same time, a well-arranged course of study, like that of the New Haven school, the Troy school, or the Institute of Technology, will include a vast deal of information and many practical exercises appropriate to the professions which the students have in view. . . .

The experimental period in the development of technical instruction in the United States is past. Henceforth the American parent who wants to give a practical education to his son may know clearly what is accessible to him as an alternative with the college. He may find at several schools a carefully arranged and comprehensive course of coordinated studies, lasting three or four years and covering the same period of life as the common college course, namely, the period from sixteen or eighteen till twenty or twenty-two. This comprehensive course of studies is generally called, in such schools as those at New Haven, Troy, and Boston, the "regular" or "general course"; and the students who follow it are the "regular students," in contradistinction to the "partial" or "special" students, who study only one subject, or a few irregularly selected subjects, among all those taught in the school. . . .

The scientific schools have been recruited in large part, of course, from that excellent and numerous class of young men who have more taste and capacity for science than for language and literature, and who have followed their natural bent in making

choice of a school and a profession; but they have also been the refuge of shirks and stragglers from the better organized and stricter colleges. This evil is a temporary one, incident to what has been the experimental condition of education through science. It will correct itself when the new system of education is as well organized as the old, and when the community understands the legitimate inlets and outlets of the new schools — how to get into them and what they lead to.

To avoid misapprehension, let it be distinctly stated that the scientific schools have already done a very timely and necessary work in this country by training, although hastily and imperfectly, a certain number of specialists, such as assayers, analysts, railroad engineers, and teachers of science, to very useful functions. And again, let it be acknowledged with thankfulness that genius, or even an unusual vigor of mind and will, often overcomes in afterlife that worst of obstacles, insuperable for common men, an inadequate or mistaken training in youth.

At present it is the wise effort of the faculties of all the leading polytechnic or scientific schools to carry as many of their pupils as possible through the "regular" course of study; in other words, they recommend their pupils to lay, during three or four years between seventeen and twenty-two, a broad and strong foundation for the strictly professional studies, of which a part are pursued in the school and a part during the apprenticeship which should follow their school life. . . .

The country will shortly need more polytechnic schools of the highest grade than it now has. The four or five existing schools will be filled, and new ones will be established. The number of trained young men entering the scientific professions every year, becoming engineers, architects, teachers of science, chemists, superintendents of mines and works, and constructors of machinery, ought to bear some comparison with the number of those who enter the professions of law and medicine. The polytechnic schools may also play an important part in the much-hoped-for reform of the civil service of the country. It is a mistake to suppose that the growth of the technical schools will injure the colleges. On the contrary, the polytechnic schools, though claiming young men of the college age and perhaps diverting a few from academic life, will do the colleges good service by relieving them of all necessity of meeting the demand for practical instruction and leaving them at ease for their legitimate work.

A polytechnic or technological school is best placed in a large city, in a great industrial center. A college needs quiet and seclusion; a technical school, on the contrary, should be within easy reach of works, mills, forges, machine shops, and mines. The professors of a scientific school have need to be brought into daily contact with practical affairs, to watch the progress of new inventions as they develop from day to day, and to know the men who are improving special industries. The students of a scientific school have a like need. They need to see as much as possible of the actual conditions of practical mining, manufacturing, constructing, and inventing while they are students, because, when they leave the school, they are almost invariably thrown directly into the vortex of business and have not that interval of little work and much leisure through which the young lawyer or doctor is gradually initiated into the practical details of his profession. . . .

Three difficulties beset the establishment of such new schools in this country. The first danger is the tendency to reckless preliminary expenditure upon buildings and mechanical fittings. Many American schools and colleges have been wrecked on this rock. The American trustee has a deplorable propensity to put what should be quick capital into more or less unsuitable bricks and mortar. This danger escaped, the second difficulty is the scarcity of teachers having the necessary training and the equally necessary enthusiasm.

There must be brought together a harmonious body of teachers, young, if possible both in years and spirit, but at any rate in spirit, allowed the leisure necessary for men to keep themselves on a level with the rapid progress of the arts and sciences, and paid enough to have a mind at ease. High reputation is not necessary; but conscientiousness in the discharge of routine duties, fair talents well improved, and a genuine enthusiasm are essential. If to these qualifications there can be added personal devotion to the head of the institution, the happiest conditions are united.

The American scientific schools and colleges and the European universities have trained a few Americans to such functions; but they are still scarce, because the active industries of the country absorb the greater number of energetic young men possessed of the requisite training. . . .

But now someone may ask: To what good end all this discourse about the improvement of technical education? Are not Americans already the most ingenious people on the earth? Have we not invented mowers and sewing machines and the best printing presses? Are we not doing countless things by machinery which other people do by hand? Is there really any need of instructing Americans in the application of science to the arts? The answers to these incredulous suggestions are not far to seek.

In the first place, it is emphatically true that Americans have invented a large number of laborsaving machines of the greatest value. They are powerfully incited to this sort of invention by the dearness of labor in this country. Second, this same scarcity of laborers, and the consequent abundance of work for all willing hands, enable an American to pursue the precarious rewards of invention, perhaps for years, with the certainty that if, after all, he wins no prize in the lottery, he can readily find some steady employment to keep his old age from absolute want. . . .

It is to be noticed that the chief American successes in invention are of one sort, machinery and mechanical appliances. In other departments of invention, which require greater knowledge, we are obviously borrowers rather than lenders. How many millions of dollars are sunk every few years in mining enterprises through sheer ignorance? Freiberg and Swansea have to be called upon to smelt American ores. The best managers of American print works receive patterns of the latest French designs by every steamer. The aniline colors are not American discoveries. There are hardly twenty miles of good road, in the European sense, in the whole United States. The various chemical industries are chiefly foreign. American ingenuity has been of more limited range than is commonly imagined. Not a few reputed American inventions are really of European origin. But, however this may be, we may zealously endeavor to strengthen the scientific professions in this country without being a whit less proud of the undisputed achievements of American ingenuity.

It is not a question of promoting fertility of invention by improving technical education. Inventors are a law unto themselves.

What the country needs is a steady supply of men well trained in recognized principles of science and art and well informed about established practice. We need engineers who thoroughly understand what is already known at home and abroad about mining, road and bridge building, railways, canals, water powers, and steam machinery; architects who have thoroughly studied their art; builders who can at least construct buildings which will not fall down; chemists and metallurgists who know what the world has done and is doing in the chemical arts and in the extraction and working of metals; manufacturers who appreciate what science and technical skill can do for the works which they superintend.

Americans must not sit down contented with their position among the industrial nations. We have inherited civil liberty, social mobility, and immense native resources. The advantages we thus hold over the European nations are inestimable. The question is not how much our freedom can do for us unaided but how much we can help freedom by judicious education. We appreciate better than we did ten years ago that true progress in this country means progress for the world. In organizing the new education, we do not labor for ourselves alone. Freedom will be glorified in her works.

37.

Henry C. Wheeler: Call for a Farmers' Convention

A revolution in agriculture accompanied the transformation of industry after the Civil War. The old subsistence economy gave way to a profit system in agriculture. Farming became mechanized and specialized. But these agricultural changes also made farming more costly. Farmers became dependent upon the railroads for transportation, upon dealers for marketing, and upon banks for credit. As transportation costs increased and ate away at their profits, farmers began to advocate cooperative action as a means of protecting their economic interests. The result was the emergence of the Granger movements and farmers' alliances. In March of 1869, Illinois farmers received the following letter from Henry C. Wheeler, a Du Page County farmer and later a member of the state legislature, who appealed for unified action against the railroads.

Source: Jonathan Periam, *The Groundswell, A History of the Origin, Aims, and Progress of the Farmers' Movement, etc., etc.,* Cincinnati, 1874, pp. 225-227.

To the Farmers of the Northwest:

Will you permit a working farmer, whose entire interest is identified with yours, to address to you a word of warning?

A crisis in our affairs is approaching, and dangers threaten.

You are aware that the price of many of our leading staples is so low that they cannot be transported to the markets of Europe, or even to our own seaboard, and leave a margin for profits, by reason of the excessive rates of transportation.

During the war but little attention was given to the great increase in the price of freights, as the price of produce was proportionately high; but we look in vain for any abatement, now that we are obliged to accept less than half the former prices for much that we raise.

We look in vain for any diminution in the carrying rates to correspond with the rapidly declining prices of the means of living and of materials for constructing boats, cars, engines, and track; but, on the other hand, we see a total ignoring of that rule of reciprocity between the carrying and producing interests which prevails in every other department of trade and commerce.

Does it not behoove us, then, to inquire earnestly how long we can stand this descending scale on the one hand and the ascending on the other, and which party must inevitably and speedily go to the wall?

I by no means counsel *hostility* to the carrying interest — it is one of the producer's best friends; but, like the fire that cooks our food and warms our dwelling, it may also become the hardest of masters. The fire fiend laughs as he escapes from our control, and in an hour licks up and sweeps away the accumulations of years of toil.

As we cherish the fire fiend, so we welcome the clangor of the carrier fiend as he approaches our dwellings, opening up communication with the busy marts of trade. But it needs no great stretch of imagination to hear also the cach! cach! cachinnations of the carrier fiend as he speeds beyond our reach and leaving no alternative but compliance with his exorbitant demands.

Many of us are not aware of the gigantic proportions the carrying interest is assuming. Less than forty years since the first railroad fire was kindled on this continent, but which now, like a mighty conflagration, is crackling and roaring over every prairie and through every mountain gorge. The first year produced 15 miles; the last, 5,000.

On the same mammoth scale goes on the work of organization and direction. By the use of almost unlimited means, it enlists in its service the finest talents of the land as officers, attorneys, agents, and lobbyists; gives free passes and splendid entertainments to the representatives of the people; and even transports whole legislatures into exceeding high mountains, showing them the kingdoms of the world, with lavish promises of reward for fealty and support. Witness its land grants and franchises secured from the powers that be, such as no similar interest ever acquired even in the Old World. In Europe every corporation returns its franchises to the Crown within a specified time, while here their titles are more secure than the farmers' warranty deeds.

Do you say that you are out of debt and can stop producing when it does not pay? I tell you, my friends, that the carrying interest, with its present momentum unchecked, will soon acquire the power to tax your unencumbered possessions into leaseholds, and you and me into tenants at will.

I fancy I hear the response: "These things are so, but what can we do?" Rather, my friends, what can we *not* do? What power can withstand the combined and concentrated force of the producing interest of this republic? But what avails our strength if, like Polyphemus in the fable, we are unable to use it for want of eyesight; or, like a mighty army without discipline, every man fighting on his own hook; or, worse, reposing in fancied security while Delilahs of the enemy have well-nigh shorn away the last lock of strength? In this respect we constitute a solitary exception, every other interest having long since protected itself by union and organization.

As a measure calculated to bring all interested, as it were, within speaking distance, and as a stepping-stone to an efficient organization, I propose that the farmers of the great Northwest concentrate their efforts, power, and means, as the great transportation companies have done theirs, and accomplish something instead of frittering away their efforts in doing nothing.

And, to this end, I suggest a convention of those opposed to the present tendency to monopoly and extortionate charges by our transportation companies, to meet at Bloomington, Illinois, on the 20th day of April next, for the purpose of discussion and the appointment of a committee to raise funds to be expended in the employment of the highest order of legal talent, to put in form of report and argument an exposition of the rights, wrongs, interests, and injuries (with their remedies) of the producing masses of the Northwest, and lay it before the authorities of each state and of the general government.

Congress is now in session, and the constitutional convention of this state will then again be convened. Farmers, now is the time for action!

38.

Charles Francis Adams, Jr.: The Struggle for Erie

Charles Francis Adams, Jr., a grandson of John Quincy Adams, gave up his law practice after 1866 to devote his full time to the study of railroads, which he regarded as "the most developing force and largest field of the day." During the latter part of the 1860s the tremendous growth and economic importance of the railroads attracted speculators who often engaged in highly unscrupulous practices at the expense of the public. The fight for the control of the Erie Railroad in 1867-1868 by a group of Wall Street bankers was especially notorious and occupied the attention of Adams, who wrote a series of articles analyzing the group's financial dealings. In July 1869, Adams published A Chapter of Erie, his classic study of the unbridled financial manipulation of corporate stocks. The work soon established him as an expert and one of the leading proponents of public regulation of the railroads.

Source: *North American Review,* July 1869: "A Chapter of Erie."

Some seventeen or eighteen years ago, Mr. Daniel Drew first made his appearance in the Board of Directors of the Erie, where he remained down to the year 1868, generally holding also the office of treasurer of the corporation. Mr. Drew is what is known as a self-made man. Born in the year 1797, as a boy he drove cattle down from his native town of Carmel, in Putnam County, to the market of New York City, and subsequently was for years proprietor of the Bull's Head Tavern. Like his contemporary, and ally or opponent, as the case might be, Cornelius Vanderbilt, he built up his fortunes in the steamboat interest, and subsequently extended his operations over the rapidly developing railroad system.

Shrewd, unscrupulous, and very illiterate — a strange combination of superstition and faithlessness, of daring and timidity, often good-natured and sometimes generous — he has ever regarded his fiduciary position of director of a railroad as a means of manipulating its stock for his own advantage. For years he has been the leading bear of Wall Street, and his favorite haunts have been the secret recesses of Erie. As treasurer of that corporation, he has, in its frequently recurring hours of need, advanced it sums which it could not have obtained elsewhere, and the obtaining of which was a necessity. His management of his favorite stock has been cunning and recondite, and his ways inscrutable.

Those who sought to follow him and those who sought to oppose him, alike, found food for sad reflection; until at last he won for himself the expressive sobriquet of the Speculative Director. Sometimes, though rarely, he suffered greatly in the complications of Wall Street; more frequently he inflicted severe damage upon others. On the whole, however, his fortunes had greatly prospered, and the outbreak of the Erie war found him the actual possessor of some millions and the reputed possessor of many more.

In the spring of 1866 Mr. Drew's manipulations of Erie culminated in an operation which was at the time regarded as a masterpiece, but which subsequent experience has so improved upon that it is now looked on as an ordinary and inartistic piece of financiering. The stock of the road was at that time selling at about 95, and the corporation was, as usual, in debt and in pressing need of money. As usual, also, it resorted to its treasurer. Mr. Drew stood ready to make the desired advances upon security. Some 28,000 shares of its own authorized stock, which had never been issued, were at the time in the hands of the company, which also claimed the right, under the statutes of New York, of raising money by the issue of bonds convertible, at the option of the holder, into stock.

The 28,000 unissued shares and bonds for $3 million, convertible into stock, were placed by the company in the hands of its treasurer, as security for a cash loan of $3,500,000. The negotiation had been quietly effected, and Mr. Drew's campaign now opened. Once more he was short of Erie. While Erie was buoyant, while it steadily approximated to par, while speculation was rampant, and that outside public, the delight and the prey of Wall Street, was gradually drawn in by the fascination of amassing wealth without labor — quietly and stealthily, through his agents and brokers, the grave, desponding operator was daily concluding his contracts for the future delivery of stock at current prices.

At last the hour had come. Erie was rising, Erie was scarce, the great bear had many contracts to fulfill, and where was he to find the stock? His victims were not kept long in suspense. Mr. Treasurer Drew laid his hands upon his collateral. In an instant the bonds for $3 million were converted into an equivalent amount of capital stock, and 58,000 shares, dumped, as it

were, by the cartload in Broad Street, made Erie as plenty as even Drew could desire. Before the astonished bulls could rally their faculties, the quotations had fallen from 95 to 50, and they realized that they were hopelessly entrapped. . . .

The case of the treasurer of a great corporation is different. He occupies a fiduciary position. He is a trustee — a guardian. Vast interests are confided to his care; every shareholder of the corporation is his ward; if it is a railroad, the community itself is his *cestui que trust.* But passing events, accumulating more thickly with every year, have thoroughly corrupted the public morals on this subject. A directorship in certain great corporations has come to be regarded as a situation in which to make a fortune, the possession of which is no longer dishonorable.

The method of accumulation is both simple and safe. It consists in giving contracts as a trustee to one's self as an individual, or in speculating in the property of one's *cestui que trust,* or in using the funds confided to one's charge, as treasurer or otherwise, to gamble with the real owners of those funds for their own property, and that with cards packed in advance. These proceedings are looked upon as hardly reprehensible. The wards themselves expect their guardians to throw the dice against them for their own property, and are surprised as well as gratified if the dice are not loaded. . . .

As a result of the transaction of 1866, Mr. Drew was looked upon as having effected a surprisingly clever operation, and he retired from the field — hated, feared, wealthy, and admired. . . .

Great events were impending; a new man was looming up in the railroad world, introducing novel ideas and principles, and it could hardly be that the new and old would not come in conflict. Cornelius Vanderbilt, commonly known as Commodore Vanderbilt, was now developing his theory of the management of railroads.

Born in the year 1794, Vanderbilt is a somewhat older man than Drew. There are several points of resemblance in the early lives of the two men, and many points of curious contrast in their characters. Vanderbilt, like Drew, was born in very humble circumstances in the state of New York, and received as little education. He began life by ferrying over passengers and produce from Staten Island to New York. Subsequently, he too laid the foundation of his great fortune in the growing steamboat navigation, and, likewise, in due course of time, transferred himself to the railroad interest. When at last, in 1868, the two came into collision as representatives of the old system of railroad management and of the new, they were each of them threescore and ten years of age, and had both been successful in the accumulation of millions — Vanderbilt even more so than Drew.

They were probably equally unscrupulous and equally selfish; but, while the cast of Drew's mind was somber and bearish, Vanderbilt was gay and buoyant of temperament, little given to thoughts other than of his world, a lover of horses and of the good things of this life. The first affects prayer meetings, and the last is a devotee of whist. Drew, in Wall Street, is by temperament a bear, while Vanderbilt could hardly be other than a bull. Vanderbilt must be allowed to be by far the superior man of the two. Drew is astute and full of resources, and at all times a dangerous opponent; but Vanderbilt takes larger, more comprehensive views, and his mind has a vigorous grasp which that of Drew seems to want. While, in short, in a wider field, the one might have made himself a great and successful despot, the other would hardly have aspired to be more than the head of the jobbing department of some corrupt government.

Accordingly, while in Drew's connection with the railroad system his operations and manipulations evince no qualities calculated to excite even a vulgar admiration or re-spect, it is impossible to regard Vanderbilt's methods or aims without recognizing the magnitude of the man's ideas and conceding his abilities. He involuntarily excites feelings of admiration for himself and alarm for the public. His ambition is a great one. It seems to be nothing less than to make himself master in his own right of the great channels of communication which connect the city of New York with the interior of the continent, and to control them as his private property.

While Drew has sought only to carry to perfection the old system of operating successfully from the confidential position of director, neither knowing anything nor caring anything for the railroad system except in its connection with the movements of the Stock Exchange, Vanderbilt has seen the full magnitude of the system, and through it has sought to make himself a dictator in modern civilization, moving forward to this end, step by step, with a sort of pitiless energy which has seemed to have in it an element of fatality.

As trade now dominates the world, and the railways dominate trade, his object has been to make himself the virtual master of all by making himself absolute lord of the railways. Had he begun his railroad operations with this end in view, complete failure would have been almost certainly his reward. Commencing as he did, however, with a comparatively insignificant objective point — the cheap purchase of a bankrupt stock — and developing his ideas as he advanced, his power and his reputation grew; until an end which it would have seemed madness to entertain at first became at last both natural and feasible.

Two great lines of railway traverse the state of New York and connect it with the West — the Erie and the New York Central. The latter communicates with the city by a great river and by two railroads. To get these two roads — the Harlem and the Hudson River — under his own absolute control, and then, so far as the connection with the Central was concerned, to abolish the river, was Vanderbilt's immediate object. First making himself master of the Harlem Road, he there learned his early lessons in railroad management, and picked up a fortune by the way. . . .

The Harlem was, after all, only a competing line, and competition was proverbially the rock ahead in all railroad enterprise. The success of Vanderbilt with the Harlem depended upon his getting rid of the competition of the Hudson River Railroad. An ordinary manager would have resorted to contracts, which are never carried out, or to opposition, which is apt to be ruinous. Vanderbilt, on the contrary, put an end to competition by buying up the competing line. . . .

By this time, Vanderbilt's reputation as a railroad manager — as one who earned dividends, invented stock, and created wealth — had become very great, and the managers of the Central brought that road to him and asked him to do with it as he had done with the Harlem and Hudson River. He accepted the proffered charge, and now, probably, the possibilities of his position and the magnitude of the prize within his grasp at last dawned on his mind. . . .

From the moment Vanderbilt stepped into the management of the Central, but a single effort seemed necessary to give the new railroad king absolute control over the railroad system, and consequently over the commerce, of New York. By advancing only one step, he could securely levy his tolls on the traffic of a continent. Nor could this step have seemed difficult to take. It was but to repeat with the Erie his successful operation with the Hudson River Road. Not only was it a step easy to take, but here again, as so many times before, a new fortune seemed ready to drop into his hand. The Erie might well yield a not less golden harvest than the Central, Hudson River, and Harlem Road; there was indeed but one obstacle in the way — the plan might not meet the views of the one man who at that time possessed the wealth, cunning, and combination of qualities which could defeat it, that man being the Speculative Director of the Erie — Mr. Daniel Drew.

The New York Central passed into Vanderbilt's hands in the winter of 1866-67, and he marked the Erie for his own in the succeeding autumn. As the annual meeting of the corporation approached, three parties were found in the field contending for control of the road. One party was represented by Drew, and might be called the party in possession — that which had long ruled the Erie and made it what it was, — the "Scarlet Woman of Wall Street." Next came Vanderbilt, flushed with success and bent upon his great idea of developing imperialism in corporate life. Lastly, a faction made its appearance composed of some shrewd and ambitious Wall Street operators and of certain persons from Boston, who sustained for the occasion the novel character of railroad reformers. This party, it is needless to say, was as unscrupulous and, as the result proved, as able as either of the others; it represented nothing but a raid made upon the Erie treasury in the interest of a thoroughly bankrupt New England corporation of which its members had the control. . . .

Of late years, under able and persevering, if not scrupulous management, the bankrupt, moribund company had been slowly struggling into new life, and in the spring of 1867 it had obtained, under certain conditions, from the commonwealth of Massachusetts, a subsidy in aid of the construction of the road. One of the conditions imposed obliged the corporation to raise a sum from other sources still larger than that granted by the state. Accordingly, those having the line in charge looked abroad for a victim, and fixed their eyes upon the Erie. . . . Meanwhile, the representatives of the Eastern interest played their part to admiration. Taking advantage of some Wall Street complications just then existing between Vanderbilt and Drew, they induced the former to ally himself with them, and the latter saw that his defeat was inevitable. . . .

On the Sunday preceding the election, Drew, in view of his impending defeat, called upon Vanderbilt. That gentleman thereupon very amicably read to him the legal documents prepared for his benefit, whereupon the ready treasurer at once turned about, and, having hitherto been hampering the Commodore by his bear operations, he now agreed to join hands with him in giving to the market a strong upward tendency. Meanwhile, the other parties to the contest were not idle. At the same house, at a later hour in the day, Vanderbilt explained to the Eastern adventurers his new plan of operations, which included the continuance of Drew in his directorship.

These gentlemen were puzzled, not to say confounded, by this sudden change of front. An explanation was demanded, some plain language followed, and the parties separated, only to meet again at a later hour at the house of Drew. There Vanderbilt brought the new men to terms by proposing to Drew a bold *coup de main*, calculated to throw them entirely out of the direction. Before the parties separated that night, a written agreement had been entered into, providing that, to save appearances, the new board should be elected without Drew, but that immediately thereafter a vacancy should be created and Drew chosen to fill it. He was therefore to go in as one of two directors in the Vanderbilt interest — that gentleman's nephew, Mr. Work, being the other.

This program was faithfully carried out, and, on the 2nd of October, Wall Street was at once astonished by the news of the defeat of the notorious leader of the bears and bewildered by the immediate resignation of a member of the new board and the election of Drew in his place. Apparently he had given in his submission, the one obstacle to success was removed, and the ever victorious Commodore had now but to close his fingers on his new prize. Virtual consolidation in the Vanderbilt interest seemed a foregone conclusion.

The reinstallment of Drew was followed by a period of hollow truce. . . . This, however, was a mere sportive interlude between the graver scenes of the drama. The real conflict was now impending.

Commodore Vanderbilt stretched out his hand to grasp Erie. Erie was to be isolated and shut up within the limits of New York; it was to be given over, bound hand and foot, to the lord of the Central. To perfect this program, the representatives of all the competing lines met, and a proposition was submitted to the Erie party looking to a practical consolidation and a division among the contracting parties of the earnings from the New York City travel. A new illustration was thus to be afforded, at the expense of the trade and travel to and from the heart of a continent, of George Stephenson's famous aphorism, that where combination is possible competition is impossible. The Erie party, however, represented that their road earned more than half of the fund of which they were to receive only one-third. They remonstrated and proposed modifications, but their opponents were inexorable. The terms were too hard; the conference led to no result; and the war broke out afresh.

Then Vanderbilt, foiled in his attempt, went into Wall Street, prepared to make himself master of the Erie, as before he had made himself master of the Hudson River Road. The task in itself was one of magnitude. The volume of stock was immense; all of it was upon the street, and the necessary expenditure involved many millions of dollars. The peculiar difficulty of the task, however, lay in the fact that it had to be undertaken in the face of antagonists so bold, so subtle, so unscrupulous, so thoroughly acquainted with Erie, as well as so

Charles Francis Adams (1835-1915), center without hat, pictured during his Civil War service, when he commanded a Negro cavalry regiment

familiar with all the devices and tricks of fence of Wall Street.

The first open hostilities took place on the 17th of February. For some time Wall Street had been agitated with forebodings of the coming hostilities, but not until that day was recourse had to the courts. Vanderbilt had two ends in view when he sought to avail himself of the processes of law. In the first place, Drew's long connection with Erie, and especially the unsettled transactions arising out of the famous corner of 1866, afforded admirable ground for annoying offensive operations; and, in the second place, these very proceedings, by throwing his opponent on the defensive, afforded an excellent cover for Vanderbilt's own transactions in Wall Street. . . .

It was, therefore, very necessary for Vanderbilt that he should, while buying Erie up with one hand in Wall Street, with the other close, so far as he could, that apparently inexhaustible spring from which such generous supplies of new stock were wont to flow. Accordingly, on the 17th of February, Mr. Frank Work, the only remaining representative of the Vanderbilt faction in the

Erie direction, accompanied by Mr. Vanderbilt's attorneys, Messrs. Rapallo and Spenser, made his appearance before Judge Barnard of the Supreme Court of New York, then sitting in chambers, and applied for an injunction against Treasurer Drew and his brother directors, restraining them from the payment of interest or principal of the $3,500,000 borrowed of the treasurer in 1866, as well as from releasing Drew from any liability or cause of action the company might have against him, pending an investigation of his accounts as treasurer. On the other hand, Drew was to be enjoined from taking any legal steps toward compelling a settlement.

A temporary injunction was granted in accordance with the petition, and a further hearing was assigned for the 21st. Two days later, however — on the 19th of the month — without waiting for the result of the first attack, the same attorneys appeared again before Judge Barnard, and now, in the name of the people, acting through the attorney general, petitioned for the removal from office of Treasurer Drew. The papers in the case set forth some of the difficulties which beset the Commodore and exposed the existence of a new fountain of Erie stock. It appeared that there was a recently enacted statute of New York which authorized any railroad company to create and issue its own stock in exchange for the stock of any other road under lease to it.

Mr. Drew, the petition then alleged, and certain of his brother directors, had quietly possessed themselves of a worthless road connecting with the Erie, and called the Buffalo, Bradford, and Pittsburg Railroad, and had then, as occasion and their own exigencies required, proceeded to supply themselves with whatever Erie stock they wanted by leasing their own road to the road of which they were directors, and then creating stock and issuing it to themselves, in exchange, under the authority vested in them by law. The history of this transaction affords, indeed, a most happy illustration of brilliant railroad financiering. The road cost the purchasers, as financiers, some $250,000; as proprietors, they then issued in its name bonds for $2 million, payable to one of themselves, who now figured as trustee. This person, then, shifting his character, drew up, as counsel for both parties, a contract leasing this road to the Erie Railway for 499 years, the Erie agreeing to assume the bonds; reappearing in their original character of Erie directors, these gentlemen then ratified the lease, and thereafter it only remained for them to relapse into the role of financiers and to divide the proceeds.

All this was happily accomplished, and the Erie Railway lost and someone gained $140,000 a year by the bargain. The skillful actors in this much-shifting drama probably proceeded on the familiar theory that exchange is no robbery; and the expedient was certainly ingenious. Commodore Vanderbilt, however, naturally desired to put some limit to the amount of the stock in existence, a majority of which he sought to control. Accordingly, it was now further ordered by Mr. Justice Barnard that Mr. Drew should show cause on the 21st why the prayer of the petitioner should not be granted, and meanwhile he was temporarily suspended from his position as treasurer and director. . . .

On the application of Work, an injunction was issued restraining the Erie board from any new issue of capital stock, by conversion of bonds or otherwise, in addition to the 251,058 shares appearing in the previous reports of the road, and forbidding the guaranty by the Erie of the bonds of any connecting line of road. While this last provision of the order was calculated to furnish food for thought to the Boston party, matter for meditation was supplied to Mr. Drew by other clauses which specially forbade him, his agents, attorneys, or brokers to have any transactions in Erie, or fulfill any of his contracts already entered into, until he had returned to the company 68,000 shares of capital stock, which were alleged to be the number involved in the unsettled transaction of 1866, and the more recent Buffalo, Bradford, and Pittsburg exchange. A final hearing was fixed for the 10th of March on both injunctions.

Things certainly did not now promise well for Treasurer Drew and the bear party. Vanderbilt and the bulls seemed to have it all their own way. If any virtue existed in the processes of law, if any authority was wielded by a New York court, it now seemed as if the very head of the bear faction must needs be converted into a bull in his own despite, and to his manifest ruin. He, in this hour of his trial, was to be forced by his triumphant opponent to make Erie scarce by returning into its treasury 68,000 shares — one-fourth of its whole capital stock of every description. So far from manufacturing fresh Erie and pouring it into the street, he was to be cornered by a writ and forced to work his own ruin in obedience to an injunction. Appearances are, however, proverbially deceptive, and all depended on the assumption that some virtue did exist in the processes of law, and that some authority was wielded by a New York court.

In spite of the threatening aspect of his affairs, it was very evident that the nerves of Mr. Drew and his associates were not seriously affected. Wall Street watched him with curiosity not unmingled with alarm; for this was a conflict of Titans. Hedged all around with orders of the court; suspended, enjoined, and threatened with all manner of unheard-of processes; with Vanderbilt's wealth standing like a lion in his path; and all Wall Street ready to turn upon him and rend him — in presence of all these accumulated terrors of the courtroom and of the exchange — the Speculative Director was not less speculative than his wont. He seemed rushing on destruction. Day after day he pursued the same "short" tactics; contract after contract was put out for the future delivery of stock at current prices, and this, too, in the face of a continually rising market. Evidently he did not yet consider himself at the end of his resources.

It was equally evident, however, that he had not much time to lose. It was now the 3rd of March, and the anticipated "corner" might be looked for about the 10th. As usual, some light skirmishing took place as a prelude to the heavy shock of decisive battle. The Erie party very freely and openly expressed a decided lack of respect, and something approaching contempt, for the purity of that particular fragment of the judicial ermine which — figuratively — adorned the person of Mr. Justice Barnard. They did not pretend to conceal their conviction that this magistrate was a piece of the Vanderbilt property, and they very plainly announced their intention of seeking for justice elsewhere. With this end in view they betook themselves to their own town of Binghamton, in the county of Broome,

where they duly presented themselves before Mr. Justice Balcom of the Supreme Court.

The existing judicial system of New York divides the state into eight distinct districts, each of which has an independent Supreme Court of four judges, elected by the citizens of that district. The first district alone enjoys five judges, the fifth being the Judge Barnard already referred to. These local judges, however, are clothed with certain equity powers in actions commenced before them which run throughout the state. As one subject of litigation, therefore, might affect many individuals, each of whom might initiate legal proceedings before any of the thirty-three judges, which judge, again, might forbid proceedings before any or all of the other judges, or issue a stay of proceedings in suits already commenced, and then proceed to make orders, to consolidate actions, and to issue process for contempt — it was not improbable that, sooner or later, strange and disgraceful conflicts of authority would arise, and that the law would fall into contempt.

Taking advantage of the extreme complication in practice of a system so simple in its theory, the Erie party broke ground in a new suit. The injunction was no sooner asked of Judge Balcom than it was granted; and Mr. Frank Work, the attorney general, and all other parties litigant, were directed to show cause at Courtlandville on the 7th of March; and meanwhile, Mr. Director Work, accused of being a spy of the enemy in the councils of Erie, was temporarily suspended from his position and all proceedings in the suits commenced before Judge Barnard were stayed. The moment, however, that this order became known in New York, a new suit was commenced by the Vanderbilt interest in the name of Richard Schell; and Judge Ingraham cried check to the move of Judge Balcom by forbidding any meeting of the Erie board or the transaction of any business by it unless Director Work was at full liberty to participate therein. The first move of the Drew faction did not seem likely to result in any signal advantage to their cause.

All this, however, was mere skirmishing, and now the decisive engagement was near at hand. The plans of the Erie ring were matured, and if Commodore Vanderbilt wanted the stock of their road, they were prepared to let him have all that he desired. As usual, the Erie treasury was at this time deficient in funds. As usual, also, Daniel Drew stood ready to advance all the funds required on proper security. One kind of security, and only one, the company was disposed at this time to offer — their convertible bonds under a pledge of conversion. The company could not issue stock outright, in any case, at less than par; its bonds bore interest and were useless on the street; an issue of convertible bonds was another name for an issue of stock to be sold at market rates. The treasurer readily agreed to find a purchaser, and, in fact, he himself was just then in pressing need of some scores of thousands of shares.

Already at the meeting of the Board of Directors, on the 19th of February, a very deceptive account of the condition of the road, jockied out of the general superintendent, had been read and made public; the increased depot facilities, the projected double track, and the everlasting steel rails, had been made to do vigorous duty; and the board had duly authorized the Executive Committee "to borrow such sums as might be necessary, and to issue therefor such security as is provided for in such cases by the laws of this state." Immediately after the Board of Directors adjourned, a meeting of the Executive Committee was held, and a vote to issue at once convertible bonds for $10 million gave a meaning to the very ambiguous language of the directors' resolve; and thus, when apparently on the very threshold of his final triumph, this mighty mass of 100,000 shares of new stock was hanging like an avalanche over the head of Vanderbilt.

The Executive Committee had voted to sell the entire amount of these bonds at not less than 72½. Five million were placed upon the market at once, and Mr. Drew's broker became the purchaser — Mr. Drew giving him a written guaranty against loss and being entitled to any profit that might arise. It was all done in ten minutes after the Committee adjourned — the bonds issued, their conversion into stock demanded and complied with, and certificates for 50,000 shares deposited in the broker's safe, subject to the orders of Daniel Drew. There they remained until the 29th, when they were issued, on his requisition, to certain others of that gentleman's army of brokers, much as ammunition might be issued before a general engagement. Three days later came the Barnard injunction, and Erie suddenly rose in the market. Then it was determined to bring up the reserves and let the eager bulls have the other $5 million.

The history of this second issue was, in all respects, an episode worthy of Erie, and deserves minute relation. It was decided upon on the 3rd, but, before the bonds were converted, Barnard's injunction had been served on everyone connected with the Erie Road or with Daniel Drew. The 10th was the return day of the writ, but the Erie operators needed even less time for their deliberations. Monday, the 9th, was settled upon as the day upon which to defeat the impending "corner." The night of Saturday, the 7th, was a busy one in the Erie camp. While one set of counsel and clerks were preparing affidavits and prayers for strange writs and injunctions, the enjoined vice-president of the road was busy at home signing certificates of stock, to be ready for instant use in case a modification of the injunction could be obtained, and another set of counsel was in immediate attendance on the leaders themselves.

Mr. Groesbeck, the chief of the Drew brokers, being himself enjoined, secured elsewhere, after one or two failures, a purchaser of the bonds and took him to the house of the Erie counsel, where Drew and other directors and brokers then were. There the terms of the nominal sale were agreed upon and a contract drawn up transferring the bonds to this man of straw — Mr. Groesbeck meanwhile, with the fear of injunctions before his eyes, prudently withdrawing into the next room. After the contract was closed, the purchaser was asked to sign an affidavit setting forth his ownership of the bonds and the refusal of the corporation to convert them into stock in compliance with their contract, upon which affidavit it was in contemplation to seek from some justice a writ of mandamus to compel the Erie Railway to convert them, the necessary papers for such a proceeding being then in course of preparation elsewhere.

This the purchaser declined to do. One of the lawyers present then said: "Well, you can make the demand now; here is Mr. Drew, the treasurer of the company, and Mr. Gould, one of the Executive Committee." In accordance with this suggestion, a demand for the stock was then made, and, of course, at once refused; thereupon the scruples of the man of straw being all removed, the desired affidavit was signed. All business having now been disposed of, the parties separated; the legal papers were ready, the convertible bonds had been disposed of, and the certificates of stock for which they were to be exchanged were signed in blank and ready for delivery.

Early on Monday morning the Erie people were at work. Mr. Drew, the director and treasurer, had agreed to sell on that day 50,000 shares of the stock, at 80, to the firms of which Mr. Fisk and Mr. Gould were members, these gentlemen also being Erie directors and members of the Executive Committee. The new certificates, made out in the names of these firms on Saturday

night, were in the hands of the secretary of the company, who was strictly enjoined from allowing their issue. On Monday morning this official directed an employee of the road to carry these books of certificates from the West Street office of the company to the transfer clerk in Pine Street, and there to deliver them carefully. The messenger left the room, but immediately returned empty-handed and informed the astonished secretary that Mr. Fisk had met him outside the door, taken from him the books of unissued certificates, and "run away with them." It was true; one essential step toward conversion had been taken; the certificates of stock were beyond the control of an injunction. A day or two later the convertible bonds were found upon the secretary's desk, conveyed thither by an unknown hand; the certificates were next seen in Broad Street.

Before launching the bolt thus provided, the conspirators had considered it not unadvisable to cover their proceedings, if they could, with some form of law. This probably was looked upon as an idle ceremony, but it could do no harm; and perhaps their next step was dictated by what has been called "a decent respect for the opinions of mankind," combined with a profound contempt for judges and courts of law.

Early on the morning of the 9th, Judge Gilbert, a highly respected magistrate of the Second Judicial District, residing in Brooklyn, was waited upon by one of the Erie counsel, who desired to initiate before him a new suit in the Erie litigation, this time in the name of the Saturday evening purchaser of bonds and maker of affidavits. A writ of mandamus was asked for. This writ clearly did not lie in such a case; the magistrate very properly declined to grant it, and the only wonder is that counsel should have applied for it. New counsel were then hurriedly summoned, and a new petition, in a fresh name, was presented. This petition was for an injunction, in the name of one

Belden, the business partner of Mr. Fisk, and the documents then and there presented were probably as eloquent an exposure of the lamentable condition into which the once-honored judiciary of New York had fallen as could possibly have been penned.

The petition alleged that sometime in February certain persons, among whom was especially named George G. Barnard, the justice of the Supreme Court of the First District, had entered into a combination to speculate in the stock of the Erie Railway and to use the process of the courts for the purpose of aiding their speculation; "and that, in furtherance of the plans of this combination," the actions in Work's name had been commenced before Barnard. It is impossible by any criticism to do justice to such audacity as this; the dumb silence of amazement is the only fitting commentary. Apparently, however, nothing that could be stated of his colleague across the river exceeded the belief of Judge Gilbert; for, after some trifling delays and a few objections on the part of the judge to the form of the desired order, the Erie counsel returned to New York with a new injunction, restraining all the parties to all the other suits from further proceedings and from doing any acts in "furtherance of said conspiracy"; in one paragraph ordering the Erie directors, except Work, to continue in the discharge of their duties in direct defiance of the injunction of Judge Ingraham, and in another, with an equal disregard of Judge Barnard, forbidding the directors to desist from converting bonds into stock. . . .

All was now ready. The Drew party was enjoined in every direction. One magistrate had forbidden them to move, and another magistrate had ordered them not to stand still. If the Erie board held meetings and transacted business, it violated one injunction; if it abstained from so doing, it violated another. By the further conversion of bonds into stock, pains and penalties would be incurred at the hands of Judge Barnard;

the refusal to convert would be an act of disobedience to Judge Gilbert. Strategically considered, the position could not be improved, and Mr. Drew and his friends were not the men to let the golden moment escape them.

At once, before even in New York a new injunction could be obtained, 50,000 shares of new Erie stock were flung upon the market. That day, Erie was buoyant — Vanderbilt was purchasing. His agents caught at the new stock as eagerly as at the old, and the whole of it was absorbed before its origin was suspected, and almost without a falter in the price. Then the fresh certificates appeared, and the truth became known. Erie had that day opened at 80 and risen rapidly to 83, while its rise even to par was predicted; suddenly it faltered, fell off, and then dropped suddenly to 71. . . . The attempted "corner" was a failure, and Drew was victorious. . . .

The morning of the 11th found the Erie leaders still transacting business at the office of the corporation in West Street. . . . They were speedily roused from their real or affected tranquillity by trustworthy intelligence that processes for contempt were already issued against them and that their only chance of escape from incarceration lay in precipitate flight. At 10 o'clock the astonished police saw a throng of panic-stricken railway directors . . . dash off in the direction of the Jersey ferry. In their hands were packages and files of papers, and their pockets were crammed with assets and securities. One individual bore away with him in a hackney coach bales containing $6 million in greenbacks. Other members of the board followed under cover of the night; some of them, not daring to expose themselves to the publicity of a ferry, attempted to cross in open boats concealed by the darkness and a March fog. Two directors who lingered were arrested; but a majority of the Executive Committee collected at the Erie station in Jersey City, and there, free from any apprehension of Judge Barnard's pursuing wrath, proceeded to the transaction of business.

Meanwhile, on the other side of the river, Vanderbilt was struggling in the toils. As usual in these Wall Street operations, there was a grim humor in the situation. Had Vanderbilt failed to sustain the market, a financial collapse and panic must have ensued which would have sent him to the wall. He had sustained it and had absorbed 100,000 shares of Erie. Thus, when Drew retired to Jersey City, he carried with him $7 million of his opponent's money, and the Commodore had freely supplied the enemy with the sinews of war. He had grasped at Erie for his own sake, and now his opponents promised to rehabilitate and vivify the old line with the money he had furnished them, so as more effectually to compete with the lines which he already possessed.

Nor was this all. Had they done as they loudly claimed they meant to do, Vanderbilt might have hugged himself in the faith that, after all, it was but a question of time and the prize would come to him in the end. He, however, knew well enough that the most pressing need of the Erie people was money with which to fight him. With this he had now furnished them abundantly, and he must have felt that no scruples would prevent their use of it.

Vanderbilt had, however, little leisure to devote to the enjoyment of the humorous side of his position. The situation was alarming. His opponents had carried with them in their flight $7 million in currency, which were withdrawn from circulation. An artificial stringency was thus created in Wall Street; and, while money rose, stocks fell, and unusual margins were called in. Vanderbilt was carrying a fearful load, and the least want of confidence, the faintest sign of faltering might well bring on a crash. He already had 100,000 shares of Erie, not one of which he could sell. He was liable at any time to be called upon to carry as much

more as his opponents, skilled by long practice in the manufacture of the article, might see fit to produce. Opposed to him were men who scrupled at nothing, and who knew every in and out of the money market. With every look and every gesture anxiously scrutinized, a position more trying than his then was can hardly be conceived.

It is not known from what source he drew the vast sums which enabled him to surmount his difficulties with such apparent ease. His nerve, however, stood him in at least as good stead as his financial resources. Like a great general in the hour of trial, he inspired confidence. While fighting for life, he could "talk horse" and play whist. The manner in which he then emerged from his troubles, serene and confident, was as extraordinary as the financial resources he commanded. Such a concentration of power in the hands of a single individual is one significant feature of the times. . . .

As to the useless lumber of conflict, consisting chiefly of the numerous judges of the Supreme Court of New York and their conflicting processes of law, this can be quickly disposed of. . . . It reads like some monstrous parody of the forms of law; some saturnalia of bench and bar. The magistrate became more partisan than were the paid advocates before him, and all seemed to vie with one another in their efforts to bring their common profession into public contempt. Day and night, detectives in the pay of suitors dogged the steps of the magistrate; and their sworn affidavits, filed in his own court, sought to implicate him in an attempt to kidnap Drew by means of armed ruffians and to bring the fugitive by violence within reach of his process. Then, in retaliation, the judge openly avowed from the bench that his spies had penetrated into the consultations of the litigants, and he astonished a witness by angrily interrogating him as to an affidavit reflecting upon himself, to which that witness had declined to make oath. At one moment he wept, as counsel detailed before him the story of his own grievances and the insults to which he had been subjected, and then again he vindicated his purity with select specimens of Tammany rhetoric. . . .

All the scandals of the practice of the law and the private immoralities of lawyers were dragged into the broad light of day; the whole system of favored counsel, of private argument, or referees, and of unblushing extortion was freely discussed. . . .

All this time injunctions were flying about like hailstones; but the crowning injunction of all was one issued by Judge Clerke, a colleague of Judge Barnard, at the time sitting as a member of the Court of Appeals at Albany, in reference to the appointment of a receiver. The Gilbert injunction had gone, it might have seemed, sufficiently far in enjoining Barnard the individual, while distinctly disavowing all reference to him in his judicial functions. Judge Clerke made no such exception. He enjoined the individual and he enjoined the judge; he forbade his making any order appointing a receiver, and he forbade the clerks of his court from entering it if it were made, and the receiver from accepting it if it were entered. . . .

Finally, the maze had become so intricate and the whole litigation so evidently endless and aimless that, by a sort of agreement of parties, Judge Ingraham, another colleague of Judge Barnard, issued a final injunction of universal application, as it were, and to be held inviolable by common consent, under which proceedings were stayed, pending an appeal. It was high time. Judges were becoming very shy of anything connected with the name of Erie, and Judge McCunn had in a lofty tone informed counsel that he preferred to subject himself to the liability of a fine of $1,000 rather than, by issuing a writ of habeas corpus, to allow his court "to have anything to do with the scandal."

The result of this extraordinary litigation may be summed up in a few words. It had two branches: one, the appointment of a receiver of the proceeds of the 100,000 shares of stock issued in violation of an injunction; the other, the processes against the persons of the directors for a contempt of court. As for the receiver, every dollar of the money this officer was intended to receive was well known to be in New Jersey, beyond his reach. Why one party cared to insist on the appointment, or why the other party objected to it, is not very apparent. Mr. Osgood, the son-in-law of Vanderbilt, was appointed and immediately enjoined from acting; subsequently he resigned when Mr. Peter B. Sweeney, the head of the Tammany ring, was appointed in his place, without notice to the other side. Of course he had nothing to do, as there was nothing to be done, so he was subsequently allowed by Judge Barnard $150,000 for his services.

The contempt cases had even less result than that of the receivership. The settlement subsequently effected between the litigants seemed also to include the courts. The outraged majesty of the law, as represented in the person of Mr. Justice Barnard, was pacified. . . . The penalty for violating an injunction in the manner described was finally fixed at the not unreasonable sum of $10, except in the cases of Mr. Drew and certain of his more prominent associates; their contumacy His Honor held to be too great to be estimated in money, and so they escaped without any punishment at all. The legal profession alone had cause to regret the cessation of this litigation; and as the Erie counsel had $150,000 divided among them in fees, it may be presumed that even they were finally comforted. . . .

Early in April, Mr. Drew took advantage of that blessed immunity from arrest which the Sabbath confers on the hunted of the law, to revisit the familiar scenes across the river. His visits soon resulted in conferences between himself and Vanderbilt, and these conferences naturally led to overtures of peace. Though the tide was turning against the great railroad king, though an uncontrollable popular feeling was fast bearing down his schemes of monopoly, yet he was by no means beaten or subdued. His plans, however, had evidently failed for the present. It was now clearly his interest to abandon his late line of attack and to bide his time patiently, or to possess himself of his prey by some other method. The wishes of all parties, therefore, were fixed on a settlement, and no one was disposed to stand out except in order to obtain better terms. The interests, however, were multifarious. There were four parties to be taken care of, and the depleted treasury of the Erie Railway was doomed to suffer. . . .

The details of the treaty which had been concluded between the high contracting parties were not divulged to the Board of Directors until the 2nd of July. Upon that day, Mr. Eldridge announced the following terms of settlement: Commodore Vanderbilt was to be relieved of 50,000 shares of Erie stock at 70, receiving therefore $2,500,000 in cash and $1,250,000 in bonds of the Boston, Hartford, and Erie at 80. He was also to receive a further sum of $1 million outright, as a consideration for the privilege the Erie Road thus purchased of calling upon him for his remaining 50,000 shares at 70 at any time within four months. He was also to have two seats in the Board of Directors, and all suits were to be dismissed and offenses condoned. . . .

While Vanderbilt and his friends were thus provided for, Mr. Drew was to be left in undisturbed enjoyment of the fruits of his recent operations, but was to pay into the treasury $540,000 and interest, in full discharge of all claims and causes of action which the Erie Company might have against him. The Boston party, as represented by Mr. Eldridge, was to be relieved of $5 million of their Boston, Hartford, and Erie bonds, for which they were to receive $4 million of Erie acceptances. . . .

Messrs. Gould and Fisk still remained to be provided for, and to them their associates left — the Erie Railway. These gentlemen subsequently maintained that they had

vehemently opposed this settlement and had denounced it in the secret councils as a fraud and an outrage. This would seem in no way improbable. The rind of the orange is not generally considered the richest part of the fruit; a corporation on the verge of bankruptcy is less coveted, even by operators in Wall Street, than one rich in valuable assets. However, the voice of a clear majority was for peace.

Mr. Eldridge counted out his bonds and received his acceptances, which latter were cashed at once to close up the transaction, and thereupon he resigned his positions as director and president. The Boston raiders then retired, heavy with spoil, into their own North country, where, doubtless, in good time, they will introduce the more highly developed civilization of the land of their temporary adoption. Mr. Vanderbilt apparently ceased to concern himself with Erie; and Daniel Drew, released from the anxieties of office, assumed for a space the novel character of a disinterested observer of the operations of Wall Street. . . .

Comment would only weaken the force of this narrative. It sufficiently suggests its own moral. The facts which have been set forth cannot but have revealed to every observant eye the deep decay which has eaten into every part of our social edifice. No portion of our system was left untested, and no portion showed itself to be sound. The Stock Exchange revealed itself as a haunt of gamblers and a den of thieves; the offices of our great corporations appeared as the secret chambers in which trustees plotted the spoliation of their wards; the law became a ready engine for the furtherance of wrong, and the ermine of the judge did not conceal the eagerness of the partisan; the halls of legislation were transformed into a mart in which the price of votes was higgled over, and laws, made to order, were bought and sold; while, under all and through all, the voice of public opinion was silent or was disregarded. . . .

Modern society has created a class of artificial beings who bid fair soon to be the masters of their creator. It is but a very few years since the existence of a corporation controlling a few millions of dollars was regarded as a subject of grave apprehension, and now this country already contains single organizations which wield a power represented by hundreds of millions. These bodies are the creatures of single states; but in New York, in Pennsylvania, in Maryland, in New Jersey, and not in those states alone, they are already establishing despotisms which no spasmodic popular effort will be able to shake off. Everywhere, and at all times, however, they illustrate the truth of the old maxim of the common law, that corporations have no souls.

Even now the system threatens the central government. The Erie Railway represents a weak combination compared to those which day by day are consolidating under the unsuspecting eyes of the community. A very few years more and we shall see corporations as much exceeding the Erie and the New York Central in both ability and will for corruption as they will exceed those roads in wealth and in length of iron track. We shall see these great corporations spanning the continent from ocean to ocean — single, consolidated lines, not connecting Albany with Buffalo, or Lake Erie with the Hudson, but uniting the Atlantic and the Pacific, with *termini* at New York and San Francisco. Already the disconnected members of these future leviathans have built up states in the wilderness and chosen their attorneys senators of the United States.

Now their power is in its infancy; in a very few years they will reenact, on a larger theater and on a grander scale, with every feature magnified, the scenes which were lately witnessed on the narrow stage of a single state. The public corruption is the foundation on which corporations always depend for their political power. There is a natural tendency to coalition between them

and the lowest strata of political intelligence and morality; for their agents must obey, not question. The lobby is their home, and the lobby thrives as political virtue decays. The ring is their symbol of power, and the ring is the natural enemy of political purity and independence. . . .

It is a new power for which our language contains no name. We know what aristocracy, autocracy, democracy are; but we have no word to express government by moneyed corporations. Yet the people already instinctively seek protection against it, and look for such protection, significantly enough, not to their own legislature but to the single, autocratic feature retained in our system of government — the veto by the Executive. Through this, Governor Hoffman won and lost his reputation in New York, and it is to the possible use of this same power by President Grant, in Washington, that the people look for security from the misdeeds of their own representatives done under the influence of corporate wealth.

The next step will be interesting. As the Erie ring represents the combination of the corporation and the hired proletariat of a great city, as Vanderbilt embodies the autocratic power of Caesarism introduced into corporate life, and as neither alone can obtain complete control of the government of the state, it, perhaps, only remains for the coming man to carry the combination of elements one step in advance and put Caesarism at once in control of the corporation and of the proletariat, to bring our vaunted institutions within the rule of all historic precedent.

It is not pleasant to take such views of the future; yet they are irresistibly suggested by the events which have been narrated. They seem to be in the nature of direct inferences. The only remedy lies in a renovated public opinion; but no indication of that has as yet been elicited.

"Amphitheatrum Johnsonianum — Massacre of the Innocents at New Orleans, 1866"; from "Harper's"

THE RECONSTRUCTION ERA

Postwar Southern Reconstruction was clearly guaranteed to revive issues supposedly settled by the Northern victory. In most Southern states the coalition of the army, the Freedmen's Bureau, and the radicals immediately removed and replaced the old governing class. But in states like Mississippi and Louisiana, the government rapidly returned to virtual prewar status, with repressive Black Codes to keep former slaves on the plantation and "in their place." But whether open or covert, the general policy of the South was non-cooperation with Reconstruction. Abolitionism, the war, and now Radicalism all served to harden the South's already firm resolve not to reform its social and political structure to please the North.

Andrew Johnson tried in his own bumbling way to carry out the Reconstruction plans of Lincoln; but with neither Lincoln's political ability nor his public appeal, Johnson was simply overwhelmed by the strong-willed Radical Republicans. The congressional election of 1866 settled the question of the North's attitude — in the wake of riots in New Orleans and Memphis in which hundreds of African Americans were killed, the Radicals won sufficient strength to override any veto.

With the new Congress began the infamous Reconstruction of political vengeance and corruption. New constitutions were written and new governments elected; the electorate was reconstituted and the states readmitted. Yet Reconstruction was temporary; as federal control faded, the old Southern system slowly revived.

Shooting down African Americans during riots in Memphis, Tenn., May 1866. Sketch from "Harper's Weekly"

(Above left) Andrew Johnson; photo by Brady; (above right) Thaddeus Stevens, leader of the Radical Republicans; (below) steamboat "Brazil" fired upon by guerrillas along the Mississippi

18. *How the President went into the excursion.*   *How he came out of the excursion.*
N. B.—This is meant Allegorical.

"Andy's Trip West" by Petroleum V. Nasby lampooned an abortive trip to gain support

(Left) Gen. O. O. Howard, Freedmen's Bureau commissioner; (right) Sen. Edmund Ross, who cast the deciding vote against Johnson's conviction; (below) farming without a mule

(Left) Maximilian, emperor of Mexico and brother of Francis Joseph I; (right) Benito Juarez, leader of the reform movement and president of Mexico before and after Maximilian's brief reign

THE CRIPPLED AMERICAN EAGLE, THE COCK, AND THE LION

Lion. "Why, Brother Jonathan, you don't look so fierce as you used. How about the Monroe Doctrine now?"

Cock. "Yes, my good Jonatan, what you tink of Privateering under de present circumstance?"

The Monroe Doctrine had gone by the board during the Civil War, but with the surrender of Lee came the opportunity to reassert American purpose in the hemisphere. The first such occasion was in Mexico where Napoleon III of France had sponsored the Emperor Maximilian against President Juarez. The withdrawal of French troops in 1867 at the insistence of Secretary of State Seward doomed Maximilian. Grant rather strongly favored expansionism, and his election in 1868 led to greater American involvement in Caribbean and Central American affairs; Grant and Senator Charles Sumner soon collided over expansionist plans.

(Left) Cartoon from "Harper's" depicting America's inability to enforce Monroe Doctrine during Civil War; (below) execution of Maximilian

(Above) U. S. Grant; (right) in anti-Democratic cartoon by Nast, Francis Blair, vice-presidential candidate, joins an Irish thug and a capitalist in oppressing African Americans, 1868

(Above) James Fisk, stock speculator; (right) stock brokers, 1868; (below) parade in honor of adoption of the 15th Amendment

"If He Can't Respect Our Flag, Send Him Where He Belongs," cartoon from "Harper's Weekly" urging support for the Cuban rebels

Hamilton Fish was easily the most capable Cabinet member of the twenty-five that Grant had. As secretary of state, Fish maintained an intelligent policy which was almost the only positive aspect of Grant's administrations. When Congress and the President ordered a recognition of belligerency for Cuban rebels, Fish pocketed the order; such recognition would very likely have led to war with Spain and seriously prejudiced American claims against Britain for premature recognition of the Confederacy. In 1871 Fish negotiated the Treaty of Washington which established arbitration for the "Alabama" claims.

(Above) Hamilton Fish, secretary of state under Grant, who persuaded the President not to become involved in the Cuban uprising; (right) pro-Cuban sentiments were openly expressed in "Harper's Weekly," 1868

HARPER'S WEEKLY.

A JOURNAL OF CIVILIZATION.

Vol. XII.—No. 622.]   NEW YORK, SATURDAY, NOVEMBER 28, 1868.   [SINGLE COPIES, TEN CENTS. $4.00 PER YEAR IN ADVANCE.

CUBAN AFFAIRS.

Library of Congress

(Left) Pro-Grant cartoon lampoons Charles Sumner and his Radical Republican friends for jumping into the Democrats' domain. Sumner, chairman of the Senate Foreign Affairs Committee, asserted Congress' policy-making role at every opportunity. His exposure of speculators behind Grant's treaty to annex Santo Domingo allied him with the Democrats in opposition to Grant. Sumner also clashed with Hamilton Fish, whose efforts to settle the disputes with Britain by diplomacy and arbitration did not satisfy the senator's rage against British "perfidy" during the Civil War

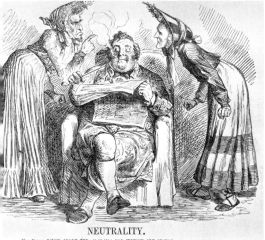

NEUTRALITY.

Mrs. North. "HOW ABOUT THE ALABAMA, YOU WICKED OLD MAN?"
Mrs. South. "WHERE'S MY RAMS? TAKE BACK YOUR PRECIOUS CONSULS—THERE!!!"

Library of Congress

General Aniline and Film Corp.

1862 cartoon shows Britain's purported disinterest in the war; John Chandler Bancroft Davis argued the U.S. position at the "Alabama" arbitration; (below) World Peace Jubilee, Boston, 1872

Library of Congress

(Left) Gen. William Belknap, Grant's secretary of war, whose misuse of the office forced his resignation; (right) Nast cartoon depicting Belknap's fate, 1876

The stain of corruption, already noticeable in Grant's first term, became glaring in 1873. Belknap, Grant's secretary of war, was impeached for accepting bribes, but resigned and thus escaped conviction. Gen. Orville Babcock, Grant's private secretary, who had worked diligently for annexation of Santo Domingo to further private American interests there, was among those involved in the "whiskey ring" frauds against federal revenue collection. Numerous congressmen appear to have sold their votes regularly to the highest bidder.

Orville Babcock, Grant's secretary involved in a "whiskey ring" defrauding the government

Nast cartoons supporting Grant: (Left) "The crowning insult to him who occupies the Presidential chair"; liberal Republicans with the aid of Democrats blaming Grant for their party's corruption; (right) "Great Expectations"; reaction to the Liberal Republicans, and later the Democrats, nominating Horace Greeley for President, and Gratz Brown for Vice=President in 1872

"CHILDREN CRY FOR IT."

(Left) "A Burden He Has to Shoulder"; cartoon by Nast; (right) Nast chides Congress for their insincere demand for civil service reforms

When the nominating conventions met in 1872, Liberal Republicans repudiated the Grant administration and nominated Horace Greeley, counting on the Democrats to support their choice in spite of Greeley's long-standing opposition to the Democratic Party. The coalition candidate ran a poor campaign, alienating all the professional politicians, and Grant was swept back into office. Following hard on his reelection came the Panic of 1873, largely brought on by railroad speculation, which stretched into a five-year depression.

(Right) Horace Greeley, unsuccessful candidate for President; (below) the president of the New York Stock Exchange announcing the suspension of Jay Cooke and Co., precipitating the Panic of 1873

(Left) Samuel Tilden and (right) Rutherford B. Hayes, candidates in the disputed election of 1876. By bargaining with Southern Democrats, Republicans achieved the needed electoral votes

The Hayes-Tilden election of 1876 marked the end of Reconstruction. Although Tilden held a clear majority, Republicans disputed the results from three Southern states and Oregon. A special electoral commission with an 8-7 Republican majority gave all the disputed states to Hayes. A political bargain had been struck: the Democrats accepted the commission verdict, while Hayes abolished the last vestiges of Reconstruction.

(Left) "Caught in a Trap"; downfall of the Republicans; (right) Peter Cooper, 1876

Hayes had pledged in advance to serve only one term as President, and kept his pledge. This left the Republican nomination in 1880 in the air. The "Stalwarts," who had made a good thing of Grant's regime, wanted him to run again, but there was strong opposition from James Blaine. Garfield, though somewhat sullied by the scandals of 1872-73, was the successful candidate, edging out the Democrat, Gen. Winfield Scott Hancock. But Garfield served only six months before his death put Chester A. Arthur in the White House.

(Top) **Republican national nominating convention held in Chicago, 1880, was photographed while Garfield was speaking;** (center) **James Garfield, 1881;** (bottom) **the attack on the President's life by a disappointed office-seeker, July 1881. Garfield died two months later**

William Sylvis, early labor organizer, was elected president of the National Labor Union, 1868; (center) communist Henri Rochefort speaking in New York; (right) Terence V. Powderly

The long depression of 1873-78 brought about much labor unrest, most notably the massive railway strike of 1877. President Hayes used federal troops against the strikers in St. Louis and Pittsburgh. For the first time a fairly strong national labor organization, the Knights of Labor, came to the fore. Organized in 1869, the Knights became an all-embracing union of skilled and unskilled workers under Terence Powderly achieving total membership of nearly 700,000 before their collapse following the Haymarket riots of 1886.

Strikers stop a train in strike on Erie R.R.; an 8 hour day was a prime labor aim. Grant gave support by decreeing this for government workers

39.

HENRY ENO: Silver in Nevada

During the three decades following the Civil War wave after wave of pioneers swept over the Missouri, bent on gaining wealth in the new Western territories. The miners were first on the scene, and, after their disappointment when the California gold rush of 1849 subsided, many headed East again and found rich gold and silver deposits in Nevada and Colorado. Usually, as with the case of the fabulous "Comstock Lode" at the Ophir mine, Nevada, prospectors were looking for gold and found silver as an accidental by-product of this search. Henry Eno, who was present at the height of Nevada's fame as mining territory, wrote to his brother William, on August 21, 1869, describing the activity at Hamilton White Pine.

Source: *Twenty Years on the Pacific Slope; Letters of Henry Eno from California and Nevada, 1848-1871.* W. Turrentine Jackson, ed., New Haven, 1965.

Dear Brother:

Yours of the 11th August was received yesterday. Have now been here since the 3rd of July. I came here expecting to find a rich mineral country, also to find much such a population as California had in 1849 and '50. The great mineral wealth of eastern Nevada has not been exaggerated. In fact I did not expect to find so rich or so many silver mines. There is not so much wild reckless extravagance among the people of the towns and the miners as in the early days of California. There are not as many homicides according to the numbers, but there is perhaps more highway robberies committed. We have here, as twenty years ago, numbers too lazy to work but not too lazy to steal, and some too proud to work and not afraid to steal. The laws of Nevada license gambling, and here at Hamilton, in Treasure City, and Shermantown are some ten or twelve licensed gambling tables. The next session of the legislature may perhaps license highway robbery.

There are two banking establishments, two express offices. Wells Fargo and Union Express, some ten or twelve assay offices, and a small army of lawyers. The District Court has been in session ever since I arrived. A trial often occupies ten or twelve days. A very few lawyers are doing well. From what I can discover I believe that lawyers depend more upon perjury and subornation of perjury than upon principles of law or precedents. Experts in mining do a thriving business as witnesses.

There are, I judge, nearly 200 paying mines within four miles square. There ought to be a dozen more quartz mills erected and would find full employment. The price of crushing and working ores is too high for low grade ores. The common price is $30 per ton. Under ordinary circumstances free ores yielding $15 per ton can be worked at a fair profit. There are very many mining districts within 80 and 100 miles that are now attracting attention of miners and capitalists. The merchants of Chicago are turning their attention to this silver country and will enter into competition with San Francisco, and I should not be surprised if they succeed in establishing and building up a heavy business and a profitable one. The money market in California as well as in Nevada is very stringent. There is much financial distress. Very many men reputed to be worth their many thousands last spring are now reputed worthless. But in no country that I have ever seen (not even in California) do I believe that well-directed industry and judiciously invested capital would meet with richer rewards.

It will never be considered a good grain country, but as a pastoral country it is unquestionably a good one. Millions of sheep can be kept here and without cutting hay for winter. It is also a good dairy country. There is a great scarcity of water, it is true, but artesian wells can supply it. It is also a healthy country: no fever and ague. At this high elevation, persons of weak lungs are subject to pneumonia, but a little care will prevent it. It is *no money,* not *pneumonia,* that I am troubled about and am afraid it will become chronic.

I went out a few days ago with a young fellow on a prospecting trip, about four or five miles from here. Went over as rough a country as I ever traveled over. Stiping Mountain is but a molehill compared with ours. On our return, struck a silver lode. Brought home some specimens and had them assayed. Send you the assay, so that you may see how we manage here. Intend to prospect it further.

Have made up my mind to go to Iowa and St. Louis, if I can possibly raise the means, the forepart of October and return in the spring. I made the acquaintance of Judge G. C. Bates of Chicago who was here a short time since. I formerly knew him in Sacramento. He tells me I can make money by lecturing, advises me to make my debut at Chicago, and that he will introduce me. And also at Detroit. Am now busily engaged in preparing several lectures, but I labor under many disadvantages. Still hope to overcome them. If I can but put my foot on the lower round of fortune's ladder and grasp with my hand another, I have faith to believe I can yet climb it.

Was pleased to hear about your farming operations. Reapers, mowing machines, gang plows, and the threshers have found their way to the Pacific Coast. Between Elko and Hamilton there are several mowing machines at work. Almost all the wheat of California is harvested by machines. Last year a Mr. Mitchell on the San Joaquin plains raised 14,000 acres of wheat, and this year Bidwell of the Sacramento Valley, candidate for governor last year, raised 27,000 acres of wheat. Last year, in June, I was in San Francisco. A farmer living near Sacramento River told me that he had 1,500 acres of wheat which would yield, on an average, 30 bushels to the acre. He said he could harvest it, thrash it, put in sacks, and store it in a warehouse in San Francisco within a fortnight's time. There have been fifty-six harvesting machines employed this year on the Salinas Plains. I crossed them in 1850, and there was not a furrow turned.

Our markets here are well supplied with everything man wants to sustain life and some of the luxuries. Flour, $8 per hundredweight; beef and mutton, 15 to 20 cents per lb.; sugar, 3 lbs. for $1; bacon, 30 cents per lb.; apples, peaches, apricots, nectarines, and grapes from California in abundance, all about 25 cents per lb.; potatoes, 10 cents per lb.; beans the same; and water, 12½ cents a bucket; $7 a day for a horse to ride — I find it cheaper to go afoot — wood, $6 per cord. Rents all the way from $40 to $400 per month for one or two rooms. Plenty of good air but of rather a light quality, nothing.

I think you would like a trip to this wild country and to the more civilized portions of California. It would give materials for thought and reflection and would in all probability enable you to enjoy with a greater zest the comforts of a quiet home. As for me, I feel as if I had no country and no home, but try to make the best of it wherever I am.

40.

William H. Seward: The Promise of Alaska

The idea of purchasing Alaska from Russia had been discussed as early as 1859, but the Civil War hindered any useful negotiations. Commercial interests on the West Coast were especially desirous of obtaining fishing and trading rights in the territory, which was governed by the Russian-American Company, a commercial monopoly that ruled Alaska on behalf of the Russian imperial government. Because the company's monopoly was unprofitable, and the territory was too distant from St. Petersburg to be governed or protected adequately, the Russian minister to Washington conferred in March 1867 with Secretary of State William H. Seward over the possible purchase of Alaska by the United States. Seward, always an ardent expansionist, eagerly negotiated a treaty that was ratified by the Senate on April 9. The United States paid $7,200,000 for what came to be called "Seward's Folly" or "Seward's Arctic Province." After Seward left office he made a world tour and included a visit to Alaska to see his purchase at firsthand. On August 12, 1869, he made the following speech at Sitka, in which he looked forward to the time when Alaska would take its place as a state in the Union.

Source: OSL 133.

Citizens of Alaska, Fellow Citizens of the United States:

You have pressed me to meet you in public assembly once before I leave Alaska. It would be sheer affectation to pretend to doubt your sincerity in making this request, and capriciously ungrateful to refuse it, after having received so many and varied hospitalities from all sorts and conditions of men. It is not an easy task, however, to speak in a manner worthy of your consideration while I am living constantly on shipboard, as you all know, and am occupied intently in searching out whatever is sublime, or beautiful, or peculiar, or useful.

On the other hand, it is altogether natural on your part to say, "You have looked upon Alaska; what do you think of it?" Unhappily, I have seen too little of Alaska to answer the question satisfactorily. The entire coastline of the United States, exclusive of Alaska, is 10,000 miles, while the coastline of Alaska alone, including the islands, is 26,000 miles. The portion of the territory which lies east of the peninsula, including islands, is 120 miles wide. The western portion, including Aleutian Islands, expands to a breadth of 2,200 miles. The entire land area, including islands, is 577,390 statute square miles.

We should think a foreigner very presumptuous who should presume to give the world an opinion of the whole of the United States of America after he had merely looked in from his steamer at Plymouth and Boston Harbor, or had run up the Hudson River to the Highlands, or had ascended the Delaware to Trenton, or the James River to Richmond, or the Mississippi no farther than Memphis. My observation thus far has hardly been more comprehensive.

I entered the Territory of Alaska at the Portland Canal, made my way through the narrow passages of the Prince of Wales Archipelago, thence through Peril and Chatham Straits and Lynn Channel, and up the Chilcat River to the base of Fairweather, from which latter place I have returned through Clarence Straits, to sojourn a few days in your beautiful bay, under the shadows of the Baranoff Hills and Mount Edgecombe. . . .

Alaska has been as yet but imperfectly explored; but enough is known to assure us that it possesses treasures of what are called the baser ores equal to those of any other region of the continent. We have Copper Island and Copper River, so named as the places where the natives, before the period of the Russian discovery, had procured the pure metal from which they fabricated instruments of war and legendary shields.

In regard to iron, the question seems to be not where it can be found but whether there is any place where it does not exist. Mr. Davidson of the Coast Survey invited me to go up to him at the station he had taken up the Chilcat River to make his observations of the eclipse, by writing me that he had discovered an iron mountain there. When I came there, I found that, very properly, he had been studying the heavens so busily that he had but cursorily examined the earth under his feet; that it was not a single iron mountain he had discovered but a range of hills the very dust of which adheres to the magnet; while the range itself, 2,000 feet high, extends along the east bank of the river thirty miles.

Limestone and marble crop out on the banks of the same river and in many other places. Coal beds, accessible to navigation, are found at Kootznoo. It is said, however, that the concentrated resin which the mineral contains renders it too inflammable to be safely used by steamers. In any case, it would seem calculated to supply the fuel requisite for the manufacture of iron. What seems to be excellent cannel coal is also found in the Prince of Wales Archipelago. There are also mines at Cook's Inlet. Placer and quartz gold mining is pursued under many social disadvantages upon the Stickeen and elsewhere, with a degree of success which, while it does not warrant us in assigning a superiority in that respect to the territory, does nevertheless warrant us in regarding gold mining as an established and reliable resource.

It would argue inexcusable insensibility if I should fail to speak of the scenery which, in the course of my voyage, has seemed to pass like a varied and magnificent panorama before me. The exhibition did not, indeed, open within the territory. It broke upon me first when I had passed Cape Flattery and entered the Straits of Fuca, which separate British Columbia from Washington Territory. It widened as I passed along the shore of Puget Sound, expanded in the waters which divide Vancouver from the continent, and finally spread itself out into a magnificent archipelago, stretching through the entire Gulf of Alaska and closing under the shade of Mounts Fairweather and St. Elias. Nature has furnished to this majestic picture the only suitable border which could be conceived by lifting the coast range mountains to an exalted height, and clothing them with eternal snows and crystalline glaciers.

It remains only to speak of man and of society in Alaska. Until the present moment the country has been exclusively inhabited and occupied by some thirty or more Indian tribes. I incline to doubt the popular classification of these tribes upon the assumption that they have descended from diverse races. Climate and other circumstances have indeed produced some differences of manners and customs between the Aleuts, the Koloschians, and the interior continental tribes. But all of them are manifestly of

Mongol origin. Although they have preserved no common traditions, all alike indulge in tastes, wear a physiognomy, and are imbued with sentiments peculiarly noticed in Japan and China.

Savage communities, no less than civilized nations, require space for subsistence, whether they depend for it upon the land or upon the sea — in savage communities especially; and increase of population disproportioned to the supplies of the country occupied necessitates subdivision and remote colonization. Oppression and cruelty occur even more frequently among barbarians than among civilized men. Nor are ambition and faction less inherent in the one condition than in the other. From these causes it has happened that the 25,000 Indians in Alaska are found permanently divided into so many insignificant nations.

These nations are jealous, ambitious, and violent; could in no case exist long in the same region without mutually affording what, in every case, to each party seems just cause of war. War between savages becomes the private cause of the several families which are afflicted with the loss of their members. Such a war can never be composed until each family which has suffered receives an indemnity in blankets, adjusted according to an imaginary tariff, or, in the failure of such compensation, secures the death of one or more enemies as an atonement for the injury it has sustained. The enemy captured, whether by superior force or strategy, either receives no quarter or submits for himself and his progeny to perpetual slavery.

It has thus happened that the Indian tribes of Alaska have never either confederated or formed permanent alliances, and that even at this late day, in the presence of superior power exercised by the United States government, they live in regard to each other in a state of enforced and doubtful truce. It is manifest that, under these circumstances, they must steadily decline in numbers; and, unhappily, this decline is accelerated by their borrowing ruinous vices from the white man.

Such as the natives of Alaska are, they are, nevertheless, in a practical sense, the only laborers at present in the territory. The white man comes among them from London, from St. Petersburg, from Boston, from New York, from San Francisco, and from Victoria, not to fish (if we except alone the whale fishery) or to hunt but simply to buy what fish and what peltries, ice, wood, lumber, and coal the Indians have secured under the superintendence of temporary agents or factors.

When we consider how greatly most of the tribes are reduced in numbers and how precarious their vocations are, we shall cease to regard them as indolent or incapable; and, on the contrary, we shall more deeply regret than ever before that a people so gifted by nature, so vigorous and energetic, and withal so docile and gentle in their intercourse with the white man, can neither be preserved as a distinct social community nor incorporated into our society. The Indian tribes will do here as they seem to have done in Washington Territory and British Columbia — they will merely serve their turn until civilized white men come.

You, the citizens of Sitka, are the pioneers, the advanced guard of the future population of Alaska; and you naturally ask when, from whence, and how soon reenforcements shall come, and what are the signs and guarantees of their coming. This question, with all its minute and searching interrogations, has been asked by the pioneers of every state and territory of which the American Union is now composed; and the history of those states and territories furnishes the complete, conclusive, and satisfactory answer. Emigrants go to every infant state and territory in obedience to the great natural law that obliges needy men to seek subsistence, and invites adventurous men to seek fortune where it is most easily obtained; and this is always in the new and uncultivated regions. They go from every state and territory, and from every foreign nation in America, Europe, and Asia, because no established and populous state or nation can guarantee subsistence and fortune to all who demand them among its inhabitants.

The guarantees and signs of their coming to Alaska are found in the resources of the territory, which I have attempted to describe, and in the condition of society in other parts of the world. Some men seek other climes for health and some for pleasure. Alaska invites the former class by a climate singularly salubrious and the latter class by scenery which surpasses in sublimity that of either the Alps, the Apennines, the Alleghenies, or the Rocky Mountains. Emigrants from our own states, from Europe, and from Asia will not be slow in finding out that fortunes are to be gained by pursuing here the occupations which have so successfully sustained races of untutored men.

Civilization and refinement are making more rapid advances in our day than at any former period. The rising states and nations on this continent, the European nations, and even those of eastern Asia, have exhausted, or are exhausting, their own forests and mines, and are soon to become largely dependent upon those of the Pacific. The entire region of Oregon, Washington Territory, British Columbia, and Alaska seem thus destined to become a shipyard for the supply of all nations.

I do not forget on this occasion that British Columbia belongs within a foreign jurisdiction. That circumstance does not materially affect my calculations. British Columbia, by whomsoever possessed, must be governed in conformity with the interests of her people and of society upon the American continent. If that territory shall be so governed, there will be no ground of complaint anywhere. If it shall be governed so as to conflict with the interests of the inhabitants of that territory and of the United States, we all can easily foresee what will happen in that case. You will ask me, however, for guarantees that the hopes I encourage will not be postponed. I give them.

Within the period of my own recollection, I have seen twenty new states added to the eighteen which before that time constituted the American Union; and I now see, besides Alaska, ten territories in a forward condition of preparation for entering into the same great political family. I have seen in my own time, not only the first electric telegraph but even the first railroad and the first steamboat invented by man. And even on this present voyage of mine, I have fallen in with the first steamboat, still afloat, that thirty-five years ago lighted her fires on the Pacific Ocean. These, citizens of Sitka, are the guarantees, not only that Alaska has a future, but that that future has already begun.

I know that you want two things just now, when European monopoly is broken down and United States free trade is being introduced within the territory: these are military protection while your number is so inferior to that of the Indians around you, and you need also a territorial civil government. Congress has already supplied the first of these wants adequately and effectually. I doubt not that it will supply the other want during the coming winter. It must do this because our political system rejects alike anarchy and executive absolutism. Nor do I doubt that the political society to be constituted here, first as a territory and ultimately as a state or many states will prove a worthy constituency of the republic.

To doubt that it will be intelligent, virtuous, prosperous, and enterprising is to doubt the experience of Scotland, Denmark, Sweden, Holland, and Belgium, and of New England and New York. Nor do I doubt that it will be forever true in its republican instincts and loyal to the American Union; for the inhabitants will be both mountaineers and seafaring men. I am not among those who apprehend infidelity to liberty and the Union in any quarter hereafter; but I am sure that, if constancy and loyalty are to fail anywhere, the failure will not be in the states which approach nearest to the North Pole.

Fellow citizens, accept once more my thanks, from the heart of my heart, for kindness which can never be forgotten, and suffer me to leave you with a sincere and earnest farewell.

41.

Samuel L. Clemens ("Mark Twain"): Spirit of the Tennessee Press

From the time he was eighteen in 1853, Samuel L. Clemens traveled the country as a journeyman printer and wandering journalist, contributing letters and sketches to newspapers in St. Louis, New York, Philadelphia, and Cincinnati. He worked as a pilot on a Mississippi riverboat and followed the miners to California and Nevada. These experiences provided material for his humorous sketches and lectures. His first book, The Celebrated Jumping Frog of Calaveras County, And Other Sketches, *was published in 1867 under the pseudonym "Mark Twain" and met with great success. The following selection, "Journalism in Tennessee," was written around 1869 and was included in a collection published in 1875.*

Source: *Sketches New and Old*, New York, 1875.

I was told by the physician that a Southern climate would improve my health, and so I went down to Tennessee and got a berth on the *Morning Glory and Johnson County War-Whoop* as associate editor. When I went on duty I found the chief editor sitting tilted back in a three-legged chair with his feet on a pine table. There was another pine table in the room and another afflicted chair, and both were half buried under newspapers and scraps and sheets of manuscript. There was a wooden box of sand sprinkled with cigar stubs and "old soldiers," and a stove with a door hanging by its upper hinge.

The chief editor had a long-tailed black cloth frock coat on and white linen pants. His boots were small and neatly blacked. He wore a ruffled shirt, a large seal ring, a standing collar of obsolete pattern, and a checkered neckerchief with the ends hanging down. Date of costume about 1848. He was smoking a cigar and trying to think of a word, and in pawing his hair he had rumpled his locks a good deal. He was scowling fearfully, and I judged that he was concocting a particularly knotty editorial. He told me to take the exchanges and skim through them and write up the "Spirit of the Tennessee Press," condensing into the article all of their contents that seemed of interest.

I wrote as follows:

Spirit of the Tennessee Press

The editors of the *Semi-Weekly Earthquake* evidently labor under a misapprehension with regard to the Ballyhack Railroad. It is not the object of the company to leave Buzzardville off to one side. On the contrary, they consider it one of the most important points along the line, and consequently can have no desire to slight it. The gentlemen of the *Earthquake* will, of course, take pleasure in making the correction.

John W. Blossom, Esq., the able editor of the Higginsville *Thunderbolt and Battle Cry of Freedom*, arrived in the city yesterday. He is stopping at the Van Buren House.

We observe that our contemporary of the Mud Springs *Morning Howl* has fallen into the error of supposing that the election of Van Werter is not an established fact, but he will have discovered his mistake before this reminder reaches him, no doubt. He was doubtless misled by incomplete election returns.

It is pleasant to note that the city of Blathersville is endeavoring to contract with some New York gentlemen to pave its well-nigh impassable streets with the Nicholson pavement. The *Daily Hurrah* urges the measure with ability, and seems confident of ultimate success.

I passed my manuscript over to the chief editor for acceptance, alteration, or destruction. He glanced at it and his face clouded. He ran his eye down the pages, and his countenance grew portentous. It was easy to see that something was wrong. Presently he sprang up and said:

"Thunder and lightning! Do you suppose I am going to speak of those cattle that way? Do you suppose my subscribers are going to stand such gruel as that? Give me the pen!"

I never saw a pen scrape and scratch its way so viciously, or plow through another man's verbs and adjectives so relentlessly. While he was in the midst of his work, somebody shot at him through the open window and marred the symmetry of my ear.

"Ah," said he, "that is that scoundrel Smith, of the *Moral Volcano* — he was due yesterday." And he snatched a navy revolver from his belt and fired. Smith dropped, shot in the thigh. The shot spoiled Smith's aim, who was just taking a second chance, and he crippled a stranger. It was me. Merely a finger shot off.

Then the chief editor went on with his erasures and interlineations. Just as he finished them a hand grenade came down the stovepipe, and the explosion shivered the stove into a thousand fragments. However, it did no further damage, except that a vagrant piece knocked a couple of my teeth out.

"That stove is utterly ruined," said the chief editor.

I said I believed it was.

"Well, no matter — don't want it this kind of weather. I know the man that did it. I'll get him. Now, *here* is the way this stuff ought to be written."

I took the manuscript. It was scarred with erasures and interlineations till its mother wouldn't have known it if it had had one. It now read as follows:

Spirit of the Tennessee Press

The inveterate liars of the *Semi-Weekly Earthquake* are evidently endeavoring to palm off upon a noble and chivalrous people another of their vile and brutal falsehoods with regard to that most glorious conception of the nineteenth century, the Ballyhack Railroad. The idea that Buzzardville was to be left off at one side originated in their own fulsome brains — or rather in the settlings which *they* regard as brains. They had better swallow this lie if they want to save their abandoned reptile carcasses the cowhiding they so richly deserve.

That ass, Blossom, of the Higginsville *Thunderbolt and Battle Cry of Freedom*, is down here again sponging at the Van Buren.

We observe that the besotted black-

Mark Twain (center) with Petroleum V. Nasby (left) and Josh Billings (right)

guard of the Mud Springs *Morning Howl* is giving out, with his usual propensity for lying, that Van Werter is not elected. The heaven-born mission of journalism is to disseminate truth; to eradicate error; to educate, refine, and elevate the tone of public morals and manners, and make all men more gentle, more virtuous, more charitable, and in all ways better, and holier, and happier; and yet this black-hearted scoundrel degrades his great office persistently to the dissemination of falsehood, calumny, vituperation, and vulgarity.

Blathersville wants a Nicholson pavement — it wants a jail and a poorhouse more. The idea of a pavement in a one-horse town composed of two gin mills, a blacksmith shop, and that mustard plaster of a newspaper, the *Daily Hurrah!* The crawling insect, Buckner, who edits the *Hurrah*, is braying about this business with his customary imbecility, and imagining that he is talking sense.

"Now *that* is the way to write — peppery and to the point. Mush-and-milk journalism gives me the fan-tods."

About this time a brick came through the window with a splintering crash and gave me a considerable of a jolt in the back. I moved out of range — I began to feel in the way.

The chief said, "That was the Colonel, likely. I've been expecting him for two days. He will be up now right away."

He was correct. The Colonel appeared in the door a moment afterward with a dragoon revolver in his hand.

He said, "Sir, have I the honor of addressing the poltroon who edits this mangy sheet?"

"You have. Be seated, sir. Be careful of the chair, one of its legs is gone. I believe I have the honor of addressing the putrid liar, Colonel Blatherskite Tecumseh?"

"Right, sir, I have a little account to settle with you. If you are at leisure we will begin."

"I have an article on the 'Encouraging Progress of Moral and Intellectual Development in America' to finish, but there is no hurry. Begin."

Both pistols rang out their fierce clamor at the same instant. The chief lost a lock of his hair, and the Colonel's bullet ended its career in the fleshy part of my thigh. The Colonel's left shoulder was clipped a little. They fired again. Both missed their men this time, but I got my share, a shot in the arm. At the third fire both gentlemen were wounded slightly, and I had a knuckle chipped. I then said I believed I would go out and take a walk, as this was a private matter, and I had a delicacy about participating in it further. But both gentlemen begged me to keep my seat, and assured me that I was not in the way.

They then talked about the elections and the crops while they reloaded, and I fell to tying up my wounds. But presently they opened fire again with animation, and every shot took effect — but it is proper to remark that five out of the six fell to my share. The sixth one mortally wounded the Colonel, who remarked, with fine humor, that he would have to say good morning now, as he had business uptown. He then inquired the way to the undertaker's and left.

The chief turned to me and said, "I am expecting company to dinner and shall have to get ready. It will be a favor to me if you will read proof and attend to the customers."

I winced a little at the idea of attending to the customers, but I was too bewildered by the fusillade that was still ringing in my ears to think of anything to say.

He continued, "Jones will be here at three — cowhide him. Gillespie will call earlier, perhaps — throw him out of the window. Ferguson will be along about four — kill him. That is all for today, I believe. If you have any odd time, you may write a blistering article on the police — give the chief inspector rats. The cowhides are under the table; weapons in the drawer — ammunition there in the corner — lint and bandages up there in the pigeonholes. In case of accident, go to Lancet, the surgeon, downstairs. He advertises — we take it out in trade."

He was gone. I shuddered. At the end of the next three hours I had been through perils so awful that all peace of mind and all cheerfulness were gone from me. Gillespie had called and thrown *me* out of the window. Jones arrived promptly, and when I got ready to do the cowhiding he took the job off my hands. In an encounter with a stranger, not in the bill of fare, I had lost my scalp. Another stranger by the name of Thompson left me a mere wreck and ruin of chaotic rags. And at last, at bay in the corner and beset by an infuriated mob of editors, blacklegs, politicians, and desperadoes, who raved and swore and flourished their weapons about my head till the air shimmered with glancing flashes of steel, I was in the act of resigning my berth on the paper when the chief arrived, and with him a rabble of charmed and enthusiastic friends.

Then ensued a scene of riot and carnage such as no human pen, or steel one either, could describe. People were shot, probed, dismembered, blown up, thrown out of the window. There was a brief tornado of murky blasphemy, with a confused and frantic war dance glimmering through it, and then all was over. In five minutes there was silence, and the gory chief and I sat alone and surveyed the sanguinary ruin that strewed the floor around us.

He said, "You'll like this place when you get used to it."

I said, "I'll have to get you to excuse me; I think maybe I might write to suit you after awhile; as soon as I had had some practice and learned the language, I am confident I could. But, to speak the plain truth, that sort of energy of expression has its inconveniences, and a man is liable to interruption. You see that yourself. Vigorous writing is calculated to elevate the public, no doubt, but then I do not like to attract so much attention as it calls forth. I can't write with comfort when I am interrupted so much as I have been today.

"I like this berth well enough, but I don't like to be left here to wait on the customers. The experiences are novel, I grant you, and entertaining, too, after a fashion, but they are not judiciously distributed. A gentleman shoots at you through the window and cripples *me*; a bombshell comes down the stovepipe for your gratification and sends the stove door down *my* throat; a friend drops in to swap compliments with you, and freckles *me* with bullet holes till my skin won't hold my principles; you go to dinner, and Jones comes with his cowhide, Gillespie throws me out of the window, Thompson tears all my clothes off, and an entire stranger takes my scalp with the easy freedom of an old acquaintance; and in less than five minutes all the blackguards in the country arrive in their war paint and proceed to scare the rest of me to death with their tomahawks. Take it altogether, I never had such a spirited time in all my life as I have had today.

"No; I like you, and I like your calm unruffled way of explaining things to the customers, but you see I am not used to it. The Southern heart is too impulsive; Southern hospitality is too lavish with the stranger. The paragraphs which I have written today, and into whose cold sentences your masterly hand has infused the fervent spirit of Tennesseean journalism, will wake up another nest of hornets. All that mob of editors will come — and they will come hungry, too, and want somebody for breakfast. I shall have to bid you adieu. I decline to be present at these festivities. I came South for my health, I will go back on the same errand, and suddenly. Tennesseean journalism is too stirring for me."

After which we parted with mutual regret, and I took apartments at the hospital.

42.

CHARLES W. ELIOT: The Elective Curriculum

Charles W. Eliot became president of Harvard University on October 19, 1869. His inaugural address, in which he outlined the progress he envisioned for the university, reflected an understanding of the nature of education gained during his teaching career at Harvard and the Massachusetts Institute of Technology. In the following selection from the address, Eliot proposed an elective curriculum as a resolution of the age-old controversy over classical versus practical education.

Source: *Educational Reform, Essays and Addresses,* New York, 1901, pp. 1-38.

THE ENDLESS CONTROVERSIES whether language, philosophy, mathematics, or science supplies the best mental training, whether general education should be chiefly literary or chiefly scientific, have no practical lesson for us today. This university recognizes no real antagonism between literature and science, and consents to no such narrow alternatives as mathematics or classics, science or metaphysics. We would have them all, and at their best. To observe keenly, to reason soundly, and to imagine vividly are operations as essential as that of clear and forcible expression; and to develop one of these faculties, it is not necessary to repress and dwarf the others.

A university is not closely concerned with the applications of knowledge until its general education branches into professional. Poetry and philosophy and science do indeed conspire to promote the material welfare of mankind; but science, no more than poetry, finds its best warrant in its utility. Truth and right are above utility in all realms of thought and action.

It were a bitter mockery to suggest that any subject whatever should be taught less than it now is in American colleges. The only conceivable aim of a college government in our day is to broaden, deepen, and invigorate American teaching in all branches of learning. It will be generations before the best of American institutions of education will get growth enough to bear pruning.

The descendants of the Pilgrim fathers are still very thankful for the parched corn of learning.

Recent discussions have added pitifully little to the world's stock of wisdom about the staple of education. Who blows today such a ringing trumpet call to the study of language as Luther blew? Hardly a significant word has been added in two centuries to Milton's description of the unprofitable way to study languages. Would any young American learn how to profit by travel, that foolish beginning but excellent sequel to education, he can find no apter advice than Bacon's. The practice of England and America is literally centuries behind the precept of the best thinkers upon education. A striking illustration may be found in the prevailing neglect of the systematic study of the English language. How lamentably true today are these words of Locke:

> If anyone among us have a facility or purity more than ordinary in his mother tongue, it is owing to chance, or his genius, or anything rather than to his education or any care of his teacher.

The best result of the discussion which has raged so long about the relative educational value of the main branches of learning is the conviction that there is room for them all in a sound scheme, provided that right methods of teaching be employed. It is not because of the limitation of their faculties that boys of eighteen come to college, having mastered nothing but a few score pages of Latin and Greek and the bare elements of mathematics. Not nature but an unintelligent system of instruction from the primary school through the college is responsible for the fact that many college graduates have so inadequate a conception of what is meant by scientific observation, reasoning, and proof. . . .

With good methods, we may confidently hope to give young men of twenty to twenty-five an accurate general knowledge of all the main subjects of human interest, besides a minute and thorough knowledge of the one subject which each may select as his principal occupation in life. To think this impossible is to despair of mankind; for unless a general acquaintance with many branches of knowledge, good so far as it goes, be attainable by great numbers of men, there can be no such thing as an intelligent public opinion; and in the modern world the intelligence of public opinion is the one indispensable condition of social progress.

What has been said of needed reformation in methods of teaching the subjects which have already been nominally admitted to the American curriculum applies not only to the university but to the preparatory schools of every grade down to the primary. The American college is obliged to supplement the American school. Whatever elementary instruction the schools fail to give, the college must supply. The improvement of the schools has of late years permitted the college to advance the grade of its teaching and adapt the methods of its later years to men instead of boys. This improvement of the college reacts upon the schools to their advantage; and this action and reaction will be continuous. A university is not built in the air, but on social and literary foundations which preceding generations have bequeathed. If the whole structure needs rebuilding, it must be rebuilt from the foundation. Hence, sudden reconstruction is impossible in our high places of education.

Such inducements as the college can offer for enriching and enlarging the course of study pursued in preparatory schools, the faculty has recently decided to give. The requirements in Latin and Greek grammar are to be set at a thorough knowledge of forms and general principles; the lists of classical authors accepted as equivalents for the regular standards are to be enlarged; an acquaintance with physical geography is to be required; the study of elementary mechanics is to be recommended, and prizes are to be offered for reading aloud, and for the critical analysis of passages from English authors. At the same time the university will take to heart the counsel which it gives to others.

In every department of learning the university would search out by trial and reflection the best methods of instruction. The university believes in the thorough study of language. It contends for all languages — Oriental, Greek, Latin, Romance, German, and especially for the mother tongue; seeing in them all one institution, one history, one means of discipline, one department of learning. In teaching languages, it is for this American generation to invent, or to accept from abroad, better tools than the old; to devise, or to transplant from Europe, prompter and more comprehensive methods than the prevailing; and to command more intelligent labor in order to gather rapidly and surely the best fruit of that culture and have time for other harvests.

The university recognizes the natural and physical sciences as indispensable branches of education, and has long acted upon this opinion; but it would have science taught in a rational way, objects and instruments in hand — not from books merely, not through the memory chiefly, but by the seeing eye and the informing fingers. Some of the scientific scoffers at gerund grinding and nonsense verses might well look at home; the prevailing methods of teaching science the world over are, on the whole, less intelligent than the methods of teaching language.

The university would have scientific studies in school and college and professional school develop and discipline those powers of the mind by which science has been created and is daily nourished — the powers of observation, the inductive faculty, the sober imagination, the sincere and proportionate judgment. A student in the elements gets no such training by studying even a good textbook, though he really master it, nor yet by sitting at the feet of the most admirable lecturer.

If there be any subject which seems fixed and settled in its educational aspects, it is the mathematics; yet there is no department of the university which has been, during the last fifteen years, in such a state of vigorous experiment upon methods and appliances of teaching as the Mathematical Department. It would be well if the primary schools had as much faith in the possibility of improving their way of teaching multiplication.

The important place which history, and mental, moral, and political philosophy should hold in any broad scheme of education is recognized of all; but none know so well how crude are the prevailing methods of teaching these subjects as those who teach them best. They cannot be taught from books alone, but must be vivified and illustrated by teachers of active, comprehensive, and judicial mind. To learn by rote a list of dates is not to study history.

Mr. Emerson says that history is biography. In a deep sense this is true. Certainly, the best way to impart the facts of history to the young is through the quick interest they take in the lives of the men and women who fill great historical scenes or epitomize epochs. From the centers so established, their interest may be spread over great areas. For the young, especially, it is better to enter with intense sympathy into the great moments of history than to stretch a thin attention through its weary centuries.

Philosophical subjects should never be taught with authority. They are not established sciences; they are full of disputed matters, open questions, and bottomless speculations. It is not the function of the teacher to settle philosophical and political controversies for the pupil, or even to recommend to him any one set of opinions as better than another. Exposition, not imposition, of opinions is the professor's part. The student should be made acquainted with all sides of these controversies, with the salient points of each system; he should be shown what is still in force of institutions or philosophies mainly outgrown, and what is new in those now in vogue.

The very word "education" is a standing protest against dogmatic teaching. The notion that education consists in the authoritative inculcation of what the teacher deems true may be logical and appropriate in a convent or a seminary for priests, but it is intolerable in universities and public schools, from primary to professional. The worthy fruit of academic culture is an open mind, trained to careful thinking, instructed in the methods of philosophic investigation, acquainted in a general way with the accumulated thought of past generations, and penetrated with humility. It is thus that the university in our day serves Christ and the church.

THE INCREASING WEIGHT, range, and thoroughness of the examination for admission to college may strike some observers with dismay. The increase of real requisitions is hardly perceptible from year to year; but on looking back ten or twenty years, the changes are marked and all in one direction. The dignity and importance of this examination have been steadily rising, and this rise measures the improvement of the preparatory schools. When the gradual improvement of American schools has lifted them to a level with the German gymnasia, we may expect to see the American college bearing a nearer resemblance to the German faculties of philosophy than it now does.

The actual admission examination may best be compared with the first examination of the University of France. This examination, which comes at the end of a French boy's school life, is for the degree of Bachelor of Arts or of Sciences. The degree is given to young men who come fresh from school and have never been under university teachers; a large part of the recipients never enter the university. The young men who come to our examination for admission to college are older than the average of French Bachelors of Arts. The examination tests not only the capacity of the candidates but also the quality of their school instruction; it is a great event in their lives, though not, as in France, marked by any degree. The examination is conducted by college professors and tutors who have never had any relations whatever with those examined. It would be a great gain if all subsequent college examinations could be as impartially conducted by competent examiners brought from without the college and paid for their services.

When the teacher examines his class, there is no effective examination of the teacher. If the examinations for the scientific, theological, medical, and dental degrees were conducted by independent boards of examiners, appointed by professional bodies of dignity and influence, the significance of these degrees would be greatly enhanced. The same might be said of the degree of Bachelor of Laws, were it not that this degree is, at present, earned by attendance alone and not by attendance and examination.

The American practice of allowing the teaching body to examine for degrees has been partly dictated by the scarcity of men outside the faculties who are at once thoroughly acquainted with the subjects of examination and sufficiently versed in teaching to know what may fairly be expected of both students and instructors. This difficulty could now be overcome. The chief reason, however, for the existence of this practice is that the faculties were the only bodies that could confer degrees intelligently when degrees were obtained by passing through a prescribed course of study without serious checks, and completing a certain term of residence without disgrace. The change in the manner of earning the university degrees ought, by right, to have brought into being an examining body distinct from the teaching body. . . .

The rigorous examination for admission has one good effect throughout the college course: it prevents a waste of instruction upon incompetent persons. A school with a low standard for admission and a high standard of graduation, like West Point, is obliged to dismiss a large proportion of its students by the way. Hence much individual distress and a great waste of resources, both public and private. But, on the other hand, it must not be supposed that every student who enters Harvard College necessarily graduates. Strict annual examinations are to be passed. More than a fourth of those who enter the college fail to take their degree.

Only a few years ago, all students who graduated at this college passed through one uniform curriculum. Every man studied the same subjects in the same proportions, without regard to his natural bent or preference. The individual student had no choice of either subjects or teachers. This system is still the prevailing system among American colleges and finds vigorous defenders. It has the merit of simplicity. So had the school methods of our grandfathers — one primer, one catechism, one rod for all children. On the whole, a single common course of studies, tolerably well-selected to meet the average needs, seems to most Americans a very proper and natural thing, even for grown men.

As a people, we do not apply to mental activities the principle of division of labor; and we have but a halting faith in special training for high professional employments. The vulgar conceit that a Yankee can turn his hand to anything we insensibly carry into high places, where it is preposterous and criminal. We are accustomed to seeing men leap from farm or shop to courtroom or pulpit, and we half believe that common men can safely use the seven-league boots of genius.

What amount of knowledge and experience do we habitually demand of our law-givers? What special training do we ordinarily think necessary for our diplomatists although in great emergencies the nation has known where to turn? Only after years of the bitterest experience did we come to believe the professional training of a soldier to be of value in war. This lack of faith in the prophecy of a natural bent, and in the value of a discipline concentrated upon a single object, amounts to a national danger.

In education, the individual traits of different minds have not been sufficiently attended to. Through all the period of boyhood the school studies should be representative; all the main fields of knowledge should be entered upon. But the young man of nineteen or twenty ought to know what he likes best and is most fit for. If his previous training has been sufficiently wide, he will know by that time whether he is most apt at language or philosophy or natural science or mathematics. If he feels no loves, he will at least have his hates. At that age the teacher may wisely abandon the schooldame's practice of giving a copy of nothing but zeros to the child who alleges that he cannot make that figure.

When the revelation of his own peculiar taste and capacity comes to a young man, let him reverently give it welcome, thank God, and take courage. Thereafter he knows his way to happy, enthusiastic work, and, God willing, to usefulness and success. The civilization of a people may be inferred from the variety of its tools. There are thousands of years between the stone hatchet and the machine shop. As tools multiply, each is more ingeniously adapted to its own exclusive purpose. So with the men that make the state. For the individual, concentration and the highest development of his own peculiar faculty is the only prudence. But for the state, it is variety, not uniformity, of intellectual product which is needful.

These principles are the justification of the system of elective studies which has been gradually developed in this college during the past forty years. At present the freshman year is the only one in which there is a fixed course prescribed for all. In the other three years, more than half the time allotted to study is filled with subjects chosen by each student from lists which comprise six studies in the sophomore year, nine in the junior year, and eleven in the senior year. The range of elective studies is large, though there are some striking deficiencies. The liberty of choice of subject is wide, but yet has very rigid limits.

There is a certain framework which must be filled; and about half the material of the filling is prescribed. The choice offered to the student does not lie between liberal studies and professional or utilitarian studies. All the studies which are open to him are liberal and disciplinary, not narrow or special. Under this system the college does not demand, it is true, one invariable set of studies of every candidate for the first degree in Arts; but its requisitions for this degree are nevertheless high and inflexible, being nothing less than four years devoted to liberal culture.

It has been alleged that the elective system must weaken the bond which unites members of the same class. This is true; but in view of another much more efficient cause of the diminution of class intimacy, the point is not very significant. The increased size of the college classes inevitably works a great change in this respect. One hundred and fifty young men cannot be so intimate with each other as fifty used to be. This increase is progressive. Taken in connection with the rising average age of the students, it would compel the adoption of methods of instruction different from the old, if there were no better motive for such change.

The elective system fosters scholarship because it gives free play to natural preferences and inborn aptitudes, makes possible enthusiasm for a chosen work, relieves the professor and the ardent disciple of the presence of a body of students who are compelled to an unwelcome task, and enlarges instruction by substituting many and various lessons given to small, lively classes, for a few lessons many times repeated to different sections of a numerous class. The college therefore proposes to persevere in its efforts to establish, improve, and extend the elective system. Its administrative difficulties, which seem formidable at first, vanish before a brief experience. . . .

HARVARD COLLEGE has always attracted and still attracts students in all conditions of life. From the city trader or professional man, who may be careless how much his son spends at Cambridge, to the farmer or mechanic, who finds it a hard sacrifice to give his boy his time early enough to enable him to prepare for college, all sorts and conditions of men have wished and still wish to send their sons hither. There are always scores of young men in this university who earn or borrow every dollar they spend here. Every year many young men enter this college without any resources whatever. If they prove themselves men of capacity and character, they never go away for lack of money. More than $20,000 a year is now devoted to aiding students of narrow means to compass their education, besides all the remitted fees and the numerous private benefactions. These latter are unfailing. Taken in connection with the proceeds of the funds applicable to the aid of poor students, they enable the corporation to say that no good student need ever stay away from Cambridge or leave college simply because he is poor.

There is one uniform condition, however, on which help is given: the recipient must be of promising ability and the best character. The community does not owe superior education to all children, but only to the elite — to those who, having the capacity, prove by hard work that they have also the necessary perseverance and endurance. The process of preparing to enter college under the difficulties which poverty entails is just such a test of worthiness as is needed.

At this moment there is no college in the country more eligible for a poor student than Harvard on the mere ground of economy. The scholarship funds are mainly the fruit of the last fifteen years. The future will take care of itself; for it is to be expected that the men who in this generation have had the benefit of these funds, and who succeed in afterlife, will pay manifold to their successors in need the debt which they owe, not to the college but to benefactors whom they cannot even thank, save in heaven.

No wonder that scholarships are founded. What greater privilege than this of giving young men of promise the coveted means of intellectual growth and freedom? The angels of heaven might envy mortals so fine a luxury. The happiness which the winning of a scholarship gives is not the recipient's alone: it flashes back to the home whence he came and gladdens anxious hearts there. The good which it does is not his alone but descends, multiplying at every step, through generations. Thanks to the beneficent mysteries of hereditary transmission, no capital earns such interest as personal culture. The poorest and the richest students are equally welcome here, provided that with their poverty or their wealth they bring capacity, ambition, and purity.

The poverty of scholars is of inestimable worth in this money-getting nation. It maintains the true standards of virtue and honor. The poor friars, not the bishops, saved the church. The poor scholars and preachers of duty defend the modern community against its own material prosperity. Luxury and learning are ill bedfellows. Nevertheless, this college owes much of its distinctive character to those who, bringing hither from refined homes good breeding, gentle tastes, and a manly delicacy, add to them openness and activity of mind, intellectual interests, and a sense of public duty. It is as high a privilege for a rich man's son as for a poor man's to resort to these academic halls and so to take his proper place among cultivated and intellectual men.

To lose altogether the presence of those who in early life have enjoyed the domestic and social advantages of wealth would be as great a blow to the college as to lose the sons of the poor. The interests of the college and the country are identical in this regard. The country suffers when the rich are ignorant and unrefined. Inherited wealth is an unmitigated curse when divorced from culture. Harvard College is sometimes reproached with being aristocratic. If by aristocracy he meant a stupid and pretentious caste, founded on wealth, and birth, and an affectation of European manners, no charge could be more preposterous: the college is intensely American in affection and intensely democratic in temper.

But there is an aristocracy to which the sons of Harvard have belonged and, let us hope, will ever aspire to belong — the aristocracy which excels in manly sports, carries off the honors and prizes of the learned professions, and bears itself with distinction in all fields of intellectual labor and combat; the aristocracy which in peace stands firmest for the public honor and renown, and in war rides first into the murderous thickets.

THE ATTITUDE OF THE UNIVERSITY in the prevailing discussions touching the education and fit employments of women demands brief explanation. America is the natural arena for these debates; for here the female sex has a better past and a better present than elsewhere. Americans, as a rule, hate disabilities of all sorts, whether religious, political, or social. Equality between the sexes, without privilege or oppression on either side, is the happy custom of American homes. While this great discussion is going on, it is the duty of the university to maintain a cautious and expectant policy.

The corporation will not receive women as students into the college proper, nor into any school whose discipline requires residence near the school. The difficulties involved in a common residence of hundreds of young men and women of immature character and marriageable age are very grave. The necessary police regulations are exceedingly burdensome. The corporation are not influenced to this decision, however, by any crude notions about the innate capacities of women. The world knows next to nothing about the natural mental capacities of the female sex. Only after generations of civil freedom and social equality will it be possible to obtain the data necessary for an adequate discussion of woman's natural tendencies, tastes, and capabilities.

Again, the corporation do not find it necessary to entertain a confident opinion upon the fitness or unfitness of women for professional pursuits. It is not the business of the university to decide this mooted point. In this country the university does not undertake to protect the community against incompetent lawyers, ministers, or doctors. The community must protect itself by refusing to employ such. Practical, not theoretical, considerations determine the policy of the university. Upon a matter concerning which prejudices are deep and opinion inflammable and experience scanty, only one course is prudent or justifiable when such great interests are at stake — that of cautious and well-considered experiment.

The practical problem is to devise a safe, promising, and instructive experiment. Such an experiment the corporation have meant to try in opening the newly established University Courses of Instruction to competent women. In these courses the university offers to young women, who have been to good schools, as many years as they wish of liberal culture in studies which have no direct professional value, to be sure, but which enrich and enlarge both intellect and character.

The university hopes thus to contribute to the intellectual emancipation of women. It hopes to prepare some women better than they would otherwise have been prepared for the profession of teaching, the one learned profession to which women have already acquired a clear title. It hopes that the proffer of this higher instruction will have some reflex influence upon schools for girls — to discourage superficiality and to promote substantial education. . . .

WHAT CAN THE COMMUNITY DO for the university? It can love, honor, and cherish it. Love it and honor it. The university is upheld by this public affection and respect. In the loyalty of her children she finds strength and courage. The corporation, the overseers, and the several faculties need to feel that the leaders of public opinion, and especially the sons of the college, are at their back, always ready to give them a generous and intelligent support. Therefore we welcome the chief magistrate of the commonwealth, the senators, judges, and other dignitaries of the state, who by their presence at this ancient ceremonial bear witness to the pride which Massachusetts feels in her eldest university. Therefore we rejoice in the presence of this throng of the alumni testifying their devotion to the college which, through all changes, is still their home. Cherish it.

This university, though rich among American colleges, is very poor in comparison with the great universities of Europe.

The wants of the American community have far outgrown the capacity of the university to supply them. We must try to satisfy the cravings of the select few as well as the needs of the average many. We cannot afford to neglect the fine arts. We need groves and meadows as well as barracks; and soon there will be no chance to get them in this expanding city. But, above all, we need professorships, books, and apparatus, that teaching and scholarship may abound.

And what will the university do for the community? First, it will make a rich return of learning, poetry, and piety. Second, it will foster the sense of public duty — that great virtue which makes republics possible. The founding of Harvard College was an heroic act of public spirit. For more than a century the breath of life was kept in it by the public spirit of the province and of its private benefactors. In the last fifty years the public spirit of the friends of the college has quadrupled its endowments.

And how have the young men nurtured here in successive generations repaid the founders for their pious care? Have they honored freedom and loved their country? For answer we appeal to the records of the national service; to the lists of the Senate, the Cabinet, and the diplomatic service, and to the rolls of the army and navy. Honored men, here present, illustrate before the world the public quality of the graduates of this college. Theirs is no mercenary service. Other fields of labor attract them more and would reward them better; but they are filled with the noble ambition to deserve well of the republic.

There have been doubts, in times yet recent, whether culture were not selfish; whether men of refined tastes and manners could really love liberty and be ready to endure hardness for her sake; whether, in short, gentlemen would in this century prove as loyal to noble ideas as in other times they had been to kings. In yonder old playground, fit spot whereon to commemorate the manliness which there was nurtured, shall soon rise a noble monument which for generations will give convincing answer to such shallow doubts; for over its gates will be written: "In memory of the sons of Harvard who died for their country." The future of the university will not be unworthy of its past.

———◆———

There is a sumptuous variety about the New England weather that compels the stranger's admiration — and regret. The weather is always doing something there; always attending strictly to business; always getting up new designs and trying them on the people to see how they will go. But it gets through more business in spring than in any other season. In the spring I have counted one hundred and thirty-six different kinds of weather inside of four-and-twenty hours.

SAMUEL L. CLEMENS ("MARK TWAIN")

43.

HENRY ADAMS: The Constitution and Civil Service Reform

It was a common political practice throughout the nineteenth century to make political appointments on the basis of party affiliation after an election was won. The practice, which came to be called the "spoils system" (perhaps because of the famous remark of Senator William Marcy of New York in 1832, that "to the victor belong the spoils"), enabled parties to build the strong political machines that became so familiar as the century wore on. Despite its practical advantages for the support of the party system, the possibilities for scandal and corruption in such a practice were — and of course still are — enormous. Abuses in the patronage system had become so obvious by the Civil War that reform groups throughout the country began to call for legislation that would place the civil service on a merit basis. One of the voices heard was that of Henry Adams, who wrote an article on the subject for the North American Review *in 1869. Portions of the article are reprinted here.*

Source: *North American Review,* October 1869: "Civil-Service Reform."

"IN THE GOVERNMENT of this commonwealth, the legislative department shall never exercise the executive and judicial powers, or either of them; the executive shall never exercise the legislative and judicial powers, or either of them; the judicial shall never exercise the legislative and executive powers, or either of them: *to the end it may be a government of laws and not of men.*"

The Massachusetts Bill of Rights, which contains this article, inimitable for grasp and conciseness, adds elsewhere the warning that among the precautions absolutely necessary for the maintenance of a free government is a frequent recurrence to the fundamental principles of the Constitution. Laying aside, therefore, the usual arguments in favor of civil service reform — arguments drawn from finance or from administrative convenience — this essay will attempt to show that the soundness and vigor, nay, even the purpose, of the reform movement must depend upon its recurrence to the fundamental principles of the Constitution.

When President Grant took the oath of office, he held in his hands a greater power than any President chosen for many years past, or likely to be chosen for many years to come. Turn which way he liked, it was supposed that a majority of the people was ready to lend him its support. . . . It was commonly supposed that the new President had determined, even before the inauguration, on his course in regard to the civil service. . . .

A stranger, who looked at the national institutions with the old assumption that the voice of the people guides the course of the government, would have thought nothing more easy than for the President to lift his administration, by a single touch, out of the mire of political corruption. Perhaps the President himself shared in this belief.

At all events, the most natural explanation of his first proceedings is to be found in some such idea. He selected a Cabinet which seemed to have but one bond of sympathy, and this one bond the common freedom from political entanglement. The wish to escape party dictation was more evident than the means of doing so were well chosen. The attempt failed, and the President yielded to political pressure so far as to make a new selection; but even after this partial check, the Cabinet contained only one member who was distinctly a representative rather of the Republican Party than of the Republican sentiment of the country.

The Cabinet once formed, it became necessary to establish a rule in regard to inferior appointments. Here, too, the popular expectation turned out to be well-founded. Instructions were duly given to the effect that there should be no sweeping and partisan changes. Removals from office might indeed be made in cases of incompetence or misbehavior, or for reasons of economy, or even where extreme partisanship had compromised the loyalty due to the government, but no general proscription on account of political opinions was to be authorized. This was the principle laid down by the President to the members of his Cabinet for the rule of the departments — a principle sound, just, and popular, which deserved and in the end would probably have received universal applause.

How was it that this rule was not carried into effect? . . . Nothing could be easier than to announce that faithful and competent servants of the government should not be disturbed, but nothing was more difficult than to maintain the promise. In the struggle which followed, the President stood alone. The great mass of his friends, who cared nothing for office or patronage, could neither see what was going forward nor could they lend him encouragement or support. They only knew that General Grant, penned up in the White House, was surrounded by a hungry army of political adventurers whose trade was an object of popular odium or contempt.

Had the army of office seekers marched alone against the White House, General Grant would probably have routed it, large as it was, with the utmost ease. Such men might fret him, but they would have found

him a difficult instrument to play upon. They came, therefore, supported on one side by all the personal influence, on the other by all the political power they could control; and day after day the whole phalanx flung itself upon the President. Escape was impossible.

There are many things that a President cannot evade and among the first of these is the duty of listening with patience and replying with courtesy to the leading men of his party. A senator may be tedious, ill-mannered, and a notorious rogue, but the double majesty of state and Senate speaks from his lips and commands a hearing. . . .

The early administrations, from the time of Washington to the time of Jackson, were, in spite of all political differences, practically one continuous government; that is, the President, whoever he might be, stood as regarded the legislature and the political parties as merely the temporary head of a permanent executive system, which was meant to furnish, and did in fact furnish, the necessary solidity and continuity without which no government can last. The President represented not a party nor even the people, either in a mass or in any of its innumerable divisions, but an essential part of the frame of government; that part which was neither legislature nor judiciary; a part which, in the nature of society, must of necessity exist — which in the United States was intentionally and wisely made a system by itself in order to balance the other portions of the structure.

The President might die, but the office could not be vacant. He might be sent back to private life, but his successor took up the instruments which he laid down. He might be incompetent as a British king, but the permanent system of which he represented the power and the wisdom would save him from contempt. He might be unprincipled as a French emperor, but the established courses of administration, more powerful than mere law, would hold his hand. The five early Presidents accepted and maintained this position to their own advantage and to that of the country.

Nor did President Jackson essentially change it. He introduced, it is true, the rule of punishing officials whose only duty was to the government for holding opinions which were hurtful only to himself, if they were hurtful at all; but his very attitude toward the Senate implied a high sense of his official duty, and so long as his strong hand guided the executive system it was maintained in all its power, if not in all its dignity. When he passed away, however, and a succession of weaker men assumed his place, the effects of his example were little by little drawn into service to break down this bulwark of the executive.

By an unwritten law of the Constitution, which has seldom been found at fault, the nervous system of the great extra-constitutional party organizations finds its center in the United States Senate. As the party organizations grew in development and strength, the Senate became more and more the seat of their intrigues; and when the party organizations discovered that their power would be greatly increased by controlling the executive patronage, the Senate lent all its overruling influence to effect this result, and soon became, through its individual members, the largest dispenser of this patronage.

This was, however, only the first step. Mr. Marcy's celebrated declaration, drawn from the sink of New York politics, "To the victor belong the spoils," was mischievous, but it was not fatal. The President had always been in the habit of consulting friendly senators and representatives in regard to special appointments, and when he now broke down the permanence and dignity of that administrative system of which he ought to have been the champion, he only admitted individual members of the legislature to a wider influence in executive patronage than they had hitherto enjoyed.

But the movement could not stop here. When it was that Congress first began to claim as a right the nominating power which it had until then held as a favor is a question difficult to answer with exactness, but at all events the concession has been made within the last ten years. It may be safe to say, on the authority of a person well informed as to the history of times in which he has acted a great part, that the assumption by members of Congress of local patronage as a right was first conceded in principle by the first administration of Mr. Lincoln, in 1861. . . . Mr. Lincoln's death was the accidental cause of bringing the evil to a head, and if anyone is curious to follow the exact process by which this poison of executive power works in corrupting a legislature and a people, it is only necessary to watch what has since occurred.

Since the foundation of the government, there has been no scandal and no corruption which could be compared in its mischievous effects to the disgraceful bargaining for office which took place between President Johnson and the Senate. Even the men who shared in it were ashamed. No one has a word of defense for it. This attempt on the part of the legislature to exercise the executive power has produced in Congress and in the country an indifference to strict rules of wrong and right, a contempt for personal dignity, a cynical assumption of official dishonesty, and a patient assent to the supposed necessity of corruption, which nothing but a great popular reaction can overcome. . . .

Thus, when General Grant came into power, the executive, which had originally been organized as a permanent system with a permanent and independent existence and a temporary head, was wholly changed in its nature. . . . General Grant, therefore, whether he knew it or not, was attempting a far more serious reform than any mere improvement of the civil service implies, a reform in comparison with which the proposed saving of $100 million a year to the treasury was but a trifle. . . .

Before a week had passed it had become clear that the President's perseverance in his attempt would provoke a personal rupture with so many members of the legislature, and secret hostility in so many more, as to endanger the success of the administration. The President gave way. Then began those cruel scenes which for months reduced the city of Washington to such a condition as is caused by an ordinary pestilence or famine. . . .

The Grand Army of the Republic was not perhaps organized as a political association. Its nominal object was rather one of charity, and it is believed to have proved useful in lending its protection or assistance to soldiers and soldiers' families in distress. As a charitable and useful society, it contains many members of the highest character; and its chief, General Logan, has done good service to the country, and deserves respect for it. But whether the original organization was intended to be political or not, it certainly plunged into politics very soon after its existence began; and by the time General Grant entered office, it had already reached the lowest level of political activity.

Under the pretense of clearing Rebels from the public service, it organized within the departments an elaborate system of espionage, such as the American government had never yet been degraded enough to cover with its protection. The history of every clerk, from the highest to the lowest, was ransacked to obtain evidence of his political opinions; and everyone who fell under suspicion was watched, his words taken down, even his looks carefully noted. The evidence thus collected was duly reported to the proper authorities of the organization, and the officers of the Grand Army of the Republic, on the strength of this testimony,

secretly acquired by means which were once thought disgraceful, then made a formal demand upon the United States government, through the heads of departments, denouncing, like Jacobins of the Reign of Terror, the criminals thus condemned without a hearing, and demanding their removal for the benefit of soldiers of the Grand Army. . . .

[The] difficulty of dividing responsibility between the executive and the legislature is one which is too serious to exist long. The country has now arrived at a point where it must either go back or go forward. The great executive authority established by the Constitution as the counterpoise of the great legislative authority has gradually abandoned, first, that character as a permanent and regular system which served as the defense of weak Presidents; second, the right of nomination to executive offices which belong within the constituencies of members of the legislature; and finally, it only remains to adopt a measure, formally urged in the last session of Congress, by which the entire patronage of the executive may be allotted between the several states in *pro rata* proportions, and then the legislature will have grasped the whole executive power, leaving in its place only the empty honor of a name.

The experience of the present government has shown that even a President so determined in character and so strong in popular support as General Grant shrank from the attempt to reform the civil service as one which was beyond his powers. Not only has this opportunity been lost — an opportunity which may never occur again — but the Republican Party by its action in this case seems to have shut the door to reform. Had General Grant succeeded in carrying out his original purpose, public opinion might have been roused to enforce the precedent on future administrations.

But it is difficult to understand how any

Republican member of Congress can now propose a measure of reform, which, if worth consideration at all, must, by securing the permanence of present officeholders, practically jockey any future administration out of its power. And it is equally difficult to see why any future Democratic President should consider himself bound by such a law. Nothing remains but to act outside of all party organizations and to appeal with all the earnestness that the emergency requires, not to Congress nor to the President but to the people, to return to the first principles of the government and to shut off forever this source of corruption in the state.

44.

Against Religious Exercises in Public Schools

The case of John D. Minor et al. *v.* The Board of Education of the City of Cincinnati et al. *was instituted in the Superior Court of Cincinnati on November 26, 1869. The case stemmed from a motion put to the Board of Education to suspend the practice of daily readings from the King James Bible in the public schools of that city. A campaign of public pressure against the motion quickly developed, but the Board passed it by a vote of 23 to 15 at its November meeting. Protestants immediately filed an injunction to restrain the Board. The document that follows is the Board's reply to the suit. The Superior Court, in a 2 to 1 decision, issued the injunction against the Board. In a dissenting opinion, Judge Alphonso Taft answered Protestant charges that the Board of Education had showed itself hostile to the Bible: "The Bible is not banished, nor is religion degraded or abused," he declared. "The Board have simply aimed to free the common schools from any just conscientious objections, by confining them to secular instruction." Taft's opinion was sustained by the Ohio Supreme Court in 1873.*

Source: *The Bible in the Public Schools. Arguments in the Case of John D. Minor et al., etc. etc.,* Cincinnati, 1870, pp. 12-15.

THE BOARD OF EDUCATION of the city of Cincinnati, the city of Cincinnati and W. J. O'Neil *et al.,* defendants in the above-entitled action, in answer to the petition, say:

That it is true that on the 1st day of November, 1869, said Board of Education passed the resolutions in said petition set forth; that these defendants also believe it to be true that the rule abrogated by said resolutions was adopted by the Board of Trustees and Visitors of the Common Schools in 1852.

That it is also true that the version of the Bible generally in use in the common schools of Cincinnati is that known as King James' Version; that these defendants are not informed as to the truth of the allegation in the petition respecting the action of the School Board in 1842, but that if said allegation be true, the rule claimed in the petition to have been adopted in 1842 has long since ceased to be acted upon or to be recognized as of binding force, the same not being found among the standing rules published and promulgated by the School

Board, or Board of Education, during the last twenty-five years; that the sole version of the Bible which has been read in the common schools at any time within the knowledge of the defendants is that known and described in the petition as the King James' Version.

That it is true that there are books other than the Bible now in use in the common schools of Cincinnati which contain passages and selections from the Bible, and from writings inculcating truths which by many persons are designated as religious truths, but that such books are not religious books and are not used for the purpose of conveying religious instruction; that these defendants believe it to be true that a number of children who are educated in the common schools receive no religious instruction or knowledge of the Bible except that communicated in said schools; that while the defendants do not deny that religious instruction is necessary and indispensable to fit said children to be good citizens of the state of Ohio and of the United States, they deny that such instruction can or ought to be imparted in the schools established by the state.

And these defendants say that it is true that the individuals named as defendants, are, with the exception of W. F. Hurlbut, members of said Board of Education, duly elected and qualified, and that said W. F. Hurlbut is clerk of said Board, and that his duties are correctly described in the petition; and these defendants deny each and every other allegation of the petition which is not hereinbefore admitted.

And said defendants, further answering, say that the citizens of Cincinnati, who are taxed for the support of the schools under the management of said Board of Education, and all of whom are equally entitled to the benefits thereof by having their children instructed therein, are very much divided in opinion and practice upon matters connected with religious belief, worship, and education; that a considerable number

thereof are Israelites, who reject the Christian religion altogether and believe only in the inspired truth of what is known as the Old Testament, and this only in the original Hebrew tongue, and such other religious truths and worship as are perpetuated in their body by tradition.

That, also, many of said citizens do not believe the writings embraced in the Bible to be entitled to be considered as containing an authoritative declaration of religious truth; that a still greater number of said citizens, together with their children, are members of the Roman Catholic Church and conscientiously believe in its doctrines, faith, and forms of worship; and that by said church the version of the Scriptures referred to in the petition is taught and believed to be incorrect as a translation and incomplete by reason of its omission of a part of the books held by such church to be an integral portion of the inspired canon.

And, furthermore, that the Scriptures ought not to be read indiscriminately, inasmuch as said church has divine authority as the only infallible teacher and interpreter of the same, and that the reading of the same without note or comment and without being properly expounded by the only authorized teachers and interpreters thereof is not only not beneficial to the children in said schools but likely to lead to the adoption of dangerous errors, irreligious faith, practice, and worship.

And that by reason thereof the practice of reading the King James' Version of the Bible, commonly and only received as inspired and true by the Protestant religious sects, in the presence and hearing of Roman Catholic children, is regarded by the members of the Roman Catholic Church as contrary to their rights of conscience; and that such practice as heretofore pursued has had the necessary effect to prevent the attendance of large numbers of children of those who are members of said church, who, in consequence thereof, have erected and now maintain separate schools at their own expense, in which there are enrolled and taught a number — about two-thirds of the number of those who are enrolled and taught in the schools under the management of said Board of Education.

That also there are other religious sects and denominations and bodies of citizens who either do not regard the Bible as the authoritative source of religious truth or who regard themselves as possessed of the only true sense thereof; that, furthermore, a large number of persons in this community who are ready and qualified to act as teachers in said public schools object to the reading of the Bible in the version in use (or, indeed, in any version without note or comment) on conscientious grounds and are thereby precluded from employment as teachers in said schools.

That in consideration of these facts, said Board of Education has concluded that it was not possible for it to take upon itself any instruction in religion, and that it is neither right nor expedient to continue in use in said public schools the reading of any version of the Bible as a religious exercise, or any other religious exercise whatever, and, therefore, has passed the resolutions now complained of by the plaintiffs.

These defendants pray to be dismissed with their costs.

45.

FRANCIS PARKMAN: The Diffusion of Education and the Degradation of Culture

Francis Parkman, member of a distinguished New England family, was educated at Harvard University and then attempted to improve his frail health by undertaking a strenuous journey over the Oregon Trail. The trip led him to write what was to become the classic account of the trail. The work, which was followed by his histories of the French and English struggles in the New World, established him as one of America's greatest historians. Parkman championed the values of traditional education in the following essay, written in response to charges by exponents of popular culture that scholarship was unproductive.

Source: *Nation*, December 23, 1869: "The Tale of the 'Ripe Scholar.'"

NOT MANY YEARS AGO, a certain traditional prestige, independent of all considerations of practical utility, attached to the scholastic character, at least in New England where the clergy long held a monopoly of what passed for learning. New England colleges were once little more than schools for making ministers. As the clergyman has lost in influence, so the scholar has lost in repute, and the reasons are not hard to find. The really good scholars were exceptions, and very rare ones. In the matter of theology some notable results were produced, but secular scholarship was simply an exotic and a sickly one. It never recovered from its transplantation and drew no vital juices from the soil. The climate was hostile to it.

All the vigor of the country drifted into practical pursuits, and the New England man of letters, when he happened not to be a minister, was usually some person whom constitutional defects, bodily or mental, had unfitted for politics or business. He was apt to be a recluse, ignorant of the world, bleached by a close room and an iron stove, never breathing the outer air when he could help it, and resembling a medieval monk in his scorn of the body, or rather in his utter disregard of it. Sometimes he was reputed a scholar merely because he was nothing else. The products of his mind were as pallid as the hue of his face, and, like their parent, void of blood, bone, sinew, muscle, and marrow.

That he should be provincial was, for a long time, inevitable; but that he was emasculate was chiefly his own fault. As his scholarship was not fruitful of any very valuable results, as it did not make itself felt in the living world that ranged around it, as, in short, it showed no vital force, it began at length to be regarded as a superfluous excrescence. Nevertheless, like the monkish learning of the Middle Ages, it served a good purpose in keeping alive the tradition of liberal culture against a future renaissance.

We shall be told that we exaggerate, and, in one sense, this is true; for we describe not an individual but a type, from which, however, the reality was rarely very remote and with which it was sometimes identified. The most finished and altogether favorable example of this devitalized scholarship, with many graceful additions, was Edward Everett; and its echoes may still be heard in the halls of Congress, perplexing Western members with Latin quotations — profuse, if not always correct.

As the nation grew in importance and in sensitiveness, the want of intellectual productiveness began to trouble the popular pride, and an impatient public called on its authors to be "original." Spasmodic efforts were made to respond, and the results were such as may be supposed. The mountain went into convulsions of labor and produced a mouse, or something as ridiculous. After an analogous fashion, some of the successors of our pallid, clerical scholars

raise the cry, "Let us be strong," and fall into the moral and physical gymnastics of muscular Christianity. This, certainly, is no bad sign, insofar as it indicates the consciousness of a want; but neither originality nor force can be got up to order. They must spring from a deeper root and grow by laws of their own. Happily, our soil has begun to put forth such a growth, promising in quality but as yet, in quantity and in maturity, wholly inadequate to the exigent need.

In times of agitation, alive with engrossing questions of pressing moment, when all is astir with pursuit and controversy, when some are mad for gold, and some are earnest and some rabid for this cause or for that, the scholarship of the past is naturally pronounced not up with the times. Despite his manifold failings, "the self-made man," with his palatial mansion, his exploits in the gold room, in the caucus, on the stump, in Congress, and in the presidential chair, flatters popular self-love and fills the public eye. Only a slight reason is wanted for depreciating the scholar, and a strong one is offered. Because the culture which our colleges supplied, and which too many of them still supply, was weak, thin, and unsuitable, it was easy to depreciate all culture. By culture we mean development, not polish or adornment, though these are its natural and by no means useless belongings.

Using the word, then, in this sense, culture is with us a supreme necessity, not for the profit of a few but of all. The presence of minds highly and vigorously developed is the most powerful aid to popular education and the necessary condition of its best success. In a country where the ruling power is public opinion, it is above all things necessary that the best and maturest thought should have a fair share in forming it. Such thought cannot exist in any force in the community without propagating its own image, and a class of strong thinkers is the palladium of democracy. They are the natural enemies of ignorant, ostentatious, and

Daguerreotype of Francis Parkman

aggressive wealth, and the natural friends of all that is best in the popular heart. They are sure of the hatred of charlatans, demagogues, and political sharpers. They are the only hope of our civilization; without them it is a failure, a mere platitude of mediocrity, stagnant or turbid, as the case may be.

The vastest aggregate of average intelligences can do nothing to supply their place, and even material growth is impeded by an ignorance of its conditions and laws. If we may be forgiven the metaphor, our civilization is at present a creature with a small and feeble head, a large, muscular, and active body, and a tail growing at such a rate that it threatens to become unmanageable and shake the balance of the vital powers.

The tendency of a partial education, such as the best popular education must of necessity be, is to produce an excess of self-confidence; and one of its results in this country is a prodigious number of persons who think, and persuade others to think, that they know everything necessary to be known and are fully competent to form opinions and make speeches upon all questions whatever. As these are precisely the persons who make the most noise on the most momentous questions of the day, who have the most listeners and admirers, and who hold each other up as shining examples for imitation, their incompetency becomes a public evil of the first magnitude. If rash and ignorant theorizing, impulsive outcries, and social and political charlatanry of all sorts are to have the guiding of our craft, then farewell to the hope that her voyage will be a success.

The remedy is to infuse into the disordered system the sedative and tonic of a broad knowledge and a vigorous reason. This means to invigorate and extend the higher education; to substitute for the effete and futile scholasticism which the popular mind justly holds in slight account, an energetic and manly development, trained to grapple with the vast questions of the present, and strong enough in numbers as well as quality to temper with its mature thought the rashness of popular speculation. Our best colleges are moving hopefully in this direction; none of them with more life and vigor than the oldest of them all. The present generation will see an increase in the number of our really efficient thinkers, but it is a positive not a relative increase, and is far behind the fast increasing need. Powerful causes are at work against it, and we will try to explain what, to our thinking, some of these causes are.

Perhaps the most obvious of them is the ascendancy of material interests among us. To the great mass of our population, the clearing of lands, the acquiring of new territory, the building of cities, the multiplication of railroads, steamboats, and telegraph lines, the growth of trade and manufactures, the opening of mines, with the resulting fine houses, fine clothes, and sumptuous fare, constitute the real sum and substance of progress and civilization. Art, literature, philosophy, and science — so far as science has no direct bearing on material interests — are regarded as decorations, agreeable and creditable but not essential. In other words, the material basis of civilization is accepted for the entire structure.

A prodigious number of persons think that money-making is the only serious business of life, and there is no corresponding number who hold a different faith. There are not a few among us who would "improve" our colleges into schools of technology, where young men may be trained with a view mainly to the production of more steamboats, railroads, and telegraphs; more breadstuffs; more iron, copper, silver, and gold; more cottons and woolens; and, consequently, more fine houses and fine clothes. All this is very well, but it does not answer the great and crying need of the time. The truth is, our material growth so greatly exceeds our other growth that the body politic suffers from diseases of repletion. A patient bloated with generous living, and marked already with the eruptions of a perverted, diseased blood, is not to be cured solely by providing him with more food.

The drift toward material activity is so powerful among us that it is very difficult for a young man to resist it; and the difficulty increases in proportion as his nature is active and energetic. Patient and devoted study is rarely long continued in the vortex of American life. The dusty arena of competition and strife has fascinations almost irresistible to one conscious of his own vigor. Intellectual tastes may, however, make a compromise. Journalism and the lecture room offer them a field midway between the solitude of the study and the bustle of the world of business; but the journal and the lecture room have influences powerfully adverse to solid, mature, and independent thinking. There, too, is the pulpit, for those who have a vocation that way; but in this, also, a mighty and increasing temptation besets the conscientious student. As for politics, they have fallen to such a pass that the men are rare who can mingle in them without deteriorating.

Paradoxical as it may seem, the diffusion of education and intelligence is at present acting against the free development of the highest education and intelligence. Many have hoped and still hope that by giving a partial teaching to great numbers of persons, a stimulus would be applied to the best minds among them and a thirst for knowledge awakened which would lead to high results; but thus far these results have not equaled the expectation. There has been a vast expenditure of brick and mortar for educational purposes, and, what is more to the purpose, many excellent and faithful teachers of both sexes have labored diligently in their vocation; but the system of competitive cramming in our public schools has not borne fruits on which we have much cause to congratulate ourselves. It has produced an immense number of readers; but what thinkers are to be found may be said to exist in spite of it.

The public school has put money in abundance into the pockets of the dealers in sensation stories, sensation illustrated papers, and all the swarm of trivial, sickly, and rascally literature. From this and cheap newspapers, thousands — nay, millions — draw all their mental improvement and pamper their mental stomachs with adulterated, not to say poisoned, sweetmeats, till they have neither desire nor digestion for strong and wholesome food. But we would speak rather of that truly intelligent and respectable public which forms the auditories of popular preachers and popular lecturers, which is the lavish patron of popular periodical literature, which interests itself in the questions of the day, and has keen mental appetites of a certain kind. This public is strong in numbers and very strong in collective wealth. Its voice can confer celebrity, if not reputation; and it can enrich those who win its favor. In truth, it is the American people.

Now, what does this great public want? It is, in the main, busied with the active work of life, and though it thinks a little and feels a great deal on matters which ought to engage the attention of every self-governing people, yet it is impatient of continuous and cool attention to anything but its daily business, and sometimes even to that. Indeed, the exciting events of the last ten years, joined to the morbid stimulus applied to all departments of business, have greatly increased this tendency; and today there are fewer serious and thoughtful readers than in the last decade. More than ever before, the public demands elocution rather than reason of those who address it; something to excite the feelings and captivate the fancy rather than something to instruct the understanding. It rejoices in sweeping statements, confident assertions, bright lights, and black shadows alternating with something funny.

Neither does it care much for a terse, idiomatic, and pointed diction, but generally prefers the flatulent periods of the ready writers. On matters of the greatest interest it craves to be excited or amused. Lectures professing to instruct are turned to a tissue of jokes, and the pulpit itself is sometimes enlivened after a similar fashion. The pill must be sugared and the food highly seasoned, for the public mind is in a state of laxity and needs a tonic. But the public taste is very exacting, and it offers great and tempting rewards to those who please it.

That which pleases it pays so much better in money and notoriety, and is so much cheaper of production, than the better article which does not please it that the temptation to accept light work and high wages in place of hard work and low wages is difficult to resist. Nothing but a deep love of truth or of art can stand unmoved against it. In our literary markets, educated tastes are completely outridden by uneducated or half-educated tastes, and the commodity is debased accordingly. Thus, the editor of a magazine may be a man of taste and talents; but his interests as a man of letters and his interests as a man of business are not the same. "Why don't you make your magazine what it ought to be?" we once asked of a well-known editor. "Because," he replied, "if we did, we should lose four-fifths of our circulation." A noted preacher not long ago confessed to us that the temptation to give his audience the sort of preaching which they liked to hear, instead of that which it was best that they should hear, was almost irresistible.

The amount of what we have been saying is that the public which demands a second-rate article is so enormously large in comparison with the public which demands a first-rate article that it impairs the quality of literary production and exercises an influence adverse to the growth of intellectual eminence. Now, what is the remedy? It seems to us to be twofold. First, to direct popular education, not to stuffing the mind with crude aggregations of imperfect knowledge but rather to the development of its powers of observation, comparison, analysis, and reasoning; to strengthening and instructing its moral sense, and leading it to self-knowledge and consequent modesty. All this, no doubt, is vastly more difficult and far less showy in its results than the present system of competitive cramming, and requires in its teachers a high degree of good sense and sound instruction.

The other remedy consists in a powerful reenforcement of the higher education and the consequent development of a class of persons, whether rich or poor, so well-instructed and so numerous as to hold their ground against charlatanry, and propagate sound and healthy thought through the community. He who gives or bequeaths money to a well-established and wisely conducted university confers a blessing which radiates through all the ranks of society. He does a service eminently practical and constitutes himself the patron of the highest and best utilitarianism.

1870

46.

Negro National Labor Union Platform

At the third annual convention of the National Labor Union, held in Philadelphia in August 1869, nine African American delegates made a strong appeal for including the protection of African American workers in the Union's program. One of the men, Isaac Myers, of the Colored Caulkers' Trades' Union Society, made a plea for unity among white and black workers. Since no real action followed the rather mild resolutions of the meeting, there was formed in Washington, D.C., in December 1869, a Negro National Labor Union with Myers as its president. The new union issued the following platform on January 1, 1870, closely following the resolutions of the National Labor Union, but with greater emphasis on education and on equal rights of black and white laborers to jobs.

Source: *Working Man's Advocate*, January 1, 1870 [Commons, IX, pp. 247-253].

Whereas, labor has its privileges no less than its duties, one of which is to organize, and, if need be, to furnish reasons for its organization; therefore,

Resolved, that labor was instituted by Almighty God as a means of revealing the rich endowments of inanimate creation to be understood and used by man, and that labor is a duty common to and the natural heritage of the human family, each person having a natural right to labor in any field of industry for which he or she is capacitated, the rights to be governed and restricted only by laws of political economy.

Resolved, that capital is an agent or means used by labor for its development and support, and labor is an agent or means used by capital for its development and general enhancement; and that for the well-being and productiveness of capital and labor, the best harmony of fellowship and action should at all times prevail, that "strikes" may be avoided and the workman convinced that justice is done him, and that he is receiving an equivalent for the labor performed.

Resolved, that there should be a frequent interchange of opinions upon all questions affecting alike the employer and employed, and that cooperation for the purpose of protection and the better remuneration of labor is a sure and safe method, invading no specific rights, but is alike beneficial to the whole community and tends to elevate the working classes to higher achievements and positions in society; presents the necessity of and increases the desire to give their children a more liberal education; induces the practice of economy in the distribution of their earnings; and accelerates the accumulation of wealth, with all the happiness which must necessarily ensue therefrom.

Resolved, that intemperance is the natural foe and curse of the American family, especially the working classes, its terrible effects being to disease, corrupt, and otherwise disfigure and destroy the constitution, producing vice, crime, and poverty where peace and plenty would otherwise exist.

Resolved, that education is one of the strongest safeguards of the Republican Party, the bulwark of American citizens, and a defense against the invasion of the rights of man; its liberal distributions to all, without regard to race, creed, or sex, is necessary for the well-being and advancement of society, and that all should enjoy its blessing alike in each of the states and territories of the United States; that educated labor is more productive, is worth and commands higher rates of wages, is less dependent upon capital; therefore, it is essentially necessary to the rapid and permanent development of the agricultural, manufacturing, and mechanical growth and interests of the nation that there shall be a liberal free-school system enacted by the legislatures of the several states for the benefit of all the inhabitants thereof.

Resolved, that the government of the United States, republican in form, is a government of the people, for the people, and by the people; and that all men are equal in political rights and entitled to the largest political and religious liberty compatible with the good order of society; as, also, the use and enjoyment of the fruits of their labor and talents; and that no laws should be made by any legislative body to the advantage of one class and against the interest and advantage of the other, but that all leg-islation for the benefit of all the people of any particular state, and of the United States, to the end that loyalty to and love for the institutions and the government of the United States should be a permanent consideration with all the citizens thereof.

Resolved, that we return our thanks to Divine Providence for the immense natural resources that are within the geographical limits of the United States of America, whereby the application of diligent and patient labor is capable of producing from our earth all the necessities for human existence and the comfort of man, and from its vast and unbounded supply has become the greatest moral agent known to man, in that it affords a refuge for the oppressed of all lands to improve their condition, and, by the influence of our institutions, elevate them to their proper standard of manhood; its rebounding influence is to destroy the tyranny and despotism of the Old World.

Resolved, that we feel it to be a duty that we owe to ourselves, to society, and to our country to encourage by all means within our reach industrial habits among our people, the learning of trades and professions by our children without regard to sex; to educate and impress them with the fact that all labor is honorable and a sure road to wealth; that habits of economy and temperance combined with industry and education are the great safeguard of free republican institutions, the elevator of the condition of man, the motive power to increase trade and commerce, and to make the whole of this land the wealthiest and happiest on the face of the globe.

Resolved, that regarding the labor of the country, the common property of the people, no portion should be excluded therefrom because of the geographical division of the globe in which they or their forefathers were born, or on account of status or color, but that every man or woman should receive employment according to his or her ability to perform the labor required, without any other test; that the exclusion of colored men and apprentices from the right to labor in any department of industry or workshops, in any of the states and territories of the United States, by what is known as "trade unions," is an insult to God, injury to us, and disgrace to humanity; while we extend a free and welcome hand to the free immigration of labor of all nationalities, we emphatically deem imported, contract, coolie labor to be a positive injury to the working people of the United States — is but the system of slavery in a new form — and we appeal to the Congress of the United States to rigidly enforce the act of 1862 prohibiting coolie importations, and to enact such other laws as will best protect and free American labor against this or any similar form of slavery.

Resolved, that we do not regard capital as the natural enemy of labor; that each is dependent on the other for its existence; that the great conflict daily waged between them is for want of a better understanding between the representatives of capital and labor; and we therefore recommend the study of political economy in all of our labor organizations as a means to understand the relationships of labor to capital and as a basis for the adjournment of many of the disputes that arise between employer and employee.

Resolved, that we recommend the establishment of cooperative workshops, land, building and loan associations among our people as a remedy against their exclusion from other workshops on account of color, as a means of furnishing employment as well as a protection against the aggression of capital and as the easiest and shortest method of enabling every man to procure a homestead for his family. And to accomplish this end we would particularly impress the greatest importance of the observance of diligence in business and the practice of rigid economy in our social and domestic arrangements.

Resolved, that we regard the use of intoxicating liquors as the most damaging and damnable habits practised by the human family; that we denounce the infamous practice planters have of drenching their employees with this poisonous drug (with or without cost), intended to stupefy their brain and incapacitate them to know the condition of their accounts, the value of their labor, and to rob them of their sense and feelings of humanity; that we appeal to our people to discountenance the use of intoxicating liquors because of its effects to shorten life and because it is the great cause of so much misery and poverty among the working classes of the country; and we advise the organization of temperance associations as a necessary instrument for the speedy and permanent elevation of our people.

Resolved, that we regard education as one of the greatest blessings that the human family enjoys, and that we earnestly appeal to our fellow citizens to allow no opportunity, no matter how limited and remote, to pass unimproved, that the thanks of the colored people of this country is due to the Congress of the United States for the establishment and maintenance of the Freedmen's Bureau, and to Maj. Gen. O. O. Howard, commissioner; Rev. J. W. Alvord and John M. Langston, Esq., general inspectors, for their cooperative labors in the establishment and good government of hundreds of schools in the Southern states, whereby thousands of men, women, and children have been and are now being taught the rudiments of an English education.

The thanks of the whole people are due to these philanthropists and friends to the benevolent institution of this and other countries for the means and efforts in money and teachers furnished, whereby our race is being elevated to the proper standard of intelligent American citizens; and we appeal to the friends of progress and to our citizens of the several states to continue their efforts to the various legislatures until every state can boast of having a free-school system, that knows no distinction in dissemination of knowledge to its inhabitants on account of race, color, sex, creed, or previous condition; and:

Resolved, that we recommend a faithful obedience to the laws of the United States and of the several states in which we may reside; that the Congress and the courts of the United States have ample power to protect its citizens. All grievances, whether personal or public, should be carried to the proper tribunal, and from the lowest to the highest, until justice is granted; that armed resistance against the laws is treason against the United States and ought to be summarily punished. We further appeal to the colored workingmen to form organizations throughout every state and territory that they may be able in those districts far removed from courts of justice to communicate with the Bureau of Labor to be established by the National Labor Union, and that justice may be meted out to them as though they lived in the large cities, where justice is more liberally distributed; that loyalty and love for the government may be fostered and encouraged, and prosperity and peace may pervade the entire land.

47.

Frederick Law Olmsted: The Unplanned Growth of Cities

Between 1860 and 1910 American cities underwent dramatic growth of population. The historian Arthur M. Schlesinger, Sr., has said that during this period "urbanization for the first time became a controlling factor in national life." But urban growth was chaotic and created miserable living conditions. Many leaders sought ways to make the city a more secure and comfortable place to live. Frederick Law Olmsted, a landscape architect and engineer, pioneered in the development of the idea of city planning. He was a leader of the public park movement and the architect of park systems in several cities: his most famous creation is New York's Central Park. Olmsted's main point was that urban areas should incorporate natural settings, a theme he advanced in the following address delivered at Boston on February 25, 1870.

Source: *Journal of Social Science,* No. 3, 1871: "Public Parks and the Enlargement of Towns."

We began experimentally with street railways twenty years ago. At present, in New York, one pair of horses serves to convey one hundred people, on an average, every day at a rate of fare about one-fiftieth of the old hackney coach rates; and the total number of fares collected annually is equal to that of the population of the United States. And yet thousands walk a number of miles every day because they cannot be seated in the cars. It is impossible to fix a limit to the amount of travel which really ample, convenient, and still cheap means of transportation for short distances would develop. Certain improvements have caused the whole number of people seeking conveyances in London to be doubled in the last five years, and yet the supply keeps nowhere near the demand.

See how rapidly we are really gaining

and what we have to expect. Two recent inventions give us the means of reducing by a third, under favorable circumstances, the cost of good McAdam roads. There have been sixteen patents issued from one office for other new forms of perfectly smooth and nearly noiseless street pavement, some of which, after two or three years' trial, promise so well as to render it certain that some improvement will soon come by which more than one of the present special annoyances of town life will be abated. An improvement in our sewer system seems near at hand, also, which will add considerably to the comparative advantages of a residence in towns, and especially the more open town suburbs.

Experiments indicate that it is feasible to send heated air through a town in pipes like water; and that it may be drawn upon; and the heat which is taken, measured and paid for according to quantity required. Thus may come a great saving of fuel and trouble in a very difficult department of domestic economy. No one will think of applying such a system to farmhouses.

Again, it is plain that we have scarcely begun to turn to account the advantages offered to townspeople in the electric telegraph; we really have not made a beginning with those offered in the pneumatic tube, though their substantial character has been demonstrated. By the use of these two instruments, a tradesman ten miles away on the other side of a town may be communicated with, and goods obtained from him by a housekeeper, as quickly and with as little personal inconvenience as now if he were in the next block. A single tube station for 500 families, acoustic pipes for the transmission of orders to it from each house, with a carriers' service for local distribution of packages, is all that is needed for this purpose.

As to the economy which comes by systematizing and concentrating, by the application of a large apparatus, of processes which are otherwise conducted in a desultory way, wasteful of human strength, as by public laundries, bakeries, and kitchens, we are yet, in America, even in our larger cities, far behind many of the smaller towns of the Old World. . . .

As railroads are improved, all the important stations will become centers or subcenters of towns, and all the minor stations suburbs. For most ordinary, everyday purposes, especially housekeepers' purposes, these will need no very large population before they can obtain urban advantages. I have seen a settlement, the resident population of which was under 300, in which there was a public laundry, bathhouse, barber's shop, billiard room, beer garden, and bakery. Fresh rolls and fresh milk were supplied to families before breakfast time every morning; fair fruit and succulent vegetables were delivered at house doors not half an hour after picking; and newspapers and magazines were distributed by a carrier. I have seen a town of not more than 1,200 inhabitants, the streets and the yards, alleys, and places of which were swept every day as regularly as the house floors, and all dust removed by a public dustman.

The construction of good roads and walks, the laying of sewer, water, and gas pipes, and the supplying of sufficiently cheap, rapid, and comfortable conveyances to town centers is all that is necessary to give any farming land in a healthy and attractive situation the value of town lots. And whoever has observed in the French agricultural colonies how much more readily and cheaply railroads, telegraph, gas, water, sewer, and nearly all other advantages of towns may be made available to the whole population than under our present helter-skelter methods of settlement, will not believe that even the occupation of a farm laborer must necessarily and finally exclude his family from a very large share of urban conveniences. . . .

It is hardly a matter of speculation, I am disposed to think, but almost of demonstration that the larger a town becomes because simply of its advantages for commercial purposes, the greater will be the convenience available to those who live in and near it for cooperation, as well with reference to the accumulation of wealth in the higher forms — as in seats of learning, of science, and of art — as with reference to merely domestic economy and the emancipation of both men and women from petty, confining, and narrowing cares.

It also appears to be nearly certain that the recent rapid enlargement of towns and withdrawal of people from rural conditions of living is the result mainly of circumstances of a permanent character.

We have reason to believe, then, that towns which of late have been increasing rapidly on account of their commercial advantages are likely to be still more attractive to population in the future; that there will, in consequence, soon be larger towns than any the world has yet known; and that the further progress of civilization is to depend mainly upon the influences by which men's minds and characters will be affected while living in large towns.

Now, knowing that the average length of the life of mankind in towns has been much less than in the country, and that the average amount of disease and misery and of vice and crime has been much greater in towns, this would be a very dark prospect for civilization, if it were not that modern science has beyond all question determined many of the causes of the special evils by which men are afflicted in towns and placed means in our hands for guarding against them. It has shown, for example, that under ordinary circumstances, in the interior parts of large and closely built towns, a given quantity of air contains considerably less of the elements which we require to receive through the lungs than the air of the country or even of the outer and more open parts of a town; and that instead of them it carries into the lungs highly corrupt and irritating matters, the action of which tends strongly to vitiate all our sources of vigor — how strongly may perhaps be indicated in the shortest way by the statement that even metallic plates and statues corrode and wear away under the atmospheric influences which prevail in the midst of large towns more rapidly than in the country. . . .

It has happened several times within the last century, when old artificial obstructions to the spreading out of a city have been removed, and especially when there has been a demolition of and rebuilding on a new ground plan of some part which had previously been noted for the frequency of certain crimes, the prevalence of certain diseases, and the shortness of life among its inhabitants, that a marked improvement in all these respects has immediately followed and has been maintained, not alone in the dark parts but in the city as a whole.

But although it has been demonstrated by such experiments that we have it in our power to greatly lessen and counteract the two classes of evils we have had under consideration, it must be remembered that these means are made use of only with great difficulty. . . .

It must be within the observation of most of us that where, in the city, wheelways originally twenty feet wide were with great difficulty and cost enlarged to thirty, the present width is already less nearly adequate to the present business than the former was to the former business; obstructions are more frequent, movements are slower and oftener arrested, and the liability to collision is greater. The same is true of sidewalks. Trees have been cut down, porches, bow windows, and other encroachments removed; but every year the walk is less sufficient for the comfortable passing of those who wish to use it.

It is certain that as the distance from the interior to the circumference of towns shall increase with the enlargement of their population, the less sufficient relatively to the service to be performed will be any given space between buildings. In like manner, every evil to which men are specially liable when living in towns is likely to be aggravated in the future unless means are devised and adapted in advance to prevent it.

Let us proceed, then, to the question of means, and with a seriousness in some degree befitting a question, upon our dealing with which we know the misery or happiness of many millions of our fellow beings will depend.

We will, for the present, set before our minds the two sources of wear and corruption which we have seen to be remediable and therefore preventible. We may admit that commerce requires that in some parts of a town there shall be an arrangement of buildings and a character of streets and of traffic in them which will establish conditions of corruption and of irritation, physical and mental. But commerce does not require the same conditions to be maintained in all parts of a town,

Air is disinfected by sunlight and foliage. Foliage also acts mechanically to purify the air by screening it. Opportunity and inducement to escape at frequent intervals from the confined and vitiated air of the commercial quarter, and to supply the lungs with air screened and purified by trees and recently acted upon by sunlight, together with opportunity and inducement to escape from conditions requiring vigilance, wariness, and activity toward other men — if these could be supplied economically, our problem would be solved. . . .

Now that our towns are built without walls and we can have all the room that we like, is there any good reason why we should not make some similar difference between parts which are likely to be dwelt in and those which will be required exclusively for commerce?

Would trees, for seclusion and shade and beauty, be out of place, for instance, by the side of certain of our streets? It will, perhaps, appear to you that it is hardly neces-

Biltmore Estate, Asheville, N.C.
Frederick Law Olmsted by John Singer Sargent

sary to ask such a question, as throughout the United States trees are commonly planted at the sides of streets. Unfortunately they are seldom so planted as to have fairly settled the question of the desirableness of systematically maintaining trees under these circumstances. In the first place, the streets are planned, wherever they are, essentially alike. Trees are planted in the space assigned for sidewalks, where at first, while they are saplings and the vicinity is rural or suburban, they are not much in the way, but where, as they grow larger, and the vicinity becomes urban, they take up more and more space, while space is more and more required for passage. That is not all. Thousands and tens of thousands are planted every year in a manner and under conditions as nearly certain as possible either to kill them outright or to so lessen their vitality as to prevent their natural and beautiful development, and to cause premature decrepitude. Often, too, as their lower limbs are found inconvenient, no space having been provided for trees in laying out the street, they are deformed by butcherly amputations. If by rare good fortune they are suffered to become beautiful, they still stand subject to be condemned to death at any time as obstructions in the highway.

What I would ask is, whether we might not with economy make special provision in some of our streets — in a twentieth or a fiftieth part, if you please, of all — for trees to remain as a permanent furniture of the city? I mean, to make a place for them in which they would have room to grow naturally and gracefully. Even if the distance between the houses should have to be made half as much again as it is required to be in our commercial streets, could not the space be afforded? Out-of-town space is not costly when measures to secure it are taken early. The assessments for benefit where such streets were provided for would, in nearly all cases, defray the cost of the land required. The strips of ground reserved for the trees, six, twelve, twenty feet wide, would cost nothing for paving or flagging.

The change both of scene and of air which would be obtained by people engaged for the most part in the necessarily confined interior commercial parts of the town, on passing into a street of this character after the trees had become stately and graceful, would be worth a good deal. If such streets were made still broader in some parts, with spacious malls, the advantage would be increased. If each of them were given the proper capacity and laid out with laterals and connections in suitable directions to serve as a convenient trunk line of communication between two large districts of the town or the business center and the suburbs, a very great number of people might thus be placed every day under influences counteracting those with which we desire to contend. These, however, would be merely very simple improvements upon arrangements which are in common use in every considerable town. Their advantages would be incidental to the general uses of streets as they are.

But people are willing very often to seek recreation, as well as receive it by the way. Provisions may indeed be made expressly for public recreations, with certainty that, if convenient, they will be resorted to. We come then to the question: What accommodations for recreation can we provide which shall be so agreeable and so accessible as to be efficiently attractive to the great body of citizens, and which, while giving decided gratification, shall also cause those who resort to them for pleasure to subject themselves, for the time being, to conditions strongly counteractive to the special enervating conditions of the town?

In the study of this question, all forms of recreation may, in the first place, be conveniently arranged under two general heads. One will include all of which the predominating influence is to stimulate exertion of any part or parts needing it; the other, all which cause us to receive pleasure without conscious exertion. Games chiefly of mental skill, as chess, or athletic sports, as baseball, are examples of means of recreation of the first class, which may be termed that of *exertive* recreation; music and the fine arts generally of the second or *receptive* division. . . .

I do not propose to discuss this part of the subject at present, as it is only necessary to my immediate purpose to point out that if recreations requiring large spaces to be given up to the use of a comparatively small number are not considered essential, numerous small grounds so distributed through a large town that some one of them could be easily reached by a short walk from every house, would be more desirable than a single area of great extent however rich in landscape attractions it might be. Especially would this be the case if the numerous local grounds were connected and supplemented by a series of trunk roads or boulevards. . . .

There is an instinctive inclination to this social, neighborly, unexertive form of recreation among all of us. In one way or another er it is sure to be constantly operating upon those millions on millions of men and women who are to pass their lives within a few miles of where we now stand. To what extent it shall operate so as to develop health and virtue will, on many occasions, be simply a question of opportunity and inducement. And this question is one for the determination of which for a thousand years we here today are largely responsible. . . .

For this purpose neither of the forms of ground we have heretofore considered are at all suitable. We want a ground to which people may easily go after their day's work is done, and where they may stroll for an hour, seeing, hearing, and feeling nothing of the bustle and jar of the streets — where they shall, in effect, find the city put far away from them. We want the greatest possible contrast with the streets and the shops and the rooms of the town which will be consistent with convenience and the preservation of good order and neatness. We want, especially, the greatest possible contrast with the restraining and confining conditions of the town, those conditions which compel us to walk circumspectly, watchfully, jealously, which compel us to look closely upon others without sympathy. Practically, what we most want is a simple, broad, open space of clean greensward, with sufficient play of surface and a sufficient number of trees about it to supply a variety of light and shade. This we want as a central feature. We want depth of wood enough about it not only for comfort in hot weather but to completely shut out the city from our landscapes.

The word "park," in town nomenclature, should, I think, be reserved for grounds of the character and purpose thus described.

Not only as being the most valuable of all possible forms of public places but regarded simply as a large space which will seriously interrupt crosstown communication wherever it occurs, the question of the site and bounds of the park requires to be determined with much more deliberation and art than is often secured for any problem of distant and extended municipal interests. . . . The park should, as far as possible, complement the town.

Openness is the one thing you cannot get in buildings. Picturesqueness you can get. Let your buildings be as picturesque as your artists can make them. This is the beauty of a town. Consequently, the beauty of the park should be the other. It should be the beauty of the fields, the meadow, the prairie, of the green pastures, and the still waters. What we want to gain is tranquillity and rest to the mind. Mountains suggest effort. But besides this objection there are others of what I may indicate as the housekeeping class. It is impossible to give the public range over a large extent of ground of a highly picturesque character, unless under very exceptional circumstances, and sufficiently guard against the occurrence of opportunities and temptations to shabbiness, disorder, indecorum, and indecency that will be subversive of every good purpose the park should be designed to fulfill. . . .

A park, fairly well managed near a large town, will surely become a new center of that town. With the determination of location, size, and boundaries should therefore be associated the duty of arranging new trunk routes of communication between it and the distant parts of the town existing and forecasted.

These may be either narrow informal elongations of the park, varying say from 200 to 500 feet in width and radiating irregularly from it, or if, unfortunately, the town is already laid out in the unhappy way that New York and Brooklyn, San Francisco and Chicago are, and, I am glad to say, Boston is not, on a plan made long years ago by a man who never saw a spring carriage and who had a conscientious dread of the Graces, then we must probably adopt formal parkways. They should be so planned and constructed as never to be noisy and seldom crowded, and so also that the straightforward movement of pleasure carriages need never be obstructed, unless at absolutely necessary crossings, by slow-going, heavy vehicles used for commercial purposes.

If possible, also, they should be branched or reticulated with other ways of a similar class, so that no part of the town should finally be many minutes' walk from some one of them; and they should be made interesting by a process of planting and decoration, so that in necessarily passing through them, whether in going to or from the park, or to and from business, some substantial recreative advantage may be incidentally gained. It is a common error to regard a park as something to be produced complete in itself, as a picture to be painted on canvas. It should rather be planned as one to be done in fresco, with constant consideration of exterior objects, some of them quite at a distance and even existing as yet only in the imagination of the painter. . . .

The New York legislature of 1851 passed a bill providing for a park on the east side of the island. Afterward, the same legislature, precipitately and quite as an afterthought, passed the act under which the city took title to the site of the greater part of the present Central Park. . . . The question of the relative value of what is called offhand common sense, and of special, deliberate, businesslike study, must be settled in the case of the Central Park, by a comparison of benefit with cost. During the last four years, over 30 million visits have been made to the park by actual count, and many have passed uncounted. From 50,000 to 80,000 persons on foot, 30,000 in carriages, and 4,000 to 5,000 on horseback have often entered it in a day.

Among the frequent visitors, I have found all those who, a few years ago, believed it impossible that there should ever be a park in this republican country — and especially in New York of all places in this country — which would be a suitable place of resort for "gentlemen." They, their wives and daughters, frequent the park more than they do the opera or the church. There are many men of wealth who resort to the park habitually and regularly, as much so as businessmen to their places of business. Of course, there is a reason for it, and a reason based upon their experience.

As to the effect on public health, there is no question that it is already great. The testimony of the older physicians of the city will be found unanimous on this point. Says one: "Where I formerly ordered patients of a certain class to give up their business altogether and go out of town, I now often advise simply moderation and prescribe a ride in the park before going to their offices, and again a drive with their families before dinner. By simply adopting this course as a habit, men who have been breaking down frequently recover tone rapidly and are able to retain an active and controlling influence in an important business, from which they would have otherwise been forced to retire. I direct schoolgirls, under certain circumstances, to be taken wholly, or in part, from their studies and sent to spend several hours a day rambling on foot in the park."

The lives of women and children too poor to be sent to the country can now be saved in thousands of instances by making them go to the park. During a hot day in July last, I counted at one time in the park eighteen separate groups, consisting of mothers with their children, most of whom were under school age, taking picnic dinners which they had brought from home with them. The practice is increasing under medical advice, especially when summer complaint is rife.

The much greater rapidity with which patients convalesce and may be returned with safety to their ordinary occupations after severe illness, when they can be sent to the park for a few hours a day, is beginning to be understood. The addition thus made to the productive labor of the city is not unimportant.

The park, moreover, has had a very marked effect in making the city attractive to visitors, and in thus increasing its trade, and causing many who have made fortunes elsewhere to take up their residence and become taxpayers in it — a much greater effect in this way, beyond all question, than all the colleges, schools, libraries, museums, and art galleries which the city possesses. It has also induced many foreigners who have grown rich in the country, and who would otherwise have gone to Europe to enjoy their wealth, to settle permanently in the city.

48.

Concerning the Annexation of the Dominican Republic

The feelings that led Congress in 1869 to offer U.S. protection to Haiti and the Dominican Republic did not extend to approving annexation of the latter. President Grant, who was eager to acquire the Dominican Republic for the United States, sent his private secretary, Orville Babcock, there to arrange a treaty of annexation. Because Grant's Cabinet objected to Babcock's arrangements, Grant had a more formal treaty submitted to the Senate in January 1870. The Senate Committee on Foreign Relations returned an unfavorable report on the proposal, and Grant replied with the following message of May 31, explaining his position. The most formidable opposition came from Charles Sumner, whose strong stand against annexation cost him his position as chairman of the Senate Committee. Sumner's celebrated "Naboth's Vineyard" speech of December 21, 1870, is also reprinted here in part.

Source: Richardson, VII, pp. 61-63.
      The Works of Charles Sumner, Boston, 1883, Vol. XIV, pp. 94-124.

I.

ULYSSES S. GRANT:
For Annexation

I TRANSMIT TO THE SENATE, for consideration with a view to its ratification, an additional article to the treaty of the 29th of November last, for the annexation of the Dominican Republic to the United States, stipulating for an extension of the time for exchanging the ratifications thereof, signed in this city on the 14th instant by the plenipotentiaries of the parties.

It was my intention to have also negotiated with the plenipotentiary of San Domingo amendments to the treaty of annexation to obviate objections which may be urged against the treaty as it is now worded; but on reflection I deem it better to

Ulysses S. Grant

submit to the Senate the propriety of their amending the treaty as follows:

First, to specify that the obligations of this government shall not exceed the $1,500,000 stipulated in the treaty; second, to determine the manner of appointing the agents to receive and disburse the same; third, to determine the class of creditors who shall take precedence in the settlement of their claims; and finally, to insert such amendments as may suggest themselves to the minds of senators to carry out in good faith the conditions of the treaty submitted to the Senate of the United States in January last, according to the spirit and intent of that treaty.

From the most reliable information I can obtain, the sum specified in the treaty will pay every just claim against the Republic of San Domingo and leave a balance sufficient to carry on a territorial government until such time as new laws for providing a territorial revenue can be enacted and put in force.

I feel an unusual anxiety for the ratifica-

tion of this treaty, because I believe it will redound greatly to the glory of the two countries interested, to civilization, and to the extirpation of the institution of slavery.

The doctrine promulgated by President Monroe has been adhered to by all political parties, and I now deem it proper to assert the equally important principle that hereafter no territory on this continent shall be regarded as subject of transfer to a European power.

The government of San Domingo has voluntarily sought this annexation. It is a weak power, numbering probably less than 120,000 souls, and yet possessing one of the richest territories under the sun, capable of supporting a population of 10 million people in luxury. The people of San Domingo are not capable of maintaining themselves in their present condition and must look for outside support. They yearn for the protection of our free institutions and laws, our progress and civilization. Shall we refuse them?

I have information, which I believe reliable, that a European power stands ready now to offer $2 million for the possession of Samana Bay alone. If refused by us, with what grace can we prevent a foreign power from attempting to secure the prize?

The acquisition of San Domingo is desirable because of its geographical position. It commands the entrance to the Caribbean Sea and the Isthmus transit of commerce. It possesses the richest soil, best and most capacious harbors, most salubrious climate, and the most valuable products of the forest, mine, and soil of any of the West India islands. Its possession by us will in a few years build up a coastwise commerce of immense magnitude, which will go far toward restoring to us our lost Merchant Marine. It will give to us those articles which we consume so largely and do not produce, thus equalizing our exports and imports.

In case of foreign war it will give us

command of all the islands referred to, and thus prevent an enemy from ever again possessing himself of rendezvous upon our very coast.

At present our coast trade between the states bordering on the Atlantic and those bordering on the Gulf of Mexico is cut into by the Bahamas and the Antilles. Twice we must, as it were, pass through foreign countries to get by sea from Georgia to the west coast of Florida.

San Domingo, with a stable government, under which her immense resources can be developed, will give remunerative wages to tens of thousands of laborers not now on the island. This labor will take advantage of every available means of transportation to abandon the adjacent islands and seek the blessings of freedom and its sequence — each inhabitant receiving the reward of his own labor. Puerto Rico and Cuba will have to abolish slavery as a measure of self-preservation to retain their laborers.

San Domingo will become a large consumer of the products of Northern farms and manufactories. The cheap rate at which her citizens can be furnished with food, tools, and machinery will make it necessary that the contiguous islands should have the same advantages in order to compete in the production of sugar, coffee, tobacco, tropical fruits, etc. This will open to us a still wider market for our products.

The production of our own supply of these articles will cut off more than $100 million of our annual imports, besides largely increasing our exports. With such a picture it is easy to see how our large debt abroad is ultimately to be extinguished. With a balance of trade against us (including interest on bonds held by foreigners and money spent by our citizens traveling in foreign lands) equal to the entire yield of the precious metals in this country, it is not so easy to see how this result is to be otherwise accomplished.

The acquisition of San Domingo is an adherence to the Monroe Doctrine; it is a measure of national protection; it is asserting our just claim to a controlling influence over the great commercial traffic soon to flow from east to west by the way of the Isthmus of Darien; it is to build up our Merchant Marine; it is to furnish new markets for the products of our farms, shops, and manufactories; it is to make slavery insupportable in Cuba and Puerto Rico at once, and ultimately so in Brazil; it is to settle the unhappy condition of Cuba and end an exterminating conflict; it is to provide honest means of paying our honest debts without overtaxing the people; it is to furnish our citizens with the necessaries of everyday life at cheaper rates than ever before; and it is, in fine, a rapid stride toward that greatness which the intelligence, industry, and enterprise of the citizens of the United States entitle this country to assume among nations.

II.

CHARLES SUMNER:
Against Annexation

THE RESOLUTION before the Senate commits Congress to a dance of blood. It is a new step in a measure of violence. Already several steps have been taken, and Congress is now summoned to another.

Before I proceed with the merits of this question, so far as such language can be used with reference to it, and as I see the senator from Ohio [Mr. Sherman] in his seat, I wish to answer an argument of his yesterday. He said that the resolution was simply one of inquiry, and that therefore there could be no objection to it. I was astonished when I heard one of his experience in this chamber and his familiarity with legislation characterize the pending proposition simply as a resolution of inquiry. The senator is mistaken. It is a joint resolution creating three offices under the Constitution of the United States, offices contemplated in the Constitution itself, and specially mentioned by name in the Act of 1856 to regulate the diplomatic and consular systems of the United States. I read the 1st Section of that act, as follows:

> That ambassadors, envoys extraordinary and ministers plenipotentiary, ministers resident, *commissioners*, chargés d'affaires, and secretaries of legation, appointed to the countries hereinafter named in Schedule A, shall be entitled to compensation for their services, respectively, at the rates per annum hereinafter specified: that is to say, ambassadors and envoys extraordinary and ministers plenipotentiary, the full amounts specified therefor in said Schedule A; ministers resident and *commissioners, 75* percentum.

Now, sir, by this joint resolution, the President is authorized to appoint three "commissioners," and also a "secretary," the latter to be versed in the English and Spanish languages, to proceed to the island of San Domingo, and to inquire into, ascertain, and report certain things. I say this is a legislative act creating three new offices; but the senator says that it is simply a resolution of inquiry. Even suppose the offices are not diplomatic, they are nonetheless offices. . . .

The senator, it seems to me, has not comprehended the object of this resolution. To my mind it is plain. It is simply to commit Congress to the policy of annexation. I insist upon this point: the object of the resolution, and I will demonstrate it, is to commit Congress to the policy of annexation. Otherwise, why is the resolution introduced? The President does not need it. Under existing powers he is authorized to appoint agents, if he pleases, to visit foreign countries, and he is supplied with a secret-service fund by which their expenses may

be defrayed. The President does not need this resolution. It is an act of supererogation, so far as he is concerned; and it is also contrary, so far as I am informed, to the precedents of our history. . . .

I object to this proposition because it is a new stage in a measure of violence, which, so far as it has been maintained, has been upheld by violence. I use strong language, but only what the occasion requires. As senator, as patriot, I cannot see my country suffer in its good name without an earnest effort to save it.

The negotiation for annexation began with a person known as Buenaventura Baez. All the evidence, official and unofficial, shows him to be a political jockey. But he could do little alone; he had about him two other political jockeys, Cazneau and Fabens; and these three together, a precious copartnership, seduced into their firm a young officer of ours, who entitled himself "aide-de-camp to the President of the United States." Together they got up what was called a protocol, in which the young officer entitling himself "aide-de-camp to the President" proceeds to make certain promises for the President. Before I read from this document, I desire to say that there is not one word showing that at the time this "aide-de-camp" had any title or any instruction to take this step. If he had, that title and that instruction have been withheld; no inquiry has been able to penetrate it. At least the committee which brought out the protocol did not bring out any such authority.

The document is called "a protocol," which I need not remind you, sir, is in diplomatic terms the first draft of a treaty, or the memorandum between two powers in which are written down the heads of some subsequent convention; but at the time it is hardly less binding than a treaty itself, except, as you are well aware, that under the Constitution of the United States it can receive no final obligation without the consent of the Senate. This document begins as follows:

> The following bases, which shall serve for framing a definitive treaty between the United States and the Dominican Republic, have been reduced to writing and agreed upon by General Orville E. Babcock, aide-de-camp to His Excellency, General Ulysses S. Grant, President of the United States of America, and his special agent to the Dominican Republic, and Mr. Manuel Maria Gautier, secretary of state of the Departments of the Interior and of Police, charged with the foreign relations of the said Dominican Republic.

Here you see how this young officer, undertaking to represent the United States of America, entitles himself "aide-de-camp to His Excellency, General Ulysses S. Grant, President of the United States of America, and his special agent to the Dominican Republic." Sir, you have experience in the government of this country; your post is high, and I ask you — Do you know any such officer in our government as "aide-de-camp to His Excellency, the President of the United States"? Does such designation appear in the Constitution, in any statute, or in the history of this republic anywhere? If it does, your information, sir, is much beyond mine.

I have never before met any such instance. This young officer stands alone in using the lofty title. I believe, still further, that he stands alone in the history of free governments. I doubt whether you can find a diplomatic paper anywhere in which any person undertaking to represent his government has entitled himself aide-de-camp of the chief of the state. The two duties are incompatible according to all the experience of history. No aide-de-camp would be appointed commissioner; and the assumption of this exalted and exceptional character by this young officer shows at least his inexpe-

rience in diplomacy, if not his ambition to play a great part. Doubtless it had an effect with Baez, Cazneau, and Fabens, the three confederates. They were pleased with the eminence of the agent. It helped on the plan they were engineering.

The young aide-de-camp then proceeds to pledge the President as follows:

> His Excellency, General Grant, President of the United States, promises, *privately*, to use all his influence in order that the idea of annexing the Dominican Republic to the United States may acquire such a degree of popularity among members of Congress as will be necessary for its accomplishment.

Shall I read the rest of the document? It is of somewhat the same tenor. There are questions of money in it, cash down, all of which must have been particularly agreeable to the three confederates. It finally winds up as follows:

> Done in duplicate, *in good faith*, in the city of San Domingo, the 4th day of the month of September, A.D. 1869.
>
> ORVILLE E. BABCOCK
> MANUEL MARIA GAUTIER

"In good faith," if you please, sir.

I have heard it said that Orville E. Babcock did not write "aide-de-camp" against his name at the bottom of the protocol. This was not necessary. The designation of a person in such documents always appears at the beginning, as, for instance, in a deed between two parties. It is not written against the name. Therefore we have here a "protocol," so entitled, signed by a young officer who entitles himself "aide-de-camp to His Excellency, the President of the United States," and who promises for the President that he shall privately use all his influence in order that the idea of annexing the Dominican Republic to the United States may acquire such a degree of popularity among members of Congress as will be necessary for its accomplishment.

Such was the promise. Senators about me know how faithfully the President has fulfilled it, how faithfully he has labored, privately and publicly, even beyond the protocol — the protocol only required that he should work privately — privately and publicly, in order that the idea of annexing the Dominican Republic should be agreeable to Congress.

The young officer, "aide-de-camp to the President of the United States," with this important and unprecedented document in his pocket, returned to Washington. Instead of being called to account for this unauthorized transaction, pledging the chief magistrate to use his influence privately with Congress in order to cram down a measure that the confederates justly supposed to be offensive, he was sent back with directions to negotiate a treaty. I would not allude to that treaty if it had not been made the subject of discussion by the President himself in his annual message.

You know it. The treaty itself is not on your tables legislatively; it has never been communicated legislatively to Congress. The other House, which may be called to act upon this important measure, can know nothing of that treaty, and what we know of it we cannot speak of even in this debate. We can simply speak of its existence, for the President himself has imparted that to Congress and to the country. The treaty exists; and now the practical question is — By what means was it negotiated?

I have described to you the three confederates who seduced into their company the aide-de-camp of the President; and now I have to aver, and I insist that the evidence will substantiate what I say, that at the time of the signature of the treaty of annexation, Baez was sustained in power by the presence of our naval force in the waters of the Dominican government. Go to the documents and you will find that what I say is

true. Confer with naval officers, confer with honest patriot citizens who know the case, and they will all testify that without the presence of our ships-of-war in those waters Baez would have been powerless.

This is not all, sir; I broaden the allegation. Ever since the signature of the treaty, and especially since its rejection, Baez has been sustained in power by the presence of our naval force. Such I aver to be the fact. I state it with all the responsibility of my position and with full conviction of its truth. I ask you, sir, to go to the State Department and Navy Department and read the reports there on file, and I feel sure that what I state will be found to be substantially true. I ask you also to confer with any naval officer who has been there, or with any patriot citizen. . . .

There are two chieftains in Dominica: one the political jockey with whom our government has united and who is now sustained in power by our naval force; and the other is Cabral, who, as I have been assured by one who is bound to be well informed, represents the people of his country besides being *de jure* its head. Some time ago Cabral favored the sale of the Bay of Samana to the United States; but I am assured that he has never favored annexation to the United States. I am assured that his policy is to bring the two governments of Dominica and Haiti once more together, as they were down to the revolution and war which lasted from 1844 to 1848, terminating in the uncertain independence of the Dominican part of the island.

Now I have answered categorically the inquiries of my two friends. The evidence, as I have it, is not that these two chieftains are agreed. On the contrary, there is between them discord; they differ from each other — one seeking unity for these two governments, the other seeking to sell his country for a price. But whatever may be the sentiment of the people, whether Baez and Cabral agree or disagree, I come back to the single practical point that Baez has been, and is now, maintained in power by the naval force of the United States. Deny it if you can. All this is still worse when it is considered that the very constitution of Dominica, under which the adventurer professes to hold rule, provides that there shall be no transfer to any foreign power of any portion of the country. . . .

Sir, I have presented but half of this case, and perhaps the least painful part. I am now brought to another aspect of it. This naval force to which I have referred has also been directed against the neighboring Republic of Haiti (the only colored government now existing in the world, a republic seeking to follow our great example), penetrating its harbors and undertaking to dictate what it should do. If you will read again the reports at the Navy Department, you will find that I do not overstate when I say that they have undertaken to dictate to the government of Haiti what it should do. Nor is this all. In an unhappy moment, the commodore of an American fleet, going ashore, allowed himself to insult and menace the government there, saying that if it interfered in any way with the territory of Dominica, he would blow the town down. So I have been informed by one who ought to know.

You look grave, sir. Well you may. I wish I could give you the official evidence on this assumption; but I am assured, on evidence which I regard as beyond question, that this incident has occurred. In what school was our commodore reared? The prudent mother in the story cautioned her son to take care never to fight with a boy of his own size. An American commodore, in the same spirit, undertakes to insult a sister republic too weak to resist. Of course, if he did this on his own motion and without instructions from Washington, he ought to be removed — and, in my judgment, rather than carry out such instructions, he ought to have thrown his sword into the sea. . . .

Every attempt at jurisdiction in those waters was a usurpation and an act of violence; I think I should not go too far if I said it was an act of war. If a commodore leaves his quarterdeck, pulls ashore, and, with his guns commanding a town, threatens to blow it down, is not this an act of war? . . . I have called it an act of war — war, sir, made by the executive without the consent of Congress. If Congress had declared war against this feeble republic, then it would have been the part of the executive to carry that declaration into effect; but until then what right had our executive to do this thing? None which can be vindicated by the laws of our country, none except what is found in the law of force.

This outrage by our navy upon a sister republic is aggravated by the issue which the President of the United States in his annual message has directly made with the President of Haiti. Of course, sir, the President of the United States, when he prepared his message, was familiar with a document like that which I now hold in my hands, entitled "The Monitor, Official Journal of the Republic of Haiti," under date of Saturday, the 24th of September, 1870, containing the message of the President of Haiti addressed to the National Assembly. This message is divided into sections or chapters, with headings, not unlike a message or document in our own country. And now, sir, listen to what the President of Haiti in this annual message says of the project of annexation, and then in one moment listen to the issue which the President of the United States has joined with this President. I translate it literally:

> The project of annexation of the Dominican part has been rejected by the American Senate. The anxieties which this annexation caused to spring up have been dissipated before the good sense and the wisdom of the Senate at Washington.

Of course the President of the United

States was intimate with this document. He could not have undertaken to hurl his bolt against this feeble republic without knowing at least what its President had said. I will not do him the wrong to suppose him ignorant. His secretary of state must have informed him. He must have known the precise words that President Saget had employed when he said that the anxieties caused by this annexation were dissipated before the good sense and wisdom of the Senate at Washington. Our President joins issue with President Saget; he says that the rejection of the treaty was a "folly." There you have it. The President of the Black Republic calls the rejection an act of "good sense" and "wisdom"; the President of the United States calls it an act of "folly." Am I wrong? Let me read from the message of our President:

> A large commercial city will spring up, to which we will be tributary without receiving corresponding benefits, and then will be seen the folly of our rejecting so great a prize.

So the two stand — President Saget and President Grant — President Grant speaking with the voice of 40 million; and this other President, who has less than 600,000 people, all black. . . .

Nine times in this message has the President — after joining issue first with the President of Haiti — nine times has he menaced the independence of the Haitian republic. Some remarkable propositions at times are received with nine cheers. Here is a menace nine times over; and throughout the whole of that San Domingo column, written with so much intensity, we are called to consider commercial, financial, material advantages, and not one word is lisped of justice or humanity, not one word of what we owe to the neighboring Republic of Haiti, nine times menaced. . . .

Vain to set forth, as the message does, all manner of advantages, "commercially and materially." What are these if right and humanity are sacrificed? What are these without that priceless blessing, peace? I am not insensible to the commercial and material prosperity of my country. But there is something above these. It is the honor and good name of the republic, now darkened by an act of wrong. If this territory, so much coveted by the President, were infinitely more valuable than it is, I hope the Senate would not be tempted to obtain it by trampling on the weak and humble. Admit all that the advocates of the present scheme assert with regard to the resources of this territory, and then imagine its lofty mountains bursting with the precious metals, its streams flowing with amber over silver sands, where every field is a garden of the Hesperides, blooming with vegetable gold, and all this is not worth the price we are called to pay.

There is one other consideration, vast in importance and conclusive in character, to which I allude only. The island of San Domingo, situated in tropical waters, and occupied by another race of another color, never can become a permanent possession of the United States. You may seize it by force of arms or by diplomacy, where a naval squadron does more than the minister; but the enforced jurisdiction cannot endure. Already by a higher statute is that island set apart to the colored race. It is theirs by right of possession, by their sweat and blood mingling with the soil, by tropical position, by its burning sun, and by unalterable laws of climate. Such is the ordinance of nature, which I am not the first to recognize. San Domingo is the earliest of that independent group destined to occupy the Caribbean Sea, toward which our duty is plain as the Ten Commandments. Kindness, beneficence, assistance, aid, help, protection, all that is implied in good neighborhood — these we must give freely, bountifully; but their independence is as precious to them as is ours to us, and it is placed under the safeguard of natural laws which we cannot violate with impunity.

Long ago it was evident that the great republic might fitly extend the shelter of its protection to the governments formed in these tropical islands, dealing with them graciously, generously, and in a Christian spirit — helping them in their weakness, encouraging them in their trials, and being to them always a friend; but we take counsel of our supposed interests rather than theirs when we seek to remove them from the sphere in which they have been placed by Providence.

I conclude as I began. I protest against this legislation as another stage in a drama of blood. I protest against it in the name of justice outraged by violence; in the name of humanity insulted; in the name of the weak trodden down; in the name of peace imperiled; and in the name of the African race, whose first effort at independence is rudely assailed.

49.

Against the Importation of "Coolie" Labor

Chinese immigrants, who first came to America during the California gold rush of 1849, were welcomed as domestic servants, gardeners, and mine laborers. American businessmen, who thought it unlikely that the "coolie" workers would be affected by labor organizers, imported several thousand Chinese to help build the transcontinental railroads. There is also evidence that some employers used Chinese in other industries to lower wage scales and to break strikes. The Boston Transcript *reported on June 13, 1870, that Chinese laborers were transported to North Adams, Massachusetts, when the shoemakers there went on strike. Native laborers held a protest meeting in Boston and issued the following resolutions.*

Source: *Boston Investigator,* July 6, 1870 [Commons, IX, pp. 86-88].

A LARGE AND ENTHUSIASTIC meeting of the workingmen of this city was held in Tremont Temple last Wednesday afternoon and evening. Its object was to take some measures relative to the importation of coolie labor into Massachusetts. Many speeches were made, the substance of which is embodied in the following resolutions passed by the meeting:

Whereas, efforts are now being made to introduce into the manufactories of this state coolie labor from China in order to cheapen, and, if possible, degrade the intelligent, educated, loyal labor of Massachusetts; therefore, be it

Resolved, that while we welcome voluntary laborers from every clime, and pledge them the protection of our laws and the assurance of equal opportunities in every field of industry, still we cannot but deprecate all attempts to introduce into the manufactories of this state a servile class of laborers from China, or elsewhere, who come in fulfillment of contracts made on foreign soil, and with no intention to become American citizens or aid in the permanent development of American resources.

Resolved, that in the language of the Massachusetts Bill of Rights, government is instituted for the common good, for the protection, safety, and happiness of the people, and not for the profit, honor, or private interest of any one man, family, or class of men. Therefore, the people alone have an incontrovertible, unalienable, and indefeasible right to institute government, and to reform, alter, or totally change the same when their protection, safety, property, or happiness require it; and we, therefore, declare our fixed and unalterable purpose to use the power of the ballot to secure the protection, safety, property, and happiness of the working people of this commonwealth as against this new attempt of capital to cheapen labor and degrade the working classes by importing coolie slaves for that purpose.

Resolved, that we tender our thanks to the Honorable Henry Wilson for his earnest efforts to secure the passage of a law prohibiting the fulfillment on American soil of these infamous contracts for coolie labor; and we call upon our representatives in Congress to use all their influence to secure the passage of such a law as is due alike to the best interests of the country, as well as a measure of justice to the coolie, who, ignorant of the value of labor, accepts conditions degrading alike to him and to us.

Resolved, that the conduct of the Massachusetts legislature in twice refusing to take action calculated to check the introduction of the coolie system into this state deserves the rebuke and condemnation of every workingman in the state, as well as the condemnation of every man who believes in the dignity of labor or the supremacy of liberty over tyranny.

Resolved, that we ignore all elements, whether in this meeting or out, which have for their tendency the strengthening of any man's chance for political honors who is not pledged to represent the greatest number of the people for the people's good, and who is not willing to be held accountable to the people for his political actions.

Resolved, that we have voted for protection to American industry at the suggestions of the rich manufacturers who owned the protected products, thinking to help ourselves; but we now find that, under the scheme of protection, capital is to get the protection and American labor is to be reduced to the Chinese standard of rice and rats; and we cut loose, now and forever, from the false and lying knaves who have beguiled us.

Resolved, that the rights of workingmen will gain no successful foothold in Massachusetts until the workingmen repudiate those time-serving politicians who think to retain office at any price of double-dealing.

Resolved, that we cordially endorse the course of Honorable Henry K. Oliver, chief of the Bureau of Labor Statistics, and his assistants for the able report on the condition of labor in this state, and pledge ourselves all the aid in our power by collecting and placing before the people the true condition and needs of the working classes.

50.

BRET HARTE: "Plain Language from Truthful James"

Bret Harte left the East for California in 1854, when he was eighteen. He taught in a rural school, made a brief trip into the mining country that legend later expanded into an extensive participation in camp life, and worked as a Wells Fargo expressman. He became a newspaperman in 1857 and in 1868 was named editor of the Overland Monthly *magazine, to which he contributed a series of local color sketches and stories that were successful in acquainting Eastern readers with life in California. "The Luck of Roaring Camp" and "The Outcasts of Poker Flat" made him a reputation that was greatly increased by the popular poem, "Plain Language from Truthful James," which appeared in 1870. This satirical ballad on the relations between white Westerners and Asians became known as "The Heathen Chinee" when it was reprinted in pirated editions throughout the country.*

Source: *Poems*, Boston, 1871.

PLAIN LANGUAGE FROM TRUTHFUL JAMES

Which I wish to remark,
  And my language is plain,
That for ways that are dark
  And for tricks that are vain,
The heathen Chinee is peculiar.
  Which the same I would rise to
    explain.

Ah Sin was his name;
  And I shall not deny
In regard to the same
  What that name might imply;
But his smile it was pensive and childlike,
  As I frequent remarked to Bill Nye.

It was August the third,
  And quite soft was the skies;
Which it might be inferred
  That Ah Sin was likewise;
Yet he played it that day upon William
  And me in a way I despise.

Which we had a small game,
  And Ah Sin took a hand:
It was euchre. The same
  He did not understand;
But he smiled as he sat by the table,
  With the smile that was childlike and
    bland.

Yet the cards they were stocked
  In a way that I grieve,
And my feelings were shocked
  At the state of Nye's sleeve,
Which was stuffed full of aces and bowers
  And the same with intent to deceive.

But the hands that were played
  By that heathen Chinee,
And the points that he made,
  Were quite frightful to see —
Till at last he put down a right bower,
  Which the same Nye had dealt unto me.

Then I looked up at Nye,
  And he gazed upon me;
And he rose with a sigh,
  And said, "Can this be?
We are ruined by Chinese cheap labor,"
  And he went for that heathen Chinee.

In the scene that ensued
  I did not take a hand,
But the floor it was strewed,
  Like the leaves on the strand,
With the cards that Ah Sin had been
    hiding,
  In the game "he did not understand."

In his sleeves, which were long,
  He had twenty-four packs —
Which was coming it strong,
  Yet I state but the facts;
And we found on his nails, which were
    taper,
  What is frequent in tapers — that's wax.

Which is why I remark,
  And my language is plain,
That for ways that are dark,
  And for tricks that are vain,
The heathen Chinee is peculiar —
  Which the same I am free to maintain.

51.

Red Cloud: Native American Rights

Red Cloud, chief of the largest tribe of the Teton Sioux Nation, achieved early fame as a warrior and yet was one of the most influential Native American leaders to urge peace with the U.S. government. In 1870 Red Cloud visited the East, at which time he gave the following speech at a reception in his honor at Cooper Union in New York on July 16. Though a persistent critic of the government and of its Indian agents, whom he charged with graft and corruption, Red Cloud openly opposed agitation for further wars that, he knew, would only result in losses for his people.

Source: *New York Times,* July 17, 1870.

My brethren and my friends who are here before me this day, God Almighty has made us all, and He is here to bless what I have to say to you today. The Good Spirit made us both. He gave you lands and He gave us lands; He gave us these lands; you came in here, and we respected you as brothers. God Almighty made you but made you all white and clothed you; when He made us He made us with red skins and poor; now you have come.

When you first came we were very many, and you were few; now you are many, and we are getting very few, and we are poor. You do not know who appears before you today to speak. I am a representative of the original American race, the first people of this continent. We are good and not bad. The reports that you hear concerning us are all on one side. We are always well-disposed to them. You are here told that we are traders and thieves, and it is not so. We have given you nearly all our lands, and if we had any more land to give we would be very glad to give it. We have nothing more. We are driven into a very little land, and we want you now, as our dear friends, to help us with the government of the United States.

The Great Father made us poor and ignorant — made you rich and wise and more skillful in these things that we know nothing about. The Great Father, the Good Father in Heaven, made you all to eat tame food — made us to eat wild food — gives us the wild food. You ask anybody who has gone through our country to California; ask those who have settled there and in Utah, and you will find that we have treated them always well. You have children; we have children. You want to raise your children and make them happy and prosperous; we want to raise and make them happy and prosperous. We ask you to help us to do it.

At the mouth of the Horse Creek, in 1852, the Great Father made a treaty with us by which we agreed to let all that country open for fifty-five years for the transit of those who were going through. We kept this treaty; we never treated any man wrong; we never committed any murder or depredation until afterward the troops were sent into that country, and the troops killed our people and ill-treated them, and thus war and trouble arose; but before the troops were sent there we were quiet and peaceable, and there was no disturbance. Since that time there have been various goods sent from time to time to us, the only ones that ever reached us, and then after they reached us (very soon after) the government took them away. You, as good men, ought to help us to these goods.

Colonel Fitzpatrick of the government said we must all go to farm, and some of the people went to Fort Laramie and were badly treated. I only want to do that which is peaceful, and the Great Fathers know it, and also the Great Father who made us both. I came to Washington to see the Great Father in order to have peace and in

Library of Congress
Chief Red Cloud; photo by Heyn

order to have peace continue. That is all we want, and that is the reason why we are here now.

In 1868 men came out and brought papers. We are ignorant and do not read papers, and they did not tell us right what was in these papers. We wanted them to take away their forts, leave our country, would not make war, and give our traders something. They said we had bound ourselves to trade on the Missouri, and we said, no, we did not want that. The interpreters deceived us. When I went to Washington I saw the Great Father. The Great Father showed me what the treaties were; he showed me all these points and showed me that the interpreters had deceived me and did not let me know what the right side of the treaty was. All I want is right and justice. . . . I represent the Sioux Nation; they will be governed by what I say and what I represent. . . .

Look at me. I am poor and naked, but I am the Chief of the Nation. We do not want riches, we do not ask for riches, but we want our children properly trained and brought up. We look to you for your sympathy. Our riches will . . . do us no good; we cannot take away into the other world anything we have — we want to have love and peace. . . . We would like to know why commissioners are sent out there to do nothing but rob [us] and get the riches of this world away from us?

I was brought up among the traders and those who came out there in those early times. I had a good time for they treated us nicely and well. They taught me how to wear clothes and use tobacco, and to use firearms and ammunition, and all went on very well until the Great Father sent out another kind of men — men who drank whisky. He sent out whiskymen, men who drank and quarreled, men who were so bad that he could not keep them at home, and so he sent them out there.

I have sent a great many words to the Great Father, but I don't know that they ever reach the Great Father. They were drowned on the way, therefore I was a little offended with it. The words I told the Great Father lately would never come to him, so I thought I would come and tell you myself.

And I am going to leave you today, and I am going back to my home. I want to tell the people that we cannot trust his agents and superintendents. I don't want strange people that we know nothing about. I am very glad that you belong to us. I am very glad that we have come here and found you and that we can understand one another. I don't want any more such men sent out there, who are so poor that when they come out there their first thoughts are how they can fill their own pockets.

We want preserves in our reserves. We want honest men, and we want you to help to keep us in the lands that belong to us so that we may not be a prey to those who are viciously disposed. I am going back home. I am very glad that you have listened to me, and I wish you good-bye and give you an affectionate farewell.

The only good Indian is a dead Indian.
Philip H. Sheridan, 1869

Another Redskin bit the dust!
Anon., "The Nick Carter Library"

52.

Samuel L. Clemens ("Mark Twain"): My Watch

Innocents Abroad, published in 1869, had firmly established Samuel Clemens in his literary career, and in 1870 he married Olivia Langdon and settled down to write in Hartford, Connecticut. When the following instructive tale appeared in 1870, he was at the beginning of the twenty-five year period during which his greatest successes, including Tom Sawyer, Huckleberry Finn, *and* A Connecticut Yankee in King Arthur's Court, *were to be achieved.*

Source: *Sketches New and Old*, New York, 1875.

My beautiful new watch had run eighteen months without losing or gaining, and without breaking any part of its machinery or stopping. I had come to believe it infallible in its judgments about the time of day, and to consider its constitution and its anatomy imperishable. But at last, one night, I let it run down. I grieved about it as if it were a recognized messenger and forerunner of calamity. But by and by I cheered up, set the watch by guess, and commanded my bodings and superstitions to depart.

Next day I stepped into the chief jeweler's to set it by the exact time, and the head of the establishment took it out of my hand and proceeded to set it for me. Then he said, "She is four minutes slow — regulator wants pushing up." I tried to stop him — tried to make him understand that the watch kept perfect time. But no; all this human cabbage could see was that the watch was four minutes slow, and the regulator *must* be pushed up a little; and so, while I danced around him in anguish and implored him to let the watch alone, he calmly and cruelly did the shameful deed.

My watch began to gain. It gained faster and faster day by day. Within the week it sickened to a raging fever, and its pulse went up to a 150 in the shade. At the end of two months it had left all the timepieces of the town far in the rear, and was a fraction over thirteen days ahead of the almanac. It was away into November enjoying the snow while the October leaves were still turning. It hurried up house rent, bills payable, and such things in such a ruinous way that I could not abide it.

I took it to the watchmaker to be regulated. He asked me if I had ever had it repaired. I said no, it had never needed any repairing. He looked a look of vicious happiness and eagerly pried the watch open, and then put a small dice box into his eye and peered into its machinery. He said it wanted cleaning and oiling, besides regulating — come in a week.

After being cleaned, and oiled, and regulated, my watch slowed down to that degree that it ticked like a tolling bell. I began to be left by trains, I failed all appointments, I got to missing my dinner; my watch strung out three days' grace to four and let me go to protest; I gradually drifted back into yesterday, then day before, then into last week, and by and by the comprehension came upon me that, all solitary and alone, I was lingering along in week before last and the world was out of sight. I seemed to detect in myself a sort of sneaking fellow feeling for the mummy in the museum, and a desire to swap news with him.

I went to a watchmaker again. He took the watch all to pieces while I waited, and then said the barrel was "swelled." He said he could reduce it in three days. After this the watch *averaged* well, but nothing more. For half a day it would go like the very mischief and keep up such a barking, and wheezing, and whooping, and sneezing, and snorting that I could not hear myself think for the disturbance; and as long as it held out there was not a watch in the land that stood any chance against it. But the rest of the day it would keep on slowing down and fooling along, until all the clocks it had left behind caught up again. So, at last, at the end of twenty-four hours, it would trot up to the judges' stand all right and just in time. It would show a fair and square average, and no man could say it had done more or less than its duty.

But a correct average is only a mild virtue in a watch, and I took this instrument to another watchmaker. He said the kingbolt was broken. I said I was glad it was nothing more serious. To tell the plain truth, I had no idea what the kingbolt was, but I did not choose to appear ignorant to a stranger. He repaired the kingbolt, but what the watch gained in one way it lost in another. It would run awhile and then stop awhile, and then run awhile again, and so on, using its own discretion about the intervals. And every time it went off it kicked back like a musket. I padded my breast for a few days, but finally took the watch to another watchmaker. He picked it all to pieces and turned the ruin over and over under his glass; and then he said there appeared to be something the matter with the hair-trigger. He fixed it, and gave it a fresh start. It did well now, except that always at ten minutes to ten the hands would shut together like a pair of scissors, and from that time forth they would travel together.

The oldest man in the world could not make head or tail of the time of day by such a watch, and so I went again to have the thing repaired. This person said that the crystal had got bent, and that the mainspring was not straight. He also remarked that part of the works needed half-soling. He made these things all right, and then my timepiece performed unexceptionably, save that now and then, after working along quietly for nearly eight hours, everything inside would let go all of a sudden and begin to buzz like a bee, and the hands would straightway begin to spin round and round so fast that their individuality was lost completely, and they simply seemed a delicate spider's web over the face of the watch. She would reel off the next twenty-four hours in six or seven minutes, and then stop with a bang.

I went with a heavy heart to one more watchmaker, and looked on while he took her to pieces. Then I prepared to cross-question him rigidly, for this thing was getting serious. The watch had cost $200 originally, and I seemed to have paid out $2,000 or $3,000 for repairs. While I waited and looked on I presently recognized in this watchmaker an old acquaintance — steamboat engineer of other days, and not a good engineer, either. He examined all the parts carefully, just as the other watchmakers had done, and then delivered his verdict with the same confidence of manner.

He said: "She makes too much steam — you want to hang the monkey wrench on the safety valve!" I brained him on the spot and had him buried at my own expense.

My uncle William (now deceased, alas!) used to say that a good horse was a good horse until it had run away once, and that a good watch was a good watch until the repairers got a chance at it. And he used to wonder what became of all the unsuccessful tinkers, and gunsmiths, and shoemakers, and engineers, and blacksmiths; but nobody could ever tell him.

1871

53.

African Americans Appeal for Protection of Life and Property

One of the distinguishing characteristics of Southern life in the post-Civil War era was the attack on the life and property of African Americans by white Southerners. The persecution was carried out by extremists who saw no other alternative to the Reconstruction program imposed by the Radical Republicans of the North. The following petition to Congress of March 25, 1871, from African Americans of Kentucky is typical of the appeals made in response to such intimidation. Appended to the original copy of the petition is a list of 116 instances of violence to African Americans between 1867 and 1871. The most numerous are reports of African Americans hanged by lynch mobs, but there are also reports of homes, schools, and churches set afire, and whole families expelled from their homes by angry white mobs.

Source: National Archives, Record Group 46, Records of the U.S. Senate, Memorial. . . , April 11, 1871 (42 Congress).

To the Senate and House of Representatives in Congress assembled:

We the colored citizens of Frankfort and vicinity do this day memorialize your honorable bodies upon the condition of affairs now existing in this the state of Kentucky.

We would respectfully state that life, liberty, and property are unprotected among the colored race of this state. Organized bands of desperate and lawless men, mainly composed of soldiers of the late Rebel armies, armed, disciplined, and disguised, and bound by oath and secret obligations, have by force, terror, and violence subverted all civil society among colored people, thus utterly rendering insecure the safety of persons and property, overthrowing all those rights which are the primary basis and objects of the government which are expressly guaranteed to us by the Constitution of the United States as amended.

We believe you are not familiar with the description of the Ku Klux Klan's riding nightly over the country, going from county to county, and in the county towns spreading terror wherever they go by robbing,

"ONE VOTE LESS."—*Richmond Whig.*

Engraving by Thomas Nast from "Harper's Weekly"

whipping, ravishing, and killing our people without provocation, compelling colored people to break the ice and bathe in the chilly waters of the Kentucky River.

The legislature has adjourned; they refused to enact any laws to suppress Ku Klux disorder. We regard them as now being licensed to continue their dark and bloody deeds under cover of the dark night. They refuse to allow us to testify in the state courts where a white man is concerned. We find their deeds are perpetrated only upon colored men and white Republicans. We also find that for our services to the government and our race we have become the special object of hatred and persecution at the hands of the Democratic Party.

Our people are driven from their homes in great numbers, having no redress, only the U.S. courts, which is in many cases unable to reach them. We would state that we have been law-abiding citizens, pay our tax, and, in many parts of the state, our people have been driven from the polls — refused the right to vote. Many have been slaugh-

tered while attempting to vote; we ask how long is this state of things to last.

We appeal to you as law-abiding citizens to enact some laws that will protect us and that will enable us to exercise the rights of citizens. We see that the senator from this state denies there being organized bands of desperadoes in the state; for information we lay before you a number of violent acts [that] occurred during his administration. Although he, Stevenson, says half-dozen instances of violence did occur, these are not more than one-half the acts that have occurred.

The Democratic Party has here a political organization composed only of Democrats; not a single Republican can join them. Where many of these acts have been committed, it has been proven that they were the men, done with arms from the state arsenal. We pray you will take some steps to remedy these evils.

Done by a committee of grievances appointed at a meeting of all the colored citizens of Frankfort and vicinity.

54.

The Ku Klux Klan Act

The terrorist campaigns of the Ku Klux Klan prompted Congress in 1871 to establish the Congressional Ku Klux Klan Committee to investigate its activities. On April 20, Congress passed an Act to enforce the Fourteenth Amendment. This was the third of four Force Acts passed between 1870 and 1875 to buttress federal laws in the South. An unavowed, but equally important, motive for the passage of the Acts was the Republican effort to use the executive power to maintain Republican governments in the South against the resistance of the Ku Klux Klan. Some of the Force Acts were declared unconstitutional by the Supreme Court in 1883, and the remainder during the second Cleveland administration.

Source: *Statutes*, XVII, pp. 13-15.

An act to enforce the provisions of the Fourteenth Amendment to the Constitution of the United States, and for other purposes.

Be it enacted by the Senate and House of Representatives of the United States of America in Congress assembled, that any person who, under color of any law, statute, ordinance, regulation, custom, or usage of any state, shall subject, or cause to be subjected, any person within the jurisdiction of the United States to the deprivation of any rights, privileges, or immunities secured by the Constitution of the United States shall, any such law, statute, ordinance, regulation, custom, or usage of the state to the contrary notwithstanding, be liable to the party injured in any action at law, suit in equity, or other proper proceeding for redress; such proceeding to be prosecuted in the several District or Circuit courts of the United States, with and subject to the same rights of appeal, review upon error, and other remedies provided in like cases in such courts, under the provisions of the act of the 9th of April, 1866, entitled "An act to protect all persons in the United States in their civil rights, and to furnish the means of their vindication"; and the other remedial laws of the United States which are in their nature applicable in such cases.

Section 2. That if two or more persons within any state or territory of the United States shall conspire together to overthrow, or to put down, or to destroy by force the government of the United States; or to levy war against the United States; or to oppose by force the authority of the government of the United States; or by force, intimidation, or threat to prevent, hinder, or delay the execution of any law of the United States; or by force to seize, take, or possess any property of the United States contrary to the authority thereof; or by force, intimidation, or threat to prevent any person from accepting or holding any office or trust or place of confidence under the United States, or from discharging the duties thereof; or by force, intimidation, or threat to induce any officer of the United States to leave any state, district, or place where his duties as such officer might lawfully be performed; or to injure him in his person or property on account of his lawful discharge of the duties of his office, or to injure his person while engaged in the lawful discharge of the duties of his office, or to injure his property so as to molest, interrupt, hinder, or impede him in the discharge of his official duty; or by force, intimidation, or threat to deter any party or witness in any court of the United States from attending such court or from testifying in any matter pending in such court fully, freely, and truthfully; or to injure any such party or witness in his person or property on account of his having so attended or testified; or by force, intimidation, or threat to influence the verdict, presentment, or indictment, of any juror or grand juror in any court of the United States; or to injure such juror in his person or property on account of any verdict, presentment, or indictment lawfully assented to by him, or on account of his being or having been such juror; or shall conspire together or go in disguise upon the public highway or upon the premises of another for the purpose, either directly or indirectly, of depriving any person or any class of persons of the equal protection of the laws, or of equal privileges or immunities under the laws, or for the purpose of preventing or hindering the constituted authorities of any state from giving or securing to all persons within such state the equal protection of the laws; or shall conspire together for the purpose of in any manner impeding, hindering, obstructing, or defeating the due course of justice in any state or territory with intent to deny to any citizen of the United States the due and equal protection of the laws; or to injure any person in his person or his property for lawfully enforcing the right of any person or class of persons to the equal protection of the laws; or by force, intimidation, or threat to prevent any citizen of the United States lawfully entitled to vote from giving his support or advocacy in a

lawful manner toward or in favor of the election of any lawfully qualified person as an elector of President or Vice-President of the United States, or as a member of the Congress of the United States; or to injure any such citizen in his person or property on account of such support or advocacy; each and every person so offending shall be deemed guilty of a high crime, and, upon conviction thereof in any District or Circuit Court of the United States or District or Supreme Court of any territory of the United States having jurisdiction of similar offenses, shall be punished by a fine not less than $500 nor more than $5,000, or by imprisonment, with or without hard labor, as the court may determine, for a period of not less than six months nor more than six years, as the court may determine, or by both such fine and imprisonment as the court shall determine.

And if any one or more persons engaged in any such conspiracy shall do, or cause to be done, any act in furtherance of the object of such conspiracy whereby any person shall be injured in his person or property, or deprived of having and exercising any right or privilege of a citizen of the United States, the person so injured or deprived of such rights and privileges may have and maintain an action for the recovery of damages occasioned by such injury or deprivation of rights and privileges against any one or more of the persons engaged in such conspiracy; such action to be prosecuted in the proper District or Circuit Court of the United States, with and subject to the same rights of appeal, review upon error, and other remedies provided in like cases in such courts under the provisions of the act of April 9, 1866. . . .

Section 3. That in all cases where insurrection, domestic violence, unlawful combinations, or conspiracies in any state shall so obstruct or hinder the execution of the laws thereof and of the United States as to deprive any portion or class of the people of such state of any of the rights, privileges, or immunities, or protection, named in the Constitution and secured by this act; and the constituted authorities of such state shall either be unable to protect, or shall, from any cause, fail in or refuse protection of the people in such rights, such facts shall be deemed a denial by such state of the equal protection of the laws to which they are entitled under the Constitution of the United States; and in all such cases, or whenever any such insurrection, violence, unlawful combination, or conspiracy shall oppose or obstruct the laws of the United States or the due execution thereof, or impede or obstruct the due course of justice under the same, it shall be lawful for the President, and it shall be his duty to take such measures, by the employment of the militia or the land and naval forces of the United States, or of either, or by other means, as he may deem necessary for the suppression of such insurrection, domestic violence, or combinations; and any person who shall be arrested under the provisions of this and the preceding section shall be delivered to the marshal of the proper district, to be dealt with according to law.

Section 4. That whenever in any state or part of a state the unlawful combinations named in the preceding section of this act shall be organized and armed, and so numerous and powerful as to be able, by violence, to either overthrow or set at defiance the constituted authorities of such state, and of the United States within such state, or when the constituted authorities are in complicity with, or shall connive at the unlawful purposes of, such powerful and armed combinations; and whenever, by reason of either or all of the causes aforesaid, the conviction of such offenders and the preservation of the public safety shall become in such district impracticable, in every such case such combinations shall be deemed a rebellion against the government of the United States, and during the continuance of such rebellion, and within the limits of the district which shall be so under the

sway thereof, such limits to be prescribed by proclamation, it shall be lawful for the President of the United States, when in his judgment the public safety shall require it, to suspend the privileges of the writ of habeas corpus, to the end that such rebellion may be overthrown.

Provided, that all the provisions of the 2nd Section of an act entitled "An act relating to habeas corpus, and regulating judicial proceedings in certain cases," approved March 3, 1863, which relate to the discharge of prisoners other than prisoners of war, and to the penalty for refusing to obey the order of the court, shall be in full force so far as the same are applicable to the provisions of this section: *Provided further,* that the President shall first have made proclamation, as now provided by law, commanding such insurgents to disperse: *And provided also,* that the provisions of this section shall not be in force after the end of the next regular session of Congress.

Section 5. That no person shall be a grand or petit juror in any court of the United States upon any inquiry, hearing, or trial of any suit, proceeding, or prosecution based upon or arising under the provisions of this act who shall, in the judgment of the court, be in complicity with any such combination or conspiracy; and every such juror shall, before entering upon any such inquiry, hearing, or trial, take and subscribe an oath in open court that he has never, directly or indirectly, counseled, advised, or voluntarily aided any such combination or conspiracy; and each and every person who shall take this oath, and shall therein swear falsely, shall be guilty of perjury, and shall be subject to the pains and penalties declared against that crime, and the 1st Section of the act entitled "An act defining additional causes of challenge and prescribing an additional oath for grand and petit jurors in the United States courts," approved June 17, 1862, be, and the same is hereby, repealed.

Section 6. That any person or persons,

having knowledge that any of the wrongs conspired to be done and mentioned in the 2nd Section of this act are about to be committed, and having power to prevent or aid in preventing the same, shall neglect or refuse so to do, and such wrongful act shall be committed, such person or persons shall be liable to the person injured, or his legal representatives, for all damages caused by any such wrongful act which such first-named person or persons by reasonable diligence could have prevented; and such damages may be recovered in an action on the case in the proper Circuit Court of the United States; and any number of persons guilty of such wrongful neglect or refusal may be joined as defendants in such action.

55.

Federal Grand Jury Report on the Ku Klux Klan

The Ku Klux Klan, like the Knights of the White Camelia and other secret societies, attempted to restore white social and political supremacy despite the contrary provisions of the Fourteenth Amendment. The activities of the most active Klan group, in South Carolina, led President Grant to exercise his powers to enforce the Amendment. He suspended the right of habeas corpus in nine South Carolina counties in October 1871, and several military arrests followed. At the same time a grand jury was summoned in Columbia to investigate the activities of the Klan. A portion of the report of the grand jury follows, addressed to the judges of the U.S. Circuit Court.

Source: 42 Congress, 2 Session, House Report No. 22, Pt. 1, pp. 48-49.

IN CLOSING THE LABORS of the present term, the grand jury beg leave to submit the following presentment.

During the whole session we have been engaged in investigations of the most grave and extraordinary character — investigations of the crimes committed by the organization known as the Ku Klux Klan. The evidence elicited has been voluminous, gathered from the victims themselves and their families, as well as those who belong to the Klan and participated in its crimes. The jury has been shocked beyond measure at the developments which have been made in their presence of the number and character of the atrocities committed, producing a state of terror and a sense of utter insecurity among a large portion of the people, especially the colored population. The evidence produced before us has established the following facts:

1. That there has existed since 1868, in many counties of the state, an organization known as the "Ku Klux Klan," or "Invisible Empire of the South," which embraces in its membership a large proportion of the white population of every profession and class.

2. That this Klan [is] bound together by an oath, administered to its members at the time of their initiation into the order, of which the following is a copy:

OBLIGATION

I [name], before the immaculate Judge of Heaven and earth, and upon the Holy Evangelists of Almighty God, do, of my own free will and accord, subscribe to the following sacredly binding obligation:

1. We are on the side of justice, humanity, and constitutional liberty, as bequeathed to us in its purity by our forefathers.

2. We oppose and reject the principles of the Radical Party.

3. We pledge mutual aid to each other in sickness, distress, and pecuniary embarrassment.

4. Female friends, widows, and their households shall ever be special objects of our regard and protection.

Any member divulging, or causing to be divulged, any of the foregoing obligations, shall meet the fearful penalty and traitor's doom, which is Death! Death! Death!

That, in addition to this oath, the Klan has a constitution and bylaws, which provides, among other things, that each member shall furnish himself with a pistol, a Ku Klux gown, and a signal instrument. That the operations of the Klan were executed in the night, and were invariably directed against members of the Republican Party by warnings to leave the country, by whippings, and by murder.

3. That in large portions of the counties of York, Union, and Spartanburgh, to which our attention has been more particularly called in our investigations during part of the time for the last eighteen months, the civil law has been set at defiance and ceased to afford any protection to the citizens.

4. That the Klan, in carrying out the purposes for which it was organized and armed, inflicted summary vengeance on the colored citizens of these counties by breaking into their houses at the dead of night, dragging them from their beds, torturing them in the most inhuman manner, and in many instances murdering them; and this, mainly, on account of their political affilia-tions. Occasionally, additional reasons operated, but in no instance was the political feature wanting.

5. That for this condition of things, for all these violations of law and order and the sacred rights of citizens, many of the leading men of those counties were responsible. It was proven that large numbers of the most prominent citizens were members of the order. Many of this class attended meetings of the Grand Klan. At a meeting of the Grand Klan held in Spartanburgh County, at which there were representatives from the various dens of Spartanburgh, York, Union, and Chester counties, in this state, besides a number from North Carolina, a resolution was adopted that no raids should be undertaken or anyone whipped or injured by members of the Klan without orders from the Grand Klan. The penalty for violating this resolution was 100 lashes on the bare back for the first offense; and for the second, death.

This testimony establishes the nature of the discipline enforced in the order, and also the fact that many of the men who were openly and publicly speaking against the Klan, and pretending to deplore the work of this murderous conspiracy, were influential members of the order and directing its operations, even in detail.

The jury has been appalled as much at the number of outrages as at their character, it appearing that 11 murders and over 600 whippings have been committed in York County alone. Our investigation in regard to the other counties named has been less full; but it is believed, from the testimony, that an equal or greater number has been committed in Union, and that the number is not greatly less in Spartanburgh and Laurens.

We are of the opinion that the most vigorous prosecution of the parties implicated in these crimes is imperatively demanded; that without this there is great danger that these outrages will be continued, and that there will be no security to our fellow citizens of African descent.

We would say further that unless the strong arm of the government is interposed to punish these crimes committed upon this class of citizens, there is every reason to believe that an organized and determined attempt at retaliation will be made, which can only result in a state of anarchy and bloodshed too horrible to contemplate.

56.

Wendell Phillips: Resolutions Against the Profit System

Wendell Phillips worked on behalf of nearly every reform movement of the nineteenth century: abolition, temperance, women's rights, and labor. He joined the Labor Reform Party and was its unsuccessful candidate for governor of Massachusetts in 1870. He drew up the following platform for the Labor Reform Convention that met at Worcester on September 4, 1871. In a speech supporting the platform he expressed his rather strange conception of the labor reform movement in these words: "If any man asks me, therefore, what value I place first upon this movement, I should say it was the movement of humanity to protect itself; and secondly, it is the insurance of peace; and thirdly, it is a guaranty against the destruction of capital."

Source: *Speeches, Lectures, and Letters,* 2nd series, Boston, 1905, pp. 152-153.

We affirm as a fundamental principle that labor, the creator of wealth, is entitled to all it creates.

Affirming this, we avow ourselves willing to accept the final results of the operation of a principle so radical — such as the overthrow of the whole profit making system, the extinction of all monopolies, the abolition of privileged classes, universal education and fraternity, perfect freedom of exchange, and, best and grandest of all, the final obliteration of that foul stigma upon our so-called Christian civilization — the poverty of the masses. Holding principles as radical as these, and having before our minds an ideal condition so noble, we are still aware that our goal cannot be reached at a single leap. We take into account the ignorance, selfishness, prejudice, corruption, and demoralization of the leaders of the people, and, to a large extent, of the people themselves; but, still, we demand that some steps be taken in this direction; therefore,

Resolved, that we declare war with the wages system, which demoralizes alike the hirer and the hired, cheats both, and enslaves the workingman; war with the present system of finance, which robs labor and gorges capital, makes the rich richer and the poor poorer, and turns a republic into an aristocracy of capital; war with these lavish grants of the public lands to speculating companies, and, whenever in power, we pledge ourselves to use every just and legal means to resume all such grants heretofore made; war with the system of enriching capitalists by the creation and increase of public interest bearing debts. We demand that every facility and all encouragement shall be given by law to cooperation in all branches of industry and trade, and that the same aid be given to cooperative efforts that has heretofore been given to railroads and other enterprises.

We demand a ten hour day for factory work, as a first step, and that eight hours be the working day of all persons thus employed hereafter. We demand that, whenever women are employed at public expense to do the same kind and amount of work as men perform, they shall receive the same wages. We demand that all public debts be paid at once in accordance with the terms of the contract, and that no more debts be created. Viewing the contract importation of coolies as only another form of the slave trade, we demand that all contracts made relative thereto be void in this country; and that no public ship and no steamship which receives public subsidy shall aid in such importation.

57.

"The Schooner *E. A. Horton*"

The ballad reprinted below tells a true story. The E. A. Horton, *out of Gloucester, Massachusetts, was taken into custody by Canadian authorities in September 1871 (not 1861, as the song incorrectly states), for violation of an old treaty requiring U.S. fishing vessels to stay outside the three-mile limit. The* Horton *was moored and partly dismantled at Guysborough, Nova Scotia, as had been other ships seized under equally flimsy pretexts. The U.S. government, not wishing to make an international issue of the matter, ignored the plight of such ships, and the captain of the* Horton, *Harvey Knowlton, decided to free his own vessel. With the help of six of his fellow fishermen, Knowlton began to assemble supplies. The group met at night on Sunday, October 8, 1871, went aboard the* Horton, *and by 2:30* A.M. *had got her afloat. They escaped from Guysborough and out to sea, but without a compass or charts, and had to weather a gale before making their home port. The news of their daring escape was carried to other fishermen by the song.*

Source: *Ballads Migrant in New England,* Helen H. Flanders and Marguerite Olney, eds., New York, 1953.

☙ THE SCHOONER *E. A. HORTON*

Come all you sons of Uncle Sam, come listen to me awhile,
And I'll tell you of a capture that was made in Yankee style.

'Twas the schooner *E. A. Horton* in the British harbor lie,
She was taken by the *Sweepstakes* while cruising in disguise.
Our treaties they've rejected and our governments defied.
It's now you've stole our fishermen so Johnnies, mind yer eye.

'Twas the thirteenth day of October in the year of sixty-one,
Brave Knowlton and his comrades, the day it was begun
While the British thick-skulls were sleepin' with red ruin on their brain
We stole away our fisherman and brought her back again.

Says brave Knowlton to his comrades, "If you will follow me
We'll have the *Horton* home again whate'er the cost may be;
We'll stick to one another like brothers just as true,
And we'll show these Yankee thievish-men what Yankee lads can do."

'Twas early the next mornin' the news did spread about;
They found the gold prospector with the *Horton* had stepped out;
The news began to penetrate the British skulls so thick
They finally did acknowledge 'twas a bold and Yankee trick.

Now, boys, there is a jolly time in Glou-chester tonight,
For heavy guns are firin' and torches burnin' bright.
The band plays, "Yankee Doodle" and the voices loudly ring
For the Yankee boys are shoutin' that the *Horton* has got in.

Now you Dominion Canaday, I warn you to beware.
You better sign the treaty and settle this affair.
And always do to others as you'll have 'em do to you,
And don't try to treat your neighbor like old Johnny tried to do.

58.

P. S. Dorney: Anti-Chinese Rioting in Los Angeles

The number of Chinese arriving in the United States reached sizeable proportions by the middle of the nineteenth century. The need for cheap labor created by the Civil War and the construction of railroads in the West resulted in a heavy flow of Asian immigrants. By 1860, the number in California approached 35,000, most of them in San Francisco. With the completion of the Central Pacific and Union Pacific railroads, Chinese laborers flooded the labor markets in the West Coast cities. American workers, feeling threatened by the competition of the Chinese and believing that employers exploited "coolie" labor to depress wages, reacted by staging riots and resorting to violence against the "yellow peril." The most violent attack on the Chinese occurred in Los Angeles in October 1871. P. S. Dorney observed the episode and wrote the following account fifteen years later.

Source: *Overland Monthly*, March 1886: "A Prophecy Partly Verified."

As a result of the gubernatorial message of 1854, the state senate appointed a committee . . . to investigate the "Chinese evil." An exhaustive investigation was had; and, read in the light of latter days, the report of that committee proves the far-seeing judgment of those who made it. The report declared:

The Chinese are destructive to the best interests of the state and dangerous to its peace. They come not as freemen but as serfs and hirelings of a master. It needs no Solomon to predict the result: disputes will take place and blood will flow, to be followed by the expulsion of a population who will be driven from the state by violence instead of law.

Already this fearful prophecy has been partly fulfilled. In the mining troubles of Shasta, the first libation of blood reddened the path of the coming conflict; and the riot of 1871 was the next and greatest horror that took place to prove the truth of the senatorial prophecy of 1852.

For some time prior to the 28th of October, 1871, the Chinese quarter of Los Angeles had been in a state of agitation, growing out of a dispute concerning the ownership and possession of a Chinese woman. "Chinatown" was then, as now, divided between distinct clans. One of those clans claimed the woman, Quangk Cow, by name. A rival clan disputed the claim and spirited Quangk away to Santa Barbara. The first claimant, however, utilized the machinery of the courts, and the county of Los Angeles was put to the expense of bringing the woman back to answer a buncombe charge of larceny. Upon her arrival, Quangk Cow was immediately bailed out and fell into the hands of her original masters. This result created intense excitement among the Celestials, and a carriage containing the leader of the successful faction and the disputed woman was surrounded and fired upon in broad daylight and in the heart of Los Angeles by a band of infuriated highbinders.

The clan, so cruelly nonplussed by the machinery of "Mellica man's law," contained a born diplomat — a kind of guttersnipe Talleyrand — whose name was Hing Ho. To Hing a brilliant idea occurred. If the Montagues might move the machinery of the court, why may not the Capulets invoke the prestige of the church? Hing Ho resolved to woo and wed Quangk Cow. Quangk was willing, and the twain succeeded in meeting in the presence of a parson, where — backed by all the powers of

Church and State — the disputed woman was transferred to the keeping of Hing and thereby to the clan so recently overreached by the managers of the larceny scheme.

Wedded "allee same Mellica gal," Quangk Cow was firmly anchored in the clan of Hing Ho, and Chinatown prepared for war — bitter war, unending war. One side of a narrow street (Nigger Alley), flanked by low adobe houses, was seized and barricaded by those who originally claimed Quangk, while the other was fortified by the friends of Hing. Thus divided, the Celestial inhabitants of Los Angeles spent several days scowling and chattering like infuriated monkeys; as yet, however, no blood was shed.

In the meantime, the case was referred to some tribunal in San Francisco by which Hing Ho was condemned to death. To execute the sentence, two cutthroats were dispatched by steamer to Los Angeles, where they arrived on the morning of October 26. Hing had been apprised by telegraph of his sentence and of the coming of his executioners. So accurately had they been described by the 'Frisco friends of Hing that the latter pointed them out just as they stepped from the San Pedro train, and they were arrested on warrants previously sworn to by the condemned man. The two would-be executioners were immediately brought before a justice and held in $5,000 bail each. The bail was instantly furnished, and the agents of the death court were escorted in triumph to Chinatown.

The liberated assassins were lionized by their Los Angeles adherents. Their appearance in the Mongolian quarter was heralded abroad by the pounding of gongs and the crackling of crackers, accompanied by a pandemonium of guttural yells. The 'Frisco fighters were the heroes of the hour. They took immediate charge of the fighting force of their clan, and hostilities began.

For two days that portion of the city cursed by the presence of the Mongols was in a state of war. Every house was barricaded, and the crack of revolvers and the bursting of bombs reverberating throughout the city kept the people in a constant state of anxious excitement. Crowds gathered at the intersection of Commercial and Los Angeles Streets, and some of the most daring ventured as near the Mongol quarter as Carillo's or Caswell's corner; but they were quickly dispersed by a shower of bullets from the pistols of the Mongolian shooters.

Business and travel in and about the Chinese quarter being wholly suspended, the authorities resolved to quell the disorder. To this end the police made a raid upon the fighters late on the afternoon of October 28. This show of authority had a singular effect upon the Chinese. The storm of internecine fury instantly lulled. Upon all sides a peculiar cry went up; the fighters, as one man, united in opposing the police; and, taken wholly by surprise, the "peelers" were routed in a moment.

The town was now thoroughly moved. A feeling of deep alarm, not unmixed with fear, spread abroad. Places of business and residences adjacent to the scene of war were closed and abandoned, and an immense concourse of anxious spectators collected at the intersections of Main and Aliso, and of Commercial and Los Angeles Streets.

The police prepared for another charge and were joined by a few citizens, among whom was "Bob" Thompson, a well-known and very popular character. The second charge was better calculated and more determined than the first but was met as before; the police were again routed, leaving behind them Officer Bilderrain, desperately wounded, a Spanish boy shot in the foot, and citizen Thompson writhing in the agonies of death. A third charge resulted only in bearing off the wounded. The boy and Officer Bilderrain were taken to their homes, while Thompson was borne to a drugstore on Main Street. It was now between 6 and 7 o'clock in the evening, and a vast multitude were assembled in front of this store.

About 8 o'clock the death of Thompson was announced. The announcement was received in sullen silence; but in a moment the crowd melted away, and Main Street was deserted. In another moment, armed men were seen hastening, singly and in clusters, from every street and avenue, all heading toward Chinatown. The whole city seemed moved by one grim and tacit purpose — men streamed down from the hills and swarmed from the suburbs, while "Sonora" poured forth a horde of swarthy avengers. Businessmen closed their shops and joined the gathering clans, and in less than fifteen minutes after the announcement of "Bob" Thompson's death, the cracking of rifles, the roar of shotguns, and the rattle of small arms proclaimed the investment of Chinatown.

About 9 o'clock the first Chinese was captured. He was armed with a hatchet and was taken while attempting to break through the cordon of whites that surrounded the Chinese quarter. A dozen hands clutched him, and a hundred throats hoarsely shouted: "A rope! To the hill! To the hill!"

A man, then and now of standing and influence, dashed into a neighboring store and presently emerged, shaking aloft the first rope — a smooth, kinky, brand-new coil.

As the maddened men surged up the hill (Temple Street), the little ill-favored prisoner, borne bodily along, was stabbed in the back and side and was dead as a doorstep before General Baldwin's corral was reached, to the gate-beam of which the dead man was hanged. While the rope was being fastened to the neck of the corpse, two burly human beasts held it erect, while an Irish shoemaker known as "Crazy Johnson" stood guard, revolver in hand. Johnson is now a prominent leader of the San Bernardino Holiness Band.

By this time, Chinatown, wholly surrounded, was in a state of siege. Mounted men came galloping from the country —

the vaquero was in his glory, and the cry was: *"Carajo la Chino!"*

Among the Spaniards whose boldness and vigor attracted attention that night was Vasquez, afterward famous as a bandit, and Jesus Martinez, his chum and relative. Chief among the Americans, plying a Henry rifle until excessive labor clogged its mechanism, the writer observed a certain high official; and in the van of the fight, one of the city fathers — a member of the City Council and a Wells Fargo official — valiantly struck out from the shoulder. A young Israelite, heavy-framed and coarse-featured, and a German known as "Dutch Charley" were prominently active and cruel. "Crazy Johnson" seemed to represent all Ireland; while Jacques, a Frenchman, shirtless and hatless, and armed with a cleaver, reveled in the memory of the Pont Neuf and the Sans Culottes. Jacques was the fire-fiend of the occasion — time and again Chinatown was ablaze — and Jacques with his cleaver was always found pictured in the glare.

After the assault became general, the Chinese never returned shot or blow; but securely barricading every avenue of approach, each like a badger retired to his den and in sullen silence awaited his fate. But few attempted to escape, and all who made the attempt fell riddled with bullets. Not far from eleven o'clock the Main Street side of Chinatown fell into the hands of the besiegers, and, led by Jesus Martinez, the assailants scaled the low adobe walls and mounted to the asphaltum roof. This achievement was hailed with deafening cheers by the crowd below.

The condition of the Chinese had now become wretched indeed. The "Quarters," it will be remembered, were an old Spanish hacienda one story high, with an open courtyard in the center. Martinez and his companions, armed with axes as well as firearms, cut holes in the asphaltum roof, through which the cowering creatures below were shot in their hiding places or hunted from room to room out into the

open courtyard, where death from the bullets of those on the roof was certain. Within or without, death was inevitable. The alternative was terrible. As each separate wretch, goaded from his covert, sought in his despair the open space, a volley from the roof brought him down; a chorus of yells telegraphed that fact to the surrounding mob, and the yells were answered by a hoarse roar of savage satisfaction.

A simultaneous rush from Los Angeles Street forced the doors upon that side, and the work of real diabolism began. Men were dragged forth, many of them mortally wounded, and hurled headlong from a raised sidewalk to the ground. To the necks of some of the most helpless the mob fastened ropes and, with a whoop and a hurrah, rushed down Los Angeles Street to the hanging place, dragging some writhing wretch prone upon the ground. More of the doomed and bleeding miserables were jerked along by as many eager hands as could lay hold of clothing and queue, cuffed and cursed in the meantime by the infuriated multitude. A boy was thus led to the place of slaughter. The little fellow was not above twelve years of age. He had been but a month in the country and knew not a word of English. He seemed paralyzed by fear — his eyes were fixed and staring, and his face blue-blanched and idiotic. He was hanged.

Close behind the boy followed the Chinese doctor; a man of extreme age, well known, and reputed wealthy. The doctor begged piteously for his life, pleading in English and in Spanish; but he might as well have pleaded with wolves. At last he attempted to bribe those who were hurrying him to his death. He offered $1,000 — $2,000 — $3,000 — $5,000 — $10,000 — $15,000! But to no purpose. He was hanged, and his $15,000 was spirited away none the less. At his death the old man wore a valuable diamond ring upon his left index finger, but when his corpse was cut down it was found that the left index finger had been wrenched from its socket, and finger and ring were gone.

One very tall Chinaman, while being hustled to the place of execution, endeavored from time to time to strike aside the hands that clutched him, accompanying his efforts with spasmodic ejaculations, such as: "All light, me go, me no flaid!" When this man was brought to Goler's (a blacksmith and wagonmaker's shop, the awning of which served as a gallows), the mob [was] in a state of frenzy over the famine of rope. "Rope, more rope!" was hoarsely howled upon all sides, and — let humanity blush — a woman, a married one, and a mother, rushed to appease the human tigers with her clothesline. This woman kept a boarding house on Los Angeles Street, directly opposite Goler's shop.

Goler's awning being filled with pendant dead, a large wagon of prairie schooner kind was made to serve as a gallows tree. With the clothesline the tall Chinaman was swung from the driver's seat of the prairie schooner. The man being very tall, he could not be swung wholly clear; his toes still lightly touched the ground. Among oaths and derisive cries of "Rise 'em, Riley!" desperate efforts were made to swing the man clear of the ground but to no purpose. The act of sickening brutality by which — the writer being witness — the victim's death was, in the fury of the moment, compassed is not fit for these pages. The murderer, "Dutch Charley," a tinsmith by trade, was afterward sent to San Quentin from San Bernardino County for the murder of a squaw.

Charley's act was the crowning horror of that horrible night. It revolted even the baser brutes who had urged him to its commission. Brutality had sickened itself. The babel of passion was hushed and abashed, and in sullen silence the mob fell to pieces and slunk away in the night, like a gorged and tired beast.

It was midnight, and a body of men appointed by the sheriff cut down the dead — twenty-three in number. Nearly all had been dragged through the streets at the end of a rope, and all were found shot and stabbed as well as hanged. Such was the first completed act of the drama prophesied by the senate of 1854.

———————◆———————

The republican form of government is the highest form of government; but because of this it requires the highest type of human nature — a type nowhere at present existing.

HERBERT SPENCER, *The Americans*

Billboards in New York City about 1870

MONEY TO BURN

Nations that experience the trauma of war often seek to heal their psychic wounds in a postwar entertainment binge, and in this America was no exception in the aftermath of the Civil War. Indeed, the pattern was reinforced by two consequences of industrial development during and after the war: the amassing of great private wealth and the rapid growth of the cities. Private fortunes provided financial resources to support refined entertainment (opera, for instance), while the concentration of people in cities provided audiences for mass entertainment. It is probably no accident that New York's Metropolitan Museum of Art and the Kentucky Derby were both founded in the 1870s. Also involved in America's postwar entertainment boom was a great hunger for self-improvement, virtually a culture panic. This was manifested in the popularity of travel, of amateur science, and of public lectures; during this period the Chautauqua movement developed alongside the older Lyceum. The vulgar version of this impulse took the form of a taste for the exotic, the bizarre, and the spectacular.

(Above) Lester Wallack in a carriage outside his New York theater; (left) Edwin Booth as Hamlet

The American theater, though largely dependent on Europe for ideas and personalities, began to develop on its own in the decades after the war. Minstrel shows, variety shows, and musical comedy became popular and the traveling companies and circuit theaters which lasted through the days of vaudeville were built throughout the country. The cities had their theaters, of course, but it became common for even small towns to have a theater or "opera house"; these were often the sole source of entertainment for a small community.

(Below) Ada Isaaca Menken, costumed for her role in "The Child of the Sun." She gained international fame for her role in "Mazeppa"

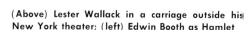

(Above) **Mrs. John Drew's Arch Street Theater in Philadelphia, 1883;** (below left) **Joe Jefferson as ''Rip Van Winkle,''** 1869; (below right) **Sarah Bernhardt in ''Le Sphinx,''** 1880

Mr. Frederick Coombs, a crackpot inventor and pitchman, who used a resemblance to Washington as a come-on for his book "Popular Phrenology"

There seemed to be a market for anything in the expansive "Gilded Age," and there were always innumerable ways to get rid of extra money. The new popularity of science opened the field of pseudo-science and quackery to enterprising men, who stood ready to cure anything with tonics and strange devices. On a slightly higher plane, horse racing, traditionally the sport of kings, became available to the masses, and great horses vied with boxing champions as the popular heroes of the day.

Advertisement for the miraculous cure and prevention of disease possible from Professor Caldwell's electric shock treatment; Signorina Maria Spelterini crossing Niagara Rapids

WONDERFUL DISCOVERY!!

Hundreds of little Nerves and Muscles respond to the action of the Wonderful Magneto-Galvanic Battery the moment it is applied. It instantly allays Pain, Strengthens the Weak and Painful parts, and draws all Poison from the Blood.

It is the best Preventive and Cure for Biliousness, Sick Headache, Skin Eruptions, Impure Blood, Fevers, Pimples on the Face, Giddiness, Feverishness, Mental Depression, Want of Appetite, Sourness of Stomach, Constipation, Vomiting, Thirst, &c., and to remove the effects of errors in Eating and Drinking.

As Lightning Purifies the Air, so must Electricity Purify The Blood.

ELECTRICITY

The Crowning Medical and Scientific Triumph of the Nineteenth Century.

The Friend of Man   *The Foe of Disease*

BEFORE USING.   AFTER USING.

The Blood is the Life !   JOY TO INVALIDS !!

AN OUNCE OF PREVENTION WORTH A POUND OF CURE !

NEARLY ALL DISEASES PREVENTED AND EFFECTUALLY CURED BY

PROFESSOR CALDWELL'S MAGNETO-GALVANIC BATTERIES.

GOOD TIDINGS FOR THE HEALTHY AND AFFLICTED.

Hammill and Brown in their great 5 mile race on the Hudson, 1867; Hammill won on a foul

(Above) The champion trotter George W. Jarvis; (below) the trotting stallion George M. Patchen, Jr. from California, victor in a match race with Commodore Vanderbilt on Long Island, 1866

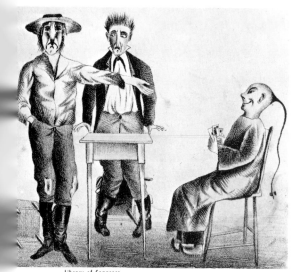

(Above) Bret Harte, photographed about 187.; (left) illustration for Harte's "Heathen Chinee" "We are ruined by Chinese cheap labor."

While American art was generally lagging and derivative, a new kind of literature was evolving in some corners of the country that, though unappreciated at the time, came eventually to be recognized as the long-awaited native literature. Drawing on the resources of local color and frontier humor — themselves both minor genres — the new literature utilized vernacular speech as a positive element suitable for protagonists. Until this period, such speech had almost invariably been used for making invidious contrasts — the villain and the boor spoke dialect, while everyone else spoke

(Left) Mark Twain and George Washington Cable (below left) "Josh Billings," Henry Wheeler Shaw (below) "Artemus Ward," Charles F. Browne

(Above) Cartoon by Thomas Nast from "Notes from Kentucky" by Petroleum V. Nasby: "Suffer Little White Children to Come Unto Me."

King's English. The workers in the vernacular were not confined to any one section: James Russell Lowell, Josh Billings, and Artemus Ward wrote of Eastern and New England characters; George W. Cable and Joel Chandler Harris worked in the South; Edward Eggleston and Mark Twain were of the Midwest. The simple use of vernacular speech did not, of course, constitute greatness in itself; but it was a necessary element for American literature, and an essential element in the truly great "Huckleberry Finn."

(Right) Santa in 1872; (below) Clement Moore, author of "The Night Before Christmas"

A rally against Chinese immigrants by the Workingmen's Trade and Labor Union in San Francisco in the 1870s

In the aftermath of the Civil War, American entertainment often dealt with the changing social and political landscape by lampooning those whose new rights and aspirations challenged the status quo. Demeaning caricatures of African Americans, Native Americans, and other minorities in illustrations, stage shows, and literature were popular with white audiences. This backlash also took more direct forms, such as public demonstrations.

(Below) During the 1880s, Currier and Ives, the most-respected publisher of commercial lithographs, carried a series of racist "Darktown" cartoons, an indication of the respectability of racial humor during the period; (left) similarly indicative is this caricature of a Native American from 1875

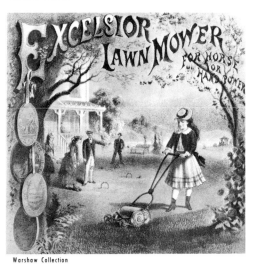

Advertisements for a variety of new, labor-saving devices, indicating the expansion both of consumer goods and of business advertising of those products: (top) a wringer washer is so practical the housewife is wearing her best dress; (left) a mower even a child can operate; (below) "Old Sachem Bitters" for what ails you, and an "Eureka" mop for floors

The beach at Atlantic City about 1865; bathing costume seems to consist of old clothes

(Above) Picnic lunch inside Mammoth Cave, Ky.;
(right) cog railway, Mt. Washington, N.H.

A group of astronomers and photographers gathered at Burlington, Iowa, August 1869, to o
record a total eclipse of the sun. Photographs of the sun's corona were obtained

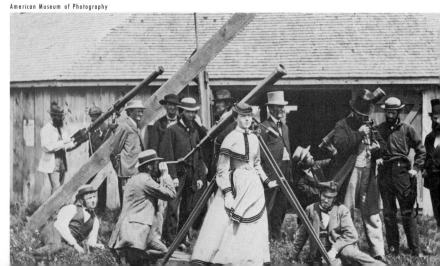

(Above) The Salt Water Floating Bath, in the Hudson River off lower Manhattan

The summer vacation became a fixture of American life in the late nineteenth century. In this, as in other forms of recreation, the mass of people sought to emulate the wealthy. For some of those who could not afford Saratoga Springs or Newport or Bar Harbor, the beaches of Atlantic City were an accessible vacation spot. And for those whose finances dictated a stay-at-home summer, there were such local attractions as zoos and swimming pavilions.

Scenes at the Philadelphia Zoo in Fairmont Park, about 1876. The zoo was opened in 1874 and is the oldest in the country. (Right) the Monkey House, and (below) the elephants bathing

Three scenes from Saratoga Springs, the most popular spa of the era: (Top) Columbian Spring, with a few couples partaking of the waters; (right) parlor of the Grand Union Hotel; (below) guests on the rear piazza, United States Hotel

59.

FREDERICK LAW OLMSTED: The Chicago Fire

By 1871 Chicago had swelled to a population of over 300,000. Two-thirds of the city's buildings as well as most of its sidewalks were constructed of wood. A concentration of wooden buildings near the mouth of the Chicago River near the center of the city was a virtual tinderbox, and few resources were available for combating fires. The weather in the summer and autumn of 1871 was exceptionally dry and hot, and Chicago fell victim to a disastrous fire on the evening of October 8. According to a local tradition of doubtful authenticity, the great fire started in the barn of a certain Mrs. O'Leary when her lamp was overturned while she milked her cow. The fire raged for the next two days, until October 10, razing an area of four square miles, including the business district. Over 18,000 buildings were destroyed, about 90,000 people were homeless, and about 250 persons lost their lives. Property damage was estimated at $200,000,000. Frederick Law Olmsted, landscape architect and city planner, recorded his observations after the great fire.

Source: *Nation,* November 9, 1871: "Chicago in Distress."

I HAVE HAD AN OPPORTUNITY of looking at Chicago at the beginning of the fourth week after the fire and, as you requested, will give you a few notes of my observation.

Chicago had a central quarter, compactly built, mostly of brick, stone, and iron, and distinguished by numerous very large and tall structures, comparable to, but often more ostentatious than, Stewart's store in New York. They were mostly lined, to the fourth, fifth, or sixth floor, with pine-wood shelves, on which, or in pine-wood cases, a fresh stock of — larger at the moment than ever before — dry goods or other inflammable materials was set up, with plentiful air space for rapid combustion. This central quarter occupied a mile and a half square of land. On one side of it was the lake; on the other three sides, for the distance of a mile, the building, though irregular, was largely of detached houses, some of the villa class, with small planted grounds about them and luxuriously furnished, but generally comfortable dwellings of moderate size set closely together.

There were also numerous churches and tall school buildings and some large factories. At a distance of two miles from the center and beyond, houses were much scattered; and within a mile of the political boundary there was much open prairie, sparsely dotted with cabins and a few larger buildings. It will be seen that a much larger part of the town proper was burned than a stranger would be led to suppose by the published maps.

The fire started half a mile southwest, which was directly to windward, of the central quarter, rapidly carried its heights, and swept down from them upon the comparatively suburban northern quarter, clearing it to the outskirts, where the few scattered houses remaining were protected by a dense grove of trees. The field of ruin is a mile in width, bounded by the lake on one side and mainly by a branch of the river on the other, and four miles in length, thus being as large as the half of New York City from the Battery to the Central Park, or as the whole of the peninsula of Boston. The houses burned, set ten feet apart, would form a row over 100 miles in length. I judge that more than a third of the roof space and fully half the floor space of the city, the population of which was 330,000, was destroyed.

Familiar with these facts and comparisons before I came here and having already seen many who had left the city since the fire, I now feel myself to have been able but slightly to appreciate the magnitude of its calamity. Besides the extent of the ruins, what is most remarkable is the completeness with which the fire did its work, as shown by the prostration of the ruins and the extraordinary absence of smoke stains, brands, and all debris, except stone, brick, and iron, bleached to an ashy pallor. . . .

Where houses stood detached, and especially where they were surrounded by tall trees, there is less evidence of intense heat, charred wood, and smoke stains being seen in the ruins. I had heard it surmised that, by furnishing numerous small brands, the planted trees of the North Division would have helped to scatter the fire; but I find them generally standing to the smallest twigs, so inclined and stiffened, however, as to show perfectly the action upon them of the wind at the moment of death. It is evident that they would have been an efficient protection to the houses they surrounded had the buildings to windward been a little less tall or the gale a degree less furious. For the wind appears not only to have been strong but gusty and whirling. . . .

Many, a moment after they had been out to observe the flames in the distance and had judged that they had still a chance to save their houses, were suddenly driven by a fierce heat, borne down upon them apparently from above, to flee, leaving even their choicest property, though previously packed and ready to be carried by hand. The radiated heat from the larger buildings was so strong that it scorched men ten rods away across the wind. Families were driven from one place of refuge to another — in several cases, to my knowledge, four times, and, finally, a few into the lake; many thousands into the open country. Some were floated or swam across the river.

Burning fragments of wooden parapets, sheets of roofing metal, signs, and scuttle doors were carried great distances, and, with blazing felt, tarred paper, and canvas, and myriads of smaller sparks, sometimes swept down upon the fugitives with a terrific roar. Very sensible men have declared that they were fully impressed at such a time with the conviction that it was the burning of the world. Loose horses and cows, as well as people of all conditions on foot and in wagons, were hurrying half-blinded through the streets together; and it often happened that husbands and wives, parents and children, even mothers and infants, were forced apart and lost to each other. Sudden desolation thus added to the previous horrors, made some frantic who would otherwise have maintained composure. In general, however, the people, especially the households of the North Side, appear to have manifested a greater degree of self-possession and of considerate thoughtfulness one for another, under these circumstances, than can be easily believed. Almost everyone holds the remembrance of some instance of quiet heroism, often flavored with humor.

The remains of only about 100 human bodies have thus far been recognized in the ruins, and the coroner and others are of the opinion that not more than 200 lives were lost. That the number should be so small can only be accounted for by the fact that there was an active volunteer rear guard of cool-headed Christians, who often entered and searched houses to which they were strangers, dragging out their inmates sometimes by main force, and often when some, caught unawares, were bewildered, fainting, or suffocating. One still sees burned garments and singed beards.

Of course, a state of mind approaching insanity followed with many. After the lost had been found, as in most cases they soon were — children, especially, having been almost invariably taken up, tenderly cared for, and advertised by strangers — and after food and rest had been had, there was a reaction from desperation. For a time men were unreasonably cheerful and hopeful; now, this stage appears to have passed. In its place there is sternness; but so narrow is the division between this and another mood, that in the midst of a sentence a change of quality in the voice occurs, and you see that eyes have moistened.

I had partly expected to find a feverish, reckless spirit, and among the less disciplined classes an unusual current setting toward turbulence, lawlessness, and artificial jollity, such as held in San Francisco for a long time after the great fire there — such as often seizes seamen after a wreck. On the contrary, Chicago is the soberest and the most clear-headed city I ever saw. . . . The clearing of the wreck goes ahead in a driving but steady, well-ordered way. . . .

There are respectable citizens who hold to the opinion that the fire was started and spread systematically by incendiaries, and I have seen one, lately from Paris, who is sure that it was part of a general war upon property. Numerous alleged facts are cited to sustain this view, but I believe them generally to be delusions growing out of the common excitement or accidental coincidences. It is certain that the origin, progress, and all the unusual general phenomena of the fire can be reasonably accounted for in other ways.

You will have heard bad symptoms reported among the workingmen since the fire, but, on the whole, their conduct seems to have been as satisfactory as could have been reasonably expected. An unusual proportion of them are Germans, Swedes, and Norwegians, and, what is of great consequence, they were the owners of a lot and cottage. There has been an advance of about 20 percent in wages, and this has occurred without strikes or any general ill-feeling. Laborers now command $2 a day, carpenters and masons, $4 to $5. Good mechanics are wanted, and many hundred more than are now here will be required in the spring.

The responsibility of leading affairs is felt to be too great to be trifled with. Even in politics this is true; perhaps on the principle of locking the stable door after the horse is stolen. City officers are to be elected next week, and citizens who have heretofore been unable to spare time for public from their private business are exhibiting some concern about the character of the candidates. The old knots of dirty, overdressed men waiting for something to turn up seem to have had enough and have disappeared. I have seen no soldiers, nor the slightest occasion for them. The police, as usual, except those regulating the passage of the crossings, seem to have nothing on their minds but a lazy looking forward to the arrival of their reliefs.

Although few of those who were men of substance yet know where they stand, and the work of general permanent reconstruction must, from loss of land titles and other reasons, be postponed till next summer, there has been no delay in deciding upon and starting efficient temporary arrangements for nearly all the old business of the city, except that of the courts. The shipping, railways, telegraphs are all doing more work than before the fire and will probably continue to. The city is again supplied with water, most of it with gas; it is as well sewered and paved as before.

Omnibuses and streetcars are running on all the old lines; newspapers are published, schools are open and full, and half the numerous churches of the past are working more than double tides — the sensible, economical Roman Catholic custom of successive congregations and relays of clergymen having been adopted; while every day in the week the most effective preaching of the gospel, in the form of bread, beef, and blankets, is uttered from each. Theaters, concerts, and lectures are advertised; and a new public library is started in the basement of a Baptist meetinghouse.

Three hundred of the burnt-out business concerns advertise themselves in new quarters, and new stocks of goods are constantly seen coming from the Eastern railway stations. In but few respects will the market a week hence be much worse, either to buy or sell in, than before. There is no difficulty in handling the crops, and, fortunately, they are large and excellent. Chicago, in short, is under jury-masts and yet carries her ensign union down; but she answers her helm, lays her course, is making fair headway, and her crew, though on short allowance and sore tried, is thoroughly sober and knows its stations.

You ask whether it is in the power of man adequately to guard against such calamities — whether other great cities are as much exposed as was Chicago? All the circumstances are not established with sufficient accuracy for a final answer, and one cannot, in the present condition of affairs, make full inquiries of men who must be best informed; but to such preliminary discussion as is in order, I can offer a certain contribution. . . .

It is to be considered that millions of acres of land hereabouts, on which trees were scarce, have been settled within thirty years by people whose habits had been formed in regions where woods abound. They have used much timber for building, for fencing, railroads, and fuel. They have grown none. They are planting none to speak of. The same is true of nearly all parts of our country in which a great destruction of forests has occurred or is occurring. If the reduction of foliage in any considerable geographical division of the world tends to make its seasons capricious, as there is much evidence, the evil both of destructive droughts and devastating floods is very likely to extend and increase until we have a government service which we dare trust with extensive remedial measures. It is not a matter which commerce can be expected to regulate. . . .

The origin of the fire was probably a commonplace accident. The fire started in a wooden building and moved rapidly from one to another, close at hand, until the extended surface of quickly burning material heated a very large volume of the atmosphere, giving rise to local currents, which, driving brands upon the heated roofs and cornices of the tall buildings to leeward, set them on fire; and through the rapid combustion of their contents, loosely piled tier upon tier, developed a degree of heat so intense that ordinary means of resistance to it proved of no avail.

Under an old law, wooden buildings had been forbidden to be erected in or moved to the locality were the fire started. In 1867, upon the motion of men who wished to dispose of buildings they had contracted to move out of the more compact part of the city, the Common Council consented to a modification of this law. The Board of Health at the time urged the danger of doing so and was told to mind its business. Underwriters, merchants, and capitalists were silent.

Chicago had a weakness for "big things" and liked to think that it was outbuilding

Chicago Historical Society

Scene from the Chicago fire, sketched by Alfred R. Waud, artist for "Harper's Weekly"

New York. It did a great deal of commercial advertising in its housetops. The faults of construction as well as of art in its great showy buildings must have been numerous. Their walls were thin and were often overweighted with gross and coarse misornamentation. Some ostensibly stone fronts had huge overhanging wooden or sheet-metal cornices fastened directly to their roof timbers, with wooden parapets above them. Flat roofs covered with tarred felt and pebbles were common. In most cases, I am told by observers, the fire entered the great buildings by their roof timbers, even common sheet metal seeming to offer but slight and very temporary protection to the wood on which it rested. Plain brick walls or walls of brick with solid stone quoins and window dressings evidently resisted the fire much better than stone-faced walls with a thin backing of brick.

There has been no court-martial called for the trial of the fire service of the city. I understand that it was under the same board with the police. Most of the so-called police force of Chicago, whom I had seen before the fire, appeared in dirty, half-buttoned uniforms, and were either leaning against a doorpost in conversation with equally disreputable-looking friends and incessantly spitting on the sidewalk or were moving with a gait and carriage which can be described by no word but "loafing."

No one can be sure that with reasonably solid brick walls, reasonably good construction, and honest architecture this fire could, once under strong headway, with the wind that was blowing, have been stopped at any point in its career, even by good generalship, directing a thoroughly well-drilled and disciplined soldierly force of firemen and police. But that the heat thrown forward would have been less intense, the advance of the fire less rapid, the destruction of buildings less complete, the salvage of their contents greater, and the loss of life smaller may be assumed with confidence. . . .

The two most important buildings in the city were the courthouse, which was also the city hall, and the pumping house of the waterworks. The courthouse was a costly structure with a stone exterior, ostensibly fireproof, standing in the midst of a public square. No respectable structure in the same situation would have been seriously injured. Large additions had been made to it two years ago, and the design for them is said to have been bargained for under such conditions that no respectable architect could have been employed. The result, architecturally, was at all events very bad.

There is much more beauty in the walls now, where they have been chipped and crumbled by the fire, than ever before. It has also been publicly charged that some of the legislators of the city were interested in the building contracts, and that much money was made on them. The first fall of snow after the roof was put on caused it to fall in, and other parts of the structure were so thoroughly shattered that it was feared that the whole would come down. A proposition to tear it down and rebuild it was seriously entertained, but, as one of the gentlemen who decided the question told me, in view of what it had already cost, the taxpayers would not have stood it, and it was determined to patch it up.

On the top of it, a tall, wooden, tin-clad cupola was set. The fire, true to its mission of instructive punishment, made a long leap forward to seize upon this; it soon fell in; and, before the nearest adjoining commercial blocks to windward had even taken fire, it had been completely burned out with all its invaluable contents.

I have neither seen the waterworks nor the justly distinguished engineer who is regarded as responsible for their construction, and who may be depended on to give the reason of their unfortunate breakdown with the utmost accuracy and candor. The roof of the pumping house, of metal, I believe, is publicly stated to have been upheld by wooden timbering, which was charred by heat from firebrands which had fallen above. Breaking down, it broke some part of the pumping engine, and thus the city was left without water. The main battle, such as it was, had been before this fought and lost; but that much might still have

been saved had the flow of water continued, a single experience will sufficiently indicate.

A friend who had, with other treasures, a choice library of several thousand volumes, tells me that he had thought much of the danger of fire and was prepared to meet it. His house stood apart from all others and was surrounded by trees. He had a strong force of instructed assistants, with private hydrants, hose, wet carpets, and buckets, well-distributed. He had horses and wagons ready, but to the last was confident in his means of resistance. All houses to windward of him had nearly burned down, and he had extinguished every spark that had fallen upon his own, when the water failed. Five minutes afterwards, his roofs and walls were on fire in a dozen places, and he had all he could do to save the lives of his household.

Considering the circumstances under which the arrangements for relief were formed, they appear to be admirably good. In the midst of the most pressing demands of their private affairs, men of great good sense and well informed have taken time to devise and bring others into a comprehensive and sufficient organization, acting under well-guarded laws. Chicago, when all did well, exceeded all in her manner of providing for the sick and wounded, prisoners and refugees, as well as friends, and now the bread she then floated is truly returning to her under natural laws. . . .

Amidst all the material prosperity of Chicago, there had always been a few of her citizens who had really bonded themselves to have no share in it, in devotion to higher pursuits. As examples of these, the Kinnicut brothers, as both are dead, may perhaps be named. There were others, their instructors, leaders, supporters, and followers, who, like them, had traveled frugally and far, studied devotedly, and who, aided by a few worthy men of greater wealth, were laying the foundations of a true seat and school of art, science, and learning.

Several special collections had already been gathered, which money can never replace. These, with libraries, many series of notes, the work of half a lifetime, and some unpublished books, more or less nearly complete, are lost; and most of those who had supplied the funds to sustain these most interesting and important bases of the higher civilization for the great Northwest are thrown back to struggle again for the decent maintenance of their families.

But great as is this loss, it will be consciously felt by comparatively few. Even more appalling, in view of the long years of weary labor of many educated men involved, is the destruction of important papers, contracts, agreements and accounts, notes of surveys, and records of deeds and mortgages. It is estimated that nine-tenths of the papers held by attorneys were kept in various patent safes on upper floors and were destroyed. The same is true of those held by surveyors, real-estate agents, etc. The city and county records were, I believe, in vaults built, like those of the custom-house and post office, on stone slabs, supported on iron columns, which, soon yielding to the heat, tumbled them into a pit of fire, and all were lost.

How the city is to recover from this blow, no one can yet see; but the difficulty is engaging the study of its best and most conservative minds; and that in some way it will recover and that it will presently advance even with greater rapidity, but with far firmer steps than ever before, those most staggered and cast down by it have not a shadow of doubt.

60.

COUNT VON HÜBNER: Observations of an Austrian Diplomat

One of the numerous European travelers who toured the United States during the nineteenth century was Joseph Alexander, Graf von Hübner, an Austrian career diplomat. After a stint as his country's ambassador to Rome he took (in 1871) a leisurely trip around the world, one of the fruits of which was a book published in Paris in 1873. Some of his impressions of American cities, taken from a translation of the work, appear in the following selection. Von Hübner was particularly interested in the Mormons of Salt Lake City; he implies that their then current practice of polygamy was not as licentious as most Americans thought at the time.

Source: *Promenade autour du monde, 1871*, Paris, 1873 [TWA, pp. 297-324].

NEW YORK IN ITS OUTWARD ASPECT reflects in a very remarkable manner the characteristics of the whole Union. One might say that the intellectual, moral, and commercial life of the American people is here condensed, to spread its rays afterwards across the immense tracts which are called the United States.

Broadway is the representative and the model of those great arteries which bind together the different portions of this great continent from ocean to ocean. The great thoroughfares of London, the boulevards of Paris, the Ringstrasse and other great streets of Vienna are as busy and as animated perhaps as Broadway; but their animation springs from the needs and the commerce of their respective cities. But this great artery of the American metropolis is more than a street; it is a royal road leading everywhere.

Certainly New York is a great capital in the European sense of the word. But it is also more than that; it is at the same time an enormous railway station, a depot, to use an American term, both of travelers and goods, where one meets a floating population large enough to give the impression of that agitation and preoccupation and that provisional state of things which is the characteristic of all the great American cities. To sum up, Broadway represents the principle of mobility.

Let us pass on to Wall Street, the center of all great financial operations. Here the resemblance with the City of London is incontestable; the buildings are nearly all banks; and the jostling crowds, the very air one breathes smells of millions! Yet even here the analogy with Europe is not complete. I will quote but one of a thousand little indications of difference. A banker will not pay you even the smallest sum at once. He sets the telegraph to work, and after a few minutes the money is brought to you from the public bank where the funds of his particular house are deposited. Nothing can be more praiseworthy than this practice, for these banks are real fortresses, to break into which would be impossible.

Now we are on Fifth Avenue and, consequently, far from the industrial quarter. Here the eye rejoices in the contemplation of all the luxury that money can bring. Do not let us be hypercritical or examine too closely the artistic taste of these pretentious buildings, which seem to parade their magnificence in pompous architecture. After all, the identical meretricious taste has spread to Europe. The Belgravia of London, the Ringstrasse of Vienna are both examples of the same style.

But what struck me most in New York is the enormous number of public buildings consecrated to divine worship. I speak not of the great Gothic cathedral which the Irish are now building, and which belongs to another date and another order of ideas, but of the innumerable little churches belonging to the different sects, built very often at great cost and with a profusion of ornament in every possible and impossible style, which attracts the attention and piques the curiosity. In Europe, the massive pile of the cathedral, and the belfries, spires, towers, and high roofs of the other churches, stand out against the sky, tower above the houses of the faithful and, seen from a distance, give to each town a particular character.

In New York it is quite the reverse. Seen from the river or from Jersey City, this huge metropolis is a great mass of red, gray, or yellowish brick. At most, one or two steeples rise above the roofs, which, from far, seem all of the same height — one long horizontal line stretching toward the plain beyond. Europeans landing for the first time cannot help wondering how two or three churches can possibly suffice for upwards of a million Christians! They learn their mistake when they walk through the town, especially along Fifth Avenue, where the commercial fever is at rest, or, at any rate, gives way to a little quiet, to study, and perhaps to meditation and prayer.

Not that all those little chapels impress one with a feeling of sanctity or fill the mind with that grave spirit of recollection which comes over one in the aisles of our great cathedrals. Far from it! The *sanctitas loci* is entirely wanting in this worldly quarter. These little buildings, each consecrated to a different form of worship, are only accessories to the whole. They are only open during their respective services on Sundays. But there they are, and however poor they may be they prove that religion persists in the hearts of these rich people, who had perhaps little or no time to think of the soul when they were making their fortunes, but now that they are millionaires begin to remember that they have one.

In a society of which the most energetic, the most important, and the youngest portion lives in a perpetual millrace, it is evident that spiritual or inner life must be stifled. Indeed, it seems dead; but it is not. From time to time there is an extraordinary awakening. Enormous sums are then given for the construction of new churches; and in revivals, great meetings in the forests and prairies of the Far West, a sudden thirst for spiritual consolation bursts out among the masses like an epidemic of extraordinary violence, producing the most fantastic scenes, now tragic, now comic. These are only different manifestations of the same spirit — the spirit of faith, kept down but not exterminated by the worship of the Golden Calf, which is the religion of the state, the only apparent religion, of the merchant, the miner, the carrier, the porter — in a word, of the fortune hunters of young America. . . .

In the West the towns are quickly seen and are all alike. One may say the same of the hotels, which play so great a part here, not only in the life of travelers but in those of the residents. A great number of families, especially newly married couples, live in hotels. This method saves expenses and the bother of housekeeping; it also makes easy the frequent moves from one town to another. But it has the inconvenience of condemning the young wife to a life of idleness and solitude. All day long the husband is at his office. He comes in only at mealtimes and then devours his food with the silence and dispatch of a starving man. Then he rushes back to his treadmill.

The children are sent to school when they are five or six years old. They go by themselves and pass the rest of their day exactly as they please, no one thinking it right to interfere with their liberty. Paternal authority is nil or, at any rate, is never exercised. There is no education in our sense of the word; but there is instruction, public, good, and accessible to all. The little gentlemen talk loudly and are as proud and sharp as the full-grown men of their nation. The young girls at eight and nine years old excel in the arts of coquetry and flirtation and promise to become "fast" young ladies; but nevertheless they make good and faithful wives. If their husband should be rich, they will help him ruin himself by extravagance in dress; yet they will accept misery calmly, and the moment there is a change in the wheel of fortune fly into the same follies as of old.

The home of the English, so dear to their hearts, is only a secondary consideration in the lives of their cousins beyond the seas. This is easily explained. In the New World man is born to conquer. Life is a perpetual struggle, a rivalry from which no one can exempt himself, a race in the open field across terrible obstacles, with the prospect of enormous rewards for reaching the goal. The American cannot keep his arms folded. He must embark on something, and once embarked he must go on and on forever; for if he stops, those who follow him would crush him under their feet. His life is one long campaign, a succession of never-ending fights, marches, and countermarches.

In such a militant existence, what place is left for the sweetness, the repose, the intimacy of home or its joys? Is he happy? Judging by his tired, sad, exhausted, anxious, and often delicate and unhealthy appearance, one would be inclined to doubt it. Such an excess of uninterrupted labor cannot be good for any man.

The woman suffers most from this regime. She sees her husband at most for half an hour, once in the day, and then in the evening, when, worn out with fatigue, he comes home to sleep. She cannot lighten his burden or share his anxiety and cares, for she knows nothing of his business; for want of time, there is little or no interchange of thought between them. As a mother, her share in the education of her children is of the smallest. As soon as her little ones can run alone, they pass their lives away from her, out of the house. They are entirely ignorant of the obedience or respect due their parents but, on the other hand, learn early to do without care or protection, to be self-sufficient. They ripen quickly and prepare themselves from their tenderest years for the fatigues and struggles of the overexciting, harsh, adventurous life which awaits them.

Besides all this, a woman boarding at one of these huge caravanseries has not even the resource and occupation which ordinary domestic details involve. Is it as a compensation for these privations that American society surrounds her with privileges and attentions unknown in the Old World? Everywhere she is the object of a respectful gallantry, which might be called chivalric were it less frivolous, and sometimes even grotesque and ridiculous. For example, I am sitting in one of these tram cars which cross all the principal streets of the great towns. A tap of a parasol or a fan rouses me from my meditations. I see standing right in front of me a young woman, who looks at me from head to foot with an imperious, haughty, even angry expression. I wake up to the situation and hasten to give her my seat, which she takes at once, without deigning to thank me, even by a look or a smile. The consequence is that I am obliged to perform the rest of my journey standing in a most uncomfortable position, and to hold on by a leather strap which is fastened for that purpose along the roof of the carriage.

On the other hand, it is the fashion to disparage American women. People call them frivolous, flirtatious, extravagant, and say that they are always running after pleasure. These accusations seem to me unjust. The American woman bears the stamp of her position and of the atmosphere around her. As a young girl she naturally follows the inclinations of her sex which are not, with us, regulated and controlled by th teaching and example of a mother. Sh wishes to please, and if she is naturally live ly she will become "fast"; that is, she w laugh loudly and by smart repartee and p quant looks will endeavor to attract th greatest possible number of young me But this vulgar coquetry, however jarring t good taste, rarely goes beyond a certai point. There is always a father, a brothe or an uncle near by, armed with revolver o Bowie knife, who is quite ready to ask you with every imaginable politeness, if your in tentions be fair and honorable.

Married women in America are, as a rul unexceptionable. If they are too fond o dress, it is generally their husbands wh wish it. If they are often seen abroad, it i because they have nothing to do at home If they are rather free and easy, such man ners are allowed in society; it is, after al bad taste — not sin. Their minds are gener ally well cultivated, for they read a grea deal, mostly novels, but also English classi authors and encyclopedias. And they atten the public lectures and literary conversation held in all the great towns of the Union.

In Salt Lake City, I turn my steps towar Main Street and find myself in a regula city of the Far West. Here there are n trees. Houses line each side of the street the greater portion built of brick, or rathe of adobe. The more modern buildings have some pretension to architecture. In all, th first floor consists of open shops. The wall are, without exception, covered from top t bottom with gaudy advertisements. Th streets are thronged with bullock wagon and carriages of every description. A stage-coach drawn by ten horses, belonging to Wells, Fargo and Company, draws a crowd and increases the confusion. Formerly, these coaches were the only resource of the impatient traveler; but they have nearly disappeared since the railroad opened. Porters, miners on foot or on donkeys — in a word, a whole body of strong, intelligent-looking men with tanned, weather-beaten faces and brawny arms, whose life is one continual fight with savage nature and who are justly termed the pioneers of civilization — jostle one another in the crowded thoroughfares.

In the forenoon, "old" Townsend, the innkeeper, took me to see the Tabernacle. This is a long, low hall, entirely bare and destitute of religious emblems, with a raised dais at one end on which are the armchairs of the prophet and bishops, the whole being covered by a heavy, oval cupola. Alongside they are building a new temple, which is to be an immense edifice of cut stone in the Roman style. But only the foundations are as yet laid; and no one hopes or seems to wish for its completion. There are scarcely any men at work on it, for both money and fervor are wanting.

The theater is far more popular. This is one of Brigham Young's thousand schemes and the great resource of the inhabitants of Salt Lake City. It is open almost every night. The house is badly decorated and still worse lit. In the pit I saw groups of children, who had evidently come all alone. On benches and in the galleries sat a number of men in blouses, each with two or three wives dressed with a certain amount of care. The offering, a sensational drama which had a great run in England some years ago and is full of English habits and institutions, contrasted singularly with the public of the New Jerusalem. Nevertheless, the play was listened to with great attention, although there was neither laughter nor clapping. Brigham Young, who is himself the censor and excludes all indecent pieces, is very anxious to encourage people to go to his theater. It is in his hands a kind of school of art, whereby he strives to refine the habits of a society which has been reduced by circumstances to a condition of perpetual forced labor.

Brigham Young is the keystone of the Mormon enterprise. To have conceived the migration, to have carried it out, with the loss of a great number of men, it is true, but without shaking the faith or confidence of a single one of the survivors, is a historical [deed] which would suffice to immortalize the name of any man, whether he be king, captain, or prophet.

Brigham Young unites in himself these three qualities. As prophet, though taking good care not to utter any prophecies, he rules over men's consciences; as sovereign, he exercises his power without the slightest check; as general, he has organized so large and respectable a militia that the central government hesitates to force this potentate to respect the law of the land.

The first three years after the exodus were very trying ones. George Smith, the historian, told me that he and his wife, as in fact everybody else, were reduced to half the food necessary for the support of animal life. For many weeks they lived entirely upon roots.

The work of preaching among the gentiles was then taken up with renewed fervor. But they did not make any proselytes except in England and Wales, in Australia, and, in a lesser degree, in Scandinavia. Brigham Young always chose his emissaries by inspiration. He has often accosted perfect strangers in the street, and by a sudden inspiration given them apostolic missions to Europe, Australia, or to the islands of the South Seas. The men thus summoned leave wife, children, and business, and start out.

The Mormon missionaries never attempt to preach to the rich, or even to those who are tolerably well off. Nor will they go near an educated man. Their proselytes are always the poorest and the most ignorant. The recruits spring either from those who have been born in misery or who have fallen into it from their own faults or the fault of circumstances, men who have nothing to lose, and who can only gain by being dragged out of the moral and physical degradation in which they exist.

It is quite impossible that doctrine alone should touch people's hearts, strike their imaginations, and attract from the worst quarters of London, from the dockyards of Liverpool, from the agricultural population of Wales, the 3,000 or 4,000 converts who arrive every year. The converts are simply men who find themselves in a state of utter destitution and want to get out of it. If Brigham Young's missioners had nothing more to offer than a continuation in another world (with a God who is like themselves) of an existence as miserable as that which has fallen to their lot here, the proselytes would not accept the Mormon teaching with such eagerness. They would at once turn their backs on the missioners.

But the envoys tell them more than that. After having promised, as all religions do, eternal felicity in a future state, they offer what no other religion does, a most brilliant prospect even in this lower world. On the single condition of moderate work they guarantee the converts the enjoyment of all the good things to which the heart of man can aspire.

How are such poor fellows to resist these brilliant promises without the restraining force of strong Christian convictions which they have not got? Besides, no sooner have they indicated their adhesion than Brigham Young's bankers at once advance to them the money necessary for the voyage. At New York they receive a pass and letters for the whole of their journey, and, unlike the majority of other immigrants, they are sure to find help and protection at the different stations of their itinerary.

Once arrived, the bishops and elders procure work for the strong, help for the sick, food for all. In fact, the church provides for the wants of the newcomers until lands are assigned them for cultivation. Young then advances money to them to build their houses — brick or adobe — boards, and tools. The value of the land and the objects furnished to the immigrants is calculated in dollars and inscribed in the creditor's books. Payment is made in installments, to which is added the tithe, a tenth of the gross rental of the farm, levied for the wants of the church.

Young thus becomes the creditor of the whole community. Few, if any, Mormons can ever clear off their debts. They gain a livelihood by dint of work; they may even become tolerably well-off, but it is extremely difficult to save and next to impossible to become rich. The rarity of specie and the difficulty of procuring ready money adds to the financial embarrassment which is the normal condition of this society.

To leave Utah, the saints must pay their debts; to pay, they must sell their farms; to sell, they must find buyers with ready United States money. Now, there is only one man in Utah in that position, and that is Brigham Young. But Brigham Young is precisely the man least interested in facilitating the sales. The great secret of his political and religious power consists, in a large measure, although not entirely, in the nature of his financial relations with the majority of the Mormons, who are all, more or less, his debtors.

But, strange to say, the immigrant, instead of independence, has found the one thing which he lacked in Europe when he embraced the religion of the saints, and that is faith! Yes, this unbeliever of yesterday, not only in the old religions but in the new, has become today the staunchest of disciples. He believes firmly, blindly, in the prophet Brigham Young. How account for this strange yet incontestable fact which everybody confirms and which, besides, bears the evidence of truth on the very face of things?

Until 1869 Brigham Young was in the zenith of his power. One may affirm without exaggeration that in the normal condition of affairs the prophet is literally the absolute master of the bodies and souls of his believers. He disposes of their wills and consciences, and even of their thoughts; for he gives them a certain direction and takes care it shall be maintained. Besides, who dares to think for himself in Utah? They believe, they work, but they do not think.

The Tabernacle on Sundays, the shop or the farm during the week, the theater and the harem every night — that is enough. There is no time left for reflection; everything is done by inspiration. God inspires, and the person who is inspired is Brigham Young. In every kind of business, trouble, difficulty, or doubt, Brigham Young is the referee. Young is not an incarnate God, but he acts as such. That is why I say that he disposes of the souls of men.

Now for their bodies. He concentrates on his own hands the strings of all their material interests. He exploits the whole territory. He likewise exploits the physical powers and the mental faculties of 200,000 people. He has, in consequence, the reputation of being one of the richest men in the United States. People say he has a fortune of more than $12 million. He rules the markets; he fixes the price of food; he makes the roads and exacts enormous tolls. After having created all these different industries, he works them all for his own benefit. With his armed force, his militia, perfectly well-exercised and equipped, his telegraph which he has carried to every point of the territory, he is master of the situation. In addition, till two years ago, he had the advantage of being geographically inaccessible. Add to this a prompt and summary execution of justice, in part occult, and you have a very fair picture of the unheard-of powers of this one man.

But there is still another element which grows out of the imposition, under cover of a pretended revelation in 1852, of the doctrine and practice of polygamy. Under the influence of Young, an Assembly of Delegates adopted the principle, which was declared a duty and a privilege; but it could not, however, be exercised without a special command of God, through the medium of his prophet Brigham Young, who, before giving his decision, examines the merits of the case or has it examined by his bishops.

The higher a man advances in the ranks of the hierarchy, the more his duty compels him to use the privilege of plurality. Brigham Young at this moment possesses sixteen wives, without counting sixteen others who are what is called "sealed." Some of these latter live with him in a conjugal fashion, but the greater part are widows or old maids, who by this means hope to become, in a future state, what they are not here below — the real wives of the prophet. George Smith, the historian, has five wives; the other apostles content themselves with four. None has less than three.

Look at it which way you will, polygamy bears within it the seeds of destruction; for the family first of all, and for society afterwards. But its first victims are the women. All those I have seen have a sad, timid look. In their homes they have not the place due a wife. The men avoid speaking of them and never allow them to appear before strangers; one would fancy they were ashamed of them, or rather of themselves. These poor women have fallen from the place they once held; they feel themselves degraded, and degradation is read on all these melancholy and faded countenances.

Labor and faith, two words forever in Brigham Young's mouth, explain these strange phenomena. But what secret motives caused the birth of this faith in the hearts of those who never possessed anything of the sort when they embraced the new doctrines? How was this transformation effected? How did men who left their native land believing in nothing, soon after reaching the Valley of the Saints, begin to believe in everything — that is, in everything which it pleased Brigham Young to make them believe? The following are the conclusions at which I arrived.

The beginnings of Mormonism are like those of any other sect. With some people, spiritual needs, the thirst for more supernatural help, the wish to draw nearer to God, from time to time, arise in a sudden and unexpected manner. The rarer these revivals, the more violent they seem; like mill dams long closed and suddenly opened. The waters at first rush out furiously, but when they have had their flow, they resume their usual calm course. This is the history of the famous religious revivals. This is also the origin of the greater part of the sects, especially in America where everyone is so occupied with material interests that there is no time for meditation or prayer. Moral wants long neglected, the voice of conscience long stifled, repentance, even despair, suddenly take possession of souls. People ask for reassurances and accept them from the first comer.

At such moments men always turn up ready to put themselves at the head of the movement, to direct, master, and, if possible, work it for their own ends. These are sometimes hypocrites, often fanatics, or a mixture of the two. But the hypocrite lacks the light of faith; the fanatic, the light of reason. Bad passions, cupidity, and sensuality mingle in the business. What wonder then that they merge into the absurd and monstrous? Under these conditions, Mormonism, like the other sects, was born.

The first founders, those influenced by Joseph Smith, were certainly in earnest; they were genuine fanatics. They were Americans and formed the moral center which afterwards received the European immigrants.

The great migration to Salt Lake marked a turning point in the history of the sect by consolidating the prestige and authority of the modern Moses. Amidst a thousand dangers and fearful privation, but under the guidance of this wonderful man, the Mormons found the spot exactly as God in His vision had revealed it to His elect. Certainly Brigham Young must be a supernatural being; if not a god, very near one. And after all, what is God? The Mormons do not trouble their heads with such inquiries; and besides, their prophet has told them that man is the equal of God. Certainly no one is so more than Young. It is evident — it is

clear — everyone thinks, repeats, and believes it.

Thus public opinion formed itself in the Valley of the Saints and was quickly imparted to the newcomers. The European immigrant had no means of defense. He was poor, ignorant, and debased; and, in declaring himself a Mormon, he had already renounced the religion in which he was born. He could not find arguments against the errors of the sect he had just embraced in the dogmas of the old faith he had denied. Moreover, he had burned his ships; he belonged body and soul to the president. He behaved, then, like everyone else, shut his eyes and became a believer, that is, a believer in Brigham Young.

Two years ago defections were very rare. Since the opening of the railroad, Anglican and Presbyterian ministers have devoted themselves to their apostolic labors in Salt Lake City without serious risk. But it has been so much lost time in the sense that the few men willing to leave the sect have been incapable of receiving any religious impressions or any moral sense. From believing Mormons and good workmen, they became, when emancipated, frank atheists and incorrigible scamps.

The influence of the railroad, of the discovery of the silver mines, and of the influx of miners in the last few months has already been felt in various ways. In the first place, the Reign of Terror, under which the few gentiles groaned, has entirely disappeared. Once helots, the Christians are now independent. Soon they will become a power. Even in the heart of the community the situation is much modified. Immigrants who are not Mormons have arrived, brought in capital, opened stores, and extend their operations every day. Everything, in fact, is changing. There is no longer talk of sudden sentences and secret executions; no more bodies of apostate Mormons; no more avenging angels! The young girls themselves are in rebellion. They openly proclaim against plurality and swear never to accept polygamist husbands. Even the Beehive has been invaded by insubordination; the eldest son has told his father that he does not consider the children by later marriages legitimate. . . .

If we, children of old Europe, who cling to the present as the logical natural continuation of the past, who cherish old recollections, traditions, and habits, if we do homage to your success, obtained under institutions which, on all essential points, are contrary to ours, this is a proof of our impartiality. For let us not deceive ourselves, America is the born antagonist of Europe. The first arrivals, the precursors of your actual greatness, those who sowed the seed, were discontented men. Intestine divisions and religious persecutions tore them from their homes and threw them on America's shores.

They brought with them and planted in the soil of their new country the principle for which they had suffered and fought — the authority of the individual. He who possesses it is free in the fullest sense of the term. And, as in that sense you are all free, each of you is the equal of every other. Your country then is the classic soil of liberty and equality and it has become so from the fact that it was peopled by the men whom Europe expelled from its bosom. That is why you, in conformity with your origin, and we, by a totally different genesis, are antagonistic.

You offer liberty and equality to everyone. It is to the magic charm of these two words, more than to your gold fields, that you owe the influx of your immigrants and the enormous and ever growing increase of your population. Russia and Hungary still have miles of uncultivated lands; Algeria needs and clamors for hands; but no one goes there. The great mass of emigrants turn their steps to North America. Why? First, to find bread, an article which in our overpopulated Europe it is no longer easy to procure; next, to obtain liberty and equality. The emigrants go to you for bread, individual liberty, and social equality, and they find space; that is, liberty to work and equality of success if they bring with them the necessary qualifications.

All the world admires you. But all the world does not love you. Those among us who judge you from an exclusively European point of view see in you nothing but enemies of the fundamental principles of society. The more they appreciate your work, the more, in fact, they admire, the less they like you. I should add that they fear you. They dread your success as a dangerous example to Europe, and as far as they can they try to stop the spread of your ideas. But they are a minority.

Your friends are more numerous. They see in you the prototype and the last fruits of civilization, and they desire to transform themselves after your example. There is a third class, those who are resigned; their opinion is the widest spread. Although they do not like you, they are willing to submit to you; to submit to your principles, your habits, your institutions. They believe that Europe will become Americanized, fatally, but inevitably.

As for me, I share neither these hopes nor these fears. I maintain that these fears, these hopes, this blind faith in imaginary decrees of Providence are founded on an imperfect knowledge of America and of the fundamental differences between the Old World and the New.

Compared to Europe, your country is as a sheet of white paper. Everything has to be begun; everything is new. In Europe one rebuilds or restores or modifies or adds (if one has space, which is more and more rare) a wing to one's house. But unless you demolish what exists, you don't rebuild the foundations; for what abounds in America is what we lack most — space. To become American would be to presuppose the entire destruction of Europe.

There is another reason why you cannot serve as a model in spite of the admiration you excite. How choose as a model a thing which is incomplete? You are at the growing age; you are not yet fully formed. What will you be when you have come to maturity? You do not know and no one can predict, for history offers no example of such a genesis. What new race will spring from this mixture of Celts, Germans, and Mongols? We cannot tell; no one can; we only know that a great change will result.

There remains also the unsolved problem as to liberty of conscience, the right of each one to worship the Supreme Being according to his own fashion. Until now, this system has worked well. Life is easy here for everybody, for everyone has space. To prevent a disagreeable meeting, one has only to cross to the other side of the street; it is wide enough for all. But the day will come, although it is now far-off, when this illimitable space will be narrowed and when it will be difficult by flight to escape those who do not share your religious convictions. Even in your country the question of liberty of conscience has not yet been definitively settled.

To sum up: You have the great advantage of space, which is wanting in Europe; and you are at the growing age. North America offers an unlimited field of liberty to the individual. It does not simply give him the opportunity; it forces him to employ all the faculties with which nature has endowed him. The arena is open. As soon as he enters it he must fight, and fight to the death. In Europe it is just the contrary. Everyone finds himself hemmed in by the narrow sphere in which he is born. To get out of his groove a man must be able to rise above his equals, to make extraordinary efforts, and he must have abilities and qualities above the average.

What with you is the rule, with us is the exception. In Europe a man works to live, or, at most, to arrive at comparative ease; here he works to become rich. Everyone does not attain this goal, but everyone tries for it. Such supreme efforts on all sides lead to extraordinary success.

This miraculous difference is due in large measure to the political institutions which govern your nation. To convince yourself of that fact you need only look at Canada. Perhaps its inhabitants are all the happier for it; but taking things altogether, in a material point of view, the British colony is incontestably inferior.

So much that is brilliant must have its dark shadow. Every mortal man is afflicted with the faults inseparable from his good qualities. And you are not exempt from this infirmity. One cause of your greatness is the unlimited expansion of individual liberty. But the liberty of the individual must necessarily be limited by the liberty of all, represented by the state. The balance of the two is the guarantee of each.

In the Old World the state claims too much and the individual obtains too little. With you, the fault is just the contrary. It is the conviction of most of your eminent men that you grant too much to the individual and too little to the state. Most of the scandals and abuses in your country arise from that source. The control of the organs of public opinion is insufficient. There is no subjection to an admitted authority recognized by everyone.

You have obtained, and are obtaining every day, enormous results; but at the cost of excessive labor, of a permanent tension of mind, and a permanent drain of physical strength. This excess of toil seems to me the source of serious evils. It produces exhaustion, lassitude, and premature old age; it deprives those who give themselves up to it, first, of time and then of the power of enjoying the results of their labors. It makes money the principal object in life, excludes gaiety, entails a sadness which is the natural consequence of overfatigue, and destroys the family ties and home joys.

1872

61.

CHARLES LORING BRACE: The Lost Children of New York

*Charles Brace, motivated by humanitarian instincts and by his theological training,
devoted himself to charitable work among the poor of New York City. In 1853 he
founded the Children's Aid Society, which built inexpensive lodging houses, trade schools,
summer camps, and sanitariums, and sent more than 100,000 city children to healthier
homes and employment in the country. Brace's principles of self-help and avoidance
of permanent dependence on charity set an example for later philanthropic efforts.
The Dangerous Classes of New York (1872) was one of the first of a large number of
works by religious leaders on urban problems. A chapter of Brace's book appears here.*

Source: *The Dangerous Classes of New York, and Twenty Years' Work Among Them,*
3rd edition, New York, 1880: "The Prolétaires of New York."

THE PROLÉTAIRES OF NEW YORK

NEW YORK is a much younger city than its
European rivals, and with perhaps one-third
the population of London; yet it presents
varieties of life among the "masses" quite as
picturesque and elements of population
even more dangerous. The throng of different nationalities in the American city gives
a peculiarly variegated air to the life beneath the surface, and the enormous over-
crowding in portions of the poor quarters
intensifies the evils, peculiar to large towns,
to a degree seen only in a few districts in
such cities as London and Liverpool.

The *mass* of poverty and wretchedness is,
of course, far greater in the English capital.

There are classes with inherited pauperism
and crime more deeply stamped in them in
London or Glasgow than we ever behold in
New York; but certain small districts can be
found in our metropolis with the unhappy
fame of containing more human beings
packed to the square yard and stained with
more acts of blood and riot, within a given
period, than is true of any other equal space
of earth in the civilized world.

There are houses, well known to sanitary
boards and the police, where fever has tak-
en a perennial lease and will obey no legal
summons to quit; where cholera — if a single germ seed of it float anywhere in American atmosphere — at once ripens a black
harvest; where murder has stained every

floor of its gloomy stories, and vice skulks or riots from one year's end to the other. Such houses are never reformed. The only hope for them is in the march of street improvements, which will utterly sweep them away.

It is often urged that the breaking-up of these "dens" and "fever nests" only scatters the pestilence and moral disease but does not put an end to them.

The objection is more apparent than real. The abolishing of one of these centers of crime and poverty is somewhat like withdrawing the virus from one diseased limb and diffusing it through an otherwise healthy body. It seems to lose its intensity. The diffusion weakens. Above all, it is less likely to become hereditary.

One of the remarkable and hopeful things about New York, to a close observer of its "dangerous classes," is . . . that they do not tend to become fixed and inherited as in European cities. But, though the crime and pauperism of New York are not so deeply stamped in the blood of the population, they are even more dangerous.

The intensity of the American temperament is felt in every fiber of these children of poverty and vice. Their crimes have the unrestrained and sanguinary character of a race accustomed to overcome all obstacles. They rifle a bank, when English thieves pick a pocket; they murder, where European *prolétaires* cudgel or fight with fists; in a riot, they begin what seems about to be the sacking of a city, where English rioters would merely batter policemen or smash lamps. The "dangerous classes" of New York are mainly American-born but the children of Irish and German immigrants. They are as ignorant as London flashmen or costermongers. They are far more brutal than the peasantry from whom they descend, and they are much banded together in associations, such as "Dead Rabbit," "Plug-ugly," and various target companies.

They are our *enfants perdus*, grown up to young manhood.

The murder of an unoffending old man, like Mr. Rogers, is nothing to them. They are ready for any offense or crime, however degraded or bloody. New York has never experienced the full effect of the nurture of these youthful ruffians as she will one day. They showed their hand only slightly in the riots during the war. At present, they are like the athletes and gladiators of the Roman demagogues. They are the "roughs" who sustain the ward politicians and frighten honest voters. They can "repeat" to an unlimited extent and serve their employers. They live on *"panem et circenses,"* or city hall places and pothouses, where they have full credit. . . .

We may say in brief that the young ruffians of New York are the products of accident, ignorance, and vice. Among a million people such as compose the population of this city and its suburbs, there will always be a great number of misfortunes; fathers die and leave their children unprovided for; parents drink and abuse their little ones, and they float away on the currents of the street; stepmothers or stepfathers drive out, by neglect and ill-treatment, their sons from home. Thousands are the children of poor foreigners who have permitted them to grow up without school, education, or religion.

All the neglect and bad education and evil example of a poor class tend to form others, who, as they mature, swell the ranks of ruffians and criminals. So, at length, a great multitude of ignorant, untrained, passionate, irreligious boys and young men are formed, who become the "dangerous class" of our city. They form the "19th Street Gangs," the young burglars and murderers, the garroters and rioters, the thieves and flashmen, the "repeaters" and ruffians, so well known to all who know this metropolis.

THE DANGERS

IT HAS BEEN COMMON, since the recent terrible Communistic outbreak in Paris, to assume that France alone is exposed to such horrors; but, in the judgment of one who has been familiar with our "dangerous classes" for twenty years, there are just the same explosive social elements beneath the surface of New York as of Paris.

There are thousands on thousands in New York who have no assignable home and "flit" from attic to attic and cellar to cellar; there are other thousands more or less connected with criminal enterprises; and still other tens of thousands, poor, hard-pressed, and depending for daily bread on the day's earnings, swarming in tenement houses, who behold the gilded rewards of toil all about them but are never permitted to touch them.

All these great masses of destitute, miserable, and criminal persons believe that for ages the rich have had all the good things of life, while to them have been left the evil things. Capital to them is the tyrant. Let but law lift its hand from them for a season, or let the civilizing influences of American life fail to reach them, and, if the opportunity offered, we should see an explosion from this class which might leave this city in ashes and blood.

To those incredulous of this, we would recall the scenes in our streets during the riots in 1863, when, for a short period, the guardians of good order, the local militia, had been withdrawn for national purposes and when the ignorant masses were excited by dread of the draft.

Who will ever forget the marvelous rapidity with which the better streets were filled with a ruffianly and desperate multitude, such as in ordinary times we seldom see — creatures who seemed to have crept from their burrows and dens to join in the plunder of the city — how quickly certain houses were marked out for sacking and ruin, and what wild and brutal crimes were committed on the unoffending Negroes? It will be recalled, too, how much women figured in these horrible scenes, as they did in the Communistic outbreak in Paris. It was evident to all careful observers then that had another day of license been given the crowd, the attack would have been directed at the apparent wealth of the city — the banks, jewelers' shops, and rich private houses.

No one doubted then, or during the Orange Riot of 1871, the existence of "dangerous classes" in New York. And yet the separate members of these riotous and ruffianly masses are simply neglected and street-wandering children who have come to early manhood.

The true preventives of social catastrophes like these are . . . Christian reformatory and educational movements. . . .

Of the number of the distinctively homeless and vagrant youth in New York, it is difficult to speak with precision. We should be inclined to estimate it, after long observation, as fluctuating each year between 20,000 and 30,000. But to these, as they mature, must be added, in the composition of the dangerous classes, all those who are professionally criminal, and who have homes and lodging places. And again to these, portions of that vast and ignorant multitude, who, in prosperous times, just keep their heads above water, who are pressed down by poverty or misfortune, and who look with envy and greed at the signs of wealth and luxury all around them, while they themselves have nothing but hardship, penury, and unceasing drudgery.

62.

Francis A. Walker: The Dilemma of Indian Policy

Westward expansion by white settlers and the resulting Native American resistance troubled the government throughout the nineteenth century. The policy of Indian removal that was consistently followed after 1825 eventually led to the confinement of Native Americans on reservations west of the Mississippi that were supposed to be permanent Indian property. By the close of the Civil War, as it became apparent that even this territory would not escape white settlement, the attitudes of white Americans toward Native Americans became, if anything, even more hardened. The "five civilized tribes" that had aligned themselves with the Confederacy were forced to submit to Reconstruction treaties that curtailed some of their rights. In 1871 Native American groups ceased to be legally considered as separate nations with which treaties could be signed. By the time Francis Walker was writing his report as Commissioner of Indian Affairs in November 1872, these policies had led to the general demoralization of Indians who were unable to retain their traditional way of life within the confines of a reservation, as well as to frequent and violent protests. The portions of Walker's report that outline a policy for these problems are presented below.

Source: *Report of the Commissioner of Indian Affairs*, Washington, 1873, pp. 391-401.

THE INDIAN POLICY

THE INDIAN POLICY, so called, of the government is a policy, and it is not a policy, or rather it consists of two policies, entirely distinct, seeming, indeed, to be mutually inconsistent and to reflect each upon the other: the one regulating the treatment of the tribes which are potentially hostile, that is, whose hostility is only repressed just so long as, and so far as, they are supported in idleness by the government; the other regulating the treatment of those tribes which, from traditional friendship, from numerical weakness, or by the force of their location are either indisposed toward, or incapable of, resistance to the demands of the government. The treatment of the feeble Poncas and of the friendly Arrickarees, Mandans, and Gros Ventres of the North is an example of the latter; while the treatment of

their insolent and semihostile neighbors, the Sioux, furnishes an example of the former. In the same way at the South, the treatment of the well-intentioned Papagoes of Arizona contrasts just as strongly with the dealings of the government by their traditional enemies, the treacherous and vindictive Apaches.

This want of completeness and consistency in the treatment of the Indian tribes by the government has been made the occasion of much ridicule and partisan abuse; and it is indeed calculated to provoke criticism and to afford scope for satire; but it is nonetheless compatible with the highest expediency of the situation. It is, of course, hopelessly illogical that the expenditures of the government should be proportioned not to the good but to the ill desert of the several tribes; that large bodies of Indians should be supported in entire indolence by the bounty of the government simply because they are audacious and insolent, while well-disposed Indians are only assisted to self-maintenance, since it is known they will not fight.

It is hardly less than absurd, on the first view of it, that delegations from tribes that have frequently defied our authority and fought our troops and have never yielded more than a partial and grudging obedience to the most reasonable requirements of the government, should be entertained at the national capital, feasted, and loaded with presents. There could be no better subject for the lively paragraphist in his best estate or for the heavy editorial writer on a dull news day than such a course on the part of the government. These things can be made to appear vastly amusing, and the unreflecting are undoubtedly influenced in a great degree to the prejudice of the Indian policy by the incessant small-arms fire of squibs and epigrams, even more perhaps than by the ponderous artillery of argument and invective directed against it. And yet, for all this, the government is right and its critics wrong; and the "Indian policy" is sound, sensible, and beneficent, because it reduces to the minimum the loss of life and property upon our frontier and allows the freest development of our settlements and railways possible under the circumstances.

The mistake of those who oppose the present Indian policy is not in erroneously applying to the course of the government the standard they have taken but in taking an altogether false standard for the purpose. It is not a whit more unreasonable that the government should do much for hostile Indians and little for friendly Indians than it is that a private citizen should, to save his life, surrender all the contents of his purse to a highwayman; while on another occasion, to a distressed and deserving applicant for charity, he would measure his contribution by his means and disposition at the time. There is precisely the same justification for

the course of the government in feeding saucy and mischievous Indians to repletion, while permitting more tractable and peaceful tribes to gather a bare subsistence by hard work, or what to an Indian is hard work.

It is not, of course, to be understood that the government of the United States is at the mercy of Indians; but thousands of its citizens are, even thousands of families. Their exposed situation on the extreme verge of settlement affords a sufficient justification to the government for buying off the hostility of the savages, excited and exasperated as they are, and most naturally so, by the invasion of their hunting grounds and the threatened extinction of game. It would require 100,000 troops, at least, to form a cordon behind which our settlements could advance with the extent of range, the unrestrained choice of location, the security of feeling, and the freedom of movement which have characterized the growth of the past three or four years. Indeed, the presence of no military force could give that confidence to pioneer enterprise which the general cessation of Indian hostilities has engendered. Men of an adventurous cast will live and work behind a line of troops with, it is possible, some exhilaration of feeling on that account; but, as a rule, men will not place women and children in situations of even possible peril, nor will they put money into permanent improvements under such circumstances.

Especially has the absence of Indian hostilities been of the highest value, within the last few years, in directing and determining to the extreme frontier the immigrants arriving in such vast numbers on our shores. Americans habituated to the contemplation of this species of danger as one of the features of pioneer life will scarcely comprehend the reluctance with which men accustomed to the absolute security of person and property in the settled countries of Europe expose themselves and their families to perils of this kind. I was informed by the late president of the Northern Pacific Railroad that it was found almost impossible to hire Swedes and Norwegians to work upon the line of that road, then under construction from the Red River to the Missouri, on account of the vague apprehension of Indian attack which prevailed in connection with the progress of the road through the past summer. As a matter of fact, no well-informed person believed that the savages would undertake any offensive operations whatever until after the Missouri had been crossed and passed at least one hundred miles. But these people, unaccustomed to regard possible torture and murder as one of the conditions of a contract to labor, would refuse high wages rather than subject themselves to the slightest risk.

The fact that Americans are more daring and adventurous in the presence of a danger more familiar to them only constitutes a stronger reason for maintaining the immunity which has, for three years now, been secured by the feeding system. There are innumerable little rifts of agricultural or mining settlements all over the western country which, if unmolested, will in a few years become self-protecting communities, but which, in the event of a general Indian war occurring at the present time, would utterly and instantly disappear, either by abandonment or massacre. The first month of hostilities would see fifty valleys, up which population is now slowly but steadily creeping under cover of the feeding system, swept bare by the horrid atrocities of Indian warfare or deserted by their affrighted inhabitants, hastily driving before them what of their stock could be gathered at a moment's notice and bearing away what of their household goods could be carried in their single wagons. Such would be the result even with the most favorable issue of military operations. It is right that those who criticize the policy of the government toward the Indians and ridicule it as undig-

nified in its concessions and unstatesmanlike in its temporizing with a recognized evil should fairly face the one alternative which is presented. There is no question of national dignity, be it remembered, involved in the treatment of savages by a civilized power. With wild men, as with wild beasts, the question whether in a given situation one shall fight, coax, or run is a question merely of what is easiest and safest. . . .

SUBMISSION THE ONLY HOPE OF THE INDIANS

No one certainly will rejoice more heartily than the present Commissioner when the Indians of this country cease to be in a position to dictate, in any form or degree, to the government; when, in fact, the last hostile tribe becomes reduced to the condition of suppliants for charity. This is, indeed, the only hope of salvation for the aborigines of the continent. If they stand up against the progress of civilization and industry, they must be relentlessly crushed. The westward course of population is neither to be denied nor delayed for the sake of all the Indians that ever called this country their home. They must yield or perish; and there is something that savors of providential mercy in the rapidity with which their fate advances upon them, leaving them scarcely the chance to resist before they shall be surrounded and disarmed.

It is not feebly and futilely to attempt to stay this tide, whose depth and strength can hardly be measured, but to snatch the remnants of the Indian race from destruction from before it, that the friends of humanity should exert themselves in this juncture and lose no time. And it is because the present system allows the freest extension of settlement and industry possible under the circumstances, while affording space and time for humane endeavors to rescue the Indian tribes from a position altogether barbarous and incompatible with civilization and social progress, that this system must be approved by all enlightened citizens.

Whenever the time shall come that the roving tribes are reduced to a condition of complete dependence and submission, the plan to be adopted in dealing with them must be substantially that which is now being pursued in the case of the more tractable and friendly Indians, as described in the portions of the report which follow. This is the true permanent Indian policy of the government.

THE CLAIMS OF THE INDIAN

THE PEOPLE OF THE UNITED STATES can never without dishonor refuse to respect these two considerations:

Francis Amasa Walker; photo by B. Kimball

1. That this continent was originally owned and occupied by the Indians, who have on this account a claim somewhat larger than the privilege of 160 acres of land and "find himself" in tools and stock, which is granted as a matter of course to any newly arrived foreigner who declares his intention to become a citizen; that something in the nature of an endowment, either capitalized or in the form of annual expenditures for a series of years for the benefit of the Indians, though at the discretion of the government as to the specific objects, should be provided for every tribe or band which is deprived of its roaming privilege and confined to a diminished reservation — such an endowment being not in the nature of a gratuity but in common honesty the right of the Indian on account of his original interest in the soil.

2. That inasmuch as the progress of our industrial enterprise has cut these people off from modes of livelihood entirely sufficient for their wants and for which they were qualified, in a degree which has been the wonder of more civilized races, by inherited aptitudes and by long pursuit, and has left

them utterly without resource, they have a claim on this account again to temporary support and to such assistance as may be necessary to place them in a position to obtain a livelihood by means which shall be compatible with civilization.

Had the settlements of the United States not been extended beyond the frontier of 1867, all the Indians of the continent would to the end of time have found upon the plains an inexhaustible supply of food and clothing. Were the westward course of population to be stayed at the barriers of today, notwithstanding the tremendous inroads made upon their hunting grounds since 1867, the Indians would still have hope of life. But another such five years will see the Indians of Dakota and Montana as poor as the Indians of Nevada and Southern California; that is, reduced to a habitual condition of suffering from want of food.

The freedom of expansion which is working these results is to us of incalculable value. To the Indian it is of incalculable cost. Every year's advance of our frontier takes in a territory as large as some of the kingdoms of Europe. We are richer by hundreds of millions; the Indian is poorer by a large part of the little that he has. This growth is bringing imperial greatness to the nation; to the Indian it brings wretchedness, destitution, beggary. Surely there is obligation found in considerations like these, requiring us in some way, and in the best way, to make good to these original owners of the soil the loss by which we so greatly gain.

Can any principle of national morality be clearer than that, when the expansion and development of a civilized race involve the rapid destruction of the only means of subsistence possessed by the members of a less fortunate race, the higher is bound as of simple right to provide for the lower some substitute for the means of subsistence which it has destroyed. That substitute is, of course, best realized, not by systematic gratuities of food and clothing continued beyond a present emergency, but by directing these people to new pursuits which shall be consistent with the progress of civilization upon the continent; helping them over the first rough places on "the white man's road," and, meanwhile, supplying such subsistence as is absolutely necessary during the period of initiation and experiment.

A LEGALIZED REFORMATORY CONTROL NECESSARY

THE ASSISTANCE DUE to the Indians from the government in the discharge of those obligations which have been adverted to should not much longer be irrespective of their own efforts. Just so soon as these tribes cease to be formidable, they should be brought distinctly to the realization of the law that if they would eat they must also work. Nor should it be left to their own choices how miserably they will live in order that they may escape work as much as possible. The government should extend over them a rigid reformatory discipline to save them from falling hopelessly into the condition of pauperism and petty crime.

Merely to disarm the savages and to surround them by forces which it is hopeless in them to resist, without exercising over them for a series of years a system of paternal control, requiring them to learn and practise the arts of industry, at least until one generation has been fairly started on a course of self-improvement, is to make it pretty much a matter of certainty that by far the larger part of the now-roving Indians will become simply vagabonds in the midst of civilization, forming little camps here and there over the face of the Western states, which will be festering sores on the communities near which they are located; the men resorting for a living to basket making and hog stealing; the women to fortune telling and harlotry.

No one who looks about him and observes the numbers of our own race who, despite our strong constitutional disposition to labor, the general example of industry, the possession of all the arts and appliances which diminish effort while they multiply results, and the large rewards offered in the constitution of modern society for success in industrial effort, yet sink to the most abject condition from indolence or from vice, can greatly doubt that, unless prompt and vigorous measures are taken by the government, something like what has been described is to be the fate of the now-roving Indians, when they shall be surrounded and disarmed by the extension of our settlements and deprived of their traditional means of subsistence through the extinction of game.

Unused to manual labor and physically disqualified for it by the habits of the chase, unprovided with tools and implements, without forethought and without self-control, singularly susceptible to evil influences, with strong animal appetites and no intellectual tastes or aspirations to hold those appetites in check, it would be to assume more than would be taken for granted of any white race under the same conditions, to expect that the wild Indians will become industrious and frugal except through a severe course of industrial instruction and exercise, under restraint. The reservation system affords the place for thus dealing with tribes and bands, without the access of influences inimical to peace and virtue.

It is only necessary that federal laws, judiciously framed to meet all the facts of the case and enacted in season, before the Indians begin to scatter, shall place all the members of this race under a strict reformatory control by the agents of the government. Especially is it essential that the right of the government to keep Indians upon the reservations assigned to them and to arrest and return them whenever they wander away should be placed beyond dispute. Without this, whenever these people become restive under compulsion to labor, they will break away in their old roving spirit and stray off in small bands to neighboring communities, upon which they will prey in a petty fashion, by begging and stealing, until they have made themselves so much of a nuisance that the law is invoked against them or their apprehensions of violence become excited, when they will pass on, to become the pests of other and more distant communities.

In a word, in the 275,000 Indians west of the Mississippi, the United States have all the elements of a large gypsy population, which will inevitably become a sore, a well-nigh intolerable, affliction to all that region, unless the government shall provide for their instruction in the arts of life, which can only be done effectually under a pressure not to be resisted or evaded. The right of the government to do this cannot be seriously questioned. Expressly excluded by the Constitution from citizenship, the government is only bound in its treatment of them by considerations of present policy and justice. Even were the constitutional incapacity of these people not what it is and

were there nothing in the history of the dealings of the United States with them to form a precedent for their being placed under arbitrary control, still, the manifest necessity of self-protection would amply justify the government in any and all measures required to prevent the miserable conclusion I have indicated.

THE PRACTICAL SIDE OF THE INDIAN QUESTION

I HAVE PURPOSELY DIVESTED these remarks of what is commonly known as "sentiment" and have refrained from appealing to the higher considerations of human and Christian charity, not because I have not respect for such considerations nor because sentiment is out of place in dealing with such a question but because I believe that the Indian policy of the government, past and prospective, can be fully justified before the country by arguments addressed solely to self-interest, and because it has appeared to me that a certain class of the community have become a little wearied of appeals, in behalf of the Indians, to sentiments which are, perhaps, rather too fine for popular daily use. Nothing that the government is doing toward the Indians but can be vindicated on grounds of practical usefulness and economy as completely as the expenditures of our American communities for the education of the young.

I know of no stronger proof that could be offered for the satisfaction of the country that the Indian policy of the government, notwithstanding so much about it that appears whimsical and contradictory, is really to be justified on common sense principles, than the fact that for several years bills making appropriations for the necessarily heavy expenditures involved have run the gauntlet of the Appropriation Committees of both House and Senate, without losing a single original feature of value. No one who understands the constitution of those committees and knows their readiness to slaughter any provision for any service which cannot give an unmistakable reason for itself, will need stronger assurance that, when the details of the Indian policy come to be explained, point by point, to men versed in public affairs and in the methods of business, they are found to be based upon good practical reasons, and not upon theories or sentiments.

THE ENDOWMENT OF INDIAN TRIBES

I CANNOT ADMIT that there is any reason for the apprehensions which many persons feel, that when the Indians cease to be formidable, they will be neglected. It is certainly desirable on all grounds, not merely to avoid the possibility of an occasional failure in the provision for their wants but also for the sake of securing comprehensiveness and consistency in the treatment of the subject, that the endowments for the several tribes and bands be capitalized and placed in trust for their benefit, out of the reach of accident or caprice. The proceeds arising from sales, as their reservations are from time to time diminished by authority of law, for the sake of securing a higher culture of the portions remaining, ought, if the Indians are honestly treated in the transaction, to be sufficient to provide for all ordinary beneficial expenditures in behalf of tribes and bands having lands secured to them by treaty.

The reservations granted heretofore have generally been proportioned, and rightly so, to the needs of the Indians in a roving state, with hunting and fishing as their chief means of subsistence, which condition implies the occupation of a territory far exceeding what could possibly be cultivated. As they change to agriculture, however rude and primitive at first, they tend to contract the limits of actual occupation.

With proper administrative management, the portions thus rendered available for cession or sale can be so thrown together as in no way to impair the integrity of the reservation. Where this change has taken place, there can be no question of the expediency of such sale or cession. The Indian Office has always favored this course, and, notwithstanding the somewhat questionable character of some of the resulting transactions, arising especially out of violent or fraudulent combinations to prevent a fair sale, it can be confidently affirmed that the advantage of the Indians has generally been subserved thereby.

For those tribes and bands which have no reservations secured to them by treaty, from which they can hope in the course of time to realize a civilization and improvement fund, provision will still require to be made by law. Their right to endowment is none the less clear than the right of other tribes whose fortune it was to deal with the United States by treaty, before Congress put an end to the treaty system with its many abuses and absurdities. We have received the soil from them; and we have extinguished their only means of subsistence. Nothing in the history of the United States justifies the belief that either Congress or the country will be wanting in justice or generosity in dealing with the necessities of a people who have been impoverished that we might be rich.

Our national charity has sought the objects of its benefactions at the ends of the earth. Americans will never be wanting in simple justice to helpless dependents at home. I have, therefore, no fear for the future of the Indians of this continent when once the arms of their resistance are laid down, and Indian outrages are no longer reported to inflame the hostility of the border states and to mingle doubt and misgivings with the philanthropic intentions of the charitable and humane.

1873

63.

Francis Ellingwood Abbot: Nine Demands of Liberalism for Separation of Church and State

The Free Religious Association was founded in 1867 to propound a religion of humanity, guided by reason, and to provide an organizational home for those who regarded themselves as too enlightened to remain within the confines of splintered sectarian Christianity. One of the association's leaders was Francis Ellingwood Abbot, who directed his energies against the National Reform Association (founded by Presbyterians and Episcopalians) that was attempting to amend the Constitution to endorse Christianity officially. Abbot called for complete separation of church and state. His beliefs were briefly expressed in "The Demands of Liberalism," which he published on the front page of his weekly paper, The Index.

Source: *The Index*, January 1, 1874.

1. We demand that churches and other ecclesiastical property shall no longer be exempt from just taxation.

2. We demand that the employment of chaplains in Congress, in state legislatures, in the navy and militia, and in prisons, asylums, and all other institutions supported by public money shall be discontinued.

3. We demand that all public appropriations for sectarian educational and charitable institutions shall cease.

4. We demand that all religious services now sustained by the government shall be abolished; and especially that the use of the Bible in the public schools, whether ostensibly as a textbook or avowedly as a book of religious worship, shall be prohibited.

5. We demand that the appointment by the President of the United States or by the governors of the various states of all religious festivals and fasts shall wholly cease.

6. We demand that the judicial oath in the courts and in all other departments of the government shall be abolished, and that simple affirmation under the pains and penalties of perjury shall be established in its stead.

7. We demand that all laws directly or indirectly enforcing the observance of Sunday as the Sabbath shall be repealed.

8. We demand that all laws looking to the enforcement of "Christian" morality shall be abrogated, and that all laws shall be conformed to the requirements of natural morality, equal rights, and impartial liberty.

9. We demand that, not only in the constitutions of the United States and of the several states but also in the practical administration of the same, no privilege or advantage shall be conceded to Christianity or any other special religion; that our entire political system shall be founded and administered on a purely secular basis; and that whatever changes shall prove necessary to this end shall be consistently, unflinchingly, and promptly made.

64.

"John Henry"

"America's greatest ballad," as it has been called, celebrates an African American railroad worker named John Henry who is supposed to have met his death during the construction of the Big Bend Tunnel, in West Virginia, sometime around 1873. John Henry's job was to drive the steel drills into the rock to make holes for the blasting charges. He "drove steel with a twelve-pound sheep-nose hammer with a regular-size switch handle four feet long. . . . He drove steel from his left shoulder and would make a stroke of more than nineteen and a half feet. . . . And he could drive ten hours without turning a stroke. He was the steel-driving champion of the country and his record has never been equaled." They sang of the glint of his hammer in the murky darkness of the tunnel, saying that it rang like silver and shone like gold. One day the boss came around with a new steam-driven hammer, a machine which John Henry confronted as a personal challenge.

❦ JOHN HENRY

When John Henry was a little baby,
Sitting on his pappy's knee,
He grabbed a hammer and a little piece of steel,
Said, "This hammer'll be the death of me, Lord, Lord,
This hammer'll be the death of me."

Now the captain said to John Henry,
"I'm gonna bring that steam drill around,
I'm gonna take that steam drill out on the job,
I'm gonna whop that steel on down, Lord, Lord,
Gonna whop that steel on down."

John Henry told his captain,
"A man ain't nothing but a man,
But before I'll let that steam drill beat me down
I'll die with my hammer in my hand, Lord, Lord,
I'll die with my hammer in my hand."

John Henry said to his shaker,
"Now shaker, why don't you sing?
'Cause I'm throwing twelve pounds from my hips on down,
Just listen to that cold steel ring, Lord, Lord,
Just listen to that cold steel ring."

The man that invented the steam drill,
He thought he was mighty fine,
But John Henry he made fourteen feet
While the steam drill only made nine, Lord, Lord,
The steam drill only made nine.

John Henry hammered on the mountain
Till his hammer was striking fire.
He drove so hard he broke his poor heart,
Then he laid down his hammer and he died, Lord, Lord,
He laid down his hammer and he died.

They took John Henry to the graveyard,
And they buried him in the sand,
And every locomotive comes rolling by
Says, "There lies a steel-driving man, Lord, Lord,
There lies a steel-driving man."

Now some say he was born in Texas,
And some say he was born in Maine,
But I don't give a damn where that poor boy was born.
He was a steel-driving man, Lord, Lord,
He was a steel-driving man.

65.

SAMUEL F. MILLER AND STEPHEN J. FIELD:
Slaughter-House Cases

If the Radical Republicans hoped that the "due process" clause of the Fourteenth Amendment would protect private enterprise from the vagaries of interfering state legislation, they were disappointed by the U.S. Supreme Court's decision in the Slaughter-House cases of 1873. Louisiana's legislature had granted to one corporation a monopoly of the slaughtering business in New Orleans. This monopoly was challenged on the ground that it violated the First Section of the Fourteenth Amendment. The Court stated in its majority opinion that the Amendment applied to the status of African Americans only, and was not meant to confer federal protection over all possible areas of civil rights. The following selection contains portions of Justice Miller's opinion and of Justice Field's dissent.

Source: 16 Wallace 36.

Mr. Justice Miller: These cases are brought here by writs of error to the Supreme Court of the state of Louisiana. They arise out of the efforts of the butchers of New Orleans to resist the Crescent City Live-Stock Landing and Slaughter-House Company in the exercise of certain powers conferred by the charter which created it and which was granted by the legislature of that state. . . .

It cannot be denied that the statute under consideration is aptly framed to remove from the more densely populated part of the city, the noxious slaughter-houses, and large and offensive collections of animals necessarily incident to the slaughtering business of a large city, and to locate them where the convenience, health, and comfort of the people require they shall be located. And it must be conceded that the means adopted by the act for this purpose are appropriate, are stringent, and effectual. But it is said that in creating a corporation for this purpose, and conferring upon it exclusive privileges — privileges which it is said con-

stitute a monopoly — the legislature has exceeded its power. If this statute had imposed on the city of New Orleans precisely the same duties, accompanied by the same privileges, which it has on the corporation which it created, it is believed that no question would have been raised as to its constitutionality. In that case the effect on the butchers in pursuit of their occupation and on the public would have been the same as it is now.

Why cannot the legislature confer the same powers on another corporation, created for a lawful and useful public object, that it can on the municipal corporation already existing? That wherever a legislature has the right to accomplish a certain result, and that result is best attained by means of a corporation, it has the right to create such a corporation and to endow it with the powers necessary to effect the desired and lawful purpose, seems hardly to admit of debate. The proposition is ably discussed and affirmed in the case of *M'Culloch* v. *The State of Maryland*, in relation to the power of Congress to organize the Bank of the United States to aid in the fiscal operations of the government.

It can readily be seen that the interested vigilance of the corporation created by the Louisiana legislature will be more efficient in enforcing the limitation prescribed for the stock-landing and slaughtering business for the good of the city than the ordinary efforts of the officers of the law.

Unless, therefore, it can be maintained that the exclusive privilege granted by this charter to the corporation is beyond the power of the legislature of Louisiana, there can be no just exception to the validity of the statute. And in this respect we are not able to see that these privileges are especially odious or objectionable. The duty imposed as a consideration for the privilege is well defined, and its enforcement well guarded. The prices or charges to be made by the company are limited by the statute, and we are not advised that they are on the whole exorbitant or unjust. . . .

It may, therefore, be considered as established that the authority of the legislature of Louisiana to pass the present statute is ample, unless some restraint in the exercise of that power be found in the constitution of that state or in the amendments to the Constitution of the United States adopted since the date of the decisions we have already cited. If any such restraint is supposed to exist in the constitution of the state, the Supreme Court of Louisiana having necessarily passed on that question, it would not be open to review in this Court.

The plaintiffs in error accepting this issue allege that the statute is a violation of the Constitution of the United States in these several particulars:

That it creates an involuntary servitude forbidden by the 13th Article of amendment; that it abridges the privileges and immunities of citizens of the United States; that it denies to the plaintiffs the equal protection of the laws; and that it deprives

them of their property without due process of law, contrary to the provisions of the 1st Section of the 14th Article of amendment.

This Court is thus called upon for the first time to give construction to these articles. . . .

Twelve articles of amendment were added to the federal Constitution soon after the original organization of the government under it in 1789. Of these, all but the last were adopted so soon afterwards as to justify the statement that they were practically contemporaneous with the adoption of the original; and the 12th, adopted in 1803, was so nearly so as to have become, like all the others, historical and of another age. But within the last eight years, three other articles of amendment of vast importance have been added by the voice of the people to that now venerable instrument.

The most cursory glance at these articles discloses a unity of purpose, when taken in connection with the history of the times, which cannot fail to have an important bearing on any question of doubt concerning their true meaning. Nor can such doubts, when any reasonably exist, be safely and rationally solved without a reference to that history; for in it is found the occasion and the necessity for recurring again to the great source of power in this country — the people of the states — for additional guarantees of human rights; additional powers to the federal government; additional restraints upon those of the states. Fortunately, that history is fresh within the memory of us all, and its leading features, as they bear upon the matter before us, free from doubt. . . .

The process of restoring to their proper relations with the federal government and with the other states those which had sided with the rebellion, undertaken under the proclamation of President Johnson in 1865, and before the assembling of Congress, developed the fact that, notwithstanding the formal recognition by those states of the abolition of slavery, the condition of the slave race would, without further protection of the federal government, be almost as bad as it was before. Among the first acts of legislation adopted by several of the states in the legislative bodies which claimed to be in their normal relations with the federal government, were laws which imposed upon the colored race onerous disabilities and burdens, and curtailed their rights in the pursuit of life, liberty, and property to such an extent that their freedom was of little value, while they had lost the protection which they had received from their former owners from motives both of interest and humanity.

They were in some states forbidden to appear in the towns in any other character than menial servants. They were required to reside on and cultivate the soil without the right to purchase or own it. They were excluded from many occupations of gain and were not permitted to give testimony in the courts in any case where a white man was a party. It was said that their lives were at the mercy of bad men, either because the laws for their protection were insufficient or were not enforced.

These circumstances, whatever of falsehood or misconception may have been mingled with their presentation, forced upon the statesmen who had conducted the federal government in safety through the crisis of the rebellion, and who supposed that by the 13th Article of amendment they had secured the result of their labors, the conviction that something more was necessary in the way of constitutional protection to the unfortunate race who had suffered so much. They accordingly passed through Congress the proposition for the 14th Amendment; and they declined to treat as restored to their full participation in the government of the Union the states which had been in insurrection, until they ratified that article by a formal vote of their legislative bodies. . . .

We repeat, then, in the light of this reca-

pitulation of events, almost too recent to be called history but which are familiar to us all, and on the most casual examination of the language of these amendments, no one can fail to be impressed with the one pervading purpose found in them all, lying at the foundation of each, and without which none of them would have been even suggested; we mean the freedom of the slave race, the security and firm establishment of that freedom, and the protection of the newly made freeman and citizen from the oppressions of those who had formerly exercised unlimited dominion over him. It is true that only the 15th Amendment, in terms, mentions the Negro by speaking of his color and his slavery. But it is just as true that each of the other articles was addressed to the grievances of that race and designed to remedy them as the 15th. . . .

The 1st Section of the 14th Article, to which our attention is more specially invited, opens with a definition of citizenship — not only citizenship of the United States but citizenship of the states. No such definition was previously found in the Constitution, nor had any attempt been made to define it by act of Congress. It had been the occasion of much discussion in the courts, by the executive departments, and in the public journals. It had been said by eminent judges that no man was a citizen of the United States except as he was a citizen of one of the states composing the Union. Those, therefore, who had been born and resided always in the District of Columbia or in the territories, though within the United States, were not citizens. Whether this proposition was sound or not had never been judicially decided.

But it had been held by this Court, in the celebrated Dred Scott case, only a few years before the outbreak of the Civil War, that a man of African descent, whether a slave or not, was not and could not be a citizen of a state or of the United States. This decision, while it met the condemnation of some of the ablest statesmen and constitutional lawyers of the country, had never been overruled; and if it was to be accepted as a constitutional limitation of the right of citizenship, then all the Negro race who had recently been made freemen were still, not only not citizens but were incapable of becoming so by anything short of an amendment to the Constitution.

To remove this difficulty primarily, and to establish a clear and comprehensive definition of citizenship which should declare what should constitute citizenship of the United States and also citizenship of a state, the first clause of the 1st Section was framed. "All persons born or naturalized in the United States, and subject to the jurisdiction thereof, are citizens of the United States and of the state wherein they reside." . . .

Of the privileges and immunities of the citizen of the United States, and of the privileges and immunities of the citizen of the state, and what they respectively are, we will presently consider; but we wish to state here that it is only the former which are placed by this clause under the protection of the federal Constitution; and that the latter, whatever they may be, are not intended to have any additional protection by this paragraph of the amendment.

If, then, there is a difference between the privileges and immunities belonging to a citizen of the United States as such and those belonging to the citizen of the state as such, the latter must rest for their security and protection where they have heretofore rested; for they are not embraced by this paragraph of the amendment. . . .

It would be the vainest show of learning to attempt to prove by citations of authority that up to the adoption of the recent amendments no claim or pretense was set up that those rights depended on the federal government for their existence or protection, beyond the very few express limitations which the federal Constitution imposed upon the states, such, for instance, as the prohibition against ex post facto laws,

bills of attainder, and laws impairing the obligation of contracts. But with the exception of these and a few other restrictions, the entire domain of the privileges and immunities of citizens of the states, as above defined, lay within the constitutional and legislative power of the states, and without that of the federal government.

Was it the purpose of the 14th Amendment, by the simple declaration that no state should make or enforce any law which shall abridge the privileges and immunities of *citizens of the United States,* to transfer the security and protection of all the civil rights which we have mentioned from the states to the federal government? And where it is declared that Congress shall have the power to enforce that article, was it intended to bring within the power of Congress the entire domain of civil rights heretofore belonging exclusively to the states?

All this and more must follow if the proposition of the plaintiffs in error be sound. For not only are these rights subject to the control of Congress whenever in its discretion any of them are supposed to be abridged by state legislation, but that body may also pass laws in advance limiting and restricting the exercise of legislative power by the states, in their most ordinary and usual functions, as in its judgment it may think proper on all such subjects. And still further, such a construction followed by the reversal of the judgments of the Supreme Court of Louisiana in these cases would constitute this Court a perpetual censor upon all legislation of the states, on the civil rights of their own citizens, with authority to nullify such as it did not approve as consistent with those rights, as they existed at the time of the adoption of this amendment.

The argument, we admit, is not always the most conclusive which is drawn from the consequences urged against the adoption of a particular construction of an instrument. But when, as in the case before us, these consequences are so serious, so far reaching and pervading, so great a departure from the structure and spirit of our institutions; when the effect is to fetter and degrade the state governments by subjecting them to the control of Congress, in the exercise of powers heretofore universally conceded to them of the most ordinary and fundamental character; when, in fact, it radically changes the whole theory of the relations of the state and federal governments to each other and of both these governments to the people; the argument has a force that is irresistible, in the absence of language which expresses such a purpose too clearly to admit of doubt.

We are convinced that no such results were intended by the Congress which proposed these amendments, nor by the legislatures of the states which ratified them.

Having shown that the privileges and immunities relied on in the argument are those which belong to citizens of the states as such, and that they are left to the state governments for security and protection and not by this article placed under the special care of the federal government, we may hold ourselves excused from defining the privileges and immunities of citizens of the United States which no state can abridge, until some case involving those privileges may make it necessary to do so.

Mr. Justice Field: In the law in question there are only two provisions which can properly be called police regulations — the one which requires the landing and slaughtering of animals below the city of New Orleans; and the other, which requires the inspection of the animals before they are slaughtered. When these requirements are complied with, the sanitary purposes of the act are accomplished. In all other particulars the act is a mere grant to a corporation created by it of special and exclusive privileges by which the health of the city is in no way promoted.

It is plain that if the corporation can, without endangering the health of the public, carry on the business of landing, keeping, and slaughtering cattle within a district below the city embracing an area of over a thousand square miles, it would not endanger the public health if other persons were also permitted to carry on the same business within the same district under similar conditions as to the inspection of the animals. The health of the city might require the removal from its limits and suburbs of all buildings for keeping and slaughtering cattle, but no such object could possibly justify legislation removing such buildings from a large part of the state for the benefit of a single corporation. The pretense of sanitary regulations for the grant of the exclusive privileges is a shallow one which merits only this passing notice.

It is also sought to justify the act in question on the same principle that exclusive grants for ferries, bridges, and turnpikes are sanctioned. But it can find no support there. Those grants are of franchises of a public character appertaining to the government. Their use usually requires the exercise of the sovereign right of eminent domain. It is for the government to determine when one of them shall be granted and the conditions upon which it shall be enjoyed. It is the duty of the government to provide suitable roads, bridges, and ferries for the convenience of the public; and if it chooses to devolve this duty to any extent or in any locality upon particular individuals or corporations, it may of course stipulate for such exclusive privileges connected with the franchise as it may deem proper without encroaching upon the freedom or the just rights of others. The grant, with exclusive privileges, of a right thus appertaining to the government is a very different thing from a grant, with exclusive privileges, of a right to pursue one of the ordinary trades or callings of life, which is a right appertaining solely to the individual.

Nor is there any analogy between this act of Louisiana and the legislation which confers upon the inventor of a new and useful improvement an exclusive right to make and sell to others his invention. The government in this way only secures to the inventor the temporary enjoyment of that which, without him, would not have existed. It thus only recognizes in the inventor a temporary property in the product of his own brain.

The act of Louisiana presents the naked case, unaccompanied by any public considerations, where a right to pursue a lawful and necessary calling, previously enjoyed by every citizen and in connection with which a thousand persons were daily employed, is taken away and vested exclusively for twenty-five years, for an extensive district and a large population, in a single corporation, or its exercise is for that period restricted to the establishments of the corporation, and there allowed only upon onerous conditions.

If exclusive privileges of this character can be granted to a corporation of seventeen persons, they may, in the discretion of the legislature, be equally granted to a single individual. If they may be granted for twenty-five years, they may be equally granted for a century, and in perpetuity. If they may be granted for the landing and keeping of animals intended for sale or slaughter, they may be equally granted for the landing and storing of grain and other products of the earth, or for any article of commerce. If they may be granted for structures in which animal food is prepared for market, they may be equally granted for structures in which farinaceous or vegetable food is prepared. They may be granted for any of the pursuits of human industry, even in its most simple and common forms. Indeed, upon the theory on which the exclusive privileges granted by the act in question are sustained, there is no monopoly, in the most odious form, which may not be upheld.

The question presented is, therefore, one of the gravest importance, not merely to the parties here but to the whole country. It is nothing less than the question whether the recent amendments to the federal Constitution protect the citizens of the United States against the deprivation of their common rights by state legislation. In my judgment, the 14th Amendment does afford such protection and was so intended by the Congress which framed and the states which adopted it. . . .

The first clause of the 14th Amendment . . . recognizes in express terms, if it does not create, citizens of the United States; and it makes their citizenship dependent upon the place of their birth, or the fact of their adoption, and not upon the constitution or laws of any state or the condition of their ancestry. A citizen of a state is now only a citizen of the United States residing in that state. The fundamental rights, privileges, and immunities which belong to him as a free man and a free citizen now belong to him as a citizen of the United States and are not dependent upon his citizenship of any state.

The exercise of these rights and privileges, and the degree of enjoyment received from such exercise, are always more or less affected by the condition and the local institutions of the state or city or town where he resides. They are thus affected in a state by the wisdom of its laws, the ability of its officers, the efficiency of its magistrates, the education and morals of its people, and by many other considerations. This is a result which follows from the constitution of society and can never be avoided, but in no other way can they be affected by the action of the state, or by the residence of the citizen therein. They do not derive their existence from its legislation and cannot be destroyed by its power.

The amendment does not attempt to confer any new privileges or immunities upon citizens, or to enumerate or define those already existing. It assumes that there are such privileges and immunities which belong of right to citizens as such and ordains that they shall not be abridged by state legislation. . . .

The privileges and immunities designated are those *which of right belong to the citizens of all free governments.* Clearly among these must be placed the right to pursue a lawful employment in a lawful manner, without other restraint than such as equally affects all persons. . . .

It will not be pretended that under the 4th Article of the Constitution any state could create a monopoly in any known trade or manufacture in favor of her own citizens, or any portion of them, which would exclude an equal participation in the trade or manufacture monopolized by citizens of other states. She could not confer, for example, upon any of her citizens the sole right to manufacture shoes or boots or silk, or the sole right to sell those articles in the state so as to exclude nonresident citizens from engaging in a similar manufacture or sale. The nonresident citizens could claim equality of privilege under the provisions of the 4th Article with the citizens of the state exercising the monopoly as well as with others, and thus, as respects them, the monopoly would cease. If this were not so, it would be in the power of the state to exclude at any time the citizens of other states from participation in particular branches of commerce or trade and extend the exclusion from time to time so as effectually to prevent any traffic with them.

Now, what the clause in question does for the protection of citizens of one state against the creation of monopolies in favor of citizens of other states, the 14th Amendment does for the protection of every citizen of the United States against the creation of any monopoly whatever. The privileges and immunities of citizens of the United States, of every one of them, is secured against abridgment in any form by any state. The 14th Amendment places them under the guardianship of the national authority. All monopolies in any known trade or manufacture are an invasion of these privileges, for they encroach upon the liberty of citizens to acquire property and pursue happiness. . . .

This equality of right, with exemption from all disparaging and partial enactments in the lawful pursuits of life throughout the whole country, is the distinguishing privilege of citizens of the United States. To them, everywhere, all pursuits, all professions, all avocations are open without other restrictions than such as are imposed equally upon all others of the same age, sex, and condition. The state may prescribe such regulations for every pursuit and calling of life as will promote the public health, secure the good order, and advance the general prosperity of society, but when once prescribed, the pursuit or calling must be free to be followed by every citizen who is within the conditions designated and will conform to the regulations. This is the fundamental idea upon which our institutions rest, and unless adhered to in the legislation of the country our government will be a republic only in name.

The 14th Amendment, in my judgment, makes it essential to the validity of the legislation of every state that this equality of right should be respected. How widely this equality has been departed from, how entirely rejected and trampled upon by the act of Louisiana, I have already shown. And it is to me a matter of profound regret that its validity is recognized by a majority of this Court, for by it the right of free labor, one of the most sacred and imprescriptible rights of man, is violated. As stated by the Supreme Court of Connecticut, in the case cited, grants of exclusive privileges, such as is made by the act in question, are opposed to the whole theory of free government, and it requires no aid from any bill of rights to render them void. That only is a free government, in the American sense of the term, under which the inalienable right of every citizen to pursue his happiness is unrestrained, except by just, equal, and impartial laws.

66.

The Farmers' Declaration of Independence

In 1873, the National Granger movement, responding to the farmers' complaints of high costs and small profits, had spread to all but four states and claimed a membership of about 800,000. Originally organized as an educational and social society, the Grange had by the mid-1870s become far more political than educational in nature and was lobbying for state regulation of railroads and grain elevators. So many farmers made Independence Day, 1873, an occasion for airing their complaints that it became known as the "Farmers' Fourth of July." The problems of the farmers were summed up in the following "Farmers' Declaration of Independence." The agitation led to temporary relief in the form of state "Granger Laws" that regulated railroad and warehouse rates.

Source: *Prairie Farmer*, July 12, 1873.

WHEN IN THE COURSE of human events, it becomes necessary for a class of people, suffering from long-continued systems of oppression and abuse, to rouse themselves from an apathetic indifference to their own interests, which has become habitual; to assume among their fellow citizens that equal station and demand from the government they support those equal rights to which the laws of nature and of nature's God entitles them; a decent respect for the opinions of mankind requires that they should declare the causes that impel them to a course so necessary to their own protection.

We hold these truths to be self-evident: That all men are created equal; that they are endowed by their Creator with certain inalienable rights; that among these are life, liberty, and the pursuit of happiness. That to secure these rights governments are instituted among men, deriving their just powers from the consent of the governed; that whenever the powers of a government become destructive of these, either through the injustice or inefficiency of its laws or through the corruption of its administrators, it is the right of the people to abolish such laws and institute such reforms as to them shall seem most likely to effect their safety and happiness.

Prudence indeed will dictate that laws long established shall not be changed for light and trifling causes, and, accordingly, all experience hath shown that mankind are more disposed to suffer while evils are sufferable than to right themselves by abolishing the laws to which they are accustomed. But when a long train of abuses and usurpations, pursuing invariably the same object, evinces a desire to reduce a people under the absolute despotism of combinations that, under the fostering care of government and with wealth wrung from the people, have grown to such gigantic proportions as to overshadow all the land and wield an almost irresistible influence for their own selfish purposes in all its halls of legislation, it is their right — it is their duty — to throw off such tyranny and provide new guards for their future security.

Such has been the patient sufferance of the producing classes of these states, and such is now the necessity which compels them to declare that they will use every means save a resort to arms to overthrow this despotism of monopoly, and to reduce all men claiming the protection of American laws to an equality before those laws, making the owner of a railroad as amenable thereto as the "veriest beggar that walks the streets, the sun and air his sole inheritance."

The history of the present railway monopoly is a history of repeated injuries and oppressions, all having in direct object the establishment of an absolute tyranny over the people of these states unequaled in any monarchy of the Old World, and having its only parallel in the history of the medieval ages, when the strong hand was the only law and the highways of commerce were taxed by the feudal barons, who, from their strongholds, surrounded by their armies of vassals, could levy such tribute upon the traveler as their own wills alone should dictate. To prove this, let facts be submitted to a candid world:

They have influenced our executive officers to refuse their assent to laws the most wholesome and necessary for the public good; and when such laws have been passed, they have utterly refused to obey them.

They have procured the passage of other laws for their own benefit alone, by which they have put untold millions into their own coffers, to the injury of the entire commercial and industrial interests of the country.

They have influenced legislation to suit themselves by bribing venal legislators to betray the true interests of their constituents, while others have been kept quiet by the compliment of free passes.

They have repeatedly prevented the reelection of representatives for opposing with manly firmness their invasion of the people's rights.

They have by false representations and subterfuge induced the people to subscribe funds to build roads, whose rates, when built, are so exorbitant that in many instances transportation by private conveyance is less burdensome.

They have procured charters by which they condemn and appropriate our lands without adequate compensation therefor and arrogantly claim that by virtue of these charters they are absolutely above the control of legal enactments.

They have procured a law of Congress by which they have dispossessed hundreds of farmers of the homes that by years of toil they have built up; have induced others to mortgage their farms for roads never intended to be built, and, after squandering the money thus obtained, have left their victims to the mercy of courts over which they have held absolute sway.

They have obstructed the administration of justice by injunctions procured from venal judges by legal quibbles and appeals from court to court, with intent to wear out or ruin the prosecutor, openly avowing their determination to make it so terrible for the public to prosecute them that they will not dare undertake it.

They have virtually made judges dependent on their will alone and have procured their appointment for the express purpose of reversing a decision of the highest court of the nation by which millions were gained to them, to the injury of the holders of the bonds and the breaking down of this last safeguard of American freemen.

They have affected to render themselves independent of and superior to the civil power by ordering large bodies of hirelings to enforce their unlawful exactions and have protected them from punishment for an injury they might inflict upon peaceful citizens, while ejecting them from their conveyances for refusing to pay more than the rate of fare prescribed by laws.

They have arrested and summoned from their homes for trial, at distant points, other citizens for the same offense of refusing to pay more than the legal fare, putting them to as great inconvenience and expense as possible, and still further evincing their determination to make it too terrible for the people to dare engage in any legal conflict with them.

They have combined together to destroy competition and to practise an unjust discrimination, contrary to the expressed provisions of our Constitution and the spirit of our law.

They have virtually cut off our trade with distant parts of the world by their unjust discriminations and by their exorbitant rates of freights, forcing upon us the alternative of accumulating upon our hands a worthless surplus, or of giving three-fourths of the price our customers pay for their products for their transportation.

Under the false and specious pretense of developing the country, they have obtained enormous grants of public lands from Congress and now retard rather than develop its settlement by the high prices charged for such land.

They have converted the bonds fraudulently obtained from the government into a great corruption fund, with which they are enabled to bribe and control legislatures and subvert every branch of government to their own base and sordid purpose.

They have increased the already intolerable burden of taxation which the people have to endure, compared with which the Tea and Stamp Tax which precipitated the War of the Revolution seems utterly insignificant, by the appropriation of money from the public treasury, while they have escaped taxation themselves by evading and violating the expressed provisions of their charters.

In every stage of these oppressions we have petitioned our legislatures for redress in the most humble terms. Our repeated petitions have been answered only by silence or by attempts to frame laws that shall seem to meet our wants, but that are, in fact, only a legal snare for courts to disagree upon and for corporations to disobey.

Nor have we been wanting in attempts to obtain redress through Congress. We have warned them from time to time of these various and repeated encroachments upon our rights; we have reminded them of the circumstances of our emigration and settlement here; we have appealed to them as the administrators of a free and impartial government to protect us from these encroachments, which, if continued, would inevitably end in the utter destruction of those liberties for which our fathers gave their lives, and the reinstatement of privileged classes and an aristocracy of wealth, worse than that from which the War of the Revolution freed us. They too have been deaf to the voice of justice and of duty. We must therefore acquiesce in the necessity which compels us to denounce their criminal indifference to our wrongs and hold them as we hold our legislators — enemies to the producer — to the monopolists, friends.

We, therefore, the producers of this state in our several counties assembled, on this the anniversary of that day that gave birth to a nation of freemen and to a government of which, despite the corruption of its officers, we are still so justly proud, appealing to the Supreme Judge of the world for the rectitude of our intentions, do solemnly declare that we will use all lawful and peaceable means to free ourselves from the tyranny of monopoly, and that we will never cease our efforts for reform until every department of our government gives token that the reign of licentious extravagance is over and something of the purity, honesty, and frugality with which our fathers inaugurated it has taken its place.

That to this end we hereby declare ourselves absolutely free and independent of all past political connections, and that we will give our suffrage only to such men for office, from the lowest officer in the state to the President of the United States, as we have good reason to believe will use their best endeavors to the promotion of these ends; and for the support of this declaration, with a firm reliance on Divine Providence, we mutually pledge to each other our lives, our fortunes, and our sacred honor.

1874

67.

Declaration of Purpose of the National Grange

The Granger movement promoted the development of farmers' cooperatives to combat the vast business interests by which the farmers were victimized. The cooperatives usually met with small success because competition was too powerful; but there was some political benefit to the farmers in the form of state laws regulating privately owned shipping companies and grain elevators. The official policy of the Patrons of Husbandry, or National Grange, was proclaimed in the following resolution, adopted at the organization's seventh annual meeting in early February 1874. Every state, except Maine and Delaware, was represented.

Source: Jonathan Periam, *The Groundswell, A History of the Origin, Aims, and Progress of the Farmers' Movement, etc., etc.,* Cincinnati, 1874, pp. 572-574.

PROFOUNDLY IMPRESSED with the truth that the National Grange of the United States should definitely proclaim to the world its general objects, we hereby unanimously make this declaration of purposes of the Patrons of Husbandry.

First. United by the strong and faithful tie of agriculture, we mutually resolve to labor for the good of our Order, our country, and mankind.

Second. We heartily endorse the motto: "In essentials, Unity; in non-essentials, Liberty; in all things, Charity."

Third. We shall endeavor to advance our cause by laboring to accomplish the following objects: To develop a better and higher manhood and womanhood among ourselves; to enhance the comforts and attraction of our homes, and strengthen our attachments to our pursuits; to foster mutual understanding and cooperation; to maintain inviolate our laws, and to emulate each other to labor to hasten the good time coming; to reduce our expenses, both individual and corporate; to buy less and produce more in order to make our farms self-supporting; to diversify our crops and plant no more than we can cultivate; to condense the weight of our exports, selling less in the bushel and more on the hoof and in fleeces; to systematize our work and calculate intelligently on the probabilities; to discountenance the credit system, the mortgage system, the fashion system, and every other system tending to prodigality and bankruptcy.

We propose meeting together, talking together, working together, buying together, selling together, and generally acting together for our mutual protection and advancement, as occasion may require. We shall avoid litigation as much as possible by arbitration in the Grange. We shall constantly strive to secure entire harmony, goodwill, and vital brotherhood among ourselves, and to make order perpetual. We shall earnestly endeavor to suppress personal, local, sectional, and national prejudices, all unhealthy rivalry and all selfish ambition. Faithful adherence to these principles will ensure our mental and moral, social and material advancement.

Fourth. For our business interests, we desire to bring producers and consumers, farmers and manufacturers into the most intimate relations possible. Hence, we must dispense with a surplus of middlemen: not that we are unfriendly to them, but we do not need them. Their surplus and their exactions diminish our profits. We wage no aggressive warfare against any other interests whatever. On the contrary, all our acts and all our efforts, so far as business is concerned, are not only for the benefit of producers but also for all other interests that try to bring those two parties into speedy and economical contact. Hence, we hold that transportation companies of every kind are necessary to our success; that their interests are intimately connected with our interests, and that harmonious action is mutually advantageous.

Keeping in view the first sentence in our declaration of principles of action, that "individual happiness depends upon the general prosperity," we shall therefore advocate for every state the increase, in every practicable way, of all facilities for transporting cheaply to the seaboard, or between home producers and consumers, all the productions of our country. We adopt it as our fixed purpose to open out the channel in nature's great arteries that the lifeblood of commerce may flow freely. We are not enemies of railroads, navigable and irrigating

canals, nor of any corporation that will advance our industrial interests, nor of the laboring classes.

In our noble Order there is no communism, no agrarianism. We are opposed to such spirit and management of any corporation or enterprise as tends to oppress people and rob them of their just profits. We are not enemies to capital, but we oppose tyranny of monopolies. We long to see the antagonism between capital and labor removed by common consent and by an enlightened statesmanship worthy of the nineteenth century. We are opposed to excessive salaries, high rates of interest, and exorbitant percent profits in trade. They greatly increase our burdens, and do not bear a proportion to the profits of producers. We desire only self-protection and the protection of every true interest of our land by legitimate transactions, legitimate trade, and legitimate profits.

We shall advance the cause of education among ourselves and for our children by all just means within our power. We especially advocate for our agricultural and industrial colleges that practical agriculture, domestic science, and all the arts which adorn the home be taught in their courses of study.

Fifth. We emphatically and sincerely assert the oft-repeated truth taught in our organic law, that the Grange — National, State or subordinate — is not a political or party organization. No Grange, if true to its obligations, can discuss political or religious questions, nor call political conventions, nor nominate candidates, nor even discuss their merits in its meetings; yet the principles we teach underlie all true politics, all true statesmanship, and, if properly carried out, will tend to purify the whole political atmosphere of our country, for we seek the greatest good of the greatest number.

But we must always bear it in mind that no one, by becoming a Grange member, gives up that inalienable right and duty which belongs to every American citizen to take a proper interest in the politics of his country. On the contrary, it is right for every member to do all in his power legitimately to influence for good the action of any political party to which he belongs. It is his duty to do all he can in his party to put down bribery, corruption, and trickery; to see that none but competent, faithful, and honest men, who will unflinchingly stand by our industrial interests, are nominated for all positions of trust, and to have carried out the principles which should always characterize every Grange member — that the office should seek the man and not the man the office.

We acknowledge the broad principle that difference of opinion is not crime, and hold that progress toward truth is made by differences of opinion, while the fault lies in the bitterness of controversy. We desire a proper equality, equity, and fairness; protection for the weak, restraint upon the strong — in short, justly distributed burdens and justly distributed power. These are American ideas, the very essence of American independence, and to advocate the contrary is unworthy of the sons and daughters of an American republic.

We cherish the belief that sectionalism is, and of right should be, dead and buried with the past. Our work is for the present and the future. In our Agricultural Brotherhood and its purposes, we shall recognize no North, no South, no East, no West. It is reserved by every Patron, as his right as a freeman, to affiliate with any party that will best carry out his principles.

Sixth. Ours being peculiarly a farmer's institution, we cannot admit all to our ranks. Many are excluded by the nature of our organization, not because they are professional men, or artisans, or laborers, but because they have not a sufficient direct interest in tilling or pasturing the soil, or may have some interest in conflict with our purposes; but we appeal to all good citizens for their cordial cooperation to assist in our efforts toward reform, that we may eventually remove from our midst the last vestige of tyranny and corruption. We hail the general desire for fraternal harmony, equitable compromise, and earnest cooperation as an omen of our future success.

Seventh. It shall be an abiding principle with us to relieve any of our oppressed and suffering brotherhood by any means at our command.

Last, but not least, we proclaim it among our purposes to inculcate a proper appreciation of the abilities and sphere of woman, as is indicated by admitting her to membership and position in our Order.

Imploring the continued assistance of our Divine Master to guide us in our work, we here pledge ourself to faithfully and harmoniously labor for all future time to return by our united efforts to the wisdom, justice, fraternity, and political purity of our forefathers.

GLORIOUS OPPORTUNITY TO GET RICH — We are starting a cat ranch in Lacon with 100,000 cats. Each cat will average twelve kittens a year. The cat skins will sell for thirty cents each. One hundred men can skin 5,000 cats a day. We figure a daily profit of over $10,000. Now what shall we feed the cats? We will start a rat ranch next door with 1,000,000 rats. The rats will breed twelve times faster than the cats. So we will have four rats to feed each day to each cat. Now what shall we feed the rats? We will feed the rats the carcasses of the cats after they have been skinned. Now get this! We feed the rats to the cats and the cats to the rats and get the skins for nothing.

ANON., Prospectus of Lacon, Illinois, Cat-and-Rat Ranch.
This hoax was carried by every newspaper in the U.S., 1875.

68.

Sidney Lanier: "Corn"

Sidney Lanier was born in Macon, Georgia, served in the Confederate Army, and spent all of his life writing and teaching in the South. Much of his work was based on Southern themes, and he wrote a number of poems about the suffering caused by the Civil War, and by the conflict between the old and the new way of life. "Perhaps you know," he wrote to a friend, "that with us of the younger generation in the South, since the war pretty much of the whole of life has been merely not dying." "Corn," composed in 1874, contains some fine writing about this plant that is one of America's greatest gifts to mankind, but it also has an economic theme: The latter half of the poem is an attack on the cotton trader's "games of Buy-and-Sell."

Source: *Poems*, Mary D. Lanier, ed., New edition, New York, 1899.

CORN

Today the woods are trembling through and through
With shimmering forms, that flash before my view,
Then melt in green as dawn-stars melt in blue.
　　The leaves that wave against my cheek caress
　　Like women's hands; the embracing boughs express
　　　　A subtlety of mighty tenderness;
　　The copse-depths into little noises start,
　　That sound anon like beatings of a heart,
　　Anon like talk 'twixt lips not far apart.
　　The beech dreams balm, as a dreamer hums a song;
　　Through that vague wafture, expirations strong
　　Throb from young hickories breathing deep and long
With stress and urgence bold of prisoned spring
　　　　And ecstasy of burgeoning.
　　Now, since the dew-plashed road of morn is dry,
　　Forth venture odors of more quality
　　And heavenlier giving. Like Jove's locks awry,
　　　　　　Long muscadines
Rich-wreathe the spacious foreheads of great pines,
And breathe ambrosial passion from their vines.
　　I pray with mosses, ferns, and flowers shy
　　That hide like gentle nuns from human eye
　　To lift adoring perfumes to the sky.

I hear faint bridal sighs of brown and green
Dying to silent hints of kisses keen
As far lights fringe into a pleasant sheen
 I start at fragmentary whispers, blown
 From undertalks of leafy souls unknown,
 Vague purports sweet, of inarticulate tone.

Dreaming of gods, men, nuns, and brides, between
Old companies of oaks that inward lean
To join their radiant amplitudes of green
 I slowly move, with ranging looks that pass
 Up from the matted miracles of grass
Into yon veined complex of space
Where sky and leafage interlace
 So close, the heaven of blue is seen
 Inwoven with a heaven of green.

I wander to the zigzag-cornered fence
Where sassafras, entrenched in brambles dense,
Contests with stolid vehemence
 The march of culture, setting limb and thorn
 As pikes against the army of the corn.

There, while I pause, my fieldward-faring eyes
Take harvests, where the stately corn-ranks rise,
  Of inward dignities
And large benignities and insights wise,
  Graces and modest majesties.
Thus, without theft, I reap another's field;
Thus, without tilth, I house a wondrous yield,
And heap my heart with quintuple crops concealed.

Look, out of line one tall corn-captain stands
Advanced beyond the foremost of his bands,
 And waves his blades upon the very edge
 And hottest thicket of the battling hedge.
Thou lustrous stalk, that ne'er mayst walk nor talk,
 Still shalt thou type the poet-soul sublime
 That leads the vanward of his timid time
 And sings up cowards with commanding rhyme—

Soul calm, like thee, yet fain, like thee, to grow
By double increment, above, below;
 Soul homely, as thou art, yet rich in grace like thee,
 Teaching the yeomen selfless chivalry
 That moves in gentle curves of courtesy;
Soul filled like thy long veins with sweetness tense,

By every godlike sense
Transmuted from the four wild elements.
        Drawn to high plans,
    Thou lift'st more stature than a mortal man's,
Yet ever piercest downward in the mold
        And keepest hold
    Upon the reverend and steadfast earth
        That gave thee birth;
    Yea, standest smiling in thy future grave,
        Serene and brave,
    With unremitting breath
    Inhaling life from death,
Thine epitaph writ fair in fruitage eloquent,
        Thyself thy monument.

            As poets should,
    Thou hast built up thy hardihood
    With universal food,
        Drawn in select proportion fair
        From honest mold and vagabond air;
    From darkness of the dreadful night,
            And joyful light;
        From antique ashes, whose departed flame
        In thee has finer life and longer fame;
    From wounds and balms,
    From storms and calms,
    From potsherds and dry bones
            And ruin-stones.

    Into thy vigorous substance thou has wrought
    Whate'er the hand of Circumstance hath brought;
        Yea, into cool solacing green hast spun
        White radiance hot from out the sun.
    So thou dost mutually leaven
    Strength of earth with grace of Heaven;
        So thou dost marry new and old
        Into a one of higher mold;
        So thou dost reconcile the hot and cold,
            The dark and bright,
    And many a heart-perplexing opposite,
            And so,
        Akin by blood to high and low,
    Fitly thou playest out thy poet's part,
    Richly expending thy much-bruiséd heart
        In equal care to nourish lord in hall
            Or beast in stall:
        Thou took'st from all that thou mightst give to all.

O steadfast dweller on the selfsame spot
Where thou wast born, that still repinest not—
Type of the home-fond heart, the happy lot!
   Deeply thy mild content rebukes the land
   Whose flimsy homes, built on the shifting sand
Of trade, for ever rise and fall
With alternation whimsical,
   Enduring scarce a day,
   Then swept away
By swift engulfments of incalculable tides
Whereon capricious Commerce rides.
Look, thou substantial spirit of content!
Across this little vale, thy continent,
   To where, beyond the moldering mill,
   Yon old deserted Georgian hill
Bares to the sun his piteous aged crest
        And seamy breast,
   By restless-hearted children left to lie
   Untended there beneath the heedless sky,
   As barbarous folk expose their old to die.
Upon that generous-rounding side,
      With gullies scarified
   Where keen Neglect his lash hath plied,
Dwelt one I knew of old, who played at toil,
And gave to coquette Cotton soul and soil.
   Scorning the slow reward of patient grain,
   He sowed his heart with hopes of swifter gain,
   Then sat him down and waited for the rain.
He sailed in borrowed ships of usury —
A foolish Jason on a treacherous sea,
Seeking the Fleece and finding misery.
   Lulled by smooth-rippling loans, in idle trance
   He lay, content that unthrift Circumstance
   Should plough for him the stony field of Chance.
Yea, gathering crops whose worth no man might tell,
He staked his life on games of Buy-and-Sell,
And turned each field into a gambler's hell.
   Aye, as each year began,
   My farmer to the neighboring city ran;
Passed with a mournful anxious face
Into the banker's inner place;
Parleyed, excused, pleaded for longer grace;
   Railed at the drought, the worm, the rust, the grass;
   Protested ne'er again 'twould come to pass;
   With many an *oh* and *if* and *but alas*
Parried or swallowed searching questions rude,
And kissed the dust to soften Dives's mood.

At last, small loans by pledges great renewed,
   He issues smiling from the fatal door,
   And buys with lavish hand his yearly store
   Till his small borrowings will yield no more.
Aye, as each year declined,
With bitter heart and ever brooding mind
He mourned his fate unkind.
   In dust, in rain, with might and main,
   He nursed his cotton, cursed his grain,
   Fretted for news that made him fret again,
Snatched at each telegram of Future Sale,
And thrilled with Bulls' or Bears' alternate wail —
In hope or fear alike forever pale.
   And thus from year to year, through hope and fear,
   With many a curse and many a secret tear,
   Striving in vain his cloud of debt to clear,
         At last
He woke to find his foolish dreaming past,
   And all his best-of-life the easy prey
   Of squandering scamps and quacks that lined his way
       With vile array,
From rascal statesman down to petty knave;
Himself, at best, for all his bragging brave,
A gamester's catspaw and a banker's slave.
   Then, worn and gray, and sick with deep unrest,
   He fled away into the oblivious West,
       Unmourned, unblest.

Old hill! old hill! thou gashed and hairy Lear
Whom the divine Cordelia of the year,
E'en pitying Spring, will vainly strive to cheer —
   King, that no subject man nor beast may own,
   Discrowned, undaughtered, and alone —
Yet shall the great God turn thy fate,
And bring thee back into thy monarch state
      And majesty immaculate.
   Lo, through hot waverings of the August morn,
   Thou givest from thy vasty sides forlorn
   Visions of golden treasuries of corn —
Ripe largesse lingering for some bolder heart
That manfully shall take thy part,
      And tend thee,
      And defend thee,
With antique sinew and with modern art.

69.

Samuel Ab Thomas: Wage Slaves in Pennsylvania Coal Mines

Samuel Ab Thomas, a Welsh immigrant miner in the anthracite coal district of eastern Pennsylvania, wrote the following letter a few months before the miners' "long strike" (December 1874 - June 1875) over long hours and low wages, compulsory patronage of company housing and company stores, and production of 3,000 pounds to a "ton." The union was broken during the strike, and the miners came under the domination of a secret terrorist society, the Molly Maguires. When the Maguires were finally crushed in the fall of 1875 — twenty-four members were indicted for murder — the miners were left without any representation or organization. Most eventually joined the Knights of Labor, but not until the Knights relinquished certain secret rituals too strongly reminiscent of the Maguires.

Source: *The Welsh in America: Letters from the Immigrants*, Alan Conway, ed., Minneapolis, 1961, pp. 194-196.

THERE ARE FOUR LARGE COAL WORKS in Tioga County by the names of Morris Run, Fallbrook, Antrim, and Arnot. You all know about the bankers' debts a few months ago which caused the new railroads to be stopped, mills and furnaces to be blown out, and the coal works to be stopped, etc., so that thousands of craftsmen, puddlers, and laborers have been thrown out of work to live or die as best as they can.

We in this country have had to bend to the ground under the burdens placed on us by the avaricious, tyrannical masters. We were forced throughout the years to work for low wages which were hardly enough to keep body and soul together; to accept those wages in script which was worthless outside the local trading circle of the company; and to buy all our goods from their store and pay 25 percent more than we could get in other places; together with robbing us of half of our coal, taxed for what we knew not, without any receipt.

Also, to show us their power, they forced us to sign the contract law, which was against the law of the state government, that is that if any misunderstanding occurred between master and workman, the latter had to leave his house with ten-days' notice according to the contract law, whereas the state government allowed three months.

But, although we suffered the above without grumbling throughout the years, it was not enough to satisfy the greed of our masters, for early this winter they rushed on us with the fierceness of a lion on its prey, lowering us to 20 percent and also threatening us with 10 percent and forcing us to bind ourselves not to accept money for our labor until May 20, 1874.

In the face of such tyranny and oppression, we called a meeting of the workmen for the purpose of drawing up some plan to withstand the continuance of such tyranny and oppression. We resolved to form a branch of the National Miners and Laborers Benevolent Association of Pennsylvania, which was backed by the government a few years ago and gave it a charter. As I understand it, this same union pays well throughout the country, and we hope it will be the same here.

But when the company heard that we had formed a union, they stopped the works to kill it in its infancy, and so it has been for two months. They put a notice on the wall containing the conditions under which we could restart working. (1) Are you a member of the union of miners in the county of Tioga or of any like society? (2) If you are not a member, will you undertake not to join such a society in the future? (3) If you are a member, will you undertake to break your connection with that society and not to join such a thing again?

When they understood that one and all we refused the above terms, they put the screw to work, that is, warning us to leave our houses within ten days; and when the time came and we had not left our houses, they summoned us before the judge to demand why we refused to obey the warnings. The cruel judge would not listen to us, as he had been bought body and soul by the company, and gave judgment against us, together with having to pay all costs. So hundreds and hundreds of families were forced to leave their houses and to look for fresh houses amid the snow and ice. What a terrible sight it was to see hundreds of innocent men, women, and children having to break up their comfortable homes without knowing where to go.

But Providence worked for us, opening up the hearts of the farmers and tradesmen to take pity on us by opening their doors and taking us in, together with helping with our keep. Also, the union has played its part wonderfully, and the country generally feels for us and sends contributions; to crown it all, Providence has given us a milder winter than they have had in these parts. All the costs charged to us have been returned, as costs cannot be charged unless the person is worth $300.

P.S. In the circumstances, I thought it better to send my family back to Wales. I heard that the ship had left, but nothing more, and if anyone reads these lines, news of them would be welcome, whether they are dead or alive.

Working miners are hooted by strikers and their wives at the Mahanoy City mine in Pennsylvania

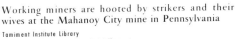

Tamiment Institute Library

70.

James S. Pike: African American Legislators of South Carolina

The newly freed and enfranchised African Americans in the South used their power of the vote during Reconstruction with varying results. From 1869 to 1877, fourteen African Americans — some of the stature of Blanche K. Bruce and Hiram Revels — were elected to Congress. Most of them served ably and promoted progressive legislation. On the state level, however, many black legislators became targets of jealous and displaced whites. In South Carolina, enough African Americans were voted in to attain majority control of the legislature. Their record is detailed in the following report of the 1873 session by James S. Pike, a Northern journalist generally sympathetic to African Americans. The alleged corruption of African American politicians became a rallying cry of white Southerners to return to power and continued to serve as a motivating factor behind Jim Crow laws and disfranchisement into the twentieth century.

Source: *The Prostrate State: South Carolina Under Negro Government*, New York, 1874, pp. 9-23.

YESTERDAY, about 4 P.M., the assembled wisdom of the state, whose achievements are illustrated on that theater, issued forth from the state house. About three-quarters of the crowd belonged to the African race. They were of every hue, from the light octoroon to the deep black. They were such a looking body of men as might pour out of a market house or a courthouse at random in any Southern state. Every Negro type and physiognomy was here to be seen, from the genteel serving man to the rough-hewn customer from the rice or cotton field. Their dress was as varied as their countenances. There was the secondhand black frock coat of infirm gentility, glossy and threadbare. There was the stovepipe hat of many ironings and departed styles. There was also to be seen a total disregard of the proprieties of costume in the coarse and dirty garments of the field — the stub jackets and slouch hats of soiling labor. In some instances, rough woolen comforters embraced the neck and hid the absence of linen. Heavy brogans and short, torn trousers it was impossible to hide. The dusky tide flowed out into the littered and barren grounds, and, issuing through the coarse wooden fence of the enclosure, melted away into the street beyond. These were the legislators of South Carolina. . . .

Here sit 124 members. Of these, 23 are white men, representing the remains of the old civilization. These are good-looking, substantial citizens. They are men of weight and standing in the communities they represent. They are all from the hill country. The frosts of sixty and seventy winters whiten the heads of some among them. There they sit, grim and silent. They feel themselves to be but loose stones, thrown in to partially obstruct a current they are powerless to resist. They say little and do little as the days go by. They simply watch the rising tide, and mark the progressive steps of the inundation. They hold their places reluctantly. They feel themselves to be in some sort martyrs, bound stoically to suffer in behalf of that still great element in the state whose prostrate fortunes are becoming the sport of an unpitying fate. Grouped in a corner of the commodious and well-furnished chamber, they stolidly survey the noisy riot that goes on in the great black left and center, where the business and debates of the House are conducted, and where sit the strange and extraordinary guides of the fortunes of a once proud and haughty state.

In this crucial trial of his pride, his manhood, his prejudices, his spirit, it must be said of the Southern Bourbon of the legislature that he comports himself with a dignity, a reserve, and a decorum that command admiration. He feels that the iron hand of destiny is upon him. He is gloomy, disconsolate, hopeless. The gray heads of this generation openly profess that they look for no relief. They see no way of escape. The recovery of influence, of position, of control in the state is felt by them to be impossible. They accept their position with a stoicism that promises no reward here or hereafter. They are the types of a conquered race. They staked all and lost all. Their lives remain, their property and their children do not. War, emancipation, and grinding taxation have consumed them. Their struggle now is against complete confiscation. They endure, and wait for the night.

This dense Negro crowd they confront do the debating, the squabbling, the lawmaking, and create all the clamor and disorder of the body. These 23 white men are but the observers, the enforced auditors of the dull and clumsy imitation of a deliberative body, whose appearance in their present capacity is at once a wonder and a shame to modern civilization.

Deducting the 23 members referred to, who comprise the entire strength of the opposition, we find 101 remaining. Of this 101, 94 are colored, and 7 are their white allies. Thus the blacks outnumber the whole body of whites in the House more than three to one. On the mere basis of numbers in the state, the injustice of this disproportion is manifest, since the black population is relatively four to three of the whites. A just rectification of the disproportion, on the basis of population merely, would give 54 whites to 70 black members. And the line of race very nearly marks the line of hostile politics.

As things stand, the body is almost literally a Black Parliament, and it is the only one on the face of the earth which is the representative of a white constituency and the professed exponent of an advanced type of modern civilization. But the reader will find almost any portraiture inadequate to give a vivid idea of the body, and enable him to comprehend the complete metamorphosis of the South Carolina legislature, without observing its details. The speaker is black, the clerk is black, the doorkeepers are black, the little pages are black, the chairman of the Ways and Means is black, and the chaplain is coal black. At some of the desks sit colored men whose types it would be hard to find outside of the Congo; whose costume, visages, attitudes, and expression only befit the forecastle of a buccaneer.

It must be remembered, also, that these men, with not more than half a dozen exceptions, have been themselves slaves, and that their ancestors were slaves for generations. Recollecting the report of the famous schooner *Wanderer*, fitted out by a Southern slaveholder twelve or fifteen years ago, in ostentatious defiance of the laws against the slave trade, and whose owner and master boasted of having brought a cargo of slaves from Africa and safely landed them in South Carolina and Georgia, one thinks it must be true, and that some of these representatives are the very men then stolen from their African homes. If this be so, we will not now quarrel over their presence. It would be one of those extraordinary coincidences that would of itself almost seem to justify the belief of the direct interference of the hand of Providence in the affairs of men.

ONE OF THE THINGS that first strike a casual observer in this Negro assembly is the fluency of debate, if the endless chatter that goes on there can be dignified with this term. The leading topics of discussion are all well understood by the members, as they are of a practical character, and appeal directly to the personal interests of every legislator, as well as to those of his constituents. When an appropriation bill is up to raise money to catch and punish the Ku Klux, they know exactly what it means. They feel it in their bones. So, too, with educational measures. The free school comes right home to them; then the business of arming and drilling the black militia. They are eager on this point. Sambo can talk on these topics and those of a kindred character, and their endless ramifications, day in and day out. There is no end to his gush and babble. The intellectual level is that of a bevy of fresh converts at a Negro camp meeting.

Of course, this kind of talk can be extended indefinitely. It is the doggerel of debate, and not beyond the reach of the lowest parts. Then the Negro is imitative in the extreme. He can copy like a parrot or a monkey, and he is always ready for a trial of his skill. He believes he can do anything, and never loses a chance to try, and is just as ready to be laughed at for his failure as applauded for his success. He is more vivacious than the white, and, being more volatile and good-natured, he is correspondingly more irrepressible. His misuse of language in his imitations is at times ludicrous beyond measure. He notoriously loves a joke or an anecdote, and will burst into a broad guffaw on the smallest provocation. He breaks out into an incoherent harangue on the floor just as easily, and being without practice, discipline, or experience, and wholly oblivious of Lindley Murray, or any other restraint on composition, he will go on repeating himself, dancing as it were to the music of his own voice, forever. He will speak half a dozen times on one question, and every time say the same things without knowing it. . . .

But the old stagers admit that the colored brethren have a wonderful aptness at legislative proceedings. They are "quick as lightning" at detecting points of order, and they certainly make incessant and extraordinary use of their knowledge. No one is allowed to talk five minutes without interruption, and one interruption is the signal for another and another, until the original speaker is smothered under an avalanche of them. Forty questions of privilege will be raised in a day. At times, nothing goes on but alternating questions of order and of privilege. The inefficient colored friend who sits in the speaker's chair cannot suppress this extraordinary element of the debate. Some of the blackest members exhibit a pertinacity of intrusion in raising these points of order and questions of privilege that few white men can equal. Their struggles to get the floor, their bellowings and physical contortions, baffle description. The speaker's hammer plays a perpetual tattoo all to no purpose. The talking and the interruptions from all quarters go on with the utmost license. Everyone esteems himself as good as his neighbor, and puts in his oar, apparently as often for love of riot and confusion as for anything else.

It is easy to imagine what are his ideas of propriety and dignity among a crowd of his own color, and these are illustrated without reserve. The speaker orders a member whom he has discovered to be particularly unruly to take his seat. The member obeys, and, with the same motion that he sits down, throws his feet onto his desk, hiding himself from the speaker by the soles of his boots. In an instant he appears again on the floor. After a few experiences of this sort, the speaker threatens, in a laugh, to call "the gemman" to order. This is considered a capital joke, and a guffaw follows. The laugh goes round, and then the peanuts are cracked and munched faster than ever; one hand being employed in fortifying the inner man with this nutriment of universal use, while the other enforces the views of the orator. This laughing propensity of the sable crowd is a great cause of disorder. They laugh as hens cackle — one begins and all follow.

But underneath all this shocking burlesque upon legislative proceedings, we must not forget that there is something very real to this uncouth and untutored multitude. It is not all sham, nor all burlesque. They have a genuine interest and a genuine earnestness in the business of the assembly, which we are bound to recognize and respect, unless we would be accounted shallow critics. They have an earnest purpose, born of a conviction that their position and condition are not fully assured, which lends a sort of dignity to their proceedings. The barbarous, animated jargon in which they so often indulge is on occasion seen to be so transparently sincere and weighty in their own minds that sympathy supplants disgust.

The whole thing is a wonderful novelty to them as well as to observers. Seven years ago these men were raising corn and cotton under the whip of the overseer. Today they are raising points of order and questions of privilege. They find they can raise one as well as the other. They prefer the latter. It is easier, and better paid. Then, it is the evidence of an accomplished result. It means escape and defense from old oppressors. It means liberty. It means the destruction of prison walls only too real to them. It is the sunshine of their lives. It is their day of jubilee. It is their long-promised vision of the Lord God Almighty.

71.

Militant White Supremacy

Southern reaction to Reconstruction laws and programs often led to the extreme measures taken by such organizations as the Knights of the White Camelia and the Ku Klux Klan. The following editorial, from the Atlanta News *of September 10, 1874, expresses the point of view of white supremacy advocates at a time when they were trying to regain their political power.*

Source: 43 Congress, 2 Session, House Report No. 261.

EVERY RADICAL CONVENTION that has been held this year has demanded the passage of the civil rights bill; every Radical politician of any prominence has advocated it; and President Grant, in yielding to the clamors of a few scoundrelly politicians and sending troops to the South, ostensibly to preserve order but really to control the elections in the interest of the Negroes and their allies, has demonstrated that we have nothing to hope from him in the shape of a veto of the bill. What, then, are the facts?

Radicalism has declared a war of extermination against the whites of the South. It proposes to punish rebels and make "treason odious" by the most vindictive measures its malignity can conceive. Our fate is to be less merciful than that of the Trojans, less sublime than that of the Carthaginians. We are not to perish by the sword as these people perished; we are to live, and live in degradation. Our helots and serfs of yesterday are to rule us politically and to sit beside us on terms of equality socially. All pride of race is to be crushed within us. We are to be the slave; the Negro is to be the master.

History gives no precedent for this monstrous program; its pages teem with the stories of conquered and oppressed people; but not one story is akin to this. It was left for the fertile brain of a New England Yankee to conceive the punishment. Nor will it end in this civil rights bill. The next thing on the program will be to enact a compulsory education law, and compel us to send our children to public schools, there to herd with Negroes. This is not a gratuitous proposition. It has already been made and favorably received.

Against the fate that confronts us, what have the Southern people? Is it that "prudence" which such papers as the *Louisville Courier-Journal* advocates, but which men less gifted than the editor of that paper call a dastardly submission? No. Our only hope is *in a stern, resolute resistance — a resistance to the death, if necessary, with arms in our hands.*

Let there be *White Leagues formed in every town, village, and hamlet of the South;* and let us organize for the great struggle which seems to be inevitable. If the October elections which are to be held at the North are favorable to the Radicals, the time will have arrived for us to prepare for the very worst. The radicalism of the Republican Party must be met by the radicalism of white men. We have no war to make against the United States government, but against the Republican Party *our hate must be unquenchable, our war interminable and merciless.* Fast fleeting away is the day for wordy protests and idle appeals to the magnanimity of the Republican Party. By brute force they are endeavoring to force us into acquiescence to their hideous program.

We have submitted long enough to indignities, and *it is time to meet brute force with brute force. Every Southern state should swarm with White Leagues, and we should stand ready to act* the moment Grant signs the civil rights bill. It will not do to wait until radicalism has fettered us to the car of social equality before we make an effort to resist it. The signing of the bill will be a declaration of war against the Southern whites. It is our duty to ourselves, it is our duty to our children, it is our duty to the white race whose prowess subdued the wilderness of this continent, whose civilization filled it with cities and towns and villages, whose mind gave it power and grandeur, and whose labor imparted to it prosperity, and whose love made peace and happiness dwell within its homes, to take the gauge of battle the moment it is thrown down.

If the white Democrats of the North are men, they will not stand idly by and see us borne down by Northern Radicals and half-barbarous Negroes. But no matter what they may do, it is time for us to organize. We have been temporizing long enough. Let Northern Radicals understand that military supervision of Southern elections and the civil rights bill mean war, that war means bloodshed, and that we are terribly in earnest; and even they, fanatical as they are, may retrace their steps before it is too late.

72.

Revival Songs

In the quarter of a century following the Civil War, religious revivals occurred in many communities, and "Gimme That Old-Time Religion" became the classic hymn of restatement of religious faith. It was an expression of the direct relation between man and God, as well as an affirmation of fundamentalist dogma. "She'll Be Comin' 'Round the Mountain" was also a revival song, but it was born among the railroaders and was influenced by such spirituals as "The Old Ship of Zion" and "When the Chariot Comes." Track foremen were often hired for their singing ability, since singing made the work go smoother and kept the men in good spirits, and it was natural to convert such a rousing song to religious ends.

GIMME THAT OLD-TIME RELIGION

Gimme that old-time religion,
Gimme that old-time religion,
Gimme that old-time religion,
  It's good enough for me.

It is good in time of trouble,
It is good in time of trouble,
It is good in time of trouble,
  It's good enough for me.

It was good for Paul and Silas, etc.

It'll make you love your neighbor, etc.

It'll make you love your brother, etc.

It'll take you home to Heaven, etc.

It was good for the Hebrew children, etc.

It'll be good when I am dying, etc.

SHE'LL BE COMIN' 'ROUND THE MOUNTAIN

She'll be comin' 'round the mountain when she comes,
She'll be comin' 'round the mountain when she comes,
She'll be comin' 'round the mountain,
She'll be comin' 'round the mountain,
She'll be comin' 'round the mountain when she comes.

She'll be drivin' six white horses when she comes, etc.

She'll be shinin' just like silver when she comes, etc.

Oh we'll all go out to meet her when she comes, etc.

She'll be breathin' smoke an' fire when she comes, etc.

We'll be singin' "Hallelujah" when she comes, etc.

We will kill the old red rooster when she comes, etc.

We'll all have chicken an' dumplin's when she comes, etc.

73.

Charles W. Eliot: Concerning Property Exempt from Taxation

Charles W. Eliot, educational and civic leader and president of Harvard University, directed the following paper of December 12, 1874, to the commissioners of the Commonwealth of Massachusetts, in response to their request for his views concerning properties exempt from taxation. The report, in which Eliot argued for a tax-exempt status for educational institutions, also reflects his views on the value of education to the whole of society. Excerpts from the report appear here.

Source: *American Contributions to Civilization, and Other Essays and Addresses,* New York, 1897: "The Exemption From Taxation."

THE PROPERTY which has been set apart for religious, educational, and charitable uses is not to be thought of or dealt with as if it were private property; for it is completely unavailable for all the ordinary purposes of property so long as the trusts endure. It is like property of a city or state which is essential for carrying on the work of the city or state, and so cannot be reckoned among the public assets; it is irrecoverable and completely unproductive. The capital is sunk, so to speak, just as the cost of a sewer or a highway is capital sunk. There is a return, both from a church or a college, and from a sewer or a highway, in the benefit secured to the community; but the money which built them is no longer to be counted as property, in the common sense. It can never again be productive, except for the purposes of the trust for which it was set apart. . . .

When a church or a college or a hospital buys land and erects buildings thereon, the state does not sacrifice the value of the land or the money spent upon the buildings; private persons make these sacrifices; but the state does sacrifice, by the exemption statute, the opportunity to tax in the future the improvements which might have been put upon that land if it had not been converted to religious, educational, or charitable uses, and all the indirect taxable benefits which might have been derived from the use for productive purposes of the land, and of the money which the buildings cost.

This is the precise burden of the exemption upon the state. Why does the state assume it? For a reason similar to, though much stronger than, its reason for building a new road and losing that area forever for taxation. The state believes that the new road will be such a convenience to the community that the indirect gain from making it will be greater than the direct and indirect loss. In the same way the state believes, or at least believed when the exemption statute was adopted, that the indirect gain to its treasury which results from the establishment of the exempted institutions is greater than the loss which the exemption involves. If this belief is correct, in the main, though not perhaps universally and always, the exemption can hardly be described as a burden to the state at large. . . .

If it be granted that the religious, educational, or charitable use is a public use, like the use of a sewer or a highway, there is no more reason for taxing the church, the academy, or the hospital than for annually taxing the abutters on a sewer or a highway on the cost of that sewer, or on the cost of the highway and its value considered as so many feet of land, worth, like the adjoining lots, so many dollars a foot. The community is repaid for the loss of the taxable capital sunk in the sewer by the benefit to the public health and the resulting enhancement of the value of all its territory. In like manner, it is repaid for the loss of the capital set apart for religious, educational, and charitable uses by the increase of morality, spirituality, intelligence, and virtue, and the general well-being which results therefrom. . . .

Exemption from taxation is not then a form of state aid in the usual sense of those words; it is an inducement or encouragement held out by the state to private persons, or private corporations, to establish or maintain institutions which are of benefit to the state. The answer to the question — Why should the state give encouragement, in any form, to private corporations which support churches, academies, colleges, hospitals, asylums, and similar institutions of learning, advanced education, and public charity? — involves, therefore, an exposition of the public usefulness of these corporations. I say advanced education because the lower grades of education are already provided for at the public charge, and there seems to be little disposition to question the expediency and rightfulness of this provision.

The reason for treating these institutions in an exceptional manner is that, having no selfish object in view or purpose of personal gain, they contribute to the welfare of the state. Their function is largely a public function; their work is done primarily, indeed, for individuals, but ultimately for the public good. It is not enough to say of churches and colleges that they contribute to the welfare of a state; they are necessary to the existence of a free state. They form and mold the public character; and that public character is the foundation of everything which is precious in the state, including even its material prosperity. To develop noble human character is the end for which states themselves exist, and civil liberty is not a good in itself, but only a means to that good end.

The work of churches and institutions of education is a direct work upon human character. The material prosperity of every improving community is a fruit of character; for it is energetic, honest, and sensible men that make prosperous business, and not prosperous business that makes men. Who have built up the manufactures and trade of this bleak and sterile Massachusetts? A few men of singular sagacity, integrity, and courage, backed by hundreds of thousands of men and women of common intelligence and honesty. The roots of the prosperity are in the intelligence, courage, and honesty. Massachusetts today owes its mental and moral characteristics, and its wealth, to eight generations of people who have loved and cherished church, school, and college. . . .

To tax such endowments is to reduce the good work done by them and, therefore, to increase the work to be done by direct appropriation of government money, unless the people are willing to accept the alternative of having less work of the kind done. If the state wants the work done, it has but two alternatives — it can do it itself, or it can encourage and help benevolent and public-spirited individuals to do it. There is no third way. . . .

There are, nevertheless, some cases in which a new exemption involves a real loss, though not without compensations, to the town or city from which the property was abstracted; and there are also cases in which the restoration of an exempted piece of property to taxation might be a real gain, in spite of considerable losses. When a benevolent citizen of one town gives $100,000 of personal property to an exempted institution situated in another town, the first town loses so much property which was there taxable, and the second town has the local benefit of the institution, if there be any. On the other hand, the town which loses in this case has similar chances of gaining local benefits by gifts to institutions situated within its limits from citizens of other towns. Again, it by no means follows that the citizen who gave this $100,000 would have kept it in a taxable form at his place of residence if he had not given it to an exempted institution.

Such gifts are often — perhaps generally — made out of annual earnings or sudden profits; and if the $100,000 had not been given to an exempted institution, it might have been unprofitably consumed, or lost, or given away to individuals resident elsewhere. A good deal of the personal property which now goes to churches, colleges, and hospitals would be consumed outright if it were not so saved. If the gift is made by will instead of during life, there are more chances that the $100,000 would, in the distribution of the property, have been carried away from the testator's place of residence at any rate. When a piece of estate is transferred to an exempted institution for its own proper use, the local benefits of the institution, if there be any, are for the same town which gives up the taxes on the piece of real estate, and the withdrawal of that piece from productive uses probably brings some other piece into use at once, or at least sooner than would otherwise have happened. . . .

It has been often asserted that to exempt an institution from taxation is the same thing as to grant it money directly from the public treasury. This statement is sophistical and fallacious. . . .The exemption method is comprehensive, simple, and automatic; the grant method as it has been exhibited in this country requires special legislation of a peculiarly dangerous sort, a legislation which inflames religious quarrels, gives occasion for acrimonious debates, and tempts to jobbery. The exemption method leaves the trustees of the fostered institutions untrammeled in their action and untempted to unworthy acts or mean compliances. The grant method, as practised here, puts them in the position of importunate suitors for the public bounty, or, worse, converts them into ingenious and unscrupulous assailants of the public treasury.

Finally and chiefly — and to this point I ask special attention — the exemption method fosters public spirit, while the grant method, persevered in, annihilates it. The state says to the public-spirited benefactor, "You devote a part of your private property forever to certain public uses; you subscribe to build a church, for example, or you endow an academy; we agree not to take a portion of the income of that property every year for other public uses, such as the maintenance of schools, prisons, and highways." That is the whole significance of the exemption of any endowment from taxation. . . .

In this country, when one wishes to scoff at endowments, he must draw on his imagination for his facts. There is but one well-founded charge to bring against our countrymen in this matter of setting apart private property for public uses of religion, education, and charity. They scatter their gifts too widely; so that a greater number of institutions are started than can be well maintained. But the remedy for this evil is to consolidate endowments, not to tax them. This consolidation has already begun and will be brought about by the gradual enlightenment of public opinion on this subject.

To draw a vivid picture of alleged scandals and abuses, and then propose some action of an irrelevant nature, desired for other reasons, as if it were a remedy for those scandals and abuses, is a well-known device of ingenious disputants; but it is a device which ought not to impose on clear-headed people. To prejudice the mass of the people against endowments is the part of a demagogue, for it is to induce them to act ignorantly in direct opposition to their own real interests; since endowments exist for the benefit of the great mass of the people, while they are a matter of but slight concern to the rich.

The rich man does not care whether education be dear or cheap; he does not want the scholarships of a college; he does not need to send his children to a hospital; he could afford to keep a clergyman in his own family, if he cared to. It is the poor man who needs the church which others have built; the college which, because it has endowments, is able to offer his ambitious son a liberal education; the hospital which will give him, when disabled, attendance as skillful and careful as the rich man can buy. Moreover, the poor man has no direct interest in this proposed taxation of the institutions now exempted; it will not help him pay his poll tax, nor lessen the amount of it; it will help no one but the property holders.

It is natural enough that a property holder who has no public spirit should desire to escape his share of the charge of supporting institutions of public utility on the ground that he feels no personal need of them. But that a man of property feels no want of institutions which are necessary to the security of the community and does not believe in them are no reasons for excusing him from his share in the support of these institutions. The doctrine that a citizen can justly be called upon to contribute to the support of those things only which he approves or which are of direct benefit to him would cripple our public schools as well as our colleges, and, in fact, would destroy the basis of almost all taxation. . . .

No exempted institution can hold real estate free of taxes except that which is fairly necessary for the purposes of the religious, educational, or charitable trust. It would be a dishonorable evasion of the real intent of the statute to claim exemption on real estate which was bought with the intention of selling it again at a profit; and if any addition could be made to the statute which would make such a practice impossible, or would subject to penalties any institution which should be guilty of it, such an addition would be an improvement; although it is altogether likely that the offense contemplated has never, as a matter of fact, been committed. Of course, the mere fact that an institution has made a sale of exempted land is not in itself evidence of an evasion of the statute; for poverty may compel an institution to part with land which it ought, in the real interest of the trust, to keep.

It is also a perfectly legitimate transaction for an exempted institution to sell one site in order to occupy another. One cause of the agitation for the abolition of the exemption has been the distrust awakened by sales of church property at large profit in the older parts of our growing cities. But these sales are perfectly legitimate. Those who believe in the public utility of churches need only to be assured that the proceeds of these advantageous sales must be invested in new churches — that none of the property can relapse into the condition of private property. . . .

Those who advocate limiting the amount of the exempted property which may be held for a religious, educational, or charitable trust seem to forget that it is the public which is the real enjoyer of all such property, and that it is the public only which is really interested in its increase, except as gratitude, affection, or public spirit may prompt individuals to share this public interest. . . .

Now, for the public to make laws which tend to discourage private persons from giving property to the public for its own uses is as unwise as for the natural heir to put difficulties in the way of a well-disposed relative who is making his will. The fact that the property of these public trusts is administered by persons who are not immediately chosen or appointed by the public obscures to some minds the essential principle that the property is really held and used for the public benefit; but the mode of administration does not alter the uses, or make the property any less property held for the public. . . .

It remains to consider the effect of abolishing the exemption. No church could be maintained upon ground which would be very valuable for other purposes, and costly church edifices would be out of the question. A society whose land and building were worth $300,000 would have to pay $4,500 a year in taxes, besides all the proper expenses of a church. The burden would be intolerable. The loss to the community, in that pure pleasure which familiar objects of beauty give, would be unspeakable. The village could spare its spired wooden church as ill as the city its cathedral. . . .

The abolition of the exemption would reduce the service of all the institutions of advanced education in the state from 20 to 25 percent at present, and this diminution of efficiency would grow greater year by year. All the academies, colleges, professional schools, and scientific or technical schools,

all the libraries not town libraries, all the museums of art or natural history would see from one-fifth to one-quarter of their income diverted from education and applied to ordinary city and town expenditures. An extravagant city or town government might at any time demand much more than one-fourth of their income. Precious institutions which render great services to the whole state, or perhaps to the nation, would be at the mercy of a single local government. . . .

If abuses have crept in, let them be reformed. If institutions which are really not of a public character get exempted, cut them off; if greater publicity is desirable in regard to the condition and affairs of the institutions exempted, provide for annual published returns; if there be fear of improper sales of land long exempted to the private advantage of the trustees or proprietors of the moment, enact that all sales of such property shall be by order of a court, and that the court shall take cognizance of the investment of the proceeds. But while we reform the abuses, let us carefully preserve the precious uses of the exemption statute. That statute is an essential part of our existing system of taxation. It may be expedient that the whole system should be reconstructed; but the exemption of religious, educational, and charitable property is certainly not the point at which the reconstruction should begin.

Let us transmit to our descendants, in long generations, the invaluable institutions of religion, education, and charity which we inherited from our fathers, and transmit them, not merely as strong and ample as ever but multiplied, beautified, and enriched by our loving care.

1875

74.

Secret Labor Organizations

Early trade and labor organizations adopted secret rituals and induction practices as a defense against employer opposition. Prospective members were first cleared by investigating committees, then presented to the society by a sponsor posing as another initiate. Thus, if the proposed member refused to join the organization, he would not know that his sponsor was already a member. The following National Labor Tribune *editorial of April 24, 1875, attempted to justify the secret rituals — many of them adopted from the Masonic Order — practised by labor societies.*

Source: *National Labor Tribune*, April 24, 1875.

WHEN MEN cannot assert their rights and resist a wrong perpetrated by an employer for fear of discharge, it is time to devise some plan for the better protection of our labor.

When men are persecuted for unionism, when they are robbed of the true value of their labor, when they feel it unsafe to speak in their interest, it is time to look farther and deeper for some means of defense.

When monopolies become stronger than the law, when legislatures become the servants of monopolies, when corporations can successfully bid defiance to public good and trample on individual rights, it is time for the people to come together to erect defenses for personal rights and public safety.

When the commercial interests combine to exact the greatest share of profits of labor and give labor the least, even to the verge of starvation, when all attempts of labor to openly oppose and defeat the efforts of these combinations are made the pretext for still further oppression and persecution, it is time for the people to unite together for their individual and common safety.

That municipal, state, and national interests are not administered for the greatest good of the greatest number, all of us know by sad experience. That our labor has become a commodity out of which we are not able to earn enough to live in the comfort we should enjoy is a fact apparent to any man. These considerations have prompted men in all trades to have recourse to secret organization, not for wrongdoing but to bring about a better state of affairs.

We have noticed from time to time the

growth of one of the most powerful of these orders. It is especially deserving of notice and confidence as being exclusively composed of workingmen. Its numbers and the harmony and unity produced entitle it to our attention. It is rapidly extending and will, ere long, number its hundreds of thousands, all guided by one common impulse and for one common end. It numbers in its ranks our best men. In it all are equal. In it all are heard, respected, and benefited.

We learn that it is rapidly becoming a national organization. Cost of membership is little, to let in all good men. If ever an order turned bad men into good ones, this one does. If there is a spark of manhood in a man, this order will kindle it into a flame of genial warmth for all who toil. We are glad to see the spread of this order. Its objects are noble and holy. It makes every man in it purer and better. It widens his comprehension, lifts his conceptions, widens his understanding, deepens his affections, and ennobles his whole nature.

The order is moving westward. It has a solid footing in Pittsburgh, at which place officers are receiving applications for its extension further west. All enquiries receive proper attention, but from the nature of the order the replies cannot be as full as some would like. To such we say, "Enter the holy of holies and know all."

75.

Edward King: Postwar Plantation Life

Edward King became a skilled journalist and social observer through early jobs as a reporter on the Springfield (Massachusetts) Daily Union *and* Springfield Republican. *His assignments included reporting the Paris Exposition of 1867, the Franco-Prussian War, the Paris Commune, and the Carlist Wars. At the request of* Scribner's Monthly *magazine, King traveled through the South in 1873 and 1874 to report on the economic potential of the area. The articles, collected in* The Great South *(1875), are one of the best accounts of the postwar South. The selection reprinted here is from his work.*

Source: *The Great South,* Hartford, 1875, Ch. 31.

During my stay in Natchez, one of the many gentlemen interested in cotton planting on the west, or Louisiana, side of the river invited me to accompany him on a tour of inspection. The rapidly rising river threatened to inundate the lands on which hundreds of Negroes had been expending weeks of patient care, and the planter felt it his duty to take a horseback ride over the trio of plantations under his charge; so we crossed the Mississippi and rode twelve miles into the interior of Louisiana.

On the road, which led along the lovely banks of Lake Concordia, the planter chatted of some of the vexations by which he is daily beset, and spoke rather hopelessly of the labor problem. The condition of society, too, he thought very bad, and that it was an actual hindrance to the development of the section.

"Are the Negroes," I asked him, "aggressive and insolent toward the white people?"

But as the planter was about to answer this question, we approached a ferryboat, or barge, in which we were to cross an arm of the lake to the island on which my friend's plantations were situated. An old Negro man, much the worse for liquor, was preparing to monopolize the boat with his mule team, but held back the mules and touched his hat with drunken courtesy as we came up.

"Stand aside, uncle," said the planter firmly, but very politely; "we wish to cross at once, and there is not room for us all."

"Yas, sah; yas, Colonel," said the old man. "I's willin' to wait on you gemmen, 'cause you is gemmen; but ef yer was no count folks, I'd go for yer. Ride in, Colonel."

When we were some distance from shore, the planter said:

"That old man made way for us simply out of deference to our social position. The Negroes are courteous enough to us; it has been their habit so long that they cannot forget it. But they will kill our deer and steal our poultry and bacon, and we have no redress."

After an hour or two of journeying over rough roads, we came to one of the plantations. A host of Negroes were busily filling a breach in a dike which the treacherous water might sweep away if rains came to swell the already ominous floods of the Mississippi. A pack of hounds came yelping to meet the planter; and the black women in the cabin curtsied obsequiously.

We crossed the field, bordered by noble cypresses and oaks, stopping now and then to watch the Negroes as they carefully prepared the ground which an inundation might, in less than a day, reduce to a hopeless wilderness of mud. Entering the house of the overseer, we found that functionary

smoking his pipe and reposing after a long ride over the plantation. He was a rough, hearty, good-natured man, accustomed to living alone and faring rudely. I asked him what he thought of the Negro as a free laborer.

"He works well, mostly, sir. These yer Alabama niggers that's workin' on our plantations now do well on wages. They make some little improvements around their cabins, but mighty little, sir. Ef politics would only let 'em alone, they'd get along well enough, I reckon."

"Do the Negroes on this plantation vote?"

"I reckon not (laughing). I don't want my niggers to have anything to do with politics. They can't vote as long as they stay with us, and these Alabama boys don't take no interest in the elections here."

"What do they receive as monthly wages?"

"From $10 to $16. It costs us about $15 per head to bring 'em from Alabama. These niggers likes wages better than shares. We keep a store here, and Saturday nights, most of the money they have earned comes back to us in trade. They're fond o' whiskey and good things to eat."

"What is the routine of your work on a large plantation like this, and those adjoining it, throughout the year?"

"Wal, sir, I reckon that's a long story. We don't have much spare time, and mighty little amusement. Wal, sir, the first thing we do, sir, we begin early in January, a few weeks after the old crop is all gathered in, to repair fences and clean out all the ditches, sir. Then we pull down the old stalks and start the plows to throw quadruple furrows in the fields. Then we throw out the 'middles.'"

"What are they?"

"Wal, sir, we throw out soil at the sides so as to leave a slope bed of fresh ground to plant on, and loose earth to cover it with. If the spring freshet breaks onto this yer prepared earth, we've got to begin over again, and that makes the season very late.

"Planting begins about the last of March, or very early in April. Piles of cottonseed are laid along some ways apart on the field, and then the niggers sow it along the beds, a ton of seed to eight acres. Then it is 'barred off' — covered up, that means.

"Ez soon as the cotton stalks begin to peep up, 'scraping' begins. The hands weed every row carefully and don't leave any weakly plants. That, and looking after the caterpillars, keeps 'em busy till July. Caterpillars ain't the only danger we have to fight against. Thar's a hundred others. Cotton's a ticklish plant to raise. You've got to watch it mighty close, and then the worms and the weather will sometimes ruin the crop.

"Between July and September we keep the hands busy getting out baskets and setting things in order; then we pile in new help, and for the rest of the season employ three times as many hands as thar's in the fields now. Up to Christmas it's picking and ginning, and it's right lively, you can be sure."

From the overseer's conversation, I learned that cotton picking is done quite as thoroughly under the system of free labor as in the days when slave driving was permissible, but that the "niggers" require constant watching. On many plantations where the yield is abundant, it is difficult to concentrate labor enough at the proper time to get the cotton into the gin house the same year that it is planted. I have seen cotton fields still white with their creamy fleeces late in December, because the Negroes were either too lazy or too busily engaged in their annual merrymakings to gather the harvest. But on the large lowland plantations along the Mississippi, the crop is usually gathered early and the picking is very thorough. I could not discover that there was any system of "forced labor" now in use, and I thought the overseer's statement

that a "good field hand nowadays would pick 250 pounds of cotton daily" was excellent testimony in favor of free labor. He added, however, that on many plantations the average hands would not pick more than 100 pounds per day.

The laborers were coming in from the field in a long picturesque procession. As it was springtime, many of them had been plowing and were mounted upon the backs of the stout mules which had been their companions all day. Some of the men were singing rude songs, others were shouting boisterously and scuffling as they went their way along the broad pathway bordered by giant cypresses and noble oaks. The boys tumbling and wriggling in the grass perpetually exploded into guffaws of contagious laughter. Many of the men were tall and finely formed. They had an intelligent look and were evidently not so degraded as those born on the Louisiana lowlands. The overseer sat on the veranda of his house, now and then calling out a sharp command or a caution, the Negroes looking up obsequiously and touching their hats as they heard his voice.

When the mules were stabled, the men came lounging back to the cabins, where the women were preparing their homely supper; and an hour afterward we heard the tinkle of banjos, the pattering of feet, and uproarious laughter. The interiors of the Negro cabins were of the rudest description. The wretched huts in which the workmen live seem to them quite comfortable, however. I saw no one who appeared discontented with his surroundings. Few of these laborers could read at all. Even those who had some knowledge of the alphabet did not seem to be improving it.

Late in the evening, as the planter, with his heavy cloak thrown about his shoulders, was reposing from the fatigues of a wearisome ride over the broad acres, a delegation of field hands came to see him, all to ask favors of "de Cunnel" — to get him to write a few letters, or bring some tiny parcel from the town on his next visit to the plantation. The men came huddling in, bowing awkwardly, and stood with their caps in their hands as near the door as possible, as if ready to run on the slightest provocation. If I looked at them steadily, they burst into uneasy laughter and moved away, while the black women in the doorway and on the porch reechoed the merriment. Meantime, the planter listened to one after another of the delegation. Charles, a black boy, six feet tall and with sinews strong as steel, stepped forward to the flickering light given by the candles and the burning logs in the fireplace.

"Cunnel, I wish you read me dat letter, please, sah."

The "Cunnel" read it, Charles meantime standing erect, with his great arms folded across his mighty chest and the massive column of his throat throbbing with scornful emotion. There was a strange, baffled expression in his face; a look of contempt for his own helplessness, which was painful.

The letter was commonplace enough, reproaching Charles for having left Alabama before liquidating the pressing claims of certain swarthy creditors. Having, after some trouble, deciphered the letter's meaning, the Colonel said, gently but coldly:

"Stand aside, Charles. Andy, who is the likeliest Negro from Alabama now on the plantation?"

No answer for a minute. Andy stepped forward into the light, looking first into the fireplace, then at the deer's horns over the mantel, then at the shining revolver on the rough wooden table, while his immense lips worked nervously, as if endeavoring to draw in inspiration from the air.

"Did you hear me, Andy?"

"Cunnel, I's a-studyin', sah."

After having studied some time, Andy darted out without a word and presently returned with three hulking black giants, who huddled together in the same helpless way that the first arrivals did. They held their shapeless felt hats in their enormous hands, glancing from them into the faces of the white men; then, exchanging significant looks with each other, burst into the regulation laugh.

"Did the colored politicians try to keep you from leaving Alabama to come here with me, boys?" inquired the Colonel.

Intense surprise on the part of the Negroes.

"No, sah; reckon not, sah."

"Did you vote in Alabama?"

"Yas, Cunnel; yas, sah, always voted, sah."

"Can you do better here than in Alabama?"

After mature reflection, the trio responded in the affirmative.

"Would you care to vote here?"

Hesitatingly, "No, sah"; whereupon the three Negroes were dismissed into the darkness.

The Alabama papers at the beginning of the current year reported that the colored laborers were leaving that state in troops of thousands. They were nearly all en route for the cotton plantations of Mississippi and on the Louisiana bank of the Father of Waters. Central Alabama appeared at that time to be undergoing rapid depopulation for the benefit of the richer lands along the Mississippi bottom. It was estimated in the spring of 1874 that Alabama had already lost from $700,000 to $1 million in her labor element alone. How long the influx of the freedmen into Mississippi and Louisiana from the South Atlantic states and from Alabama will continue is uncertain. In 1873 Georgia lost fully 20,000 of her able-bodied colored laborers and gained but little in white immigration to balance it.

The women and children on the cotton plantations near the Mississippi River do not work in the fields as much as they used. Rude as are their surroundings in the little cabins which they now call their own, they are beginning to take an interest in their homes, and the children spend some time each year at school. The laborers on the plantations in Louisiana have sometimes been paid as high as $30 per month, and furnished with a cabin, food, and a plot of ground for a garden; but this is exceptional.

While supper was being prepared, the master of the plantation apologized for what he called the homely fare which, he said, was all that he could set before us.

"We are so far from town here," he said, "that we can offer you only plantation fare — rough meat and eggs, with bacon, a loaf of baker's bread, and some bottles of claret which I brought from Vidalia."

I ventured to suggest that on the plantation he had every facility for a superb garden, and to wonder that the overseers did not employ some of the Negroes to cultivate a plot of ground that its fruits might appear on the table.

"Oh, oh," laughed the overseer. "Make a garden here; reckon it would have to have a mighty high wall; the niggers would steal everything in it as fast as it was ripe."

But I suggested that if each of the Negroes had a small garden, which he seemed to have ample time after hours to cultivate, he would not desire to steal.

The Colonel smiled gravely, and the overseer shook his head incredulously, adding: "These is good niggers, but stealing is as natural as eating to them"; and, with this remark, we were ushered into the supper room, where two black servant girls ran nimbly about bringing in plain but substantial fare, which our hard riding made thoroughly palatable.

There was no white lady on the plantation. The overseer and his two assistants were busy from dawn till dark, and when night threw its shadows over the great cypress-bordered aisles of the forest and the wide expanse of the fields they dismissed the Negroes about the store and the stables and retired to rest. But on the occasion of our visit we saw unusual activity. A violent storm arose while we were at supper, and the overseers mounted their horses and rode off in different directions to inspect the levees. Troops of Negroes were dispatched in skiffs along the lake with hundreds of sacks, which they were instructed to fill with sand and place at weak points on the levees. All night they fought the slowly but steadily rising waters, while my companion and I slept on a mattress on the floor of the overseer's room, undisturbed by anything save the sighing of the winds through the noble trees surrounding the house and the clatter of rain upon the shingles.

With early morning, back came the Colonel, pale and worn with a night of battle with the steadily rising water; and, as he laid aside his heavy cloak, placed his revolver on the table, and sat down with a weary sigh, he said it was hardly worthwhile to try to be a successful cotton planter nowadays; things human and things divine seemed to conspire to make it impossible to succeed. I thought of his sigh and of his helpless look a day or two afterward when I was told that 1,000 acres of his plantation had been flooded and badly injured by the offensive policy of a neighbor planter who had cut the Colonel's levees to save his own.

With daylight, also, although the rain was steadily falling, the plantation blossomed into activity. The overseers had arisen long before the dim streaks of the dawn were seen on the lowland horizon; had galloped over many a broad acre, but returned gloomily, announcing that the land was too wet to work that day. The Negroes slouchingly disposed themselves about the store and the overseer's "mansion," keeping at a respectful distance from the kitchen, where sat the overseer himself, surrounded by his dogs. Nothing more dispiriting could be imagined than the atmosphere of this lowland plantation over which imminent disaster seemed breaking. From right and left came stories of trouble and affliction. Here and there a planter had made a good crop and had laid aside a little money, but the evidences of material prosperity were painfully few. The overseers, while doggedly persistent in working the plantations up to their full capacity, still seemed to have a grim sense of a fate which overhung the whole locality and which would not permit consecutive years of prosperity and plenty.

There is still much on one of these remote and isolated plantations to recall the romance which surrounded them during the days of slavery. The tall and stalwart women, with their luxuriant wool carefully wrapped in gaily colored handkerchiefs; the picturesque and tattered children, who have not the slightest particle of education and who have not been reached, even since the era of Reconstruction, by the influences of schools and teachers; the groups of venerable darkies, with their gray slouch hats and impossible garments, who chatter for hours together on the sunny side of some outbuildings; and the merrymakings at night, all recall a period which, the planter will tell you with a mournful look, comprised the halcyon days of Louisiana.

The thing which struck me as most as-tonishing here, in the cotton lands, as on the rice plantations of South Carolina, was the absolute subjection of the Negro. Those with whom I talked would not directly express any idea. They gave a shuffling and grimacing assent to whatever was suggested; or, if they dissented, would beg to be excused from differing verbally and seemed to be much distressed at being required to express their opinions openly. Of course, having the most absolute political liberty, because in that section they were so largely in the majority numerically, that no intimidation could have been practised, it seemed astonishing that they should be willing to forgo the right to vote and to willingly isolate themselves from their fellows.

I could not discover that any of the Negroes were making a definite progress, either manifested by a subscription to some newspaper or by a tendency to discussion; and while the planter gave me the fullest and freest account of the social status of the Negroes employed by him, he failed to mention any sign of a definite and intellectual growth. The only really encouraging sign in their social life was the tendency to create for themselves homes and now and then to cultivate the land about them.

76.

William Tecumseh Sherman: Military Lessons of the War

William T. Sherman, who was, next to Grant, the best-known Union general in the Civil War, remained in the U.S. Army after the war was over. Between 1866 and his retirement in 1884, Sherman served as lieutenant general of the Army, headed an expedition to Mexico in 1867, and became general commander of the Army upon Grant's election to the presidency. Sherman's concern with proper military education, first as superintendent of Louisiana Military Academy (now Louisiana State University) and then as founder of the Army school at Fort Leavenworth, is reflected in the following selection from his Memoirs.

Source: *Memoirs of General William T. Sherman*, New York, 1875, Vol. II, Ch. 25.

No ARMY CAN BE EFFICIENT unless it be a unit for action; and the power must come from above, not from below. The President usually delegates his power to the commander in chief, and he to the next, and so on down to the lowest actual commander of troops, however small the detachment. No matter how troops come together, when once united, the highest officer in rank is held responsible, and should be consequently armed with the fullest power of the executive, subject only to law and existing orders. The more simple the principle, the greater the likelihood of determined action; and the less a commanding officer is circumscribed by bounds or by precedent, the greater is the probability that he will make the best use of his command and achieve the best results.

The regular army and the Military Academy at West Point have in the past provided, and doubtless will in the future provide, an ample supply of good officers for future wars; but, should their numbers be insufficient, we can always safely rely on the great number of young men of education and force of character throughout the country to supplement them. At the close of our Civil War, lasting four years, some of our best corps and division generals as well as staff officers were from civil life; but I cannot recall any of the most successful who did not express a regret that he had not received, in early life, instruction in the elementary principles of the art of war, instead of being forced to acquire this knowledge in the dangerous and expensive school of actual war.

But the real difficulty was, and will be again, to obtain an adequate number of good soldiers. We tried almost every system known to modern nations, all with more or less success — voluntary enlistments, the draft, and bought substitutes — and I think that all officers of experience will confirm my assertion that the men who voluntarily enlisted at the outbreak of the war were the best, better than the conscript, and far better than the bought substitute.

When a regiment is once organized in a state and mustered into the service of the United States, the officers and men become subject to the same laws of discipline and government as the regular troops. They are in no sense "militia," but compose a part of the Army of the United States, only retain their state title for convenience, and yet may be principally recruited from the neighborhood of their original organization. Once organized, the regiment should be kept full by recruits; and when it becomes difficult to obtain more recruits, the pay should be raised by Congress instead of tempting new men by exaggerated bounties. I believe it would have been more economical to have raised the pay of the soldier to $30 or even $50 a month than to have held out the promise of $300 and even $600 in the form of bounty.

Toward the close of the war, I have often heard the soldiers complain that the "stay-at-home" men got better pay, bounties, and food than they who were exposed to all the dangers and vicissitudes of the battles and marches at the front. The feeling of the soldier should be that, in every event, the sympathy and preference of his government is for him who fights, rather than for him who is on provost or guard duty to the rear, and, like most men, he measures this by the amount of pay. Of course, the soldier must be trained to obedience and should be "content with his wages"; but whoever has commanded an army in the field knows the difference between a willing, contented mass of men and one that feels a cause of grievance. There is a soul to an army as well as to the individual man, and no general can accomplish the full work of his army unless he commands the soul of his men, as well as their bodies and legs.

The greatest mistake made in our Civil War was in the mode of recruitment and promotion. When a regiment became reduced by the necessary wear and tear of service, instead of being filled up at the bottom and the vacancies among the officers filled from the best noncommissioned officers and men, the habit was to raise new regiments with new colonels, captains, and men, leaving the old and experienced battalions to dwindle away into mere skeleton organizations. I believe with the volunteers this matter was left to the states exclusively; and I remember that Wisconsin kept her regiments filled with recruits, whereas other states generally filled their quotas by new regiments; and the result was that we estimated a Wisconsin regiment equal to an ordinary brigade. I believe that 500 new men added to an old and experienced regiment were more valuable than 1,000 men in the form of a new regiment; for the former, by association with good, experienced captains, lieutenants, and noncommissioned officers, soon became veterans, whereas the latter were generally unavailable for a year. . . .

The "feeding" of an army is a matter of the most vital importance and demands the earliest attention of the general entrusted with a campaign. To be strong, healthy, and capable of the largest measure of physical effort, the soldier needs about three pounds gross of food per day, and the horse or mule about twenty pounds. When a general first estimates the quantity of food and forage needed for an army of 50,000 or 100,000 men, he is apt to be dismayed, and here a good staff is indispensable, though the general cannot throw off on them the responsibility. He must give the subject his personal attention, for the army reposes in him alone, and should never doubt the fact that their existence overrides in importance all other considerations. Once satisfied of this, and that all has been done that can be, the soldiers are always willing to bear the largest measure of privation. Probably no army ever had a more varied experience in this regard than the one I commanded in 1864-1865. . . .

Wounds, which in 1861 would have sent a man to the hospital for months, in 1865 were regarded as mere scratches, rather the subject of a joke than of sorrow. To new soldiers the sight of blood and death always has a sickening effect, but soon men become accustomed to it, and I have heard them exclaim on seeing a dead comrade borne to the rear, "Well, Bill has turned up *his* toes to the daisies." Of course, during a skirmish or battle, armed men should *never* leave their ranks to attend a dead or wounded comrade — this should be seen to in advance by the colonel, who should designate his musicians or company cooks as hospital attendants, with a white rag on their arm to indicate their office. A wounded man should go himself (if able) to the surgeon near at hand, or, if he need help, he should receive it from one of the attendants and not a comrade. It is wonderful how soon the men accustom themselves to these simple rules.

In great battles these matters call for a more enlarged attention, and then it becomes the duty of the division general to see that proper stretchers and field hospitals are ready for the wounded and trenches are dug for the dead. There should be no real neglect of the dead, because it has a bad effect on the living; for each soldier values himself and comrade as highly as though he were living in a good house at home.

The regimental chaplain, if any, usually attends the burials from the hospital, should make notes, and communicate details to the captain of the company and to the family at home. Of course, it is usually impossible to mark the grave with names, dates, etc., and consequently the names of the "unknown" in our national cemeteries equal about one-half of all the dead.

Very few of the battles in which I have participated were fought as described in European textbooks, viz., in great masses, in perfect order, maneuvering by corps, divisions, and brigades. We were generally in a wooded country, and, though our lines were deployed according to tactics, the men generally fought in strong skirmish lines, taking advantage of the shape of ground and of every cover. We were generally the assailants, and in wooded and broken countries the "defensive" had a positive advantage over us; for they were always ready, had cover, and always knew the ground to their immediate front, whereas we, their assailants, had to grope our way over unknown ground, and generally found a cleared field or prepared entanglements that held us for a time under a close and withering fire.

Rarely did the opposing lines in compact order come into actual contact, but when, as at Peach Tree Creek and Atlanta, the lines did become commingled, the men fought individually in every possible style, more frequently with the musket clubbed than with the bayonet, and in some instances the men clinched like wrestlers and went to the ground together. Europeans frequently criticized our war because we did not always take full advantage of a victory; the true reason was that habitually the woods served as a screen, and we often did not realize the fact that our enemy had retreated till he was already miles away and was again entrenched, having left a mere skirmish line to cover the movement, in turn to fall back to the new position.

Our war was fought with the muzzle-loading rifle. Toward the close I had one brigade (Walcutt's) armed with breech-loading "Spencers"; the cavalry generally had breech-loading carbines, "Spencers" and "Sharps," both of which were good arms.

The only change that breech-loading arms will probably make in the art and practice of war will be to increase the amount of ammunition to be expended and necessarily to be carried along; to still further "thin out" the lines of attack and to reduce battles to short, quick, decisive conflicts. It does not in the least affect the grand strategy or the necessity for perfect organization, drill, and discipline. The companies and battalions will be more dispersed, and the men will be less under the immediate eye of their officers, and therefore a higher order of intelligence and courage on the part of the individual soldier will be an element of strength.

When a regiment is deployed as skirmishers and crosses an open field or woods under heavy fire, if each man runs forward from tree to tree, or stump to stump, and yet preserves a good general alignment, it gives great confidence to the men themselves, for they always keep their eyes well to the right and left and watch their comrades; but when some few hold back, stick too close or too long to a comfortable log, it often stops the line and defeats the whole object. Therefore, the more we improve the firearm, the more will be the necessity for good organization, good discipline, and intelligence on the part of the individual soldier and officer.

There is, of course, such a thing as individual courage, which has a value in war, but familiarity with danger, experience in war and its common attendants, and personal habit are equally valuable traits, and these are the qualities with which we usually have to deal in war. All men naturally shrink from pain and danger and only incur their risk from some higher motive, or from habit; so that I would define true courage to be a perfect sensibility of the measure of danger and a mental willingness to incur it, rather than that insensibility to danger of which I have heard far more than I have seen. The most courageous men are generally unconscious of possessing the quality; therefore, when one professes it too openly, by words or bearing, there is reason to mistrust it. I would further illustrate my meaning by describing a man of true courage to be one who possesses all his faculties and senses perfectly when serious danger is actually present.

Modern wars have not materially changed the relative values or proportions of the several arms of service: infantry, artillery, cavalry, and engineers. If anything, the infantry has been increased in value. The danger of cavalry attempting to charge infantry armed with breech-loading rifles was fully illustrated at Sedan, and with us very frequently. So improbable has such a thing become that we have omitted the infantry square from our recent tactics. Still, cavalry against cavalry, and as auxiliary to infantry, will always be valuable, while all great wars will, as heretofore, depend chiefly on the infantry. Artillery is more valuable with new and inexperienced troops than with veterans.

In the early stages of the war the field guns often bore the proportion of 6 to 1,000 men; but toward the close of the war 1 gun, or at most 2 to 1,000 men, was deemed enough. Sieges, such as characterized the wars of the last century, are too slow for this period of the world, and the Prussians recently almost ignored them altogether, penetrated France between the forts and left a superior force "in observation" to watch the garrison and accept its surrender when the greater events of the war ahead made further resistance useless; but earth forts, and especially fieldworks, will hereafter play an important part in wars because they enable a minor force to hold a superior one in check for a *time,* and time is a most valuable element in all wars.

It was one of Professor Mahan's maxims that the spade was as useful in war as the musket, and to this I will add the axe. The habit of entrenching certainly does have the effect of making new troops timid. When a line of battle is once covered by a good parapet, made by the engineers or by the labor of the men themselves, it does require an effort to make them leave it in the face of danger; but when the enemy is entrenched, it becomes absolutely necessary to permit each brigade and division of the troops immediately opposed to throw up a corresponding trench for their own protection in case of a sudden sally. We invariably did this in all our recent campaigns, and it had no ill effect, though sometimes our troops were a little too slow in leaving their well-covered lines to assail the enemy in position or on retreat. Even our skirmishers were in the habit of rolling logs together, or of making a lunette of rails with dirt in front to cover their bodies; and, though it revealed their position, I cannot say that it worked a bad effect; so that, as a rule, it may safely be left to the men themselves. On the defensive, there is no doubt of the propriety of fortifying; but in the assailing army the general must watch closely to see that his men do not neglect an opportunity to drop his precautionary defenses and act promptly on the offensive at every chance.

I have many a time crept forward to the skirmish line to avail myself of the cover of the pickets' "little fort" to observe more closely some expected result; and always talked familiarly with the men, and was astonished to see how well they comprehended the general object and how accurately they were informed of the state of facts existing miles away from their particular corps. Soldiers are very quick to catch the general drift and purpose of a campaign, and are always sensible when they are well commanded or well cared for. Once impressed with this fact, and that they are making progress, they bear cheerfully any amount of labor and privation.

In camp, and especially in the presence of an active enemy, it is much easier to maintain discipline than in barracks in time of peace. Crime and breaches of discipline are much less frequent, and the necessity for court-martials far less. The captain can usually inflict all the punishment necessary, and the colonel *should* always. The field officers' court is the best form for war, viz., one of the field officers — the lieutenant colonel or major — can examine the case and report his verdict, and the colonel should execute it. Of course, there are statutory offenses which demand a general court-martial, and these must be ordered by the division or corps commander; but the presence of one of our regular civilian judge advocates in an army in the field would be a first-class nuisance, for technical courts always work mischief. Too many court-martials in any command are evidence of poor discipline and inefficient officers. . . .

To be at the head of a strong column of troops, in the execution of some task that requires brain, is the highest pleasure of war — a grim one and terrible, but which leaves on the mind and memory the strongest mark; to detect the weak point of an enemy's line; to break through with vehemence and thus lead to victory; or to discover some key point and hold it with tenacity; or to do some other distinct act which is afterward recognized as the real cause of success. These all become matters that are never forgotten. Other great difficulties, experienced by every general, are to measure truly the thousand-and-one reports that come to him in the midst of conflict; to preserve a clear and well-defined purpose at every instant of time; and to cause all efforts to converge to that end.

To do these things he must know perfectly the strength and quality of each part of his own army as well as that of his opponent, and must be where he can personally see and observe with his own eyes and judge with his own mind. No man can properly command an army from the rear; he must be "at its front"; and when a detachment is made, the commander thereof should be informed of the object to be accomplished and left as free as possible to execute it in his own way; and when an army is divided up into several parts, the superior should always attend that one which he regards as most important.

Some men think that modern armies may be so regulated that a general can sit in an office and play on his several columns as on the keys of a piano; this is a fearful mistake. The directing mind must be at the very head of the army — must be seen there, and the effect of his mind and personal energy must be felt by every officer and man present with it to secure the best results. Every attempt to make war easy and safe will result in humiliation and disaster.

Lastly, mail facilities should be kept up with an army if possible that officers and men may receive and send letters to their friends, thus maintaining the home influence of infinite assistance to discipline. Newspaper correspondents with an army, as a rule, are mischievous. They are the world's gossips, pick up and retail the camp scandal, and gradually drift to the headquarters of some general, who finds it easier to make reputation at home than with his own corps or division. They are also tempted to prophesy events and state facts which, to an enemy, reveal a purpose in time to guard against it. Moreover, they are always bound to see facts colored by the partisan or political character of their own patrons, and thus bring army officers into the political controversies of the day, which are always mischievous and wrong. Yet, so greedy are the people at large for war news that it is doubtful whether any army commander can exclude all reporters without bringing down on himself a clamor that may imperil his own safety. Time and moderation must bring a just solution to this modern difficulty.

77.

Thomas P. Westendorf: "I'll Take You Home Again, Kathleen"

The population of the United States doubled in the years between 1860 and 1890, and of the 63,000,000 inhabitants at the latter date, some 10,000,000 were immigrants. They came willingly and with hope, of course, but they often had to leave loved ones behind, and many new Americans never got over their homesickness for the old country they had left. "I'll Take You Home Again, Kathleen" was written by Thomas P. Westendorf, a public school music teacher in Plainfield, Indiana, and introduced in a school show or pageant in 1876. Westendorf's wife was away on a trip, and he is said to have expressed his loneliness and tender feelings for her in the song, which included a promise to take her back to the old country, where she presumably wanted to go. The song, which may have been influenced by another popular ballad of the period, "Barney, Take Me Home Again," was a favorite of Thomas Alva Edison, and Henry Ford liked it so much that he placed an autographed copy in his Detroit museum.

❧ I'LL TAKE YOU HOME AGAIN, KATHLEEN

I'll take you home again, Kathleen,
Across the ocean, wild and wide,
To where your heart has ever been
Since first you were my bonny bride.

The roses all have left your cheek—
I've watched them fade away and die.
Your voice is sad whene'er you speak,
And tears bedim your loving eyes.

I know you love me, Kathleen dear,
Your heart was ever fond and true;
I always feel when you are near
That life holds nothing, dear, but you.
The smiles that once you gave to me
I scarcely ever see them now,
Though many many times I see
A darkening shadow on your brow.

To that dear home beyond the sea
My Kathleen shall again return,
And when thy old friends welcome thee
Thy loving heart will cease to yearn.
Where laughs the little silver stream
Beside your mother's humble cot
And brightest rays of sunshine gleam —
There all your grief will be forgot.

Chorus:
Oh I will take you back, Kathleen,
To where your heart will feel no pain,
And when the fields are fresh and green
I'll take you to your home again.

78.

Samuel L. Clemens ("Mark Twain"): The Curious Republic of Gondour

Mark Twain's experiences as pilot, printer, miner, reporter, lecturer, foreign traveler, and would-be capitalist shaped his attitudes toward the "Gilded Age," and he reflected, in many works, on the problems that confronted the era from the point of view of an average man. He was furthermore a product of the frontier, and as such encumbered by few traditional values; he was a hater of sham wherever found, and he unleashed the fury of his satiric powers on the pomposity of the "better" classes. "The Curious Republic of Gondour" is an example of his social criticism, dealing, as it does, with the plight of an imaginary nation that is edging toward oligarchy. The story was first published anonymously in the Atlantic Monthly.

Source: *Atlantic Monthly*, October 1875.

As soon as I had learned to speak the language a little, I became greatly interested in the people and the system of government.

I found that the nation had at first tried universal suffrage pure and simple, but had thrown that form aside because the result was not satisfactory. It had seemed to deliver all power into the hands of the ignorant and non-taxpaying classes; and of a necessi-

ty the responsible offices were filled from these classes also.

A remedy was sought. The people believed they had found it; not in the destruction of universal suffrage but in the enlargement of it. It was an odd idea, and ingenious. You must understand, the constitution gave every man a vote; therefore that vote was a vested right and could not be taken away. But the constitution did not say that certain individuals might not be given two votes, or ten! So an amendatory clause was inserted in a quiet way; a clause which authorized the enlargment of the suffrage in certain cases to be specified by statute. To offer to "limit" the suffrage might have made instant trouble; the offer to "enlarge" it had a pleasant aspect.

But of course the newspapers soon began to suspect; and then out they came! It was found, however, that for once — and for the first time in the history of the republic — property, character, and intellect were able to wield a political influence; for once, money, virtue, and intelligence took a vital and a united interest in a political question. For once these powers went to the "primaries" in strong force; for once the best men in the nation were put forward as candidates for that parliament whose business it should be to enlarge the suffrage. The weightiest half of the press quickly joined forces with the new movement, and left the other half to rail about the proposed "destruction of the liberties" of the bottom layer of society, the hitherto governing class of the community.

The victory was complete. The new law was framed and passed. Under it every citizen, howsoever poor or ignorant, possessed one vote, so universal suffrage still reigned; but if a man possessed a good common-school education and no money, he had two votes; a high-school education gave him four; if he had property likewise, to the value of 3,000 *sacos*, he wielded one more vote; for every 50,000 *sacos* a man added to his property, he was entitled to another vote; a university education entitled a man to nine votes, even though he owned no property. Therefore, learning being more prevalent and more easily acquired than riches; educated men became a wholesome check upon wealthy men, since they could outvote them. Learning goes usually with uprightness, broad views, and humanity; so the learned voters, possessing the balance of power, became the vigilant and efficient protectors of the great lower rank of society.

And now a curious thing developed itself — a sort of emulation whose object was voting power! Whereas formerly a man was honored only according to the amount of money he possessed, his grandeur was measured now by the number of votes he wielded. A man with only one vote was conspicuously respectful to his neighbor who possessed three. And if he was a man above the commonplace, he was as conspicuously energetic in his determination to acquire three for himself. This spirit of emulation invaded all ranks. Votes based upon capital were commonly called "mortal" votes, because they could be lost; those based upon learning were called "immortal," because they were permanent, and because of their customarily imperishable character they were naturally more valued than the other sort. I say "customarily" for the reason that these votes were not absolutely imperishable, since insanity could suspend them.

Under this system, gambling and speculation almost ceased in the republic. A man honored as the possessor of great voting power could not afford to risk the loss of it upon a doubtful chance.

It was curious to observe the manners and customs which the enlargement plan produced. Walking the street with a friend one day, he delivered a careless bow to a passerby, and then remarked that that person possessed only one vote and would probably never earn another; he was more respectful to the next acquaintance he met; he explained that this salute was a four-vote bow. I tried to "average" the importance of the people he accosted after that by the nature of his bows, but my success was only partial, because of the somewhat greater homage paid to the immortals than to the mortals.

My friend explained. He said there was no law to regulate this thing, except that most powerful of all laws, custom. Custom had created these varying bows, and in time they had become easy and natural. At this moment he delivered himself of a very profound salute, and then said, "Now there's a man who began life as a shoemaker's apprentice and without education; now he swings twenty-two mortal votes and two immortal ones; he expects to pass a high-school examination this year and climb a couple of votes higher among the immortals; mighty valuable citizen."

By and by my friend met a venerable personage, and not only made him a most elaborate bow but also took off his hat. I took off mine, too, with a mysterious awe. I was beginning to be infected.

"What grandee is that?"

"That is our most illustrious astronomer. He hasn't any money, but is fearfully learned. Nine immortals is *his* political weight! He would swing 150 votes if our system were perfect."

"Is there any altitude of mere moneyed grandeur that you take off your hat to?"

"No. Nine immortal votes is the only power we uncover for — that is, in civil life. Very great officials receive that mark of homage, of course."

It was common to hear people admiringly mention men who had begun life on the lower levels and in time achieved great voting power. It was also common to hear youths planning a future of ever so many votes for themselves. I heard shrewd mammas speak of certain young men as good "catches" because they possessed such-and-such a number of votes. I knew of more than one case where an heiress was married to a youngster who had but one vote; the argument being that he was gifted with such excellent parts that in time he would acquire a good voting strength, and perhaps in the long run be able to outvote his wife, if he had luck.

Competitive examinations were the rule in all official grades. I remarked that the questions asked the candidates were wild, intricate, and often required a sort of knowledge not needed in the office sought.

"Can a fool or an ignoramus answer them?" asked the person I was talking with.

"Certainly not."

"Well, you will not find any fools or ignoramuses among our officials."

I felt rather cornered, but made shift to say —

"But these questions cover a good deal more ground than is necessary."

"No matter; if candidates can answer these it is tolerably fair evidence that they can answer nearly any other question you choose to ask them."

There were some things in Gondour which one could not shut his eyes to. One was that ignorance and incompetence had no place in the government. Brains and property managed the state. A candidate for office must have marked ability, education, and high character, or he stood no sort of chance of election. If a hod carrier possessed these, he could succeed; but the mere fact that he was a hod carrier could not elect him, as in previous times.

It was now a very great honor to be in the parliament or in office; under the old system such distinction had only brought suspicion upon a man and made him a helpless mark for newspaper contempt and scurrility. Officials did not need to steal now, their salaries being vast in comparison with the pittances paid in the days when parliaments were created by hod carriers, who viewed official salaries from a hod-carrying point of view and compelled that view to be respected by their obsequious servants. Justice was wisely and rigidly administered; for a judge, after once reaching his place through the specified line of promotions, was a permanency during good behavior. He was not obliged to modify his judgments according to the effect they might have upon the temper of a reigning political party.

The country was mainly governed by a ministry which went out with the administration that created it. This was also the case with the chiefs of the great departments. Minor officials ascended to their several positions through well-earned promotions and not by a jump from gin-mills or the needy families and friends of members of parliament. Good behavior measured their terms of office.

The head of the government, the Grand Caliph, was elected for a term of twenty years. I questioned the wisdom of this. I was answered that he could do no harm, since the ministry and the parliament governed the land, and he was liable to impeachment for misconduct. This great office had twice been ably filled by women, women as aptly fitted for it as some of the sceptered queens of history. Members of the cabinet, under many administrations, had been women.

I found that the pardoning power was lodged in a court of pardons, consisting of several great judges. Under the old *régime,* this important power was vested in a single official, and he usually took care to have a general jail delivery in time for the next election.

I inquired about public schools. There were plenty of them, and of free colleges, too. I inquired about compulsory education. This was received with a smile, and the remark —

"When a man's child is able to make himself powerful and honored according to the amount of education he acquires, don't you suppose that that parent will apply the compulsion himself? Our free schools and free colleges require no law to fill them."

There was a loving pride of country about this person's way of speaking which annoyed me. I had long been unused to the sound of it in my own. The Gondour national airs were forever dinning in my ears; therefore I was glad to leave that country and come back to my dear native land, where one never hears that sort of music.

Let no guilty man escape.

ULYSSES S. GRANT, when it was discovered that his personal secretary and other friends were involved in the Whisky Ring scandal, 1875

That party never had but two objects — grand and petty larceny.

ROBERT G. INGERSOLL, of the Democratic Party, speech, Indianapolis, 1876

When I want to buy up any politicians I always find the anti-monopolist the most purchasable. They don't come so high.

WILLIAM H. VANDERBILT, interview aboard his special train approaching Chicago, Oct. 8, 1882

1876

79.

BLANCHE K. BRUCE: African American Hopes for Assimilation

Blanche Bruce was one of the two African Americans elected to the U.S. Senate during the Reconstruction period. Born in Prince Edward County, Virginia, Bruce attended Oberlin College and later became a successful planter at Floreyville, Mississippi. His political abilities were soon recognized, and newly franchised African Americans elected him to several state offices and, finally, in 1874, to the Senate, where he served one term. His record there was commendable. Bruce was mainly concerned with exposing election fraud and battling for civil rights in the South. In the following selection from a speech delivered to the Senate on March 31, 1876, Bruce expressed remarkable tolerance toward those who were feverishly working to undo the recently won political power of African Americans. After his Senate term ended in 1881 he became a political appointee for numerous Republican administrations.

Source: *Record*, 44 Cong., 1 Sess., pp. 2101-2105.

WE WANT PEACE AND GOOD ORDER at the South; but it can only come by the fullest recognition of the rights of all classes. The opposition must concede the necessity of change, not only in the temper but in the philosophy of their party organization and management. The sober American judgment must obtain in the South as elsewhere in the republic, that the only distinctions upon which parties can be safely organized and in harmony with our institutions are differences of opinions relative to principles and policy of government, and that differences of religion, nationality, or race can neither with safety nor propriety be permitted for a moment to enter into the party contests of the day.

The unanimity with which the colored voters act with a party is not referable to any race prejudice on their part. On the contrary, they invite the political cooperation of their white brethren, and vote as a unit because proscribed as such. They deprecate the establishment of the color line by the opposition, not only because the act is unwise and wrong in principle but because it isolates them from the white men of the South, and forces them, in sheer self-protection and against their inclination, to act seemingly upon the basis of a race prejudice that they neither respect nor entertain.

As a class they are free from prejudices and have no uncharitable suspicions against their white fellow citizens, whether native-born or settlers from the Northern states. They not only recognize the equality of citizenship and the right of every man to hold, without proscription, any position of honor and trust to which the confidence of the people may elevate him; but, owing nothing to race, birth, or surroundings, they, above all other classes in the community, are interested to see prejudices drop out of both politics and the business of the country, and success in life proceed only upon the integrity and merit of the man who seeks it. They are also appreciative — feeling and exhibiting the liveliest gratitude for counsel and help in their new career, whether they come from the men of the North or of the South.

But withal, as they progress in intelligence and appreciation of the dignity of their prerogatives as citizens, they, as an evidence of growth, begin to realize the significance of the proverb, "When thou doest well for thyself, men shall praise thee"; and are disposed to exact the same protection and concession of rights that are conferred upon other citizens by the Constitution, and that, too, without the humiliation involved in the enforced abandonment of their political convictions.

We simply demand the practical recognition of the rights given us in the Constitution and laws, and ask from our white fellow citizens only the consideration and fairness that we so willingly extend to them. Let them generally realize and concede that citizenship imports to us what it does to them, no more and no less, and impress the colored people that a party defeat does not imperil their political franchise. Let them cease their attempts to coerce our political cooperation, and invite and secure it by a policy so fair and just as to commend itself to our judgment, and resort to no motive or measure to control us that self-respect would preclude their applying to themselves. When we can entertain opinions and select party affiliations without proscription, and cast our ballots as other citizens and without jeopardy to person or privilege, we can safely afford to be governed by the considerations that ordinarily determine the political action of American citizens.

But we must be guaranteed in the unproscribed exercise of our honest convictions and be absolutely, from within or without, protected in the use of our ballot before we can either wisely or safely divide our vote. In union, not division, is strength, so long as White League proscription renders division of our vote impracticable by making a difference of opinion opprobrious and an antagonism in politics a crime. On the other hand, if we should, from considerations of fear, yield to the shotgun policy of our opponents, the White League might win a temporary success, but the ultimate result would be disastrous to both races, for they would first become aggressively turbulent, and we, as a class, would become servile, unreliable, and worthless.

It has been suggested, as the popular sentiment of the country, that the colored citizens must no longer expect special legislation for their benefit, nor exceptional interference by the national government for their protection. If this is true, if such is the judgment relative to our demands and needs, I venture to offset the suggestion, so far as it may be used as reason for a denial of the protection we seek, by the statement of another and more prevalent popular conviction. Back of this, and underlying the foundations of the republic itself, there lies deep in the breasts of the patriotic millions of the country the conviction that the laws must be enforced, and life, liberty, and property must, alike to all and for all, be protected. But I allege that we do not seek special action in our behalf, except to meet special danger, and only then such as all classes of

Blanche K. Bruce, senator from Mississippi

citizens are entitled to receive under the Constitution. We do not ask the enactment of new laws, but only the enforcement of those that already exist.

The vicious and exceptional political action had by the White League in Mississippi has been repeated in other contests and in other states of the South, and the colored voters have been subjected therein to outrages upon their rights similar to those perpetrated in my own state at the recent election. Because violence has become so general a quality in the political canvasses of the South and my people the common sufferers in each instance, I have considered this subject more in detail than would, under other circumstances, have been either appropriate or necessary. As the proscription and violence toward the colored voters are special and almost exclusive, and seem to proceed upon the assumption that there is something exceptionally offensive and unworthy in them, I have felt, as the only representative of my race in the Senate of the United States, that I was placed, in some sort, upon the defensive; and I have consequently endeavored to show how aggravated and inexcusable were the wrongs worked upon us, and have sought to vindicate our title to both the respect and goodwill of the just people of the nation.

The gravity of the issues involved has demanded great plainness of speech from me. But I have endeavored to present my views to the Senate with the moderation and deference inspired by the recollection that both my race and myself were once bondsmen, and are today debtors largely to the love and justice of a great people for the enjoyment of our personal and political liberty. While my antecedents and surroundings suggest modesty, there are some considerations that justify frankness, and even boldness of speech. . . .

I have confidence, not only in my country and her institutions but in the endurance, capacity, and destiny of my people. We will, as opportunity offers and ability serves, seek our places, sometimes in the field of letters, arts, sciences, and the professions. More frequently mechanical pursuits will attract and elicit our efforts; more still of my people will find employment and livelihood as the cultivators of the soil. The bulk of this people — by surroundings, habits, adaptation, and choice — will continue to find their homes in the South and constitute the masses of its yeomanry. We will there, probably, of our own volition and more abundantly than in the past, produce the great staples that will contribute to the basis of foreign exchange, aid in giving the nation a balance of trade, and minister to the wants and comfort and build up the prosperity of the whole land.

Whatever our ultimate position in the composite civilization of the republic and whatever varying fortunes attend our career, we will not forget our instincts for freedom nor our love of country. Guided and guarded by a beneficent Providence, and living under the genial influence of liberal institutions, we have no apprehensions that we shall fail from the land from attrition with other races, or ignobly disappear from either the politics or industries of the country.

Mr. President, allow me here to say that, although many of us are uneducated in the schools, we are informed and advised as to our duties to the government, our state, and ourselves. Without class prejudice or animosities, with obedience to authority as the lesson and love of peace and order as the passion of our lives, with scrupulous respect for the rights of others, and with the hopefulness of political youth, we are determined that the great government that gave us liberty and rendered its gift valuable by giving us the ballot shall not find us wanting in a sufficient response to any demand that humanity or patriotism may make upon us; and we ask such action as will not only protect us in the enjoyment of our constitutional rights but will preserve the integrity of our republican institutions.

80.

An Act to Keep Children off the Stage

Child labor flourished relatively unopposed through the early history of America, increasing dramatically with the growth of textile mills, canneries, and other factory operations. By 1870 the employment of children between the ages of ten and fifteen years reached 750,000. As the rate of employment kept increasing, the Knights of Labor and other labor organizations launched a campaign for state regulation of child labor. New York, among other states, passed legislation prohibiting certain occupations as "wrongs to children." The following New York State law, passed in 1876, forbade employment of children less than sixteen years old in musical and theatrical productions.

Source: *General Statutes of New York*, 1876, Ch. 122.

THE PEOPLE OF THE STATE of New York, represented in Senate and Assembly, do enact as follows:

Section 1. Any person having the care, custody, or control of any child under the age of sixteen years who shall exhibit, use, or employ, or who shall in any manner or under any pretense sell, apprentice, give away, let out, or otherwise dispose of any such child to any person in or for the vocation, occupation, service, or purpose of singing, playing on musical instruments, rope or wire walking, dancing, begging or peddling, or as a gymnast, contortionist, rider, or acrobat, in any place whatsoever; or for or in any obscene, indecent, or immoral purpose, exhibition, or practice whatsoever; or for or in any business, exhibition, or vocation injurious to the health or dangerous to the life or limb of such child; or who shall cause, procure, or encourage any such child to engage therein, shall be guilty of a misdemeanor.

Nothing in this section contained shall apply to or affect the employment or use of any such child as a singer or musician in any church, school, or academy, or the teaching or learning the science or practice of music; nor the employment of any child as a musician at any concert or entertainment, on the written consent of the mayor of the city or president of the board of trustees of the village where such concert or entertainment shall take place.

Section 2. Every person who shall take, receive, hire, employ, use, exhibit or have in custody any child under the age, and for any of the purposes mentioned in the 1st Section of this act shall be guilty of a misdemeanor.

Section 3. When, upon examination before any court or magistrate, it shall appear that any child, within the age previously mentioned in this act, was engaged or used for, or in any business, or exhibition or vocation, or purpose specified and as mentioned in this act; and when, upon the conviction of any person of a criminal assault upon a child in his or her custody, the court or magistrate before whom such conviction is had shall deem it desirable for the welfare of such child that the person so convicted should be deprived of its custody thereafter, such court or magistrate may commit such child to an orphan asylum, charitable or other institution, or make such other disposition thereof as now is or hereafter may be provided by law in cases of vagrant, truant, disorderly, pauper, or destitute children.

Section 4. Whoever, having the care or custody of any child, shall willfully cause or permit the life of such child to be endangered, or the health of such child to be injured; or who shall willfully cause or permit such child to be placed in such a situation that its life may be endangered, or its health shall be likely to be injured, shall be guilty of a misdemeanor.

Section 5. All fines, penalties, and forfeitures imposed and collected in any county in this state, under the provisions of this and of every act passed, or which may be passed, relating to or affecting children, in every case where the prosecution shall be instituted or conducted by a society incorporated pursuant to the provisions of Chapter 130 of the laws of 1875, being an act entitled "An act for the incorporation of societies for the prevention of cruelty to children," shall, except where otherwise provided, enure to such society in aid of the purposes for which it was incorporated.

Section 6. Nothing herein contained shall be construed as affecting the punishment of offenses under Chapter 116 of the laws of 1874, entitled "An act in relation to mendicant and vagrant children."

———————◆———————

Every crowd has a silver lining.
PHINEAS TAYLOR BARNUM

Torch of the Statue of Liberty on display at the Philadelphia International Exhibition, 1876

GROWTH AND CONSOLIDATION

In addition to the torch of Liberty, the 1876 centennial exhibition in Philadelphia featured such new inventions as the typewriter, the telephone, and the Westinghouse air brake. The celebration of one hundred years of independence coincided with the greatest period of expansion and innovation America had yet seen. With the war over, with land and resources and money seemingly endless, American industry took advantage of every new development in technique and organization to expand and consolidate. The result was the huge, efficient corporations and trusts.

The oil industry, delayed in its infancy by the war, became one of the largest; steel developed the Bessemer and open-hearth processes; the railroads spread into new markets and spanned the continent. On a smaller scale but perhaps more symbolic, Joseph Glidden invented barbed wire in 1874 — even the West was beginning to organize, to fence itself in, and thereby more freely to exploit its vast resources. The Philadelphia centennial was, on the one hand, an extravagant celebration of material "progress"; on the other, it was only a bare hint of things to come.

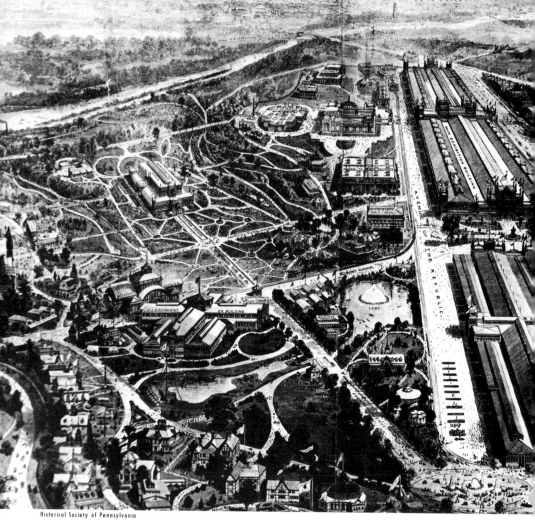

(Above) Balloon view of the grounds at the centennial exhibition; engraving made for "Harper's Weekly," 1876; (below) centennial horticultural hall which housed plants from all sections of the earth; the exposition's purpose and design were influenced by the Crystal Palace Exposition in London

(Above) Interior of agricultural hall; (below left) the Corliss steam engine which generated all the power for the fair; (below) the Campbell printing press on exhibit

The interdependent coal and steel industries were the center of the American industrial complex. The introduction of the new Bessemer and open-hearth processes for producing medium- and high-grade steel for construction opened a vast market for bituminous coal. Mining for bituminous spread into Michigan, Minnesota, Wisconsin, and Alabama; anthracite, virtually limited to eastern Pennsylvania, could not compete. The common objective of coal and steel and of industry generally was to produce always more, faster, cheaper, and better. The national development that came with the boom was accompanied, incidentally, by huge personal fortunes.

(Left) Converters in operation making Bessemer steel at Pittsburgh mill, 1886; (below) Glendon Iron Works, Pennsylvania, about 1875

(Top) View of the exterior of an anthracite coal breaker in Buck Mountain, Pa., 1880; (center) entrance to an anthracite coal mine at Buck Mountain, 1880; (bottom) "Waiting for the Blast"; engraving from a series on coal mining operations in "Leslie's Illustrated," 1871

(Above) **First oil wells pumping in the United States; owned by the Venango Co., Titusville, Pa., 1860; (left) "Band of Bummers"; photo by J. C. Goetchius, Titusville, about 1875**

From the discovery of the first oil well in 1859 until 1870, the annual production of oil in the United States increased from about 2,000 barrels to nearly 10,000,000. In 1870 John D. Rockefeller formed the Standard Oil Co., which eventually controlled virtually the entire industry. The Standard, while ruthless in business methods, was largely responsible for the rapid growth of refining and distribution techniques.

Pioneer Run, 1865; a year later, the completion of Lady Brooks well increased the importance of this region for oil production

(Above left) Flowing well; from a stereograph by Detlor & Waddell; (above right) view of an oil fire; from a stereograph by Frank Robbins, 1880; (below) view of Oil City, Pa.

The railroad industry mirrored the growth of others; trackage increased from 35,000 to 93,000 miles between 1863 and 1880. Refrigerator cars, Pullmans, safety couplers, air brakes all added impetus; wild speculation presided over by the inevitable tycoons brought the capital, and Europe supplied the labor. Competing corporations learned to supplement rate-juggling, rebates, and outright warfare with industry-wide agreements on standard rail gauge and handling facilities.

(Top) Baltimore and Ohio engine house at Piedmont, 1866; (center) certificate for twenty shares of stock in a railroad, 1871; (bottom) Pennsylvania Railroad shops at Altoona, Pa., 1860s

(Top) Railroad bridge over the Ohio River, Bellaire, Ohio, 1872; (center) B&O's rolling mills, Cumberland, Md.; (bottom) first passenger train over the Ohio River Bridge, Louisville, Ky., 1870

Vanderbilt and James Fisk were in competition for control of western railroads

Though few would admit it publicly, most "captains of industry" agreed with railroad magnate William Vanderbilt's famed expletive: "The public be damned!" The huge corporations and incredible personal power and wealth that were the hallmark of the laissez faire Gilded Age became further and further removed from the hardware of industry; capitalists became financiers and paper became the symbol and tool of wealth.

(Right) Cornelius Vanderbilt; (below) Jay Gould (left) and Daniel Drew, who employed stock manipulation and bribery of state politicians to block Vanderbilt's efforts to take the Erie R.R.; Gould later defrauded Erie stockholders, engaged in numerous stock manipulations, and caused the crash of 1869 speculating in gold

81.

ULYSSES S. GRANT: The Separation of Church and School

Several church bodies, notably Catholics and Lutherans, developed extensive systems of parochial education in the latter half of the nineteenth century. The parochial school was based on the conviction that "secular" education was inadequate, even dangerous, for children of church affiliation. The churches that were engaged in education argued that they had a right to some of the public funds that were devoted to schools. Bishops Michael Corrigan of Newark and John Ireland of St. Paul both actively sought public funds for Catholic schools. In Illinois, it was feared that the combined vote of the Catholic and Lutheran electorate would endanger the very existence of the public school system. With such issues as these in mind, President Grant made the following remarks at Des Moines, Iowa, in 1876.

Source: Rena M. Atchison, *Un-American Immigration: Its Present Effects and Future Perils*, Chicago, 1894, pp. 90-91.

I DO NOT BRING into this assemblage politics, certainly not partisan politics, but it is a fair subject for soldiers in their deliberations to consider what may be necessary to secure the prize for which they battled in a republic like ours; where the citizen is the sovereign and the official the servant; where no power is exercised except by the will of the people. It is important that the sovereign, the people, should foster intelligence and the promoter of that intelligence which is to preserve us as a nation. If we are to have another contest in the near future for our national existence, I predict that the dividing line will not be Mason and Dixon's Line but between patriotism and intelligence on the one side, and superstition, ambition, and ignorance on the other.

Now, the centennial year of our national existence, I believe, is a good time to begin the work of strengthening the foundations of the structure commenced by our patriotic fathers a hundred years ago at Lexington.

Let us labor to add all needful guarantees for the greater security of free thought, free speech, a free press, pure morals, unfettered religious sentiments, and equal rights and privileges to all men, irrespective of nationality, color, or religion. Encourage free schools and resolve that not one dollar of the money appropriated to their support shall be appropriated to the support of any sectarian school; that neither the state or nation, nor both combined, shall support institutions of learning other than those sufficient to afford to every child in the land the opportunity of a good common-school education, unmixed with sectarian, pagan, or atheistical dogma.

Leave the matter of religion to the family altar, the church, and private schools entirely supported by private contributions. Keep the church and state forever separate. With these safeguards I believe the battles which created the Army of the Tennessee will not have been fought in vain.

82.

ALEXANDER LYMAN HOLLEY: Theory and Practice in Industrial Engineering

The mechanical engineer Alexander Lyman Holley was responsible for bringing the Bessemer steel-making process to the United States. The process, modified and improved by him, became the basis for the entire American steel industry, and he spent the years after 1868 designing steel plants in all parts of the country. As president of the American Institute of Mining Engineers, Holley delivered an address on February 22, 1876, entitled "The Inadequate Union of Engineering Science and Art," from which the excerpt below is taken.

Source: *Memorial of Alexander Lyman Holley,* New York, 1884, pp. 205-222.

THE APPLICATION of scientific methods to the investigation of natural laws and to the conduct of the useful arts which are founded upon them is year by year mitigating the asperity and enlarging the outcome of human endeavor. More notably, perhaps, are these the facts in that system of productive and constructive arts of which Engineering is the general name. In metallurgical engineering especially, within the period of our own recollection, how rapid has been the rate and how wide the scope of progress — the scientific discovery and mining of metalliferous veins; the economical separation and reduction of ores of every grade; the production and regulation of high temperatures; the varied improvements in the manufacture of iron, in saved heat and work, in uniformity and range of products; and most important of all, the creation and the utilization, to be counted by the million tons a year, of the cheap constructive steels!

Wonderful as this range and degree of development may appear to the public eye, the close and thoughtful observer must nevertheless conclude that neither the profession nor the craft of engineering may con-gratulate themselves too complacently, but that they should rather acknowledge to each other the embarrassing incompleteness of the union between engineering science and art.

There is a small but most truly scientific and most truly practical school of philosophers whom we may designate as original investigators — men who come close to nature, who search into first principles, and who follow in all things that scientific, and therefore fruitful, method by which the relations of matter and force are discovered, classified, and brought within the reach of practice. These wonderful men do not indeed create the laws of nature, as they sometimes almost seem to, but they go up into the trembling mountain and the thick darkness and bring down the tables upon which they are written.

There is a large class of men whom we may designate as the schoolmen — a class popularly, and, to a great extent, correctly recognized as the scientific element of human progress — men who are learned in the researches and conclusions of others and skilled in reasoning or speculating from these or from abstract data upon the certain or probable results of physical and chemical combinations.

And there is the great army of practicians, almost infinite in its degrees of quality, ranging from the mere human mechanism by which mind lays hold of matter and force, through all the grades of practical judgment and power — an indispensable link between nature's forces, as the philosopher thinks they are, and nature's materials, as the practician knows they are.

As the art precedes the science (however the science may afterward revolutionize the art), let us first consider the matter from the artisan's — the "practical" man's — standpoint. While every day's experience could teach him a more helpful lesson, it could hardly teach him one of greater general importance than that the men who speculate, from secondhand data, upon the probable results of combinations of forces and materials, are not the men who can best make these combinations in practice, who intuitively know all the concealed pitfalls, such as friction — that trick of nature, which, like the thousandth part of phosphorus, alters all the conditions of use in iron — nor are they the men who can determine the completeness of these combinations or read the record of their results, as in the character of a flame, in the feeling of a refractory mixture in the behavior of a metal under treatment; nor are they the men who, by familiarity with objects and phenomena, are best fitted to pursue that original investigation which is the foundation of even theoretical progress.

The expert who delights to call himself "practical" is honestly amazed at the attempts of experts of school graduation, who have not been graduated in works, to solve the engineering problems of the day. And, from his standpoint, there are numerous and conspicuous illustrations. While metallurgists are still disputing over the nature and sequence of reactions in combustion and reduction, the practical iron smelter has

felt his way from the barbarous practice of a century ago to the vast and economical production of today. The attainment of powerful and sufficiently hot blast by means of waste heat, the adaptation of shape and proportion of stack to different fuels and ores, laborsaving appliances and arrangements — all these have grown out of the constant handling, not of books but of furnaces. . . .

Mere familiarity with steam engines is not, indeed, a *cause* of improved steam engineering but it is a *condition*. The mechanical laws of heat were not developed in an engine house, yet, without the mechanism which the knowledge, derived *through this familiarity,* has created and adapted, the study of heat would have been an ornamental rather than a useful pursuit. So in other departments. When one can feel the completion of a Bessemer "blow" without looking at the flame or number the remaining minutes of a Martin steel charge from the bubbling of the bath or foretell the changes in the working of a blast furnace by watching the colors and structure of the slag or note the carburization of steel by examining its fracture or say what an ore will yield from its appearance and weight in the hand or predict the lifetime of a machine by feeling its pulse; when one in any art can make a diagnosis by looking the patient in the face rather than by reading about similar cases in a book, then only may he hope to practically apply such improvements as theory may suggest or to lead in those original investigations upon which successful theories shall be founded.

These are the conclusions of the "practical" man, and they are none the less true because they are not the whole truth. That they are too little considered by the schoolmen and the graduates of schools is also true, but, happily, less conspicuously so as the years advance.

The evil consequences of this mistake develop themselves in various ways. The recent graduates of schools do not, indeed, expect immediate positions of responsibility and authority, but they often demand them after too short a term of object teaching. Perhaps the greatest advantage of their scientific training is that they can learn from objects and phenomena faster than can the mere workman, who, although full of the elements of new and useful conclusions, lacks, if I may so say, the scientific reagent which precipitates the rubbish and leaves a clear solution of the problem.

It is, however, true — in the iron manufacture, perhaps, especially true — that men of wide learning and of great mental dexterity, unless they have studied at least as many years in the works as they have in the school, do not successfully compete for the desirable places with the men that have come up from the ranks. Narrow, unsystematic, and fruitless of new results as his knowledge may be, he who has grown up steadily from the position even of puddler's helper, will be selected to take the manager's post in preference to him whose reputation is founded solely on the school.

Nor does this prove, as the schoolmen too often believe, that the owners and directors of metallurgical enterprises are always unappreciative of scientific culture. It rather proves that the lowest functions, as in the case of pure humanity, must first be considered; that the conditions of maintenance and regular working, which constant familiarity with objects and phenomena alone can provide, are earliest in order. Conservation first and improvement afterward.

Another consideration in this connection is that scientific aid appears to be more readily provided for the "practical" man than practical aid for the "scientific" man. The trained scholar can the more readily adapt himself to the situation. He should suggest many more improvements than would ever crystallize in an equally good but undisciplined mind. Yet his attempt, with mere scholastic aids, to carry these improvements out might disorganize a whole establishment. As there must be one final authority, judgment founded on experience almost universally ranks the wider and more fruitful culture of the school.

And if we ask those great masters, whose experimental knowledge is as wide as their scientific culture, they will tell us that as the inert and clumsy flywheel, that typical conservator, is more helpful to a steam engine in the long run than a valve gear, so highly organized that it seems to know what it ought to do — so in their own undertakings, plodding, practical economics must sit in judgment upon theory and limit the reaches of imagination.

Another evil growing out of the inadequate regard of mere schoolmen for practice is the frequent failure of their works or their inability to complete them. Inventions and constructions designed after a scientific method and under the light of organized facts and detailed history as laid down in books may fail simply in default of a practical knowledge of how far the capital at hand will reach or what the means at hand will do or what the materials at hand will stand or what the labor and assistance at hand can be relied on to accomplish. A vast number of facts about the operation of forces in materials are so subtle, or so incompletely revealed or disentangled from groups of phenomena, that they cannot be defined in words nor understood if they could be formulated. But after long familiarity with the general behavior of materials under stress, a practical expert can, by a process more like instinct than reason, judge how far and in what directions he may safely push his new combinations.

Thus, while the unschooled practician usually wastes his energies in unscientific methods and on impossible combinations, but generally carries into successful use his comparatively few well-founded attempts, the student merely of principles and abstract facts usually originates the ideas upon which progress is founded and rarely clothes them with practical bodies. In this chasm between science and art, how much effort and treasure, and even life, are swallowed up year by year! . . .

I hope it may not seem that the dignity of abstract scientific investigation is undervalued by the utilizers of nature's powers and materials or that any considerations of profit obscure even in the average commercial mind the splendor of those achievements made in the mere love of truth, with thought of neither commercial application nor pecuniary reward — achievements which distinguish such names as Faraday, Bunsen, Leverrier, Mayer, Joule, Henry, Darwin, and Tyndall. Do not their successes rather encourage us, in our lower sphere, to more persistently pursue the method of these great discoverers — the original investigation of nature's truths? . . .

But the undervaluation of the study of objects and phenomena by schoolmen is not the principal hindrance to the complete union of science and art. A greater obstacle is the combined misapprehension and ignorance on the part of a large class of "practical" men, of what they are pleased to call "theory," meaning by theory something which is likely to be discordant with fact — or possibly with the interests of the craft.

There is also a class of practicians who do secretly and abstractly respect the labors of the scientific investigator and are unwillingly governed, more or less, by his conclusions; but their minds are so barren of general facts and so untrained in the scientific methods of utilizing facts and, hence, so distrustful of any ideas which reach beyond their own practice that they, also, are impediments rather than helpers in the union of science and art. . . .

In the enlargement of this method of mutual respect and instruction, to a certain ex-

Alexander L. Holley, foremost designer of steel plants in the United States

tent, lies the solution of the problem under consideration; but it is a complex method, only actively operative under several important conditions, such as:

1. A *public opinion* among schoolmen that a course of object and phenomena study in works is not to be reckoned a matter of mere business sequence, but a large and equal feature of that curriculum which is essential to a degree of professional graduation.

2. A diffusion, among the class which we have termed the "practical" class, of a real appreciation of an organized system of information and of the scientific method of making this information useful to all classes of men and noxious or unimportant to none; such a general explanation to that vast, preponderating class of workmen and of foremen and managers who are foremen and managers simply because they have been efficient workmen, as will ever prevent their indiscriminate and contemptuous application of the term "theory" to whatever a schoolman proposes.

3. An understanding among the owners,

directors, and commercial managers of engineering enterprises that it is not a matter of favor but a matter of as much interest to themselves as to any class that young men of suitable ability and of suitable preliminary culture, however acquired, should have opportunity and encouragement to master the practical feature of technical education in works, not as mere apprentices but under reasonable facilities for economy of time and completeness of research.

But these conditions do not largely exist and are only growing with general civilization. They must be hastened and magnified by some better means than merely stating the case again and again, as some of us, I confess, are too fond of doing, perpetually repeating, in a manner more sentimental than efficient, that scientists should appreciate practice, and practicians should appreciate science, and capital should join the hands of science and practice, saying, "Bless you, my children," in the expectation that this will prove a fruitful union. Let us rather inquire if some new order of procedure in *technical education,* some revolutionary innovation, if need be, will not put the coming race of engineers on a plane which is lifted above the embarrassments from which we are slowly emerging.

First, in order that the technical school should be in the highest degree useful, fruitful, and economical, it must instruct, not *men* of good general education but *artisans* of good general education. The art must precede the science. The man must first feel the necessity and know the direction of a larger knowledge, and then he will master it through and through. . . .

Undoubtedly, there may be extremes in any form of educational method. For a youth to begin the special business of technical education by any method, practical or otherwise, before he has acquired not only a common-school education, but, at least, such a knowledge of polite literature and general science, including, of course, mathe-matics, as would fit him to enter one of the classical universities, should be strongly discouraged for various reasons. It is useless to disguise the fact that the want, not of high scholarship but of liberal and general education, is today the greatest of all the embarrassments which the majority of existing engineering experts and managers encounter. This statement cannot be deemed uncomplimentary to the class, seeing that they have risen to power despite the embarrassment. At the present day, the high-school systems founded by states and by private enterprise bring such an education within the reach of everyone; and it seems of the first importance to promote, if not almost to create, a public opinion that liberal and general culture is as high an element of success in engineering as it is in any profession or calling. . . .

It may be urged in favor of beginning in the technical school rather than in the works that mental capacity for the after acquisition and application of facts and principles is thus developed. But mental training is not the product of the technical school alone. Habits of logical thinking and power of analysis and generalization may be acquired in any school. And a positive objection to beginning with the technical school is that it cannot stop at logical methods and sciences which are essentially abstract. It also attempts to teach about objects and phenomena, the first knowledge of which, if it is to be broad and genuine, must come from the fountainhead.

These considerations may be further illustrated by the course of the inexpert graduate when he enters work as a matter of business or of study. We have seen that the practical man can, at least, keep the wheels running and the fires burning; and that when he is of a certain grade of ability and ambition, he will most rapidly acquire the scientific knowledge and culture which, joined to his practical judgment, make him a master. The unpracticed graduate, however, can keep neither wheels turning nor fires burning — he has not even the capacity of a conservator. Nor can he for a long time recognize, in the whirl and heat of full-sized practice, the course and movement of those forces about which his abstract knowledge may be profound. The youngest apprentices are more useful in an emergency. He must begin with the lowest manual processes, not indeed to become simply dexterous but, as it were, to learn the alphabet of a new language. He has started in the middle of his course instead of at the beginning. He must go back before he can advance, while the practician goes straight on.

The knowledge of the schoolman about physical science, however often he may have visited works and mines and engines during school excursions, is essentially abstract; it no more stimulates desire and power of practical research than the calculus creates a passion or a capacity for studying the actual work of steam in an engine or the actual endurance of a truss in a bridge.

The disappointment of inexpert graduates at finding themselves so far from being experts, their inability ofttimes to pay for further schooling, the necessity that they should now begin to earn money, as they had persuaded themselves they could so readily do upon graduation, discourage many from pursuing engineering and what is worse, send many out into practice, who never do complete their technical education, but who, by the character of their work, lower the professional standard.

It can hardly be urged against the precedence of practical culture that the student will get "out of practice" while he is in the school. He may indeed lose dexterity, but not the better fruits of experience. In fact, those who begin as practicians almost instinctively keep up their intimacy with the current practice.

A most signal advantage of beginning technical education in the works is that the mind is brought into early and intimate consideration of those great elements of success which cannot be imparted in any other way — the management of labor and the general principles of economy in construction, maintenance, and working. An early knowledge of these subjects molds the whole character of subsequent education and practice. There seems to be no corresponding advantage in beginning with the technical school. The fundamental mathematics and general information on physical science may be acquired in the preliminary school.

There is little doubt that the managers of technical schools will favor this order of study. They want to graduate not half-educated men but experts. They desire of all qualifications in the student that enthusiasm which can only spring from a well-defined want of specific knowledge.

Second, but the *order* of education is not the only desirable change. Whether before or after their course in the school, the hundreds of young men who are every year entering engineering pursuits are wasting their time in bad methods of practical study, or, if after the school course, they are more frequently doing bad work as engineers, when they should still be only students. While the teaching of general facts and principles and of scientific method is highly developed, there is no organized system for guiding students to direct knowledge of objects and phenomena. . . .

The only alternative is to establish organized schools in the various existing engineering works. At first, this idea would seem subversive of all discipline and economy, but I am assured by experts in several branches of engineering that such would not be the case. Let us take, for example, a Bessemer works. A score of students under the discipline, as well as under the technical guidance, of a master could be distributed among its various departments, not only without detriment but with some immediate advantage to the owner; for while receiving no pay, they would become skillful, at least as soon as the common laborers who form the usual reinforcement. Students should, of course, be expected not to work when and in what manner they might choose, but to do good and full work during specific hours. This responsibility, as workmen, would rapidly impart not only the knowledge sought in the works but a desire for higher knowledge and culture. . . .

It should thus appear that these somewhat radical changes in the curriculum of engineering study — first, a hand-to-hand knowledge, acquired not desultorily but by an organized system; and, afterward, the investigation of abstract and general facts and their relations — would largely economize the student's time and better the quality of his knowledge. The novice is nearly as valuable a student in works as the graduate, but he is a vastly less apt scholar in the school. My own belief, founded on the study of many typical cases, is that this order of procedure would produce a better class of experts in little more than half the time required by the reverse order; that it would always make *experts*; that it would discourage none from finishing an engineering education which would be complete in its parts, even if insufficient time were taken to fully develop it. A well-balanced culture will naturally grow in scope and in fruitfulness.

83.

Work Songs

Work songs are among the most popular forms of American folk music. They come from all professions and occupations. In the decade after the Civil War, the buffalo herds were still thick, and a government bounty on hides brought hunters to swarm over the plains. Buffalo hunters (the first song reprinted here describes their life) were generally shunned; according to a cowboy saying, "if them buffalo hunters don't kill ye for money, they'll kill ye for meanness." "Drill, Ye Tarriers, Drill!" was a stage song first, but it came to stand for the work of the railroader and was adopted into folk music because of its theme. In the East, much of the work was done in factories, and by women. Their loathing of the New England textile mills is expressed in "Factory Girl."

Source: Allen.

🎵 BUFFALO SKINNERS

'Twas in the town of Jacksboro in the spring of seventy-three,
A man by the name of Crego came stepping up to me,
Saying, "How do you do, young fellow, and how would you like to go
And spend the summer pleasantly on the range of the buffalo?"

And me not having any job, to old Crego I did say,
"This going out on the buffalo range depends upon the pay.
But if you will pay good wages, give transportation too,
I think that I will go with you to the range of the buffalo."

"Yes, I will pay good wages, give transportation too,
Provided you will go with me and stay the summer through;
But if you should grow homesick, come back to Jacksboro,
I won't pay transportation from the range of the buffalo."

Our meat it was of buffalo hump, like iron was our bread,
And all we had to sleep on was a buffalo for a bed;
The fleas and gray-backs worked on us, and boys, they were not slow;
I tell you there's no worse hell on earth than the range of the buffalo.

Our hearts were cased with buffalo hocks, our souls were cased with steel;
The hardships of that summer would nearly make us reel.
While skinning the damned old stinkers, our lives they had no show,
For the Indians waited to pick us off on the hills of Mexico.

The season being over, old Crego he did say
The crowd had been extravagant, was in debt to him that day.
We coaxed him and we begged him and still it was no go —
We left old Crego's bones to bleach on the range of the buffalo.

It's now we've crossed Pease River and homeward we are bound.
No more in that hell-fired country shall ever we be found —
Go home to our wives and sweethearts, tell others not to go —
For God's forsaken the buffalo range and the damned old buffalo.

DRILL, YE TARRIERS, DRILL!

Well, every morning at seven o'clock
There were twenty tarriers a-workin' at the rock,
And the boss comes around and he says "Kape still!
And come down heavy on the cast iron drill,
And drill, ye tarriers, drill!"

Chorus:
Drill, ye tarriers, drill!
For its work all day for sugar in your tay,
Down behind of the railway and,
Drill, ye tarriers, drill!
  And blast!
  And fire!

Now the foreman he was Jim McCann,
By God he was a blame mean man;
Last week a premature blast went off
And a mile in the air went big Jim Goff,
And drill, ye tarriers, drill!

The next time pay day comes around
Jim Goff a dollar short was found;
When he asked, "What for?" came this reply:
"You're docked for the time you was up in the sky,
And drill, ye tarriers, drill!"

The boss was a fine man down to the ground,
And he married a lady six feet 'round;
She baked good bread and she baked it well,
But she baked it hard as the holes of hell,
And drill, ye tarriers, drill!

FACTORY GIRL

No more shall I work in the fact'ry,
Greasy up my clothes;
No more shall I work in the fact'ry
With splinters in my toes.

No more shall I hear the bosses say,
"Boys, you'd better daulf,"
No more shall I hear those bosses say,
"Spinners, you'd better clean off."

No more shall I hear the drummer wheels
A-rolling over my head,
When factories are hard at work,
I'll be in my bed.

No more shall I hear the whistle blow,
To call me up so soon;
No more shall I hear the whistle blow,
To call me from my home.

No more shall I see the super come,
All dressed up so proud;
For I know I'll marry a country boy
Before the year is out.

No more shall I wear the old black dress,
Greasy all around;
No more shall I wear the old black bonnet
With holes all in the crown.

Chorus:
Pity me my darling,
Pity me, I say;
Pity me my darling,
And carry me away.

1877

84.

On Permitting Women to Preach

The Methodist, Unitarian, and Universalist churches all had women preachers by 1877, but unlike the other two bodies, the Methodist Church refused to ordain or license women in the ministry. Opposition to such ordination could be heard, as in the following debate, reported in the Syracuse (New York) Sunday Morning Courier *of March 4, 1877. The Miss Oliver quoted in the text appealed to the General Conference of the Methodist Episcopal Church in session at Cincinnati in May 1880, saying: "I am so thoroughly convinced that the Lord has laid commands upon me in this direction, that it becomes with me a question of my own soul's salvation." The Council denied her appeal in a resolution stating that "women have already all the rights and privileges in the Methodist Church that are good for them."*

Source: *History of Woman Suffrage*, Elizabeth C. Stanton *et al.*, eds., New York, 1881, Vol. I, pp. 784-785.

THE SUBJECT OF PERMITTING WOMEN TO preach in Methodist pulpits was incidentally, but rather racily, discussed at the Methodist ministers' meeting in New York City a few days since. A Miss Oliver, a more or less reverend lady, had been invited to preach to the ministers at their next meeting, and the question was raised, by what authority she was invited? Thereupon Brother Buckley took the floor and gave expression to his dissent in the following terms:

"I am opposed to inviting any woman to preach before this meeting. If the mother of our Lord were on earth, I should oppose her preaching here. *Sensation and murmurs of disapproval.* Oh, I do not mind that. I like at the beginning of a speech to find that there are two sides to my question. There is no power in the Methodist Church by which a woman can be licensed to preach; this is history, this is the report made at the last General Conference. It is, therefore, not legal for any quarterly conference to license a woman to preach, nevertheless here is a woman who claims to have such a license, and we are asked to invite her to preach."

A Brother: We have the right!

Brother Buckley: Oh, you have the right to believe the moon is made of green cheese, but yet have no right to commit the ministers of this city on an unsettled Church question. *Laughter and applause.* The tendency of men — now here is a chance to hiss — the tendency of men to endeavor to force female preachers on the Church and the desire to run after female preachers is, as Dr. Finney said to the students at Oberlin, an aberration of amativeness. *Roars of laughter and applause.* When men are [more] moved by women than by men under the same circumstances, it is certainly due to an aberration of amativeness. *Applause and more laughter.* For some time the male and female students at Oberlin used to have their prayer meetings together, but after a time they divided, and the young men complained to Dr. Finney that the Holy Ghost no longer came with equal force. Dr. Finney said this showed amativeness, or that the men were backsliding. *Applause.*

Brother Dickinson: As to the talk of ama-tiveness, what about our holiness meetings and seaside meetings, where we go to hear woman and to be moved by her words and her personality? *Applause.* Why are there so many women in the Church? It must be amativeness which urges them to go and hear men preach. *Laughter.*

Dr. Roach: If this meeting has any dignity, has any Christian intelligence, has any weight of character, it ought not to take this action. *Laughter.* What wildness, what fanaticism, what strange freaks will we not take on next? *Laughter and applause.*

Brother McAllister and others took part in the discussion, and finally, amid cries of "Motion," "Question," points of order, and the utmost confusion, the question was put, and the meeting refused to invite Miss Oliver to preach by a vote of 46 to 38. The result was received with ejaculations of "Amen" and "Thank God" and "God bless Brother Buckley." The Chair announced that Brother Kittrell will preach next Monday on "Entire Satisfaction," and the meeting adjourned.

———◆———

I can retire to private life with the consciousness that I shall receive from posterity the credit of having been elected to the highest position in the gift of the people, without any of the cares and responsibilities of the office.

SAMUEL TILDEN, when informed that though he had won the popular vote over Hayes he would not be President, 1877. The votes of the Electoral Commission were in favor of Hayes, and no one wished to fight another Civil War over the question.

85.

Morrison R. Waite and Stephen J. Field: *Munn* v. *Illinois*

This case, like the Slaughter-House cases of 1873, arose from a conflict between the "police power" of the states and the rights of business. At issue were the prices charged by a Chicago grain elevator combine, Munn and Scott, for storing and handling grain — prices that were in excess of the maximum allowed by Illinois law. Upon their conviction under the statute, certain members of the firm, relying on Justice Field's dissent in the Slaughter-House cases, appealed on the grounds that the price-fixing legislation violated the Fourteenth Amendment and deprived them of their property without due process of law. The Court's opinion of 1877, written by Chief Justice Waite, upheld the conviction, but it did not focus on the issue of private property alone; it argued, rather, that private property, if sufficiently involved with the public interest, should be subject to public control. However, Justice Field's dissent, in which he argued that mere procedural due process was inadequate protection for property rights, became the Court's prevailing view in later decisions involving the regulatory power of the states. Portions of the opinion of Chief Justice Waite and of the dissent by Justice Field are reprinted below.

Source: 94 U.S. 113.

Mr. Chief Justice Waite: When one becomes a member of society, he necessarily parts with some rights or privileges which, as an individual not affected by his relations to others, he might retain. "A body politic," as aptly defined in the preamble of the constitution of Massachusetts, "is a social compact by which the whole people covenants with each citizen, and each citizen with the whole people, that all shall be governed by certain laws for the common good." This does not confer power upon the whole people to control rights which are purely and exclusively private . . . but it does authorize the establishment of laws requiring each citizen to so conduct himself and so use his own property as not unnecessarily to injure another.

This is the very essence of government and has found expression in the maxim *sic utere tuo ut alienum non laedas.* From this source come the police powers, which, as

was said by Mr. Chief Justice Taney in the *License Cases* . . . "are nothing more or less than the powers of government inherent in every sovereignty . . . that is to say . . . the power to govern men and things." Under these powers the government regulates the conduct of its citizens one toward another and the manner in which each shall use his own property, when such regulation becomes necessary for the public good. . . .

From this it is apparent that, down to the time of the adoption of the 14th Amendment, it was not supposed that statutes regulating the use, or even the price of the use, of private property necessarily deprived an owner of his property without due process of law. Under some circumstances they may, but not under all. The amendment does not change the law in this particular; it simply prevents the states from doing that which will operate as such a deprivation. . . .

Chief Justice Morrison R. Waite

It remains only to ascertain whether the warehouses of these plaintiffs in error and the business which is carried on there come within the operation of this principle. . . .

We also are not permitted to overlook the fact that, for some reason, the people of Illinois, when they revised their constitution in 1870, saw fit to make it the duty of the General Assembly to pass laws "for the protection of producers, shippers, and receivers of grain and produce " . . . and . . . to require all railroad companies receiving and transporting grain in bulk or otherwise to deliver the same at any elevator to which it might be consigned, that could be reached by any track that was or could be used by such company; and that all railroad companies should permit connections to be made with their tracks so that any public warehouse, etc., might be reached by the cars on their railroads. This indicates very clearly that during the twenty years in which this peculiar business had been assuming its present "immense proportions," something had occurred which led the whole body of the people to suppose that remedies such as are usually employed to prevent abuses by virtual monopolies might not be inappropriate here.

For our purposes we must assume that, if a state of facts could exist that would justify such legislation, it actually did exist when the statute now under consideration was passed. For us the question is one of power, not of expediency. If no state of circumstances could exist to justify such a statute, then we may declare this one void, because in excess of the legislative power of the state. But if it could, we must presume it did. Of the propriety of legislative interference within the scope of legislative power, the legislature is the exclusive judge.

Neither is it a matter of any moment that no precedent can be found for a statute precisely like this. It is conceded that the business is one of recent origin, that its growth has been rapid, and that it is already of great importance. And it must also be conceded that it is a business in which the whole public has a direct and positive interest. It presents, therefore, a case for the application of a long-known and well-established principle in social science, and this statute simply extends the law so as to meet this new development of commercial progress. There is no attempt to compel these owners to grant the public an interest in their property but to declare their obligations if they use it in this particular manner.

It matters not in this case that these plaintiffs in error had built their warehouses and established their business before the regulations complained of were adopted. What they did was from the beginning subject to the power of the body politic to require them to conform to such regulations as might be established by the proper authorities for the common good. They entered upon their business and provided themselves with the means to carry it on subject to this condition. If they did not wish to submit themselves to such interference, they should not have clothed the public with an interest in their concerns. . . .

It is insisted, however, that the owner of property is entitled to a reasonable compensation for its use, even though it be clothed with a public interest, and that what is reasonable is a judicial and not a legislative question. . . . The practice has been otherwise. In countries where the common law prevails, it has been customary from time immemorial for the legislature to declare what shall be a reasonable compensation under such circumstances, or, perhaps more properly speaking, to fix a maximum beyond which any charge made would be unreasonable. Undoubtedly, in mere private contracts relating to matters in which the public has no interest, what is reasonable must be ascertained judicially. But this is because the legislature has no control over such a contract.

So, too, in matters which do affect the public interest and as to which legislative control may be exercised, if there are no statutory regulations upon the subject, the courts must determine what is reasonable. The controlling fact is the power to regulate at all. If that exists, the right to establish the maximum of charge, as one of the means of regulation, is implied. In fact, the common-law rule which requires the charge to be reasonable is itself a regulation as to price. Without it the owner could make his rates at will and compel the public to yield to his terms or forgo the use. . . .

We know that this is a power which may be abused; but that is no argument against its existence. For protection against abuses by legislatures the people must resort to the polls, not to the courts. . . .

We come now to consider the effect upon this statute of the power of Congress to regulate commerce.

It was very properly said in the case of the *State Tax on Railway Gross Receipts*, that "it is not everything that affects commerce that amounts to a regulation of it within the meaning of the Constitution." The warehouses of these plaintiffs in error are situated and their business carried on exclusively within the limits of the state of Illinois. They are used as instruments by those engaged in state as well as those engaged in interstate commerce, but they are no more necessarily a part of commerce itself than the dray or the cart by which, but for them, grain would be transferred from one railroad station to another. Incidentally, they may become connected with interstate commerce, but not necessarily so.

Their regulation is a thing of domestic concern, and, certainly, until Congress acts in reference to their interstate relations, the state may exercise all the powers of government over them, even though in so doing it may indirectly operate upon commerce outside its immediate jurisdiction. We do not say that a case may not arise in which it will be found that a state, under the form of regulating its own affairs, has encroached upon the exclusive domain of Congress in respect to interstate commerce, but we do say that, upon the facts as they are represented to us in this record, that has not been done.

Mr. Justice Field: The question presented . . . is one of the greatest importance — whether it is within the competency of a state to fix the compensation which an individual may receive for the use of his own property in his private business and for his services in connection with it.

The declaration of the constitution of 1870, that private buildings used for private purposes shall be deemed public institutions, does not make them so. The receipt and storage of grain in a building erected by private means for that purpose does not constitute the building a public warehouse. There is no magic in the language, though used by a constitutional convention, which can change a private business into a public one or alter the character of the building in

Chicago Board of Trade
Portrait of Ira Y. Munn

which the business is transacted. A tailor's or a shoemaker's shop would still retain its private character even though the assembled wisdom of the state should declare, by organic act or legislative ordinance, that such a place was a public workshop and that the workmen were public tailors or public shoemakers.

One might as well attempt to change the nature of colors by giving them a new designation. The defendants were no more public warehousemen, as justly observed by counsel, than the merchant who sells his merchandise to the public is a public merchant, or the blacksmith who shoes horses for the public is a public blacksmith; and it was a strange notion that by calling them so they would be brought under legislative control.

The Supreme Court of the state — divided, it is true, by three to two of its members — has held that this legislation was a legitimate exercise of state authority over private business; and the Supreme Court of the United States, two only of its members

dissenting, has decided that there is nothing in the Constitution of the United States or its recent amendments which impugns its validity. It is, therefore, with diffidence I presume to question the soundness of the decision.

The validity of the legislation was, among other grounds, assailed in the state court as being in conflict with that provision of the state constitution which declares that no person shall be deprived of life, liberty, or property without due process of law, and with that provision of the 14th Amendment of the federal Constitution which imposes a similar restriction upon the action of the state. The state court held, in substance, that the constitutional provision was not violated so long as the owner was not deprived of the title and possession of his property; and that it did not deny to the legislature the power to make all needful rules and regulations respecting the use and enjoyment of the property, referring, in support of the position, to instances of its action in prescribing the interest on money, in establishing and regulating public ferries and public mills, and fixing the compensation in the shape of tolls, and in delegating power to municipal bodies to regulate the charges of hackmen and draymen and the weight and price of bread.

In this court the legislation was also assailed on the same ground, our jurisdiction arising upon the clause of the 14th Amendment ordaining that no state shall deprive any person of life, liberty, or property without due process of law. But it would seem from its opinion that the court holds that property loses something of its private character when employed in such a way as to be generally useful. The doctrine declared is that property "becomes clothed with a public interest when used in a manner to make it of public consequence, and affect the community at large"; and from such clothing the right of the legislature is deduced to control the use of the property, and to determine the compensation which the owner may receive for it.

When Sir Matthew Hale and the sages of the law in his day spoke of property as affected by a public interest and ceasing from that cause to be *juris privati* solely, that is, ceasing to be held merely in private right, they referred to property dedicated by the owner to public uses, or to property the use of which was granted by the government, or in connection with which special privileges were conferred. Unless the property was thus dedicated, or some right bestowed by the government was held with the property, either by specific grant or by prescription of so long a time as to imply a grant originally, the property was not affected by any public interest so as to be taken out of the category of property held in private right.

But it is not in any such sense that the terms "clothing property with a public interest" are used in this case. From the nature of the business under consideration — the storage of grain — which, in any sense in which the words can be used, is a private business in which the public are interested only as they are interested in the storage of other products of the soil or in articles of manufacture, it is clear that the court intended to declare that, whenever one devotes his property to a business which is useful to the public — "affects the community at large" — the legislature can regulate the compensation which the owner may receive for its use and for his own services in connection with it.

"When, therefore," says the court, "one devotes his property to a use in which the public has an interest, he, in effect, grants to the public an interest in that use and must submit to be controlled by the public for the common good, to the extent of the interest he has thus created. He may withdraw his grant by discontinuing the use; but, so long as he maintains the use, he must submit to the control." The building

used by the defendants was for the storage of grain; in such storage, says the court, the public has an interest; therefore the defendants, by devoting the building to that storage, have granted the public an interest in that use and must submit to have their compensation regulated by the legislature.

If this be sound law, if there be no protection, either in the principles upon which our republican government is founded or in the prohibitions of the Constitution against such invasion of private rights, all property and all business in the state are held at the mercy of a majority of its legislature. The public has no greater interest in the use of buildings for the storage of grain than it has in the use of buildings for the residences of families, nor, indeed, anything like so great an interest; and, according to the doctrine announced, the legislature may fix the rent of all tenements used for residences without reference to the cost of their erection. If the owner does not like the rates prescribed, he may cease renting his houses. He has granted to the public, says the court, an interest in the use of the buildings, and "he may withdraw his grant by discontinuing the use; but, so long as he maintains the use, he must submit to the control."

The public is interested in the manufacture of cotton, woolen, and silken fabrics, in the construction of machinery, in the printing and publication of books and periodicals, and in the making of utensils of every variety, useful and ornamental; indeed, there is hardly an enterprise or business engaging the attention and labor of any considerable portion of the community in which the public has not an interest in the sense in which that term is used by the court in its opinion; and the doctrine which allows the legislature to interfere with and regulate the charges which the owners of property thus employed shall make for its use, that is, the rates at which all these different kinds of business shall be carried on, has never before been asserted, so far as I am aware, by any judicial tribunal in the United States.

The doctrine of the state court that no one is deprived of his property, within the meaning of the constitutional inhibition, so long as he retains its title and possession, and the doctrine of this court that whenever one's property is used in such a manner as to affect the community at large, it becomes by that fact clothed with a public interest and ceases to be *juris privati* only, appear to me to destroy, for all useful purposes, the efficacy of the constitutional guaranty. All that is beneficial in property arises from its use, and the fruits of that use; and whatever deprives a person of them deprives him of all that is desirable or valuable in the title and possession.

If the constitutional guaranty extends no further than to prevent a deprivation of title and possession and allows a deprivation of use and the fruits of that use, it does not merit the encomiums it has received. Unless I have misread the history of the provision now incorporated into all our state constitutions, and by the 5th and 14th Amendments into our federal Constitution, and have misunderstood the interpretation it has received, it is not thus limited in its scope and thus impotent for good. It has a much more extended operation than either court, state or federal, has given to it.

The provision, it is to be observed, places property under the same protection as life and liberty. Except by due process of law, no state can deprive any person of either. The provision has been supposed to secure to every individual the essential conditions for the pursuit of happiness; and for that reason has not been heretofore, and should never be, construed in any narrow or restricted sense. . . .

The same liberal construction which is required for the protection of life and liberty, in all particulars in which life and liberty are of any value, should be applied to the protection of private property. If the legisla-ture of a state, under pretense of providing for the public good, or for any other reason, can determine, against the consent of the owner, the uses to which private property shall be devoted, or the prices which the owner shall receive for its uses, it can deprive him of the property as completely as by a special act for its confiscation or destruction.

If, for instance, the owner is prohibited from using his building for the purposes for which it was designed, it is of little consequence that he is permitted to retain the title and possession; or, if he is compelled to take as compensation for its use less than the expenses to which he is subjected by its ownership, he is, for all practical purposes, deprived of the property, as effectually as if the legislature had ordered his forcible dispossession. If it be admitted that the legislature has any control over the compensation, the extent of that compensation becomes a mere matter of legislative discretion.

The amount fixed will operate as a partial destruction of the value of the property if it fall below the amount which the owner would obtain by contract, and, practically, as a complete destruction if it be less than the cost of retaining its possession. There is, indeed, no protection of any value under the constitutional provision which does not extend to the use and income of the property, as well as to its title and possession. . . .

It is true that the legislation which secures to all protection in their rights, and the equal use and enjoyment of their property, embraces an almost infinite variety of subjects. Whatever affects the peace, good order, morals, and health of the community comes within its scope; and everyone must use and enjoy his property subject to the restrictions which such legislation imposes. What is termed the police power of the state, which, from the language often used respecting it, one would suppose to be an undefined and irresponsible element in government, can only interfere with the conduct of individuals in their intercourse with each other and in the use of their property, so far as may be required to secure these objects. The compensation which the owners of property, not having any special rights or privileges from the government in connection with it, may demand for its use, or for their own services in union with it, forms no element of consideration in prescribing regulations for that purpose. . . .

Indeed, there is no end of regulations with respect to the use of property which may not be legitimately prescribed, having for their object the peace, good order, safety, and health of the community, thus securing to all the equal enjoyment of their property; but in establishing these regulations it is evident that compensation to the owner for the use of his property, or for his services in union with it, is not a matter of any importance. Whether it be one sum or another does not affect the regulation, either in respect to its utility or mode of enforcement.

86.

BRIGHAM YOUNG: Riches of the Desert

From the beginning the Mormons aroused bitterness and hatred among the people with whom they settled. From 1833 until July 1847, when Brigham Young settled the Mormons in Salt Lake City, they were constantly persecuted and driven from their lands. Once secure in their new settlement, Young, echoing many a founder in our history, declared: "The only fear I have is that we will not do right; if we do we will be like a city set on a hill, our light will not be hid." When Young died in the summer of 1877, the Mormons had been in Utah for thirty years. The text, reprinted below, in which Young reflects on the accomplishments of his people in making the desert bloom, is not a single discourse but a compilation of paragraphs from many discourses written over several years. The conflicting dates are owing to this arrangement.

Source: *Discourses of Brigham Young*, John A. Widtsoe, ed., Salt Lake City, 1925, pp. 738-743.

SEVEN YEARS AGO TOMORROW, about 11 o'clock, I crossed the Mississippi River with my brethren for this place, not knowing, at that time, whither we were going, but firmly believing that the Lord had in reserve for us a good place in the mountains, and that He would lead us directly to it. It is but seven years since we left Nauvoo, and we are now ready to build another temple. I look back upon our labors with pleasure.

Here are hundreds and thousands of people that have not had the privileges that some of us have had. Do you ask, what privileges? Why, of running the gauntlet, of passing through the narrows. They have not had the privilege of being robbed and plundered of their property, of being in the midst of mobs and death, as many of us have.

When the pioneers came into these valleys, we knew nearly all the families which composed the settlements in Upper and Lower California.

The most of the people called Latter-day Saints have been taken from the rural and manufacturing districts of this and the old countries, and they belonged to the poorest of the poor. Many of them, I may say the great majority, never had anything around them to make life very desirable; they have been acquainted with poverty and wretchedness, hence it cannot be expected that they should manifest that refinement and culture prevalent among the rich. Many and many a man here, who is now able to ride in his wagon and perhaps in his carriage, for years before he started for Zion never saw daylight. His days were spent in the coal mines, and his daily toil would commence before light in the morning and continue until after dark at night.

Now, what can be expected from a community, so many of whose members have been brought up like this, or, if not just like this, still under circumstances of poverty and privation? Certainly not what we might expect from those reared under more favorable circumstances. But I will tell you what we have in our mind's eye with regard to these very people and what we are trying to make of them.

We take the poorest we can find on earth who will receive the truth, and we are trying to make ladies and gentlemen of them. We are trying to educate them, to school their children, and to so train them that they may be able to gather around them the comforts of life that they may pass their lives as the human family should do — that their days, weeks, and months may be pleasant to them. We prove that this is our design, for the result, to some extent, is already before us.

Talk about these rich valleys, why there is not another people on the earth that could have come here and lived. We prayed over the land and dedicated it and the water, air, and everything pertaining to them

unto the Lord; and the smiles of Heaven rested on the land, and it became productive and today yields us the best of grain, fruit, and vegetables.

There never has been a land, from the days of Adam until now, that has been blessed more than this land has been blessed by our Father in Heaven; and it will still be blessed more and more, if we are faithful and humble and thankful to God for the wheat and the corn, the oats, the fruit, the vegetables, the cattle, and everything He bestows upon us, and try to use them for the building up of His kingdom on the earth.

You inquire if we shall stay in these mountains. I answer, yes, as long as we please to do the will of God, our Father in Heaven. If we are pleased to turn away from the holy commandments of the Lord Jesus Christ, as ancient Israel did, every man turning to his own way, we shall be scattered and peeled, driven before our enemies and persecuted, until we learn to remember the Lord our God and are willing to walk in His ways.

Many may inquire, "How long shall we stay here?" We shall stay here just as long as we ought to. "Shall we be driven, when we go?" If we will so live as to be satisfied with ourselves and will not drive ourselves from our homes, we shall never be driven from them. Seek for the best wisdom you can obtain, learn how to apply your labor, build good houses, make fine farms, set out apple, pear, and other fruit trees that will flourish here, also the mountain currant and raspberry bushes, plant strawberry beds, and build up and adorn a beautiful city.

The question now arises — "Do you think it best for us to live in cities?" Lay out your cities, but not so large that you cannot readily raze the whole city should an enemy come upon you.

I do not know that I have prayed for rain since I have been in these valleys, until this year, during which I believe that I have prayed two or three times for rain, and then with a faint heart, for there is plenty of water flowing down these canyons in crystal streams as pure as the breezes of Zion, and it is our business to use them.

When water is brought to the termination of the canal, which we can accomplish in a few days, I presume that the reservoirs on the line of the work and those portions which are excavated in full will contain water enough to allow the people to irrigate when necessary and thus do away with the practice of watering only two hours a week on a city lot, and much of that to be done in the night. And that is not all, for by the time the water is fairly on a lot it is taken by the next person whose right it is to use it. And lots which have had thousands of dollars expended on them, and which would yield more than $1,000 worth of fruit and vegetables, could they be properly irrigated, are only allowed a small stream of water for two hours once a week; and, at the same time, an adjoining lot planted with corn, the hills six feet apart and one stalk in a hill, comparatively speaking, the balance of the ground being covered with weeds, is allotted the same time and amount of water as the one on which the fruit trees and other choice vegetation are worth thousands of dollars.

There ought to be a reformation in the distribution of the water. The man who will not raise $5 worth of produce on his lot has the same water privilege as the man who could raise $1,000 worth. For instance, brother Staines gets the water for two hours in a week, and what are his fruit trees worth? He could make his $1,000 a year from them, if he were disposed to sell the fruit instead of giving it away, could he have a fair portion of water. I have a lot just below him well-cultivated in fruit trees, a nursery, and choice vegetables; I also can only have the water on my lot for two hours in a week; when lots nearby, with but little on them except weeds, get the same water privilege, and that too in the daytime,

while we have to use it in the night. Water masters ought to look to this matter until they have arranged a more just distribution.

The River Jordan will be brought out and made to flow through a substantial canal to Great Salt Lake City. When this is done, it will not only serve as a means of irrigating but it will form a means of transportation from the south end of Utah Lake to Great Salt Lake City. As soon as that is completed from Big Cottonwood to this city, we expect to make a canal on the west side of Jordan and take its water along the east base of the west mountains, as there is more farming land on the west side of that river than on the east. When that work is accomplished we shall continue our exertions until Provo River runs to this city. We intend to bring it around the point of the mountain to Little Cottonwood, from that to Big Cottonwood, and lead its waters upon all the land from Provo Canyon to this city, for there is more water runs in that stream alone than would be needed for that purpose.

Until the Latter-day Saints came here, not a person among all the mountaineers and those who had traveled here, so far as we could learn, believed that an ear of corn would ripen in these valleys. We know that corn and wheat produce abundantly here, and we know that we have an excellent region wherein to raise cattle, horses, and every other kind of domestic animal that we need. We also knew this when we came here thirteen years ago this summer. Bridger said to me, "Mr. Young, I would give $1,000 if I knew that an ear of corn could be ripened in these mountains. I have been here twenty years and have tried it in vain, over and over again." I told him if he would wait a year or two we would show him what could be done. A man named Wells, living with Miles Goodyear, where now is Ogden City, had a few beans growing and carried water from the river in a pail to irrigate them.

87.

EDWIN R. MEADE: Chinese Immigration to the United States

Chinese immigration to the United States increased steadily during the second half of the nineteenth century, encouraged by American businessmen who found the "coolies" ideal laborers: neat, patient workers, indifferent to union organizers. The American working class, however, did not appreciate competition from the Chinese laborers and expressed its aversion by means of resolutions in Massachusetts (1870) and riots in California (1871 and 1877). In the following address, delivered September 7, 1877, before the Social Science Association of America, Congressman Edwin Meade of New York proposed limiting immigration of Asians as a solution to the "coolie question."

Source: *Chinese Immigration; Its Social, Moral, and Political Effect*, Sacramento, 1878, pp. 293-302.

THE TOTAL CHINESE POPULATION of California at present is fairly estimated at from 150,000 to 200,000 and, in San Francisco, fluctuating from 30,000 to 60,000, according to the season for labor in the country. These coolies are chiefly males, between the ages of twenty and forty years. The coolie women arriving in this country are for the most part prostitutes and number about 4,000. The Page Bill, so-called, prohibiting the importation of women for immoral purposes, passed by the 43rd Congress, together with the adverse sentiment of the Chinese merchants in this country, substantially preclude further arrivals of this class. During the year ending June . . . 1876, only 259 females were landed, and, since that time, their coming has practically ceased. There are now here about 100 respectable Chinese families, all of whom belong to the merchant class, and the children in the country number from 3,000 to 4,000, of which above 2,000 are in San Francisco.

These statistics plainly indicate the nature and extent of the great wave of coolie immigration which is with so great confidence predicted. China is the most densely settled country on the globe, and with its outlying and tributary provinces comprises something over 500 million population, or about one-third of the world's mankind. It is largely overpopulated, especially with the labor element, and, considering the shortness of the time its ports have been open, its people have proved themselves the most migratory of any nation. They are already to be found in nearly every country on the earth and in this country have pitched a residence in every considerable town. Their passage to this country varies in expense per capita from $12 to $400.

They follow the great lines of travel, thus making their way to our Eastern Seaboard as fast as means and opportunities permit. New York City now contains about 2,000 coolies, while opium dens and a joss house already mark the eastward march of their peculiar civilization. In the Pacific states, Australia, Luzon, Java, Straits Settlements, Borneo, Peru, Cuba, and British Guiana, the coolie face and dress have become as familiar as those of the white laborer. From their Asiatic hive they still come pouring forth, and it is fair to presume will increase in volume as the advantages offered by the outside world in wages and liberal government become better known, accelerated, too, by the famines, internal wars, and pestilence which so frequently devastate their own country.

The term "coolie," however, does not imply a condition of servitude, as various public accounts, including the platforms of both political parties in 1876 would indicate. This popular error arose from the traffic formerly carried on by the Portuguese from the Ports of Macao and Swatow with Peru and Cuba, which had all the worst features of the African slave trade. Coolie women are, it is true, bought and sold for purposes of prostitution, but the men are free and their immigration entirely voluntary. All Chinese bound for this country take passage at the English port of Hongkong and come from the districts adjacent to Kwontong (or Canton). All accounts of contracts binding these coolies to conditions of servitude are incorrect, as to either the American or English immigrants; nor are they at this day permitted anywhere, though some irritation continues between the Spanish and Chinese governments by reason of the treatment of coolies in Spanish colonies, whose contract services have not yet expired or are perhaps forcibly continued.

The position of the Chinese six companies . . . has been misunderstood to be that of contractors for coolie labor. They possess some of the features of employment agencies, as known in our large cities, but nothing worse. They advance no money to immigrants and usually have no act or part in their coming here. They are organized in accordance with the various dialects spoken by these immigrants, and their offices are places for the registering of new arrivals, especially those desiring work. Besides this, they act as arbitrators between white employers and coolies and between the coolies themselves. It is not shown that they usurp any of the functions of government, and

there is reason to believe they are, in their way, as proper and beneficial as any of our employment agencies or boards of exchange, to which they bear much resemblance.

It does not simplify the question or render it less serious to know that the coolie comes to our shores voluntarily. As a slave, or one held under conditions of servitude, he would be subject to ordinary methods of legislation, and public sentiment would scarcely be divided respecting him; but, as now presented, he becomes a question of desirability, and the proper course at issue to prevent his further introduction becomes a very serious problem.

As suggested, he comes here as a laborer. He personifies the character in its absolutely menial aspect — what the operation of fifty centuries of paganism, poverty, and oppression have made him — a mere animal machine, performing the duties in his accepted sphere, punctually and patiently, but utterly incapable of any improvement; and in this aspect of the question the most serious phase of the problem is presented.

The qualities of coolie labor mentioned, and the fact that it can be secured in any desired amount and discharged without controversy, renders it especially attractive to capitalists and contractors. African slave labor presented to some extent the same features, but in a marked degree coolie labor is cheaper and therefore competitive with white labor. . . .

Recent disturbances in regard to labor show the importance of this aspect of the question and irresistibly awaken the conviction that cheap labor is not desirable in this country; and whatever folly there may be in the idea of establishing a minimum of wages by the government, it may properly withdraw encouragement from cheap labor even at the expense of dividends on diluted capital, as represented in watered stock. We require liberal wages to meet high tariffs, high taxes, and heavy charges of transportation. Coolie labor means to white labor starvation, almshouses, prisons filled, and, lastly, capital wasting itself. Liberal wages and white labor mean prosperity for all classes and progress in the ways of Christian civilization. All fancied advantages which have followed the introduction of coolies in this country disappear before the prospects to which their future in this country would invite us.

The coolie deserves the most serious consideration, and a more extended one than these limits admit. He invites the same antagonism of race which even now wars for supremacy on the banks of the Danube, as it has for centuries past, and which manifests itself wherever they come in contact. The Mongol entertains a feeling of profound contempt for other civilizations. Founded as our society is upon the Christian religion, he for that reason alone thoroughly rejects it. . . .

A republican or even liberal government of any form is to them quite incomprehensible. Government to their minds is a despotic power, in which they have no lot or part except unqualified obedience. If sufficiently intelligent, they point to the duration, the extent, and the achievements of the Celestial Empire and contrast them with our own country of a hundred years only of existence. Their superstitions, prejudices, and opinions have become as fixed as their habits of life, and their observations only disclose the apparent defects, contradictions, and inconsistencies in our government and religion, which to their minds is radical evidence of their general character. . . .

If he seems to conform to our ways, it is only to get a better foothold for money-making. He professes friendship, of which sentiment he has not the remotest conception. He is cruel and unrelenting, only waiting the opportunity in which he may safely strike the object of his spite, cupidity, or superstition. . . .

The people on the Pacific Coast describe the coolie as devoid of conscience. He has evidently never made sufficient use of one

to cause it to be a prominent element of his character, or, at least, he manifests it after a different manner from ourselves. He has no respect for our form of oath; and no other form has been devised which reaches his mythical conscience or makes him tell the truth further than he regards it for his interest so to do. This was quite the uniform testimony; and Police Judge Louderback, a man of great moderation and excellent judgment, testified that, in his opinion, in respect "to honesty and reliability, the Chinese (meaning coolies) were the lowest in the scale of humanity." . . .

But that we are bound to receive this alien influx is, I fancy, a piece of sentimentalism, which will not be accepted. Our social nature repels the idea, and our political system revolts at the reception of such a strange, unamalgamating, unassimilating, unnatural element. Of different planes, possessing widely divergent characteristics, we but invite the irrepressible conflict of races by recognizing for the time the equality of this Asiatic invasion. We boast that the Anglo-Saxon conquers or absorbs but never recognizes equality in other races; but we cannot overlook the fact that the Chinese nation has lasted from the dawn of centuries; that its government and people have witnessed the birth, decay, and dissolution of the greatest empires and republics that have existed; and that they now confront us upon the shores of the Pacific with a host which, by force of numbers alone, is able to convert this broad land into a Chinese colony, and the valley of the Mississippi a new battlefield of the races.

To accord the coolies only an inferior social position conflicts both with their and our own ideas; and since we have recognized the political equality of the Negro, we are, by that, if for no other reason, well-nigh estopped from denying the same privileges to the yellow man. Just now, however, by our laws, citizenship is denied him. The laws of the United States do not admit of the naturalization of Mongolians. A brief allusion to the statutes will relieve this branch of the subject of some obscurity.

By the act of 1804, naturalization was confined to aliens, being free white persons, and so the law stood until 1871, when it was amended by adding "aliens of African nativity and persons of African descent." Upon the adoption of the Revised Statutes in 1873, the words "aliens being free white persons" were altogether omitted, and thereby it was claimed that naturalization was restricted to aliens of African nativity or descent. This omission of free white persons is alleged to have been a clerical error, but a construction became necessary which allowed the naturalization of all aliens, including persons of African nativity and descent; and, so as to give the statute a restrictive sense, Congress, in 1875, and for the purpose it is said of excluding Mongolians, restored the omitted words, so that now our naturalization laws apply to aliens being free white persons and aliens of African nativity, and to persons of African descent. Citizenship can therefore only benefit Chinese actually born in this country. A few hundred children have been born here, but that small number will eventually form the nucleus for a sentiment in favor of Mongol naturalization, and the absurdity of existing laws may be some day proved by the immigration of Mongols born in African colonies, who, thereby, being persons of African nativity, will be entitled to American citizenship.

The assertion that Chinese will not bring their families here is abundantly refuted in the exceptions which already exist, and also is an error the further statement that they do not desire citizenship. In conversation with their more intelligent people, they distinctly stated their desire to become citizens, which has doubtless been increased by observing the influence which their natural enemy, the "hoodlum," possesses, and as a protection from his indignities. The Chinese are, moreover, subjected to all the taxation of whites and, in instances, taxes discriminating against them. To be sure their taxable property, especially real estate, is comparatively small, but we must recognize the principle which extends the privilege of suffrage to all who bear taxation, unless we propose to erect a caste in our midst. Indeed the arguments are so strong in favor of citizenship, if we allow unrestricted immigration, that common justice, even if disguising the partisan seeking mere party ends, will succeed in making our naturalization laws, at least, as liberal toward the Chinaman as the wild African fresh from his native jungles.

It is true that ethnologists declare that a brain capacity of less than eighty-five inches is unfit for free government, which is considerably above that of the coolie as it is below the Caucasian, but, whatever its merits, the statement will scarce stand in the way of either the demands of a justice recognized in the case of the Negro or where party advantages demand the concession. These coolies are, as mentioned, generally made up of males of voting age. Their number is already sufficient, if voters acting together, to now control the politics of the Pacific states, and there is good reason to believe that they would thus act, and under direction of their headmen.

The inference would seem, therefore, irresistible that the coolie, if permitted to immigrate here, must be received as an equal factor in our social policy and system, including the elective franchise, or else we must turn back the hands on the dial plate and reestablish a caste approaching servitude. The latter, I believe, utterly inadmissible, as, I believe, the former fraught with evils to our race and civilization, the like of which have not been chronicled in all the broad pages of the history of man.

An embarrassment in the way of a proper treatment of this subject is our generally declared policy in favor of unrestricted immigration and the right of self-expatriation. The error in this respect lies in classing this exceptional and peculiar people along with those of other countries and the white race; but, however much at variance with such a policy, we cannot afford to hesitate in the application of necessary measures to prevent this hurtful immigration. To accomplish this, without disturbing our valuable and growing commercial relations with the Chinese empire, requires careful consideration. For this purpose alone the treaty-making branch of government is preferable to Congress. Many of the alleged difficulties in the way disappear upon investigation.

For instance, we find that the influential Chinese in this country favor either prohibition or a large restriction of coolie immigration, and such a course the Chinese merchants in San Francisco have, on several occasions, advised. This they are led to do by way of accommodating public sentiment, in which they concur, and because of the disadvantages to prosperous relations between the two countries if this irritating cause be not removed before it shall have been become firmly established. The Chinese national policy is also opposed to the emigration of its subjects. "To stay at home and mind their own business, and let other people do the same" has for centuries been the maxim of Chinese statesmen and sages, and the edicts against emigration have never been repealed, notwithstanding their repugnance to the provisions of their treaties with "the barbarians," as they are wont to style us. It is not unlikely, however, that a discrimination by us against their people, and without the assent of the Pekin government, would be received with disfavor and result in counteraction on the part of the Chinese.

The Burlingame Treaty recognizes in broad terms the right of the citizens of both countries to migrate, and guarantees the protection of the respective nations to citizens of the other, either in regard to trade, travel, or residence. If the Pekin government insists upon holding us to this bargain, our friendly relations and business interests may be preserved by recourse to that cooperative system through which the relations of foreign nations with China are in a large degree regulated. Already, in various English colonies, especially Queensland and other provinces of the proposed Australian federation, coolie immigration has become almost unendurable, the opposition to it there even exceeding that on the Pacific Coast.

The English government, as well as ourselves, must meet the question face to face, and neither of the other great powers can be presumed to have any serious objection to a restrictive or even prohibitive policy. Cooperation, too, is the more desirable, because in a simple modification of the Burlingame Treaty we would not possibly be able to cover the vessels of other nations bringing coolies here, nor would we exclude that indirect immigration which is liable to reach us from the overstocked British colonies and the islands of the Pacific.

These suggestions are only made to show that the difficulty is not insurmountable, as some would have it.

Other modes for accomplishing the desired result doubtless exist. Whatever is done should be done without further delay; for delay will only fasten the evil of coolie population upon us. Chinese merchants, capitalists, and students, as well as those representing the Pekin government, deserve our kindest encouragement and protection. A Chinese embassy, soon to be permanently established here, and a Chinese consulship in San Francisco will tend to a better understanding of the character of that remarkable people and the resources of their country, while a professorship of Chinese literature, just established by one of our leading colleges, will explain the mysteries of its philosophy, science, and art; but the dignity of American labor and citizenship, and the welfare and renown of the white race, and an elevated and Christian civilization, alike, demand the exclusion of coolie immigrants.

1878

88.

The Knights of Labor

The traditional premium placed upon craftsmanship in handwork was rapidly supplanted during the Industrial Revolution by new demands for efficiency in mass production. Skilled workmen such as shoemakers, machinists, molders, coopers, garment workers, and cigar makers seemed most likely to be replaced by machines and were most amenable to the protection offered by trade unions. The Noble Order of the Knights of Labor, founded in 1869 by Uriah Stephens, enlisted the garment workers of Philadelphia into a common cause under the motto, "An injury to one is the concern of all." The Constitution of the Knights of Labor was written in 1874; the Preamble, reprinted below, drafted by Terence V. Powderly and Robert Schilling, was adopted January 3, 1878.

Source: Terence V. Powderly, *Thirty Years of Labor, 1859 to 1889*, Columbus, Ohio, 1889, pp. 243-245.

THE RECENT ALARMING DEVELOPMENT and aggression of aggregated wealth, which, unless checked, will invariably lead to the pauperization and hopeless degradation of the toiling masses, render it imperative, if we desire to enjoy the blessings of life, that a check should be placed upon its power and upon unjust accumulation, and a system adopted which will secure to the laborer the fruits of his toil. And as this much-desired object can only be accomplished by the thorough unification of labor and the united efforts of those who obey the divine injunction that "In the sweat of thy brow shalt thou eat bread," we have formed the ——— with a view of securing the organization and direction, by cooperative effort, of the power of the industrial classes; and we submit to the world the objects sought to be accomplished by our organization, calling upon all who believe in securing "the greatest good to the greatest number" to aid and assist us:

1. To bring within the folds of organization every department of productive industry, making knowledge a standpoint for action and industrial and moral worth, not wealth, the true standard of individual and national greatness.

2. To secure to the toilers a proper share of the wealth that they create; more of the leisure that rightfully belongs to them; more societary advantages; more of the benefits, privileges, and emoluments of the world; in a word, all those rights and privileges necessary to make them capable of en-

joying, appreciating, defending, and perpetuating the blessings of good government.

3. To arrive at the true condition of the producing masses in their educational, moral, and financial condition by demanding from the various governments the establishment of Bureaus of Labor Statistics.

4. The establishment of cooperative institutions, productive and distributive.

5. The reserving of the public lands — the heritage of the people — for the actual settler — not another acre for railroads or speculators.

6. The abrogation of all laws that do not bear equally upon capital and labor; the removal of unjust technicalities, delays, and discriminations in the administration of justice; and the adopting of measures providing for the health and safety of those engaged in mining, manufacturing, or building pursuits.

7. The enactment of laws to compel chartered corporations to pay their employees weekly, in full, for labor performed during the preceding week, in the lawful money of the country.

8. The enactment of laws giving mechanics and laborers a first lien on their work for their full wages.

9. The abolishment of the contract system on national, state, and municipal work.

10. The substitution of arbitration for strikes, whenever and wherever employers and employees are willing to meet on equitable grounds.

11. The prohibition of the employment of children in workshops, mines, and factories before attaining their fourteenth year.

12. To abolish the system of letting out by contract the labor of convicts in our prisons and reformatory institutions.

13. To secure for both sexes equal pay for equal work.

14. The reduction of the hours of labor to eight per day, so that the laborers may have more time for social enjoyment and intellectual improvement and be enabled to reap the advantages conferred by the labor-saving machinery which their brains have created.

15. To prevail upon governments to establish a purely national circulating medium, based upon the faith and resources of the nation and issued directly to the people, without the intervention of any system of banking corporations, which money shall be a legal tender in payment of all debts, public or private.

89.

WILLIAM GLADSTONE: A Comparison of American and British Institutions

William Gladstone, four times prime minister and the leading British statesman of the nineteenth century, retired to study and write for five years after the dissolution of his first cabinet in 1874. (He had once remarked that "public life is full of snares and dangers, and I think it a fearful thing for a Christian to look forward to closing his life in the midst of its . . . essentially fevered activity.") One of the works of this brief period, before British policies in the Middle East drew him back to active politics in 1879, was a comparative study of American and British political institutions. The following is an abridged version of the work.

Source: *North American Review*, September-October 1878: "Kin Beyond Sea."

IT IS NOW nearly half a century since the works of De Tocqueville and De Beaumont, founded upon personal observation, brought the institutions of the United States effectually within the circle of European thought and interest. They were cooperators but not upon an equal scale. De Beaumont belongs to the class of ordinary though able writers; De Tocqueville was the Burke of his age, and his treatise upon America may well be regarded as among the best books hitherto produced for the political student of all times and countries.

But higher and deeper than the concern of the Old World at large in the thirteen colonies, now grown into thirty-eight states, besides eight territories, is the special interest of England in their condition and prospects.

I do not speak of political controversies between them and us, which are happily, as I trust, at an end. I do not speak of the vast contribution which from year to year, through the operations of a colossal trade, each makes to the wealth and comfort of the other; nor of the friendly controversy, which in its own place it might be well to raise, between the leanings of America to protectionism and the more daring reliance of the Old Country upon free and unrestricted intercourse with all the world; nor of the menace which, in the prospective development of her resources, America offers to the commercial preeminence of England. On this subject I will only say that it is she alone who, at a coming time, can, and probably will, wrest from us that commercial primacy.

We have no title, I have no inclination, to murmur at the prospect. If she acquires it, she will make the acquisition by the right of the strongest; but, in this instance, the strongest means the best. She will probably become what we are now, the head servant in the great household of the world, the employer of all employed, because her service will be the most and ablest. We have no more title against her than Venice, or Genoa, or Holland has had against us. One great duty is entailed upon us, which we unfortunately neglect — the duty of preparing, by a resolute and sturdy effort, to reduce our public burdens in preparation for a day when we shall probably have less capacity than we have now to bear them.

Passing by all these subjects with their varied attractions, I come to another which lies within the tranquil domain of political philosophy. The students of the future, in this department, will have much to say in the way of comparison between American and British institutions. The relationship between these two is unique in history. It is always interesting to trace and to compare constitutions as it is to compare languages; especially in such instances as those of the Greek states and the Italian republics, or the diversified forms of the feudal system in the different countries of Europe. But there is no parallel in all the records of the world to the case of that prolific British mother who has sent forth her innumerable children over all the earth to be the founders of half a dozen empires. She, with her progeny, may almost claim to constitute a kind of universal church in politics.

But among these children, there is one whose place in the world's eye and in history is superlative: it is the American republic. She is the eldest born. She has, taking the capacity of her land into view as well as its mere measurement, a natural base for the greatest continuous empire ever established by man. And it may be well here to mention what has not always been sufficiently observed, that the distinction between continuous empire and empire severed and dispersed over sea is vital. The development which the republic has effected has been unexampled in its rapidity and force. While other countries have doubled, or at most trebled, their population, she has risen, during one single century of freedom, in round numbers, from 2 million to 45 million.

As to riches, it is reasonable to establish, from the decennial stages of the progress thus far achieved, a series for the future; and, reckoning upon this basis, I suppose that the very next census, in the year 1880, will exhibit her to the world as certainly the wealthiest of all the nations. The huge figure of £1 billion, which may be taken roundly as the annual income of the United Kingdom, has been reached at a surprising rate; a rate which may perhaps be best expressed by saying that, if we had started forty or fifty years ago from zero, at the rate of our recent annual increment we should now have reached our present position. But while we have been advancing with this portentous rapidity, America is passing us by in a canter. Yet even now the work of searching the soil and the bowels of the territory, and opening out her enterprise throughout its vast expanse, is in its infancy.

The England and the America of the present day are probably the two strongest nations of the world. But there can hardly be a doubt as between the America and the England of the future, that the daughter, at some no very distant time, will, whether fairer or less fair, be unquestionably yet stronger than the mother — "O matre forti filia fortior."

But all this pompous detail of material triumphs, whether for the one or for the other, is worse than idle unless the men of the two countries shall remain, or shall become, greater than the mere things that they produce and shall know how to regard those things simply as tools and materials for the attainments of the highest purposes of their being. Ascending then, from the ground floor of material industry toward the regions in which these purposes are to be wrought out, it is for each nation to consider how far its institutions have reached a state in which they can contribute their maximum to the store of human happiness and excellence. And for the political student all over the world, it will be beyond anything curious as well as useful to examine with what diversities, as well as what resemblances, of apparatus the two greater branches of a race born to command have been minded, or induced, or constrained, to work out in their sea-severed seats their political destinies according to their respective laws.

No higher ambition can find vent in a paper such as this than to suggest the position and claims of the subject and slightly to indicate a few outlines, or at least fragments, of the working material.

In many and the most fundamental respects, the two still carry in undiminished, perhaps in increasing, clearness the notes of resemblance that beseem a parent and a child. Both wish for self-government; and however grave the drawbacks under which in one or both it exists, the two have, among the great nations of the world, made the most effectual advances toward the true aim of rational politics.

They are similarly associated in their fixed idea that the force in which all government takes effect is to be constantly backed and, as it were, illuminated, by thought in speech and writing. The ruler of St. Paul's time "bare the sword" (Rom. 13:4). Bare it, as the apostle says, with a mission to do right; but he says nothing of any duty or any custom to show by reason that he was doing right. Our two governments, whatsoever they do, have to give reasons for it; not reasons which will convince the unreasonable but reasons which, on the whole, will convince the average mind and carry it unitedly forward in a course of action, often though not always wise, and bearing within itself provisions, where it is unwise, for the correction of its own unwisdom before it grow to an intolerable rankness. They are governments, not of force only but of persuasion.

Many more are the concords, and not less vital than these, of the two nations as expressed in their institutions. They alike prefer the practical to the abstract. They tolerate opinion, with only a reserve on behalf of decency; and they desire to confine coercion to the province of action and to leave thought, as such, entirely free. They set a high value on liberty for its own sake. They desire to give full scope to the principles of self-reliance in the people, and they deem self-help to be immeasurably superior to

help in any other form — to be the only help, in short, which ought not to be continually or periodically put upon its trial and required to make good its title.

They mistrust and mislike the centralization of power; and they cherish municipal, local, even parochial liberties, as nursery grounds, not only for the production here and there of able men but for the general training of public virtue and independent spirit. They regard publicity as the vital air of politics, through which alone, in its freest circulation, opinions can be thrown into common stock for the good of all and the balance of relative rights and claims can be habitually and peaceably adjusted. It would be difficult, in the case of any other pair of nations, to present an assemblage of traits at once so common and so distinctive as has been given in this probably imperfect enumeration.

There were, however, the strongest reasons why America could not grow into a reflection or repetition of England. Passing from a narrow island to a continent almost without bounds, the colonists at once and vitally altered their conditions of thought, as well as of existence, in relation to the most important and most operative of all social facts, the possession of the soil. In England, inequality lies imbedded in the very base of the social structure; in America, it is a late, incidental, unrecognized product, not of tradition but of industry and wealth, as they advance with various and, of necessity, unequal steps. Heredity, seated as an idea in the heart's core of Englishmen and sustaining far more than it is sustained by those of our institutions which express it, was as truly absent from the intellectual and moral store with which the colonists traversed the Atlantic as if it had been some forgotten article in the bills of lading that made up their cargoes.

Equality combined with liberty and renewable at each descent from one generation to another, like a lease with stipulated breaks, was the groundwork of their social creed. In vain was it sought by arrangements such as those concocted with the name of Baltimore or of Penn to qualify the action of those overpowering forces which so determined the case. Slavery itself, strange as it now must seem, failed to impair the theory, however it may have imported into the practice a hideous solecism. No hardier republicanism was generated in New England than in the slave states of the South, which produced so many of the great statesmen of America.

It may be said that the North and not the South had the larger number of colonists and was the center of those commanding moral influences which gave to the country as a whole its political and moral atmosphere. The type and form of manhood for America was supplied neither by the Recusant in Maryland nor by the Cavalier in Virginia but by the Puritan of New England; and it would have been a form and type widely different could the colonization have taken place a couple of centuries, or a single century, sooner. Neither the Tudor nor even the Plantagenet period could have supplied its special form. The Reformation was a cardinal factor in its production; and this in more ways than one. . . .

One whose life has been greatly absorbed in working with others, the institutions of his own country has not had the opportunities necessary for the careful and searching scrutiny of institutions elsewhere. I should feel, in looking at those of America, like one who attempts to scan the stars with the naked eye. My notices can only be few, faint, and superficial; they are but an introduction to what I have to say of my own country. A few sentences will dispose of them.

America, whose attitude toward England has always been masculine and real, has no longer to anticipate at our hands the frivolous and offensive criticisms which were once in vogue among us. But neither nation prefers (and it would be an ill sign if either did prefer) the institutions of the other; and we certainly do not contemplate the great republic in the spirit of mere optimism. We see that it has a marvelous and unexampled adaptation for its peculiar vocation; that it must be judged, not in the abstract but under the foreordered laws of its existence; that it has purged away the blot with which we brought it into the world; that it bravely and vigorously grapples with the problem of making a continent into a state; and that it treasures with fondness the traditions of British antiquity, which are in truth unconditionally its own as well and as much as they are ours.

The thing that perhaps chiefly puzzles the inhabitants of the Old Country is why the American people should permit their entire existence to be continually disturbed by the business of the presidential elections; and, still more, why they should raise to its maximum the intensity of this perturbation by providing, as we are told, for what is termed a clean sweep of the entire civil service, in all its ranks and departments, on each accession of a chief magistrate. We do not perceive why this arrangement is more rational than would be a corresponding usage in this country on each change of Ministry. Our practice is as different as possible. We limit to a few scores of persons the removals and appointments on these occasions; although our Ministries seem to us, not unfrequently, to be more sharply severed from one another in principle and tendency, than are the successive Presidents of the great Union.

It would be out of place to discuss in this article occasional phenomena of local corruption in the United States, by which the nation at large can hardly be touched; or the mysterious manipulations of votes for the presidency, which are now understood to be under examination; or the very curious influences which are shaping the politics of the Negroes and of the South. These last are corollaries to the great slave question; and it seems very possible that after a few years we may see most of the laborers, both in the Southern states and in England, actively addicted to the political support of that section of their countrymen who to the last had resisted their emancipation.

But if there be those in this country who think that American democracy means public levity and intemperance, or a lack of skill and sagacity in politics, or the absence of self-command and self-denial, let them bear in mind a few of the most salient and recent facts of history, which may profitably be recommended to their reflections. We emancipated 1 million Negroes by peaceful legislation; America liberated 4 or 5 million by a bloody civil war; yet the industry and exports of the Southern states are maintained, while those of our Negro colonies have dwindled; the South enjoys all its franchises, but we have, *proh pudor!* found no better method of providing for peace and order in Jamaica, the chief of our islands, than by the hard and vulgar, even where needful, expedient of abolishing entirely its representative institutions.

The Civil War compelled the states, both North and South, to train and embody 1,500,000 men and to present to view the greatest, instead of the smallest, armed forces in the world. Here there was supposed to arise a double danger. First, that, on a sudden cessation of the war, military life and habits could not be shaken off, and having become rudely and widely predominant would bias the country toward an aggressive policy or still worse, would find vent in predatory or revolutionary operations. Second, that a military caste would grow up with its habits of exclusiveness and command and would influence the tone of politics in a direction adverse to republican freedom.

But both apprehensions proved to be wholly imaginary. The innumerable soldiery was at once dissolved. Cincinnatus, no longer a unique example, became the commonplace of every day, the type and mold of a nation. The whole enormous mass quietly

resumed the habits of social life. The generals of yesterday were the editors, the secretaries, and the solicitors of today. The just jealousy of the state gave life to the now-forgotten maxim of Judge Blackstone, who denounced as perilous the erection of a separate profession of arms in a free country. The standing army, expanded by the heat of civil contest to gigantic dimensions, settled down again into the framework of a miniature with the returning temperature of civil life and became a power well-nigh invisible, from its minuteness, amid the powers which sway the movements of a society exceeding 40 million.

More remarkable still was the financial sequel to the great conflict. The internal taxation for federal purposes, which before its commencement had been unknown, was raised in obedience to an exigency of life and death so as to exceed every present and every past example. It pursued and worried all the transactions of life. The interest of the American debt grew to be the highest in the world, and the capital touched £560 million. Here was provided for the faith and patience of the people a touchstone of extreme severity.

In England, at the close of the great French war, the propertied classes, who were supreme in Parliament, at once rebelled against the Tory government and refused to prolong the income tax even for a single year. We talked big, both then and now, about the payment of our national debt; but sixty-three years have now elapsed, all of them except two called years of peace, and we have reduced the huge total by about one-ninth; that is to say, by little over £100 million, or scarcely more than £1,500,00 a year. This is the conduct of a state elaborately digested into orders and degrees, famed for wisdom and forethought, and consolidated by a long experience.

But America continued long to bear, on her unaccustomed and still smarting shoulders, the burden of the war taxation. In twelve years she has reduced her debt by £158 million, or at the rate of £13 million for every year. In each twelve months she has done what we did in eight years; her self-command, self-denial, and wise forethought for the future have been, to say the least, eightfold ours. These are facts which redound greatly to her honor; and the historian will record with surprise that an enfranchised nation tolerated burdens which in this country a selected class, possessed of the representation, did not dare to face, and that the most unmitigated democracy known to the annals of the world resolutely reduced at its own cost prospective liabilities of the state, which the aristocratic, and plutocratic, and monarchical government of the United Kingdom has been contented ignobly to hand over to posterity. And such facts should be told out. It is our fashion so to tell them, against as well as for ourselves; and the record of them may some day be among the means of stirring us up to a policy more worthy of the name and fame of England.

It is true, indeed, that we lie under some heavy and, I fear, increasing disadvantages, which amount almost to disabilities. Not, however, any disadvantage respecting power as power is commonly understood. But while America has a nearly homogeneous country and an admirable division of political labor between the states individually and the federal government, we are, in public affairs, an overcharged and overweighted people. . . .

The main and central point of interest, however, in the institutions of a country is the manner in which it draws together and compounds the public forces in the balanced action of the state. It seems plain that the formal arrangements for this purpose in America are very different from ours. It may even be a question whether they are not, in certain respects, less popular; whether our institutions do not give more rapid effect than those of the Union to any

formed opinion and resolved intention of the nation.

In the formation of the federal government we seem to perceive three stages of distinct advancement: (1) the formation of the Confederation under the pressure of the War of Independence; (2) the Constitution, which placed the federal government in defined and direct relation with the people inhabiting the several states; (3) the struggle with the South, which, for the first time, and definitely, decided that to the Union, through its federal organization and not to the state governments, were reserved all the questions not decided and disposed of by the express provisions of the Constitution itself. The great *arcanum imperii*, which with us belongs to the three branches of the legislature and which is expressed by the current phrase, "omnipotence of Parliament," thus became the acknowledged property of the three branches of the federal legislature; and the old and respectable doctrine of state independence is now no more than an archaeological relic, a piece of historical antiquarianism.

Yet the actual attributions of the state authorities cover by far the largest part of the province of government; and by this division of labor and authority, the problem of fixing for the nation a political center of gravity is divested of a large part of its difficulty and danger, in some proportion to the limitations of the working precinct. Within that precinct the initiation, as well as the final sanction in the great business of finance, is made over to the popular branch of the legislature, and a most interesting question arises upon the comparative merits of this arrangement and of our own method, which theoretically throws upon the Crown the responsibility of initiating public charge, and under which, until a recent period, our practice was in actual and even close correspondence with this theory.

We next come to a difference still more marked. The federal executive is born anew of the nation at the end of each four years and dies at the end. But during the course of those years it is independent, in the person both of the President and of his ministers, alike of the people, of their representatives, and of that remarkable body, the most remarkable of all the inventions of modern politics, the Senate of the United States. In this important matter, whatever be the relative excellences and defects of the British and American systems, it is most certain that nothing would induce the people of this country, or even the Tory portion of them, to exchange our own for theirs. . . .

The power of the American executive resides in the person of the actual President and passes from him to his successor. His ministers, grouped around him, are the servants not only of his office but of his mind. The intelligence which carries on the government has its main seat in him. The responsibility of failures is understood to fall on him; and it is round his head that success sheds its halo.

90.

"Here Rattler Here"

"Here Rattler Here" tells the story of the escape from a Southern prison camp of a man named Riley, who hears that his woman has died. Riley tells his friends that, if the captain asks if he is running, they should say that he is flying; if the captain asks if he is laughing, they should say that he is crying. Riley makes his escape, pursued by a posse and the dog Rattler, who could "trail you 'cross a live oak log." It has been contended that Riley was a real person, but in fact the song, with its terrifying refrain, has been found in many forms, some of which suggest that the original Riley might even have been a slave in antebellum times.

Source: *Negro Folk Music, U.S.A.*, Harold Courlander, ed., New York, 1963.

⚭ HERE RATTLER HERE

Why don't you here, Rattler, here,
Oh, don't you here, Rattler, here.
This Old Rattler was a walker dog,
Says he'll trail you 'cross a live oak log.
Says Old Rattler hit the man's trail,
Says he run and bit him on the heel,
And you oughta heard that man squeal.
You holler, here, here, Rattler,
Hollerin' here, here, Rattler.
Says Old Rattler was a walking dog,
He could trail you 'cross a live oak log.

Says the captain come a-riding,
Asking where is that sergeant,
Says I believe there's a man gone.
Says the sergeant come riding,
Popping his whip upon the ground,
And Old Rattler turning round and round.
He said here Old Rattler,
Says Old Rattler, here's a marrow bone,
You can eat it, you can leave it alone.
I don't want no marrow bone,
I just want the man that's long gone.
Says Old Rattler went skipping through the morning dew,
And Old Rattler went to skipping through the morning dew,
And the sergeant pop the whip upon the ground,
And Old Rattler begin to turn round and round.
He cried, here Old Rattler,
Crying, here Old Rattler.

Says Old Riley got worried,
He come running with a letter,
Says you ought to heard what that letter read.
Says Old Riley says that Irene's dead,
Say come home, pretty papa,
Yes, come home, pretty papa.
Says Old Riley he got worried,
Says to the captain that you was a-running,
You just tell him I was flying.
If he asks you was I laughing,
You can tell him I was crying.

And it's here, Old Rattler,
And it's here, Old Rattler,
And Old Rattler got to the Brazos,
Well he left him there a-howling.
Old Rattler hollered, oooh, ooh, ooh, ooh!
He hollered, ooh, ooh, ooh, ooh!
And I heard the sergeant blowing his horn,
Oughta heard that sergeant blowing his horn,
Blowed it doo, doo, doo, doo!
Blowed it oo, oo, oo, oo!
Says I believe he crossed the river,
Believe he crossed the big Brazos.
He gonna give up Old Riley,
Take another day back on the way.
I'm going to call Old Rattler,
Hollering here, Rattler, here,
Won't you here, Rattler, here, here,
Won't you here, Old Rattler.

1879

91.

EDWIN L. GODKIN: Communism in California

In 1878 a constitutional convention was called in California to remedy a number of problems that were unsettling the state. The issues causing public discontent were many: a confused system of land tenure and uncertain property titles going back to days of Mexican rule; the influx of Chinese immigrants; railroad monopoly and consequent high shipping rates; domination of the state legislature by the powerful railroad interests. The new constitution was completed in March 1879 and submitted for ratification. Because it incorporated compromise rather than radical solutions of several issues, it was attacked by many who would have preferred either a more extreme or a more moderate approach. One such attack came from Edwin L. Godkin, editor of the Nation, *who characterized the California constitution as a foolish and unfortunate departure from traditional American constitution making.*

Source: *Nation,* April 3, 1879: "A New Kind of State Constitution."

THE CONVENTION which has recently completed its work in California has reported a new constitution, which will be voted upon on the first Wednesday of May next. The work of the Convention deserves more than ordinary attention, because it is the result of a movement new in American politics. Hitherto, constitutional conventions have generally been in the hands of a very conservative class and usually have been controlled by lawyers. In California, the anti-Chinese party, combined with the Communists under Kearney, have exercised such an influence in politics during the past year or two that a powerful minority of the Convention was led by statesmen of the Kearney order. Antecedently, therefore, it might be expected that the new instrument would be somewhat unlike those drawn up for American states hitherto, and such is most certainly the fact.

A state constitution may be regarded as the most complete expression by an American community of its fundamental and permanent ideas of law and government. The constitutions of the Revolutionary and pre-Revolutionary period may be said, in a general way, to have consisted of three parts: first, provisions relating to the formal organization of the government; second, a definition of the powers of the three branches of the government; third, a few positive provisions for the protection of the person and property of the citizen, including habeas corpus, trial by jury, etc. These provisions, however, were not at all new but drawn directly from the same source from which the common law of the various states came — the English statute book.

Indeed, with regard to them, it would not be unfair to say, considering the supposed revolutionary origin of American constitutional law, that what is most remarkable about them is not their novelty but their antiquity, the great body of them having been taken from English statutes passed in the reigns of Charles II and James II, while some of the most important of them go back to the time of John. These safeguards of life, liberty, and the pursuit of happiness had already proved their value to so many generations of Englishmen and Americans that it was by no figure of speech that they were generally termed then, as they have ever since been, a common birthright.

In the hundred years which have elapsed since the Revolution, the spirit of constitution making in the various states has undergone several marked changes, which have attracted more or less attention and criticism. The first serious change, of course, was that which swept through all the states thirty years ago, and introduced universal suffrage and an elective judiciary. Whether this be regrettable or no, it is impossible to deny that the men who were responsible for the change sincerely believed in it. They were drawn, too, as a general thing, from a class competent to form an opinion on the basis of suffrage; and the conventions which incorporated the change into the fundamental law were guided by the same traditions and notions of the foundations on which society rests as their predecessors had been.

The next change in the spirit of constitution making which attracted notice was that

Library of Congress

Edwin L. Godkin, editor of the "Nation"

which made its appearance in several constitutions ten years or more ago — most noticeable, perhaps, in the constitution of Illinois of 1870 — in the direction of placing great restrictions upon the power of the legislature and upon the sovereign right through the legislature to incur debt. In the old constitutions the branch of the government which had been restricted in its functions was the executive. Almost all the grievances from which the American colonies had suffered in the last century (as may be seen from the long list of the "repeated injuries and usurpations" which are enumerated with each recurring Fourth of July by every village orator who is charged with the duty of reading the Declaration of Independence to his fellow townsmen) were laid by them at the door of the King, and consequently, in the old constitutions, the official who was most hedged about with definitions and restrictions was the governor. The purpose in view was entirely accomplished.

There has probably never been in the history of the world any executive who has made so few encroachments upon popular rights as the governor of the American state. But in carefully guarding these rights from encroachments in one quarter they had omitted to protect them from assaults in another; and it soon became clear that the legislature might become by means of special legislation, and its power of saddling the state with debts, quite as dangerous to popular government, although in a different way, as kings had been in their own. Consequently, in the later constitutions, of which the Illinois constitution is a type, the power of incurring indebtedness and of special legislation is limited in every way. These new safeguards have been found to work well, and in the states in which they have been longest in operation have improved the tone and character of legislation and strengthened the public credit.

A comparison of the earlier constitutions with those recently adopted, however, shows that in one important respect there has been a decline in the art of constitution making. The point to which we refer is this: In the older constitutions, as has been shown, the framers of the instrument were always careful to incorporate provisions affecting life, liberty, and property, which formed a fundamental part of the common laws of England and America; and the great advantage which was gained by incorporating them into a written constitution was that they were removed from the power of the legislature and made irrepealable except by constitutional amendment. They became part of a law which is superior to all mere legislative acts, and, in case of conflict, overrides them.

Of late years, however, it has become more and more common for demagogues to attempt to make use of constitutional conventions, just as the legislature is made use of every year, by getting them to adopt, for the purpose of appeasing some popular cry, a mass of heterogeneous provisions applicable to the law of persons and property, concocted on the spur of the moment and em-

bodying no fundamental economical or legal principle tested by the experience of generations, but forming a sort of popular pronunciamento on a half-understood subject, the actual effect of which the framers themselves cannot foresee. Illustrations of this tendency might be taken from several of the recent constitutions, but that just drawn up in California is the first one in which it has reached a dangerous climax.

The evils and abuses which the Convention undertook to cure and abate were, first, of course, the Chinese difficulty; second, a number of evils which are not peculiar to California, but have appeared in half the states of the Union within the past ten or twelve years, *e.g.,* the escape of large amounts of personal property from taxation, secret combinations by powerful corporations adverse to public interests, the delay of justice owing to the crowded calendars of the courts, excessive rates of toll or service by railroad, telegraph, and gas corporations, corruption in the legislature, gambling in shares of mining companies. When we examine the new constitution to see how the California Convention has dealt with these questions, we find that its most marked characteristic is that it contains some novel and ingenious provision with regard to each of them.

In the first place, it proposes to bring stock gambling to an end by giving to the legislature power to pass laws either to regulate "or *prohibit* the buying and selling of the shares of the capital stock of corporations in any stock board, stock exchange, or stock market under the control of any association." Excessive charges by gas and telegraph companies are brought to an end by directing the legislature to pass laws "for the regulation and limitation of the charges for services performed and commodities furnished" by such corporations. Even charges for "storage and wharfage" are provided for in a similar way, whether made by corporations or *individuals.* Section 35 of the same article brings the corruption of the legislature to an end by declaring "lobbying" (which is made to embrace the somewhat vague offense of seeking to influence the votes of legislators by "intimidation") a felony.

The judiciary article contains a section intended to prevent any further delay or denial of justice in California. It provides that no judge of either Supreme or Superior Court shall draw his monthly salary unless he make oath that no cause remains in his court undecided *which has been submitted for decision for the period of ninety days.* The labor question is disposed of by making eight hours a legal day's work on all public works. Finally, corporations "other than municipal" are handled without gloves. Stock watering is prevented by declaring any stock issued except for value of some kind received to be "void." For the regulation of railroads, a board of commissioners is created with a general power "to establish freight and passenger rates for all transportation companies"; anyone who charges more than the rate established is liable to a fine of $5,000 or imprisonment for a year.

Citizenship is, of course, restricted to natives or foreigners not of Mongolian blood, and corporations are prohibited from employing Chinese labor. The old provision that taxation shall be "equal and uniform" is struck out, apparently for the purpose of enabling the legislature to impose an income tax increasing with the income. As the new constitution does not prevent the imposition of taxes upon the principal as well, it looks as if the "money kings" of "Nob Hill," as Kearney calls them, would certainly catch it this time. Many of the sections directed against abuses by corporations are so worded as to be almost unintelligible. Railroad companies, for instance, are forbidden to make contracts with vessels plying to California ports, "by which the earnings of

one doing the carrying are to be shared by the other not doing the carrying." Whenever a railroad lowers its rates of transportation for the purpose of competing with another railroad, there is to be no increase of rates afterward without the consent of the government.

Such a farrago as this is a novelty in American constitutional law. Of course, it is not difficult to see that much of it will never have any lasting effect upon the social and legal machinery in California, because much of it cannot be carried into effect in any civilized country. Some of it will be explained away by the courts, some of it will be rendered null by the corruption of the officials who are elected to execute it. But as it stands it is not the constitution of a civilized state but of a civilized state, the management of whose affairs has partly fallen into the hands of barbarians. Instead of confining itself, with regard to the ordinary rights of person and property, to a simple declaration of those permanent and settled principles to which, as we have shown, the earlier constitutions always confined themselves, it has embodied in the fundamental law of the state a mass of heterogeneous and confused edicts, representing nothing more substantial than those gusts of popular passion which hitherto have spent themselves in primaries or in the election of party candidates, or at most in laws passed *subject* to overruling by the judicial interpretation of a constitution based on fixed principles.

That they should now have reached and so largely controlled the action of a constitutional convention is a bad sign. So far as such a constitution as that proposed in California fails of the evident objects of its authors, it tends to bring all laws and constitutions into contempt. So far as it succeeds, it marks the first incorporation into American constitutional law of pure communism.

92.

McGuffey's Lessons

For the better part of a century the McGuffey Readers were widely used in school systems across the country. One of the great "best sellers" of U.S. publishing history — more than 122 million copies were printed — the Readers owed their origin to William H. McGuffey and his brother Alexander, who brought out the first of them in 1836 and issued revised editions in each of the next twenty-one years. The underlying premise of the Readers was that education is primarily a moral and only secondarily an intellectual matter — witness the examples chosen in the following selection, which always have a small moral lesson to inculcate — but they also put great emphasis on the imitation of "good" linguistic models. Millions of children copied out sentences from the "best" authors, and, if they did not learn to think any better than their twentieth-century grandchildren, they at least learned to write the English language. Such at least is the theory of some modern educators, who have put the McGuffey Readers back into the elementary school curriculum in a few states. The following selection, dealing with two elements of "Elocution" traditionally called "Articulation" and "Gesture," is taken from the Sixth Reader, as revised in 1879.

Source: *McGuffey's Sixth Eclectic Reader*, Revised edition, Cincinnati, 1879.

THE SUBJECT OF ELOCUTION, so far as it is deemed applicable to a work of this kind, will be considered under the following heads, viz.:

1. ARTICULATION.
2. INFLECTION.
3. ACCENT AND EMPHASIS.
4. READING VERSE.
5. THE VOICE.
6. GESTURE.

I. ARTICULATION.

Articulation is the utterance of the elementary sounds of a language, and of their combinations.

As words consist of one or more elementary sounds, the first object of the student should be to acquire the power of uttering those sounds with *distinctness, smoothness,* and *force.* This result can be secured only by careful practice, which must be persevered in until the learner has acquired a perfect control of his organs of speech.

ELEMENTARY SOUNDS.

An elementary sound is a simple, distinct sound made by the organs of speech.

The elementary sounds of the English language are divided into *Vocals, Subvocals,* and *Aspirates.*

VOCALS.

Vocals are sounds which consist of pure tone only. They are the most prominent elements of all words, and it is proper that they should first receive attention. A vocal may be represented by one letter, as in the word *hat*, or by two or more letters, as in *heat, beauty*. A *diphthong* is a union of two vocals, commencing with one and ending with the other. It is usually represented by two letters, as in the words *oil, boy, out, now*.

Each of these can be uttered with great force, so as to give a distinct expression of its sound, although the voice be suddenly suspended, the moment the sound is produced. This is done by putting the lips, teeth, tongue, and palate in their proper position, and then expelling each sound from the throat in the same manner that the syllable "ah!" is uttered in endeavoring to deter a child from something it is about to do; thus, a'—a'—a'—.

Let the pupil be required to utter every one of the elements . . . with all possible suddenness and percussive force, until he is able to do it with ease and accuracy. This must not be considered as accomplished until he can give each sound with entire clearness, and with all the suddenness of the "crack" of a rifle. Care must be taken that the *vocal alone* be heard; there must be no consonantal sound, and no vocal sound other than the one intended.

At first, the elementary sounds may be repeated by the class in concert; then separately. . . .

SUBVOCALS AND ASPIRATES.

Subvocals are those sounds in which the vocalized breath is more or less obstructed.

Aspirates consist of breath only, modified by the vocal organs.

Words ending with subvocal sounds should be selected for practice on the subvocals; words beginning or ending with aspirate sounds may be used for practice on the aspirates. Pronounce these words forcibly and distinctly, several times in succession; then drop the other sounds, and repeat the subvocals and aspirates alone. Let the class repeat the words and elements, at first, in concert; then separately. . . .

FAULTS TO BE REMEDIED.

The most common faults of articulation are dropping an unaccented vowel, sounding incorrectly an unaccented vowel, suppressing final consonants, omitting or mispronouncing syllables, and blending words.

1. Dropping an unaccented vocal.

EXAMPLES.

Correct.	Incorrect.		Correct.	Incorrect.
Gran´a-ry	gran'ry.		a-ban´don	a-ban-d'n.
im-mor´tal	im-mor-t'l.		reg´u-lar	reg'lar.
in-clem´ent	in-clem'nt.		par-tic´u-lar	par-tic'lar.
des´ti-ny	des-t'ny.		cal-cu-la´tion	cal-cl'a-sh'n.
un-cer´tain	un-cer-t'n.		oc-ca´sion	oc-ca-sh'n.
em´i-nent	em'nent.		ef´fi-gy	ef'gy.
ag´o-ny	ag'ny.		man´i-fold	man'fold.
rev´er-ent	rev'rent.		cul´ti-vate	cult'vate.

2. Sounding incorrectly an unaccented vowel.

EXAMPLES.

Correct.	Incorrect.		Correct.	Incorrect.
Lam-en-ta´-tion	lam-*un*-ta-tion.		ter´ri-ble	ter-*rub*-ble.
e-ter´nal	e-ter-n*u*l.		fel´o-ny	fel-*er*-ny.
ob´sti-nate	ob-st*un*-it.		fel´low-ship	fel-*ler*-ship.
e-vent´	*uv*-ent.		cal´cu-late	cal-k*er*-late.
ef´fort	*uf*-fort.		reg´u-lar	reg-*gy*-l*ur*.

EXERCISES.

The vocals most likely to be dropped or incorrectly sounded are italicized.

He *a*ttended div*i*ne service reg*u*larly.
This is my p*a*rticular request.
She *is* un*i*versally *e*steemed.
George *is* sens*i*ble *o*f his fault.
This calc*u*lation *is* inc*o*rrect.
What a terr*i*ble calam*i*ty.
His eye through vast *i*mmens*i*ty c*a*n pierce.
*O*bserve these nice dep*e*ndencies.
He *is* form*i*dable adversary.
He *is* gen*e*rous to his friends.
A temp*e*st des*o*lated the land.
He pr*e*ferred death to serv*i*tude.
God *is* the auth*o*r *o*f all things vis*i*ble *a*nd invis*i*ble.

3. Suppressing the final subvocals or aspirates.

EXAMPLES.

John an' James are frien's o' my father.
Gi' me some bread.
The want o' men is occasioned by the want o' money.
We seldom fine' men o' principle to ac' thus.
Beas' an' creepin' things were foun' there.

EXERCISES.

He learn*ed* to write.
The mas*ts* of the ship were cas*t* down.
He entered the lis*ts* at the head of his troo*ps*.
He is the merries*t* fellow in existence.
I regard not the worl*d's* opinion.
He has three assistan*ts*.
The dep*ths* of the sea.
She trus*ts* too much to servan*ts*.
His attemp*ts* were fruitless.
He chanc*ed* to see a bee hovering over a flower.

4. Omitting or mispronouncing whole syllables.

EXAMPLES.

Lit′er-a-ry is *improperly pronounced* lit-rer-ry.
co-tem′po-ra-ry   ″   ″   co-tem-po-ry.
het-er-o-ge′ne-ous   ″   ″   het-ro-ge-nous.
in-quis-i-to′ri-al   ″   ″   in-quis-i-to-ral.
mis′er-a-ble   ″   ″   mis-rer-ble.
ac-com′pa-ni-ment   ″   ″   ac-comp-ner-ment.

EXERCISES.

He devoted his attention chiefly to lit*er*ary pursuits.
He is a mis*er*able creature.
His faults were owing to the degen*er*acy of the times.
The manuscript was undeciph*er*able.
His spirit was unconqu*er*able.
Great industry was nec*ess*ary for the performance of the task.

5. Blending the end of one word with the beginning of the next.

EXAMPLES.

I court thy gif *s*no more.
The grove *s*were God *s*fir *s*temples.
My hear *t*was a mirror, that show′ *d*every treasure.
It reflecte *d*each beautiful blosso *m*of pleasure.
Han *d*′me the slate.
This worl *d*is all a fleeting show,
    For man′ *s*illusion given.

EXERCISES.

The magistrate*s* ought to arrest the rogue*s* *s*peedily.
The whirlwind*s* *s*weep the plain.
Link*ed* to thy side, through every chan*ce* I go.
But ha*d* he seen a*n* actor i*n* our days enacting Shakespeare.
Wha*t* awful sound*s* assail my ears?
We caug*h*t a glimp*se* of her.
Old age ha*s* on their temple*s* *s*hed her silver frost.
Our eagle shall rise mid the whirlwind*s* of war,
    And dart through the dun clou*d* of battle hi*s* eye.
Then honor shall wea*ve* of the laurel a crown,
    That beauty shall bin*d* on the brow of the brave.

IV. INSTRUCTIONS FOR READING VERSE.

INFLECTIONS.

In reading verse, the inflections should be *nearly* the same as in reading prose; the chief difference is, that in poetry, the *monotone* and *rising inflection* are more frequently used than in prose. The greatest difficulty in reading this species of composition, consists in giving it that measured flow which distinguishes it from prose, without falling into a *chanting* pronunciation.

If, at any time, the reader is in doubt as to the proper inflection, let him reduce the passage to earnest conversation, and pronounce it in the most familiar and prosaic manner, and thus he will generally use the proper inflection.

EXERCISES IN INFLECTION.

1. Meanwhile the south wind rose, and with black wings
   Wide hovering´, all the clouds together drove
   From under heaven` : the hills to their supply´,
   Vapor and exhalation dusk and moist
   Sent up amain` : and now, the thickened sky
   Like a dark ceiling stood` : down rushed the rain
   Impetuous´, and continued till the earth
   No more was seen` : the floating vessel swam
   Uplifted´, and, secure with beakèd prow´,
   Rode tilting o'er the waves`.

2. My friend´, adown life's valley´, hand in hand´,
      With grateful change of grave and merry speech
      Or song´, our hearts unlocking each to each´,
   We'll journey onward to the silent land` ;
   And when stern death shall loose that loving band,
      Taking in his cold hand, a hand of ours´,
      The one shall strew the other's grave with flowers´,
   Nor shall his heart a moment be unmanned`.
   My friend and brother´! if thou goest first´,
      Wilt thou no more revisit me below´?
   Yea, when my heart seems happy causelessly´,
      And swells´, not dreaming why´, my soul shall know
   That thou´, unseen´, art bending over me`.

3. Here rests his head upon the lap of earth´,
      A youth, to fortune and to fame unknown` ;
   Fair Science frowned not on his humble birth´,
      And Melancholy marked him for her own`.

4. Large was his bounty´, and his soul sincere`,
      Heaven did a recompense as largely send` ;
   He gave to misery (all he had) a tear`,
      He gained from heaven´ ('t was all he wished´) a friend`.

5. No further seek his merits to disclose´,
   Or draw his frailties from their dread abode´;
   (There they alike´ in trembling hope repose´,)
   The bosom of his Father, and his God`.

ACCENT AND EMPHASIS.

In reading verse, every syllable must have the same accent, and every word the same emphasis as in prose; and whenever the *melody* or *music* of the verse would lead to an *incorrect* accent or emphasis, this must be disregarded.

If a poet has made his verse deficient in melody, this must not be remedied by the reader, at the expense of sense or the established rules of accent and quantity. Take the following:

EXAMPLE.

O'er shields, and helms, and helmèd heads he rode,
Of thrones, and mighty Seraphim pros*trate.*

According to the *metrical* accent, the last word must be pronounced "pros-*trate´* " But according to the authorized pronunciation it is "*pros´* trate." Which shall yield, the poet or established usage? Certainly not the latter.

Some writers advise a compromise of the matter, and that the word should be pronounced without accenting either syllable. Sometimes this may be done, but where it is not practised, the prosaic reading should be preserved.

In the following examples, the words and syllables which are *improperly accented* or *emphasized* in the poetry, are marked in *italics*. According to the principle stated above, the reader should avoid giving them that pronunciation which the correct reading of the *poetry* would require, but should read them as prose, except where he can throw off all accent and thus compromise the conflict between the poetic reading and the correct reading. That is, he must read the poetry *wrong,* in order to read the language *right.*

EXAMPLES.

1. Ask *of* thy mother earth why oaks are made
   Tal*ler* and stronger than the weeds they shade.

2. Their praise is still, "the style is excel*lent,*"
   The sense they humbly take upon content.

3. False elo*quence,* like *the* prismatic glass,
   Its fairy colors spreads on every place.

4. To do aught good, nev*er* will be our task,
   But ever *to* do ill is our sole delight.

5. Of all the causes which combine to blind
   Man's erring judgment, *and* mislead the mind,
   What *the* weak head with strongest bias rules,
   Is pride, the never-failing vice of fools.

6. Eye Nature's walks, shoot folly *as* it flies,
   And catch the manners living *as* they rise.

7. To whom then, first incensed, Ad*am* replied,
   "Is this thy love, is this the recompense
   Of mine to thee, ungrateful Eve?"

8. We may, with more successful hope, resolve
   To wage, by force or guile, successful war,
   Irreconcilable to our grand foe,
   Who now tri*umphs*, and in excess of joy
   Sole reigning holds the tyranny of Heaven.

9. Which, when Beëlzebub perceived (than whom,
   Satan except, none higher sat), with grave
   A*spect*, he rose, and in his rising seemed
   A pillar of state.

10. Thee, Sion, and the flowery brooks beneath,
    That wash thy hallowed feet, and warbling flow,
    Nightly I visit: nor sometimes forget
    Those other two *equaled* with me in fate.

NOTE. — Although it would be necessary, in these examples, to violate the laws of accent or emphasis, to give perfect rhythm, yet a careful and well-trained reader will be able to observe these laws and still give the rhythm in such a manner that the defect will scarcely be noticed.

POETIC PAUSES.

In order to make the measure of poetry perceptible to the ear, there should generally be a *slight pause* at the end of each line, even where the sense does not require it.

There is, also, in almost every line of poetry, a pause at or near its middle, which is called the *caesura.*

This should, however, never be so placed as to injure the sense of the passage. It is indeed reckoned a great beauty, where it naturally coincides with the pause required by the sense. The caesura, though *generally* placed near the middle, may be placed at other intervals.

There are sometimes, also, two additional pauses in each line, called demi-caesuras.

The caesura is marked (II), and the demi-caesura thus, (I), in the examples given.

There should be a marked accent upon the long syllable next preceding the caesura, and a slighter one upon that next before each of the demi-caesuras. When made too prominent, these pauses lead to a singsong style, which should be carefully avoided.

In the following examples, the caesura is marked in each line; the demi-caesura is not marked in every case.

EXAMPLES.

1. Nature I to all things II fixed I the limits fit,
   And wisely I curbed II proud man's I pretending wit.

2. Then from his closing eyes ‖ thy form shall part,
   And the last pang ‖ shall tear thee from his heart.

3. Warms in the sun, ‖ refreshes in the breeze,
   Glows in the stars, ‖ and blossoms in the trees.

4. There is a land ‖ of every land the pride,
   Beloved by Heaven ‖ o'er all the world beside,
   Where brighter suns ‖ dispense serener light,
   And milder moons ‖ imparadise the night;
   Oh, thou shalt find, ‖ howe'er thy footsteps roam,
   That land — thy country, ‖ and that spot — thy home.

5. In slumbers ǀ of midnight ‖ the sailor ǀ boy lay;
   His hammock ǀ swung loose ‖ at the sport ǀ of the wind
   But, watch-worn ǀ and weary, ‖ his cares ǀ flew away,
   And visions ǀ of happiness ‖ danced ǀ o'er his mind.

6. She said, ǀ and struck; ‖ deep entered ǀ in her side
   The piercing steel ‖ with reeking purple dyed:
   Clogged ǀ in the wound ‖ the cruel ǀ weapon stands,
   The spouting blood ‖ came streaming o'er her hands.
   Her sad attendants ‖ saw the deadly stroke,
   And with loud cries ‖ the sounding palace shook.

SIMILE.

Simile is the likening of anything to another object of a different class; it is a poetical or imaginative comparison.

A simile, in poetry, should usually be read in a lower key and more rapidly than other parts of the passage — somewhat as a parenthesis is read.

EXAMPLES.

1. Part curb their fiery steeds, or shun the goal
   With rapid wheels, or fronted brigades form.
   As when, to warn proud cities, war appears,
   Waged in the troubled sky, and armies rush
   To battle in the clouds.
   Others with vast Typhoëan rage more fell,
   Rend up both rocks and hills, and ride the air
   In whirlwind. Hell scarce holds the wild uproar.
   As when Alcides felt the envenomed robe, and tore,
   Through pain, up by the roots, Thessalian pines,
   And Lichas from the top of Oeta threw
   Into the Euboic sea.

2.   Each at the head,
            Leveled his deadly aim; their fatal hands
            No second stroke intend; and such a frown
            Each cast at th' other, *as when two black clouds,*
            With heaven's artillery fraught, came rolling on
            Over the Caspian, there stand front to front,
            Hovering a space, till winds the signal blow
            To join the dark encounter, in mid-air:
            So frowned the mighty combatants.

3. Then pleased and thankful from the porch they go,
            And, but the landlord, none had cause of woe:
            His cup was vanished; for, in secret guise,
            The younger guest purloined the glittering prize.
            As one who spies a serpent in his way,
            Glistening and basking in the summer ray,
            Disordered, stops to shun the danger near,
            Then walks with faintness on, and looks with fear, —
            So seemed the sire, when, far upon the road,
            The shining spoil his wily partner showed.

VI. GESTURE.

Gesture is that part of the speaker's manner which pertains to his attitude, to the use and carriage of his person, and the movement of his limbs in delivery.

Every person, in beginning to speak, feels the natural embarrassment resulting from his new position. The novelty of the situation destroys his self-possession, and, with the loss of that, he becomes awkward, his arms and hands hang clumsily, and now, for the first time, seem to him worse than superfluous members. This embarrassment will be overcome gradually, as the speaker becomes familiar with his position; and it is sometimes overcome at once, by a powerful exercise of the attention upon the matter of the speech. When that fills and possesses the mind, the orator is likely to take the attitude which is becoming, and, at least, easy and natural, if not graceful.

1. The first general direction that should be given to the speaker is, that he should *stand erect and firm*, and in that posture which gives an expanded chest and full play to the organs of respiration and utterance.

2. Let the attitude be such that it can be *shifted easily* and *gracefully*. The student will find, by trial, that no attitude is so favorable to this end as that in which the weight of the body is thrown upon one leg, leaving the other free to be advanced or thrown back, as fatigue or the proper action of delivery may require.

The student who has any regard to grace or elegance, will of course avoid all the gross faults which are so common among public speakers, such as resting one foot upon a stool or bench, or throwing the body forward upon the support of the rostrum.

3. Next to attitude, come the movements of the person and limbs. In these, two objects are to be observed, and, if possible, combined, viz., *propriety* and *grace*. There is expression in the extended arm, the clinched hand, the open palm, and the smiting of the breast. But

let no gesture be made that is not in harmony with the thought or sentiment uttered; for it is this harmony which constitutes propriety. As far as possible, let there be a correspondence between the style of action and the train of thought. Where the thought flows on calmly, let there be grace and ease in gesture and action. Where the style is sharp and abrupt, there is propriety in quick, short, and abrupt gesticulation. Especially avoid that ungraceful sawing of the air with the arms, into which an ill-regulated fervor betrays many young speakers.

What is called a *graceful manner,* can only be attained by those who have some natural advantages of person. So far as it is in the reach of study or practice, it seems to depend chiefly upon the general cultivation of manners, implying freedom from all embarrassments, and entire self-possession. The secret of acquiring a graceful style of gesture, we apprehend, lies in the habitual practice, not only when speaking but at all times, of free and graceful movements of the limbs.

There is no limb nor feature which the accomplished speaker will not employ with effect, in the course of a various and animated delivery. The arms, however, are the chief reliance of the orator in gesture; and it will not be amiss to give a hint or two in reference to their proper use.

First — It is not an uncommon fault to use one arm exclusively, and to give that a uniform movement. Such movement may, sometimes, have become habitual from one's profession or employment; but in learners, also, there is often a predisposition to this fault.

Second — It is not unusual to see a speaker use only the lower half of his arm. This always gives a stiff and constrained manner to delivery. Let the whole arm move, and let the movement be free and flowing.

Third — As a general rule, let the hand be open, with the fingers slightly curved. It then seems liberal, communicative, and candid; and, in some degree, gives that expression to the style of delivery. Of course there are passages which require the clinched hand, the pointed finger, etc., etc.; but these are used to give a particular expression.

Fourth — In the movements of the arm, study variety and the grace of curved lines.

When a gesture is made with one arm only, the *eye* should be cast in the direction of that arm; not *at* it, but *over* it.

All speakers employ, more or less, the motions of the head. In reference to that member, we make but one observation. Avoid the continuous shaking and bobbing of the head, which is so conspicuous in the action of many ambitious public speakers.

The beauty and force of all gesture consist in its timely, judicious, and natural employment, when it can serve to illustrate the meaning or give emphasis to the force of an important passage. The usual fault of young speakers is too much action. To emphasize all parts alike, is equivalent to no emphasis; and by employing forcible gestures on unimportant passages, we diminish our power to render other parts impressive.

ELOCUTION AND READING.

The business of training youth in elocution, must be commenced in childhood. The first school is the nursery. There, at least, may be formed a distinct articulation, which is the first requisite for good speaking. How rarely is it found in perfection among our orators.

"Words," says one, referring to articulation, should "be delivered out from the lips, as beautiful coins, newly issued from the mint; deeply and accurately impressed, perfectly finished; neatly struck by the proper organs, distinct, in due succession, and of due weight." How rarely do we hear a speaker whose tongue, teeth, and lips, do their office so perfectly as to answer to this beautiful description! And the common faults in articulation, it should be remembered, take their rise from the very nursery.

Grace in eloquence, in the pulpit, at the bar, cannot be separated from grace in the ordinary manners, in private life, in the social circle, in the family. It cannot well be superinduced upon all the other acquisitions of youth, any more than that nameless, but invaluable, quality called good breeding. Begin, therefore, the work of forming the orator with the child; not merely by teaching him to declaim, but what is of more consequence, by observing and correcting his daily manners, motions, and attitudes. You can say, when he comes into your apartment, or presents you with something, a book or letter, in an awkward and blundering manner, "Return, and enter this room again," or, "Present me that book in a different manner," or, "Put yourself in a different attitude." You can explain to him the difference between thrusting or pushing out his hand and arm, in straight lines and at acute angles, and moving them in flowing circular lines, and easy graceful action. He will readily understand you. Nothing is more true than that the motions of children are originally graceful; it is by suffering them to be perverted, that we lay the foundation of invincible awkwardness in later life.

In schools for children, it ought to be a leading object to teach the art of reading. It ought to occupy *threefold more time* than it does. The teachers of these schools should labor to improve *themselves*. They should feel that to them, for a time, are committed the future orators of the land.

It is better that a girl should return from school a first-rate *reader,* than a first-rate performer on the pianoforte. The accomplishment, in its perfection, would give more pleasure. The voice of song is not sweeter than the voice of eloquence; and there may be eloquent *readers,* as well as eloquent *speakers.* We speak of *perfection* in this art: and it is something, we must say in defense of our preference, which we have never yet seen. Let the same pains be devoted to reading, as are required to form an accomplished performer on an instrument; let us have, as the ancients had, the formers of the voice, the music masters of the *reading* voice; let us see years devoted to this accomplishment, and then we should be prepared to stand the comparison.

Reading is, indeed, a most intellectual accomplishment. So is music, too, in its perfection. We do by no means undervalue this noble and most delightful art, to which Socrates applied himself even in his old age. But one recommendation of the art of reading is, that it requires a constant exercise of mind. It involves, in its perfection, the whole art of criticism on language. A man may possess a fine genius without being a perfect reader; but he cannot be a perfect reader without genius.

93.

Henry James: Things Present and Absent in American Life

Henry James spent most of his adult life in Europe, and this virtual expatriation not only affected his own writing but also allowed him to view the work of his countrymen with a foreigner's eyes. As early as 1879, when James was only thirty-six and when he wrote the book on Hawthorne from which the following selection is taken, he had "thrown in his lot," as he later put it, with England — he became a British subject in 1915. The passages reprinted deal not only with Hawthorne but also with the special problems that, in James's opinion, faced all American writers.

Source: *Hawthorne*, English Men of Letters Series, London, 1883, pp. 40-51.

I HAVE SAID THAT HAWTHORNE was an observer of small things, and indeed he appears to have thought nothing too trivial to be suggestive. His Note Books give us the measure of his perception of common and casual things, and of his habit of converting them into memoranda. These Note Books, by the way — this seems as good a place as any other to say it — are a very singular series of volumes; I doubt whether there is anything exactly corresponding to them in the whole body of literature. They were published — in six volumes, issued at intervals — some years after Hawthorne's death, and no person attempting to write an account of the romancer could afford to regret that they should have been given to the world. There is a point of view from which this may be regretted; but the attitude of the biographer is to desire as many documents as possible. I am thankful, then, as a biographer, for the Note Books, but I am obliged to confess that, though I have just reread them carefully, I am still at a loss to perceive how they came to be written — what was Hawthorne's purpose in carrying on for so many years this minute and often trivial chronicle. For a person desiring information about him at any cost, it is valuable; it sheds a vivid light upon his character, his habits, the nature of his mind. But we find ourselves wondering what was its value to Hawthorne himself. It is in a very partial degree a register of impressions, and in a still smaller sense a record of emotions. Outward objects play much the larger part in it; opinions, convictions, ideas pure and simple, are almost absent. He rarely takes his Note Books into his confidence or commits to its pages any reflections that might be adapted for publicity; the simplest way to describe the tone of these extremely objective journals is to say that they read like a series of very pleasant, though rather dullish and decidedly formal, letters, addressed to himself by a man who, having suspicions that they might be opened in the post, should have determined to insert nothing compromising. They contain much that is too futile for things intended for publicity; whereas, on the other hand, as a receptacle of private impressions and opinions, they are curiously cold and empty. They widen, as I have said, our glimpse of Hawthorne's mind (I do not say that they elevate our estimate of it), but they do so by what they fail to contain, as much as by what we find in them. Our business for the moment, however, is not with the light that they throw upon his intellect but with the information they offer about his habits and his social circumstances.

I know not at what age he began to keep a diary; the first entries in the American volumes are of the summer of 1835. There is a phrase in the preface to his novel of *Transformation*, which must have lingered in the minds of many Americans who have tried to write novels and to lay the scene of them in the Western world. "No author, without a trial, can conceive of the difficulty of writing a romance about a country where there is no shadow, no antiquity, no mystery, no picturesque and gloomy wrong, nor anything but a commonplace prosperity, in broad and simple daylight, as is happily the case with my dear native land." The perusal of Hawthorne's American Note Books operates as a practical commentary upon this somewhat ominous text. It does so at least to my own mind; it would be too much perhaps to say that the effect would be the same for the usual English reader. An American reads between the lines — he completes the suggestions — he constructs a picture. I think I am not guilty of any gross injustice in saying that the picture he constructs from Hawthorne's American diaries, though by no means without charms of its own, is not, on the whole, an interesting one. It is characterized by an extraordinary blankness — a curious paleness of color and paucity of detail. Hawthorne, as I have said, has a large and healthy appetite for detail, and one is therefore the more struck with the lightness of the diet to which his observation was condemned.

For myself, as I turn the pages of his journals, I seem to see the image of the crude and simple society in which he lived. I use these epithets, of course, not invidiously but descriptively; if one desire to enter as closely as possible into Hawthorne's

situation, one must endeavor to reproduce his circumstances. We are struck with the large number of elements that were absent from them, and the coldness, the thinness, the blankness, to repeat my epithet, present themselves so vividly that our foremost feeling is that of compassion for a romancer looking for subjects in such a field. It takes so many things, as Hawthorne must have felt later in life, when he made the acquaintance of the denser, richer, warmer European spectacle — it takes such an accumulation of history and custom, such a complexity of manners and types, to form a fund of suggestion for a novelist.

If Hawthorne had been a young Englishman or a young Frenchman of the same degree of genius, the same cast of mind, the same habits, his consciousness of the world around him would have been a very different affair; however obscure, however reserved, his own personal life, his sense of the life of his fellow mortals would have been almost infinitely more various. The negative side of the spectacle on which Hawthorne looked out, in his contemplative saunterings and reveries, might, indeed, with a little ingenuity, be made almost ludicrous; one might enumerate the items of high civilization as it exists in other countries which are absent from the texture of American life, until it should become a wonder to know what was left. No state, in the European sense of the word, and indeed barely a specific national name. No sovereign, no court, no personal loyalty, no aristocracy, no church, no clergy, no army, no diplomatic service, no country gentlemen, no palaces, no castles, nor manors, nor old country houses, nor parsonages, nor thatched cottages, nor ivied ruins; no cathedrals, nor abbeys, nor little Norman churches; no great universities nor public schools — no Oxford, nor Eton, nor Harrow; no literature, no novels, no museums, no pictures, no political society, no sporting class — no Epsom nor Ascot! Some such list as that might be drawn up of the absent things in American life — especially in the American life of forty years ago, the effect of which, upon an English or a French imagination, would probably as a general thing be appalling. The natural remark, in the almost lurid light of such an indictment, would be that if these things are left out, everything is left out. The American knows that a good deal remains; what it is that remains — that is his secret, his joke, as one may say. It would be cruel, in this terrible denudation, to deny him the consolation of his national gift, that "American humor" of which of late years we have heard so much.

But in helping us to measure what remains, our author's diaries, as I have already intimated, would give comfort rather to persons who might have taken the alarm from the brief sketch I have just attempted of what I have called the negative side of the American social situation, than to those reminding themselves of its fine compensations. Hawthorne's entries are to a great degree accounts of walks in the country, drives in stagecoaches, people he met in taverns. The minuteness of the things that attract his attention and that he deems worthy of being commemorated is frequently extreme, and from this fact we get the impression of a general vacancy in the field of vision. "Sunday evening, going by the jail, the setting sun kindled up the windows most cheerfully; as if there were a bright, comfortable light within its darksome stone wall." "I went yesterday with Monsieur S ——— to pick raspberries. He fell through an old log bridge, thrown over a hollow; looking back, only his head and shoulders appeared through the rotten logs and among the bushes. — A shower coming on, the rapid running of a little barefooted boy, coming up unheard, and dashing swiftly past us and showing us the soles of his naked feet as he ran adown the path and up the opposite side." In another place he de-

votes a page to a description of a dog whom he saw running round after its tail; in still another he remarks, in a paragraph by itself — "The aromatic odor of peat smoke, in the sunny autumnal air, is very pleasant." The reader says to himself that when a man turned thirty gives a place in his mind — and his inkstand — to such trifles as these, it is because nothing else of superior importance demands admission. Everything in the Notes indicates a simple, democratic, thinly composed society; there is no evidence of the writer finding himself in any variety or intimacy of relations with anyone or with anything. . . .

In fact Hawthorne appears to have ignored the good society of his native place almost completely; no echo of its conversation is to be found in his tales or his journals. Such an echo would possibly not have been especially melodious, and if we regret the shyness and stiffness, the reserve, the timidity, the suspicion, or whatever it was, that kept him from knowing what there was to be known, it is not because we have any very definite assurance that his gains would have been great. Still, since a beautiful writer was growing up in Salem, it is a pity that he should not have given himself a chance to commemorate some of the types that flourished in the richest soil of the place. Like almost all people who possess in a strong degree the storytelling faculty, Hawthorne had a democratic strain in his composition and a relish for the commoner stuff of human nature. Thoroughly American in all ways, he was in none more so than in the vagueness of his sense of social distinctions and his readiness to forget them if a moral or intellectual sensation were to be gained by it. He liked to fraternize with plain people, to take them on their own terms, and put himself if possible into their shoes. His Note Books, and even his tales, are full of evidence of this easy and natural feeling about all his unconventional fellow mortals — this imaginative interest and contemplative curiosity — and it sometimes takes the most charming and graceful forms. Commingled as it is with his own subtlety and delicacy, his complete exemption from vulgarity, it is one of the points in his character which his reader comes most to appreciate — that reader I mean for whom he is not as for some few, a dusky and malarious genius. . . .

Hawthorne appears on various occasions to have absented himself from Salem and to have wandered somewhat through the New England states. But the only one of these episodes of which there is a considerable account in the Note Books is a visit that he paid in the summer of 1837 to his old college mate Horatio Bridge, who was living upon his father's property in Maine in company with an eccentric young Frenchman, a teacher of his native tongue, who was looking for pupils among the Northern forests. I have said that there was less psychology in Hawthorne's journals than might have been looked for; but there is nevertheless a certain amount of it, and nowhere more than in a number of pages relating to this remarkable "Monsieur S." (Hawthorne, intimate as he apparently became with him, always calls him "Monsieur," just as throughout all his diaries he invariably speaks of all his friends, even the most familiar, as "Mr." He confers the prefix upon the unconventional Thoreau, his fellow woodsman at Concord, and upon the emancipated brethren at Brook Farm.)

These pages are completely occupied with Monsieur S., who was evidently a man of character, with the full complement of his national vivacity. There is an elaborate effort to analyze the poor young Frenchman's disposition, something conscientious and painstaking, respectful, explicit, almost solemn. These passages are very curious as a reminder of the absence of the offhand element in the manner in which many Americans, and many New Englanders especially, make up their minds about people whom

they meet. This, in turn, is a reminder of something that may be called the importance of the individual in the American world; which is a result of the newness and youthfulness of society and of the absence of keen competition. The individual counts for more, as it were, and, thanks to the absence of a variety of social types and of settled heads under which he may be easily and conveniently pigeonholed, he is to a certain extent a wonder and a mystery.

An Englishman, a Frenchman — a Frenchman above all — judges quickly, easily, from his own social standpoint, and makes an end of it. He has not that rather chilly and isolated sense of moral responsibility which is apt to visit a New Englander in such processes; and he has the advantage that his standards are fixed by the general consent of the society in which he lives. A Frenchman, in this respect, is particularly happy and comfortable, happy and comfortable to a degree which I think is hardly to be overestimated; his standards being the most definite in the world, the most easily and promptly appealed to, and the most identical with what happens to be the practice of the French genius itself. The Englishman is not quite so well off, but he is better off than his poor interrogative and tentative cousin beyond the seas. He is blessed with a healthy mistrust of analysis, and hairsplitting is the occupation he most despises. There is always a little of the Dr. Johnson in him, and Dr. Johnson would have had woefully little patience with that tendency to weigh moonbeams which in Hawthorne was almost as much a quality of race as of genius; albeit that Hawthorne has paid to Boswell's hero (in the chapter on "Lichfield and Uttoxeter," in his volume on England) a tribute of the finest appreciation. American intellectual standards are vague, and Hawthorne's countrymen are apt to hold the scales with a rather uncertain hand and a somewhat agitated conscience.

94.

Walt Whitman: The Great American Landscape

Walt Whitman, sixty years old and famed, thanks to his friends, as "the Good Gray Poet," made a trip to Colorado in 1879. He was amazed and pleased, as he probably expected to be, by the grandeur of the mountains and plains, and he wrote a series of descriptions of the people and places that he saw on the journey. The selection below consists of short pieces published in 1882 in Specimen Days and Collect.

Source: *Complete Prose Works*, Boston, 1898, pp. 141-144.

THE PRAIRIES AND GREAT PLAINS IN POETRY

GRAND AS IS THE THOUGHT that doubtless the child is already born who will see a hundred millions of people, the most prosperous and advanced of the world, inhabiting these prairies, the Great Plains, and the valley of the Mississippi, I could not help thinking it would be grander still to see all those inimitable American areas fused in the alembic of a perfect poem, or other aesthetic work, entirely Western, fresh, and limitless — altogether our own, without a trace or taste of Europe's soil, reminiscence, technical letter or spirit. My days and nights, as I travel here — what an exhilaration! — not the air alone and the sense of vastness but every local sight and feature. Everywhere something characteristic — the cactuses, pinks, buffalo grass, wild sage; the receding perspective, and the far circle-line of the horizon all times of day, especially forenoon; the clear, pure, cool, rarefied nutriment for the lungs, previously quite unknown; the black patches and streaks left by surface conflagrations; the deep plowed furrow of the "fire-guard"; the slanting snow racks built all along to shield the railroad from winter drifts; the prairie dogs and the herds of antelope; the

curious "dry rivers"; occasionally a "dug-out" or corral; Fort Riley and Fort Wallace; those towns of the Northern plains (like ships on the sea) Eagle-Tail, Coyote, Cheyenne, Agate, Monotony, Kit Carson — with ever the anthill and the buffalo wallow; ever the herds of cattle and the cowboys ("cowpunchers"), to me a strangely interesting class, bright-eyed as hawks, with their swarthy complexions and their broad-brimmed hats, apparently always on horseback, with loose arms slightly raised and swinging as they ride.

THE SPANISH PEAKS — EVENING ON THE PLAINS

BETWEEN PUEBLO AND BENT'S FORT, southward, in a clear afternoon sun-spell, I catch exceptionally good glimpses of the Spanish peaks. We are in southeastern Colorado — pass immense herds of cattle as our first-class locomotive rushes us along — two or three times crossing the Arkansas, which we follow many miles, and of which river I get fine views, sometimes for quite a distance, its stony, upright, not very high, palisade banks, and then its muddy flats. We pass Fort Lyon — lots of adobe houses, limitless pasturage, appropriately flecked with those herds of cattle — in due time the declining sun in the west, a sky of limpid pearl over all, and so evening on the Great Plains. A calm, pensive, boundless landscape; the perpendicular rocks of the North Arkansas, hued in twilight; a thin line of violet on the southwestern horizon; the palpable coolness and slight aroma; a belated cowboy with some unruly member of his herd; an emigrant wagon toiling yet a little further, the horses slow and tired; two men, apparently father and son, jogging along on foot — and around all the indescribable *chiaroscuro* and sentiment (profounder than anything at sea) athwart these endless wilds.

AMERICA'S CHARACTERISTIC LANDSCAPE

SPEAKING GENERALLY as to the capacity and sure future destiny of that plain and prairie area (larger than any European kingdom), it is the inexhaustible land of wheat, maize, wool, flax, coal, iron, beef and pork, butter and cheese, apples and grapes; land of ten million virgin farms, to the eye at present wild and unproductive — yet experts say that upon it, when irrigated, may easily be grown enough wheat to feed the world. Then, as to scenery (giving my own thought and feeling), while I know the standard claim is that Yosemite, Niagara Falls, the Upper Yellowstone, and the like afford the greatest natural shows, I am not so sure but the prairies and the Plains, while less stunning at first sight, last longer, fill the aesthetic sense fuller, precede all the rest, and make North America's characteristic landscape.

Indeed, through the whole of this journey, with all its shows and varieties, what most impressed me and will longest remain with me are these same prairies. Day after day, and night after night, to my eyes, to all my senses — the aesthetic one most of all — they silently and broadly unfolded. Even their simplest statistics are sublime.

EARTH'S MOST IMPORTANT STREAM

THE VALLEY of the Mississippi River and its tributaries (this stream and its adjuncts involve a big part of the question) comprehends more than twelve hundred thousand square miles, the greater part prairies. It is by far the most important stream on the globe and would seem to have been marked out by design, slow-flowing from north to south, through a dozen climates, all fitted for man's healthy occupancy, its outlet unfrozen all the year, and its line forming a safe, cheap continental avenue for commerce and passage from the north temperate to the torrid zone. Not even the mighty Amazon (though larger in volume) on its line of east and west, not the Nile in Africa, nor the Danube in Europe, nor the three great rivers of China, compare with it. Only the Mediterranean Sea has played some such part in history, and all through the past, as the Mississippi is destined to play in the future.

By its demesnes, watered and welded by its branches, the Missouri, the Ohio, the Arkansas, the Red, the Yazoo, the St. Francis, and others, it already compacts twenty-five millions of people, not merely the most peaceful and moneymaking but the most restless and warlike on earth. Its valley, or reach, is rapidly concentrating the political power of the American Union. One almost thinks it *is* the Union, or soon will be. Take it out, with its radiations, and what would be left?

From the car windows through Indiana, Illinois, Missouri, or stopping some days along the Topeka and Santa Fe road, in southern Kansas, and indeed wherever I went, hundreds and thousands of miles through this region, my eyes feasted on primitive and rich meadows, some of them partially inhabited, but far, immensely far more untouched, unbroken; and much of it more lovely and fertile in its unplowed innocence than the fair and valuable fields of

New York's, Pennsylvania's, Maryland's, or Virginia's richest farms.

PRAIRIE ANALOGIES — THE TREE QUESTION

THE WORD "PRAIRIE" is French and means, literally, meadow. The cosmical analogies of our North American plains are the steppes of Asia, the pampas and llanos of South America, and perhaps the Saharas of Africa. Some think the plains have been originally lake beds; others attribute the absence of forests to the fires that almost annually sweep over them (the cause, in vulgar estimation, of Indian summer). The tree question will soon become a grave one. Although the Atlantic slope, the Rocky Mountain region, and the southern portion of the Mississippi Valley are well-wooded, there are here stretches of hundreds and thousands of miles where either not a tree grows, or often useless destruction has prevailed; and the matter of the cultivation and spread of forests may well be pressed upon thinkers who look to the coming generations of the prairie states.

MISSISSIPPI VALLEY LITERATURE

LYING BY ONE RAINY DAY in Missouri to rest after quite a long exploration, first trying a big volume I found there of "Milton, Young, Gray, Beattie and Collins" but giving it up for a bad job, enjoying however for awhile, as often before, the reading of Walter Scott's poems, "Lay of the Last Minstrel," "Marmion," and so on, I stopped and laid down the book and pondered the thought of a poetry that should in due time express and supply the teeming region I was in the midst of and have briefly touched upon. One's mind needs but a moment's deliberation anywhere in the United States to see clearly enough that all the prevalent book and library poets, either as imported from Great Britain or followed and *doppel-ganged* here, are foreign to our states, copiously as they are read by us all. But to fully understand, not only how absolutely in opposition to our times and lands and how little and cramped, and what anachronisms and absurdities many of their pages are, for American purposes, one must dwell or travel awhile in Missouri, Kansas, and Colorado, and get rapport with their people and country.

Will the day ever come, no matter how long deferred, when those models and lay figures from the British islands — and even the precious traditions of the classics — will be reminiscences, studies only? The pure breath, primitiveness, boundless prodigality and amplitude, strange mixture of delicacy and power, of continence, of real and ideal, and of all original and first-class elements, of these prairies, the Rocky Mountains, and of the Mississippi and Missouri Rivers — will they ever appear in, and in some sort form a standard for our poetry and art? . . .

Subtler and wider and more solid . . . than the laws of the states, or the common ground of Congress, or the Supreme Court, or the grim welding of our national wars, or the steel ties of railroads, or all the kneading and fusing processes of our material and business history, past or present, would in my opinion be a great throbbing, vital, imaginative work, or series of works, or literature, in constructing which the Plains, the prairies, and the Mississippi River, with the demesnes of its varied and ample valley, should be the concrete background, and America's humanity, passions, struggles, hopes, there and now — an *eclaircissement* as it is and is to be, on the stage of the New World, of all time's hitherto drama of war, romance, and evolution — should furnish the lambent fire, the ideal.

Riverboats docked at the levee in St. Louis, c. 1880

GROWTH AND RECOVERY

The Civil War devastated the South. The traditional economy and social pattern were entirely dislocated; the system of large plantations and slave labor, the neo-feudal social structure, gave way to small farms, one-man holdings, tenancy, and large numbers of dispossessed. African Americans, released from slavery, most often found nowhere to go and nothing to do with liberty; many elected to remain field hands for their former owners, their freedom little more than a technicality; others moved on but to little purpose. The small farmers and businessmen, accustomed to a marginal but respectable life, became the original "poor white trash" — landless whites subsisting by share-cropping or day labor. They were self-supporting, but had lost all status and dignity in the social order that was passionately defended against all change, despite the outcome of the war. The traditional forms of society became the last refuge of the "old South," and it was often the very people most disadvantaged by it who defended the system most strongly.

By contrast, money was to be had by serving commercial interests. The Mississippi River was opened as a major transportation artery and river trade transformed many small towns. St. Louis, on both the Mississippi and Missouri rivers, was central to the shipping of the entire region, and became the commercial linchpin between East and West.

Riverboats along a Mississippi River dock. In the post-Civil War period, these boats were the primary means of North-South transportation in the Midwest

There were attempts to break the one-crop economy of the South, especially since the loss of slave labor had made cotton production less profitable. Efforts were made to establish industries in textiles, steel, tobacco, and lumbering. But tradition and ignorance combined to perpetuate "King Cotton" as the sole crop of most farmers; no other markets had been developed and were not likely to be in an area where ready cash for cotton was the determinant. Such measures as crop rotation or diversification, economical in the long run but expensive to start, would have to wait for a less desperate day.

(Left) The Exchange Building in Savannah, Ga., photo by J. N. Wilson, 1875; (below) shipping cotton from Savannah

"San Francisco," a prewar plantation house in Louisiana, shows the effects of neglect

(Above) Primitive cotton press in Alabama, about 1875; (below) unloading a cotton dray at the wharf in Savannah, about 1880; photo by O. P. Havens

View of Commercial Street in Montgomery, Ala., with the State House in the distance; from a stereograph of the 1860s

(Right) "Chimney Sweeps"; from a stereograph by J. A. Palmer of Aiken, S.C.; (below) the John Ross House in Rossville, Ga.; photographed by George Barnard

Langley Cotton Mill in South Carolina, about 1880; photo by Palmer

(Above) Girl selling firewood in Raleigh, N.C., 1875; (below) view of a high school graduating class, place unknown, about 1870

(Above) Broad Street in
Charleston, S.C., about
1875; photo by Barnard

(Right) Main Street of
Charlotte, N.C., showing a
mixed team of oxen and
horses that is peculiar to
this region; (below) North
Carolina turpentine dis-
tillery, c. 1875

The "J. M. White," Mississippi steamboat operating from New Orleans to Vicksburg, 1878-86

Maintaining the social structure of the prewar South was at best extremely difficult in straitened times. The elegance and opulence of Southern aristocracy was expensive to keep up; nonetheless the attempt was made. Despite the new realities of life, "graceful living" still far outranked "sordid commerce" on the official scale of values.

Interior of the "J. M. White": (right) view of the ladies parlor, used for after-dinner conversation; (below) the salon, running nearly the length of the boat on the second level

(Above) Col. Charles B. Lamborn and his friends on the riverbank at St. Louis; photo by Gardner; (below) view of grain elevators and railroad yards at the mouth of the river, Chicago

Union Stock Yards, Chicago, 1866; lithograph from "Chicago Illustrated"

In the Midwest, postwar economic expansion resulted chiefly from two developments: the establishment of transcontinental railways and the agricultural exploitation of the prairies. These developments also gave rise to the emergence of great cities such as Chicago, Minneapolis, and St. Louis on the margins of the prairie. Chicago's growth was further sparked by the invention of the refrigerator car, which made it possible to ship perishable meat over long distances. This innovation, coupled with Chicago's strategic location, led to the city's preeminance as slaughterhouse to the nation.

(Above and below) Steps in pork processing, 1873

View from the dome of City Hall, Chicago, looking to the northeast; from a stereograph by Carbutt taken before the fire

(Above left) Chicago City Hall, photo by Carbutt; (above right) John Jones, prominent free-born African American who worked for equal rights in Chicago and Illinois; (below) McVickers Theater, 1866

Chicago Fire, 1871; sketch by Waud of the view from the lakefront just north of the river

Ruins of the Farwell Building and Courthouse; photographed immediately after the 1871 fire

Calumet Avenue looking north from 23rd Street; photo by Lovejoy and Foster, 1874

(Above) Real estate broadside encouraging the settlement of Humboldt, a Chicago suburb in 1871-73; (below left) Racine Marble Works in Wisconsin; (below right) James Garside's meat market

(Above) Advertisement for H. & F. Blandy Co., 1867

(Left) Display of agricultural equipment at a fair in 1875

Midwestern store selling household goods. Small enterprises such as this were basic to the economies of countless small towns across the country

(Above) Cartoon deriding the educational atmosphere of rural schools

(Right) "Will it Pay"; lithograph depicting Dr. D. L. Moody and J. V. Farwell with their first Sunday School class in North Market Hall, Chicago, 1876; (below) Third Ward school, Des Moines, Iowa; from a stereograph by Everett & Co.

University of Wisconsin in Madison during the early 1880s

The success of American technology in the late 19th century helped create a consciousness of the power of knowledge as a catalyst to commerce, industry, and agriculture. Compulsory school attendance had been initiated in Massachusetts in 1852 and continued to spread, as did the secondary school movement. The Morrill Act of 1862 helped states establish colleges "to teach such branches of knowledge as are related to agriculture and the mechanic arts." Federal aid was extended to agricultural research by the Hatch Act of 1887.

(Right) Justin Morrill, responsible for making public lands available to states for establishing agricultural colleges; (below) State Normal College in southwestern Pennsylvania for the training of teachers

95.

ROBERT LOUIS STEVENSON: Fellow Travelers

America, the great "melting pot," was challenged to assimilate a large number of strange and foreign groups in the years following the Civil War, among them the newly freed slaves, immigrants from Europe and Asia, and various tribes of American Indians. The egalitarianism professed by "native" Americans (often immigrants of a generation or two earlier) sometimes ran afoul of an intolerance derived from latent racism and fear of economic competition. Robert Louis Stevenson, who traveled from New York to San Francisco in 1879, witnessed the effects of American intolerance on the emigrant train that carried him across the country. He recorded his impressions in Across the Plains *(1892). Early editions were heavily censored; the passages reprinted below are therefore taken from a modern, restored text of the work.*

Source: *From Scotland to Silverado,* James D. Hart, ed., Cambridge, 1966: "Fellow-Passengers" and "Despised Races."

AT OGDEN WE CHANGED CARS from the Union Pacific to the Central Pacific line of railroad. The change was doubly welcome; for, first, we had better cars on the new line; and, second, those in which we had been cooped for more than ninety hours had begun to stink abominably. Several yards away, as we returned, let us say from dinner, our nostrils were assailed by air. I have stood on a platform while the whole train was shunting; and as the dwelling cars drew near, there would come a whiff of pure menagerie, only a little sourer, as from men instead of monkeys.

I think we are human only in virtue of open windows. Without fresh air, you only require a bad heart and a remarkable command of the Queen's English to become such another as Dean Swift; a kind of leering, human goat, leaping and wagging your scut on mountains of offense. I do my best to keep my head the other way and look for the human rather than the bestial in this Yahoo-like business of the emigrant train. But one thing I must say: the car of the Chinese was notably the least offensive, and that of the women and children by a good way the worst — a stroke of nature's satire.

The cars on the Central Pacific were nearly twice as high, and so proportionally airier; they were freshly varnished, which gave us all a sense of cleanliness, as though we had bathed; the seats drew out and joined in the center, so that there was no more need for bed boards; and there was an upper tier of berths which could be closed by day and opened at night. Thus in every way the accommodation was more cheerful and comfortable, and everyone might have a bed to lie on if he pleased. The company deserve our thanks. It was the first sign I could observe of any kindly purpose toward the emigrant.

For myself, it was, in some ways, a fatal change; for it fell to me to sleep in one of the lofts; and that I found to be impossible.

The air was always bad enough at the level of the floor. But my bed was four feet higher, immediately under the roof, and shut into a kind of Saratoga trunk with one side partly open. And there, unless you were the Prince of Camby, it were madness to attempt to sleep. Though the fumes were narcotic and weighed upon the eyelids, yet they so smartly irritated the lungs that I could only lie and cough. I spent the better part of one night walking to and fro and envying my neighbors.

I had by this time some opportunity of seeing the people whom I was among. They were in rather marked contrast to the emigrants I had met on board ship while crossing the Atlantic. There was both less talent and less good manners; I believe I should add less good feeling, though that is implied. Kindness will out; and a man who is gentle will contrive to be a gentleman. They were mostly lumpish fellows, silent and noisy, a common combination; somewhat sad, I should say, with an extraordinary poor taste in humor and little interest in their fellow creatures beyond that of a cheap and merely external curiosity. If they heard a man's name and business, they seemed to think they had the heart of that mystery; but they were as eager to know that much as they were indifferent to the rest.

Some of them were on nettles till they learned your name was Dickson and you a journeyman baker; but beyond that, whether you were Catholic or Mormon, dull or clever, fierce or friendly, was all one to them. Others who were not so stupid gossiped a little and, I am bound to say, unkindly. A favorite witticism was for some lout to raise the alarm of "All aboard!" while the rest of us were dining, thus contributing his mite to the general discomfort. Such a one was always much applauded for his high spirits.

When I was ill coming through Wyoming, I was astonished — fresh from the eager humanity on board ship — to meet with little but laughter. One of the young men even amused himself by incommoding me, as was then very easy; and that not from ill-nature but mere clodlike incapacity to think, for he expected me to join the laugh. I did so, but it was phantom merriment. Later on, a man from Kansas had three violent epileptic fits, and though, of course, there were not wanting some to help him, it was rather superstitious terror than sympathy that his case evoked among his fellow passengers. "Oh, I hope he's not going to die!" cried a woman; "it would be terrible to have a dead body!" And there was a very general movement to leave the man behind at the next station. This, by good fortune, the conductor negatived.

There was a good deal of storytelling in some quarters; in others, little but silence. In this society, more than any other that ever I was in, it was the narrator alone who seemed to enjoy the narrative. It was rarely that anyone listened for the listening. If he lent an ear to another man's story, it was because he was in immediate want of a hearer for one of his own. Food and the progress of the train were the subjects most generally treated; many joined to discuss these who otherwise would hold their tongues.

One small knot had no better occupation than to worm out of me my name; and the more they tried, the more obstinately fixed I grew to baffle them. They assailed me with artful questions and insidious offers of correspondence in the future; but I was perpetually on my guard and parried their assaults with inward laughter. I am sure Dubuque would have given me ten dollars for the secret. He owed me far more, had he understood life, for thus preserving him a lively interest throughout the journey. I met one of my fellow passengers months after, driving a street tramway car in San Francisco; and, as the joke was now out of season, told him my name without subterfuge. You never saw a man more chapfallen. But had my name been Demogorgon, after so prolonged a mystery, he had still been disappointed.

There were no emigrants direct from Europe, save one German family and a knot of Cornish miners who kept grimly by themselves, one reading the New Testament all day long through steel spectacles, the rest discussing privately the secrets of their Old World, mysterious race. Lady Hester Stanhope believed she could make something great of the Cornish; for my part, I can make nothing of them at all. A division of races, older and more original than that of Babel, keeps this close, esoteric family apart from neighboring Englishmen. Not even a red Indian seems more foreign in my eyes. This is one of the lessons of travel — that some of the strangest races dwell next door to you at home.

The rest were all American-born, but they came from almost every quarter of that continent. All the states of the North had sent out a fugitive to cross the Plains with me. From Virginia, from Pennsylvania, from New York, from far-western Iowa and Kansas, from Maine, that borders on the Canadas, and from the Canadas themselves — some one or two were fleeing in quest of a better land and better wages. The talk in the train, like the talk I heard on the steamer, ran upon hard times, short commons, and hope that moves ever westward.

I thought of my shipful from Great Britain with a feeling of despair. They had come 3,000 miles and yet not far enough. Hard times bowed them out of the Clyde and stood to welcome them at Sandy Hook. Where were they to go? Pennsylvania, Maine, Iowa, Kansas? These were not places for immigration but for emigration, it appeared; not one of them but I knew a man who had lifted up his heel and left it for an ungrateful country.

And it was still westward that they ran. Hunger, you would have thought, came out of the East like the sun, and the evening was made of edible gold. And, meantime, in the car in front of me, were there not half a hundred emigrants from the opposite quarter? Hungry Europe and hungry China, each pouring from their gates in search of provender, had here come face to face. The two waves had met; East and West had alike failed; the whole round world had been prospected and condemned; there was no El Dorado anywhere; and till one could emigrate to the moon, it seemed as well to stay patiently at home.

Nor was there wanting another sign, at once more picturesque and more disheartening; for as we continued to steam westward toward the land of gold, we were continually passing other emigrant trains upon the journey east; and these were as crowded as our own. Had all these return voyagers made a fortune in the mines? Were they all bound for Paris, and to be in Rome by Easter? It would seem not, for, whenever we met them, the passengers ran on the platform and cried to us through the windows, in a kind of wailing chorus, to "come back." On the plains of Nebraska, in the mountains of Wyoming, it was still the same cry, and dismal to my heart, "Come back!" That was what we heard by the way "about the good country we were going to." And at the very hour the Sandlot of San Francisco was crowded with the unemployed, and the echo from the other side of Market Street was repeating the rant of demagogues.

If in truth it were only for the sake of wages that men emigrate, how many thousands would regret the bargain! But wages, indeed, are only one consideration out of many; for we are a race of Gypsies and love change and travel for themselves.

OF ALL STUPID ILL-FEELINGS, the sentiment of my fellow Caucasians toward our companions in the Chinese car was the most stupid and the worst. They seemed never to have looked at them, listened to them, or thought of them, but hated them *a priori*. The Mongols were their enemies in that cruel and treacherous battlefield of money. They could work better and cheaper in half a hundred industries, and hence there was no calumny too idle for the Caucasians to repeat and even to believe. They declared them hideous vermin and affected a kind of choking in the throat when they beheld them. Now, as a matter of fact, the young Chinese man is so like a large class of European women that, on raising my head and suddenly catching sight of one at a considerable distance, I have for an instant been deceived by the resemblance. I do not say it is the most attractive class of our women, but for all that many a man's wife is less pleasantly favored.

Again, my emigrants declared that the Chinese were dirty. I cannot say they were clean, for that was impossible upon the journey; but in their efforts after cleanliness they put the rest of us to shame. We all pigged and stewed in one infamy, wet our hands and faces for half a minute daily on the platform, and were unashamed. But the Chinese never lost an opportunity and you would see them washing their feet — an act not dreamed of among ourselves — and going as far as decency permitted to wash their whole bodies. I may remark, by the way, that the dirtier people are in their persons the more delicate is their sense of modesty. A clean man strips in a crowded boathouse; but he who is unwashed slinks in and out of bed without uncovering an inch of his skin. Lastly, these very foul and malodorous Caucasians entertained the surprising illusion that it was the Chinese wagon, and that alone, which stank. I have said already that it was the exception and notably the freshest of the three.

These judgments are typical of the feeling in all Western America. The Chinese are considered stupid because they are imperfectly acquainted with English. They are held to be base because their dexterity and frugality enable them to underbid the lazy, luxurious Caucasian. They are said to be thieves; I am sure they have no monopoly of that. They are called cruel; the Anglo-Saxon and the cheerful Irishman may each reflect before he bears the accusation. I am told, again, that they are of the race of river pirates and belong to the most despised and dangerous class in the Celestial Empire. But if this be so, what remarkable pirates have we here! And what must be the virtues, the industry, the education, and the intelligence of their superiors at home!

A while ago it was the Irish, now it is the Chinese that must go. Such is the cry. It seems, after all, that no country is bound to submit to immigration any more than to invasion; each is war to the knife, and resistance to either but legitimate defense. Yet we may regret the free tradition of the republic, which loved to depict herself with open arms, welcoming all unfortunates. And certainly, as a man who believes that he loves freedom, I may be excused some bitterness when I find her sacred name misused in the contention. It was but the other day that I heard a vulgar fellow in the Sandlot, the popular tribune of San Francisco, roaring for arms and butchery. "At the call of Abreham Lincoln," said the orator, "ye rose in the name of freedom to set free the Negroes; can ye not rise and liberate yourselves from a few dhirty Mongolians?"

For my own part, I could not look but with wonder and respect on the Chinese. Their forefathers watched the stars before mine had begun to keep pigs. Gunpowder and printing, which the other day we imitated, and a school of manners which we never had the delicacy so much as to desire to imitate, were theirs in a long-past antiquity. They walk the earth with us, but it seems they must be of different clay. They hear the clock strike the same hour, yet surely of a different epoch. They travel by steam conveyance, yet with such a baggage of old Asiatic thoughts and superstitions as might check the locomotive in its course. Whatever is thought within the circuit of the Great Wall; what the wry-eyed, spectacled schoolmaster teaches in the hamlets round Pekin; religions so old that our language looks a halfling boy alongside; philosophy so wise that our best philosophers find things therein to wonder at; all this traveled alongside of me for thousands of miles over plain and mountain.

Heaven knows if we had one common thought or fancy all that way, or whether our eyes, which yet were formed upon the same design, beheld the same world out of the railway windows. And when either of us turned his thoughts to home and childhood, what a strange dissimilarity must there not have been in these pictures of the mind — when I beheld that old, gray, castled city, high throned above the firth, with the flag of Britain flying, and the redcoat sentry pacing over all; and the man in the next car to me would conjure up some junks and a pagoda and a fort of porcelain, and call it, with the same affection, home.

Another race shared among my fellow passengers in the disfavor of the Chinese; and that, it is hardly necessary to say, was the noble red man of old story — he over whose own hereditary continent we had been steaming all these days. I saw no wild or independent Indian; indeed, I hear that such avoid the neighborhood of the train; but now and again, at waystations, a husband and wife and a few children, disgracefully dressed out with the sweepings of civilization, came forth and stared upon the emigrants. The silent stoicism of their conduct and the pathetic degradation of their appearance would have touched any thinking creature; but my fellow passengers danced and jested round them with a truly Cockney baseness. I was ashamed for the thing we call civilization. We should carry upon our consciences so much, at least, of our forefathers' misconduct as we continue to profit by ourselves.

If oppression drives a wise man mad, what should be raging in the hearts of these poor tribes who have been driven back and back, step after step, their promised reservations torn from them one after another as the states extended westward, until at length they are shut up into these hideous mountain deserts of the center — and even there find themselves invaded, insulted, and hunted out by ruffianly diggers? The eviction of the Cherokees (to name but an instance), the extortion of Indian agents, the outrages of the wicked, the ill-faith of all, nay, down to the ridicule of such poor beings as were here with me upon the train, make up a chapter of injustice and indignity such as a man must be in some ways base if his heart will suffer him to pardon or forget.

These old, well-founded, historical hatreds have a savor of nobility for the independent. That the Jew should not love the Christian, nor the Irishman love the English, nor the Indian brave tolerate the thought of the American is not disgraceful to the nature of man; rather, indeed, honorable, since it depends on wrongs ancient, like the race, and not personal to him who cherishes the indignation.

96.

HENRY GEORGE: Progress and Civilization

Henry George wondered, as he observed the American economy of the 1870s, why it was that the increasing wealth of the country seemed always to be accompanied by increasing poverty. He thought he had found the answer to his question in his study of price rises in California land as the result of the building of the transcontinental railroad, and he devoted the rest of his life to advocating, as the essential one among other social reforms, a tax on land that would discourage monopolies based on the rapid appreciation of land values. In his view, such a "single tax" would have the double value of equalizing wealth and paying the total cost of government. His economic ideas were explained in Progress and Poverty *(1879), one of the most famous volumes of social protest ever written in the United States. The portion of the book reprinted below discusses, among other matters, its author's theory of progress.*

Source: *Progress and Poverty,* New edition, 1900, pp. 3-13, 503-549.

COULD . . . A FRANKLIN or a Priestley have seen in a vision of the future, the steamship taking the place of the sailing vessel, the railroad train of the wagon, the reaping machine of the scythe, the threshing machine of the flail; could he have heard the throb of the engines that in obedience to human will, and for the satisfaction of human desire, exert a power greater than that of all the men and all the beasts of burden of the earth combined; could he have seen the forest tree transformed into finished lumber — into doors, sashes, blinds, boxes or barrels — with hardly the touch of a human hand; the great workshops where boots and shoes are turned out by the case with less labor than the old-fashioned cobbler could have put on a sole; the factories where, under the eye of a girl, cotton becomes cloth faster than hundreds of stalwart weavers could have turned it out with their handlooms; could he have seen steam hammers shaping mammoth shafts and mighty anchors, and delicate machinery making tiny watches; the diamond drill cutting through the heart of the rocks, and coal oil sparing the whale; could he have realized the enormous saving of labor resulting from improved facilities of exchange and communication — sheep killed in Australia, eaten fresh in England, and the order, given by the London banker in the afternoon, executed in San Francisco in the morning of the same day — could he have conceived of the hundred thousand improvements which these only suggest, what would he have inferred as to the social condition of mankind?

It would not have seemed like an inference; further than the vision went it would have seemed as though he saw; and his heart would have leaped and his nerves would have thrilled, as one who from a height beholds just ahead of the thirst-stricken caravan the living gleam of rustling woods and the glint of laughing waters. Plainly, in the sight of the imagination, he would have beheld these new forces elevating society from its very foundations, lifting the very poorest above the possibility of want, exempting the very lowest from anxiety for the material needs of life; he would have seen these slaves of the lamp of knowledge taking on themselves the traditional curse, these muscles of iron and sinews of steel making the poorest laborer's life a holiday, in which every high quality and noble impulse could have scope to grow.

And out of these bounteous material conditions he would have seen arising, as necessary sequences, moral conditions realizing the golden age of which mankind have always dreamed. Youth no longer stunted and starved; age no longer harried by avarice; the child at play with the tiger; the man with the muckrake drinking in the glory of the stars. Foul things fled, fierce things tame; discord turned to harmony! For how could there be greed where all had enough? How could the vice, the crime, the ignorance, the brutality that spring from poverty and the fear of poverty exist where poverty had vanished? Who should crouch where all were freemen; who oppress where all were peers?

More or less vague or clear, these have been the hopes, these the dreams born of the improvements which give this wonderful century its preeminence. They have sunk so deeply into the popular mind as radically to change the currents of thought, to recast creeds and displace the most fundamental conceptions. The haunting visions of higher possibilities have not merely gathered splendor and vividness but their direction has changed — instead of seeing behind the faint tinges of an expiring sunset, all the glory of the daybreak has decked the skies before.

It is true that disappointment has followed disappointment, and that discovery upon discovery and invention after invention have neither lessened the toil of those who most need respite nor brought plenty to the poor. But there have been so many things to which it seemed this failure could be laid that up to our time the new faith has hardly weakened. We have better appreciated the difficulties to be overcome; but not the less trusted that the tendency of the times was to overcome them.

Now, however, we are coming into collision with facts which there can be no mistaking. From all parts of the civilized world come complaints of industrial depression; of labor condemned to involuntary idleness; of capital massed and wasting; of pecuniary distress among businessmen; of want and suffering and anxiety among the working classes. All the dull, deadening pain, all the keen, maddening anguish, that to great masses of men are involved in the words "hard times," afflict the world today. This state of things, common to communities differing so widely in situation, in political institutions, in fiscal and financial systems, in density of population and in social organization can hardly be accounted for by local causes: There is distress where large standing armies are maintained, but there is also distress where the standing armies are nominal; there is distress where protective tariffs stupidly and wastefully hamper trade, but there is also distress where trade is nearly free; there is distress where autocratic government yet prevails, but there is also distress where political power is wholly in the hands of the people; in countries where paper is money, and in countries where gold and silver are the only currency. Evidently, beneath all such things as these, we must infer a common cause.

That there is a common cause, and that it is either what we call material progress or something closely connected with material progress, becomes more than an inference when it is noted that the phenomena we class together and speak of as industrial depression are but intensifications of phenomena which always accompany material progress, and which show themselves more clearly and strongly as material progress goes on. Where the conditions to which material progress everywhere tends are most fully realized — that is to say, where population is densest, wealth greatest, and the machinery of production and exchange most highly developed — we find the deepest poverty, the sharpest struggle for existence, and the most of enforced idleness.

It is to the newer countries — that is, to the countries where material progress is yet in its earlier stages — that laborers emigrate in search of higher wages and capital flows in search of higher interest. It is in the older countries — that is to say, the countries where material progress has reached later stages — that widespread destitution is found in the midst of the greatest abundance. Go into one of the new communities where Anglo-Saxon vigor is just beginning the race of progress; where the machinery of production and exchange is yet rude and inefficient; where the increment of wealth is not yet great enough to enable any class to live in ease and luxury; where the best house is but a cabin of logs or a cloth and paper shanty, and the richest man is forced to daily work; and though you will find an absence of wealth and all its concomitants, you will find no beggars. There is no luxury, but there is no destitution. No one makes an easy living, nor a very good living; but everyone *can* make a living, and no one able and willing to work is oppressed by the fear of want.

But just as such a community realizes the conditions which all civilized communities are striving for and advances in the scale of material progress; just as closer settlement and a more intimate connection with the rest of the world and greater utilization of laborsaving machinery make possible greater economies in production and exchange, and wealth in consequence increases, not merely in the aggregate but in proportion to population, so does poverty take a darker aspect. Some get an infinitely better and easier living, but others find it hard to get a living at all. The "tramp" comes with the locomotive, and almshouses and prisons are as surely the marks of "material progress" as are costly dwellings, rich warehouses, and magnificent churches. Upon streets lighted with gas and patrolled by uniformed policemen, beggars wait for the passerby, and in the shadow of college and library and museum are gathering the more hideous Huns and fiercer Vandals of whom Macaulay prophesied.

This fact — the great fact that poverty and all its concomitants show themselves in communities just as they develop into the conditions toward which material progress tends — proves that the social difficulties existing wherever a certain stage of progress has been reached do not arise from local circumstances but are, in some way or another, engendered by progress itself.

And, unpleasant as it may be to admit it, it is at last becoming evident that the enormous increase in productive power which has marked the present century and is still going on with accelerating ratio, has no tendency to extirpate poverty or to lighten the burdens of those compelled to toil. It simply widens the gulf between Dives and Lazarus, and makes the struggle for existence more intense. The march of invention has clothed mankind with powers of which a century ago the boldest imagination could not have dreamed. But in factories where laborsaving machinery has reached its most wonderful development, little children are at work; wherever the new forces are anything like fully utilized, large classes are maintained by charity or live on the verge of recourse to it; amid the greatest accumulations of wealth, men die of starvation and puny infants suckle dry breasts; while everywhere the greed of gain, the worship of wealth shows the force of the fear of want. The promised land flies before us like the mirage. The fruits of the tree of knowledge turn, as we grasp them, to apples of Sodom that crumble at the touch.

It is true that wealth has been greatly increased and that the average of comfort, leisure, and refinement has been raised; but these gains are not general. In them the lowest class do not share. I do not mean that the condition of the lowest class has nowhere nor in anything been improved; but that there is nowhere any improvement which can be credited to increased productive power. I mean that the tendency of what we call material progress is in nowise to improve the condition of the lowest class in the essentials of healthy, happy human life. Nay, more, that it is still further to depress the condition of the lowest class. The new forces, elevating in their nature though they be, do not act upon the social fabric from underneath, as was for a long time hoped and believed, but strike it at a point intermediate between top and bottom. It is as though an immense wedge were being forced, not underneath society but through society. Those who are above the point of separation are elevated, but those who are below are crushed down.

This depressing effect is not generally realized, for it is not apparent where there has long existed a class just able to live. Where the lowest class barely lives, as has been the case for a long time in many parts of Europe, it is impossible for it to get any lower, for the next lowest step is out of existence, and no tendency to further depression can readily show itself. But in the progress of new settlements to the conditions of older communities it may clearly be seen that material progress does not merely fail to relieve poverty; it actually produces it. In the United States it is clear that squalor and misery, and the vices and crimes that spring from them, everywhere increase as the village grows to the city, and the march of development brings the advantages of the improved methods of production and exchange. It is in the older and richer sections of the Union that pauperism and distress among the working classes are becoming most painfully apparent. If there is less deep poverty in San Francisco than in New York, is it not because San Francisco is yet behind New York in all that both cities are striving for? When San Francisco reaches the point where New York now is, who can doubt that there will also be ragged and barefooted children on her streets?

This association of poverty with progress is the great enigma of our times. It is the central fact from which spring industrial, social, and political difficulties that perplex the world, and with which statesmanship and philanthropy and education grapple in vain. From it come the clouds that overhang the future of the most progressive and self-reliant nations. It is the riddle which the Sphinx of Fate puts to our civilization, and which not to answer is to be destroyed. So long as all the increased wealth which modern progress brings goes but to build up great fortunes, to increase luxury, and make sharper the contrast between the House of Have and the House of Want, progress is not real and cannot be permanent. The reaction must come. The tower leans from its foundations, and every new story but hastens the final catastrophe. . . .

What, then, is the law of human progress — the law under which civilization advances? . . .

It is not difficult to discover such a law. We have but to look and we may see it. I do not pretend to give it scientific precision but merely to point it out.

The incentives to progress are the desires inherent in human nature — the desire to gratify the wants of the animal nature, the wants of the intellectual nature, and the wants of the sympathetic nature; the desire to be, to know, and to do — desires that short of infinity can never be satisfied, as they grow by what they feed on.

Mind is the instrument by which man advances and by which each advance is secured and made the vantage ground for new advances. Though he may not by taking thought add a cubit to his stature, man may by taking thought extend his knowledge of the universe and his power over it, in what, so far as we can see, is an infinite degree. The narrow span of human life allows the individual to go but a short distance, but though each generation may do but little, yet generations, succeeding to the gain of their predecessors, may gradually elevate the status of mankind, as coral polyps, building one generation upon the work of the other, gradually elevate themselves from the bottom of the sea.

Mental power is therefore the motor of progress, and men tend to advance in proportion to the mental power expended in progression — the mental power which is devoted to the extension of knowledge, the improvement of methods, and the betterment of social conditions.

Now mental power is a fixed quantity — that is to say, there is a limit to the work a man can do with his mind, as there is to the work he can do with his body; therefore, the mental power which can be devoted to progress is only what is left after what is required for nonprogressive purposes.

These nonprogressive purposes in which mental power is consumed may be classified as maintenance and conflict. By maintenance I mean, not only the support of existence but the keeping up of the social condition and the holding of advances already gained. By conflict I mean, not merely warfare and preparation for warfare but all expenditure of mental power in seeking the gratification of desire at the expense of others and in resistance to such aggression.

To compare society to a boat. Her progress through the water will not depend upon the exertion of her crew but upon the exertion devoted to propelling her. This will be lessened by any expenditure of force required for bailing, or any expenditure of force in fighting among themselves or in pulling in different directions.

Now, as in a separated state the whole powers of man are required to maintain existence, and mental power is set free for higher uses only by the association of men in communities, which permits the division of labor and all the economies which come with the cooperation of increased numbers, association is the first essential of progress. Improvement becomes possible as men come together in peaceful association, and the wider and closer the association, the greater the possibilities of improvement. And as the wasteful expenditure of mental power in conflict becomes greater or less as the moral law which accords to each an equality of rights is ignored or is recognized, equality (or justice) is the second essential of progress.

Thus association in equality is the law of progress. Association frees mental power for expenditure in improvement, and equality, or justice, or freedom — for the terms here signify the same thing, the recognition of the moral law — prevents the dissipation of this power in fruitless struggles.

Here is the law of progress, which will explain all diversities, all advances, all halts and retrogressions. Men tend to progress just as they come closer together, and by cooperation with each other increase the mental power that may be devoted to improvement, but just as conflict is provoked, or association develops inequality of condition and power, this tendency to progression is lessened, checked, and finally reversed. . . .

But the great cause of inequality is in the natural monopoly which is given by the possession of land. The first perceptions of men seem always to be that land is common property; but the rude devices by which this is at first recognized — such as annual partitions or cultivation in common — are consistent with only a low stage of development. The idea of property, which naturally arises with reference to things of human production, is easily transferred to land, and an institution which when population is sparse merely secures to the improver and user the due reward of his labor, finally, as population becomes dense and rent arises, operates to strip the producer of his wages. Not merely this, but the appropriation of rent for public purposes, which is the only way in which, with anything like a high development, land can be readily retained as common property, becomes, when political and religious power passes into the hands of a class, the ownership of the land by that class, and the rest of the community become merely tenants. And wars and conquests, which tend to the concentration of political power and to the institution of slavery, naturally result where social growth has given land a value, in the appropriation of the soil.

A dominant class who concentrate power in their hands will likewise soon concentrate ownership of the land. To them will fall large partitions of conquered land, which the former inhabitants will till as tenants or serfs, and the public domain, or common lands, which in the natural course of social growth are left for awhile in every country, and in which state the primitive system of village culture leaves pasture and woodland, are readily acquired, as we see by modern instances. And inequality once established, the ownership of land tends to concentrate as development goes on.

I am merely attempting to set forth the general fact that, as a social development goes on, inequality tends to establish itself, and not to point out the particular sequence, which must necessarily vary with different conditions. But this main fact makes intelligible all the phenomena of petrifaction and retrogression. The unequal distribution of the power and wealth gained by the integration of men in society tends to check, and finally to counterbalance, the force by which improvements are made and society advances. On the one side, the masses of the community are compelled to expend their mental powers in merely maintaining existence. On the other side, mental power is expended in keeping up and intensifying the system of inequality, in ostentation, luxury, and warfare.

A community divided into a class that rules and a class that is ruled — into the very rich and the very poor — may "build like giants and finish like jewelers"; but it will be monuments of ruthless pride and barren vanity, or of a religion turned from its office of elevating man into an instrument for keeping him down. Invention may for awhile to some degree go on; but it will be the invention of refinements in luxury, not the inventions that relieve toil and increase power.

In the arcana of temples or in the chambers of court, physicians' knowledge may still be sought; but it will be hidden as a secret thing, or if it dares come out to elevate common thought or brighten common life, it will be trodden down as a dangerous innovator. For as it tends to lessen the mental power devoted to improvement, so does inequality tend to render men adverse to improvement. How strong is the disposition to adhere to old methods among the classes who are kept in ignorance by being compelled to toil for a mere existence is too well known to require illustration; and, on the other hand, the conservatism of the classes to whom the existing social adjustment gives special advantages is equally apparent.

This tendency to resist innovation, even though it be improvement, is observable in every special organization — in religion, in law, in medicine, in science, in trade guilds; and it becomes intense just as the organization is close. A close corporation has always an instinctive dislike of innovation and innovators, which is but the expression of an instinctive fear that change may tend to throw down the barriers which hedge it in from the common herd and so rob it of importance and power; and it is always disposed to guard carefully its special knowledge or skill.

It is in this way that petrifaction succeeds progress. The advance of inequality necessarily brings improvement to a halt, and as it still persists or provokes unavailing reactions, draws even upon the mental power necessary for maintenance, and retrogression begins. These principles make intelligible the history of civilization.

97.

Rutherford B. Hayes: Veto of the Army Appropriation Act

From his election in 1876, President Hayes's relations with Congress were strained. The opposition of the Democratic majority was manifested in congressional attempts to enact laws objectionable to the President by attaching them as "riders" to necessary appropriation acts. Hayes vetoed six appropriation bills with "riders," the intent of which was to annul the Force Acts of 1870-1875. On the occasion of one such bill, the Army Appropriation Act of 1879, Hayes dealt forcefully with the problem of "riders" in the following veto message of April 29. For his strong exercise of presidential authority against congressional encroachment, Hayes won widespread public support.

Source: Richardson, VII, pp. 523-532.

UPON THE ASSEMBLING of this Congress, in pursuance of a call for an extra session, which was made necessary by the failure of the Forty-fifth Congress to make the needful appropriations for the support of the government, the question was presented whether the attempt made in the last Congress to ingraft by construction a new principle upon the Constitution should be persisted in or not. This Congress has ample opportunity and time to pass the appropriation bills, and also to enact any political measures which may be determined upon in separate bills by the usual and orderly methods of proceeding.

But the majority of both houses have deemed it wise to adhere to the principles asserted and maintained in the last Congress by the majority of the House of Representatives. That principle is that the House of Representatives has the sole right to originate bills for raising revenue and therefore has the right to withhold appropriations upon which the existence of the government may depend unless the Senate and the President shall give their assent to any legisla-tion which the House may see fit to attach to appropriation bills. To establish this principle is to make a radical, dangerous, and unconstitutional change in the character of our institutions. The various departments of the government and the army and the navy are established by the Constitution or by laws passed in pursuance thereof. Their duties are clearly defined and their support is carefully provided for by law.

The money required for this purpose has been collected from the people and is now in the treasury, ready to be paid out as soon as the appropriation bills are passed. Whether appropriations are made or not, the collection of the taxes will go on. The public money will accumulate in the treasury. It was not the intention of the framers of the Constitution that any single branch of the government should have the power to dictate conditions upon which this treasure should be applied to the purpose for which it was collected. Any such intention, if it had been entertained, would have been plainly expressed in the Constitution.

That a majority of the Senate now concurs in the claim of the House adds to the gravity of the situation but does not alter the question at issue. The new doctrine, if maintained, will result in a consolidation of unchecked and despotic power in the House of Representatives. A bare majority of the House will become the government. The executive will no longer be what the framers of the Constitution intended — an equal and independent branch of the government. It is clearly the constitutional duty of the President to exercise his discretion and judgment upon all bills presented to him without constraint or duress from any other branch of the government. To say that a majority of either or both of the houses of Congress may insist upon the approval of a bill under the penalty of stopping all of the operations of the government for want of the necessary supplies is to deny to the executive that share of the legislative power which is plainly conferred by the 2nd Section of the 7th Article of the Constitution. It strikes from the Constitution the qualified negative of the President.

It is said that this should be done because it is the peculiar function of the House of Representatives to represent the will of the people. But no single branch or department of the government has exclusive authority to speak for the American people. The most authentic and solemn expression of their will is contained in the Constitution of the United States. By that Constitution they have ordained and established a government whose powers are distributed among coordinate branches, which, as far as possible consistently with a harmonious cooperation, are absolutely independent of each other. The people of this country are unwilling to see the supremacy of the Constitution replaced by the omnipotence of any one department of the government.

The enactment of this bill into a law will establish a precedent which will tend to destroy the equal independence of the several branches of the government. Its principle places not merely the Senate and the executive but the judiciary also under the coercive dictation of the House. The House alone will be the judge of what constitutes a grievance, and also of the means and measure of redress. An act of Congress to protect elections is now the grievance complained of; but the House may on the same principle determine that any other act of Congress, a treaty made by the President with the advice and consent of the Senate, a nomination or appointment to office, or that a decision or opinion of the Supreme Court is a grievance, and that the measure of redress is to withhold the appropriations required for the support of the offending branch of the government.

Believing that this bill is a dangerous violation of the spirit and meaning of the Constitution, I am compelled to return it to the House in which it originated without my approval. The qualified negative with which the Constitution invests the President is a trust that involves a duty which he cannot decline to perform. With a firm and conscientious purpose to do what I can to preserve unimpaired the constitutional powers and equal independence, not merely of the executive but of every branch of the government, which will be imperiled by the adoption of the principle of this bill, I desire earnestly to urge upon the House of Representatives a return to the wise and wholesome usage of the earlier days of the republic, which excluded from appropriation bills all irrelevant legislation.

By this course you will inaugurate an important reform in the method of congressional legislation; your action will be in harmony with the fundamental principles of the Constitution and the patriotic sentiment of nationality which is their firm support, and you will restore to the country that feeling of confidence and security and the repose which are so essential to the prosperity of all of our fellow citizens.

1880

98.

WILLIAM MCELROY: Advice to a Young Politician

The following satirical look at politics was written at a time when big city machines were notorious for deep-seated corruption. Though published anonymously in the Atlantic Monthly, *the article has since been ascribed to journalist William McElroy. Written in the form of a letter, it was originally titled "An Old War Horse to a Young Politician."*

Source: *Atlantic Monthly*, June 1880.

My Dear Nephew,

I was seventy years old yesterday, and although I feel as young as I ever did, I cannot shut my eyes to the fact that, in spite of my feelings, I really am an old man. So, since I must soon pass off the stage on which — if I say it who shouldn't — I have long been a prominent figure, it is only natural that I should desire, in the absence of a son of my own, that my mantle should fall to a son of one of my blood.

I believe you have good stuff in you. Your valedictory when you graduated last summer, although containing too little that was practical to suit my taste, would have done credit to the average cong — I was going to write congressman; but I can justly go further than that. It would have done credit to the Washington journalists, who sometimes compose — that is to say, revise — speeches for some of us congressmen. This, however, like the rest of my communication, is strictly between ourselves.

When I left you on Commencement Day, I urged you to lose no time in getting into politics, promising that I would help you push your fortunes as occasion offered. Since then I have received a letter from you in which you write that you have read *Story on the Constitution*, Benton's *Thirty Years in the United States Senate*, Greeley's *American Conflict*, two or three works on political economy, and De Tocqueville on America. I suppose there can be no objection to such reading. Likely enough it has its value.

But what I particularly desire, my dear nephew, is that you should become a practical politician, a thoroughly practical politician. I never remember reading any of the works you have mentioned, or any like them, unless, indeed, you call Barnum's *How to Make Money* a treatise on finance. And yet, cast your eyes over the salient points of my career. I have been alderman, supervisor, mayor, state representative, state senator, and congressman. For many years I have been chairman of our state and county committees. I can hardly remember the time when I didn't carry the vote of my own ward in my vest pocket and of my own city in my trousers' pocket, and I've got them there yet.

For going on half a century I have had things pretty much my own way in caucuses and primaries, and the like. What has been the secret of my unusual success? I will try — in strict confidence, as you will understand — to give you some plain, blunt, nonpartisan hints for your guidance in politics which may serve to answer the question.

1. Never allow yourself to lose sight of the fact that politics, and not poker, is our great American game. If this could be beaten into the heads of some presumably well-meaning but glaringly unpractical people, we should hear less idiotic talk about reform in connection with politics. Nobody ever dreams of organizing a reform movement in poker. How droll it would sound to read that "Hon. John Oakhurst, Hon. William Nye, and Hon. Ah Sin, in connection with other well-known citizens of California, are engaged in endeavoring to reform poker from the inside!"

And yet political reform clubs, designed to reform politics from the inside or the outside, are springing up on all sides. Of course, it is just as well not to attempt to argue the masses out of their deeply rooted notion that politics is what Noah Webster defines it to be, "that part of *ethics* which has to do with the regulation and government of a nation or state." Ethics is very good in connection with politics. But then Webster, it must be remembered, was simply a learned lexicographer, and not a practical politician. No, no. Don't try to reason with the masses in this matter. The public has no head for such things. It will not understand.

2. Mr. Lincoln, a very estimable and justly popular, but in some respects an imprac-

ticable, man, formulated another widely diffused error in regard to politics. He held that ours is a government of the people, by the people, for the people. I maintain, on the contrary, that it is a government of politicians, by politicians, for politicians. If your political career is to be a success, you must understand and respect this distinction with a difference.

3. Not a few capable but unpractical people, when they fall to discussing our governmental system, argue that the existence of parties is necessary to the welfare of our country. But long experience has taught me that the more sensible way for a practical politician to look at it is that the existence of the country is necessary to the welfare of parties. Thank Heaven, my dear nephew, that we have a country!

4. You have received your commission as postmaster of your village. A post office is a capital political opening for a young man who has sense enough to discover how to make the right use of it. You will of course leave all matters touching the postal service to your deputy. Never forget that your pivotal duty as postmaster will be to nurse the party in your section. As a practical man, you must see, if you reflect a moment, that postmaster and local partymaster must be convertible terms with you if you expect to be approved by the great party leaders, and to become a great leader yourself, some day. To be sure, if you find leisure, there can be nothing indelicate in your appearing at the post office now and then and doing a few strokes of purely postal work. But take care that such service does not encroach upon the hours when you ought to be fostering the party boom.

In your selection of clerks you will be guided primarily by a determination to have only such men around you as will register your will every time at caucuses and conventions. Should it turn out in any instance that you have been deceived in your man, be nice about the phrase with which you discharge him. I submit a formula which has been repeatedly tried, and generally found to work well. We will suppose the clerk who won't answer is named John Doe. You will call him into your private office and address him substantially as follows: "Mr. Doe, I am compelled with all reluctance, at the call of duty, to dissever our relations, and must request you to file your resignation forthwith. During your connection with this office as letter carrier, you have displayed an ability and a fidelity, a grace of manner and a strength of character that have endeared you to all your associates and done not a little to elevate the tone of the entire American postal service. If I have brought myself to part with you, it is solely to the end that there may be greater homogeneousness of view, so to speak, in the office."

One of your predecessors used this formula with great satisfaction to himself, and apparently to those whom he decapitated. He always found, he told me, that the first part of it put the clerk to whom it was addressed in capital humor, while the "homogeneousness" dazed him to that extent that he walked out of the office minus his head, not appreciating what had been the matter, but having a nebulous impression that he had been killed by kindness.

5. I sincerely hope it is not necessary that I should counsel you always to vote the regular ticket, the whole regular ticket, and nothing but the regular ticket. Hold fast, I beseech you, to the doctrine of the infallibility of your party in convention assembled. Delegates, like kings, "can do no wrong." The voters who scratch ballots or bolt nominations are to be regarded as the bane of politics, just as certain other reformers have been the bane of religion. They all belong in the same category, and all are equally deserving of the execration of every practical man, as exponents of the pestiferous doctrine of the right of private judgment.

And just here a word in reply to the familiar question, Would you vote for the devil if he received the party's regular nomination? I have no hesitation in affirming that I certainly would. Let's look at it. If the day ever comes when the devil is nominated, the other side will be pretty sure to run Gabriel against him. Of the two, my choice would be the devil. To be sure, it would not be an ideal nomination, but, then, neither is ours an ideal world. I am aware that the devil has split hoofs, pronounced horns, and a bifurcated tail. But do we choose candidates for their good looks? As to his moral character, I frankly admit it is not all I could desire; but after criticism has exhausted itself, the fact remains, conceded by both parties, that he is not as black as he is painted.

On the other hand, he has many qualities that ought to commend him to practical men. He is self-made, he is thoroughly in earnest in all he undertakes, he is an untiring worker, he is one of the shrewdest of wire-pullers, he possesses vast and versatile accomplishments, he is unsurpassed in ability to find and manipulate the springs that move men, he has a positive genius for making friends. Gifted, popular, magnetic, at home in all circles, from the highest to the lowest, he would be certain to make a splendid run.

As for Gabriel, I have only to say that, while his intellectual and moral endowments are undoubtedly of the highest order, there is great reason to fear that he would not succeed in the realm of practical politics. If elected to office, it is more than likely that he would prove more of a botheration than a boon to his party. He would be living up to the promises made during the canvass; he would resolutely decline to let well enough alone. Let me not be misunderstood. I yield to no one in my regard for Gabriel. But, as a practical man, I would feel called upon to vote against him, and do all I could for his opponent. In my own ward, where my influence is most potent and my political theories most approved of, I feel convinced that the devil would have a very large majority.

This hypothetical case is, of course, an extreme one, and is never likely to occur. I have dealt with it simply for the sake of showing you that the position of those who insist upon the invariable support of regular nominations is sound in the last analysis.

6. How are scratchers and bolters to be dealt with? It is an exceedingly difficult question. I myself am at a loss to determine whether it is better to be extremely tender or awfully rough with them. Each policy is good at times, and in making a choice you must be guided by circumstances. In a sterner age than ours, an age that had less stomach for nonsense, gentlemen who were convicted of the crime of private judgment were burned at the stake. It is not permitted us in these latter, laxer days to make it as warm for scratchers and bolters as it was once made for John Huss; still we can show that we possess the sturdy practical views of those who flung Huss to the fagots, by pelting the scratchers and bolters with jeers, sneers, and innuendoes, by crediting them with the meanest of motives, and insisting that they are either traitorous, inconsequential knaves, or silly, inconsequential fools.

As for those upon whom such treatment is lost (and I confess that I suspect it fails with the majority of scratchers and bolters), try what is known to practical politicians as the postponement treatment. By the skillful use of this treatment I kept Vandyke Podgers from scratching or bolting for thirty-six consecutive years, and then, just before the state election, he died, and there was an end of that embarrassment. When I began to reason with him there was a presidential canvass on. "Podgers," said I, "as you love your country, do not scratch this year. Consider the far-reaching and vital importance of the issues involved." Podgers concluded to postpone. The following year I accomplished my purpose by reminding him that "this is the first and therefore the most critical year of an administration which upon the whole you endorse, Podgers, and which it is incumbent upon you to make some sacrifices heartily to sustain." He concluded to postpone.

The next year my argument took the shape of, "My dear Podgers, let me beg of you to vote a straight ticket this year. Do you realize what year it is, Podgers? Of course you do. I need not remind a gentleman of your exceptional intelligence that this election is but the prelude to the presidential election of next year, with its issues of far-reaching and vital importance." Podgers concluded to postpone.

The next year was the presidential year, when I repeated the argument first mentioned. The others in turn again did service, and so on for thirty-six years. And that's the way I kept persuading Podgers to postpone. He never was, but always to be, a scratcher or a bolter. At the elections at which no national or state ticket was run, and only minor local offices were to be filled, I pointed out to Podgers the necessity of keeping the party organization intact; and when all other arguments failed, I insisted that of two evils he should always choose the least and that, admitting that our ticket was evil, it was the least of the two.

Even this brief and inadequate account of its application will make sufficiently clear to you, I think, the true inwardness of the postponement treatment. Just one word more about it. Those who employ it with the most gratifying results allow the impression to be produced in the patient's mind at the outset that, although they have never happened to find an election at which scratching or bolting could be indulged in without perfectly harrowing injury to public interests of colossal moment, yet, nevertheless, they heartily and unreservedly approve of scratching and bolting in the abstract. Such an attitude on my part toward poor

Podgers won his confidence at our first political conference on this subject, and produced in him a mood hospitable to all my subsequent arguments and admonitions.

This communication has already exceeded reasonable limits, and yet I have only touched upon a few points. But perhaps I have written enough to start you right, to make you understand the nature of our great American game, and to put you in possession of the clue to the secret of playing it successfully. Be it yours to consult the expedient, leaving it to the purists of the party to consult the highly proper.

Beware of those who take sentimental views of unsentimental matters. A man who would "rather be right than be president" by all means ought to decline a presidential nomination, and run for a position in a theological seminary, a Sunday school, or Vassar College; while he who holds that "one with God is a majority" antagonizes the system of reckoning which has come down to us from the fathers, and which has the approval of every practical inspector of American elections. Be practical in your politics, be practical, ever more be practical.

99.

James Baird Weaver: The Greenback Party

The Greenback Party was a minor political party that flourished in the period from 1874 to 1884, following the hard times brought on by the Panic of 1873. The party received its name from its proposal in 1876 that the federal government issue large amounts of "greenbacks," or U.S. Treasury notes, a device first used during the Civil War to raise revenues but now fallen into disuse. Peter Cooper was the party's first presidential candidate, in 1876. Two years later the party merged with various labor groups, winning in the congressional election of 1878 more than a million votes and electing fourteen congressmen. In 1880, with the prospect of becoming a major U.S. political party, the Greenbackers ran James B. Weaver of Iowa on a platform advocating, among other things, woman suffrage, a graduated income tax, and welfare legislation of many kinds. Weaver, a nominal Republican who returned to that party after 1884, spelled out some of the issues of his candidacy in a letter accepting the nomination, dated July 3, 1880. His letter appears below.

Source: *The Platform of the National Greenback Labor Party and the Letter of Acceptance of General J. B. Weaver,* n.p., n.d.

It is my pleasure to acknowledge the receipt of your letter of June 23, 1880, formally notifying me of my nomination for the office of President of the United States, by the united Greenback Labor Party, whose representatives convened at Chicago, June 9th, 1880.

I am profoundly grateful for the honor

conferred. Fully realizing the high responsibility to which I have been called, and conscious that the position was unsought by me, I accept the nomination as a solemn duty. The convention is to be congratulated upon the great work accomplished in the unification of the various Greenback and Labor elements into one compact organization. This was of first importance, and thoroughly prepares our forces to strike a decisive blow for industrial emancipation during the impending struggle.

Our party has this significance: it is a great labor movement, composed of earnest people who earn their bread by honest toil, whether of hand, head, or heart; and as the world depends for the comforts of life upon the various departments of human toil, so will every part of society feel the vivifying influence of the grand achievements of our organization that lie just in the future; for when labor is prosperous, every other element of society feels the impulse of vigorous life.

The three great political parties have each selected their candidates and made formal declaration of their principles. It is now the high duty of every citizen of the United States to judge between them; and after careful inquiry into the aims and purposes of each, to determine the organization with which duty calls him to act.

The admirable platform adopted by the convention meets my cordial approval. It is comprehensive, reasonable, and progressive, containing those principles of economic reform essential to the preservation of the liberty and the prosperity of the whole people.

It being the duty of man to earn his bread in the sweat of his face, it becomes the first duty of civil government to foster industry. All laws, therefore, which place a premium upon idleness, whether of men or money, unjustly discriminate in favor of capital or withhold from honest men the full and just reward of their labor, are simply monstrous. Capital should be the servant of labor rather than its master.

This great truth can never be realized until there is an adequate circulating medium. Inasmuch as this circulating medium is for the benefit of all, its issue and volume should be sacredly kept under the control of the people without the intervention of banking corporations. All money, whether gold, silver, or paper, should be issued by the supreme authority of the nation, and be made a full legal tender in payment of all debts, public and private.

The system which now prevails gives into the hands of banking corporations absolute control over the volume of the currency, and through this they have the power to fix the price of the labor and property of 50 million people. By provision of law the method is clearly defined whereby they may, without limit, inflate or contract the currency at will. Cognate to this, and a part of the same scheme, stands the system of funding the public debt. Like national banking, this was borrowed from the English monarchy. By this system an enormous nontaxable, interest-bearing debt is to be perpetuated. The bonds support the banks and the banks foster the public debt. If you pay off the bonds, the banks must cease to exist. Hence, if the national banks are to continue, we must have a perpetual bonded debt. Both patriotism and sound statesmanship loudly call for the abolition of banks of issue and the substitution of legal tender treasury notes for their circulation. Pay the bonds according to contract, and as rapidly as possible.

Seven hundred million of the public debt become redeemable, at the option of the government, during this and the ensuing year. Two funding bills are now pending before Congress — one introduced by the Democratic and the other by the Republican leader of the House, whereby it is proposed to deprive the people for twenty and thirty years of the lawful right to pay said bonds. This is a crime against the laborer and the taxpayer and should cause widespread alarm among all classes.

The annual surplus revenues and the idle coin now in the treasury, and that which must continue to accumulate if the silver law approved February 28, 1878, shall be honestly enforced, are ample to pay every dollar of the $700 million, both principal and interest, within the next six years. There is not the slightest excuse for funding these bonds, except to perpetuate the debt as the basis of an iniquitous banking monopoly. It must be apparent to all that the moneyed institutions and other corporations now have control of nearly every department of our government and are fast swallowing up the profits of labor and reducing the people to a condition of vassalage and dependence. These monopolies, of whatever class, headed by the associated banks, are interlocked in purpose and always act in closest sympathy.

There are three industrial classes in America: first, the producers; second, those who manufacture our raw materials and prepare them for use; third, the distributors of these products. Each should be protected in the legitimate fruits and profits of their labor, but should not be permitted to extort from and enslave the others.

The great problem of our civilization is how to bring the producer and consumer together. This can only be done by providing an adequate circulating medium and by rigid regulation of interstate commerce and transportation. This was wisely foreseen by the framers of the Constitution, and, accordingly, by the 8th Section of Article I, Congress is clothed with power "to regulate commerce with foreign nations and among the states." This power imposes a corresponding duty upon Congress to see that it is enforced.

The two great agents of commerce are money and transportation. It is undeniable that both of these agents are under absolute control of monopolies. By controlling the volume of money, the banks fix the price of all labor and property; and the railroads, by combination, render competition impossible and control absolutely the price of transportation.

This places the people between the upper and nether millstones, and grinds them to poverty and ruin. It results in the wholesale robbery of both producer and consumer. Who is able to controvert this stupendous fact? Farmers, planters, and laboring men of the United States, I beseech you to open your eyes at once to this alarming condition of things.

I am especially thankful that the platform of the party which placed me in nomination is open, bold, and unmistakable on these great questions.

The Republican and Democratic platforms are either silent with regard to these vital issues or they have pronounced in favor of the monopolies and against the people. With 50 million people looking them in the face and pleading for relief, they utter not one word of promise or hope. Their leaders and platform makers are in the toils of the syndicate, gigantic bank corporations and railroad monopolies, and have neither the disposition nor the courage to strike one generous blow for industrial emancipation.

An area of our public domain, larger than the territory occupied by the great German Empire, has been wantonly donated to wealthy corporations; while a bill introduced by Honorable Hendrick B. Wright, of Pennsylvania, to enable our poor people to reach and occupy the few acres remaining, has been scouted, ridiculed, and defeated in Congress. In consequence of this stupendous system of land grabbing, millions of the young men of America, and millions more of industrious people from abroad seeking homes in the New World, are left homeless and destitute. The public domain must be sacredly reserved to actual settlers, and where corporations have not complied strictly with the terms of their grants, the land should be at once reclaimed.

The immigration of persons from foreign countries seeking homes and desiring to become citizens of the United States should be encouraged; but the importation of Chinese servile laborers should be prohibited by stringent laws.

While the bondholder has been paid gold in return for his depreciated currency, the soldiers and sailors who saved our Union, our homes, our money, and our altars, and whose blood consecrated every battlefield from Belmont and Donelson to Gettysburg and Appomattox, are denied the pittance justly due them under their contract with the government — as though soldiers and sailors could live on gratitude alone.

By the answer of Secretary Sherman of June 10, 1880, to the Senate resolution of inquiry, it appears that the government paid the soldiers in greenbacks during the War of the Rebellion $1,249,519,135.16. The total interest paid in gold on the public debt from July 1, 1861, to June 30, 1879, is $1,809,301,485.19, and still we owe the principal of the debt. The soldier has been taxed to pay this interest, while the bondholder, as usual, has gone free.

During the present Congress it has been impossible to induce the committee to report a single bill to remedy existing evils. The important committees of the House are so constituted, and the despotic rules of that body so interpreted, as to render relief impossible. Under these rules the speaker is as much the dictator of the country as though he were an emperor and ruling in the most despotic government on the globe.

One of the grand missions of our party is to banish forever from American politics that deplorable spirit of sectional hatred, which, for base purposes, has been fostered by the leaders of the old parties. This has greatly deceived and embittered the public mind, both North and South.

Our civilization demands a new party, dedicated to the pursuits of peace, and which will not allow the war issues ever to be reopened, and will render the military strictly subordinate to the civil power. The war is over, and the sweet voice of peace, long neglected, calls us to worship at her altars. Let us crowd her temples with willing votaries. Let us have a free ballot, a fair count, and equal rights for all classes — for the laboring man in Northern manufactories, mines, and workshops, and for the struggling poor, both white and black, in the cotton fields of the South.

I most earnestly and solemnly invoke united action of all industrial classes, irrespective of party, that we may make a manly struggle for the independence of labor, and to reestablish in the administration of public affairs the old-time Democracy of Jefferson and Jackson, and the pure Republicanism of Abraham Lincoln and Thaddeus Stevens.

In consequence of the great avenue to public opinion — the press, and the bar, and the pulpit — being mainly under the control of the enemies of our movement, your convention thought proper to request its candidates to visit the various sections of the Union and talk to the people. It is my intention to comply with this request to the extent of my ability.

And, now, eschewing all violence and tumults as unworthy of the cause we represent, and relying upon Divine Providence and the justice of our cause, let us go forth in the great struggle for human rights.

The best system is to have one party govern and the other party watch.
THOMAS B. REED, speech in the House, April 22, 1880

100.

David A. Wells: The Communism of a Discriminating Income Tax

Economist David A. Wells served as a special advisor to the federal government on several occasions and was for a time chairman of the New York State Tax Commission. He was opposed to the theory of taxation that holds that everyone ought to bear the burden of taxes according to his ability to pay. Thus he was against any kind of graduated income tax, such as had been used by the government from 1863 to 1872. Wells's views on taxation are summed up in the following article of 1880.

Source: *North American Review*, March 1880.

As a ready and elastic method of raising revenue, the theory of an income tax always commands a certain degree of popular favor; and that, under the pressure of financial necessity, governments are inclined to make such a tax a part of their fiscal policy the experience of recent years abundantly demonstrates. Income taxes are at present levied in Great Britain, Austria, Germany, and Italy. They were enacted in the United States by the federal government in 1863 as one of a series of measures which a condition of war was held to justify, and continued in force with various modifications until 1872.

All modern systems of income taxation have recognized the principle of discriminating in favor of persons in the receipt of comparatively small incomes; and have provided, as a fundamental feature of their policy, that all incomes below a certain sum (usually a small amount) should be exempted from assessment. Thus, for example, the existing income tax of Great Britain commences with its assessment on incomes of £150 ($750) and upward, and exempts all incomes of a smaller amount. In Germany,

the income exemption being very small, nearly the whole population of the country, male and female, are made subject to the provisions of the income tax. All incomes subject to taxation in any European country are invariably assessed at one and the same rate.

In the United States, on the other hand, the income tax, as first enacted in 1863, exempted $600 annual income for each person, together with whatever was paid annually for rent and repairs of residence. Five percent per annum was then levied on all incomes above $600 and not in excess of $5,000; 7 percent on all incomes above $5,000 and not in excess of $10,000; and 10 percent on all incomes in excess of $10,000. In the income tax of the United States as it existed at one period, there was, therefore, recognized the principle, not only of exempting incomes below a certain amount from all taxation, which amount, in order to keep up an appearance of equity, was allowed to be equally deducted from all larger incomes, but, in addition, the further one — not recognized in any other existing income tax — of graduating the assessment by increasing the rate or percentage of taxation on the larger incomes.

This system was accordingly exceptional and peculiar; but as on first presentation and superficial examination it seems to embody an ingenious and equitable method of equalizing the burdens of the state between the rich and the poor, and also finds special favor with persons of a communistic turn of mind, by whom, with the discriminations largely increased, it is frequently recommended for reenactment, it is proposed in the interests of political and economic science to here subject it to analysis, with a view to determine whether any income tax which discriminates in any degree is likely, as is often claimed, to constitute the one perfect form of taxation of the future. And, at the outset, attention is asked to the following proposition:

Any income tax which permits of any exemption whatever is a graduated income tax. Any form of income tax which permits of exemption is graduated, not by the rate of the tax, but by the amount of the exemption, which is equally effective in producing discrimination and inequality, because all incomes below an arbitrary line are entirely exempt from the tax. Again, in treating of an income tax, it should be always borne in mind that, when a government *taxes the income of property,* it in reality taxes the property from which the income is derived.

In England and on the continent of Europe, land is taxed on its yearly revenue or income value, and these taxes are always considered as land taxes. Alexander Hamilton, in discussing the taxation of incomes derived directly from property, used this language: "What, in fact, is property but a fiction, without the beneficial use of it? In many instances, indeed, the income is the property itself." . . .

If the law exempts from taxation income from property to the extent of $2,000, it in effect exempts property of the capital value of $50,000 from taxation; for, at present, 4 percent is about the average profit of money, land, or other property, over and above all charges and taxes; and, at that rate of profit, $2,000 will be the annual income value of $50,000. Furthermore, if we assume that the annual income of realized property is 4 percent, that the exemption to each person is $2,000, and that the rate of the tax is 5 percent, then a person who owns only $50,000 in value of property will pay no tax; he who owns $60,000 in capital value of like property will pay on its entire income 1.2 percent, or 5 percent on the income of the capital value in excess of $50,000; he who owns $100,000 of property will pay on its income 2.5 percent; while he who owns $250,000 of property will pay on its income 4 percent; and thus the tax will be, in effect, graduated in rate and continually approximating, but never quite reaching a rate of 5 per cent — the property paying income being assumed to be always of the same and competing class.

In the case of the recent income tax of the United States, the number of persons who paid this tax when the exemption (in 1868) was $1,000 was 259,385; and when the amount of exemption was raised to $2,000, the number of taxable persons was reduced to 116,000, and subsequently ran down to 71,000 out of a total population of about 40 million. Experience, therefore, demonstrates that an exemption in the United States of $2,000 of income accredited to each individual owner of property will exempt *more than nine-tenths of the entire property* of this country and *more than ninety-nine-hundredths of the property owners* from this tax. Under such circumstances, it is a misnomer to call such an exaction taxation. It is unmasked confiscation and a burlesque on taxation.

Nor can an income tax which exempts $2,000 of income be defended under any rule or doctrine of *de minimis,* or rejection of fractions; for the property and income exempted are infinitely greater in the aggregate than the property and income of the same class made subject to the tax. Under this form of an income tax there can be no equality between taxed producers and untaxed producers, and more especially as the untaxed producers will be the most numerous, and the greatest producers in quantity as a body. No man is a free man the fruits of whose industry and capital are subject to surcharged (overburdened) exactions to an unlimited degree, and from which his immediate competitors are entirely exempt.

Equality of taxation of all persons and property brought into open competition under like circumstances is necessary to produce equality of condition for all, in all production, and in all the enjoyments of life, liberty, and property. Any government, whatever name it may assume, is a despotism and commits acts of flagrant spoliation if it grants exemptions or exacts a greater or less rate of tax from one man than from another man on account of his owning or having in his possession more or less of the same class of property which is the subject of the tax. M. Thiers in his work on the *Rights of Property* thus forcibly condemns confiscation under the name and form of a graduated income tax: "Proportionality," he says, "is a principle, but progression is a hateful despotism. . . . To exact a tenth from one, a fifth from another, and a third from another is pure despotism — it is robbery."

If it were proposed to levy a tax of 5 percent on annual incomes below $2,000 in amount and to exempt all incomes above that sum, the unequal and discriminating character of the exemption would be at once apparent; and yet an income tax exempting all incomes below $2,000 is equally unjust and discriminating. In either case the exemption cannot be founded or defended on any sound principles of free constitutional government. It is a simple manifestation of tyrannical power, under whatever form of government it may be enforced.

An exemption from taxation for a private (not public) purpose and taxation for private purposes alike violate the rights of property and of equal competition. "An exemption is freedom from a burden or service to which others are liable"; but an exemption for a public purpose or a valid consideration is not an exemption except in name, for the valid and full consideration, or public purpose promoted, is received in lieu of the tax. Nor is an exemption from taxation a discriminating burden on those who pay the tax, provided the person or institution benefited by the exemption is a pauper or a public charitable institution; for then there is a consideration for the exemption, and it is justified as a matter of economy and to prevent an expensive circuity of action in levying the tax with the sole purpose of giving it back to the intended beneficiary of the government.

The avoidance of this unnecessary circuity of action is not an injury but a gain to those who pay the tax. It cannot, however, be seriously claimed that a man having $50,000 in value of productive capital and receiving from it $2,000 of annual income is entitled to receive support from the government as a public pauper. Our governments, state or national, cannot impose taxes for the purpose of fostering any particular *private* business or enterprise. . . . Taxes can only be imposed for public purposes, and when they are imposed for any other purpose, the government acts the part of a highwayman and takes forcibly the property of A and gives it to B.

In fact, there is the same reason why all exemptions of like property from taxation should be based solely on the ground of a public purpose in the exemption as that all taxes collected should be for a public purpose. A tax upon the property of A and an exemption of the property of B, of the same competing class, will enhance the value of B's property and diminish the value of A's property to the extent of the tax. A, under the circumstances, will not be able to sell on terms of equality his *taxed* property in competition with the *untaxed* property of B; and this is equivalent to taking a certain amount of property or value from A and giving it to B. An exemption of any property, or income of the same competing class of property, made subject to taxation, is a form of charity or donation to the favored person who receives the advantages of the exemption. It cannot, moreover, be claimed that a public purpose will be promoted by collecting a given tax exclusively from persons who each own property in excess of $50,000, or in excess of the annual value of $2,000.

It may, however, be conceded that private property dedicated to a public use, like railroads, bridges, or ferryboats, may in the discretion of the legislative power be exempted to promote a public purpose and to prevent the expense of the collection of a tax which would be immediately given back to the parties paying it. The power to exempt obviously involves the power to make a donation of the tax to the exempted persons; and, if the power of exempting property of the class taxed exists at all, it is also clear that it exists without any limitation. If Congress has the power to levy 5 percent on incomes above $2,000 and to exempt all less incomes, it can make the discriminating rate 100 percent of the income, and thus confiscate, under the name of taxation, all property in any one man's hands in excess of the yearly value of $2,000, or of any other sum.

The tax advancer usually not the primary tax payer. Taxes, in all conceivable or known systems of taxation, are not at first paid but advanced to the government as a kind of forced loan, with an implied obligation on the part of the government to give the person making the advance the power and ability to collect the tax from consumption and expense in the price of things consumed, where all taxes finally fall. It is im-

practicable for the government to tax property in its infinitesimal forms of consumption at the time of consumption. This would require an assessor and tax collector at the elbow of every person all the time, and hence the government proceeds against property *in invitam* (or by force) where found at a given time, or when produced or imported, and compels the owner or possessor to advance the tax to the state. But if the government fails to give the power and means of reimbursing the tax in the price and then submits the owner to the open competition of similar untaxed property, the forced loan becomes repudiated, and the tax advancer is despoiled of his property without compensation.

Taxes advanced uniformly on all property of the same competing class are circuitous means of reaching all expense and consumption, and will be apportioned and adjusted in the regulation of prices by the natural laws of open competition. Taxes will be thus advanced by those who hold the property in block, and will be primarily paid by those who consume or use the taxed property, and who, in turn, controlled by the natural law of competition, will add or diffuse a part of the tax in the cost of their salable productions, and thus all expense and consumption will finally bear the entire burden. Taxes uniformly advanced on all like competing property will always tend to equate themselves and will never be a special burden to those who originally made the advances to the government. Such persons will sell the tax in the price, rent, or use of the taxed property.

But, on the other hand, if the immediate competitors of those who have advanced taxes are untaxed on their competing property or income, then the tax advancer will be unable to sell or collect the taxes which he has been by force compelled to advance, for his untaxed competitors — especially if they are numerous and their untaxed property large in amount — will undersell him;

and the forced loan will thus be entirely re-pudiated. Hence the act of the English Parliament in the fourth year of the reign of William and Mary which imposed double rates of taxation on the income of Catholics; hence any income tax which exempts any income derived from property of the competing class made subject to the tax, or any tax imposed by any arbitrary rule of residence or nonresidence, nativity, color, or religious persuasion; any tax on contracts after they are made and not provided for in the contract; or upon business or property beyond the jurisdiction of the taxing power; or any form of tax which compels a person to advance taxes in gross to the government without some appropriate legislation to protect and enable such tax advancers to collect the tax from those who use and consume, should be regarded not as taxation but as spoliation and an invasion of the rights of property.

Direct and indirect taxes. There is a marked distinction, founded on sound philosophy, between a direct and an indirect tax. An indirect tax, whoever may first advance it, is paid voluntarily and primarily by the consumer of the taxed article; but a direct tax, on the contrary, always has in it an element of compulsion, not necessarily on the person who advances the tax in block but on the person who is compelled to use or consume the taxed property or its product. A tax upon land *compels* all persons to pay a direct tax, for no one can live except upon land or its products, and a tax upon land is therefore a direct tax. *(A land tax has been conceded by the United States Supreme Court to be a direct tax, Hylton* v. *The United States . . . .)*

A tax upon a few articles, like whisky, tobacco, licenses upon certain classes of business, can always be avoided as a primary tax, or can be paid at discretion; but there is nothing voluntary in a tax upon *all* real and personal property or their income. Human beings cannot subsist without some form of personal property, and therefore a tax upon *all* personal property or its income is of necessity compulsory and not voluntary. Any general assessment of personal property on its income must also, as well as assessments on real estate, constitute a direct tax. . . .

There is nothing compulsory or unequal in an ordinary license tax. If the license is high, no one is compelled by law, or the laws of competition, to engage in the business, and but few persons will engage in it; and thus the average profits of the taxed business, by the regular laws of competition, will finally reach the average profits of other like employments or investments. But an income tax is always compulsory, for it is imposed on income from *all* sources. Some form of property is a necessity, and therefore a tax upon all forms of property or its income is a *direct* or unavoidable tax, and not a voluntary tax.

Now, the Constitution of the United States requires that all direct taxes shall be uniform throughout the United States; and territorial uniformity of indirect taxation must imply and involve absolute uniformity and equality of these taxes on like values and quantities. But, under the operation of natural laws, larger quantities will be owned and produced by one person in one state than in another. Colorado and Texas have large herds of cattle; Illinois has large cornfields and large distilleries; Louisiana, large sugar plantations; and New England, large factories owned by single persons. Two states may, and in some instances do, have equal per capita wealth in the aggregate, but, in the one, the wealth may be made up of capital invested in numerous small industries adapted to its soil and climate; while, in the other, owing to different natural conditions, there may be great concentrations of capital in a few hands and in a few industries.

Thus, in the case of our late income tax, seven states, in the year 1869 — Massachusetts, New York, New Jersey, Pennsylvania, Ohio, Illinois, and California — possessed 40 percent of the assessed property of the United States, and had just about 40 percent also of our population. But, at the same time, these same seven states paid full three-fourths of the entire income tax levied by the federal government upon the people of the whole country; or, to put it differently, the states which had 60 percent of the wealth and population of the country paid only about one-fourth of the income tax. A violation, therefore, of the rule of uniformity in taxes on incomes from the same class of property in the hands of a single person becomes a warfare on the natural resources and natural abilities of some states, and a warfare upon property beyond a certain amount in one man's hands.

Thus, for example, two farms, wherever situated, owned by two persons and producing a profit of $2,000, will produce the same competition in the sales of products as one farm owned by one man producing $4,000 of profit. The profits of the two farms and two persons, under an exemption of $2,000, would, however, be free from all taxation; while the profit of the competing farm, producing the same income as the two other farms, would be subject to a burden on its income of 2½ percent if the farm happens to be in the hands of a single owner. The aggregate of the value of the property is the same in both cases; but the incidence of taxation is made dependent upon the circumstance of making the assessment upon two persons rather than one. This is not equality of burden on competing property or on immediate competitors; but, as M. Thiers says, "it is robbery."

A graduated income tax, to the extent of its discrimination, is an act of confiscation. The federal Constitution further provides that private property shall not be taken for public use except upon compensation. It is conceded that this is a limitation on the power of Congress. There must be a line between

the taking of private property for public use and taxation; but how can that line be drawn except by the rule that taxation means uniformity of burden on competing avocations and competing property? A recent decision of the Supreme Court of New Jersey seems to be direct upon the unconstitutionality of discriminating burdens on the same class of persons or property. Thus the New Jersey Court said:

> A tax upon the person or property of A, B, and C, individually, whether designated by name or in any other way, which is in excess of an equal apportionment among the persons or property of the class of persons or kind of property subject to the taxation, is, to the extent of such excess, the taking of private property for a public use without compensation. The process is one of confiscation and not of taxation. . . .

It only remains, to complete this argument, to consider what is meant by property of the same class. The answer to this is, obviously, property which immediately or directly competes in open market. The force of competition is not dependent upon the quantity owned or produced by few or many persons but upon the aggregate quantity of similar property offered in market, whether produced or owned by few or many persons.

It may also be pertinent in conclusion to say that $2,000 is a larger exemption than has ever been allowed in any income tax system in any country except the United States, where, owing to comparative equality of fortunes, the exemption, if any exemption is to be permitted, should be extremely low. Wherever the line of exemption may be drawn, an act of discrimination is instituted against all those who own property producing income in excess of the line of the exemption. In England, where business, to a greater extent than in any other country, is conducted by large capitalists, where the soil is owned by a comparatively few persons, and where the entire property of the nation is greatly concentrated, an exemption of $750, under the income tax there allowed to each person, is of much less practical importance than a similar exemption would be in the United States, where it would remove a large portion of all incomes derived from property from the burden of the tax.

In France, owing to the very great and minute subdivisions of the ownership of the soil, a small exemption would also take from the income list a large proportion of the owners of real estate in that country. Leroy Beaulieu, indeed, estimates that an exemption of 2,500 fr. ($500) would exempt from three-fourths to four-fifths of the entire income of France; and accordingly, when in 1848 the enactment of an income tax was debated in France, it was proposed to put the exemption as low as 250 fr., or $50.

Any judicious system of taxation in any country will have reference to its natural products; its extent of territory; its contiguity to competing nations; the density or sparseness of its population; the habits of the people and the comparative equality of their fortunes. The United States can conveniently, economically, and uniformly collect its revenues from a few domestic articles, like whisky and tobacco, manufactured in large amounts at one place by one person or firm; and on imports, like sugars, tea, and coffee, introduced into the country, to a great extent, in large vessels and in large quantities at a few ports.

With the limitation of our revenues to such few sources, economy of assessment and collection will be insured, unnecessary inquisition and loss of time — a form of unproductive taxation — will be avoided, and only a comparatively few persons will feel the direct hand of the tax gatherer; while all will cheerfully pay taxes in regulated prices on their expense and consumption, where, by the operation of natural laws, all taxation must finally rest.

But any attempt to collect an income tax which is equal and has none of the features of spoliation or confiscation from our sparse population, extending from Florida to Alaska, is entirely unpractical; and, unless the rate is excessive, the taxes received would not pay the cost of assessment and collection; while, as before shown, the rights of property, the great republican principle of equality before the law, and constitutional law itself will alike preclude any exemption of any income derived from like property.

It is a vital and constitutional question, demanding absolute equality, that is here involved and at stake. Any exemption whatever, small or great, except to the absolutely indigent, is purely arbitrary; and the principle, once allowed, may obviously be carried to any extent. Any exemption of any portion of the same class of property or incomes is an act of charity which every American ought to reject upon principle and with scorn, except under circumstances of great want and destitution. Equality and manhood, therefore, demand and require uniformity of burden in whatever is the subject of taxation.

———————◆———————

In a republic like ours, where all men are equal, this attempt to array the rich against the poor or the poor against the rich is socialism, communism, devilism.
    SENATOR JOHN SHERMAN, of the income tax, which, in the 1890s, was being suggested as a means of shifting some of the burden of taxation from the poor to the rich

101.

Sidney Lanier: The Development of Small Farming in the South

In most of the literary works of Sidney Lanier's short life there is reflected the deep love for the South of a native son, and a real concern for the economic plight of the Southern people. Among Lanier's poems, "Corn," "The Jacquerie," "The Raven Days," and "Thar's More in the Man Than Thar Is in the Land," all deal with the condition of the South during and after the Civil War. The following paper, written only a year before his death in 1881, heralds the emergence of a "new South" predicated on small farming.

Source: *Retrospects and Prospects,* 2nd edition, New York, 1899: "The New South."

It would seem that facts may now be arrayed which leave no doubt that upon the general cycle of American advance the South has described such an epicycle of individual growth that no profitable discussion of that region is possible at present which does not clearly define at the outset whether it is to be a discussion of the Old South or the New South. Although the movement here called by the latter name is originally neither political, social, moral, nor aesthetic, yet the term in the present instance connotes all these with surprising completeness. The New South means small farming.

What Southern small farming really signifies, and how it has come to involve and determine the whole compass of civilization in that part of the republic, this paper proposes to show, (1) by briefly pointing out its true relation, in its last or (what one may call) its poetic outcome, to the "large farming" now so imminent in the Northwest; (2) by presenting some statistics of the remarkable increase in the number of Southern small farms from 1860 to 1870, together with some details of the actual cultures and special conditions thereof. . . .

Indeed, one has only to recall how the connection between marriage and the price of corn is but a crude and partial statement of the intimate relation between politics, social life, morality, art, on the one hand, and the bread-giver earth, on the other; one has only to remember that, particularly here in America, whatever crop we hope to reap in the future — whether it be a crop of poems, of paintings, of symphonies, of constitutional safeguards, of virtuous behaviors, of religious exaltations — we have got to bring it out of the ground with palpable plows and with plain farmer's forethought; in order to see that a vital revolution in the farming economy of the South, if it is actually occurring, is necessarily carrying with it all future Southern politics and Southern social relations and Southern art, and that, therefore, such an agricultural change is the one substantial fact upon which any really New South can be predicated.

Approached from this direction, the quiet rise of the small farmer in the Southern states during the last twenty years becomes the notable circumstance of the period, in comparison with which noisier events signify nothing.

I

As just now hinted, small farming in the South becomes clear in its remoter bearings when seen over against the precisely opposite tendency toward large farming in the West. Doubtless, recent reports of this tendency have been sometimes exaggerated. In reading them, one has been obliged to remember that small minds love to bring large news, and, failing a load, will make one. But certainly enough appears, if only in the single apparently well-authenticated item of the tempting profits realized by some of the great Northwestern planters, to authorize the inference that the tendency to cultivate wheat on enormous farms, where the economies possible only to corporation-management can secure the greatest yield with the least expense, is a growing one.

And, this being so, the most rapid glance along the peculiar details of the Northwestern large farm opens before us a path of thought which quickly passes beyond wheat raising and leads among all those other means of life which appertain to this complex creature who cannot live by bread alone. For instance, classify, as a social and moral factor, a farm like the Grandin place, near Fargo, where 4,855 acres are sown in wheat; where 5 hands do all the work during the six winter months, while as many as 250 must be employed in midsummer; where the day's work is nearly 13 hours; where, out of the numerous structures for farm purposes, but two have any direct relation to man — one a residence for the superintendent and foreman, the other a boardinghouse for the hands; where no women, children, nor poultry are to be seen; where the economies are such as are wholly out of the power of the small wheat raisers, insomuch that even the railways can give special rates for grain coming in such convenient large quantities; where the steam machine, the telephone, and the telegraph are brought to the last degree of skillful service; where, finally, the net profits for the current year are $52,239.

It appears plainly enough from these details that, looked upon from the midst of all those associations which cluster about the idea of the farm, large farming is not farming at all. It is mining for wheat.

Or a slight change in the point of view presents it as a manufacturing business in which clods are fed to the mill and grain appears in carloads at Chicago. And perhaps the most exact relations of this large farming to society in general are to be drawn by considering such farmers as corporations, their laborers as mill operatives for six months in each year and tramps for the other six, their farms as mills where nature mainly turns the wheel, their investment as beyond the reach of strikes or fires, foreign distress their friend, and the world's hunger their steady customer.

It appears further that, while such agricultural communities are so merely in name and are manufacturing communities in fact, they are manufacturing communities only as to the sterner features of that guild — the order, the machine, the minimum of expense, the maximum of product; and not as to those pleasanter features, the schoolhouse, the church, the little workingmen's library, the sewing class, the cookery class, the line of promotion, the rise of the bright boy and the steady workman — all the gentler matters which will spring up, even out of the dust heaps, about any spot where men have the rudest abiding place. On the large farm is no abiding place; the laborer must move on; life cannot stand still, to settle and clarify.

It would not seem necessary to disclaim any design to inveigh against the owners of these great factory farms, if indignation had not been already expressed in such a way as to oblige one to declare that no obligations can be cited, as between them and their laborers, which would not equally apply to every manufacturer. If it is wrong to discharge all but ten laborers when only ten are needed, then the mill owners of Massachusetts must be held bound to run day and night when the market is overstocked because they ran so when it was booming; and if it is criminal to pay the large farmhands no more than will hardly support them for thirteen hours' work, every mill company in the world which pays market rates for work is *particeps*. But, with the coast thus cleared of personality; with the large farm thus classed as a manufacturing company in all its important incidents; and recognizing in the fullest manner that, if wheat can be made most cheaply in this way, it must be so made: a very brief train of thought brings us upon a situation, as between the small farmer on the one hand and the corporation on the other, which reveals them as embodying two tendencies in the republic at this moment whose relations it is the business of statesmanship and of citizenship to understand with the utmost clearness, since we are bound to foster both of them.

For, if we stop our ears to the noisy child's play of current politics, and remember (1) that in all ages and countries two spirits, or motives, or tendencies exist which are essentially opposed to each other, but both of which are necessary to the state; (2) that the problem of any given period or society is to recognize the special forms in which these two tendencies are then and there embodying themselves, and to keep them in such relations that neither shall crush, while each shall healthily check, the other; (3) that these tendencies may be called the spirit of control and the spirit of independence, and that they are so intimately connected with the two undeniable facts which lie at the bottom of moral behavior — namely, the facts of influence from without, on the one hand, and free will, on the other — that the questions of morals and of politics coalesce at their roots; (4) that these two tendencies are now most tangibly embodied among us in the corporation and the small farmer — the corporation representing the spirit of control, and the small farmer representing, in many curious ways, the spirit of independence; (5) that our republic vitally needs the corporation for the mighty works which only the corporation can do, while it as vitally needs the small farmer for the pure substance of individual and self-reliant manhood which he digs out of the ground, and which, the experience of all peoples would seem to show, must primarily come that way and no other — we are bound to conclude that the practical affair in the United States at the present juncture is to discover how we may cherish at once the corporation and the small farmer into the highest state of competitive activity, less by constitution straining laws which forbid the corporation to do this and that, or which coddle the small farmer with sop and privilege, than by affording free scope for both to adjust themselves, and by persistently holding sound moral principles to guide the adjustment.

When, therefore, we behold the large farm as a defection from the farm party in general — which represents individuality in the state — over to the corporation party, whose existence is necessarily based upon such relations to employees as impair their individuality, we regard with all the more interest the rise of the small farmer, now occurring in an opposite direction so opportunely as to seem as if nature herself were balancing the Northwest with the Southeast.

II

THE PHRASE "SMALL FARMING," used of the South, crops out in directions curious enough to one unacquainted with the special economies and relations of existence in that part of our country. While large farming in the South means exclusive cotton growing — as it means in the West exclusive wheat growing or exclusive corn growing — small farming means *diversified farm products*. And a special result of the Southern conditions of agriculture has brought about a still more special sense of the word; so that in Georgia, for example, the term "small farmer" brings up to every native mind the idea of a farmer who, besides his cotton crop, raises corn enough to "do" him. But again, the incidents hinging upon this apparently simple matter of making corn enough to do him are so numerous as, in turn, to render *them* the distinctive feature of small farming.

Small farming means, in short, meat and bread for which there are no notes in bank; pigs fed with homemade corn, and growing of themselves while the corn and cotton were being tended; yarn spun, stockings knit, butter made and sold (instead of bought); eggs, chickens, peaches, watermelons, the four extra sheep and a little wool, two calves and a beef, all to sell every year, besides a colt who is now suddenly become, all of himself, a good, serviceable horse; the four oxen, who are as good as gifts made by the grass; and a hundred other items, all representing income from a hundred sources to the small farmer, which equally represent outgo to the large farmer — items, too, scarcely appearing at all on the expense side of the strictest account book, because they are either products of odd moments which, if not so applied, would not have been at all applied, or products of natural animal growth, and grass at nothing a ton. All these ideas are inseparably connected with that of the small farmer in the South. . . .

Fortunately, we have means for reducing to very definite figures the growth of small farming in the South since the war, and thus of measuring the substance of the New South. A row of columns in the eighth and ninth census reports of the United States is devoted to enumerations of the number of farms in each state and county of given sizes; and a proper comparison thereof yields us facts of great significance to the present inquiry. For example, taking the state of Georgia, we find that, while in 1860 it had but 906 farms of under ten acres, in 1870 it had 3,527 such farms; in 1860, but 2,803 farms of over ten acres and under twenty

acres, in 1870, 6,942 such farms; in 1860, but 13,644 farms of over twenty and under fifty acres, in 1870, 21,971 such farms; in 1860, but 14,129 farms of over fifty and under one hundred acres, in 1870, 18,371 such farms. Making a total of all these subclasses, considered as small farms in general, and subtracting that for 1860 from that for 1870, we reach the instructive fact that, in some five years preceding 1870, the increase in the number of small farms in the state of Georgia was 19,329.

In the state of Mississippi the increase is in some particulars more striking than that in Georgia. By the census report, Mississippi had in 1860 only 563 farms of over three but under ten acres, 2,516 of over ten but under twenty, 10,967 of between twenty and fifty, and 9,204 of between fifty and one hundred; while in 1870 it had 11,003 farms of the first mentioned size, 8,981 of the second, 26,048 of the third, and 11,967 of the fourth; in short, a total gain of 34,749 small farms between 1860 and 1870.

The political significance of these figures is great. To a large extent — exactly how large I have in vain sought means to estimate — they represent the transition of the Negro from his attitude as Negro to an attitude as small farmer — an attitude in which his interests, his hopes, and, consequently, his politics become identical with those of all other small farmers, whether white or black.

Nothing seems more sure than that an entirely new direction of cleavage in the structure of Southern polity must come with the wholly different aggregation of particles implied in this development of small farming.

In the identical aims of the small farmer class, whatever now remains of the color line must surely disappear out of the Southern political situation. This class, consisting as it already does of black small farmers and white small farmers, must necessarily be a body of persons whose privileges, needs, and relations are *not* those which exist as between the black man on the one hand and the white man on the other, but those which exist as between the small farmer on the one hand and whatever affects small farming on the other. For here — as cannot be too often said — the relation of politics to agriculture is that of the turnip top to the turnip. . . .

It must be said that the stern experiences of the last fifteen years have inclined the New South to be, in general, doubtful of anything which holds out great promises at first. A cunning indication of such tendencies comes — upon the principle of like master, like man — in one of the cuttings before me (from the Atlanta *Constitution*), which records the practical views of Uncle Remus, a famous colored philosopher of Atlanta, who is a fiction so founded upon fact and so like it as to have passed into true citizenship and authority, along with Bottom and Autolycus. This is all the more worth giving since it is real Negro talk, and not that supposititious Negro minstrel talk which so often goes for the original. It is as nearly perfect as any dialect can well be; and if one had only some system of notation by which to convey the *tones* of the speaking voice in which Brer Remus and Brer Ab would say these things, nothing could be at once more fine in humor and pointed in philosophy. Negroes on the corner can be heard any day engaged in talk that at least makes one think of Shakespeare's clowns; but half the point and flavor is in the subtle tone of voice, the gesture, the glance, and these, unfortunately, cannot be read between the lines by anyone who has not studied them in the living original.

"Brer Remus, is you heern tell er deze doin's out here in de udder end er town?"

"W'at doin's is dat, Brer Ab?"

"Deze yer signs an' wunders whar dat cullud lady died day fo' yistiddy. Mighty

quare goin's on out dar, Brer Remus, sho's you bawn."

"Sperrits?"

"Wuss 'n dat, Brer Remus. Some say dat jedgment day aint fur off, an' de folks is flockin' roun' de house, a-hollerin' an' a-shoutin' like dey wuz in er revival. In de winder-glass dar you kin see de flags a-flyin', an' Jacob's ladder is dar, an' dar's writin' on de pane what no man can't read — leastwise, dey aint none read it yet."

"W'at kinder racket is dis youer givin' me now, Brer Ab?"

"I done bin dur, Brer Remus; I done seed um wid bofe my eyes. Cullud lady what was intranced done woke up an' say dey aint much time fer ter tarry. She say she meet er angel in de road, an' he p'inted straight fur de mornin' star an' tell her fer ter prepar'. Hit look mighty cu'us, Brer Remus."

"Come down ter dat, Brer Ab," said Uncle Remus, wiping his spectacles carefully and readjusting them, — "cum down ter dat, an' dey aint nuthin' that aint cu'us. I aint no 'spicious nigger myse'f, but I 'spizes fer ter hear dogs a-howlin' an' squinch owls havin' de ager out in de woods, an' w'en a bull goes a-bellerin' by de house, den my bones git cole an' my flesh commences fer ter creep; but w'en it comes ter deze yer sines in de a'r an' deze yer sperrits in de woods, den I'm out — den I'm done. I is, fer a fac'. I been livin' yer more 'n seventy year, an' I hear talk er niggers seein' ghos'es all times er night an' all times er day, but I aint never seed none yit; an' deze yer flags and Jacob's lathers, I aint seed dem, nudder."

"Dey er dar, Brer Remus."

"Hit 's des like I tell you, Brer Ab. I aint 'sputin' 'bout it, but I aint seed um, an' I don't take no chances, deze days, on dat w'at I don't see, an' dat w'at I sees I gotter 'zamine mighty close. Lemme tell you dis, Brer Ab. Don't you let deze sines onsettle you. W'en ole man Gabrile toot his ho'n, he aint gwinter hang no sine out in de winder-panes, an' w'en ole Fadder Jacob lets down dat lather er hisn you'll be mighty ap' fer ter hear de racket. An' don't you bodder wid jedgment-day. Jedgment-day is lierbul fer ter take keer un itse'f."

"Dat 's so, Brer Remus."

"Hit 's bleedzed ter be so, Brer Ab.
Hit don't bother me. Hit's done got so
now dat w'en I gotter pone er bread, an'
a rasher er bacon, an' nuff grease ter
make gravy, I aint keerin' fer much wed-
der folks sees ghos'es or no."

These concluding sentiments of Brer Remus would serve very accurately as an expression of the attitude of the small farmer
— not only in the South, but elsewhere —
toward many of the signs and ghosts and
judgment days with which the careful politician must fight the possible loss of public
attention. There may be signs of danger to
the republic; there may be ghosts of dreadful portent stalking around the hustings and
through the Capitol corridors; and judgment day may be coming — to this or that
representative or functionary — but meantime it is clear that we small farmers will
have nothing to eat unless we go into the
field and hoe the corn and feed the hogs.
By the time this is done, night comes on,
and, being too tired to sit up until 12
o'clock for a sight of the ghost, we go to
bed soon after supper and sleep without
sign or dream till the sun calls us forth
again to the corn and the hogs. . . .

It is impossible to end without adverting
to a New South which exists in a far more
literal sense than that of small farming.
How much of this gracious land is yet new
to all real cultivation, how much of it lies
groaning for the muscle of man, and how
doubly mournful is this newness, in view of
the fair and fruitful conditions which here
hold perpetual session, and press perpetual
invitation upon all men to come and have
plenty! Surely, along that ample stretch of
generous soil where the Appalachian rug-
gednesses calm themselves into pleasant hills
before dying quite away into the seaboard
levels, a man can find such temperances of
Heaven and earth — enough of struggle
with nature to draw out manhood, with
enough of bounty to sanction the struggle
— that a more exquisite coadaptation of all

blessed circumstances for man's life need
not be sought.

It is with a part of that region that this
writer is most familiar, and one cannot but
remember that, as one stands at a certain
spot thereof and looks off up and across the
Ocmulgee River, the whole prospect seems
distinctly to yearn for men. Everywhere the
huge and gentle slopes kneel and pray for
vineyards, for cornfields, for cottages, for
spires to rise up from beyond the oak
groves. It is a land where there is never a
day of summer nor of winter when a man
cannot do a full day's work in the open
field; all the products meet there, as at nature's own agricultural fair; rice grows
alongside of wheat, corn alongside of sugar-
cane, cotton alongside of clover, apples
alongside of peaches, so that a small farm
may often miniature the whole United
States in growth; the little valleys everywhere run with living waters, asking grasses
and cattle and quiet gristmills; all manner
of timbers for economic uses and trees for
finer arts cover the earth; in short, here is
such a neighborly congregation of climates,
soils, minerals, and vegetables, that within
the compass of many a hundred acre farm a
man may find wherewithal to build his
house of stone, of brick, of oak, or of pine,
to furnish it in woods that would delight
the most curious eye, and to supply his
family with all the necessaries, most of the
comforts, and many of the luxuries of the
whole world. It is the country of homes.

And, as said, it is because these blissful
ranges are still clamorous for human friendship; it is because many of them are actually virgin to plow, pillar, axe, or mill wheel,
while others have known only the insulting
and mean cultivation of the earlier immigrants who scratched the surface for cotton
a year or two, then carelessly abandoned all
to sedge and sassafras, and sauntered on toward Texas — it is thus that these lands
are, with sadder significance than that of
small farming, also a New South.

102.

Barbed Wire Fences

The Washburn and Moen Manufacturing Company of Worcester, Massachusetts, filed fourteen suits between 1876 and 1880 to enforce its barbed wire patents. On December 15, 1880, a decision in favor of the company was handed down in the U.S. Circuit Court for the Northern District of Illinois. At the time the decision was called "one of the most important opinions ever delivered in this country." To arrive at an opinion it was necessary for the Court to decide what the nature of a patentable invention was. The following letter in the Chicago Tribune *of December 22, 1880, describes the litigation connected with the decision.*

Source: *A Manual of the Fence*, Worcester, Mass., 1881.

THE MOST EXTRAORDINARY and sweeping decision of the United States court in your city, in the barbed wire cases, affects immense manufacturing and farming interests in this country. The case being one of law and possessing peculiar surroundings, your correspondent has been to considerable pains to learn all the facts in this most remarkable case, in order to present them to the readers of the *Tribune.*

To get at the essence and effects of this decision of the court, it will be necessary to go back to the first idea of a barbwire fence, so far as it appears on record in the Patent Office, and trace it up to the commencement of these suits. Wire fence as such is not new. Plain unbarbed wire for fence purposes has been used with varying success for a long period of time. But the expansion and contraction of a single wire soon broke it, and its smooth surface was no preventive to its being broken down by stock.

The Washburn & Moen Manufacturing Company, of Worcester, Mass., are the largest manufacturers of wire of all kinds in the United States and are a wealthy corporation. The demand for wire for fences was a new outlet for their product, and, being sagacious businessmen, they began to investigate the merits of a barbed fence wire and the probable future of it in the country. They very soon saw that there must be something discovered very soon to take the place of the short-lived and expensive wood fences. Barbed wire was effectual for all purposes of a fence, and was fully one-half cheaper in first cost than the cheapest wood fence that could be built. In it were all the elements of success. They then began to look around for the several patents on barbed fence wire, and came to the conclusion that, if they could get the Hunt patent, reissue it, and leave out the "wheel with spurs" and claim "spurs on a fence wire," it would cover all patents of a subsequent issue "with spurs on."

The Hunt patent had been transferred by assignment to one Charles Kennedy, from whom the Washburn & Moen Manufacturing Company purchased it. But the Hunt patent covered only one wire, while the Kelly patent covered two; hence, in order to be able to use two wires, they bought the Kelly patent. But, up to this time, these two patents embraced only "spurs" made of sheet metal. Next in order was the Glidden patent for a *wire* barb wound around the strand. This patent was in the hands of J. L. Ellwood, of DeKalb, Ill.; and an arrangement was effected between him and the Washburn & Moen Manufacturing Company whereby they became in some manner jointly interested in all these patents.

While all these things were being consummated, barbed wire was coming into general use, and, as innumerable new patents had been granted, barbed wire factories sprang up all over the country, generally, each one making its own peculiar device as patented. By the Hunt patent, Washburn & Moen claimed that any kind of a sharp point in the shape of a barb on fence wires was the "equivalent" of "spurs on a fence wire," as claimed by Hunt in the reissue, and therefore was an infringement. Those who were making barbed wire under patents granted subsequent to the Glidden contended that Hunt's first claim was for a "wheel with spurs on, strung on a fence wire"; and that the reissue of it, leaving out the word "wheel" and claiming "spurs on a wire" was a fraud, and the courts would never sustain it. They claimed that the Hunt patent was good only for that particular device, and that each patent granted since then was good only for the device patented; and on this question the issue was made up and the suits commenced.

When issue was joined on the legal question of "the broad claim," as the Hunt patent was called, the question arose whether the placing of a spur on a strand of wire came under the head of "mechanical skill" or "invention." As to where the first leaves off and the second begins depends upon the state of the art, the proof of expert mechanics, and the opinions of the courts.

The state of the art would suggest these reflections: A single wire (or more) to be used as a fence certainly is not patentable; a "wheel with spurs on" is not in and of itself a patentable device; but when the two are combined and create a new article of manufacture of great utility and value, then it comes under the head of "mechanical

United States Steel

Advertisement for Haish barbed wire used around 1880

skill," or a "patentable invention." Was it the latter? One party says it is patentable, for the United States Patent Office has so declared it. The others reply that "sharp prongs or spurs to protect a fence" are as old as the civilization of man. Europe is full of stone walls with cement tops into which are placed pricks, prongs, broken glass, etc. Sharp iron prongs on the top of garden fences, and even in the center and projecting from the sides, are common both in this country and Europe; hence Hunt did not discover "spurs on a fence" but a "spur wheel on a wire" to be used as a fence. His discovery was only a mechanical way of doing something that had been done for ages past. Hence the state of the art was such, claim the defendants, that the "broad claim patent" should not be sustained.

For nearly or quite three years the contest has gone on, and money has been poured out like water on both sides. The great case came to a final trial last May in the Circuit Court of the United States before Judges Drummond and Blodgett. The Washburn & Moen Manufacturing Company and J. L. Ellwood had the ablest and the largest array of legal talent that probably ever fought side by side for the same client in a single suit in this country; and to that is attributed their success in this suit.

The decision was made by Judge Blodgett — Judge Drummond concurring — fully sustaining "the broad claim," under the Hunt and other patents, that any kind of a sharp spur placed upon a fence is an infringement. The sweeping nature of the decision has taken the whole country by surprise, and it is doubtful if the plaintiff's counsel would have dared to have themselves written a stronger one, or made it more sweeping in its terms and effects. The public seem to be the more surprised from the fact that Judge Drummond had repeatedly, during the trial and motions, expressed himself as decidedly adverse to "the broad claim"; and that, if barbed wire came within the rule of an "invention," he could not see how a patentee could claim more than his peculiar or particular way of doing it. What has happened to change the opinion then expressed by the learned judge is what staggers the public.

The full effect of the decision is very difficult to see at present, and will in a great measure depend upon what the victorious side propose doing with it, and how they use it. Good management can win lawsuits; but it takes more brains than a majority of men possess to know how to use a victory wisely and well. The decisions of courts in this country can have and will inconvenience and ruin many an interest and people; but the final arbiter is an enlightened public sentiment; and, to this, courts, judges, corporations, and gigantic monopolies must finally submit.

There are scores of manufacturers engaged in the making of barbed wire, and the capital invested in it is immense. Not all of these, however, have been sued, and many were, and have been all along, in favor of sustaining all the patents, pooling them, with a view of putting the business on a fair basis, getting a reasonable profit, and preventing the manufacture of inferior fencing. Many holding these views have held aloof from the contest and have taken no part in it.

If Washburn & Moen are willing to settle up for the past and license for the future all who desire to go on, and on such terms as they can pay, then the general verdict is that the result of the suit will be beneficial in the end. On the contrary, if they are arbitrary and use their great victory — for certainly such it is — to crush out those who are in the business, and create a personal or small ring monopoly of it, it will create an intense feeling all over the country; and, as wire fence touches the great farming interest, it will do much to fan into a flame a growing feeling that the patent business is a tool in the hands of monopolies, and a demand will be made that it shall be abolished.

But, from all your correspondent can learn of the gentlemen who have won this suit, they are not the kind of men to oppress anybody. I learn that they have been ready, willing, and even anxious to settle the matter and stop litigation, and have been very liberal in their terms; and had it not been for the obstinacy of one or two of those who were fighting the patents, the whole matter would have been settled long ago. Until the purposes of the winning side are known, the business will be demoralized. The factories here, in Chicago, and in Joliet, so far as I can learn, will respect the decision, and stop making wire until it can be learned what is to be done about past infringements and a license for the future.

All concede that barbed wire is to be the fence of the future, both in this country and

Europe; and, when we take into consideration the fact that the fences of America alone cost the vast sum of $2 billion, and that it costs 10 percent annually, or $200 million, to keep them in repair, to say nothing of the new fences built and the export trade to foreign countries, we can see what a vast interest is affected by this remarkable decision.

It is estimated that had there been no interruption in the barbed wire trade by this decision, the product and sale for 1881 would have been not far from 100 carloads daily. Supposing the royalty on it to be one-half a cent a pound, the vast sum accruing to the holders of these patents would be $10,000 a day, or say *$3 million annually.*

Until a settlement can be made and those in the business licensed to go ahead, there must of necessity be great loss, inconvenience, a short supply of barbed wire, and distress by throwing a vast number of laborers out of work in the middle of winter; but most manufacturers are unwilling to contest the matter any further, preferring to close up and wait developments. Most of them believe that Messrs. Washburn, Moen & Co., and J. L. Ellwood, the successful litigants, will use the great power placed in their hands by the courts in a lenient manner, and so as not to arouse the indignation of the dealers in and the consumers of barbed wire. They can well afford to, for in any event, "There's millions in it."

103.

Cowboy Songs

Between 1870 and 1890, about 10 million longhorn cattle were driven, in herds of from 2,000 to 5,000, from the Texas range to railheads in Kansas and other states for shipment to Eastern markets. The herds were driven by groups of cowboys, who rode round and round the milling cattle, keeping them moving steadily and heading off strays and runaways. At night, the cowboys crooned songs, to drown out disturbing noises and avert stampedes. These songs, like the cowboy himself, have become perhaps the richest element in America's folklore. "The Dying Cowboy" tells of the cowboy's desire to escape in death the loneliness he battled in life. "Cowboy's Life" describes the rigors of life on the plains; lumberjacks and sailors sang other words to the same tune. "The Old Chisholm Trail" celebrates one of the most used trails from Texas to Kansas. And "Good-bye, Old Paint" may be the oldest cowboy song of all. It was often played at the end of square dances to say goodnight. "Paint" is Western jargon for a pinto horse.

Source: Allen.

THE DYING COWBOY

"O bury me not on the lone prairie!"
These words came low and mournfully
From the pallid lips of a youth who lay
On his dying bed at the close of day.

"O bury me not on the lone prairie
Where the wild coyotes will howl o'er me,
In a narrow grave just six by three;
O bury me not on the lone prairie!

"O bury me not on the lone prairie,
Where the wild coyotes will howl o'er me,
Where the buzzard beats and the wind
     goes free;
O bury me not on the lone prairie!

"O bury me not on the lone prairie,
In a narrow grave six foot by three,
Where the buffalo paws o'er a prairie sea;
O bury me not on the lone prairie!

"O bury me not on the lone prairie,
Where the wild coyotes will howl o'er me,
Where the rattlesnakes hiss and the crow
     flies free;
O bury me not on the lone prairie!"

"O bury me not," and his voice failed there,
But we took no heed of his dying prayer;
In a narrow grave just six by three
We buried him there on the lone prairie.

🎵 COWBOY'S LIFE

A cowboy's life is a dreary, dreary life;
Some say it's free from care,
Rounding up the cattle from morning till night,
On the bald prairie so bare.

Just about four o'clock old cook will holler out,
"Roll out, boys, it's almost day."
Through his broken slumbers the puncher he will ask,
"Has the short summer night passed away?"

The cowboy's life is a dreary, dreary life,
He's driven through the heat and cold;
While the rich man's a-sleeping on his velvet couch,
Dreaming of his silver and gold.

When the spring work sets in, then our troubles will begin,
The weather being fierce and cold;
We're almost froze, with the water in our clothes,
And the cattle we can scarcely hold.

The cowboy's life is a dreary, weary one,
He works all day to the setting of the sun;
And then his day's work is not done,
For there's his night guard to go on.

"Saddle up! Saddle up!" the boss will holler out,
When camped down by the Pecos stream,
Where the wolves and owls with their terrifying howls
Will disturb us in our midnight dream.

You are speaking of your farms, you are speaking of your charms,
You are speaking of your silver and gold;
But a cowboy's life is a dreary, dreary life,
He's driven through the heat and cold.

Once I loved to roam, but now I stay at home:
All you punchers take my advice;
Sell your bridle and your saddle, quit your roaming and your travels,
And tie on to a cross-eyed wife.

THE OLD CHISHOLM TRAIL

Well, come along, boys, and listen to my tale;
I'll tell you of my troubles on the Old Chisholm Trail.

Chorus:
Coma ti yi yippy, yippy yay, yippy yay,
Coma ti yi yippy, yippy yay.

I woke up one morning on the Old Chisholm Trail,
Rope in my hand and a cow by the tail.

I jumped in the saddle and grabbed holt the horn,
Best damn cowboy that ever was born.

I'm up in the mornin' before daylight,
And before I sleep the moon shines bright.

Oh, it's bacon and beans 'most every day,
I'd as soon be eatin' prairie hay.

I went to the boss, and we had a little chat;
I slapped him in the face with my big slouch hat.

So I sold my rope and I sold my saddle,
'Cause I'm tired of punchin' them goddam cattle.

Goin' back to town to draw my money,
Goin' back home to see my honey.

I'll ride my horse to the top of the hill;
I'll kiss that gal, guldurn, I will.

My seat's in the saddle and my saddle's in the sky;
And I'll quit punchin' cows in the sweet by and by.

GOOD-BYE, OLD PAINT

My foot in the stirrup, I'm a-leavin' Cheyenne,
My pony won't stand, I'm off to Montan'.

Chorus:
Good-bye, Old Paint, I'm a-leavin' Cheyenne.
Good-bye, Old Paint, I'm a-leavin' Cheyenne.
With my feet in the stirrup I'm off to Montana,
Good-bye, Old Paint, I'm a-leavin' Cheyenne.

I'm a-ridin' Old Paint, I'm a-leadin' Old Fan,
Good bye, little Annie, I'm off to Cheyenne.

Old Paint's a good pony, he paces when he can,
Good morning, young lady, my horses won't stand.

I'm a-ridin' Old Paint, I'm a-leadin' Old Dan,
I'm off to Montana to throw the hoolihan.

They feed in the coolies, they water in the draw,
Their tails are all matted, their backs are all raw.

Old Bill Jones had two daughters and a song:
One went to Denver, and the other went wrong.

His wife she died in a pool-room fight,
And still he sings from morning 'til night.

Oh when I die, take my saddle from the wall
Put it on my pony and lead him from the stall.

Tie my bones to his back, turn our faces to the west,
And we'll ride the prairie that we love the best.

1881

104.

George M. Beard: Modern Civilization and American Nervousness

George Beard, physician and contributor to medical literature, became interested in the study of nervous disorders soon after his graduation from the New York College of Physicians and Surgeons in 1866. A pioneer in the study of neurology, Beard made notable contributions to research on "neurasthenia" and, as a delegate to international meetings of physicians, frequently propounded the theory that Americans possessed a peculiar nervous organization. Beard published many articles in the popular press, as well as such works as American Nervousness, *from which the following selection is reprinted.*

Source: *American Nervousness, Its Causes and Consequences,* New York, 1881, pp. 96-133, 292-298.

THE CAUSES of American nervousness are complicated but are not beyond analysis. First of all, modern civilization. The phrase "modern civilization" is used with emphasis, for civilization alone does not cause nervousness. The Greeks were certainly civilized, but they were not nervous, and in the Greek language there is no word for that term. The ancient Romans were civilized, as judged by any standard. Civilization is therefore a relative term and, as such, is employed throughout this treatise. The modern differ from the ancient civilizations mainly in these five elements — steam power, the periodical press, the telegraph, the sciences, and the mental activity of women. When civilization, plus these five factors, invades any nation, it must carry nervousness and nervous diseases along with it.

CIVILIZATION VERY LIMITED IN EXTENT

ALL THAT IS SAID HERE of American nervousness refers only to a fraction of American society; for in America, as in all lands, the majority of the people are muscle workers rather than brain workers; have little education and are not striving for honor or expecting eminence or wealth. All our civilization hangs by a thread; the activity and force of the very few make us what we are as a nation; and, if, through degeneracy, the descendants of these few revert to the condition of their not very remote ancestors, all our haughty civilization would be wiped away. With all our numerous colleges, such as they are, it is a rarity and surprise to meet in business relations with a college-educated man.

A late writer, Dr. Arthur Mitchell, has shown that if, of the population of Scotland, a few thousands were destroyed or degenerated and their places unsupplied, the nation would fall downward to barbarism. To a somewhat less degree this is true of all lands, including our own land. Of our 50 million population, but a few millions have reached that elevation where they are likely to be nervous. In the lower orders, the classes that support our dispensaries and hospitals, in the tenements of our crowded cities, and even on farms in the country, by the mountainside — among the healthiest regions — we find, now and then, here and there, cases of special varieties of nervous disease, such as hay fever, neurasthenia, etc.; but the proportion of diseases of this kind among these people is much smaller than among the indoor-living and brain-working classes, although insanity of the incurable kind is more common among the lower or the middle than in the very highest classes.

Edison's electric light is now sufficiently advanced in an experimental direction to give us the best possible illustration of the effects of modern civilization on the nervous system. An electric machine of definite horsepower, situated at some central point, is to supply the electricity needed to run a certain number of lamps — say 1,000, more or less. If an extra number of lamps should be interposed in the circuit, then the power of the engine must be increased, else the light of the lamps would be decreased or give out. This has been mathematically calculated so that it is known, or believed to be known, by those in charge, just how much increase of horsepower is needed for each increase in the number of lamps. In all the calculations, however widely they may differ, it is assumed that the force supplied by any central machine is limited and cannot be pushed beyond a certain point; and if the number of lamps interposed in the circuit be increased, there must be a corresponding increase in the force of the machine.

The nervous system of man is the center of the nerve force supplying all the organs of the body. Like the steam engine, its force is limited, although it cannot be mathematically measured; and, unlike the steam engine, varies in amount of force with the food, the state of health, and external conditions; varies with age, nutrition, occupation, and numberless factors. The force in this nervous system can, therefore, be increased or diminished by good or evil influences, medical or hygienic, or by the natural evolutions — growth, disease, and decline. But nonetheless it is limited; and when new functions are interposed in the circuit, as modern civilization is constantly requiring us to do, there comes a period, sooner or later, varying in different individuals and at different times of life, when the amount of force is insufficient to keep all the lamps actively burning. Those that are weakest go out entirely, or, as more frequently happens, burn faint and feebly. They do not expire but give an insufficient and unstable light — this is the philosophy of modern nervousness. . . .

NECESSARY EVILS OF SPECIALIZATION

ONE EVIL, and hardly looked-for effect of the introduction of steam, together with the improved methods of manufacturing of recent times, has been the training in special departments or duties; so that artisans, instead of doing or preparing to do all the varieties of the manipulations needed in the making of any article, are restricted to a few simple exiguous movements, to which they give their whole lives — in the making of a rifle or a watch each part is constructed by experts on that part. The effect of this exclusive concentration of mind and muscle to one mode of action, through months and years, is both negatively and positively pernicious, and notably so, when reenforced, as it almost universally is, by the bad air of overheated and ill-ventilated establishments. Herein is one unanticipated cause of the increase of insanity and other diseases of the nervous system among the laboring and poorer classes.

The steam engine, which would relieve work, as it was hoped, and allow us to be idle, has increased the amount of work done a thousandfold; and with that increase in quantity there has been a differentiation of quality and specialization of function which, so far forth, is depressing both to mind and body. In the professions, the constringing power of specialization is neutralized very successfully by general culture and observation, out of which specialties spring and by which they are supported; but for the artisan there is no time, or chance, or hope for such redeeming and antidotal influences.

CLOCKS AND WATCHES — NECESSITY OF PUNCTUALITY

THE PERFECTION OF CLOCKS and the invention of watches have something to do with modern nervousness, since they compel us to be on time and excite the habit of looking to see the exact moment so as not to be late for trains or appointments. Before the general use of these instruments of precision in time, there was a wider margin for all appointments; a longer period was required and prepared for, especially in traveling — coaches of the olden period were not expected to start like steamers or trains, on the instant — men judged of the time by probabilities, by looking at the sun, and needed not, as a rule, to be nervous about the loss of a moment and had incomparably fewer experiences wherein a delay of a few

moments might destroy the hopes of a lifetime. A nervous man cannot take out his watch and look at it when the time for an appointment or train is near without affecting his pulse; and the effect on that pulse, if we could but measure and weigh it, would be found to be correlated to a loss to the nervous system. Punctuality is a greater thief of nervous force than is procrastination of time. We are under constant strain, mostly unconscious, oftentimes in sleeping as well as in waking hours, to get somewhere or do something at some definite moment.

Those who would relieve their nervousness may well study the manners of the Turks, who require two weeks to execute a promise that the Anglo-Saxon would fulfill in a moment. In Constantinople, indolence is the ideal, as work is the ideal in London and New York; the follower of the Prophet is ashamed to be in haste and would apologize for keeping a promise. There are those who prefer, or fancy they prefer, the sensations of movement and activity to the sensations of repose; but from the standpoint only of economy of nerve force, all our civilization is a mistake; every mile of advance into the domain of ideas brings a conflict that knows no rest, and all conquests are to be paid for, before delivery often, in blood and nerve and life. We cannot have civilization and have anything else, the price at which nature disposes of this luxury being all the rest of her domain.

THE TELEGRAPH

THE TELEGRAPH IS A CAUSE of nervousness, the potency of which is little understood. Before the days of Morse and his rivals, merchants were far less worried than now, and less business was transacted in a given time. Prices fluctuated far less rapidly, and the fluctuations which now are transmitted instantaneously over the world were only known then by the slow communication of sailing vessels or steamships. Hence, we might wait for weeks or months for a cargo of tea from China, trusting for profit to prices that should follow their arrival; whereas, now, prices at each port are known at once all over the globe. This continual fluctuation of values and the constant knowledge of those fluctuations in every part of the world are the scourges of businessmen, the tyrants of trade — every cut in prices in wholesale lines in the smallest of any of the Western cities becomes known in less than an hour all over the Union; thus competition is both diffused and intensified. Within but thirty years the telegraphs of the world have grown to 500,000 miles of line, and over 1 million miles of wire — or more than forty times the circuit of the globe. In the United States there were, in 1880, 170,103 miles of line, and, in that year, 33,155,991 messages were sent over them.

EFFECT OF NOISE ON THE NERVES

THE RELATION OF NOISE to nervousness and nervous diseases is a subject of not a little interest; but one which seems to have been but incidentally studied.

The noises that nature is constantly producing — the moans and roar of the wind, the rustling and trembling of the leaves and swaying of the branches, the roar of the sea and of waterfalls, the singing of birds, and even the cries of some wild animals — are mostly rhythmical to a greater or less degree and always varying if not intermittent. To a savage or to a refined ear, on cultured or uncultured brains, they are rarely distressing, often pleasing, sometimes delightful and inspiring. Even the loudest sounds in nature — the roll of thunder, the howling of storms, and the roar of a cataract like Niagara, save in the exceptional cases of idiosyncrasy — are the occasions not of pain but of pleasure; and, to observe them at their best, men will compass the globe.

Many of the appliances and accompaniments of civilization, on the other hand, are the causes of noises that are unrhythmical, unmelodious, and, therefore, annoying, if not injurious. Manufactures, locomotion, travel, housekeeping even, are noise-producing factors, and when all these elements are concentered, as in great cities, they maintain, through all the waking and some of the sleeping hours, an unintermittent vibration in the air that is more or less disagreeable to all, and in the case of an idiosyncrasy or severe illness may be unbearable and harmful. Rhythmical, melodious, musical sounds are not only agreeable but, when not too long maintained, are beneficial and may be ranked among our therapeutical agencies.

Unrhythmical, harsh, jarring sounds, to which we apply the term noise, are, on the contrary, to a greater or less degree, harmful or liable to be harmful; they cause severe molecular disturbance. . . .

RAILWAY TRAVELING AND NERVOUSNESS

WHETHER railway traveling is directly the cause of nervous disease is a question of not a little interest. Reasoning deductively, without any special facts, it would seem that the molecular disturbance caused by traveling long distances, or living on trains as an employee, would have an unfavorable influence on the nervous system.

In practice this seems to be found: that in some cases — probably a minority of those who live on the road — functional nervous symptoms are excited, and there are some who are compelled to give up this mode of life.

A German physician has given the name "Fear of Railway Traveling" to a symptom that is observed in some who have become nervously exhausted by long residence on trains; they become fearful of taking a journey on the cars, mainly from the unpleasant sensations caused by the vibrating motions of the train.

That railway travel, though beneficial to some, is sometimes injurious to the nerve system of the nervous is demonstrable all the time in my patients; many while traveling by rail suffer from the symptoms of seasickness and with increase of nervousness.

RAPID DEVELOPMENT AND ACCEPTANCE OF NEW IDEAS

THE RAPIDITY with which new truths are discovered, accepted, and popularized in modern times is a proof and result of the extravagance of our civilization.

Philosophies and discoveries as well as inventions, which in the Middle Ages would have been passed by or dismissed with the murder of the author, are in our time — and notably in our country — taken up and adopted, in innumerable ways made practical, modified, developed, actively opposed, possibly overthrown and displaced within a few years, and all of necessity at a great expenditure of force.

The experiments, inventions, and discoveries of Edison alone have made and are now making constant and exhausting drafts on the nervous forces of America and Europe and have multiplied in very many ways and made more complex and extensive the tasks and agonies, not only of practical men but of professors and teachers and students everywhere. The simple attempt to master the multitudinous directions and details of the labors of this one young man, with all his thousands and thousands of experiments and hundreds of patents, and with all the soluble and insoluble physical problems suggested by his discoveries, would itself be a sufficient task for even a genius in science; and any high school or college in which his labors were not recognized and the results of his labors were not taught would be patronized only for those who prefer the eighteenth century to the twentieth. On the mercantile or practical side, the promised discoveries and inventions of this one man have kept millions of capital and thousands of capitalists in suspense and distress on both sides of the sea.

In contrast with the gradualness of thought movement in the Middle Ages, consider the dazzling swiftness with which the theory of evolution and the agnostic philosophy have extended and solidified their conquests, until the whole world of thought seems hopelessly subjected to their autocracy. I once met in society a young man just entering the silver decade, but whose hair was white enough for one of sixty, and he said that the color changed in a single day, as a sign and result of a mental conflict in giving up his religion for science. Many are they who have passed, or are yet to pass, through such conflict and at far greater damage to the nerve centers.

INCREASE IN AMOUNT OF BUSINESS IN MODERN TIMES

THE INCREASE in the amount of business of nearly all kinds in modern times, especially in the last half century, is a fact that comes right before us when we ask the question: Why nervousness is so much on the increase?

Of business, as we moderns understand the term, the ancient world knew almost nothing; the commerce of the Greeks, of which classical histories talk so much, was more like play — like our summer yachting trips — than like the work or commerce of today.

Manufacturers, under the impulses of steam power and invention, have multiplied the burdens of mankind; and railways, telegraphs, canals, steamships, and the utilization of steam power in agriculture and in handling and preparing materials for transportation have made it possible to transact a hundredfold more business in a limited time than even in the eighteenth century; but with an increase rather than a decrease in business transactions. Increased facilities for agriculture, manufactures, and trades have developed sources of anxiety and of loss as well as profit, and have enhanced the risks of business; machinery has been increased in quantity and complexity, some parts, it is true, being lubricated by late inventions, others having the friction still more increased. . . .

REPRESSION OF EMOTION

ONE CAUSE of the increase of nervous diseases is that the conventionalities of society require the emotions to be repressed, while the activity of our civilization gives an unprecedented freedom and opportunity for the expression of the intellect — the more we feel the more we must restrain our feelings. This expression of emotion and expression of reason, when carried to a high degree, as in the most active nations, tends to exhaustion — the one by excessive toil and friction, the other by restraining and shutting up within the mind those feelings which are best relieved by expression. Laughter and tears are safety valves; the savage and the child laugh or cry when they feel like it — and it takes but little to make them feel like it. In a high civilization like the present it is not polite either to laugh or to cry in public; the emotions which would lead us to do either the one or the other thus turn in on the brain and expend themselves on its substance; the relief which should come from the movements of muscles in laughter and from the escape of tears in crying is denied us. Nature will not, however, be robbed; her loss must be paid and the force which might be expended in muscular actions of the face in laughter and on the whole body in various movements reverberates on the brain and dies away in the cerebral cells.

Constant inhibition, restraining normal feelings, keeping back, covering, holding in check atomic forces of the mind and body is an exhausting process; and to this process all civilization is constantly subjected.

A modern philosopher of the most liberal school states that he hates to hear one laugh aloud, regarding the habit, as he declares, a survival of barbarism.

DOMESTIC AND FINANCIAL TROUBLE

FAMILY AND FINANCIAL SORROWS, and secret griefs of various kinds, are very commonly indeed the exciting cause of neurasthenia. In very many cases where overwork is the assigned cause — and where it is brought prominently into notice — the true cause, philosophically, is to be found in family broils or disappointments, business failures or mishaps, or some grief that comes very near to one and, rightly or wrongly, is felt to be very serious.

The savage has no property and cannot fail; he has so little to win of wealth or possessions that he has no need to be anxious. If his wife does not suit he divorces or murders her; and if all things seem to go wrong he kills himself.

POLITICS AND RELIGION

THERE ARE TWO INSTITUTIONS that are almost distinctively American — political elections and religious revivals — for although in other countries both these institutions exist, yet they are far less numerous and far less exacting and have far less influence than in America. Politics and religion appeal mostly to the emotional nature of men and have little to do with the intellect save among the leaders; and, in consequence, the whole land is at times agitated by both these influences to a degree which, however needful it may be, is most exciting to the nervous temperament.

LIBERTY AS A CAUSE OF NERVOUSNESS

A FACTOR in producing American nervousness is, beyond dispute, the liberty allowed, and the stimulus given, to Americans to rise out of the position in which they were born, whatever that may be, and to aspire to the highest possibilities of fortune and glory. In the older countries, the existence of classes and of nobility and the general contexture and mechanism of society make necessary so much strenuous effort to rise from poverty and paltriness and obscurity that the majority do not attempt or even think of doing anything that their fathers did not do. Thus, trades, employments, and professions become the inheritance of families, save where great ambition is combined with great powers. There is a spirit of routine and spontaneous contentment and repose which in America is only found among the extremely unambitious. In traveling in Europe, one is often amazed to find individuals serving in menial, or at least most undignified, positions, whose appearance and conversation show that they are capable of nobler things than they will ever accomplish. In this land, men of that order, their ambition once aroused, are far more likely to ascend in the social scale. Thus it is that in all classes there is a constant friction and unrest — a painful striving to see who shall be highest; and, as those who are at the bottom may soon be at the very top, there is almost as much stress and agony and excitement among some of the lowest orders as among the very highest.

Consider how much nerve force the American people have expended in carrying through our late nominations and elections. . . .

PROTESTANTISM, with the subdivision into sects which has sprung from it, is an element in the causation of the nervous diseases of our time.

No Catholic country is very nervous and partly for this — that in a Catholic nation the burden of religion is carried by the Church. In Protestant countries this burden is borne by each individual for himself; hence the doubts, bickerings, and antagonisms between individuals of the same sect and between churches, most noticeable in this land where millions of excellent people are in constant disagreement about the way to Heaven.

The difference between Canadians and Americans is observed as soon as we cross the border, the Catholic Church and a limited monarchy acting as antidotes to neurasthenia and allied affections. Protestant England has imitated Catholicism, in a measure, by concentrating the machinery of religion and taking away the burden from the people. It is stated — although it is supposed that this kind of statistics [is] unreliable — that, in Italy, insanity has been on the increase during these few years in which there has been civil and religious liberty in that country.

If this statement could be mathematically proved — as probably it cannot in the face of so many sources of error to complicate the calculations — it would be a vigorous illustration of the philosophy here inculcated. Certain enough it is that, if such statement were proved to be true, it would be in unison with all that we know of the increase of insanity in those countries which have the most civil and religious liberty. . . .

HABIT OF FORETHOUGHT

MUCH OF THE EXHAUSTION connected with civilization is the direct product of the forethought and foreworry that makes civilization possible. In coming out of barbarism and advancing in the direction of enlightenment, the first need is care for the future.

There is a story of an American who, on going to an Italian bootmaker to have some slight job performed, was met with a refusal to do the work required. On being asked why he refused, he replied that he had enough money to last him that day and that he did not care to work. "Yes," said the American, "but how about tomorrow?" "Who ever saw tomorrow?" was the Italian's response.

Those who live on the philosophy suggested by that question can never be very nervous. This forecasting, this forethinking, discounting the future, bearing constantly with us not only the real but imagined or possible sorrows and distresses, and not only of our own lives but those of our families and of our descendants, which is the very essence of civilization as distinguished from barbarism, involves a constant and exhausting expenditure of force. Without this forecasting, this sacrifice of the present to the future, this living for our posterity, there can be no high civilization and no great achievement; but it is, perhaps, the chief element of expense in all the ambitious classes, in all except the more degraded orders of modern society.

We are exhorted, and on hygienic grounds, very wisely, not to borrow trouble; but were there no discounting of disappointment, there would be no progress. The barbarian borrows no trouble. Stationary people, like the Chinese, do so but to a slight degree; they keep both their nerve force and their possibilities of progress in reserve. Those who have acquired or have inherited wealth are saved an important percentage of this forecasting and foreworry; like Christian, they throw off the burden at the golden gate, but, unlike Christian, part of it they must retain; for they have still the fear that is ever with them of losing their wealth, and they have still all the ambitions and possible disappointments for themselves and for their children.

On the highly civilized man there rests at all times a threefold burden — the past, the present, and the future! The barbarian carries through life but one burden — that of the present — and, in a psychological view,

a very light one indeed. The civilized man is ever thinking of the past — representing, repeating, recasting, and projecting the experiences of bygone days to days that are to come. The savage has no future and but little of the past, and that little is usually pleasant and not burdensome. . . .

RELATION OF HEALTH TO WEALTH AND POVERTY

ACCUMULATED AND TRANSMITTED WEALTH is to be in this, as in other countries, one of the safeguards of national health. Health is the offspring of relative wealth. In civilization, abject and oppressed poverty is sickly, or liable to sickness, and on the average is short-lived; febrile and inflammatory disorders, plagues, epidemics, great accidents, and catastrophes even, visit first and last and remain longest with those who have no money. The anxiety that is almost always born of poverty; the fear of still greater poverty, of distressing want, of sickness that is sure to come; the positive deprivation of food that is convenient, of clothing that is comfortable, of dwellings that are sightly and healthful; the constant and hopeless association with misery, discomfort, and despair; the lack of education through books, schools, or travel; the absence of all but forced vacations — the result, and one of the worst results, of poverty, added to the corroding force of envy and the friction of useless struggle — all these factors that make up or attend upon simple want of money are in every feature antagonistic to health and longevity.

Only when the poor become absolute paupers and the burden of life is taken from them and put upon the state or public charity, are they in a condition of assured health and long life. For the majority of the poor, and for many of the rich, the one dread is to come upon the town; but as compared with many a home the poorhouse is a sanitarium. The inmates of our public institutions of charity of the modern kind are often the happiest of men, blessed with an environment, on the whole, far more salubrious than that to which they have been accustomed, and favorably settled for a serene longevity. Here, in a sanitary point of view, the extremes of wealth and poverty meet; both conditions being similar in this — that they remove the friction which is the main cause of ill-health and short life. For the same reasons, well-regulated jails are healthier than many homes, and one of the best prescriptions for the broken-down and distressed is for them to commit some crime.

The augmenting wealth of the American people during the last quarter of a century is already making its impress on the national constitution and in a variety of ways. A fat bank account tends to make a fat man; in all countries, amid all stages of civilization and semi-barbarism, the wealthy classes have been larger and heavier than the poor. Wealth, indeed, if it be abundant and permanent, supplies all the external conditions possible to humanity that are friendly to those qualities of the physique — plumpness, roundness, size — that are rightly believed to indicate well-balanced health; providing, in liberal variety, agreeable and nourishing food and drink, tasteful and commodious homes, and comfortable clothing; bringing, within ready and tempting access, education and the nameless and powerful diversions for muscle and mind that only a reasonable degree of enlightenment can obtain or appreciate; inviting and fortifying calmness, steadiness, repose in thought and action; inspiring and maintaining in all the relations of existence a spirit of self-confidence, independence, and self-esteem, which, from a psychological point of view, are, in the fight for life, qualities of the highest sanitary importance; in a word, minifying, along all the line of the physical functions, the processes of waste and magnifying the processes of repair.

So insalubrious are the hygienic surroundings of the abjectly poor that only a slow adaptation to those conditions makes it possible for them to retain either the power or the desire to live. In India this coincidence of corpulence and opulence has been so long observed that it is instinctively assumed; and certain Brahmins, it is said, in order to obtain the reputation of wealth, studiously cultivate a diet adapted to make them fat.

Poverty has, it is true, its good side, from a hygienic as well as from other points of view; for, practically, good and evil are but relative terms, the upper and nether sides of the same substance, and constantly tending to change places. The chief advantage of poverty as a sanitary or hygienic force is that, in some exceptional natures, it inspires the wish and supplies the capacity to escape from it, and in the long struggle for liberty we acquire the power and the ambition for something higher and nobler than wealth. The impulse of the rebound sends us farther than we had dreamed; stung by early deprivation to the painful search for gold, we often find treasures that gold cannot buy.

But for one whom poverty stimulates and strengthens, there are thousands whom it subjugates and destroys, entailing disease and an early death from generation to generation. The majority of our pilgrim fathers in New England and of the primitive settlers in the Southern and Middle states really knew but little of poverty in the sense in which the term is here used. They were an eminently thrifty people and brought with them both the habits and the results of thrift to their homes in the New World. Poverty as here described is of a later evolution, following in this country, as in all others, the pathway of a high civilization.

In the centuries to come there will probably be found in America, not only in our large cities but in every town and village, orders of financial nobility, above the need but not above the capacity or the disposition to work; strong at once in inherited wealth and inherited character; using their vast and easy resources for the upbuilding of manhood, physical and mental; and maintaining a just pride in transmitting these high ideals and the means for realizing them to their descendants. Families thus favored can live without physical discomfort and work without worrying. Their healthy and well-adjusted forces can be concentrated at will, and in the beginning of life, on those objects best adapted to their tastes and talents; thus economizing and utilizing so much that those who are born poor and sickly and ignorant are compelled to waste in oftentimes fruitless struggle.

The moral influence of such a class scattered through our society must be, on the whole, with various and obvious exceptions and qualifications, salutary and beneficent. By keeping constantly before the public high ideals of culture, for which wealth affords the means; by elevating the now dishonored qualities of serenity and placidity to the rank of virtues, where they justly belong, and by discriminatingly cooperating with those who are less favored in their toils and conflicts, they cannot help diffusing, by the laws of psychical contagion, a reverence for those same ideals in those who are able but most imperfectly to live according to them. Thus they may help to bring about that state of society where men shall no more boast of being overworked than of any other misfortune and shall no longer be ashamed to admit that they have both the leisure and the desire for thought; and the throne of honor so long held by the practical man shall be filled, for the first time in the history of this nation, by the man of ideas.

The germs of such a class have even now begun to appear, and already their power is clearly perceptible on American society. The essence of barbarism is equality, as the essence of civilization is inequality; but the increasing inequality of civilization may be in a degree corrected by scientific philanthropy.

105.

Wendell Phillips: The Scholar in a Republic

Wendell Phillips early ceased to practise law and became instead a social critic and advocate of such causes as abolition, penal reform, woman suffrage, and labor organization. His ardent espousal of several of these causes led some of his friends to conclude that he was mentally unsound, but all his life he remained the moral gadfly. In his seventieth year, he delivered the following Phi Beta Kappa Centennial Oration at Harvard University, June 30, 1881.

Source: *Speeches, Lectures, and Letters,* 2nd series, Boston, 1891.

STANDING ON SAXON FOUNDATIONS, and inspired, perhaps, in some degree by Latin example, we have done what no race, no nation, no age had before dared even to try. We have founded a republic on the unlimited suffrage of the millions. We have actually worked out the problem that man, as God created him, may be trusted with self-government. We have shown the world that a church without a bishop and a state without a king is an actual, real, everyday possibility.

Look back over the history of the race; where will you find a chapter that precedes us in that achievement? Greece had her republics, but they were the republics of a few freemen and subjects and many slaves; and "the battle of Marathon was fought by slaves, unchained from the doorposts of their masters' houses." Italy had her republics; they were the republics of wealth and skill and family, limited and aristocratic. The Swiss republics were groups of cousins. Holland had her republic, a republic of guilds and landholders, trusting the helm of state to property and education. And all these, which at their best held but a million or two within their narrow limits, have gone down in the ocean of time.

A hundred years ago our fathers announced this sublime and, as it seemed then, foolhardy declaration — that God intended all men to be free and equal: all men, without restriction, without qualification, without limit. A hundred years have rolled away since that venturous declaration; and today, with a territory that joins ocean to ocean, with 50 million people, with two wars behind her, with the grand achievement of having grappled with the fearful disease that threatened her central life and broken 4 million fetters, the great republic, stronger than ever, launches into the second century of her existence. The history of the world has no such chapter in its breadth, its depth, its significance, or its bearing on future history.

What Wycliffe did for religion, Jefferson and Sam Adams did for the state — they trusted it to the people. He gave the masses the Bible, the right to think. Jefferson and Sam Adams gave them the ballot, the right to rule. His intrepid advance contemplated theirs as its natural, inevitable result. Their serene faith completed the gift which the Anglo-Saxon race makes to humanity. We have not only established a new measure of the possibilities of the race; we have laid on strength, wisdom, and skill a new responsibility.

Grant that each man's relations to God and his neighbor are exclusively his own concern, and that he is entitled to all the aid that will make him the best judge of these relations; that the people are the source of all power, and their measureless capacity, the lever of all progress; their sense of right, the court of final appeal in civil affairs; the institutions they create the only ones any power has a right to impose; that the attempt of one class to prescribe the law, the religion, the morals, or the trade of another is both unjust and harmful — and the Wycliffe and Jefferson of history mean this if they mean anything — then, when in 1867, Parliament doubled the English franchise, Robert Lowe was right in affirming, amid the cheers of the House, "Now the first interest and duty of every Englishman is to educate the masses — our masters." Then, whoever sees farther than his neighbor is that neighbor's servant to lift him to such higher level. Then, power, ability, influence, character, virtue are only trusts with which to serve our time.

We all agree in the duty of scholars to help those less favored in life, and that this duty of scholars to educate the mass is still more imperative in a republic, since a republic trusts the state wholly to the intelligence and moral sense of the people. The experience of the last forty years shows every man that law has no atom of strength, either in Boston or New Orleans, unless, and only so far as, public opinion endorses it; and that your life, goods, and good name rest on the moral sense, self-respect, and law-abiding mood of the men that walk the streets, and hardly a whit on the provisions of the statute book. Come, any one of you, outside of the ranks of popular men, and you will not fail to find it so. Easy men dream that we live under a government of law. Absurd mistake! We live under a government of men and newspapers. Your first attempt to stem dominant and keenly cherished opinions will reveal this to you.

Wendell Phillips

But what is education? Of course it is not book learning. Book learning does not make 5 percent of that mass of common sense that "runs" the world, transacts its business, secures its progress, trebles its power over nature, works out in the long run a rough average justice, wears away the world's restraints, and lifts off its burdens. The ideal Yankee, who "has more brains in his hand than others have in their skulls," is not a scholar; and two-thirds of the inventions that enable France to double the world's sunshine, and make Old and New England the workshops of the world, did not come from colleges or from minds trained in the schools of science, but struggled up, forcing their way against giant obstacles from the irrepressible instinct of untrained natural power. Her workshops, not her colleges, made England, for a while, the mistress of the world; and the hardest job her workman had was to make Oxford willing he should work his wonders.

So of moral gains. As shrewd an observer as Governor Marcy, of New York, often said he cared nothing for the whole press of the seaboard, representing wealth and education (he meant book learning), if it set itself against the instincts of the people. Lord Brougham, in a remarkable comment on the life of Romilly, enlarges on the fact that the great reformer of the penal law found all the legislative and all the judicial power of England, its colleges and its bar, marshaled against him, and owed his success, *as all such reforms do*, says His Lordship, to public meetings and popular instinct. It would be no exaggeration to say that government itself began in usurpation, in the feudalism of the soldier and the bigotry of the priest; that liberty and civilization are only fragments of rights wrung from the strong hands of wealth and book learning.

Almost all the great truths relating to society were not the result of scholarly meditation, "hiving up wisdom with each curious year," but have been first heard in the solemn protests of martyred patriotism and the loud cries of crushed and starving labor. When common sense and the common people have stereotyped a principle into a statute, then bookmen come to explain how it was discovered and on what ground it rests. The world makes history, and scholars write it — one-half truly, and the other half as their prejudices blur and distort it.

New England learned more of the principles of toleration from a lyceum committee doubting the dicta of editors and bishops when they forbade it to put Theodore Parker on its platform; more from a debate whether the Antislavery cause should be so far countenanced as to invite one of its advocates to lecture; from Sumner and Emerson, George William Curtis, and Edwin Whipple, refusing to speak unless a Negro could buy his way into their halls as freely as any other — New England has learned more from these lessons than she has or could have done from all the treatises on free printing from Milton and Roger Williams through Locke down to Stuart Mill. . . .

In this sense the Frémont campaign of 1856 taught Americans more than a hundred colleges; and John Brown's pulpit at Harpers Ferry was equal to any 10,000 ordinary chairs. God lifted a million of hearts to his gibbet, as the Roman cross lifted a world to itself in that divine sacrifice of 2,000 years ago. As much as statesmanship had taught in our previous eighty years, that one week of intellectual watching and weighing and dividing truth taught 20 million people. Yet how little, brothers, can we claim for bookmen in that uprising and growth of 1856! And while the first of American scholars could hardly find in the rich vocabulary of Saxon scorn words enough to express, amid the plaudits of his class, his loathing and contempt for John Brown, Europe thrilled to him as proof that our institutions had not lost all their native and distinctive life. She had grown tired of our parrot note and cold moonlight reflection of older civilizations. Lansdowne and Brougham could confess to Sumner that they had never read a page of their contemporary, Daniel Webster; and you spoke to vacant eyes when you named Prescott, fifty years ago, to average Europeans; while Vienna asked, with careless indifference, "Seward, who is he?"

But long before our ranks marched up State Street to the John Brown song, the banks of the Seine and of the Danube hailed the new life which had given us another and nobler Washington. Lowell foresaw him when, forty years ago, he sang of:

Truth forever on the scaffold,
  Wrong forever on the throne;
Yet that scaffold sways the future,
  And behind the dim unknown
Standeth God, within the shadow,
  Keeping watch above His own.

And yet the bookmen, as a class, have not yet acknowledged him.

It is here that letters betray their lack of distinctive American character. Fifty million men God gives us to mold; burning questions, keen debate, great interests trying to vindicate their right to be, sad wrongs brought to the bar of public judgment — these are the people's schools. Timid scholarship either shrinks from sharing in these agitations or denounces them as vulgar and dangerous interference by incompetent hands with matters above them. A chronic distrust of the people pervades the book-educated class of the North; they shrink from that free speech which is God's normal school for educating men, throwing upon them the grave responsibility of deciding great questions, and so lifting them to a higher level of intellectual and moral life. Trust the people — the wise and the ignorant, the good and the bad — with the gravest questions, and in the end you educate the race.

At the same time you secure, not perfect institutions, not necessarily good ones, but the best institutions possible while human nature is the basis and the only material to build with. Men are educated and the state uplifted by allowing all — everyone — to broach all their mistakes and advocate all their errors. The community that will not protect its most ignorant and unpopular member in the free utterance of his opinions, no matter how false or hateful, is only a gang of slaves! . . .

It is not the masses who have most disgraced our political annals. I have seen many mobs between the seaboard and the Mississippi. I never saw or heard of any but well-dressed mobs, assembled and countenanced, if not always led in person, by respectability and what called itself education. That unrivaled scholar, the first and greatest New England ever lent to Congress, signaled his advent by quoting the original Greek of the New Testament in support of slavery and offering to shoulder his musket in its defense; and forty years later the last professor who went to quicken and lift the moral mood of those halls is found advising a plain, blunt, honest witness to forge and lie that this scholarly reputation might be saved from wreck. Singular comment on Landor's sneer, that there is a spice of the scoundrel in most of our literary men. But no exacting level of property qualification for a vote would have saved those stains. In those cases Judas did not come from the unlearned class. . . .

I urge on college-bred men that, as a class, they fail in republican duty when they allow others to lead in the agitation of the great social questions which stir and educate the age. Agitation is an old word with a new meaning. Sir Robert Peel, the first English leader who felt himself its tool, defined it to be "marshaling the conscience of a nation to mold its laws." Its means are reason and argument — no appeal to arms. Wait patiently for the growth of public opinion. That secured, then every step taken is taken forever. An abuse once removed never reappears in history. The freer a nation becomes, the more utterly democratic in its form, the more need of this outside agitation. Parties and sects laden with the burden of securing their own success cannot afford to risk new ideas. "Predominant opinions," said Disraeli, "are the opinions of a class that is vanishing." The agitator must stand outside of organizations, with no bread to earn, no candidate to elect, no party to save, no object but truth — to tear a question open and riddle it with light.

In all modern constitutional governments, agitation is the only peaceful method of progress. Wilberforce and Clarkson, Rowland Hill and Romilly, Cobden and John Bright, Garrison and O'Connell have been the master spirits in this new form of crusade. Rarely in this country have scholarly men joined, as a class, in these great popular schools, in these social movements which make the great interests of society "crash and jostle against each other like frigates in a storm."

It is not so much that the people need us or will feel any lack from our absence. They can do without us. By sovereign and superabundant strength they can crush their way through all obstacles.

> They will march prospering, — not
>   through our presence;
> Songs will inspirit them — not from our
>   lyre;
> Deeds will be done — while we boast
>   our quiescence,
> Still bidding crouch whom the rest bid
>   aspire.

The misfortune is, we lose a God-given opportunity of making the change an unmixed good, or with the slightest possible share of evil, and are recreant besides to a special duty. These "agitations" are the opportunities and the means God offers us to refine the taste, mold the character, lift the purpose, and educate the moral sense of the masses on whose intelligence and self-respect rests the state. God furnishes these texts. He gathers for us this audience, and only asks of our coward lips to preach the sermons. . . .

Thoughtful men see that up to this hour the government of great cities has been with us a failure; that worse than the dry rot of legislative corruption, than the rancor of party spirit, than Southern barbarism, than even the tyranny of incorporated wealth is the giant burden of intemperance, making universal suffrage a failure and a curse in every great city. Scholars who play statesmen and editors who masquerade as scholars can waste much excellent anxiety that clerks shall get no office until they know the exact date of Caesar's assassination, as well as the latitude of Pekin, and the Rule of Three. But while this crusade — the temperance movement — has been, for sixty years, gathering its facts and marshaling its arguments, rallying parties, besieging legislatures, and putting great states on the witness stand as evidence of the soundness of its methods, scholars have given it nothing but a sneer. But if universal suffrage ever fails here for a time — permanently it cannot fail — it will not be incapable civil service, nor an ambitious soldier, nor Southern vandals, nor venal legislatures, nor the greed of wealth, nor boy statesmen rotten before they are ripe that will put universal suffrage into eclipse: it will be rum entrenched in great cities and commanding every vantage ground.

Social science affirms that woman's place in society marks the level of civilization. From its twilight in Greece, through the Italian worship of the Virgin, the dreams of chivalry, the justice of the civil law, and the equality of French society, we trace her gradual recognition; while our common law, as Lord Brougham confessed, was, with relation to women, the opprobrium of the age and of Christianity. For forty years, plain men and women, working noiselessly, have washed away that opprobrium; the statute books of thirty states have been remodeled, and woman stands today almost face to face with her last claim — the ballot. It has been a weary and thankless, though successful, struggle. But if there be any refuge from that ghastly curse — the vice of great cities before which social science stands palsied and dumb — it is in this more equal recognition of woman. If, in this critical battle for universal suffrage — our fathers' noblest legacy to us and the greatest trust God leaves in our hands — there be any weapon, which once taken from the armory will make victory certain, it will be, as it has been in art, literature, and society, summoning woman into the political arena.

But at any rate, up to this point, putting suffrage aside, there can be no difference of opinion; everything born of Christianity, or allied to Grecian culture or Saxon law, must rejoice in the gain. The literary class, until within half a dozen years, has taken note of this great uprising only to fling every obstacle in its way. The first glimpse we get of Saxon blood in history is that line of Tacitus in his *Germany*, which reads, "In all grave matters they consult their women."

Years hence, when robust Saxon sense has flung away Jewish superstition and Eastern prejudice, and put under its foot fastidious scholarship and squeamish fashion, some second Tacitus, from the valley of the Mississippi, will answer to him of the Seven Hills, "In all grave questions we consult our women." . . .

"It is unfortunate," says Jefferson, "that the efforts of mankind to secure the freedom of which they have been deprived, should be accompanied with violence and even with crime. But while we weep over the means, we must pray for the end." Pray fearlessly for such ends; there is no risk! "Men are all Tories by nature," says Arnold, "when tolerably well-off; only monstrous injustice and atrocious cruelty can rouse them." Some talk of the rashness of the uneducated classes. Alas! Ignorance is far oftener obstinate than rash. Against one French Revolution — that scarecrow of the ages — weigh Asia, "carved in stone," and a thousand years of Europe, with her half-dozen nations meted out and trodden down to be the dull and contented footstools of priests and kings. The customs of a thousand years ago are the sheet anchor of the passing generation, so deeply buried, so fixed, that the most violent efforts of the maddest fanatic can drag it but a handbreadth.

Before the war, Americans were like the crowd in that terrible hall of Eblis which Beckford painted for us — each man with his hand pressed on the incurable sore in his bosom, and pledged not to speak of it. Compared with other lands, we were intellectually and morally a nation of cowards.

When I first entered the Roman states, a customhouse official seized all my French books. In vain I held up to him a treatise by Fénelon and explained that it was by a Catholic archbishop of Cambray. Gruffly he answered, "It makes no difference; *it is French.*" As I surrendered the volume to his remorseless grasp, I could not but honor the nation which had made its revolutionary purpose so definite that despotism feared its very language. I only wished that injustice and despotism everywhere might one day have as good cause to hate and to fear everything American.

At last that disgraceful seal of slave complicity is broken. Let us inaugurate a new departure, recognize that we are afloat on the current of Niagara, eternal vigilance the condition of our safety, that we are irrevocably pledged to the world not to go back to bolts and bars — could not if we would, and would not if we could. Never again be ours the fastidious scholarship that shrinks from rude contact with the masses. Very pleasant it is to sit high up in the world's theater and criticize the ungraceful struggles of the gladiators, shrug one's shoulders at the actors' harsh cries, and let every one know that but for "this villainous saltpeter you would yourself have been a soldier." But Bacon says, "In the theater of man's life, God and His angels only should be lookers-on." "Sin is not taken out of man as Eve was out of Adam, by putting him to sleep."

"Very beautiful," says Richter, "is the eagle when he floats with outstretched wings aloft in the clear blue; but sublime when he plunges down through the tempest to his eyrie on the cliff, where his unfledged young ones dwell and are starving." Accept proudly the analysis of Fisher Ames: "A monarchy is a man-of-war, staunch, iron-ribbed, and resistless when under full sail; yet a single hidden rock sends her to the bottom. Our republic is a raft hard to steer, and your feet always wet; but nothing can sink her." If the Alps, piled in cold and silence, be the emblem of despotism, we joyfully take the ever restless ocean for ours — only pure because never still.

Journalism must have more self-respect. Now it praises good and bad men so indiscriminately that a good word from nine-tenths of our journals is worthless. In burying our Aaron Burrs, both political parties — in order to get the credit of magnanimity — exhaust the vocabulary of eulogy so thoroughly that there is nothing left with which to distinguish our John Jays. The love of a good name in life and a fair reputation to survive us — that strong bond to well-doing — is lost where every career, however stained, is covered with the same fulsome flattery, and where what men say in the streets is the exact opposite of what they say to each other. *De mortuis nil nisi bonum,* most men translate, "Speak only good of the dead." I prefer to construe it, "Of the dead say nothing unless you can tell something good." And if the sin and the recreancy have been marked and far-reaching in their evil, even the charity of silence is not permissible.

To be as good as our fathers we must be better. They silenced their fears and subdued their prejudices, inaugurating free speech and equality with no precedent on the file. Europe shouted "Madmen!" and gave us forty years for the shipwreck. With serene faith they persevered. Let us rise to their level. Crush appetite and prohibit temptation if it rots great cities. Entrench labor in sufficient bulwarks against that wealth which, without the tenfold strength of modern incorporation, wrecked the Grecian and Roman states; and with a sterner effort still, summon women into civil life as reinforcement to our laboring ranks in the effort to make our civilization a success.

Sit not, like the figure on our silver coin, looking ever backward.

New occasions teach new duties;
Time makes ancient good uncouth;
They must upward still, and onward,
Who would keep abreast of Truth.
Lo! before us gleam her camp fires!
We ourselves must Pilgrims be,
Launch our *Mayflower,* and steer boldly
Through the desperate winter sea,
Nor attempt the Future's portal
With the Past's blood-rusted key.

106.

Carl Schurz: The Native American Dilemma — Civilization or Extinction

In the late nineteenth century a growing number of reformers, realizing that Native Americans faced a critical moment, became concerned with their condition. Carl Schurz eloquently expressed the dilemma facing Indian policy in the following article, published in July 1881. Schurz was secretary of the interior from 1877 to 1881, and his department included the Bureau of Indian Affairs. Although he and his department treated Indian tribes more humanely than many of their predecessors, many of the measures were still quite paternalistic, which caused problems later.

THAT THE HISTORY of our Indian relations presents, in great part, a record of broken treaties, of unjust wars, and of cruel spoliation is a fact too well known to require proof or to suffer denial. But it is only just to the government of the United States to say that its treaties with Indian tribes were, as a rule, made in good faith, and that most of our Indian wars were brought on by circumstances for which the government itself could not fairly be held responsible. Of the treaties, those were the most important by which the government guaranteed to Indian tribes certain tracts of land as reservations to be held and occupied by them forever under the protection of the United States, in the place of other lands ceded by the Indians. There is no reason to doubt that in most, if not all, of such cases those who conducted Indian affairs on the part of the government, not anticipating the rapid advance of settlement, sincerely believed in the possibility of maintaining those reservations intact for the Indians, and that, in this respect, while their intentions were honest, their foresight was at fault.

There are men still living who spent their younger days near the borders of "Indian country" in Ohio and Indiana; and it is a well-known fact that, when the Indian Territory was established west of the Mississippi, it was generally thought that the settlements of white men would never crowd into that region, at least not for many generations. Thus were such reservations guaranteed by the government with the honest belief that the Indians would be secure in their possession, which, as subsequent events proved, was a gross error of judgment.

It is also a fact that most of the Indian wars grew, not from any desire of the government to disturb the Indians in the territorial possessions guaranteed to them but from the restless and unscrupulous greed of frontiersmen who pushed their settlements and ventures into the Indian country, provoked conflicts with the Indians, and then called for the protection of the government against the resisting and retaliating Indians, thus involving it in the hostilities which they themselves had begun. It is true that in some instances Indian wars were precipitated by acts of rashness and violence on the part of military men without orders from the government, while the popular impression that Indian outbreaks were generally caused by the villainy of government agents, who defrauded and starved the Indians, is substantially unfounded. Such frauds and robberies have no doubt been frequently committed.

It has also happened that Indian tribes were exposed to great suffering and actual starvation in consequence of the neglect of Congress to provide the funds necessary to fulfill treaty stipulations. But things of this kind resulted but seldom in actual hostilities. To such wrongs the Indians usually submitted with a more enduring patience than they receive credit for, although, in some instances, it must be admitted, outrages were committed by Indians without provocation, which resulted in trouble on a large scale.

In mentioning these facts, it is not my purpose to hold the government entirely guiltless of the wrongs inflicted upon the Indians. It has, undoubtedly, sometimes lacked in vigor when Indian tribes needed protection. It has, in many cases, yielded too readily to the pressure of those who wanted to possess themselves of Indian lands. Still less would I justify some high-handed proceedings on the part of the government in moving peaceable Indian tribes from place to place without their consent, trying to rectify old blunders by new acts of injustice. But I desire to point out that by far the larger part of our Indian troubles have sprung from the greedy encroachments of white men upon Indian lands, and that, hostilities being brought about in this manner, in which the Indians uniformly succumbed, old treaties and arrangements were overthrown to be supplanted by new ones of a similar character, which eventually led to the same results.

In the light of events, the policy of assigning to the Indian tribes large tracts of land as permanent reservations, within the limits of which they might continue to roam at pleasure, with the expectation that they would never be disturbed thereon, appears as a grand mistake, a natural, perhaps

even an unavoidable mistake in times gone by, but a mistake for all that; for that policy failed to take into account the inevitable pressure of rapidly and irresistibly advancing settlement and enterprise. While duly admitting and confessing the injustice done, we must understand the real nature of the difficulty if we mean to solve it.

No intelligent man will today for a moment entertain the belief that there is still a nook or corner of this country that has the least agricultural or mineral value in it beyond the reach of progressive civilization. Districts which seemed to be remote wildernesses but a few years ago have been or are now being penetrated by railroads. Montana, Washington Territory, Idaho, and New Mexico are now more easily accessible than Ohio and Indiana were at the beginning of this century, and the same process which resulted in crowding the Indians out of these states has begun and is rapidly going on in those territories. The settler and miner are beginning, or at least threatening, to invade every Indian reservation that offers any attraction, and it is a well-known fact that the frontiersman almost always looks upon Indian lands as the most valuable in the neighborhood, simply because the Indian occupies them and the white man is excluded from them.

From the articles in the newspapers of those remote territories, it would sometimes appear as if, in the midst of millions of untouched acres, the white people were deprived of the necessary elbowroom as long as there is an Indian in the country. At any rate, the settlers and miners want to seize upon the most valuable tracts first, and they are always inclined to look for them among the lands of the Indians. The fact that wild Indians — and here it is proper to say that when in this discussion Indians are spoken of as "wild" and their habits of life as "savage," these terms are not used in their extreme sense, but as simply meaning "uncivilized," there being of course among them, in that respect, a difference of degrees — hold immense tracts of country which, possessed by them, are of no advantage to anybody; while, as is said, thousands upon thousands of white people stand ready to cultivate them and to make them contribute to the national wealth, is always apt to make an impression upon minds not accustomed to nice discrimination.

It is needless to say that the rights of the Indians are a matter of very small consideration in the eyes of those who covet their possessions. The average frontiersman looks upon the Indian simply as a nuisance that is in his way. There are certainly men among them of humane principles, but also many whom it would be difficult to convince that it is a crime to kill an Indian, or that to rob an Indian of his lands is not a meritorious act. This pressure grows in volume and intensity as the population increases, until finally, in some way or another, one Indian reservation after another falls into the hands of white settlers. Formerly, when this was accomplished, the Indians so dispossessed were removed to other vacant places farther westward. Now this expedient is no longer open.

The Western country is rapidly filling up. A steady stream of immigration is following the railroad lines and then spreading to the right and left. The vacant places still existing are either worthless or will soon be exposed to the same invasion. The plains are being occupied by cattle raisers, the fertile valleys and bottomlands by agriculturists, the mountains by miners. What is to become of the Indians?

In trying to solve this question, we have to keep in view the facts here recited. However we may deplore the injustice which these facts have brought, and are still bringing, upon the red men, yet with these facts we have to deal. They are undeniable. Sound statesmanship cannot disregard them. It is true that the Indian reservations now existing cover a great many millions of acres, containing very valuable tracts of agricultural, grazing, and mineral land; that the area now cultivated, or that can possibly be cultivated by the Indians, is comparatively very small; that by far the larger portion is lying waste. Is it not, in view of the history of more than two centuries, useless to speculate in our minds how these many millions of acres can be preserved in their present state for the Indians to roam upon? How the greedy push of settlement and enterprise might be permanently checked for the protection of the red man's present possessions, as hunting grounds upon which, moreover, there is now but very little left to hunt?

We are sometimes told that ours is a powerful government which might accomplish such things if it would only put forth its whole strength. Is this so? The government is, indeed, strong in some respects, but weak in others. It may be truthfully said that the government has never been intent upon robbing the Indians. It has frequently tried, in good faith, to protect them against encroachment, and almost as frequently it has failed. It has simply yielded to the pressure exercised upon it by the people who were in immediate contact with the Indians. Those in authority were, in most cases, drawn or driven into an active participation in conflicts not of their own making. When a collision between Indians and whites had once occurred, no matter who was responsible for it, and when bloody deeds had been committed and an outcry about Indian atrocities risen up, our military forces were always found on the side of the white people and against the savage, no matter whether those who gave the orders knew that the savages were originally the victims and not the assailants.

Imagine, now, the government were to proclaim that, from the many millions of acres at present covered by Indian reservations, white men should forever be excluded, and that the national power should be exerted to that end, what would be the consequence? For some time the government might succeed in enforcing such a resolution. How long would depend upon the rapidity with which the Western country is occupied by settlers. As the settlements crowd upon the reservations, the population thickens, and the demand for larger fields of agricultural and mining enterprise becomes more pressing, the government may still remain true to its purpose.

But will those who are hungry for the Indian lands sit still? It will be easy for the rough and reckless frontiersmen to pick quarrels with the Indians. The speculators, who have their eyes upon every opportunity for gain, will urge them on. The watchfulness of the government will, in the long run, be unavailing to prevent collisions. The Indians will retaliate. Settlers' cabins will be burned and blood will flow. The conflict once brought on, the white man and the red man will stand against one another, and, in spite of all its good intentions and its sense of justice, the forces of the government will find themselves engaged on the side of the white man. The Indians will be hunted down at whatever cost. It will simply be a repetition of the old story, and that old story will be eventually repeated whenever there is a large and valuable Indian reservation surrounded by white settlements. Unjust, disgraceful as this may be, it is not only probable but almost inevitable. The extension of our railroad system will only accelerate the catastrophe. . . .

What does, under such circumstances, wise and humane statesmanship demand? Not that we should close our eyes to existing facts; but that, keeping those facts clearly in view, we should discover among the possibilities that which is most just and best for the Indians. I am profoundly convinced that a stubborn maintenance of the system of large Indian reservations must eventually result in the destruction of the red men, however faithfully the government may endeavor to protect their rights. It is only a question of time. . . .

What we can and should do is, in general terms, to fit the Indians, as much as possible, for the habits and occupations of civilized life by work and education; to individualize them in the possession and appreciation of property by allotting to them lands in severalty, giving them a fee simple title individually to the parcels of land they cultivate, inalienable for a certain period, and to obtain their consent to a disposition of that part of their lands which they cannot use, for a fair compensation, in such a manner that they no longer stand in the way of the development of the country as an obstacle, but form part of it and are benefited by it.

The circumstances surrounding them place before the Indians this stern alternative — extermination or civilization. The thought of exterminating a race, once the only occupant of the soil upon which so many millions of our own people have grown prosperous and happy, must be revolting to every American who is not devoid of all sentiments of justice and humanity. To civilize them, which was once only a benevolent fancy, has now become an absolute necessity if we mean to save them.

Can Indians be civilized? This question is answered in the negative only by those who do not want to civilize them. My experience in the management of Indian affairs, which enabled me to witness the progress made even among the wildest tribes, confirms me in the belief that it is not only possible but easy to introduce civilized habits and occupations among Indians if only the proper means are employed. We are frequently told that Indians will not work. True, it is difficult to make them work as long as they can live upon hunting. But they will work when their living depends upon it, or when sufficient inducements are offered to them. Of this there is an abundance of proof. To be sure, as to Indian civilization, we must not expect too rapid progress or the attainment of too lofty a standard. We can certainly not transform them at once into great statesmen, or philosophers, or manufacturers, or merchants; but we can make them small farmers and herders. Some of them show even remarkable aptitude for mercantile pursuits on a small scale.

I see no reason why the degree of civilization attained by the Indians in the states of New York, Indiana, Michigan, and some tribes in the Indian Territory should not be attained in the course of time by all. I have no doubt that they can be sufficiently civilized to support themselves, to maintain relations of good neighborship with the people surrounding them, and altogether to cease being a disturbing element in society. The accomplishment of this end, however, will require much considerate care and wise guidance. That care and guidance is necessarily the task of the government which, as to the Indians at least, must exercise paternal functions until they are sufficiently advanced to take care of themselves.

In this respect, some sincere philanthropists seem inclined to run into a serious error in insisting that first of all things it is necessary to give to the Indian the rights and privileges of American citizenship, to treat him in all respects as a citizen, and to relieve him of all restraints to which other American citizens are not subject. I do not intend to go here into a disquisition on the legal status of the Indian, on which elaborate treatises have been written, and learned judicial decisions rendered, without raising it above dispute. The end to be reached is unquestionably the gradual absorption of the Indians in the great body of American citizenship. When that is accomplished, then, and only then, the legal status of the Indian will be clearly and finally fixed.

But we should not indulge in the delusion that the problem can be solved by merely conferring upon them rights they do not yet appreciate and duties they do not yet understand. Those who advocate this seem to think that the Indians are yearning for American citizenship, eager to take it if we will only give it to them. No mistake could be greater. An overwhelming majority of the Indians look at present upon American citizenship as a dangerous gift, and but few of the more civilized are willing to accept it when it is attainable. And those who are uncivilized would certainly not know what to do with it if they had it. The mere theoretical endowment of savages with rights which are beyond their understanding and appreciation will, therefore, help them little. They should certainly have that standing in the courts which is necessary for their protection. But full citizenship must be regarded as the terminal not as the initial point of their development.

The first necessity, therefore, is not at once to give it to them but to fit them for it. And to this end, nothing is more indispensable than the protecting and guiding care of the government during the dangerous period of transition from savage to civilized life. When the wild Indian first turns his face from his old habits toward "the ways of the white man," his self-reliance is severely shaken. The picturesque and proud hunter and warrior of the plain or the forest gradually ceases to exist. In his new occupations, with his new aims and objects, he feels himself like a child in need of leading strings. Not clearly knowing where he is to go, he may be led in the right direction, and he may also be led astray.

He is apt to accept the vices as well as the virtues and accomplishments of civilization, and the former, perhaps, more readily than the latter. He is as accessible to bad as to good advice or example, and the class of people usually living in the immediate vicinity of Indian camps and reservations is frequently not such as to exercise upon him an elevating influence. He is in danger of becoming a drunkard before he has learned to restrain his appetites, and of being tricked out of his property before he is able to appreciate its value. He is overcome by a feeling of helplessness, and he naturally looks to the "Great Father" to take him by the hand and guide him on. That guiding hand must necessarily be one of authority and power to command confidence and respect. It can be only that of the government which the Indian is accustomed to regard as a sort of omnipotence on earth. Everything depends upon the wisdom and justice of that guidance.

To fit the Indians for their ultimate absorption in the great body of American citizenship, three things are suggested by common sense as well as philanthropy: (1) that they be taught to work by making work profitable and attractive to them; (2) that they be educated, especially the youth of both sexes; (3) that they be individualized in the possession of property by settlement in severalty with a fee simple title, after which the lands they do not use may be disposed of for general settlement and enterprise without danger and with profit to the Indians.

This may seem a large program, strangely in contrast with the old wild life of the Indians, but they are now more disposed than ever before to accept it. Even those of them who have so far been in a great measure living upon the chase are becoming aware that the game is fast disappearing and will no longer be sufficient to furnish them a sustenance. In a few years the buffalo will be exterminated, and smaller game is gradually growing scarce, except in the more inaccessible mountain regions. The necessity of procuring food in some other way is thus before their eyes. The requests of Indians addressed to the government for instruction in agriculture, for agricultural implements and for stock cattle are in consequence now more frequent and pressing than ever before.

A more general desire for the education

of their children springs from the same source, and many express a wish for the allotment of farm tracts among them, with "the white man's paper," meaning a good, strong title like that held by white men. This progressive movement is, of course, different in degree with different tribes, but it is going on more or less everywhere. The failure of Sitting Bull's attempt to maintain himself and a large number of followers on our northern frontier in the old wild ways of Indian life will undoubtedly strengthen the tendency among the wild Indians of the Northwest to recognize the situation and to act accordingly. The general state of feeling among the red men is therefore now exceedingly favorable to the civilizing process.

Much has already been done in the direction above indicated. The area of land cultivated by Indians is steadily extended, and the quantity and value of their crops show a hopeful increase from year to year. Many Indians are already showing commendable pride in the product of their labor. Much more, however, might be done by the government to facilitate and encourage this progress by making larger appropriations for the appointment of men competent to instruct the Indians in agricultural work and for furnishing them with farming implements. Unfortunately, members of Congress are frequently more intent upon making a good record in cutting down expenses in the wrong place than upon providing the necessary money for objects the accomplishment of which would finally result in real and great economy. It may be remarked, by the way, that the promotion of agricultural work among the Indians is frequently discouraged by well-meaning men who reason upon the theory that in the transition from savage to civilized life, the pastoral state comes before the agricultural, and that the Indians, therefore, must be made herders before they can be made farmers.

This theory is supported by historical precedents. It is true that the transition from the savage state to the pastoral is less violent than that from the savage state directly to the agricultural, but this does not prove that the latter is impossible. Moreover, the former requires certain favorable conditions, one of which is not only the possession of large tracts of grazing land but also of large numbers of cattle; and another is that the transition, which would necessarily require a considerable time, be not interfered with by extraneous circumstances. There are only a few isolated instances of Indian tribes having devoted themselves successfully to the raising of herds and flocks, such as the Navajos, who have hundreds of thousands of sheep, and manufacture excellent blankets by hand. Some thrifty Indians on the Pacific coast have raised small herds of cattle, and something more has been done by the so-called civilized tribes in the Indian Territory. The rest of the Indians have only raised ponies.

To make all our wild Indians herders would require the maintenance of the system of large reservations which, as I have shown, will be a precarious thing under the pressure of advancing settlement and enterprise. It would further require the distribution among them of large numbers of stock animals. Such distributions have been gradually increased, but even among the tribes best provided for, only to the extent of giving to each family one or two cows; and I see no prospect, with the resources likely to be at the disposal of the Indian service, of carrying this practice much farther than to make it more general among all the tribes.

But the possession of a cow or two will not make a man a herder. And even if the number were increased and the cattle belonging to the members of a tribe were herded together for the purpose of regular cattle raising, that pursuit would require the constant labor of only a small number of individuals, while, under existing circumstances, it is most desirable, if not absolutely necessary, that all of them, or at least as many as possible, be actively and profitably employed so as to accelerate the civilizing process. To this end it seems indispensable that agricultural work be their principal occupation. But we need not be troubled by any misgivings on this head.

The reports of early explorers show that most of our Indian tribes, without having passed through the pastoral state, did cultivate the soil in a rough way and on a small scale when first seen by white men, and that subsequently they continued that pursuit to a greater or less extent, even while they were driven from place to place. The promotion of agricultural work among them will therefore only be a revival and development of an old practice. The progress they now make shows how naturally they take to it. And if the government, as it should, continues to furnish them with domestic animals, cattle raising in a small way may become, not their principal business but a proper and valuable addition to their agricultural work. I have no doubt, however, that young Indians may be profitably employed by the cattle raisers of the West as mounted herdsmen or cowboys. If paid reasonable wages, they would probably be found very faithful and efficient in that capacity.

Other useful occupations for which the Indians show great aptitude have been introduced with promising success. They are now doing a very large part of the freighting of government goods, such as their own supplies and annuities. Indian freighting on a large scale was introduced only a very few years ago at almost all the agencies, especially on this side of the Rocky Mountains, which are not immediately accessible by railroad or river. The Indians use their own ponies as draft animals, while the government furnishes the wagons and harness. The Indians have by this industry already earned large sums of money, and proved the most honest and efficient freighters the government ever had. There is no reason why, in the course of time, they should not be largely engaged by the government, as well as private parties, in the transportation of other than Indian goods.

That Indians can be successfully employed at various kinds of mechanical work has already been sufficiently tested. A respectable number of their young men serve as apprentices in the saddler, blacksmith, shoemaker, tinsmith, and carpenter shops at the agencies in the West, as well as at the Indian schools, and their proficiency is much commended. The school at Carlisle has been able to furnish considerable quantities of tinware, harness, and shoes, all made by Indian labor, and, in some of the sawmills and gristmills on the reservations, Indians are employed as machinists with perfect safety. Many Indians who, but a few years ago, did nothing but hunting and fighting, are now engaged in building houses for their families, and, with some instruction and aid on the part of the government, they are doing reasonably well. Here and there an Indian is found who shows striking ability as a trader.

All these things are capable of large and rapid development if pushed forward and guided with wisdom and energy. All that is said here refers to the so-called wild tribes, such as the Sioux, the Shoshones, Poncas, Cheyennes, Arapahoes, Pawnees, etc. The significant point is that, recognizing the change in their situation, Indian men now almost generally accept work as a necessity, while formerly all the drudgery was done by their women. The civilized tribes in the Indian Territory and elsewhere have already proved their capacity for advancement in a greater measure.

One of the most important agencies in the civilizing process is, of course, education in schools. The first step was the establishment of day schools on the reservations for Indian children. The efforts made by the government in that direction may not always have been efficiently conducted; but it is also certain that, in the nature of things, the result of that system could not be satisfactory. With the exception of a few hours spent in school, the children remained exposed to the influence of their more or less savage home surroundings, and the indulgence of their parents greatly interfered with the regularity of their attendance and with the necessary discipline. Boarding schools at the agencies were then tried, as far as the appropriations made by Congress would permit, adding to the usual elementary education some practical instruction in housework and domestic industries. The results thus obtained were perceptibly better, but even the best boarding schools located on Indian reservations, in contact with no phase of human life except that of the Indian camp or village, still remain without those conditions of which the work of civilizing the growing Indian generation stands most in need.

The Indian, in order to be civilized, must not only learn how to read and write but how to live. On most of the Indian reservations he lives only among his own kind, excepting the teachers and the few white agency people. He may feel the necessity of changing his mode of life ever so strongly; he may hear of civilization ever so much; but as long as he has not with his own eyes seen civilization at work, it will remain to him only a vague, shadowy idea — a newfangled, outlandish contrivance, the objects of which cannot be clearly appreciated by him in detail.

He hears that he must accept "the white man's way," and, in an indistinct manner, he is impressed with the necessity of doing so. But what is the white man's way? What ends does it serve? What means does it employ? What is necessary to attain it? The teaching in a school on an Indian reservation, in the midst of Indian barbarism, answers these questions only from hearsay. The impressions it thus produces, whether in all things right or in some things wrong, will, in any event, be insufficient to give the mind of the Indian a clear conception of what "the white man's way" really is.

The school on the reservation undoubtedly does some good, but it does not enough. If the Indian is to become civilized, the most efficient method will be to permit him to see and watch civilization at work in its own atmosphere. In order to learn to live like the white man, he should see and observe how the white man lives·in his own surroundings, what he is doing, and what he is doing it for. He should have an opportunity to observe, not by an occasional bewildering glimpse, like the Indians who now and then come to Washington to see the "Great Father," but observe with the eye of an interested party, while being taught to do likewise. . . .

As the third thing necessary for the absorption of the Indians in the great body of American citizenship, I mentioned their individualization in the possession of property by their settlement in severalty upon small farm tracts with a fee simple title. When the Indians are so settled, and have become individual property owners, holding their farms by the same title under the law by which white men hold theirs, they will feel more readily inclined to part with such of their lands as they cannot themselves cultivate and from which they can derive profit only if they sell them, either in lots or in bulk, for a fair equivalent in money or in annuities.

This done, the Indians will occupy no more ground than so many white people; the large reservations will gradually be opened to general settlement and enterprise, and the Indians, with their possessions, will cease to stand in the way of the "development of the country." The difficulty which has provoked so many encroachments and conflicts will then no longer exist. When the Indians are individual owners of real property, and as individuals enjoy the protection of the laws, their tribal cohesion will

necessarily relax and gradually disappear. They will have advanced an immense step in the direction of the "white man's way."

Is this plan practicable? In this respect we are not entirely without experience. Allotments of farm tracts to Indians and their settlement in severalty have already been attempted under special laws or treaties with a few tribes; in some instances, with success; in others, the Indians, when they had acquired individual title to their land, and before they had learned to appreciate its value, were induced to dispose of it, or were tricked out of it by unscrupulous white men who took advantage of their ignorance. They were thus impoverished again and some of them fell back upon the government for support. This should be guarded against, as much as it can be, by a legal provision making the title to their farm tracts inalienable for a certain period, say twenty-five years, during which the Indians will have sufficient opportunity to acquire more provident habits, to become somewhat acquainted with the ways of the world, and to learn to take care of themselves.

In some cases where the allotment of lands in severalty and the granting of patents conveying a fee simple title to Indians was provided for in Indian treaties, the Interior Department under the last administration saw fit to put off the full execution of this provision for the reason that the law did not permit the insertion in the patent of the inalienability clause, that without such a clause the Indians would be exposed to the kind of spoliation above mentioned, and that it was hoped Congress would speedily supply that deficiency by the passage of the general Severalty Bill then under discussion. Indeed, without such a clause in the land patents, it cannot be denied that the conveyance of individual fee simple title to Indians would be a hazardous experiment, except in the case of those most advanced in civilization. . . .

The policy here outlined is apt to be looked upon with disfavor by two classes of people: on the one hand, those who think that "the only good Indian is a dead Indian," and who denounce every recognition of the Indian's rights and every desire to promote his advancement in civilization as sickly sentimentality; and, on the other hand, that class of philanthropists who, in their treatment of the Indian question, pay no regard to surrounding circumstances and suspect every policy contemplating a reduction of the Indian reservations of being a scheme of spoliation and robbery gotten up by speculators and "land grabbers." With the first class it seems useless to reason. As to the second, they do not themselves believe, if they are sensible, that twenty-five years hence millions of acres of valuable land will, in any part of the country, still be kept apart as Indian hunting grounds.

The question is whether the Indians are to be exposed to the danger of hostile collisions, and of being robbed of their lands in consequence, or whether they are to be induced by proper and fair means to sell that which, as long as they keep it, is of no advantage to anybody, but which, as soon as they part with it for a just compensation, will be of great advantage to themselves and their white neighbors alike. No true friend of the Indian will hesitate to choose the latter line of policy as one in entire accord with substantial justice, humanity, the civilization and welfare of the red men, and the general interests of the country.

107.

Helen Hunt Jackson: Indians and Whites

Helen Hunt Jackson's book, A Century of Dishonor *(1881), the concluding chapter of which is reprinted here, documented the dealings of the federal government with the various Indian nations. Theodore Roosevelt, for one, refused to accept Jackson's findings and included her among those whom he called "these foolish sentimentalists." Jackson herself felt that her efforts on behalf of Native Americans were in vain but continued in the novel* Ramona *to condemn the government's treatment of American Indians.*

Source: *A Century of Dishonor*, Boston, 1887, Ch. 10.

There are within the limits of the United States between 250,000 and 300,000 Indians, exclusive of those in Alaska. The names of the different tribes and bands, as entered in the statistical tables of the Indian Office Reports, number nearly 300. One of the most careful estimates which have been made of their numbers and localities gives them as follows: "In Minnesota and states east of the Mississippi, about 32,500; in Nebraska, Kansas, and the Indian Territory, 70,650; in the territories of Dakota, Montana, Wyoming, and Idaho, 65,000; in Nevada and the territories of Colorado, New Mexico, Utah, and Arizona, 84,000; and on the Pacific slope, 48,000."

Of these, 130,000 are self-supporting on their own reservations, "receiving nothing from the government except interest on their own moneys or annuities granted them in consideration of the cession of their lands to the United States." This fact alone would seem sufficient to dispose forever of the accusation, so persistently brought against the Indian, that he will not work.

Of the remainder, 84,000 are partially supported by the government — the interest money due them and their annuities, as provided by treaty, being inadequate to their subsistence on the reservations where they are confined. In many cases, however, these Indians furnish a large part of their support — the White River Utes, for instance, who are reported by the Indian Bureau as getting 66 percent of their living by "root digging, hunting, and fishing"; the Squaxin band, in Washington Territory, as earning 75 percent, and the Chippewas of Lake Superior as earning 50 percent in the same way. These facts also would seem to dispose of the accusation that the Indian will not work.

There are about 55,000, who never visit an agency, over whom the government does not pretend to have either control or care. These 55,000 "subsist by hunting, fishing, on roots, nuts, berries, etc., and by begging and stealing"; and this also seems to dispose of the accusation that the Indian will not "work for a living." There remains a small portion, about 31,000, that are entirely subsisted by the government.

There is not among these 300 bands of Indians one which has not suffered cruelly at the hands either of the government or of white settlers. The poorer, the more insignificant, the more helpless the band, the more certain the cruelty and outrage to which they have been subjected. This is especially true of the bands on the Pacific slope. These Indians found themselves of a sudden surrounded by and caught up in the great influx of gold-seeking settlers, as helpless creatures on a shore are caught up in a tidal wave. There was not time for the government to make treaties; not even time for communities to make laws. The tale of the wrongs, the oppressions, the murders of the Pacific-slope Indians in the last thirty years

would be a volume by itself and is too monstrous to be believed.

It makes little difference, however, where one opens the record of the history of the Indians; every page and every year has its dark stain. The story of one tribe is the story of all, varied only by differences of time and place; but neither time nor place makes any difference in the main facts. Colorado is as greedy and unjust in 1880 as was Georgia in 1830 and Ohio in 1795; and the United States government breaks promises now as deftly as then, and with an added ingenuity from long practice.

One of its strongest supports in so doing is the widespread sentiment among the people of dislike to the Indian, of impatience with his presence as a "barrier to civilization," and distrust of it as a possible danger. The old tales of the frontier life, with its horrors of Indian warfare, have gradually, by two or three generations' telling, produced in the average mind something like a hereditary instinct of unquestioning and unreasoning aversion which it is almost impossible to dislodge or soften.

There are hundreds of pages of unimpeachable testimony on the side of the Indian; but it goes for nothing, is set down as sentimentalism or partisanship, tossed aside and forgotten.

President after President has appointed commission after commission to inquire into and report upon Indian affairs and to make suggestions as to the best methods of managing them. The reports are filled with eloquent statements of wrongs done to the Indians, of perfidies on the part of the government. They counsel, as earnestly as words can, a trial of the simple and unperplexing expedients of telling truth, keeping promises, making fair bargains, dealing justly in all ways and all things. These reports are bound up with the Government's Annual Reports, and that is the end of them. It would probably be no exaggeration to say that not 1 American citizen out of

10,000 ever sees them or knows that they exist, and yet any one of them, circulated throughout the country, read by the right-thinking, right-feeling men and women of this land, would be of itself a "campaign document" that would initiate a revolution which would not subside until the Indians' wrongs were, so far as is now left possible, righted.

In 1869, President Grant appointed a commission of nine men, representing the influence and philanthropy of six leading states, to visit the different Indian reservations and to "examine all matters appertaining to Indian affairs."

In the report of this commission are such paragraphs as the following:

To assert that "the Indian will not work" is as true as it would be to say that the white man will not work.

Why should the Indian be expected to plant corn, fence lands, build houses, or do anything but get food from day to day when experience has taught him that the product of his labor will be seized by the white man tomorrow? The most industrious white man would become a drone under similar circumstances. Nevertheless, many of the Indians (the commissioners might more forcibly have said 130,000 of the Indians) are already at work and furnish ample refutation of the assertion that "the Indian will not work." There is no escape from the inexorable logic of facts.

The history of the government connections with the Indians is a shameful record of broken treaties and unfulfilled promises. The history of the border white man's connection with the Indians is a sickening record of murder, outrage, robbery, and wrongs committed by the former, as the rule, and occasional savage outbreaks and unspeakably barbarous deeds of retaliation by the latter, as the exception.

Taught by the government that they had rights entitled to respect, when those rights have been assailed by the rapacity of the white man, the arm which should have been raised to protect them has ever been ready to sustain the aggressor.

The testimony of some of the highest military officers of the United States is on record to the effect that, in our Indian wars, almost without exception, the first aggressions have been made by the white man; and the assertion is supported by every civilian of reputation who has studied the subject. In addition to the class of robbers and outlaws who find impunity in their nefarious pursuits on the frontiers, there is a large class of professedly reputable men who use every means in their power to bring on Indian wars for the sake of the profit to be realized from the presence of troops and the expenditure of government funds in their midst. They proclaim death to the Indians at all times in words and publications, making no distinction between the innocent and the guilty. They irate the lowest class of men to the perpetration of the darkest deeds against their victims, and, as judges and jurymen, shield them from the justice due to their crimes. Every crime committed by a white man against an Indian is concealed or palliated. Every offense committed by an Indian against a white man is borne on the wings of the post or the telegraph to the remotest corner of the land, clothed with all the horrors which the reality or imagination can throw around it. Against such influences as these the people of the United States need to be warned.

To assume that it would be easy, or by any one sudden stroke of legislative policy possible, to undo the mischief and hurt of the long past, set the Indian policy of the country right for the future, and make the Indians at once safe and happy, is the blunder of a hasty and uninformed judgment. The notion which seems to be growing more prevalent, that simply to make all Indians at once citizens of the United States would be a sovereign and instantaneous panacea for all their ills and all the government's perplexities, is a very inconsiderate one. To administer complete citizenship of a sudden, all round, to all Indians, barbarous and civilized alike, would be as grotesque a blunder as to dose them all round with any one medicine, irrespective of the symptoms and needs of their diseases. It would kill more than it would cure.

Nevertheless, it is true, as was well stated by one of the superintendents of Indian Affairs in 1857, that,

> so long as they are not citizens of the United States, their rights of property must remain insecure against invasion. The doors of the federal tribunals being barred against them while wards and dependents, they can only partially exercise the rights of free government, or give to those who make, execute, and construe the few laws they are allowed to enact, dignity sufficient to make them respectable. While they continue individually to gather the crumbs that fall from the table of the United States, idleness, improvidence, and indebtedness will be the rule, and industry, thrift, and freedom from debt, the exception. The utter absence of individual title to particular lands deprives everyone among them of the chief incentive to labor and exertion — the very mainspring on which the prosperity of a people depends.

All judicious plans and measures for their safety and salvation must embody provisions for their becoming citizens as fast as they are fit and must protect them till then in every right and particular in which our laws protect other "persons" who are not citizens.

There is a disposition in a certain class of minds to be impatient with any protestation against wrong which is unaccompanied or unprepared with a quick and exact scheme of remedy. This is illogical. When pioneers in a new country find a tract of poisonous and swampy wilderness to be reclaimed, they do not withhold their hands from fire and axe till they see clearly which way roads should run, where good water will spring, and what crops will best grow on the redeemed land. They first clear the swamp. So with this poisonous and baffling part of the domain of our national affairs — let us first "clear the swamp."

However great perplexity and difficulty there may be in the details of any and every plan possible for doing at this late day anything like justice to the Indian, however

Library of Congress

Helen Hunt Jackson in 1885

hard it may be for good statesmen and good men to agree upon the things that ought to be done, there certainly is, or ought to be, no perplexity whatever, no difficulty whatever, in agreeing upon certain things that ought not to be done and which must cease to be done before the first steps can be taken toward righting the wrongs, curing the ills, and wiping out the disgrace to us of the present condition of our Indians.

Cheating, robbing, breaking promises — these three are clearly things which must cease to be done. One more thing, also, and that is the refusal of the protection of the law to the Indian's rights of property, "of life, liberty, and the pursuit of happiness."

When these four things have ceased to be done, time, statesmanship, philanthropy, and Christianity can slowly and surely do the rest. Till these four things have ceased to be done, statesmanship and philanthropy alike must work in vain, and even Christianity can reap but small harvest.

108.

James G. Blaine: A Congress of Nations of North and South America

James G. Blaine, as secretary of state in 1881, promoted the idea of Pan-American cooperation that had failed to attract adherents since the administration of John Quincy Adams. Blaine was allowed by President Chester A. Arthur to issue invitations to Latin-American states to meet in a congress at Washington in 1882. But by the end of December, Blaine had been replaced by Frederick T. Frelinghuysen, who disapproved of the plan and immediately withdrew the invitations. Such a congress of American nations did meet in 1889, however, and, coincidentally, it was James Blaine, again secretary of state, who presided over it. In its limited way, the work of Blaine for Pan-American cooperation was a forerunner of the Good Neighbor Policy of the 1930s and the Alliance for Progress of the 1960s. The following letter extending an invitation to Argentina was addressed to Thomas O. Osborn at the U.S. legation in Buenos Aires on November 29, 1881.

Source: PRFA, 1881, pp. 13-15.

Sir: The attitude of the United States with respect to the question of general peace on the American continent is well known through its persistent efforts for years to avert the evils of warfare, or, these efforts failing, to bring positive conflicts to an end through pacific counsels or the advocacy of impartial arbitration.

This attitude has been consistently maintained, and always with such fairness as to leave no room for imputing to our government any motive except the humane and disinterested one of saving the kindred states of the American continent from the burdens of war. The position of the United States as the leading power of the New World might well give to its government a claim to authoritative utterance for the purpose of quieting discord among its neighbors, with all of whom the most friendly relations exist. Nevertheless, the good offices of this government are not and have not at any time been tendered with a show of dictation or compulsion, but only as exhibiting the solicitous goodwill of a common friend.

For some years past a growing disposition has been manifested by certain states of Central and South America to refer disputes affecting grave questions of international relationship and boundaries to arbitration rather than to the sword. It has been on several such occasions a source of profound satisfaction to the government of the United States to see that this country is in a large measure looked to by all the American powers as their friend and mediator. The just and impartial counsel of the President in such cases has never been withheld, and his efforts have been rewarded by the prevention of sanguinary strife or angry contentions between peoples whom we regard as brethren.

The existence of this growing tendency convinces the President that the time is ripe for a proposal that shall enlist the goodwill and active cooperation of all the states of the Western Hemisphere, both north and south, in the interest of humanity and for the commonweal of nations. He conceives that none of the governments of America can be less alive than our own to the dangers and horrors of a state of war, and especially of war between kinsmen. He is sure that none of the chiefs of governments on the continent can be less sensitive than he is to the sacred duty of making every endeavor to do away with the chances of fratricidal strife. And he looks with hopeful confidence to such active assistance from them as will serve to show the broadness of our common humanity and the strength of the ties which bind us all together as a great and harmonious system of American commonwealths.

Impressed by these views, the President extends to all the independent countries of North and South America an earnest invitation to participate in a general congress to be held in the city of Washington on the 24th day of November, 1882, for the purpose of considering and discussing the methods of preventing war between the nations of America. He desires that the attention of the congress shall be strictly confined to this one great object; that its sole aim shall be to seek a way of permanently averting the horrors of cruel and bloody combat between countries, oftenest of one blood and speech, or the even worse calamity of internal commotion and civil strife; that it shall regard the burdensome and far-reaching consequences of such struggles, the legacies of exhausted finances, of oppressive debt, of onerous taxation, of ruined cities, of paralyzed industries, of devastated fields, of ruthless conscription, of the slaughter of men, of the grief of the widow and the orphan, of embittered resentment that long survive those who provoked them and heavily afflict the innocent generations that come after.

The President is especially desirous to have it understood that, in putting forth this invitation, the United States does not assume the position of counseling or attempting, through the voice of the congress, to counsel any determinate solution of existing questions which may now divide any of the countries of America. Such questions cannot properly come before the congress. Its mission is higher. It is to provide for the interests of all in the future, not to settle the individual differences of the present. For this reason especially the President has indicated a day for the assembling of the congress so far in the future as to leave good ground for hope that by the time named the present situation on the South Pacific Coast will be happily terminated, and that those engaged in the contest may take peaceable part in the discussion and solution of the general question affecting in an equal degree the well-being of all.

It seems also desirable to disclaim in advance any purpose on the part of the United States to prejudge the issues to be presented to the congress. It is far from the intent of this government to appear before the congress as in any sense the protector of its neighbors or the predestined and necessary arbitrator of their disputes. The United States will enter into the deliberations of the congress on the same footing as the other powers represented, and with the loyal determination to approach any proposed solution, not merely in its own interest, or with a view to asserting its power, but as a single member among many coordinate and coequal states. So far as the influence of this government may be potential, it will be exerted in the direction of conciliating whatever conflicting interests of blood, or government, or historical tradition may necessarily come together in response to a call embracing such vast and diverse elements.

You will present these views to the minister of foreign relations of the Argentine Republic, enlarging, if need be, in such terms as will readily occur to you, upon the great mission which it is within the power of the proposed congress to accomplish in the interest of humanity.

1882

109.

Standard Oil Trust Agreement

The Standard Oil Company was incorporated in Ohio in January 1870 to supplant the previous firm of Rockefeller, Andrews & Flagler. The new corporation launched an expansion program, and by 1873 it controlled all the refineries in the Cleveland area, as well as oil transport and refining companies in the state of New York and in Louisville, Kentucky. The firm acquired the main refineries in Pittsburgh and Philadelphia in 1874-1876 and took control of the Empire Transportation Company pipelines in 1877. Two years later Standard Oil owned or controlled nearly 95 percent of the refining facilities in the United States, in addition to pipelines, storage tanks, and transportation facilities in the United States and Europe. To provide administrative centralization for this vast empire, the Standard Oil Trust Agreement was set up on January 2, 1882, as the first trust-monopoly in American history, bringing Standard Oil's holdings under control of an able management team headed by John D. Rockefeller. The following selection is the trust agreement of January 2, plus the supplemental agreement of January 4.

Source: Horace L. Wilgus, *A Study of the United States Steel Corporation in its Industrial and Legal Aspects*, Chicago, 1901, Appendix.

THIS AGREEMENT, made and entered upon this 2nd day of January, A.D. 1882, by and between all the persons who shall now or may hereafter execute the same as parties thereto, witnesseth:

I. It is intended that the parties to this agreement shall embrace three classes, to wit:

1. All the stockholders and members of the following corporations and limited partnerships, to wit: Acme Oil Company (New York); Acme Oil Company (Pennsylvania); Atlantic Refining Company, of Philadelphia; Bush & Co., Limited; Camden Consolidated Oil Company; Elizabethport Acid Works; Imperial Refining Company, Limited; Chas. Pratt & Co.; Paine, Ablett & Co., Limited; Standard Oil Company (Ohio); Standard Oil Company (Pittsburgh); Smith's Ferry Oil Trans. Company; Solar Oil Company, Limited; Sone & Fleming Manufacturing Company, Limited.

Also, all the stockholders and members of such other corporations and limited partnerships as may hereafter join in this agreement at the request of the trustees herein provided for.

2. The following individuals, to wit: W. C. Andrews; Jno. D. Archbold; Lide K. Arter; J. A. Bostwick; Benj. Brewster; D. Bushnell; Thos. C. Bushnell; J. N. Camden; Henry L. Davis; H. M. Flagler; Mrs. H. M. Flagler; H. M. Harma; and Geo. W. Chapin; D. M. Harkness, D. H. Harkness, trustee; S. V. Harkness; John Huntington; H. A. Hutchins; Chas. F. G. Heye; O. B. Jennings; Chas. Lockhart; A. M. McGregor; Wm. H. Macy; Wm. H. Macy, Jr.; estate of Josiah Macy, Jr., Wm. H. Macy, Jr., executor; O. H. Payne, O. H. Payne, trustee; Chas. Pratt; Horace A. Pratt; C. M. Pratt; A. J. Pouch; John D. Rockefeller; Wm. Rockefeller; Henry H. Rogers; W. P. Thompson; J. J. Vandegrift; William T. Wardwell; W. G. Warden; Jos. L. Warden; Warden, Frew & Co., Louise C. Wheaton; Julia H. York; Geo. H. Vilas, M. R. Keith, Geo. F. Chester, trustees.

Also, all such individuals as may hereafter join in this agreement at the request of the trustees herein provided for.

3. A portion of the stockholders and members of the following corporations and limited partnerships, to wit: American Lubricating Oil Co.; Baltimore United Oil Co.; Beacon Oil Co.; Bush & Denslow Manufacturing Co.; Central Refining Co., of Pittsburgh; Chesebrough Manufacturing Co.; Chess-Carley Co.; Consolidated Tank Line Co.; Inland Oil Co.; Keystone Refining Co.; Maverick Oil Co.; National Transit Co.; Portland Kerosene Oil Co.; Producers' Consolidated Land and Petroleum Co.; Signal Oil Works, Limited; Thompson & Bedford Co., Limited; Devoe Manufacturing Co.; Eclipse Lubricating Oil Co., Limited; Empire Refining Co., Limited; Franklin Pipe Co., Limited; Galena Oil Works, Limited; Galena Farm Oil Co., Limited; Germania Mining Co.; Vacuum Oil Co.; H. C. Van Tine & Co., Limited; Waters-Pierce Oil Co.

Also, stockholders and members (not being all thereof) of other corporations and limited partnerships who may hereafter join in this agreement at the request of the trustees herein provided for.

II. The parties hereto do covenant and agree to and with each other, each in consideration of the mutual covenants and agreements of the others, as follows:

1. As soon as practicable, a corporation shall be formed in each of the following states, under the laws thereof, to wit: Ohio, New York, Pennsylvania, and New Jersey; provided, however, that instead of organizing a new corporation, any existing charter and organization may be used for the purpose when it can advantageously be done.

2. The purposes and powers of said corporation shall be to mine for, produce, manufacture, refine, and deal in petroleum and all its products and all the materials used in such businesses, and transact other business collateral thereto. But other purposes and powers shall be embraced in the several charters, such as shall seem expedient to the parties procuring the charter, or, if necessary to comply with the law, the powers aforesaid may be restricted and reduced.

3. At anytime hereafter, when it may seem advisable to the trustees herein provided for, similar corporations may be formed in other states and territories.

4. Each of said corporations shall be known as the Standard Oil Company of ——— (and here shall follow the name of the state or territory by virtue of the laws of which said corporation is organized).

5. The capital stock of each of said corporations shall be fixed at such an amount as may seem necessary and advisable to the parties organizing the same in view of the purpose to be accomplished.

6. The shares of stock of each of said

corporations shall be issued only for money, property, or assets equal at a fair valuation to the par value of the stock delivered therefor.

7. All of the property, real and personal, assets, and business of each and all of the corporations and limited partnerships mentioned or embraced in class 1 shall be transferred to and vested in the said several Standard Oil companies. All of the property, assets, and business in or of each particular state shall be transferred to and vested in the Standard Oil Company of that particular state, and in order to accomplish such purpose the directors and managers of each and all of the several corporations and limited partnerships mentioned in class 1 are hereby authorized and directed by the stockholders and members thereof (all of them being parties to this agreement) to sell, assign, transfer, convey, and make over, for the consideration hereinafter mentioned, to the Standard Oil Company or companies of the proper state or states as soon as said corporations are organized and ready to receive the same, all the property, real and personal, assets, and business of said corporations and limited partnerships. Correct schedules of such property, assets, and business shall accompany each transfer.

8. The individuals embraced in class 2 of this agreement do, each for himself, agree, for the consideration hereinafter mentioned, to sell, assign, transfer, convey, and set over all the property, real and personal, assets, and business mentioned and embraced in schedules accompanying such sale and transfer to the Standard Oil Company or companies of the proper state or states as soon as the said corporations are organized and ready to receive the same.

9. The parties embraced in class 3 of this agreement do covenant and agree to assign and transfer all of the stock held by them in the corporations or limited partnerships herein named to the trustees herein provid-ed for, for the consideration and upon the terms hereinafter set forth. It is understood and agreed that the said trustees and their successors may hereafter take the assignment of stocks in the same or similar companies upon the terms herein provided, and that whenever and as often as all the stocks of any corporation or limited partnership are vested in said trustees, the proper steps may then be taken to have all the money, property, real and personal, of such corporation or partnership assigned and conveyed to the Standard Oil Company of the proper state, on the terms and in the mode herein set forth, in which event the trustees shall receive stocks of the Standard Oil companies equal to the value of the money, property, and business assigned, to be held in place of the stocks of the company or companies assigning such property.

10. The consideration for the transfer and conveyance of the money, property, and business aforesaid to each or any of the Standard Oil companies shall be stock of the respective Standard Oil Company to which said transfer or conveyance is made, equal at par value to the appraised value of the money, property, and business so transferred. Said stock shall be delivered to the trustees hereinafter provided for, and their successors, and no stock of any of said companies shall ever be issued except for money, property, or business equal at least to the par value of the stock so issued; nor shall any stock be issued by any of said companies for any purpose except to the trustees herein provided for, to be held subject to the trusts hereinafter specified. It is understood, however, that this provision is not intended to restrict the purchase, sale, and exchange of property by said Standard Oil companies as fully as they may be authorized to do by their respective charters, provided only that no stock be issued therefor except to said trustees.

11. The consideration for any stocks de-

livered to said trustees as above provided for, as well as for stocks delivered to said trustees by persons mentioned or included in class 3 of this agreement, shall be the delivery by said trustees to the persons entitled thereto of trust certificates hereinafter provided for, equal at par value to the par value of the stocks of the said Standard Oil companies so received by said trustees, and equal to the appraised value of the stocks of other companies or partnerships delivered to said trustees. (The said appraised value shall be determined in a manner agreed upon by the parties in interest and the said trustees.) It is understood and agreed, however, that the said trustees may, with any trust funds in their hands, in addition to the mode above provided, purchase the bonds and stocks of other companies engaged in business similar or collateral to the business of said Standard Oil companies, on such terms and in such mode as they may deem advisable, and shall hold the same for the benefit of the owners of said trust certificates, and may sell, assign, transfer, and pledge such bonds and stocks whenever they may deem it advantageous to said trust so to do.

III. The trusts upon which said stocks shall be held, and the number, powers, and duties of said trustees shall be as follows:

1. The number of trustees shall be nine.

2. J. D. Rockefeller, O. H. Payne, and Wm. Rockefeller are hereby appointed trustees, to hold their office until the 1st Wednesday of April, A.D. 1885.

3. J. A. Bostwick, H. M. Flagler, and W. G. Warden are hereby appointed trustees, to hold their office until the 1st Wednesday of April, A.D. 1884.

4. Chas. Pratt, Benj. Brewster, and Jno. D. Archbold are hereby appointed trustees, to hold their office until the 1st Wednesday of April, A.D. 1883.

5. Elections for trustees to succeed those herein appointed shall be held annually, at which election a sufficient number of trust-ees shall be elected to fill all vacancies occurring either from expiration of the term of the office of trustee or from any other cause. All trustees shall be elected to hold their office for three years, except those elected to fill a vacancy arising from any cause, except expiration of term, who shall be elected for the balance of the term of the trustee whose place they are elected to fill. Every trustee shall hold his office until his successor is elected.

6. Trustees shall be elected by ballot by the owner of trust certificates or their proxies. At all meetings the owners of trust certificates, who may be registered as such on the books of the trustees, may vote in person or by proxy, and shall have one vote for each and every share of trust certificates standing in their names, but no such owner shall be entitled to vote upon any share which has not stood in his name thirty days prior to the day appointed for the election. The transfer books may be closed for thirty days immediately preceding the annual election. A majority of the shares represented at such election shall elect.

7. The annual meeting of the owners of said trust certificates for the election of trustees and for other business shall be held at the office of the trustees, in the city of New York, on the 1st Wednesday of April of each year, unless the place of meeting be changed by the trustees, and said meeting may be adjourned from day to day until its business is completed. Special meetings of the owners of said trust certificates may be called by the majority of the trustees at such times and places as they may appoint. It shall also be the duty of the trustees to call a special meeting of holders of trust certificates whenever requested to do so by a petition signed by the holders of 10 percent in value of such certificates. The business of such special meetings shall be confined to the object specified in the notice given therefor. Notice of the time and place

of all meetings of the owners of trust certificates shall be given by personal notice, as far as possible, and by public notice in one of the principal newspapers of each state in which a Standard Oil Company exists, at least ten days before such meeting.

At any meeting a majority in value of the holders of trust certificates represented consenting thereto, bylaws may be made, amended, and repealed relative to the mode of election of trustees and other business of the holders of trust certificates, provided, however, that said bylaws shall be in conformity with this agreement. Bylaws may also be made, amended, and repealed at any meeting, by and with the consent of a majority in value of the holders of trust certificates, which alter this agreement relative to the number, powers, and duties of the trustees, and to other matters tending to the more efficient accomplishment of the objects for which the trust is created, provided only that the essential intents and purposes of this agreement be not thereby changed.

8. Whenever a vacancy occurs in the Board of Trustees more than sixty days prior to the annual meeting for the election of trustees, it shall be the duty of the remaining trustees to call a meeting of the owners of Standard Oil Trust certificates for the purpose of electing a trustee or trustees to fill the vacancy or vacancies. If any vacancy occurs in the Board of Trustees, from any cause, within sixty days of the date of the annual meeting for the election of trustees, the vacancy may be filled by a majority of the remaining trustees, or, at their option, may remain vacant until the annual election.

9. If, for any reason, at any time, a trustee or trustees shall be appointed by any court to fill any vacancy or vacancies in said Board of Trustees, the trustee or trustees so appointed shall hold his or the respective office or offices only until a successor or successors shall be elected in the manner above provided for.

10. Whenever any change shall occur in the Board of Trustees, the legal title to the stock and other property held in trust shall pass to and vest in the successors of said trustees without any formal transfer thereof. But if at anytime such formal transfer shall be deemed necessary or advisable, it shall be the duty of the Board of Trustees to obtain the same, and it shall be the duty of any retiring trustee or the administrator or executor of any deceased trustee to make said transfer.

11. The trustees shall prepare certificates which shall show the interest of each beneficiary in said trust and deliver them to the persons properly entitled thereto. They shall be divided into shares of the par value of $100 each, and shall be known as Standard Oil Trust certificates, and shall be issued subject to all the terms and conditions of this agreement. The trustees shall have power to agree upon and direct the form and contents of said certificates, and the mode in which they shall be signed, attested, and transferred. The certificates shall contain an express stipulation that the holders thereof shall be bound by the terms of this agreement and by the bylaws herein provided for.

12. No certificates shall be issued except for stocks and bonds held in trust, as herein provided for, and the par value of certificates issued by said trustees shall be equal to the par value of the stocks of said Standard Oil companies, and the appraised value of other bonds and stocks held in trust. The various bonds, stocks, and monies held under said trust shall be held for all parties in interest jointly, and the trust certificates so issued shall be the evidence of the interest held by the several parties in this trust. No duplicate certificates shall be issued by the trustee, except upon surrender of the original certificate or certificates for cancellation, or upon satisfactory proof of the loss thereof, and in the latter case they shall require a sufficient bond of indemnity.

13. The stocks of the various Standard

Oil companies held in trust by said trustees shall not be sold, assigned, or transferred by said trustees, or by the beneficiaries, or by both combined so long as this trust endures. The stocks and bonds of other corporations, held by said trustees, may be by them exchanged or sold and the proceeds thereof distributed pro rata to the holders of trust certificates, or said proceeds may be held and reinvested by said trustees for the purposes and uses of the trust; provided, however, that said trustees may, from time to time, assign such shares of stock of said Standard Oil companies as may be necessary to qualify any person or persons chosen or to be chosen as directors and officers of any of said Standard Oil companies.

14. It shall be the duty of said trustees to receive and safely to keep all interests and dividends declared and paid upon any of the said bonds, stocks, and monies held by them in trust, and to distribute all monies received from such sources or from sales of trust property or otherwise, by declaring and paying dividends upon the Standard Trust certificates as funds accumulate, which, in their judgment, are not needed for the uses and expenses of said trust. The trustees shall, however, keep separate accounts of receipts from interest and dividends, and of receipts from sales or transfers of trust property, and in making any distribution of trust funds, in which monies derived from sales or transfers shall be included, shall render the holders of trust certificates a statement showing what amount of the fund distributed has been derived from such sales or transfers.

The said trustees may be also authorized and empowered by a vote of a majority in value of holders of trust certificates, whenever stocks or bonds have accumulated in their hands from money purchases thereof, or the stocks or bonds held by them have increased in value, or stock dividends shall have been declared by any of the companies whose stocks are held by said trustees, or

whenever, from any such cause, it is deemed advisable so to do, to increase the amount of trust certificates to the extent of such increase or accumulation of values, and to divide the same among the persons then owning trust certificates pro rata.

15. It shall be the duty of said trustees to exercise general supervision over the affairs of said several Standard Oil companies and, as far as practicable, over the other companies or partnerships, any portion of whose stock is held in said trust. It shall be their duty as stockholders of said companies to elect as directors and officers thereof faithful and competent men. They may elect themselves to such positions when they see fit so to do, and shall endeavor to have the affairs of said companies managed and directed in the manner they may deem most conducive to the best interests of the holders of said trust certificates.

16. All the powers of the trustees may be exercised by a majority of their number. They may appoint from their own number an executive and other committees. A majority of each committee shall exercise all the powers which the trustees may confer upon such committee.

17. The trustees may employ and pay all such agents and attorneys as they deem necessary in the managements of said trust.

18. Each trustee shall be entitled to a salary for his services not exceeding $25,000 per annum, except the president of the board, who may be voted a salary not exceeding $30,000 per annum, which salaries shall be fixed by said Board of Trustees. All salaries and expenses connected with, or growing out of, the trust shall be paid by the trustees from the trust fund.

19. The Board of Trustees shall have its principal office in the city of New York, unless changed by vote of the trustees, at which office or in some place of safe deposit in said city, the bonds and stocks shall be kept. The trustees shall have power to adopt rules and regulations pertaining to

the meetings of the board, the election of officers, and the management of the trust.

20. The trustees shall render at each annual meeting a statement of the affairs of the trust. If a termination of the trust be agreed upon as hereinafter provided, or within a reasonable time prior to its termination by lapse of time, the trustees shall furnish to the holders of the trust certificates a true and perfect inventory and appraisement of all stocks and other property held in trust, and a statement of the financial affairs of the various companies whose stocks are held in trust.

21. This trust shall continue during the lives of the survivors and survivor of the trustees in this agreement named, and for twenty-one years thereafter; provided, however, that, if at any time after the expiration of ten years, two-thirds of all the holders in value, or if after the expiration of one year, 90 percent of all the holders in value of trust certificates shall, at a meeting of holders of trust certificates called for that purpose, vote to terminate this trust at some time to be by them then and there fixed, the said trust shall terminate at the date so fixed. If the holders of trust certificates shall vote to terminate the trust as aforesaid, they may, at the same meeting or at a subsequent meeting for that purpose, decide by a vote of two-thirds in value of their number the mode in which the affairs of the trust shall be wound up, and whether the trust property shall be distributed or whether it shall be sold and the values thereof distributed, or whether part and, if so, what part, shall be divided and what part shall be sold, and whether such sales shall be public or private.

The trustees, who shall continue to hold their offices for that purpose, shall make the distribution in the mode directed, or, if no mode be agreed upon by two-thirds in value as aforesaid, the trustees shall make distribution of the trust property according to law. But said distribution, however made, and whether it be of property, or values, or

of both, shall be just and equitable, and such as to insure to each owner of a trust certificate his due proportion of the trust property or the value thereof.

22. If the trust shall be terminated by expiration of the time for which it is created, the distribution of the trust property shall be directed and made in the mode above provided.

23. This agreement, together with the registry of certificates, books of accounts, and other books and papers connected with the business of said trust, shall be safely kept at the principal office of said trustees.

SUPPLEMENTAL AGREEMENT

Whereas, in and by an agreement dated January 2, 1882, and known as the Standard Trust Agreement, the parties thereto did mutually covenant and agree, *inter alia,* as follows, to wit: That corporations to be known as Standard Oil companies, of various states, should be formed, and that all of the property, real and personal, assets, and business of each and all of the corporations and limited partnerships mentioned or embraced in class 1 of said agreement should be transferred to and vested in the said several Standard Oil companies; that all of the property, assets, and business in or of each particular state should be transferred to and vested in the Standard Oil Company of that particular state, and the directors and managers of each and all of the several corporations and associations mentioned in class 1 were authorized and directed to sell, assign, transfer, and convey and make over to the Standard Oil Company or companies of the proper state or states, as soon as said corporations were organized and ready to receive the same, all the property, real and personal, assets, and business of said corporations or associations; and, *whereas,* it is not deemed expedient that all of the companies and associations mentioned should transfer their property to the said Standard Oil companies at the present time, and in case of some companies and associations it may never be deemed expedient that the said transfer should be made, and said companies and associations go out of existence; and, *whereas*, it is deemed advisable that a discretionary power should be vested in the trustees as to when such transfer or transfers should take place, *if at all.*

Now, it is hereby mutually agreed between the parties to the said trust agreement, and as supplementary thereto, that the trustees named in the said agreement and their successors shall have the power and authority to decide what companies shall convey their said property as in said agreement contemplated, and when the said sales and transfers shall take place, if at all; and until said trustees shall so decide, each of said companies shall remain in existence and retain its property and business, and the trustees shall hold the stocks thereof in trust, as in said agreement provided. In the exercise of said discretion the trustees shall act by a majority of their number, as provided in said trust agreement. All portions of said trust agreement relating to this subject shall be considered so changed as to be in harmony with this supplemental agreement.

110.

"Jesse James"

Jesse James is America's Robin Hood. Like his famous predecessor in folklore (although in fact James was a real person), Jesse James robbed from the rich and was kind to the poor and was always willing to help some cowpoke who was "down on his luck." As legend has it, Jesse retired from his life of crime under the assumed name of Mr. Howard. He was at home with his family one evening when Robert and Charles Ford, members of Jesse's old gang (and, some say, guests in his house), shot him in the back for the sake of the reward. The author of the ballad is unknown.

Source: Allen.

✿ JESSE JAMES

It was on a Wednesday night, the moon was shining bright,
    They robbed the Danville train.
And the people they did say, for many miles away,
    'Twas the outlaws Frank and Jesse James.

Chorus:
Jesse had a wife to mourn for his life,
    The children they were brave.
'Twas a dirty little coward that shot Mister Howard,
    And laid poor Jesse in his grave.

Jesse was a man was a friend to the poor,
  He never left a friend in pain.
And with his brother Frank he robbed the Chicago bank
  And they held up the Glendale train.

It was Robert Ford, the dirty little coward,
  I wonder how he does feel,
For he ate of Jesse's bread and he slept in Jesse's bed,
  Then he laid Jesse James in his grave.

It was his brother Frank that robbed the Gallatin bank,
  And carried the money from the town.
It was in this very place that they had a little race,
  For they shot Captain Sheets to the ground.

They went to the crossing not very far from there,
  And there they did the same;
And the agent on his knees he delivered up the keys
  To the outlaws Frank and Jesse James.

It was on a Saturday night, Jesse was at home
  Talking to his family brave,
When the thief and the coward, little Robert Ford,
  Laid Jesse James in his grave.

How people held their breath when they heard of Jesse's death,
  And wondered how he ever came to die.
'Twas one of the gang, dirty Robert Ford,
  That shot Jesse James on the sly.

Jesse went to rest with his hand on his breast;
  He died with a smile on his face.
He was born one day in the county of Clay,
  And came from a solitary race.

———————◆———————

In Loving Memory of My Beloved Son
Jesse W. James
Died April 3, 1882
Aged 34 Years, 6 Months, 28 Days
Murdered by a Traitor and Coward Whose
Name Is Not Worthy to Appear Here
      Inscription on grave near Kearney, Missouri

"At the 100th Meridian, Oct. 1866"; photo by Carbutt of the unfinished Union Pacific Railroad

GROWTH AND EXPANSION

At the time the Civil War broke out, western settlement had reached Kansas; from there to the Rockies was a land largely unknown, the domain of the Indian. Beyond the Rockies, virtually isolated, lay the rich fields and mines of rapidly developing California. There had been talk of a transcontinental railroad in the 1850s and, after the interruption of the war, work began in earnest and the railroad was completed in 1869. The huge grants of land given the railroads by Congress as encouragement were sold to settlers, many of them former construction workers on the line. Settlement and the railroad were interdependent, and there was often a strong similarity to the colonization companies of the 17th century.

The Homestead Act of 1862 opened up other areas for settlement, and gradually the myth of the Great American Desert that had long held back would-be settlers dissipated before the advances of explorers and railroads.

Even those lands that were still unsuitable for farming were invaded as rich mineral resources were discovered. The Indians remained a problem; but determined and dangerous as they were, they were vastly outnumbered and poorly equipped, and were ultimately no match for the hordes in search of land and riches. With the crossing and holding of the West, the era of American continental expansion came to an abrupt end. The frontier was closed.

Railroad bridge across the Kansas River on the Leavenworth, Lawrence, and Galveston line, 1867

(Above) Laying steel on the Northern Pacific in Miles City, Mont., 1861; photo by Huffman; (below) Green River station on the Union Pacific Railway in Wyoming, 1871

(Right) Construction team working a deep cut west of Weber Canyon; from a stereo by A. J. Russell, 1868-69; (below) wagon train bringing supplies to a Union Pacific construction team

Library of Congress

Though the Union Pacific-Central Pacific line, completed in 1869, was the first and most famous, by 1884 three other lines had reached the west coast: the Northern Pacific from Minnesota to Portland; the Southern Pacific from New Orleans to San Francisco; and the Santa Fe from Kansas to San Diego. The Great Northern opened up the wheat regions of the Dakotas and reached the Pacific in 1893. With these arteries complete, the West was ready for the population and development that rapidly followed; for while the railroads were spectacular achievements, they were only the necessary preconditions for the real job at hand.

Union Pacific Railroad

Union Pacific Railroad Museum Coll.

(Right) Joining the track of the Union Pacific and the Central Pacific railroads to create the first transcontinental line. Ceremonies with the driving of a golden spike at Promontory, Utah, 1869

Bull train crossing the Smoky Hill River near Ellsworth, Kan., 1867

Group with a tame elk at a ranch on Clear Creek in central Kansas, 1867

Steve Young, hanged at Laramie by vigilantes; photo by A. C. Hull, 1868

Fifth Street, Leavenworth, Kan.; photo by Gardner, 1867

Post-war Kansas was typical of the Great Plains states. With less than 100 miles of railroad in 1865, it had 3,000 miles by 1880. With the railroads came the cattle towns, among them the famed Abilene, Wichita, and Dodge City. Longhorn cattle were driven north from Texas for shipment to Omaha and Chicago. Herds often wintered on the Kansas plains, and a great grazing industry grew up alongside the wheat empire. Much of America's best-known and best-loved folk lore came out of the Kansas cowtowns — the cowboys, the badmen, the gunfights — but ordinary life was generally less glamorous. Sod huts or, with luck, log houses were the rule.

(Center) Eldridge House, Lawrence, Kan.; photo by Gardner, 1867; (right) State University at Lawrence, about 1867; photo by Gardner

Captured Sioux at Ft. Snelling, Minnesota, after 1862 massacre

Native Americans were generally treated like any other obstacle to western expansion — removed or destroyed or both. The invasion of Colorado by miners brought constant skirmishing in 1861. The next year the Sioux of the Dakotas reacted against the heavy influx of settlers and began ten years of warfare. The Sioux were skilled warriors but were hampered by disunity and shortages of weapons and game. The practice of making treaties was given up in 1871 after 370 had been made and most broken. An official policy of paternalism ensued, but under the influence of wealth, practice remained the same. The gold rush to the Black Hills in 1875 finally broke the Sioux; two years later gold led the government to drive the peaceful Nez Perce out of their lands in Idaho. Chief Joseph resisted, but it was, of course, useless.

(Above) Little Crow, leader of the 1862 uprising; (below) Pawnee camp on the Platte River, 1866

(Top) Peace Conference at Ft. Laramie in 1868 between the Sioux and the United States; (center left) Gen. George Armstrong Custer, killed with more than 250 men from the Seventh Cavalry in a battle with the Sioux led by Sitting Bull at Little Big Horn, 1876; (center right) Chief Joseph of the Nez Perce tribe in Idaho; (bottom) pictograph by White Bird showing the battle at Little Big Horn. Custer is in the fringed jacket at left center

Two photographs by Timothy O'Sullivan who accompanied the Wheeler expedition; (above) ancient ruins in Canon de Chelle, New Mexico, in a niche 50 feet above present canyon bed; (right) two Indians of the Mohave tribe of southern Colorado and western Arizona

Hayden survey team camped in Cache Valley near Yellowstone Park; Jackson photo dated 1871

Beyond the railroad lines and their immediate surroundings, the West was largely unknown. In 1867 John Muir began the explorations that would lead to the creation of Yosemite National Park. Between 1870 and 1880 Clarence King led a survey of the 40th parallel and worked for the creation of Sequoia National Park. In 1871 George M. Wheeler began eight years of field work for a survey of the lands west of the 100th meridian. John Wesley Powell, who had descended the Colorado River through the Grand Canyon in 1869, continued his work in exploration and ethnology. Ferdinand Hayden explored the Great Plains and the Rockies for thirty years and was largely responsible for the creation of Yellowstone National Park.

View in Yellowstone National Park by W. H. Jackson, 1871, with the Hayden Survey

Scenes in California: (Above) Worked-out placer mines in Tuolumne County near Columbia; Lawrence and Houseworth photo, 1866; (left) hauling redwood logs to Casper River in Mendocino County; photograph by Soule in 1870; (below) Garland's Mill in Placer County

(Above) **Gould and Curry Mill in Virginia City, Nev., 1871; photo by T. O'Sullivan; (right)** view of tunnel in the Gould and Curry Mine

Gold, first in California, then in South Dakota and Idaho; silver in Nevada; copper in Arizona — thousands streamed into the West in search of the riches. The individual entrepeneur of '49 soon vanished, however, as mining followed the pattern of the age by giving birth to industrial empires. Though 15,000 miners were in the Black Hills by the fall of 1875, virtually all operations were taken over by one company, the Homestake.

Wells Fargo office in Virginia City, 1866; photo by Lawrence and Houseworth

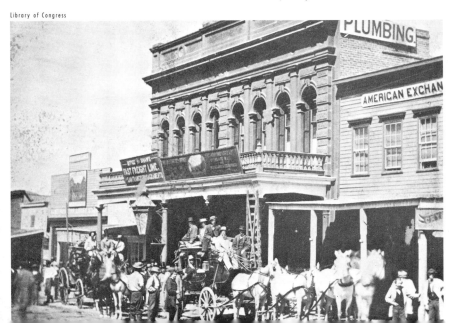

(Above) Deadwood, S.D. in 1876; from a stereograph

(Right) Black Hawk City in the Colorado Territory in 1864; photo by George Wakeley

Two views of Denver: (Left) Flood of 1864; (right) panorama by Jackson from a stereograph, 1875

111.

Samuel L. Clemens ("Mark Twain"): Political Liberty in the South

Mark Twain drew on his early experiences as a riverboat pilot for the material in
Life on the Mississippi, *first published as a series of articles in the* Atlantic
Monthly *in 1875, and in book form in 1883. "Political Liberty in the South,"
presented here, was originally Chapter 48 of* Life on the Mississippi. *Often
call "the suppressed chapter," it was set up in type with the rest of the manuscript
in 1882, then canceled in the proofs, probably because the publishers thought it
would offend many Southern readers.*

Source: The Suppressed Chapter of "Life on the Mississippi," n.p., n.d.

I MISSED ONE THING in the South — African slavery. That horror is gone, and permanently. Therefore, half the South is at last emancipated, half the South is free. But the white half is apparently as far from emancipation as ever.

The South is "solid" for a single political party. It is difficult to account for this; that is, in a region which purports to be free. Human beings are so constituted that, given an intelligent, thinking hundred of them, or thousand, or million, and convince them that they are free from personal danger or social excommunication for opinion's sake, it is absolutely impossible that they shall tie themselves in a body to any one sect, religious or political. Every thinking person in the South and elsewhere knows this: it is a truism.

Given a "solid" country, anywhere, and the ready conclusion is that it is a community of savages. But here are the facts — not conjectures, but facts — and I think they spoil that conclusion. The great mass of Southerners, both in town and country, are neighborly, friendly, hospitable, peaceable, and have an aversion for disagreements and embroilments; they belong to the church, and they frequent it; they are Sabbath observers; they are promise keepers; they are honorable and upright in their dealings; where their prejudices are not at the front, they are just, and they like to see justice done; they are able to reason, and they reason.

These characteristics do not describe a community of savages, they describe the reverse, an excellent community. How such a community should all vote one way is a perplexing problem. That such a people should all be Democrats or all Republicans seems against nature.

It may be that a minor fact or two may help toward a solution. It is imagined in the North that the South is one vast and gory murder field, and that every man goes armed, and has at one time or another taken a neighbor's life. On the contrary, the great mass of Southerners carry no arms and do not quarrel. In the city of New York, where killing seems so frightfully common, the mighty majority, the overwhelming majority of the citizens have never seen a weapon drawn in their lives. This is the case in the South; murders are much commoner there than in the North; but these killings are scattered over a vast domain; in small places, long intervals of time intervene between events of this kind; and in both small and large places it is the chance half dozen who witness the killing — the vast majority of that community are not present, and may live long lives and die without ever having seen an occurrence of the sort.

As I have said, the great mass of Southerners are not personally familiar with murder. And being peaceably disposed, and also accustomed to living in peace, they have a horror of murder and violence.

There is a superstition, current everywhere, that the Southern temper is peculiarly hot; whereas, in truth, the temper of the average Southerner is not hotter than that of the average Northerner. The temper of the Northerner, through training, heredity, and fear of the law, is kept under the better command, that is all. In a wild country where born instincts may venture to the surface, this fact shows up. In California, Nevada, and Montana, the most of the desperadoes, and the deadliest of them, were not from the South but from the North.

Now, in every community, North and South, there is one hothead, or a dozen, or a hundred, according to distribution of population; the rest of the community are quiet folk. What do these hotheads amount to in the North? Nothing. Who fears them? Nobody. Their heads never get so hot but that they retain cold sense enough to remind them that they are among a people who will not allow themselves to be walked over by their sort; a people who, although they will not insanely hang them upon suspicion and without trial, nor try them, convict them, and then let them go, but will give them a fair and honest chance in the courts, and if conviction follow will punish them with imprisonment or the halter.

In the South the case is very different. The one hothead defies the hamlet; the half

dozen or dozen defy the village and the town. In the South the expression is common that such-and-such a ruffian is the "terror of the town." Could he come North and be the terror of a town? Such a thing is impossible. Northern resolution backing Northern law was too much for even the "Molly Maguires," powerful, numerous, and desperate as was that devilish secret organization. But it could have lived a long life in the South; for there it is not the rule for courts to hang murderers.

Why? — seeing that the bulk of the community are murder-hating people. It is hard to tell. Are they torpid, merely? — indifferent? — wanting in public spirit?

Their juries fail to convict, even in the clearest cases. That this is not agreeable to the public is shown by the fact that very frequently such a miscarriage of justice so rouses the people that they rise, in a passion, and break into the jail, drag out their man, and lynch him. This is quite sufficient proof that they do not approve of murder and murderers. But this hundred or two hundred men usually do this act of public justice with masks on. They go to their grim work with clear consciences, but with their faces disguised. They know that the law will not meddle with them — otherwise, at least, than by empty form — and they know that the community will applaud their act. Still, they disguise themselves.

The other day, in Kentucky, a witness testified against a young man in court and got him fined for a violation of a law. The young man went home and got his shotgun and made short work of that witness. He did not invent that method of correcting witnesses; it had been used before in the South. Perhaps this detail accounts for the reluctance of witnesses there to testify; and also the reluctance of juries to convict; and, perhaps, also, for the disposition of lynchers to go to their gruesome labors disguised.

Personal courage is a rare quality. Everywhere in the Christian world, except, possibly, down South, the average citizen is not brave, he is timid. Perhaps he is timid down South, too. According to *The Times-Democrat,* the favorite diversion of New Orleans' hoodlums is crowding upon the late streetcars, hustling the men passengers and insulting the ladies. They smoke, they use gross language, they successfully defy the conductor when he tries to collect their fare. All this happens, and they do not get hurt. Apparently the average Southern citizen is like the average Northern citizen — does not like to embroil himself with a ruffian.

The other day, in Kentucky, a single highwayman, revolver in hand, stopped a stagecoach and robbed the passengers, some of whom were armed — and he got away unharmed. The unaverage Kentuckian, being plucky, is not afraid to attack half a dozen average Kentuckians; and his bold enterprise succeeds — probably because the average Kentuckian is like the average of the human race, not plucky, but timid.

In one thing the average Northerner seems to be a step in advance of the average Southerner, in that he bands himself with his timid fellows to support the law (at least in the matter of murder), protect judges, juries, and witnesses, and also to secure all citizens from personal danger and from obloquy or social ostracism on account of opinion, political or religious; whereas the average Southerners do not band themselves together in these high interests but leave them to look out for themselves unsupported; the results being unpunished murder, against the popular approval, and the decay and destruction of independent thought and action in politics.

I take the following paragraph from a recent article in *The Evening Post,* published at Louisville, Ky. The italics are mine:

There is no use in mincing matters. The condition of the state is worse than we have ever known it. Murders are more frequent, punishment is lighter, pardons more numerous, and abuses more flagrant than at any period within our recollection, running back fifteen years. Matters are getting worse day by day. The most alarming feature of all is the *indifference of the public.* No one seems to see the carnival of crime and social chaos to which we are rapidly drifting. No one seems to realize the actual danger which hangs over the lives of all. *Appeals to the order-loving and law-abiding element appear vain and idle. It is difficult to stir them.* Shocking tragedies at their very doors do not startle them to a realization of the evils that are cursing Kentucky, imperiling the lives of her citizens, barring us against the current of immigration and commerce, and presenting us to the eyes of the world as a reckless, God-defying, reeking band of lawbreakers and murderers.

That editor does not feel indifferent. He feels the opposite of indifferent. Does he think he is alone? He cannot be. I think that without question he is expressing the general feeling of the South. But it is not *organized,* therefore it is ineffective. Once organized it would be abundantly strong for the occasion; the condition of things complained of by the editor would cease. But it is not going to organize itself; somebody has got to take upon himself the disagreeable office of making the first move. In the Knoxville region of Tennessee that office has been assumed, and a movement is now on foot there to organize and band together the best people for the protection of courts, juries, and witnesses. There is no reason why the experiment should not succeed; and if it succeeds, there is no reason why the reform should not spread.

As to white political liberty in New Orleans. I take four pages, at random, from the city directory for the present year — 1882. It "samples" the book, and affords one a sort of bird's-eye view of the nationalities of New Orleans.

(Insert the 4 pages, 772 A B & C — reduce them in facsimile and crowd them into a single page of my book, to be read by a magnifier.)

"Many men, many minds," says the

proverb. What a lovely thing it is to see all these variegated nationalities exhibiting a miracle which makes all other miracles cheap in comparison — that is, voting and feeling all one way, in spite of an eternal law of nature which pronounces such a thing impossible. And how pretty it is to see all these Germans and Frenchmen, who bitterly differ in all things else, meet sweetly together on the platform of a single party in the free and unembarrassed political atmosphere of New Orleans. How odd it is to see the mixed nationalities of New York voting all sorts of tickets, and the very same mixed nationalities of New Orleans voting all one way — and letting on that that is just the thing they wish to do, and are entirely unhampered in the matter, and wouldn't vote otherwise, oh, not for anything. As the German phrases it, "it is not thick enough."

112.

Chinese Exclusion Act

By 1882 approximately 375,000 Chinese had immigrated to the United States. The Burlingame Treaty of 1868 provided for unlimited immigration, but denied the Chinese the right of citizenship. During the early 1870s an economic depression and the massing of cheap "coolie" labor in West Coast cities gave rise to fierce economic competition with American workers, whose demand for higher wages put them at a disadvantage. Fearing civil disorder, Congress in 1879 passed an act restricting Chinese immigration, but President Hayes vetoed it on the grounds that it violated the Burlingame Treaty. In 1880 the Treaty was revised to limit Chinese labor immigration, and on May 6, 1882, Congress passed the Chinese Exclusion Act.

Source: *Statutes*, XXII, pp. 58-61.

An act to execute certain treaty stipulations relating to Chinese

Whereas, in the opinion of the government of the United States the coming of Chinese laborers to this country endangers the good order of certain localities within the territory thereof; therefore,

Be it enacted by the Senate and House of Representatives of the United States of America in Congress assembled, that from and after the expiration of ninety days next after the passage of this act, and until the expiration of ten years next after the passage of this act, the coming of Chinese laborers to the United States be, and the same is hereby, suspended; and during such suspension it shall not be lawful for any Chinese laborer to come, or, having so come after the expiration of said ninety days, to remain within the United States.

Section 2. That the master of any vessel who shall knowingly bring within the United States on such vessel, and land or permit to be landed, any Chinese laborer from any foreign port or place shall be deemed guilty of a misdemeanor, and on conviction thereof shall be punished by a fine of not more than $500 for each and every such Chinese laborer so brought, and may be also imprisoned for a term not exceeding one year.

Section 3. That the two foregoing sections shall not apply to Chinese laborers who were in the United States on the 17th day of November, 1880, or who shall have come into the same before the expiration of ninety days next after the passage of this act, and who shall produce to such master before going on board such vessel, and shall produce to the collector of the port in the United States at which such vessel shall arrive, the evidence hereinafter in this act required of his being one of the laborers in this section mentioned; nor shall the two foregoing sections apply to the case of any master whose vessel, being bound to a port not within the United States, shall come within the jurisdiction of the United States by reason of being in distress or in stress of weather, or touching at any port of the United States on its voyage to any foreign port or place: *Provided,* that all Chinese laborers brought on such vessel shall depart with the vessel on leaving port. . . .

Section 6. That in order to the faithful execution of Articles I and II of the treaty [of 1880]. . . every Chinese person other than a laborer who may be entitled by said treaty and this act to come within the United States, and who shall be about to come to the United States, shall be identified as so entitled by the Chinese government in each case, such identity to be evidenced by a certificate issued under the authority of said government, which certificate shall be in the English language or (if not in the English language) accompanied by a translation into English, stating such right to come, and which certificate shall state the name, title, or official rank, if any, the age, height, and all physical peculiarities, former and present occupation or profession, and place of residence in China of the person to whom the certificate is issued and that such person is entitled conformably to the treaty . . . to come within the United States. Such certificate shall be prima facie evidence of the fact set forth therein, and shall be produced to the collector of cus-

toms, or his deputy, of the port in the district in the United States at which the person named therein shall arrive. . . .

Section 8. That the master of any vessel arriving in the United States from any foreign port or place shall . . . deliver and report to the collector of customs of the district in which such vessels shall have arrived a separate list of all Chinese passengers taken on board his vessel at any foreign port. . . . Any willful refusal or neglect of any such master to comply with the provisions of this section shall incur the same penalties and forfeiture as are provided for a refusal or neglect to report and deliver a manifest of the cargo. . . .

Section 11. That any person who shall knowingly bring into or cause to be brought into the United States by land, or who shall knowingly aid or abet the same, or aid or abet the landing in the United States from any vessel of any Chinese person not lawfully entitled to enter the United States, shall be deemed guilty of a misdemeanor, and shall, on conviction thereof, be fined in a sum not exceeding $1,000, and imprisoned for a term not exceeding one year.

Section 12. That no Chinese person shall be permitted to enter the United States by land without producing to the proper officer of customs the certificate in this act required of Chinese persons seeking to land from a vessel. And any Chinese person found unlawfully within the United States shall be caused to be removed therefrom to the country from whence he came, by direction of the President of the United States, and at the cost of the United States, after being brought before some justice, judge, or commissioner of a court of the United States and found to be one not lawfully entitled to be or remain in the United States.

Section 13. That this act shall not apply to diplomatic and other officers of the Chinese government traveling upon the business of that government, whose credentials shall be taken as equivalent to the certificate in this act mentioned, and shall exempt them and their body and household servants from the provisions of this act as to other Chinese persons.

Section 14. That hereafter no state court or court of the United States shall admit Chinese to citizenship; and all laws in conflict with this act are hereby repealed.

Section 15. That the words "Chinese laborers" wherever used in this act shall be construed to mean both skilled and unskilled laborers and Chinese employed in mining.

113.

"Charles Guiteau"

The nomination of James A. Garfield in 1880 caused a split in the Republican Party. Supporters of ex-President Grant hoped for a third term for the now retired general. The Grant promoters eventually gave reluctant support to the ticket. When Garfield had been in office only four months he was shot (July 2) by Charles J. Guiteau, a disappointed office seeker, who claimed to be a member of the Grant wing of the party. Garfield died September 19, 1881. The following song shows Guiteau lamenting his trial and coming execution. Guiteau, who unsuccessfully pleaded insanity at his trial, was executed on June 30, 1882.

☙ CHARLES GUITEAU

Come all you Christian people, wherever you may be,
And please pay close attention to these few lines from me.
On the thirtieth day of June, I am condemned to die
For the murder of James A. Garfield, upon the scaffold high.

Chorus:
My name is Charles Guiteau, my name I'll never deny,
To leave my aged parents in sorrow for to die,
But little did I think, while in my youthful bloom,
I'd be carried to the scaffold to meet my fatal doom.

I tried to play off insane, but found it would not do,
The people all against me, it proved to make no show.
Judge Cox he passed the sentence, and the clerk he wrote it down,
On the thirtieth day of June to die I was condemned.

And now I'm at the scaffold to bid you all adieu,
The hangman now is waiting, it's a quarter after two;
The black cap is on my face, no longer can I see,
But when I'm dead and buried, dear Lord, remember me.

114.

WILLIAM GRAHAM SUMNER: Inequality, Liberty, and Progress

From the time he accepted a professorship at Yale in 1872, William Graham Sumner did not cease to write and speak about social, political, and economic issues facing the United States. Because he regarded most reform programs as ill-conceived and poorly executed, he is usually classed as an apologist for the status quo. Sumner was a leading exponent of "Social Darwinism" and a purveyor of the thought of Herbert Spencer, whose ideas shaped the attitudes of many Americans on social and economic questions.
Sumner's opposition to socialism led him to write the following essay attacking it. The article was written sometime in the 1880s and originally titled simply "Socialism." It was not published, however, until 1914, at which time the editor of Sumner's work, Albert G. Keller, changed the title to "The Challenge of Facts." An abridgment of the essay is reprinted below.

Source: *The Challenge of Facts and Other Essays*, Albert G. Keller, ed., New Haven, 1914.

SOCIALISM IS NO NEW THING. In one form or another it is to be found throughout all history. It arises from an observation of certain harsh facts in the lot of man on earth, the concrete expression of which is poverty and misery. These facts challenge us. It is folly to try to shut our eyes to them. We have first to notice what they are, and then to face them squarely.

Man is born under the necessity of sustaining the existence he has received by an onerous struggle against nature, both to win what is essential to his life and to ward off what is prejudicial to it. He is born under a burden and a necessity. Nature holds what is essential to him, but she offers nothing gratuitously. He may win for his use what she holds, if he can. Only the most meager and inadequate supply for human needs can be obtained directly from nature. There are trees which may be used for fuel and for dwellings, but labor is required to fit them for this use. There are ores in the ground, but labor is necessary to get out the metals and make tools or weapons. For any real satisfaction, labor is necessary to fit the products of nature for human use. In this struggle every individual is under the pressure of the necessities for food, clothing, shelter, fuel, and every individual brings with him more or less energy for the conflict necessary to supply his needs. The relation, therefore, between each man's needs and each man's energy, or "individualism," is the first fact of human life.

It is not without reason, however, that we speak of a "man" as the individual in question, for women (mothers) and children have special disabilities for the struggle with nature, and these disabilities grow greater and last longer as civilization advances. The perpetuation of the race in health and vigor, and its success as a whole in its struggle to expand and develop human life on earth, therefore, require that the head of the family shall, by his energy, be able to supply not only his own needs but those of the organisms which are dependent upon him. . . .

The next great fact we have to notice in regard to the struggle of human life is that labor which is spent in a direct struggle with nature is severe in the extreme and is but slightly productive. To subjugate nature, man needs weapons and tools. These, however, cannot be won unless the food and clothing and other prime and direct necessities are supplied in such amount that they can be consumed while tools and weapons are being made, for the tools and weapons themselves satisfy no needs directly. A man who tills the ground with his fingers or with a pointed stick picked up without labor will get a small crop. To fashion even the rudest spade or hoe will cost time, during which the laborer must still eat and drink and wear, but the tool, when obtained, will multiply immensely the power to produce.

Such products of labor, used to assist production, have a function so peculiar in the nature of things that we need to distinguish them. We call them capital. A lever is capital, and the advantage of lifting a weight with a lever over lifting it by direct exertion is only a feeble illustration of the power of capital in production. The origin of capital lies in the darkness before history, and it is probably impossible for us to imagine the slow and painful steps by which the race began the formation of it. Since then it has gone on rising to higher and higher powers by a ceaseless involution, if I may use a mathematical expression. Capital is labor raised to a higher power by being constantly multiplied into itself. Nature has been more and more subjugated by the human race through the power of capital, and every human being now living shares the improved status of the race to a degree which neither he nor anyone else can measure and for which he pays nothing.

Let us understand this point, because our subject will require future reference to it. It is the most shortsighted ignorance not to see that, in a civilized community, all the advantage of capital except a small fraction is gratuitously enjoyed by the community. For instance, suppose the case of a man utterly destitute of tools who is trying to till the ground with a pointed stick. He could get something out of it. If now he should obtain a spade with which to till the ground, let us suppose, for illustration, that he could get twenty times as great a product. Could, then, the owner of a spade in a civilized state demand, as its price, from the man who had no spade nineteen-twentieths of the product which could be produced by the use of it? Certainly not. The price of a spade is fixed by the supply and demand of products in the community. A spade is bought for a dollar and the gain from the use of it is an inheritance of knowledge, experience, and skill which every man who lives in a civilized state gets for nothing.

What we pay for steam transportation is no trifle, but imagine, if you can, eastern Massachusetts cut off from steam connection with the rest of the world, turnpikes and sailing vessels remaining. The cost of food would rise so high that a quarter of the population would starve to death and another quarter would have to emigrate. Today every man here gets an enormous advantage from the status of a society on a level of steam transportation, telegraph, and machinery for which he pays nothing.

So far as I have yet spoken, we have before us the struggle of man with nature, but the social problems, strictly speaking, arise at the next step. Each man carries on the struggle to win his support for himself, but there are others by his side engaged in the same struggle. If the stores of nature were unlimited, or if the last unit of the supply she offers could be won as easily as the first, there would be no social problem. If a square mile of land could support an indefinite number of human beings, or if it cost only twice as much labor to get forty bushels of wheat from an acre as to get twenty, we should have no social problem. If a square mile of land could support millions, no one would ever emigrate and there would be no trade or commerce. If it cost only twice as much labor to get forty bushels as twenty, there would be no advance in the arts.

The fact is far otherwise. So long as the population is low in proportion to the amount of land, on a given stage of the arts, life is easy and the competition of man with man is weak. When more persons are trying to live on a square mile than it can support, on the existing stage of the arts, life is hard and the competition of man with man is intense. In the former case, industry and prudence may be on a low grade; the penalties are not severe, or certain, or speedy. In the latter case, each individual needs to exert on his own behalf every force, original or acquired, which he can command. In the former case, the average condition will be one of comfort and the population will be all nearly on the average. In the latter case, the average condition will not be one of comfort, but the population will cover wide extremes of comfort and misery. Each will find his place according to his ability and his effort. The former society will be democratic; the latter will be aristocratic.

The constant tendency of population to outstrip the means of subsistence is the force which has distributed population over the world and produced all advance in civilization. To this day the two means of escape for an overpopulated country are emigration and an advance in the arts. The former wins more land for the same people; the latter makes the same land support more persons. If, however, either of these means opens a chance for an increase of population, it is evident that the advantage so won may be speedily exhausted if the increase takes place. The social difficulty has only undergone a temporary amelioration, and when the conditions of pressure and competition are renewed, misery and poverty reappear. The victims of them are those who have inherited disease and depraved appetites, or have been brought up in vice and ignorance, or have themselves yielded to vice, extravagance, idleness, and imprudence. In the last analysis, therefore, we come back to vice in its original and hereditary forms as the correlative of misery and poverty.

The condition for the complete and regular action of the force of competition is liberty. Liberty means the security given to each man that, if he employs his energies to sustain the struggle on behalf of himself and those he cares for, he shall dispose of the product exclusively as he chooses. It is impossible to know whence any definition or criterion of justice can be derived if it is not deduced from this view of things, or if it is not the definition of justice that each shall enjoy the fruit of his own labor and self-denial, and of injustice that the idle and the industrious, the self-indulgent and the self-denying shall share equally in the product. Aside from the a priori speculations of philosophers who have tried to make equality an essential element in justice, the human race has recognized, from the earliest times, the above conception of justice as the true one and has founded upon it the right of property. The right of property, with marriage and the family, gives the right of bequest.

Monogamic marriage, however, is the most exclusive of social institutions. It contains, as essential principles, preference, superiority, selection, devotion. It would not be at all what it is if it were not for these characteristic traits, and it always degenerates when these traits are not present. For instance, if a man should not have a distinct preference for the woman he married, and if he did not select her as superior to others, the marriage would be an imperfect one according to the standard of true monogamic marriage. The family under monogamy, also, is a closed group, having special interests and estimating privacy and reserve as valuable advantages for family development. We grant high prerogatives, in our society, to parents, although our observation teaches us that thousands of human beings are unfit to be parents or to be entrusted with the care of children. It follows, therefore, from the organization of marriage and the family under monogamy that great inequalities must exist in a society based on those institutions. The son of wise parents cannot start on a level with the son of foolish ones, and the man who has had no home discipline cannot be equal to the man who has had home discipline. If the contrary were true, we could rid ourselves at once of the wearing labor of inculcating sound morals and manners in our children.

Private property, also, which we have seen to be a feature of society organized in accordance with the natural conditions of the struggle for existence, produces inequalities between men. The struggle for existence is aimed against nature. It is from her niggardly hand that we have to wrest the satisfactions for our needs, but our fellow-men are our competitors for the meager supply. Competition, therefore, is a law of nature. Nature is entirely neutral; she submits to him who most energetically and resolutely assails her. She grants her rewards to the fittest, therefore, without regard to other considerations of any kind. If, then, there be liberty, men get from her just in proportion to their works, and their having and enjoying are just in proportion to their being and their doing.

Such is the system of nature. If we do not like it and if we try to amend it, there is only one way in which we can do it. We can take from the better and give to the worse. We can deflect the penalties of those who have done ill and throw them on those who have done better. We can take the rewards from those who have done better and give them to those who have done worse. We shall thus lessen the inequalities. We shall favor the survival of the unfittest, and we shall accomplish this by destroying liberty. Let it be understood that we cannot go outside of this alternative: liberty, inequality, survival of the fittest; not-liberty, equality, survival of the unfittest. The former carries society forward and favors all its best members; the latter carries society downward and favors all its worst members.

For 300 years now men have been trying to understand and realize liberty. Liberty is not the right or chance to do what we choose; there is no such liberty as that on earth. No man can do as he chooses; the autocrat of Russia or the king of Dahomey has limits to his arbitrary will; the savage in the wilderness, whom some people think free, is the slave of routine, tradition, and superstitious fears; the civilized man must earn his living, or take care of his property, or concede his own will to the rights and claims of his parents, his wife, his children, and all the persons with whom he is connected by the ties and contracts of civilized life.

What we mean by liberty is civil liberty, or liberty under law; and this means the guarantees of law that a man shall not be interfered with while using his own powers for his own welfare. It is, therefore, a civil and political status; and that nation has the freest institutions in which the guarantees of peace for the laborer and security for the capitalist are the highest. Liberty, therefore, does not by any means do away with the struggle for existence. We might as well try to do away with the need of eating, for that would, in effect, be the same thing. What civil liberty does is to turn the competition of man with man from violence and brute force into an industrial competition under which men vie with one another for the acquisition of material goods by industry, energy, skill, frugality, prudence, temperance, and other industrial virtues. Under this changed order of things the inequalities are not done away with.

Nature still grants her rewards of having and enjoying according to our being and doing, but it is now the man of the highest training and not the man of the heaviest fist who gains the highest reward. It is impossible that the man with capital and the man without capital should be equal. To affirm that they are equal would be to say that a man who has no tool can get as much food out of the ground as the man who has a spade or a plow; or that the man who has no weapon can defend himself as well against hostile beasts or hostile men as the man who has a weapon. If that were so, none of us would work any more. We work and deny ourselves to get capital just because, other things being equal, the man who has it is superior for attaining all the ends of life to the man who has it not.

Considering the eagerness with which we all seek capital and the estimate we put upon it, either in cherishing it if we have it or envying others who have it while we have it not, it is very strange what platitudes pass current about it in our society so soon as we begin to generalize about it. If our young people really believed some of the teachings they hear, it would not be amiss to preach them a sermon once in a while to reassure them, setting forth that it is not wicked to be rich, nay, even that it is not wicked to be richer than your neighbor.

It follows from what we have observed that it is the utmost folly to denounce capital. To do so is to undermine civilization, for capital is the first requisite of every social gain, educational, ecclesiastical, political, aesthetic, or other.

It must also be noticed that the popular antithesis between persons and capital is very fallacious. Every law or institution which protects persons at the expense of capital makes it easier for persons to live and to increase the number of consumers of capital while lowering all the motives to prudence and frugality by which capital is created. Hence every such law or institution tends to produce a large population sunk in misery. All poor laws and all eleemosynary institutions and expenditures have this ten-

dency. On the contrary, all laws and institutions which give security to capital against the interests of other persons than its owners restrict numbers while preserving the means of subsistence. Hence every such law or institution tends to produce a small society on a high stage of comfort and well-being. It follows that the antithesis commonly thought to exist between the protection of persons and the protection of property is in reality only an antithesis between numbers and quality. . . .

We are told that economic causes do not correct themselves. That is true. We are told that when an economic situation becomes very grave it goes on from worse to worse and that there is no cycle through which it returns. That is not true, without further limitation. We are told that moral forces alone can elevate . . . people again. But it is plain that a people which has sunk below the reach of the economic forces of self-interest has certainly sunk below the reach of moral forces, and that this objection is superficial and shortsighted. What is true is that economic forces always go before moral forces. Men feel self-interest long before they feel prudence, self-control, and temperance. They lose the moral forces long before they lose the economic forces. If they can be regenerated at all, it must be first by distress appealing to self-interest and forcing recourse to some expedient for relief. . . .

It is by strenuous exertion only that each one of us can sustain himself against the destructive forces and the ever recurring needs of life; and the higher the degree to which we seek to carry our development, the greater is the proportionate cost of every step. For help in the struggle we can only look back to those in the previous generation who are responsible for our existence. In the competition of life, the son of wise and prudent ancestors has immense advantages over the son of vicious and imprudent ones. The man who has capital possesses immeasurable advantages for the struggle of life over him who has none. The more we break down privileges of class, or industry, and establish liberty, the greater will be the inequalities and the more exclusively will the vicious bear the penalties. Poverty and misery will exist in society just so long as vice exists in human nature.

I now go on to notice some modes of trying to deal with this problem. There is a modern philosophy which has never been taught systematically, but which has won the faith of vast masses of people in the modern civilized world. For want of a better name it may be called the sentimental philosophy. It has colored all modern ideas and institutions in politics, religion, education, charity, and industry, and is widely taught in popular literature, novels, and poetry, and in the pulpit. The first proposition of this sentimental philosophy is that nothing is true which is disagreeable. If, therefore, any facts of observation show that life is grim or hard, the sentimental philosophy steps over such facts with a genial platitude, a consoling commonplace, or a gratifying dogma. The effect is to spread an easy optimism, under the influence of which people spare themselves labor and trouble, reflection and forethought, pains and caution — all of which are hard things, and to admit the necessity for which would be to admit that the world is not all made smooth and easy for us to pass through it surrounded by love, music, and flowers.

Under this philosophy, "progress" has been represented as a steadily increasing and unmixed good; as if the good steadily encroached on the evil without involving any new and other forms of evil, and as if we could plan great steps in progress in our academies and lyceums and then realize them by resolution. To minds trained to this way of looking at things, any evil which exists is a reproach. We have only to consider it, hold some discussions about it, pass resolutions, and have done with it. Every moment of delay is, therefore, a social crime. It is monstrous to say that misery and poverty are as constant as vice and evil passions of men! People suffer so under misery and poverty! Assuming, therefore, that we can solve all these problems and eradicate all these evils by expending our ingenuity upon them, of course we cannot hasten too soon to do it.

A social philosophy consonant with this has also been taught for a century. It could not fail to be popular for it teaches that ignorance is as good as knowledge, vulgarity as good as refinement, shiftlessness as good as painstaking, shirking as good as faithful striving, poverty as good as wealth, filth as good as cleanliness — in short, that quality goes for nothing in the measurement of men, but only numbers. Culture, knowledge, refinement, skill, and taste cost labor, but we have been taught that they have only individual, not social, value, and that socially they are rather drawbacks than otherwise. In public life we are taught to admire roughness, illiteracy, and rowdyism. The ignorant, idle, and shiftless have been taught that they are "the people," that the generalities inculcated at the same time about the dignity, wisdom, and virtue of "the people" are true of them, that they have nothing to learn to be wise, but that, as they stand, they possess a kind of infallibility, and that to their "opinion" the wise must bow. It is not cause for wonder if whole sections of these classes have begun to use the powers and wisdom attributed to them for their interests, as they construe them, and to trample on all the excellence which marks civilization as an obsolete superstition.

Another development of the same philosophy is the doctrine that men come into the world endowed with "natural rights," or as joint inheritors of the "rights of man," which have been "declared" times without number during the last century. The divine rights of man have succeeded to the obsolete divine right of kings. If it is true, then, that a man is born with rights, he comes into the world with claims on somebody besides his parents. Against whom does he hold such rights? There can be no rights against nature or against God. A man may curse his fate because he is born of an inferior race, or with a hereditary disease, or blind, or, as some members of the race seem to do, because they are born females; but they get no answer to their imprecations.

But, now, if men have rights by birth, these rights must hold against their fellow-men and must mean that somebody else is to spend his energy to sustain the existence of the persons so born. What then becomes of the natural rights of the one whose energies are to be diverted from his own interests? If it be said that we should all help each other, that means simply that the race as a whole should advance and expand as much and as fast as it can in its career on earth; and the experience on which we are now acting has shown that we shall do this best under liberty and under the organization which we are now developing, by leaving each to exert his energies for his own success.

The notion of natural rights is destitute of sense, but it is captivating, and it is the more available on account of its vagueness. It lends itself to the most vicious kind of social dogmatism, for if a man has natural rights, then the reasoning is clear up to the finished socialistic doctrine that a man has a natural right to whatever he needs and that the measure of his claims is the wishes which he wants fulfilled. If, then, he has a need, who is bound to satisfy it for him? Who holds the obligation corresponding to his right? It must be the one who possesses what will satisfy that need, or else the state which can take the possession from those who have earned and saved it, and give it to him who needs it and who, by the hypothesis, has not earned and saved it.

It is with the next step, however, that we come to the complete and ruinous absurdity of this view. If a man may demand from those who have a share of what he needs and has not, may he demand the same also for his wife and for his children, and for how many children? The industrious and prudent man who takes the course of labor and self-denial to secure capital finds that he must defer marriage, both in order to save and to devote his life to the education of fewer children. The man who can claim a share in another's product has no such restraint. The consequence would be that the industrious and prudent would labor and save, without families, to support the idle and improvident who would increase and multiply, until universal destitution forced a return to the principles of liberty and property; and the man who started with the notion that the world owed him a living would once more find, as he does now, that the world pays him its debt in the state prison.

The most specious application of the dogma of rights is to labor. It is said that every man has a right to work. The world is full of work to be done. Those who are willing to work find that they have three days' work to do in every day that comes. Work is the necessity to which we are born. It is not a right but an irksome necessity, and men escape it whenever they can get the fruits of labor without it. What they want is the fruits, or wages, not work. But wages are capital which someone has earned and saved. If he and the workman can agree on the terms on which he will part with his capital, there is no more to be said. If not, then the right must be set up in a new form. It is now not a right to work, nor even a right to wages, but a right to a certain rate of wages, and we have simply returned to the old doctrine of spoliation again. It is immaterial whether the demand for wages be addressed to an individual capitalist or to a civil body, for the latter can give no wages which it does not collect by taxes out of the capital of those who have labored and saved.

Another application is in the attempt to fix the hours of labor *per diem* by law. If a man is forbidden to labor over eight hours per day (and the law has no sense or utility for the purposes of those who want it until it takes this form), he is forbidden to exercise so much industry as he may be willing to expend in order to accumulate capital for the improvement of his circumstances. . . .

The truth is that the social order is fixed by laws of nature precisely analogous to those of the physical order. The most that man can do is by ignorance and self-conceit to mar the operation of social laws. The evils of society are to a great extent the result of the dogmatism and self-interest of statesmen, philosophers, and ecclesiastics who in past time have done just what the socialists now want to do. Instead of studying the natural laws of the social order, they assumed that they could organize society as they chose; they made up their minds what kind of a society they wanted to make; and they planned their little measures for the ends they had resolved upon. It will take centuries of scientific study of the facts of nature to eliminate from human society the mischievous institutions and traditions which the said statesmen, philosophers, and ecclesiastics have introduced into it.

Let us not, however, even then delude ourselves with any impossible hopes. The hardships of life would not be eliminated if the laws of nature acted directly and without interference. The task of right living forever changes its form, but let us not imagine that that task will ever reach a final solution or that any race of men on this earth can ever be emancipated from the necessity of industry, prudence, continence, and temperance if they are to pass their lives prosperously. If you believe the contrary, you must suppose that some men can come to exist who shall know nothing of old age, disease, and death.

The socialist enterprise of reorganizing society in order to change what is harsh and sad in it at present is therefore as impossible, from the outset, as a plan for changing the physical order. . . . Socialists are filled with the enthusiasm of equality. Every scheme of theirs for securing equality has destroyed liberty.

The student of political philosophy has the antagonism of equality and liberty constantly forced upon him. Equality of possession or of rights and equality before the law are diametrically opposed to each other. The object of equality before the law is to make the state entirely neutral. The state, under that theory, takes no cognizance of persons. It surrounds all, without distinctions, with the same conditions and guarantees. If it educates one, it educates all — black, white, red, or yellow; Jew or gentile; native or alien. If it taxes one, it taxes all, by the same system and under the same conditions. If it exempts one from police regulations in home, church, and occupation, it exempts all.

From this statement it is at once evident that pure equality before the law is impossible. Some occupations must be subjected to police regulation. Not all can be made subject to militia duty even for the same limited period. The exceptions and special cases furnish the chance for abuse. Equality before the law, however, is one of the cardinal principles of civil liberty, because it leaves each man to run the race of life for himself as best he can. The state stands neutral but benevolent. It does not undertake to aid some and handicap others at the outset in order to offset hereditary advantages and disadvantages or to make them start equally. Such a notion would belong to the false and spurious theory of equality, which is socialistic. If the state should attempt this it would make itself the servant of envy. I am entitled to make the most I can of myself without hindrance from anybody, but I am not entitled to any guarantee that I shall make as much of myself as somebody else makes of himself.

The modern thirst for equality of rights is explained by its historical origin. The medieval notion of rights was that rights were special privileges, exemptions, franchises, and powers given to individuals by the king; hence each man had just so many as he and his ancestors had been able to buy or beg by force or favor, and if a man had obtained no grants, he had no rights. Hence no two persons were equal in rights, and the mass of the population had none. The theory of natural rights and of equal rights was a revolt against the medieval theory. It was asserted that men did not have to wait for a king to grant them rights; they have them by nature, or in the nature of things, because they are men and members of civil society. If rights come from nature, it is inferred that they fall like air and light on all equally. It was an immense step in advance for the human race when this new doctrine was promulgated. Its own limitations and errors need not now be pointed out. Its significance is plain, and its limits are to some extent defined when we note its historical origin.

I have already shown that where these guarantees exist and where there is liberty the results cannot be equal, but with all liberty there must go responsibility. If I take my own way I must take my own consequences; if it proves that I have made a mistake, I cannot be allowed to throw the consequences on my neighbor. If my neighbor is a free man and resents interference from me, he must not call on me to bear the consequences of his mistakes. Hence it is plain that liberty, equality before the law, responsibility, individualism, monogamy, and private property all hold together as consistent parts of the same structure of society, and that an assault on one part must sooner or later involve an assault on all the others.

To all this must be added the political element in socialism. The acquisition of some capital — the amount is of very subordinate importance — is the first and simplest proof that an individual possesses the industrial and civil virtues which make a good citizen and a useful member of society. Political power, a century ago, was associated, more or less, even in the United States, with the possession of land. It has been gradually extended until the suffrage is to all intents and purposes universal in North and South America, in Australia, and in all Europe, except Russia and Turkey. On this system, political control belongs to the numerical majority, limited only by institutions. It may be doubted, if the terms are taken strictly and correctly, whether the noncapitalists outnumber the capitalists in any civilized country, but in many cities where capital is most collected they certainly do.

The powers of government have been abused for ages by the classes who possessed them to enable kings, courtiers, nobles, politicians, demagogues, and their friends to live in exemption from labor and self-denial, that is, from the universal lot of man. It is only a continuation of the same abuse if the new possessors of power attempt to employ it to secure for themselves the selfish advantages which all possessors of power have taken. Such a course would, however, overthrow all that we think has been won in the way of making government an organ of justice, peace, order, and security, without respect of persons; and if those gains are not to be lost, they will have to be defended, before this century closes, against popular majorities, especially in cities, just as they had to be won in a struggle with kings and nobles in the centuries past.

The newest socialism is, in its method, political. The essential feature of its latest phases is the attempt to use the power of the state to realize its plans and to secure its objects. These objects are to do away with poverty and misery, and there are no socialistic schemes yet proposed, of any sort, which do not, upon analysis, turn out to be projects for curing poverty and misery by making those who have share with those who have not. Whether they are paper-money schemes, tariff schemes, subsidy schemes, internal-improvement schemes, or usury laws, they all have this in common with the most vulgar of the communistic projects; and the errors of this sort in the past which have been committed in the interest of the capitalist class now furnish precedents, illustration, and encouragement for the new category of demands. . . .

It is a matter of course that a reactionary party should arise to declare that universal suffrage, popular education, machinery, free trade, and all the other innovations of the last hundred years are all a mistake. If anyone ever believed that these innovations were so many clear strides toward the millennium, that they involve no evils or abuses of their own, that they tend to emancipate mankind from the need for prudence, caution, forethought, vigilance — in short, from the eternal struggle against evil — it is not strange that he should be disappointed. If anyone ever believed that some "form of government" could be found which would run itself and turn out the pure results of abstract peace, justice, and righteousness without any trouble to anybody, he may well be dissatisfied. To talk of turning back, however, is only to enhance still further the confusion and danger of our position. The world cannot go back. Its destiny is to go forward and to meet the new problems which are continually arising.

Under our so-called progress, evil only alters its forms, and we must esteem it a grand advance if we can believe that, on the whole and over a wide view of human affairs, good has gained a hairsbreadth over evil in a century. Popular institutions have their own abuses and dangers just as much as monarchical or aristocratic institutions. We are only just finding out what they are. All the institutions which we have inherited were invented to guard liberty against the encroachments of a powerful monarch or aristocracy, when these classes possessed land and the possession of land was the greatest social power. Institutions must now be devised to guard civil liberty against popular majorities, and this necessity arises first in regard to the protection of property, the first and greatest function of government and element in civil liberty.

There is no escape from any dangers involved in this or any other social struggle save in going forward and working out the development. It will cost a struggle and will demand the highest wisdom of this and the next generation. It is very probable that some nations — those, namely, which come up to this problem with the least preparation, with the least intelligent comprehension of the problem, and under the most inefficient leadership — will suffer a severe check in their development and prosperity; it is very probable that in some nations the development may lead through revolution and bloodshed; it is very probable that in some nations the consequence may be a reaction toward arbitrary power.

In every view we take of it, it is clear that the general abolition of slavery has only cleared the way for a new social problem of far wider scope and far greater difficulty. It seems to me, in fact, that this must always be the case. The conquest of one difficulty will only open the way to another; the solution of one problem will only bring man face to face with another. Man wins by the fight, not by the victory, and therefore the possibilities of growth are unlimited, for the fight has no end. . . .

The sound student of sociology can hold

out to mankind, as individuals or as a race, only one hope of better and happier living. That hope lies in an enhancement of the industrial virtues and of the moral forces which thence arise. Industry, self-denial, and temperance are the laws of prosperity for men and states; without them, advance in the arts and in wealth means only corruption and decay through luxury and vice. With them, progress in the arts and increasing wealth are the prime conditions of an advancing civilization which is sound enough to endure. The power of the human race today over the conditions of prosperous and happy living are sufficient to banish poverty and misery, if it were not for folly and vice. The earth does not begin to be populated up to its power to support population on the present stage of the arts; if the United States were as densely populated as the British Islands, we should have 1 billion people here.

If, therefore, men were willing to set to work with energy and courage to subdue the outlying parts of the earth, all might live in plenty and prosperity. But if they insist on remaining in the slums of great cities or on the borders of an old society, and on a comparatively exhausted soil, there is no device of economist or statesman which can prevent them from falling victims to poverty and misery or from succumbing in the competition of life to those who have greater command of capital. The socialist or philanthropist who nourishes them in their situation and saves them from the distress of it is only cultivating the distress which he pretends to cure.

115.

CARROLL D. WRIGHT: The Factory System

The economic advantages of mass production were offset in the late nineteenth century by the relatively low status to which the individual worker was relegated in society. Living and working conditions to which workers were subject did not compare favorably with the benefits that factory owners and society itself received from technological innovations in production. Whether or not the worker was better off under the factory system is analyzed in the following paper of September 8, 1882, by Carroll D. Wright, who became the first U.S. Labor Commissioner in 1885. Wright's highly optimistic view of the factory system as a civilizing force came to have more validity in the twentieth century than it did in the last two decades of the nineteenth century.

Source: *Journal of Social Science*, No. 16, December 1882: "The Factory System as an Element in Civilization."

THE INFLUENCES WHICH LED to the institution of the factory system are as diverse in their nature, almost, as the ramifications of the system itself. These influences, however, are not shrouded in any mystery but are clearly defined; and their power, not only abstractly but concretely, is fully recognizable in the origin of the system.

The factory system is of recent origin and is entirely the creation of influences existing or coming into existence during the last half of the eighteenth century. These influences were both direct and subtle in their character but all-important in their place and in their combination. As a great fact, the system originated in no preconceived plan, nor did it spring from any spasmodic exercise of human wisdom; on the contrary, "it was formed and shaped by the irresistible force of circumstances, fortunately aided and guided by men who were able to profit by circumstances." To borrow the expression of Cooke Taylor,

> Those who were called the fathers of the system were not such demons as they have sometimes been described, nor yet were they perfect angels; they were simply men of great intelligence, industry, and enterprise; they have bequeathed the system to this age with the imperfections incident to every human institution, and the task of harmonizing their innovation with existing institutions, and with the true spirit of righteousness belongs really to the great employers of labor rather than to the professed teachers of morality. It is too late to inquire whether the system ought or ought not to have been established; for established it is, and established it will remain in spite of all the schemes of the socialists or the insane panaceas of quack economists.

In its origin the factory system found its application in the textile trades of England, and we are very apt now, when the term is used, to confine it in our minds to the production of cotton and woolen goods, although it has in reality embraced nearly all lines of the products of machinery.

A factory is an establishment where several workmen are collected together for the purpose of obtaining greater and cheaper conveniences for labor than they could procure individually at their homes; for producing results by their combined efforts which they could not accomplish separately; and for saving the loss of time which the carrying of an article from place to place, during the several processes necessary to complete its manufacture, would occasion.

The principle of a factory is that each laborer, working separately, is controlled by some associating principle, which directs his producing powers to effect a common result, which it is the object of all collectively to attain. Factories are, therefore, the legitimate outgrowth of the universal tendency to association which is inherent in our nature, and by the development of which every advance in human improvement and human happiness has been gained.

The first force which tended to create this system was that of invention, and the stimulus to this grew out of the difficulty the weavers experienced in obtaining a sufficient supply of yarn to keep their looms in operation. . . .

The power loom closed the catalogue of machines essential for the inauguration of the era of mechanical supremacy; what inventions will come during the continuance of that era cannot be predicted, for we are still at the beginning of the age of invention. The wonderful results of its first twenty years of life are sufficient to indicate something of the future. . . .

Inventions were the material forces, powerful, indeed, as agents in building the factory system. What were the spiritual forces, so to speak? The inner, subtle but also powerful agencies at work to render the material forces successful? A body without a spirit is but dead matter. This is certainly true in one sense of all the mechanical bodies which have served as expressions of mind. A machine is really embodied action; a grand combination of inventions must embody not only all the actions represented but the spirit of the age, for without this they are powerless. . . .

[A] new system, which has found its most rapid extension in the United States, has enabled the manufacturers of this country, with our wonderful stores of raw materials at hand, to become the successful rivals in the mechanic arts of any country that desires to compete with them. It has changed the conditions of masses of people; it has become an active element in the processes of civilization, and has changed the character of legislation and of national policy everywhere.

Is this great, powerful, and growing system a power for good or for evil? Does it mean the elevation of the race or its retrogression?

When we speak of civilization we have in mind the progress of society toward a more perfect state, as indicated by the growth of a long period of time; we do not simply contemplate specific reforms or special evils but the trend of all social influences.

When we speak of the factory system we are apt to let our thoughts dwell upon the evils that we know or imagine belong to it; this is certainly true when civilization and the factory system are suggested in the same sentence. This is wrong, for we should contemplate the factory system in its general influence upon society and especially upon that portion of society most intimately connected with the factory.

My position is that the system has been and is a most potent element in promoting civilization. I assume, of course, and the assumption is in entire harmony with my thoughts, that the civilization of the nineteenth century is better than that of the eighteenth. An examination into the conditions existing under the factory system and those of the domestic or individual system which preceded it fully sustains this position.

None of the systems of labor which existed prior to the present or factory system were particularly conducive to a higher civilization. Wages have been paid for services rendered since the wants of men induced one to serve another, yet the wage system is of recent origin as a system. It arose out of the feudal system of labor and was the first fruits of the efforts of men to free themselves from villenage. The origin of the wage system cannot be given a birthday as can the factory system. It is true, however, that the wage system rendered the factory system possible, and they have since grown together. The first may give way to some

other method for dividing the profits of production, but the factory system perfected, must, whether under socialistic or whatever political system, remain, until disintegration is the rule in society.

The feudal and slave systems had nothing in them from which society could draw the forces necessary to growth; on the contrary, they reflected the most depressing influences and were actually the allies of retrogression. The domestic system, which claims the eighteenth century almost entirely, was woven into the two systems which existed before and came after it; in fact, it has not yet disappeared. It is simple fact, however, when we say that the factory system set aside the domestic system of industry; it is idyllic sentiment when we say that the domestic system surpassed the former, and nothing but sentiment.

There is something poetic in the idea of the weaver of old England, before the spinning machinery was invented, working at his loom in his cottage, with his family about him, some carding, others spinning the wool or the cotton for the weaver, and writers and speakers are constantly bewailing the departure of such scenes.

I am well aware that I speak against popular impression, and largely against popular sentiment, when I assert that the factory system in every respect is vastly superior as an element in civilization to the domestic system which preceded it; that the social and moral influences of the present outshine the social and moral influences of the old. The hue and cry against the prevailing system has not been entirely genuine on either side of the Atlantic. Abuses have existed, great and abominable enough, but not equal to those which have existed in the imagination of men who would have us believe that virtue is something of the past.

The condition of the workers of society has never been the ideal condition, and the worker is too often the victim of the contemptible selfishness which tempts a man to commit the crime of robbing the operative of his just share in the results of his toil. The evils of the factory system are sufficient to call out all the sentiments of justice and philanthropy which enable us to deal with wrong and oppression; all this I do not dispute, but I claim that with all its faults and attendant evils the factory system is a vast improvement upon the domestic system of industry in almost every respect, not only with reference to the individual and the family but to society and the state.

The usual mistake is to consider the factory system as the creator of evils, and not only evils, but of evil disposed persons. This can hardly be shown to be true, although it is that the system may congregate evils or evil disposed persons, and thus give the appearance of creating that which already existed.

It is difficult, I know, to establish close comparisons of the conditions under the two systems because they are not often found to be contemporaneous; yet sufficient evidence will be adduced, I think, from a consideration of the features of the two, and which I am able to present, to establish the truth of my assertions.

Do not construe what I say against the domestic system of industry as in the least antagonistic to the family, for I am one of those who believe that its integrity is the integrity of the nation; that the sacredness of its compacts is the sacredness and the preservation and the extension of the race; that the inviolability of its purity and its peace is the most emphatic source of anxiety of lawmakers; and that any tendency, whether societary or political, toward its decay or even toward its disrespect, deserves the immediate condemnation and active opposition of all citizens as the leading cause of irreligion and of national disintegration.

It should not be forgotten that

the term factory system, in technology, designates the combined operation of many orders of work people . . . in tending with assiduous skill a series of

productive machines continually propelled by a central power. This definition includes such organizations as cotton mills, flax mills, silk and woolen mills, and many other works; but it excludes those in which the mechanisms do not form a connected series, nor are dependent on one prime mover.

It involves in its strictest sense "the idea of a vast automatum, composed of various mechanical and intellectual organs, acting in uninterrupted concert for the production of a common object, all of them being subordinated to a self-regulated moving force."

So a factory becomes a scientific structure, its parts harmonious, the calculations requisite for their harmony involving the highest mathematical skill, and in the factory the operative is always the master of the machine and never the machine the master of the operative. . . .

The spasmodic nature of work under the domestic system caused much disturbance, for handworking is always more or less discontinuous from the caprice of the operative, while much time must be lost in gathering and returning materials. For these and obvious reasons a hand weaver could very seldom turn off in a week much more than one-half what his loom could produce if kept continuously in action during the working hours of the day at the rate which the weaver in his working paroxysms impelled it.

The regular order maintained in the factory cures this evil of the old system and enables the operative to know with reasonable certainty the wages he is to receive at the next payday. His life and habits become more orderly, and he finds, too, that as he has left the closeness of his home shop for the usually clean and well-lighted factory, he imbibes more freely of the health giving tonic of the atmosphere. It is commonly supposed that cotton factories are crowded with operatives. From the nature of things the spinning and weaving rooms cannot be crowded. The spinning mules, in their advancing and retreating locomotion, must have five or six times the space to work in that the actual bulk of the mechanism requires, and where the machinery stands the operative cannot.

In the weaving rooms there can be no crowding of persons. During the agitation for factory legislation in the early part of this century, it was remarked before a committee of the House of Commons "that no part of a cotton mill is one-tenth part as crowded, or the air in it one-tenth part as impure, as the House of Commons with a moderate attendance of members." This is true today; the poorest factory in this country is as good a place to breathe in as Representatives Hall during sessions, or the ordinary schoolroom. In this respect the new system of labor far surpasses the old.

Bad air is one of the surest influences to intemperance, and it is clearly susceptible of proof that intemperance does not exist, and has not existed to such alarming degrees, under the new as under the old system; certainly the influence of bad air has not been as potent.

The regularity required in mills is such as to render persons who are in the habit of getting intoxicated unfit to be employed there, and many manufacturers object to employing persons guilty of the vice; yet, notwithstanding all the efforts which have been made to stop the habit, the beer-drinking operatives of factory towns still constitute a most serious drawback to the success of industrial enterprises, but its effects are not so ruinous under the new as under the old system. . . .

What is the truth as to wages? The vast influence of wages upon social life need not be considered here, but the question whether the factory system has increased them may be. I am constantly obliged, in my everyday labors, to refute the assertion that wages under the factory system are growing lower and lower. The reverse is the truth, which is easily demonstrated; the progress of improvement in machinery may have re-

duced the price paid for a single article, yard, or pound of product, or for the services of a skilled and intelligent operative, but the same improvement has enabled the workman to produce in a greater proportion and always with a less expenditure of muscular labor and in less time, and it has enabled a low grade of labor to increase its earnings. At the same time, a greater number have been benefited, either in consumption or production, by the improvement.

Experience has not only evolved but proven a law in this respect, which is, the more the factory system is perfected, the better will it reward those engaged in it, if not in increased wages to skill, certainly in higher wages to less skill.

Better morals, better sanitary conditions, better health, better wages, these are the practical results of the factory system, as compared with that which preceded it, and the results of all these have been a keener intelligence. Under the domestic system there existed no common centers of thought and action. Religious bigotry has fought against the new order because it tends to destroy the power of the church. Association kills such power in time. . . .

The factory brings mental friction, contact, which could not exist under the old system. Take our own factories in New England, today, fed as they are by French Canadian operatives; when they go back to their own land, as many do, they carry with them the results, whatever they are, of contact with a new system, and the effects of such contact will tell upon their children if not upon themselves. The factory brings progress and intelligence; it establishes at the centers, the public hall for the lyceum and the concert; and even literary institutions have been the result of the direct influence of the system.

Such things could not, in the nature of conditions, find a lodgement under the domestic system. It is in evidence that "the book trade of Great Britain flourishes and fades with its manufactures in vital sympathy, while it is nearly indifferent to the good or bad state of its agriculture."

While the factory system is superior in almost every respect to the individual system, the former is not free from positive evils because human nature is not perfect. These evils are few compared to the magnitude of the benefits of the system, but they should be kept constantly in mind, that public sentiment may be strong enough some day to remove them, in fact, it is removing them.

Whatever there was that was good in the old household plan of labor — so far as keeping the family together at all times and working under the care of the head — was temporarily lost when the factory system took its place, insofar as the old workers entered the factories. This evil, like most others attendant upon the new order, has been greatly exaggerated. The workers under the old system strenuously opposed the establishment of the new, and this led to the employment of great numbers of parish children, a feature of employment which was eagerly fostered by parish officers. Yet, while the working of young children in mills is something to be condemned in our own time, when it began it placed them in a far better condition than they had ever been in, or could have expected to be in, for it made them self-supporting.

The children have been excluded from the factories in all countries, gradually, till the laws of most states, European and American, prohibit their employment under fourteen years of age.

A great evil which even now attracts attention, and in our own country too, is the employment of married women. This occurs more generally with Irish and Canadian women, and too often is the result of the indolence or cupidity of the father. Employers have done much to check this evil, which is not so much an evil to the present as to the future generations. It is bad enough for the present. It robs the young of

the care of their natural protectors, it demoralizes the older children, it makes home dreary and robs it of its amenities. The factory mother's hours of labor in the mills are as long as those of others, and then comes the thousand and one duties of the home, in which, although she may be aided by members of the family, there is little rest.

No ten-hour law can reach the overworked housewife in any walk of life, certainly not when she is a factory worker. Her employment in the mills is a crime to her offspring and, logically, a crime to the state; and the sooner law and sentiment make it impossible for her to stand at the loom, the sooner the character of mill operatives will be elevated. I count their employment with the consequent train of evils, the worst, and the very worst of the evils of a system which is the grandeur of the age, in an industrial point of view.

It is gratifying to know that in Massachusetts cotton mills only about 8 percent of the females employed are married women. This is equally true of English factories, and I believe that in both countries the number is gradually decreasing. So, too, the number of operatives who live in individual homes is increasing.

The employment of children is an evil which has been stimulated as much by the actions of parents as by mill owners.

These evils, however, have been the result of development rather than of inauguration, and thus will disappear as education, in its broad sense, takes the place of ignorance.

The evil effects of the kind of labor performed in mills, so far as health is concerned, have been considerable, while less than those attending the household system. All employments have features not conducive to health. These features or conditions are incidental and cannot be separated from the employment. In mining coal, for instance, the nature of the occupation is bad in nearly all respects; but coal must be had, and there is never any lack of miners. What, then, shall be done?

Operators are in duty bound, of course, to make all evils, whether incidental or artificial, as light as possible, and should introduce every improvement which will lighten the burden of any class who, by their mental incapacity or other causes, are content to seek employment in the lowest grades of labor. Machinery is constantly elevating the grades of labor and the laborer. The working of mines, even, is today an easy task compared to what it was a few years ago. The workers themselves have much responsibility on their own shoulders so far as the healthfulness or unhealthfulness of an occupation is concerned.

Let the children of factory workers everywhere be educated in the rudiments of sanitary science, and then let law say that bad air shall be prohibited, and I believe the vexed temperance question will not trouble us to the extent it has. Drunkenness and intemperance are not the necessary accompanying evils of the factory system and never have been; but wherever corporations furnish unhealthy home surroundings, there the evils of intemperance will be more or less felt in all the directions in which the results of rum find their wonderful ramifications.

The domestic system of labor could not deal with machinery; machinery really initiated the factory system; that is, the latter is the result of machinery. But machinery has done something more — it has brought with it new phases of civilization — for while it means the factory system in one sense, it is the type and representative of the civilization of this period, because it embodies, so far as mechanics are concerned, the concentrated, clearly wrought-out thought of the age. While books represent thought, machinery is the embodiment of thought.

Industry and poverty are not handmaidens, and, as poverty is lessened, good morals thrive. If labor, employment of the mind, is an essential to good morals, then the highest kind of employment, that requiring the most application and the best intellectual effort, means the best morals. This condition, I take courage to assert, is superinduced eventually by the factory system, for by it the operative is usually employed in a higher grade of labor than that which occupied him in his previous condition. For this reason the present system of productive industry is constantly narrowing the limits of the class that occupies the bottom step of social order.

One of the inevitable results of the factory is to enable men to secure a livelihood in less hours than of old; this is grand in itself, for as the time required to earn a living grows shorter, our civilization grows up. That system which demands of a man all his time for the earning of mere subsistence is demoralizing in all respects. . . .

The fact that the lowest grade of operatives can now be employed in mills does not signify more ignorance but, as I have said, a raising of the lowest to higher employments, and, as the world progresses in its refinement, the lowest, which is high comparatively, seems all the lower. Society will bring all up, unless society is compelled to take up what is called a simpler system of labor. We should not forget that growth in civilization means complication, not simplification, nor that the machine is the servant of the workman, and not his competitor.

It is obvious that the factory system has not affected society as badly as has been generally believed; and if it has, in its introduction, brought evils, it has done much to remove others. "The unheard-of power it has given labor, the wealth that has sprung from it, are not the sole property of any class or body of men. They constitute a kind of common fund, which, though irregularly divided," as are all the gifts of nature to finite understandings, "ought at least to satisfy the material, and many of the moral wants of society."

The softening of the misery caused by the change in systems has occurred, but in subtle ways. Transition stages are always harsh upon the generation that experiences them; the great point is that they should be productive of good results in the end. The mind recoils at the contemplation of the conditions which the vast increase of population would have imposed without the factory system.

> It is a sad law, perhaps, but it is an invariable law, that industry, in its march, takes no account of the positions that it overturns, nor of the destinies that it modifies. We must keep step with its progress or be left upon the road. It always accomplishes its work, which is to make better goods at a lower price, to supply more wants and also those of a better order, not with regard for any class but having in view the whole human race. Industry is this, or it is not industry; true to its instincts it has no sentiment in it, unless it is for its own interest; and yet such is the harmony of things, when they are abandoned to their natural course, notwithstanding the selfishness of industry, directed to its own good, it turns finally to secure the good of all, and while requiring service for itself, it serves at the same time by virtue of its resources and its power.

Recent writers, notwithstanding all the facts of history, find a solution for whatever difficulties result from the production of goods under the factory system, in the dispersion of congregated labor, and a return to simple methods when they would have the machines owned and manipulated as individual property, under individual enterprise; but it is safe to assert that "a people who have once adopted the large system of production, are not likely to recede from it"; labor is more productive on the system of large industrial enterprises; the produce is greater in proportion to the labor employed; the same number of persons can be supported equally well with less toil and greater leisure; and in the moral aspect of the question, something better is aimed at as the good of industrial improvement than to disperse the workers of society over the earth to be employed in pent-up houses and the sin-breeding small shops of another age, where there would be scarcely any community of interest or necessary mental communion with other human beings. "If public spirit, generous sentiments, or true justice and equality are desired, association, not isolation of interests, is the school in which these excellences are nurtured."

It is from such influences we discern the elevation of an increased proportion of working people from the position of unskilled to that of skilled laborers and the opening of an adequate field of remunerative employment to women, two of the most important improvements which could be desired in the condition of the working classes. Since, therefore, the extension of the factory system tends strongly toward both these results, it may be considered as one of the features of the present age, which is the most favorable to their more permanent advancement.

It is also true that the factory system has stamped itself most emphatically upon the written law of all countries where it has taken root, as well as upon the social and moral laws which lie at the bottom of the forces which make written law what it is. With the exception of laws relating to the purely commercial features of the factory system, the legislation which that system has produced has been stimulated by the evils which have grown with it.

It is the worst phases of society which gauge the legislation requisite for its protection. Laws other than those for the regulation of trade and the protection of rights as to property, by definition of rights, are made for the restraint of the evil disposed and do not disturb those whose motives and actions are right; so if it were not for the evils which creep into existence with every advance society makes, laws would remain unwritten because not needed. We have a way of judging by the worst examples.

The social battles which men have fought

have been among the severest for human rights, and they mark eras in social conditions as clearly as do field contests in which more human lives have been lost, perhaps, but in which no greater human interests have been involved.

At the time of the institution of the factory system, there was upon the statute books of England but few laws relating to master and man; those which did exist were largely of criminal bearing, establishing punishment for various shortcomings of the men; but with the coming of the new system, the evils of poor law abuses came into full view, and while pauper children were vastly better off in the factories than in the parish poorhouses, they attracted attention and became the subjects of parliamentary protection. For the first time, there appeared some of the consequences of congregated labor, or rather the effects of the congregation of one class of labor appeared. A whole generation of operatives were growing up under conditions of comparative physical degeneracy, of mental ignorance and moral corruption, all of which existed before, but which the factory system brought into strong light.

And now the great question began to be asked, "Has the nation any right to interfere? Shall society suffer that individuals may profit?" Shall the next and succeeding generations be weakened, morally and intellectually, that estates may be enlarged? . . .

The weal or woe of the operative population depends largely upon the temper in which the employers carry the responsibility entrusted to them. I know of no trust more sacred than that given into the hands of the captains of industry, for they deal with human beings in close relations; not through the media of speech or exhortation but of positive association, and by this they can

make or mar. Granted that the material is often poor, the intellects often dull; then all the more sacred the trust and all the greater the responsibility. The rich and powerful manufacturer with the adjuncts of education and good business training holds in his hand something more than the means of subsistence for those he employs, he holds their moral well-being in his keeping, insofar as it is in his power to mold their morals. He is something more than a producer, he is an instrument of God for the upbuilding of the race.

This may sound like sentiment; I am willing to call it sentiment, but I know it means the best material prosperity, and that every employer who has been guided by such sentiments has been rewarded twofold; first, in witnessing the wonderful improvement of his people, and, second, in seeing his dividends increase and the wages of the operatives increase with his dividends.

The factory system of the future will be run on this basis. The instances of such are multiplying rapidly now, and whenever it occurs, the system outstrips the pulpit in the actual work of the gospel, that is, in the work of humanity. It needs no gift of prophecy to foretell the future of a system which has in it more possibilities for good for the masses who must work for day wages than any scheme which has yet been devised by philanthropy alone.

To make the system what it will be, the factory itself must be rebuilt and so ordered in all its appointments that the great question for the labor reformer shall be how to get people out of their homes and into the factory. The agitation of such a novel proposition will bring all the responsibility for bad conditions directly home to the individual, and then the law can handle the difficulty.

Every force evolves a form.

Shaker proverb

1883

116.

MARY BAKER EDDY: Christian Science

Christian Science, like the Church of Jesus Christ of Latter-day Saints (the Mormons), is a purely American religious development. It owes its origin and early growth to the long, energetic career of Mrs. Mary Baker Eddy, who integrated elements of idealism with the teachings of her mentor, Dr. Phineas P. Quimby, into a system of spiritual healing that was in many ways uniquely her own. Mrs. Eddy described her system of thought in Science and Health, *which first appeared in 1875 and underwent many revisions before her death in 1910. Subsequent editions were titled* Science and Health With Key to the Scriptures; *the work, along with her* Church Manual *(1895), is held by Christian Scientists to have been divinely inspired. Mrs. Eddy founded the monthly* Christian Science Journal *in 1883, the weekly* Christian Science Sentinel *in 1898, and in 1908 the* Christian Science Monitor *(published in Boston, the home of the Mother Church), and still one of the leading daily newspapers in America. The following essay from her* Miscellaneous Writings *was probably first written in 1883, though not published until 1896.*

Source: *Miscellaneous Writings*, Boston, 1924, pp. 21-30.

CHRISTIAN SCIENCE BEGINS with the First Commandment of the Hebrew Decalogue, "Thou shalt have no other gods before Me." It goes on in perfect unity with Christ's Sermon on the Mount, and in that age culminates in the Revelation of St. John, who, while on earth and in the flesh, like ourselves, beheld "a new Heaven and a new earth" — the spiritual universe, whereof Christian Science now bears testimony.

Our Master said, "The works that I do shall ye do also"; and, "The kingdom of God is within you." This makes practical all His words and works. As the ages advance in spirituality, Christian Science will be seen to depart from the trend of other Christian denominations in nowise except by increase of spirituality.

My first plank in the platform of Christian Science is as follows: "There is no life, truth, intelligence, nor substance in matter. All is infinite Mind and its infinite manifestation, for God is All-in-all. Spirit is immortal Truth; matter is mortal error. Spirit is the real and eternal; matter is the unreal and temporal. Spirit is God, and man is His image and likeness. Therefore man is not material; he is spiritual."

I am strictly a theist — believe in one God, one Christ or Messiah.

Science is neither a law of matter nor of man. It is the unerring manifesto of Mind, the law of God, its divine Principle. Who dare say that matter or mortals can evolve Science? Whence, then, is it, if not from the divine source, and what, but the contemporary of Christianity, so far in advance of human knowledge that mortals must work for the discovery of even a portion of it? Christian Science translates Mind, God, to mortals. It is the infinite calculus defining the line, plane, space, and fourth dimension of Spirit. It absolutely refutes the amalgamation, transmigration, absorption, or annihilation of individuality. It shows the impossibility of transmitting human ills, or evil, from one individual to another; that all true thoughts revolve in God's orbits — they come from God and return to Him — and untruths belong not to His creation; therefore these are null and void. It hath no peer, no competitor, for it dwelleth in Him besides whom "there is none other."

That Christian Science is Christian, those who have demonstrated it, according to the rules of its divine Principle — together with the sick, the lame, the deaf, and the blind, healed by it — have proven to a waiting world. He who has not tested it is incompetent to condemn it; and he who is a willing sinner cannot demonstrate it.

A falling apple suggested to Newton more than the simple fact cognized by the senses, to which it seemed to fall by reason of its own ponderosity; but the primal cause, or Mind-force, invisible to material sense, lay concealed in the treasure troves of Science. True, Newton named it gravitation, having learned so much; but Science, demanding more, pushes the question: Whence or what is the power back of gravitation, the intelligence that manifests power? Is pantheism true? Does mind "sleep in the mineral, or dream in the animal and wake in man"? Christianity answers this question. The prophets, Jesus, and the apostles demonstrated a divine intelligence that subordinates so-called material laws; and

disease, death, winds, and waves obey this intelligence. Was it Mind or matter that spoke in creation, "and it was done"? The answer is self-evident, and the command remains, "Thou shalt have no other gods before Me."

It is plain that the Me spoken of in the First Commandment must be Mind; for matter is not the Christian's God and is not intelligent. Matter cannot even talk; and the serpent, Satan, the first talker in its behalf, lied. Reason and revelation declare that God is both noumenon and phenomena — the first and only cause. The universe, including man, is not a result of atomic action, material force, or energy; it is not organized dust. God, Spirit, Mind, are terms synonymous for the one God, whose reflection is creation, and man is His image and likeness. Few there are who comprehend what Christian Science means by the word "reflection." God is seen only in that which reflects good, Life, Truth, Love — yea, which manifests all His attributes and power, even as the human likeness thrown upon the mirror repeats precisely the looks and actions of the object in front of it. All must be Mind and Mind's ideas; since, according to natural science, God, Spirit, could not change its species and evolve matter.

These facts enjoin the First Commandment; and knowledge of them makes man spiritually minded. St. Paul writes: "For to be carnally minded is death; but to be spiritually minded is life and peace." This knowledge came to me in an hour of great need; and I give it to you as deathbed testimony to the daystar that dawned on the night of material sense. This knowledge is practical, for it wrought my immediate recovery from an injury caused by an accident and pronounced fatal by the physicians. On the third day thereafter, I called for my Bible, and opened it at Matt. 9:2. As I read, the healing Truth dawned upon my sense; and the result was that I rose, dressed myself, and ever after was in better health than I had before enjoyed. That short experience

Mary Baker Eddy, founder of Christian Science

included a glimpse of the great fact that I have since tried to make plain to others, namely, Life in and of Spirit; this Life being the sole reality of existence. I learned that mortal thought evolves a subjective state which it names matter, thereby shutting out the true sense of Spirit.

Per contra, Mind and man are immortal; and knowledge gained from moral sense is illusion, error, the opposite of Truth; therefore it cannot be true. A knowledge of both good and evil (when good is God, and God is All) is impossible. Speaking of the origin of evil, the Master said: "When he speaketh a lie, he speaketh of his own; for he is a liar and the father of it." God warned man not to believe the talking serpent, or rather the allegory describing it. The Nazarene Prophet declared that his followers should handle serpents; that is, put down all subtle falsities or illusions and thus destroy any supposed effect arising from false claims exercising their supposed power on the mind and body of man, against his holiness and health.

That there is but one God or Life, one cause and one effect, is the *multum in parvo*

of Christian Science; and to my understanding it is the heart of Christianity, the religion that Jesus taught and demonstrated. In divine Science it is found that matter is a phase of error and that neither one really exists, since God is Truth and All-in-all. Christ's Sermon on the Mount, in its direct application to human needs, confirms this conclusion.

Science, understood, translates matter into Mind, rejects all other theories of causation, restores the spiritual and original meaning of the Scriptures, and explains the teachings and life of our Lord. It is religion's "new tongue," with "signs following," spoken of by St. Mark. It gives God's infinite meaning to mankind, healing the sick, casting out evil, and raising the spiritually dead. Christianity is Christlike only as it reiterates the word, repeats the works, and manifests the spirit of Christ.

Jesus' only medicine was omnipotent and omniscient Mind. As *omni* is from the Latin word meaning *all,* this medicine is all-power; and omniscience means, as well, all-science. The sick are more deplorably situated than the sinful if the sick cannot trust God for help and the sinful can. If God created drugs good, they cannot be harmful; if He could create them otherwise, then they are bad and unfit for man; and if He created drugs for healing the sick, why did not Jesus employ them and recommend them for that purpose?

No human hypotheses, whether in philosophy, medicine, or religion, can survive the wreck of time; but whatever is of God hath life abiding in it and ultimately will be known as self-evident truth, as demonstrable as mathematics. Each successive period of progress is a period more humane and spiritual. The only logical conclusion is that all is Mind and its manifestation, from the rolling of worlds, in the most subtle ether, to a potato patch.

The agriculturist ponders the history of a seed and believes that his crops come from the seedling and the loam; even while the Scripture declares He made "every plant of the field before it was in the earth." The Scientist asks, Whence came the first seed, and what made the soil? Was it molecules or material atoms? Whence came the infinitesimals — from infinite Mind or from matter? If from matter, how did matter originate? Was it self-existent? Matter is not intelligent and thus able to evolve or create itself; it is the very opposite of Spirit, intelligent, self-creative, and infinite Mind. The belief of mind in matter is pantheism. Natural history shows that neither a genus nor a species produces its opposite. God is All, in all. What can be more than All? Nothing; and this is just what I call matter, *nothing*. Spirit, God, has no antecedent; and God's consequent is the spiritual cosmos. The phrase "express image," in the common version of Heb. 1:3, is, in the Greek Testament, "character."

The Scriptures name God as good, and the Saxon term for God is also good. From this premise comes the logical conclusion that God is naturally and divinely infinite good. How, then, can this conclusion change, or be changed, to mean that good is evil, or the creator of evil? What can there be besides infinity? Nothing! Therefore the Science of good calls evil *nothing*. In divine Science the terms God and good, as Spirit, are synonymous. That God, good, creates evil, or aught that can result in evil — or that Spirit creates its opposite, named matter — are conclusions that destroy their premise and prove themselves invalid. Here is where Christian Science sticks to its text and other systems of religion abandon their own logic. Here also is found the pith of the basal statement, the cardinal point in Christian Science, that matter and evil (including all inharmony, sin, disease, death) are *unreal*. Mortals accept natural science, wherein no species ever produces its opposite. Then why not accept divine Science on this ground; since the Scriptures maintain this fact by parable and proof, asking, "Do men gather grapes of thorns, or figs of thistles?" "Doth a fountain send forth at the same place sweet water and bitter?"

According to reason and revelation, evil and matter are negation; for evil signifies the absence of good, God, though God is ever present; and matter claims something besides God, when God is really *All*. Creation, evolution, or manifestation — being in and of Spirit, Mind, and all that really is — must be spiritual and mental. This is Science and is susceptible of proof.

But, say you, is a stone spiritual? To erring material sense, No! but to unerring spiritual sense, it is a small manifestation of Mind, a type of spiritual substance, "the substance of things hoped for." Mortals can know a stone as substance only by first admitting that it is substantial. Take away the mortal sense of substance and the stone itself would disappear, only to reappear in the spiritual sense thereof. Matter can neither see, hear, feel, taste, nor smell having no sensation of its own. Perception by the five personal senses is mental and dependent on the beliefs that mortals entertain. Destroy the belief that you can walk and volition ceases; for muscles cannot move without mind. Matter takes no cognizance of matter. In dreams, things are only what mortal mind makes them; and the phenomena of mortal life are as dreams; and this so-called life is a dream soon told. In proportion as mortals turn from this mortal and material dream to the true sense of reality, everlasting Life will be found to be the only Life. That death does not destroy the beliefs of the flesh, our Master proved to His doubting disciple Thomas. Also, He demonstrated that divine Science alone can overbear materiality and mortality; and this great truth was shown by His ascension after death, whereby He arose above the illusion of matter.

The First Commandment, "Thou shalt have no other gods before Me," suggests the inquiry, What meaneth this Me — Spirit or matter? It certainly does not signify a graven idol and must mean Spirit. Then the commandment means, Thou shalt recognize no intelligence nor life in matter; and find neither pleasure nor pain therein. The Master's practical knowledge of this grand verity, together with His divine Love, healed the sick and raised the dead. He literally annulled the claims of physique and of physical law by the superiority of the higher law; hence His declaration, "These signs shall follow them that believe; . . . if they drink any deadly thing, it shall not hurt them; they shall lay hands on the sick, and they shall recover."

Do you believe His words? I do, and that His promise is perpetual. Had it been applicable only to His immediate disciples, the pronoun would be *you*, not *them*. The purpose of His life work touches universal humanity. At another time He prayed, not for the twelve only but "for them also which shall believe on Me through their word."

The Christ-healing was practised even before the Christian Era; "the Word was with God, and the Word was God." There is, however, no analogy between Christian Science and spiritualism, or between it and any speculative theory.

In 1867, I taught the first student in Christian Science. Since that date I have known of but 14 deaths in the ranks of my about 5,000 students. The census since 1875 (the date of the first publication of my work, *Science and Health with Key to the Scriptures*) shows that longevity has *increased*. Daily letters inform me that a perusal of my volume is healing the writers of chronic and acute diseases that had defied medical skill.

Surely the people of the Occident know that esoteric magic and Oriental barbarisms will neither flavor Christianity nor advance health and length of days.

Miracles are no infraction of God's laws; on the contrary, they fulfill His laws; for they are the signs following Christianity, whereby matter is proven powerless and subordinate to Mind. Christians, like students in mathematics, should be working up to those higher rules of Life which Jesus taught and proved. Do we really understand the divine Principle of Christianity before we prove it, in at least some feeble demonstration thereof, according to Jesus' example in healing the sick? Should we adopt the "simple addition" in Christian Science and doubt its higher rules or despair of ultimately reaching them, even though failing at first to demonstrate all the possibilities of Christianity?

St. John spiritually discerned and revealed the sum total of transcendentalism. He saw the real earth and Heaven. They were spiritual, not material; and they were without pain, sin, or death. Death was not the door to this Heaven. The gates thereof he declared were inlaid with pearl, likening them to the priceless understanding of man's real existence, to be recognized here and now.

The great Way-shower illustrated Life unconfined, uncontaminated, untrammeled by matter. He proved the superiority of Mind over the flesh, opened the door to the captive, and enabled man to demonstrate the law of Life, which St. Paul declares "hath made me free from the law of sin and death."

The stale saying that Christian Science "is neither Christian nor science!" is today the fossil of wisdomless wit, weakness, and superstition. "The fool hath said in his heart, There is no God."

Take courage, dear reader, for any seeming mysticism surrounding realism is explained in the Scripture, "There went up a mist from the earth [matter]"; and the mist of materialism will vanish as we approach spirituality, the realm of reality; cleanse our lives in Christ's righteousness; bathe in the baptism of Spirit, and awake in His likeness.

117.

Labor and Capital

The Senate Committee on Education and Labor held a series of hearings in 1883 in the course of an investigation of the relations between labor and capital. The Committee heard testimony from representatives of many interested parties, including labor, management, the professions, and reform movements. The portions of the hearings reprinted here include testimony by Samuel Gompers, who helped reorganize the Cigarmakers' Union in the 1870s and founded the American Federation of Labor in 1886; Thomas L. Livermore, a factory manager; and Dr. Timothy D. Stow, a physician in a factory town.

Source: *Report of the Committee of the Senate Upon the Relations Between Labor and Capital,* Washington, 1885, Vol. I, pp. 270-301, 361-382, Vol. III, pp. 3-28, 407-418.

I.

SAMUEL GOMPERS:
Testimony of a Labor Leader

[*Mr. Gompers:*] Mr. Ira Steward has remarked that improvements in machinery and the fact of its invention discharges labor faster than new industries are founded and tends to increase the hours of labor; and that among the reasons for this may be named the following:

"Capital must reproduce itself and bear interest" is the first and main maxim of modern industry. What does this mean? It means that capital is the accumulated value of past labor employed in production for the purpose of further accumulation; and when invested in machinery or other enterprises must reappear in its original form as money, not alone to an amount equal to the amount invested but in an increased amount. The individual possessor of capital invested in any industry wants his interest, and the corporations have a more artificial term for it; they term it dividends. The question is how is this result to be obtained by machinework? It is a well settled fact that the only producer of value is labor; there is a well established value in labor; hence, if machinery displaces manual labor and performs the labor itself, it must create some value; but what is the amount of it, especially taking into consideration that human labor and that of machinery are always combined?

Q. You adopt that view as your own, I suppose?

A. I do. Otherwise I would not read it. I intend to speak of the hours of labor, and that is why I use this as a preliminary statement. The hours of labor have been discussed by many thinkers on the labor question and by many from different standpoints. During my attendance upon this committee I have heard a good many questions asked and answered, and in my humble opinion some of the answers were not what they ought to have been. I maintain that the hours of labor ought to be reduced. From every standpoint the hours are too long in modern industries, more especially where the individual, the worker, is but a part of the machine and is compelled to keep in motion in accordance with the velocity with which the machine turns. The production of goods is not, as many have been led to believe, lessened by a reduction of the hours of labor; but, on the contrary, the productivity of labor increases. In all countries, in all states in this country, in all factories where in certain branches of trade the experiment has been made, wherever the hours of labor have been reduced, there the productivity of labor has become greater.

By the Chairman:

Q. Absolutely, or in proportion to the time occupied?

A. Absolutely.

Q. One day with another, more goods produced?

A. More produced, one day with another. I am saying that the productivity of labor has increased, not from the desire, or probably not from the ability, of the laborer to produce more in the shorter number of hours but as a consequence of the fact that, owing to the reduction of the hours of labor, machinery has been improved, new tools have been made, and the different industries have been divided and subdivided, so that as a consequence of the reduction of the hours there has come increased production.

Q. Then the increased productivity is the result of the improved machinery and not of the shorter hours of labor?

A. But the improved machinery is the result of the reduction of the hours of labor.

Q. But we are speaking of the direct cause; and the reduction of the hours of labor is not the direct cause of the increased production, you say, but the reduction of the hours of labor has led to invention and improved machinery, and by the machinery, combined with shorter hours of labor, more is produced?

A. Decidedly.

Q. Then you attribute the invention not to genius alone but to genius and *opportunity?*

A. Yes, sir, I hold that the necessity for inventions brings them forth, and that they

do not come forth without that. A man might go to China and live there a hundred years and probably never think of a Morse telegraph machine.

Q. But do you think that the inventors of this country are stimulated to invent by reason of the reduction of the hours of labor?

A. I think that the necessity created by reduction of the hours of labor for other means of supplying wants that need to be satisfied is the cause of inventive genius becoming active.

Q. Then your ground is this, that the *immediate* result of the reduction of hours of labor is decreased production, and that that creates the necessity of supplying that deficiency of production by improved machinery?

A. Let me answer by saying, as one of our greatest economists says, that there is but one sure and permanent way by which the customs and habits of the people can be improved. Or rather that, if you wish to improve the condition of the people, you must improve their habits and customs. The reduction of the hours of labor reaches the very root of society. It gives the workingman better conditions and better opportunities, and makes of him what has been too long neglected — a consumer instead of a mere producer.

Q. You think, then, that he will consume more in consequence of the reduction of the hours of labor?

A. I do, positively.

Q. In a certain way he will have more time to consume in?

A. Yes, sir. And another thing. A man who goes to his work before the dawn of day requires no clean shirt to go to work in, but is content to go in an old overall or anything that will cover his members; but a man who goes to work at 8 o'clock in the morning wants a clean shirt; he is afraid his friends will see him, so he does not want to be dirty. He also requires a newspaper; while a man who goes to work early in the morning and stays at it late at night does not need a newspaper, for he has no time to read, requiring all the time he has to recuperate his strength sufficiently to get ready for his next day's work.

I agree with Mr. Ira Steward in his view. I have regretted very much that his work has not been so widely circulated as it deserved to be. I say this because I think it contains the fundamental truths of the labor question. The reduction in the hours of labor reaches the lowest stratum of society. I say I agree entirely with Mr. Steward, and I think he is (or rather has been, for he is dead now) the ablest thinker on the economic question, more especially in regard to the application of the reduction, of the hours of labor and to the movement and its effects upon society in general. That labor deserves a reduction of the hours of toil I believe hardly anyone will dispute, unless when he is on "the other side of the house" and labor is seeking to enforce such a reduction against his interest, as he thinks.

The general reduction of the hours of labor to eight per day would reach further than any other reformatory measure; it would be of more lasting benefit; it would create a greater spirit in the workingman; it would make him a better citizen, a better father, a better husband, a better man in general. The "voting cattle," so called, those whose votes are purchased on election day, are drawn from that class of our people whose life is one continuous round of toil. They cannot be drawn from workingmen who work only eight hours. A man who works but eight hours a day possesses more independence both economically and politically. It is the man who works like his machine and never knows when to stop, until in his case perpetual motion is almost arrived at — he is the man whose vote you can buy. The man who works longest is the first to be thrown out on the sidewalk, because his recreation is generally drink. . . .

Q. Do you believe . . . that a law of the United States or of the states reducing the hours of labor to eight per day would be or

could be actually enforced in this country?

A. For private employers, do you mean?

Q. Yes; for corporations and factories — private employers?

A. I think, first, that the general government, under the Constitution, possesses no such power. I am speaking upon this question because I believe that it is a wrong that, with all our modern inventions, the working people should be called upon to work the long hours that they do; and while in this instance I am not seeking redress from the general government, or asking it to reduce the hours of labor generally, I do say that it is more than negligence, more than wrong on the part of the government to permit its own statute on that subject to remain unenforced. The government has adopted a national eight-hour law for all government employees. If that law is wrong it should be obliterated from the statute books; but as it is good, it ought to remain; and so long as it is a law it is worse than neglect on the part of any officer of the government to set the example of ignoring or violating it.

Q. The real difficulty comes in here: government employment and other employments must have more or less relation to each other, and the government employee does not like to take eight hours' pay when another man outside may work a little longer and get ten hours' pay.

A. That may be true; but the fact is that the operatives in the government employ were paid ten hours' pay for eight hours of labor until the panic arose; and that then, for what reason I cannot say, the eight-hour law was construed to mean a reduction of wages, in spite of the fact that two proclamations of President Grant had been issued setting forth that no reduction in pay should result from the reduction of the hours of labor from ten to eight. That was during the panic and when the labor organizations were considerably crippled.

Q. I admit your point as against the apparent evasion of what would seem to be

Factory views: (top left) "Bell-time"; drawing by Winslow Homer for "Harper's Weekly"; (top right) workers in a corset factory in McGrawville, N.Y.; (right) lithograph of the Amoskeag Manufacturing Company in Manchester, N.H.

the intent of the law; but the other difficulty, which is a substantial one, still remains. Can any such law be properly enforced so as to reach the great mass of laborers or wage workers of the country in private employ?

A. I do not think it can under our present competitive system.

Q. Then the suggestion of an eight-hour law would seem to be of no use?

A. No, sir. I do not take that view. I hold that our representatives, possessing more than the average intelligence, or at least the average intelligence, should be in the van, should in a measure teach the people, and should adopt the eight-hour law for the government employees, not so much to benefit those employees as to set an example to be imitated by private employers, to be requested by the employed, to be agitated for, to be organized for, to be attained. That law ought to be enforced to

enable the workingmen to look to the government as an example and say, "Here, our government has adopted the eight-hour law, and *it* is worthy of imitation."

Q. Do you think that private employers would be much influenced by sentimental considerations of that kind?

A. Probably not all; but I know that a good many employers would.

Q. A portion of the employees would refuse to work more than eight hours probably; but would not they find as a result that they would have to take the eight hours' pay?

A. They would not refuse to work more than eight hours until the movement became somewhat general, at least in their own trades.

By Mr. Pugh:

Q. A law of Congress is an expression of public opinion. Now, would not that expression of public opinion in favor of the national eight-hour law have necessarily a great influence upon the same question between individuals?

A. Yes, sir. I think it would.

Q. That would be its moral effect, and the force of public opinion would compel conformity to it in practice in the course of time?

A. That is what I have been attempting to get at.

By the Chairman:

Q. Here is this law, more than a dozen years old, still on the statute book, but entirely disregarded; so that that theory is absolutely disproved by the fact.

A. And the national legislature is continually banged at to have that law enforced.

Q. Yes; the mass of public opinion would seem to be the other way, or else congressional action is not an expression of public opinion. But here is a law on the statute book, and yet not only is its principle not adopted among the people at large but even the government itself fails to enforce its own edict.

A. It is a very peculiar government in that respect.

Q. Now, I have suggested the question whether an eight-hour law, or any law regulating the rates of wages, in order to be of benefit must not reach not only the employer but also the employed, with penalties attached, so that no man should be allowed to work more than eight hours, under penalty of fine and imprisonment; and if an employer permitted him to work for more than eight hours he also should be subjected to punishment. With such a law enforced you would have something which would make room for this surplus labor in regard to which there has been so much testimony here. But just so long as compensation depends upon the amount of labor performed, and just so long as the individual is capable of doing his ten hours' work, he will work his ten hours, and, by private agreements between himself and his employer, they will increase wages and production by the evasion of any general law which applies only to the employer.

A. If the eight-hour law were enforced by the government, and at least it ought to enforce its own edict —

Q. [Interposing.] Do you mean that the government should go into the labor market just as any other employer does, and see what it can obtain service for; or that, finding that competent labor for ten hours a day can be obtained at a certain price, it should hire that labor, work it only eight hours, and pay it the same price as for ten hours' work? Would that be fair toward private employers?

A. I do say that the government of the United States ought to be in advance of its people. It is the duty of a legislator, as I understand it, to frame and adopt measures for the welfare of the people. I believe that the duty of the legislature is to propose laws for the benefit of the people. The Constitution of the country, I believe, does not give our national government the right to adopt a law which would be applicable to private employments; yet for its own employees it ought to be in advance; it ought not to enter the labor market, as you have suggested, Mr. Chairman, in competition with all other employers, but ought to be in advance. The selfish, mercenary, or other such motives which govern individuals in their struggle to accumulate wealth ought not to exist in our government, although they do exist to a morbid degree in too many of our employers.

The government having adopted the eight-hour law, it seems to me to be hardly a debatable question, the efficiency or the good of the reduction of the hours of labor; and the government having adopted that law, it should be faithfully executed, not as someone during the panic did construe it, or as others do now, but in accordance with its language and spirit. Of course I will bow in submission to a decision upon the law, but I cannot for the life of me see how that eight-hour law was construed to mean anything but what it plainly says on the face of it. It seems to cover and imply everything that is needed, and not only was that the first construction that was placed upon the law, but several of the executive officers were desirous of reducing the wages of the government employees when the law came into force, and President Grant, in a proclamation which he issued; quoted the law, and stated that from its plain language and meaning it was clear that no reduction of wages could or should ensue from the reduction of the hours of labor. There was a subsequent proclamation to that same effect. Yet, in violation of (1) the law and (2) the two proclamations of the President — and it is to be presumed that the President upon a question of construction of law is not going to issue a proclamation without having his legal adviser advise him as to whether the construction is correct or not — that law was disregarded!

As representatives of the organized trades and labor unions of this country we have met in council within a few days, and on next Tuesday we shall meet in our third annual session in this city. From time to time we have formulated our demands and requests for things that we thought ought to be done by legislation or otherwise. We know very well that the government of the United States and the legislative power cannot be more probably than a step in advance of the people. If they go much further they are apt to have the platform pulled away from under them, leaving them floating in the air without any support. That is not the intention of organized labor; but we do say that our legislators ought to be at least that one step in advance of the general public. Now, if they will have the national eight-hour law enforced, we do not ask anything further of them in reference to the reduction of the hours of labor. Let the question of endeavoring to enforce a reduction of the hours of

labor among private employers be a question to be settled amicably, if possible, between ourselves and our employers, and I think it will not be many years before it will be generally settled. This seems to me to be the question of questions, the reduction of the hours of labor. . . .

The remedies that I suggest, and which I think the government can and ought to adopt, are the following:

1. Strict enforcement of the national eight-hour law. The workingmen of this country, in all their organizations where they have come together, either in private or in public, either as local, state, national, or confederated unions, have set forth that demand for the enforcement of the national eight-hour law.

2. The passage of a law by Congress giving the trades and labor unions the right to become chartered under the general laws of our government. The laws written and now in operation to protect the property of the capitalist and the moneyed class generally are almost innumerable, yet nothing has been done to protect the property of the workingmen, the only property that they possess, their working power, their savings bank, their school, and trades union; and we ask that our existence as organizations may be legalized, not for the purposes of strikes, as has been said, but for such reasons and objects as have been recognized in England and France. . . .

3. We ask also, for the purpose of procuring information for the legislators of our country (who frequently find a very good excuse for nonaction by saying that they are ignorant as to the true condition of the working people), the establishment of a national bureau of labor statistics. Such a bureau would give our legislators an opportunity to know, not from mere conjecture but actually, the condition of our industries, our production and consumption, and what could be done by law to improve both. Our state governments would undoubtedly follow the lead of the national Congress and

legislate in the interest of labor; but we see that so long as our national legislators have an excuse for saying that they do not know the condition of labor, there is very little chance of obtaining legislation. . . .

There are several other measures to which I might call attention and which I might suggest as remedies, but the best organized trades unions of the world are eminently practical. They are composed of men who are desirous of obtaining reforms by gradual means, and in that spirit we ask the adoption of these measures which I have set forth here, because we believe and know that they will redound to our benefit as workingmen and to the benefit of society. If the legislators of this country are desirous of acting in this matter and alleviating the distress that is too prevalent, and if they desire to assist those who are working in this cause to mount a step higher, let them adopt these measures and they will receive the thanks of the working people of the world and of all posterity. But in any event, they ought not to continue to be so indifferent to the condition of labor as they have been in the past.

II.

Thomas L. Livermore:
Testimony of a Factory Manager

Mr. Pugh. I understand that you have been a lawyer in your time, and I wish you would now proceed, if you please, to give the committee such facts and information and such opinions as you consider pertinent to the subject of investigation . . . and without waiting for any special question. You may proceed in your own way and state anything in the shape of facts from your own personal knowledge or from information which you regard as reliable, or any opinions which your experience may suggest to you . . . first stating, if you please, your residence and occupation, and what opportunities you have had to understand the subjects under investigation, so as to give force and effect to your statements.

The Witness. I live in Manchester, N.H., and am agent in this place for the Amoskeag Manufacturing Company. I have the management of the affairs of the corporation here. I have had that management as agent for four and a half years. . . .

Q. How is it as to the supply of labor here generally, so far as you know — of manufacturing labor?

A. The supply of labor in this place, so far as I know, has generally been good; it has been sufficient. That, I have no doubt, is due in a degree to the proximity of this place to the Canadian border and to its being situated upon a railroad which brings down many Canadians; but I think it is due in a greater degree to the wages which are paid here, which are greater for the same kind of work, I am informed and believe, than are paid, for instance, in Lowell, our nearest manufacturing neighbor, in Massachusetts; and I have been led to believe that this difference is due mainly to the fact that the hours of labor are unlimited here, while in Massachusetts there is a ten-hour law, for it seems to be certain that no law can bring it about that eleven hours' pay shall be paid for ten hours' work. And very recently, in determining whether my scale of wages was one that ought to be maintained, I went to Lowell and had careful inquiry made among several of the leading manufacturing establishments there as to their rates of wages; and upon the information which I got in that way, I was led to believe that we were paying here at least an increase proportioned to the hours of labor; in some cases a little more; that is to say, we were paying wages, as compared with theirs, in the proportion of 10¾ to 10, which are the respective hours of labor in the two places. I have no doubt that the ample supply of labor here is to be attributed, in some degree, also, to the favorable character of the place for a residence and to the tenements which are kept for the people. I have been informed that during the last year, when labor was not scarce here, it was scarce in Lowell and Lawrence in reputable mills, where all conditions, excepting, perhaps, wages, were as good as those here. I attribute that to the difference in the hours of labor. . . .

By the Chairman:

Q. Suppose a system were introduced of paying, substantially, by the hour or by the piece, and it prevailed all through your entire system of work, and then the proposition was made to the operatives to absolutely limit the hours of labor to ten, nine, or eight hours. Do you think that the operatives themselves would approve of that proposition, or would they prefer to work longer and get more pay?

A. I do not think they would approve of it.

Q. If it were submitted to them, you think they would decide adversely?

A. Of course, if the operatives were persuaded that by the reduction of the hours of labor the manufacturers would be compelled to pay more per cut so that they could earn as much in the nine hours as they could in the eleven hours, I suppose they would willingly agree to it; but taking things as they are, with economic laws governing the prices to be paid, I do not think you would find one in a hundred who would agree to the reduction of hours under the circumstances which you suppose.

Q. Then in order to enact a ten-, or say, an eight-hour law — it would be a matter of indifference as to the number of hours in excess of ten — to be really enforced, the compulsion would have to extend to the operatives as well as the manufacturer, would not that be so?

A. I see no other way.

Q. No one should be allowed by law to work more than that number of hours?

A. Yes. If you were to make a thing optional with the operatives, and part of the work were piecework and part were daywork, I do not see myself how the law could result in any good, because it would

either result that all the operatives would agree that they wished to work eleven hours, supposing that be the number that was deemed advisable, or else part would want to work eleven and part eight or nine; and the manufacturer could not afford to supply the increased quantity of machinery to those who wished to work eight hours to keep up with those who wished to work eleven, I should think. That is something, however, that I have never figured out, but I should suppose that that would be so.

Q. How would it operate upon the interests of the manufacturer and how upon the working people, in your judgment, if hours could be reduced so that the machinery could be employed, say, for illustration, sixteen hours a day, and two sets of hands employed, each working eight, would such a system as that be practicable, and, if so, what would be the effect upon the wages of each individual operative do you think?

A. I do not know whether it would be practicable. I can see objections to it, but whether they would be insuperable I am really unable now to say. The three chief objections to it which I see now are these: With two sets of hands running the same set of machinery it would be very difficult to place the responsibility for the care of the machinery upon either; that is a very important factor in maintaining a mill. Then it would be very difficult to find time to repair that machinery, and it would all have to be done in the nighttime. You would have to keep a set of workmen in the nighttime, which would be more expensive and troublesome. Then the risk of fire would be increased very largely by reason of the lighting of the mills at night. At the present time the insurers object to running the mills beyond 10 o'clock at night, for instance.

Q. The danger of fire increases later in the nighttime, does it?

A. Yes, on account of the gas and the difficulty of seeing around under the machinery for hot bearings, and all that sort of thing, which induces fire. Whether those expenses would be so great as to make it too expensive to manufacture could only be told, I suppose, by trial.

Q. There would be this about it, that the machinery, which is perhaps the cheapest production in the mills, would work twice as long.

A. Not twice as long, but it would work sixteen hours a day. It would be twice as long if you worked twenty-two hours a day. Then there is this further consideration to be taken into account — whether machinery would in the course of a year do twice as much work by working twice as long. Some mechanics think that machinery needs rest; and the item of repairs of machinery is a very great item in the cost of running a mill. We read of people who make very large profits in running their mills for a year or two or three or four or five years, we will say, and then suddenly, for some reason which is not obvious to the public, the mills become bankrupt, when the real reason is that they are worn out. It is not safe to calculate that you can run a mill without spending on an average 10 percent per annum on the value of the machinery on repairs and renewals of machinery, and that is a subject which requires very careful attention in running a mill. I know a mill which ran night and day — a cotton mill — it is the only one I think, that I ever saw do it. That is the mill at Atlanta, Ga., and they thought it succeeded, but I believe the mill was not a financial success. I think it failed. Whether the failure was due to that I do not express any opinion.

Q. Is that recently?

A. Yes. I should not suppose, however, that that was the origin of the difficulty, because I think that was done after it went into the receiver's hands.

Q. Do you think it would be possible to get the necessary number of laborers to supply the working interests of the country where machinery was employed largely if more than one relay of hands was used?

A. That I do not know. Take the case of Lowell and Lawrence that I have instanced, where they have had a scarcity of labor for their present hours, it would seem as though that scarcity would be multiplied by running twice as many hours. It would be perhaps remedied by paying higher wages.

Q. But that would interfere with the marketing of the production?

A. Yes; and it is a question whether, if you paid higher wages, you could afford to run the mill.

Q. Or to employ anybody?

A. Yes.

The Chairman. I asked the question because the suggestion has been made by many labor reformers, as they are termed, that even six hours, considering the increased productive power of machinery or of the human being and machinery combined, would be as long as laboring people ought to be expected to work, as long as the interests of society require that they should; and inasmuch as there are many unemployed people, a reduction of the hours of labor would give something to others to do. The question whether it could be made to work practically is the serious thing.

The Witness. I do not believe at all in such theories. I think that at least in a free country like this, with thousands of miles of land to be taken up in a vast area of country which is inhabited by people occupied in industrial pursuits and the great variety of employments to be found in this country, it is perfectly safe for at least the lifetime of this generation to leave the question of how a man shall work, and how long he shall work, and where he shall work, and what wages he shall get to himself. It is as certain that wages in a country situated as ours is will adjust themselves to the level required by the demand and the market as it is that water will seek its level. I do not believe that anyone has ever yet seen in this country a time when distress on the part of the laboring people was universal. It has occurred in certain industries and in certain places without any question, but every time the tremendous field which is afforded to the laboring man in which to find employment has come to his relief, and, with a little foresight, a little forehandedness, and a little energy, he has been able to find some employment in which he could earn his living and a little more.

By Mr. Pugh:

Q. The complaining demand often comes for a particular kind of work in a particular place at higher wages?

A. Yes.

Q. They want to stay in the cities and do the work that they are accustomed to?

A. That is true.

Q. There is a great opposition to change; they cannot get rid of the charm of city life, although it be in tenement houses and frequently without pure air or food?

A. That is true.

By the Chairman:

Q. Won't you please tell us your experience with the question of child labor; how it is and to what extent it exists here; why it exists, and whether, as it is actually existing here, it is a hardship on a child or on a parent; or whether there is any evil in that direction that should be remedied?

A. There is a certain class of labor in the mills which, to put it in very common phrase, consists mainly in running about the floor — where there is not as much muscular exercise required as a child would put forth in play, and a child can do it about as well as a grown person can do it — not quite as much of it, but somewhere near it — and with proper supervision of older people, the child serves the purpose. That has led to the employment of children in the mills, I think. . . .

Now, a good many heads of families, without any question in my mind, were not sufficiently considerate of the mental and physical welfare of their children, and they put them to work in the mills, perhaps too early, and certainly kept them there too much of the time in former years, and the

legislature had to step in and protect the children against the parents by requiring that they should go to school a certain number of months or weeks in a year, or else they should not be allowed to work in the mills; and at the present time there is a very severe law in this state applicable to children — I think some under twelve and some under sixteen. I do not remember the terms of it, but the child has to have a certificate of the authorities in control of the schools that he has been to school the time required by the statute before the mill manager is able to employ him. I think the mill manager is subject to a very considerable penalty for noncompliance with that law.

In this city in our mills, and as far as I know in the rest of the mills, we have been very particular to observe the statute. I do not know how it is outside of the city. I suppose that it may depend a good deal upon public sentiment. If public sentiment supports the law, it will be enforced; if it does not, it will not be. I think public sentiment does support it here to an extent, although I think it extends a little too far in preventing children up to sixteen working in mills more than a given time. . . . The city authorities here have an officer who makes it his business to go through the mills to see whether the law is complied with or not.

Now, I think that when it is provided that a child shall go to school as long as it is profitable for a workman's child (who has got to be a workingman himself) to go to school, the limit has been reached at which labor in the mills should be forbidden. There is such a thing as too much education for working people sometimes. I do not mean to say by that that I discourage education to any person on earth, or that I think that with good sense any amount of education can hurt anyone, but I have seen cases where young people were spoiled for labor by being educated to a little too much refinement.

Q. You have known something of farm

life and the necessity that a boy is put under of learning to farm while he is still a boy?

A. Yes.

Q. Now, with reference to the acquirement of the necessary skill to earn a living, without which an education would amount to little — a man having enough knowledge to starve upon has not much advantage — do you think that the child should be withheld from the educating idea in the industrial line to so large an extent as the law now requires?

A. I do not.

Q. Is there danger of too much abstention from that sort of practical education which enables a child when grown to earn his living?

A. I think so. I will state that in our machine shops we take apprentices to learn the trade of a machinist, which is one of the best trades that any man in this country can have. We agree that if they will agree to serve three years for pay which enables them to live, we will teach them the trade of a machinist; and it is a curious illustration of the effect of very advanced common schools that our foremen prefer for apprentices boys from the country, who have worked on farms and been to a district school a little while, to boys that have been educated in the city. They say that the city boys do not stick to their work as the others do. They are a little above the employment.

Q. Is this employment that you speak about in the mills in which children are engaged of a character to tax their muscular or physical frame more than it ought to during their growing period?

A. No, sir; I don't know of any such employment in the mills being put upon children. . . .

By Mr. Pugh:

Q. How do you compare your ability to sustain yourself in competition with foreign manufacturers of the same kind of goods?

A. As far as I have been able to judge, there are some few kinds of goods in which the great proportion of the value consists in the material, and a small portion of the value consists in the labor, that we could compete with the foreign manufacturers in. . . . Denims . . . are perhaps an illustration of that. They are very coarse goods, into which little labor, comparatively, enters; but when it comes to finer goods, such as our ginghams, which constitute one-half of our product, I do not think we could run our mills upon them without a protective tariff.

Q. How much benefit do you get from a protective tariff in the prices? What percent is added to the price of your fabrics in the American market on account of the tariff?

A. I suppose that all our profit is due to the tariff.

Q. All your profits are derived from the tariff?

A. Yes; on that class of goods. In other words, I think if there were no tariff, there would be but little trade on that class of goods where there was a large amount of labor. We could not sell them in competition with those which could be imported.

Q. Did you express any opinion as to the power to consume in this country being equal to the power of production, with all the inducements to invest in manufacturing industries?

A. I did express an opinion. It was this: that, at the present time, the cotton mills exceed in productive capacity the power to consume.

Q. But you think the increase in population will supply that inequality?

A. Yes, very soon, as I remember it now, according to Mr. Atkinson's statistics, which appear to be well-founded, it took an increase of several hundred thousand spindles a year to keep up with the increase of population, and we exceeded that limit a little the last year or two; but it will not take more than a year or so more to restore the equilibrium.

Q. Well, will there ever be a change in the conditions of labor and capital and of consumption and production in this country from what they are now?

A. I think there will. When all the cheap lands are taken up so that there is no employment, like that of farming, into which the overflow of labor can pour; but I suppose that time will be a long time removed. As long, however, as the abundance of cheap lands affords the means of livelihood and of profit to all those who choose to engage in cultivating them, as is the case now, so long labor will always be in demand in this country and will always bring a good price, I suppose.

Q. What is your judgment as to the ability of our manufacturing industries to live without the benefit of a protective tariff?

A. I do not believe that with the labor market as it is now, and as I suppose it will be until the lands are all consumed, the cotton manufacturing industries could, in general, compete with those abroad without protection. . . .

By the Chairman:

Q. Do you know, as matter of fact, of any manufacturer in this country whose profit is beyond a reasonable return upon the capital invested and used at the present time?

A. I do not.

Q. I mean any article whatever. I use the word "manufacturer" in the broadest sense — including every kind of manufacturer of which you have knowledge.

A. As far as I have knowledge, I do not. I must qualify my answer by saying that my knowledge is confined pretty exclusively on that subject to cotton manufacture.

Q. Take the woolen trade; what is your understanding of the general condition of business in that trade in the country? Is it making large profits or excessive profits?

A. I got the impression that they were rather suffering.

Q. And the iron trade?

A. I have the same impression about the iron trade. I have heard that their mills were stopped.

By Mr. Pugh:

Q. That has been the result under the operation of a high tariff?

A. Well, that is a *sequitur* which one must draw for himself. I suppose it will be true in this country as it is in every other country where there is capital to be invested, that when it is apparent that considerable profits are made in any industry people immediately put their money into that industry, and that has a tendency to reduce profits; but I do not think the fluctuations of any industry from one year to another afford any basis for a solution of the question of tariff, because when prices are down in any one year they are up another year.

You can probably never adjust the growth of machinery to the population, sometimes one may be ahead and sometimes another. This year we may have reason to plume ourselves on profits and next year to mourn because nobody is making any. And it seems to me that he who would really draw a conclusion upon which to base an opinion to be adopted for guidance in the regulation of tariffs must look back to the operations of a long series of years.

III.

Timothy D. Stow: Testimony of a Physician

By the Chairman:

Q. You are a physician?

A. Yes.

Q. You live at Fall River?

A. Yes.

Q. Won't you state how you happen to appear before the committee, what your object is in coming here, and at whose request you come; and then give us the benefit of any observations you choose to lay before us?

A. Mr. Robert Howard, of our city, called on me yesterday and desired me to appear here today before your committee to give whatever testimony I could relating particularly to the physical and mental and perhaps the moral condition of the operatives and laboring classes of Fall River. I have made no notes, and I hardly know what your plan is; but I would as soon answer questions as to make any detailed statement.

The Chairman: We want to find out how the working people of Fall River are living and doing. You can tell us that in the way in which one gentleman would talk to another, the one understanding the subject and the other not understanding it. Just tell us the condition of the operatives there, in your own way, bearing in mind that we would rather have it without premeditation than as a prepared statement.

The Witness: I have been in Fall River about eleven years, though I have been one year absent during that time. As a physician and surgeon, of course, I have been brought into contact with all classes of people there, particularly the laboring classes, the operatives of the city.

With regard to the effect of the present industrial system upon their physical and moral welfare, I should say it was of such a character as to need mending, to say the least. It needs some radical remedy. Our laboring population is made up very largely of foreigners, men, women, and children, who have either voluntarily come to Fall River or who have been induced to come there by the manufacturers.

As a class they are dwarfed physically. Of course there are exceptions to that; some notable ones. On looking over their condition and weighing it as carefully as I have been able to, I have come to the conclusion that the character and quality of the labor which they have been doing in times past, and most of them from childhood up, has been and is such as to bring this condition upon them slowly and steadily.

They are dwarfed, in my estimation, sir, as the majority of men and women who are brought up in factories must be dwarfed under the present industrial system; because by their long hours of indoor labor and their hard work they are cut off from the benefit of breathing fresh air and from the sights that surround a workman outside a mill. Being shut up all day long in the noise and in the high temperature of these mills they become physically weak.

Then, most of them are obliged to live from hand to mouth, or, at least, they do not have sufficient food to nourish them as they need to be nourished. Those things, together with the fact that they have to limit their clothing supply — this constant strain upon the operative — all tend to make him, on the one hand, uneasy and restless, or, on the other hand, to produce discouragement and recklessness. They make him careless in regard to his own condition. All those things combined tend to produce what we have in Fall River.

Now, first, as to the moral condition of the operatives of Fall River. I think so far as crime is concerned we have quite as little crime there as in any city of its size. We have a population rising on 50,000. There is a disposition at times, and under certain pressure, for some operatives to violate the law, to pilfer, or something of that kind, and I think it grows out of not what is called "pure cussedness" but a desire to relieve some physical want. For instance, a man wants a coat and has not the means of earning it, and he is out of employment, and being pinched with the cold, and with no prospect of getting employment, or of getting a coat by honest means, he steals one. Or perhaps he steals food on the same principle.

But so far as crime is concerned, we have comparatively little. But what I do say, and what has been on my mind ever since I came to Fall River, with reference to operatives there, is the peculiar impress they seem to bear, a sort of dejected, tired, worn-out, discouraged appearance, growing out of the bad influences of long hours of labor, the close confinement of the mills, the din of the machinery, their exclusion from social intercourse, except at night.

And I think we can look for a solution of the problem which the country at large is endeavoring to solve — that with reference to the intemperate habits of the laboring classes and the operatives — in those facts that I have mentioned.

I have questioned many thoughtful men and women in regard to that. I have said, "Why is it that at night, particularly, you frequent the dram shops? Why is it that by day you drink; that you store enough even for the day in your houses?" The answer is, "Well, doctor, I tell you the fact is this, there is a sense of fatigue over us which we do not know how to overcome, and which we must overcome for the time being if we are to have any social qualities of an evening, and we can't do it without taking something which will bridge over the time and make us equal to the emergency of the evening or the occasion." For instance, the operative being in the mill all day long comes out at night, and it is the only time he has, unless he uses Sunday, and he uses that largely in which to visit his friends, who are scattered here and there all over the city.

Families are, of course, scattered in that way. They are either brought over here by the manufacturers or come of their own accord. One person finds a place in one mill and another in another mill. They have no means of communication with each other except at night or on Sunday. Now, they say to themselves, "How can we fit ourselves for this social intercourse — what we deem a necessity?" The result is that a man steps into a lager-beer saloon, or often into a place where he gets stronger liquor, and he takes a glass of it, and in a few minutes he begins to feel the stimulating influence of the liquor, and it braces him up. But I have said, "How does this make you feel? You say you have been feeling fatigued in the evening and discouraged; that your fu-

ture does not look bright; how do you feel when you get the liquor?" "Why," he will say, "it covers that all up; we lose all thought of that, and for the time being we feel well." And so they go on from day to day, and from night to night.

Now, after all, I do not know of many drunkards in Fall River, but this is true; the operative spends his 5, 10, or 15, or 25 cents a night for liquor, and it is so much lost money to him, and yet he feels impelled to it because he does not know how otherwise to adapt himself to the circumstances of the evening. It does not seem to affect his constitution, and most of them keep up pretty well, but some succumb to it. Others who cannot succumb to the influences of lager beer often resort to stronger liquors, such as brandy, whisky, and so on, to stimulate them more, because they require more and more to keep up the effect. Those go down to the drunkard's grave.

I should say that the average man there who reaches that condition gets to be a pauper at thirty-five or forty. The women, particularly the English women, brew their own beer to some extent, but they buy largely of the stores and keep beer in their houses for the day. It is a common thing for these barkeepers to peddle around beer and ale, to leave from half a dozen to a dozen bottles of ale a week at a house. Almost every Saturday some families will put in from a dozen to two dozen bottles of ale.

Now, it is invariably the testimony of the more intelligent men and women in answer to the question, "Why do you persist in drinking?" "It makes us feel better; we are relieved of the ennui of life; we are relieved of mental depression for the time being, and after the evening's social engagements are over we get home and go to bed, and think nothing of it, and next day resume our day's work." And so it goes on from day to day. . . .

Q. Are there any means taken to give them amusements in the evenings by means of lectures or libraries, or anything of that kind?

A. Not very much. We have a city library and it is frequented very much by the operatives; for even if they do not read much they are a thinking class, and they are probing this matter to the bottom, and they are the ones that are finding fault with the system.

Q. I would like to know your idea about this: Many people say that the labor agitators are a set of men who are looking for their personal aggrandizement.

A. I do not believe that that is so, sir.

Q. What would you say about that — I mean the men who are agitating the labor question?

A. I do not know any agitator in Fall River who has anything at heart except the good of his fellowmen. I think the statements of those who stigmatize them as discreditable are entirely at variance with the truth and with the fact.

Q. You have some acquaintance with them, I take it?

A. Yes.

Q. What about their intellectual qualities?

A. Well, I do not know of more than half a dozen who may be called agitators in Fall River, and, indeed, I think that number may be reduced. The most prominent man there now among the laborers, that is, a man connected with the organization of laborers, is Mr. Howard. He is a man of intelligence, and has devoted much time and study to this labor question. He is of a very nervous temperament. So far as his ideas are concerned — his wish to benefit his fellows — they are all right; but he may have some ideas that are far in advance of his fellows.

By Mr. Pugh:

Q. I do not understand that the class of men that are condemned as agitators, mischief-makers, and organizers are actual workers but men on the "make" who appeal to the prejudices of their class for their own selfish uses in some outside matter. It is not the actual workers that agitate. I do not understand that that term covers the workers.

A. Well, that class may not do very much of that sort of work, but they think and aid the others. . . .

Q. If there were not other particulars as to the conditions you might raise the question of cure, having stated the cause?

A. Well, I do not know that I have stated the cause perfectly. I may be very radical in regard to these questions, and I try to get at the bottom of things. My opinion is that three or four of the main features of our political economy require to be materially changed before you can expect to benefit the masses.

In the first place, I think monopolies should be broken up, and that the monopolies of the many should be broken up or changed so that there could be no monopolization of it; and that the monopoly of transportation should be materially changed. Many other things would be necessary, but I think those features of our political economy —

The Chairman: [Interposing.] The land, money, and transportation?

The Witness: Yes — ought to be materially changed.

Q. In what respect?

A. I think that the land belonging to the government — land not sold — should be reserved for actual settlers, in quantities sufficient for their necessities, and no more.

Q. How large lots? You know that is the law now?

A. That would depend upon the quality of the land. I should think as a rule 50 to 100 acres would be sufficient for any person to have to cultivate.

Q. Would you apply the Homestead Law, but reduce the quantity so as to have some for the future?

A. I would reduce the quantity. Of course mechanics, men who follow mechanical pursuits, do not require as much land; but every man ought to be entitled to what would be necessary for a garden and a commodious building spot, so that his house should not be so near his neighbor's as to be exposed to fire or pestilence.

That the government should see to. I do not know why this government should neglect that provision for each and every person. I think the violation of God's laws in regard to these things has brought about all our troubles, and we have attempted to adjust them by weak and human laws, frequently taking away the liberties of the people and injuring them more than anything else.

The lands which have been so profusely given to railroad corporations, which they have not earned, and which it can be shown they have not earned, and have forfeited, should be restored to the people, and my impression is that as population advances it will be necessary to fix it so that here or in New York, or anywhere in Northern states where land is high the large estates should be broken up on the death of the occupant. It is difficult for a man to go from Fall River and get cheap land anywhere this side of the Rocky Mountains, and when he has got his family there he has not got much to get along with. This idea of parental government need not be brought up. We are all here to help one another in this world, and this should be seen to, or else it is government's failure.

Q. You were going to say more about the land?

A. Nothing in particular, only about the quality of the land. Wherever in the location of land an individual strikes a valuable mine, I think there should be in the contract between him and the government a provision with reference to the sale of the land, whether he buys it or whether it is a gift to him, that the government should reserve the power and the right to hold that mining section for the benefit of the whole

people, and not allow it to pass into the hands of any individual or clique.

In regard to the matter of transportation, in order to enable the population of our great cities — these great surging masses who are crowding each other every day in order to fill their stomachs — to be relieved from the pressure, the law should be so fixed that persons wanting to go out and get upon the land so subdivided should have access to that land instead of spending all they have laid by for a few months to get there. . . .

Q. You think that labor should be well taken care of before capital gets any profit?

A. I think that all that capital gets, it gets from labor, and it is for the interest, even of capitalists, that they should first, above all things, see that the laboring classes of the country are well paid, well clothed, well housed, and made comfortable in their work; that they should have access to public libraries and to parks and public improvements of every kind. I think this is necessary for the improvement of the individual, physically, morally, and mentally.

Q. And that this, for the safety of capital itself, should be first secured?

A. Yes, I do not see how you can maintain capital in this country, as it is now getting into the hands of a few men, unless you do that thing. The tendency seems to be to the aggregation of wealth by these processes. The most wealthy men seek to rob or fleece those below them by watering stock, etc.

Q. There is a great deal of that; but, after all, is not the great mass of capital in this country dedicated to wise, conservative industrial production?

A. I presume it is; I think it is.

Q. Is there any danger that we may confound the abuses attending the exception and identify those abuses with the great mass of capital which may be more conservatively and usefully employed?

A. Well, I should have to weigh that perhaps some little time to give you a very definite answer.

The Chairman: Well, I shall not ask you to go into it.

The Witness: It seems to me, however, that the tendency of the times is to a concentration of wealth, whether that wealth consists of money or of property.

Q. Yes, but the concentration of wealth for wise purposes and conservative uses is one thing, and the concentration of wealth for speculative uses is another. Do you not think that it may be that most of the abuses that attend its use are when it is dedicated to insane, and it may be almost malicious, speculation? You speak of the large fishes devouring those of a smaller size, and those again devouring fishes of a size still smaller. Society seems inclined to consume itself?

A. Yes, I think that is the tendency, and this tendency on the part of the few who have made power by hook or by crook to do all this, unless checked by some plan which shall distribute the products of labor to the masses, will, it seems to me, eventually break up the government.

118.

JOSEPH P. BRADLEY AND JOHN M. HARLAN: Civil Rights Cases

The Civil Rights Act of March 1875 had sought to guarantee equality of access to public accommodations. Several suits were brought alleging violation of the Act. In a Supreme Court decision handed down October 15, 1883, the Act of 1875 was declared unconstitutional, on the grounds that it was not authorized under the Thirteenth or Fourteenth Amendments. The decision meant essentially that individuals were protected from federal and state infringement of their civil rights, but were not protected from such infringement by other individuals. The Court left open the question whether Congress might legislate under the commerce clause in favor of equal accommodations on public conveyances operating across state lines. Reprinted here are portions of the Court's opinion, by Justice Joseph P. Bradley, and of the dissent, by Justice John M. Harlan. Harlan's dissent, it will be noted, makes use of much of the reasoning that was used to promote the Civil Rights Act of 1965, which also contained a public accommodations section.

Source: 109 U.S. 3.

Mr. Justice Bradley: It is obvious that the primary and important question in all the cases is the constitutionality of the law; for if the law is unconstitutional none of the prosecutions can stand. . . . Has Congress constitutional power to make such a law? Of course, no one will contend that the power to pass it was contained in the Constitution before the adoption of the last three amendments. The power is sought, first, in the Fourteenth Amendment, and the views and arguments of distinguished senators, advanced while the law was under consideration, claiming authority to pass it

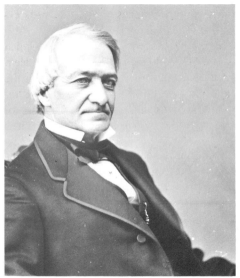

Joseph Bradley, associate justice of the Supreme Court

by virtue of that amendment, are the principal arguments adduced in favor of the power.

We have carefully considered those arguments, as was due to the eminent ability of those who put them forward, and have felt, in all its force, the weight of authority which always invests a law that Congress deems itself competent to pass. But the responsibility of an independent judgment is now thrown upon this Court; and we are bound to exercise it according to the best lights we have.

The 1st Section of the Fourteenth Amendment (which is the one relied on), after declaring who shall be citizens of the United States and of the several states, is prohibitory in its character and prohibitory upon the states. It declares that:

> No state shall make or enforce any law which shall abridge the privileges or immunities of citizens of the United States; nor shall any state deprive any person of life, liberty, or property without due process of law; nor deny to any person within its jurisdiction the equal protection of the laws.

It is state action of a particular character that is prohibited. Individual invasion of individual rights is not the subject matter of the amendment. It has a deeper and broader scope. It nullifies and makes void all state legislation and state action of every kind which impairs the privileges and immunities of citizens of the United States, or which injures them in life, liberty, or property without due process of law, or which denies to any of them the equal protection of the laws. It not only does this, but, in order that the national will, thus declared, may not be a mere *brutum fulmen*, the last section of the amendment invests Congress with power to enforce it by appropriate legislation. To enforce what? To enforce the prohibition. To adopt appropriate legislation for correcting the effects of such prohibited state laws and state acts, and thus to render them effectually null, void, and innocuous.

This is the legislative power conferred upon Congress, and this is the whole of it. It does not invest Congress with power to legislate upon subjects which are within the domain of state legislation; but to provide modes of relief against state legislation or state action of the kind referred to. It does not authorize Congress to create a code of municipal law for the regulation of private rights; but to provide modes of redress against the operation of state laws, and the action of State officers, executive or judicial, when these are subversive of the fundamental rights specified in the amendment. Positive rights and privileges are undoubtedly secured by the Fourteenth Amendment; but they are secured by way of prohibition against state laws and state proceedings affecting those rights and privileges, and by power given to Congress to legislate for the purpose of carrying such prohibition into effect; and such legislation must necessarily be predicated upon such supposed state laws or state proceedings, and be directed to the correction of their operation and effect. . . .

In this connection it is proper to state

that civil rights, such as are guaranteed by the Constitution against state aggression, cannot be impaired by the wrongful acts of individuals, unsupported by state authority in the shape of laws, customs, or judicial or executive proceedings. The wrongful act of an individual, unsupported by any such authority, is simply a private wrong, or a crime of that individual; an invasion of the rights of the injured party, it is true, whether they affect his person, his property, or his reputation; but if not sanctioned in some way by the state, or not done under state authority, his rights remain in full force and may presumably be vindicated by resort to the laws of the state for redress.

An individual cannot deprive a man of his right to vote, to hold property, to buy and sell, to sue in the courts, or to be a witness or a juror; he may, by force or fraud, interfere with the enjoyment of the right in a particular case; he may commit an assault against the person, or commit murder, or use ruffian violence at the polls, or slander the good name of a fellow citizen; but, unless protected in these wrongful acts by some shield of state law or state authority, he cannot destroy or injure the right; he will only render himself amenable to satisfaction or punishment; and amenable therefor to the laws of the state where the wrongful acts are committed.

Hence, in all those cases where the Constitution seeks to protect the rights of the citizen against discriminative and unjust laws of the state by prohibiting such laws, it is not individual offenses, but abrogation and denial of rights which it denounces and for which it clothes the Congress with power to provide a remedy. This abrogation and denial of rights, for which the states alone were or could be responsible, was the great seminal and fundamental wrong which was intended to be remedied. And the remedy to be provided must necessarily be predicated upon that wrong. It must assume that in the cases provided for, the evil or wrong actually committed rests upon some state law or state authority for its excuse and perpetration. . . .

If the principles of interpretation which we have laid down are correct, as we deem them to be (and they are in accord with the principles laid down in the cases before referred to, as well as in the recent case of *United States* v. *Harris*, 106 U.S. 629), it is clear that the law in question cannot be sustained by any grant of legislative power made to Congress by the Fourteenth Amendment. That amendment prohibits the states from denying to any person the equal protection of the laws, and declares that Congress shall have power to enforce, by appropriate legislation, the provisions of the amendment. The law in question, without any reference to adverse state legislation on the subject, declares that all persons shall be entitled to equal accommodations and privileges of inns, public conveyances, and places of public amusement, and imposes a penalty upon any individual who shall deny to any citizen such equal accommodations and privileges.

This is not corrective legislation; it is primary and direct; it takes immediate and absolute possession of the subject of the right of admission to inns, public conveyances, and places of amusement. It supersedes and displaces state legislation on the same subject, or only allows it permissive force. It ignores such legislation and assumes that the matter is one that belongs to the domain of national regulation. Whether it would not have been a more effective protection of the rights of citizens to have clothed Congress with plenary power over the whole subject is not now the question. What we have to decide is whether such plenary power has been conferred upon Congress by the Fourteenth Amendment; and, in our judgment, it has not. . . .

We must not forget that the province and scope of the Thirteenth and Fourteenth amendments are different; the former simply abolished slavery; the latter prohibited the states from abridging the privileges or immunities of citizens of the United States; from depriving them of life, liberty, or property without due process of law; and from denying to any the equal protection of the laws. The amendments are different, and the powers of Congress under them are different. What Congress has power to do under one, it may not have power to do under the other. Under the Thirteenth Amendment, it has only to do with slavery and its incidents. Under the Fourteenth Amendment, it has power to counteract and render nugatory all state laws and proceedings which have the effect to abridge any of the privileges or immunities of citizens of the United States, or to deprive them of life, liberty, or property without due process of law, or to deny to any of them the equal protection of the laws. Under the Thirteenth Amendment, the legislation, so far as necessary or proper to eradicate all forms and incidents of slavery and involuntary servitude, may be direct and primary, operating upon the acts of individuals, whether sanctioned by state legislation or not; under the Fourteenth, as we have already shown, it must necessarily be, and can only be, corrective in its character, addressed to counteract and afford relief against state regulations or proceedings.

The only question under the present head, therefore, is whether the refusal to any persons of the accommodations of an inn, or a public conveyance, or a place of public amusement, by an individual, and without any sanction or support from any state law or regulation, does inflict upon such persons any manner of servitude or form of slavery, as those terms are understood in this country? Many wrongs may be obnoxious to the prohibitions of the Fourteenth Amendment which are not, in any just sense, incidents or elements of slavery. Such, for example, would be the taking of private property without due process of law; or allowing persons who have committed certain crimes (horse stealing, for example) to be seized and hung by the *posse comitatus* without regular trial; or denying to any person, or class of persons, the right to pursue any peaceful avocations allowed to others.

What is called class legislation would belong to this category and would be obnoxious to the prohibitions of the Fourteenth Amendment but would not necessarily be so to the Thirteenth, when not involving the idea of any subjection of one man to another. The Thirteenth Amendment has respect, not to distinctions of race, or class, or color but to slavery. The Fourteenth Amendment extends its protection to races and classes, and prohibits any state legislation which has the effect of denying to any race or class, or to any individual, the equal protection of the laws.

Now, conceding, for the sake of the argument, that the admission to an inn, a public conveyance, or a place of public amusement, on equal terms with all other citizens, is the right of every man and all classes of men, is it any more than one of those rights which the states by the Fourteenth Amendment are forbidden to deny to any person? And is the Constitution violated until the denial of the right has some state sanction or authority? Can the act of a mere individual, the owner of the inn, the public conveyance, or place of amusement, refusing the accommodation be justly regarded as imposing any badge of slavery or servitude upon the applicant, or only as inflicting an ordinary civil injury, properly cognizable by the laws of the state and presumably subject to redress by those laws until the contrary appears?

After giving to these questions all the consideration which their importance demands, we are forced to the conclusion that such an act of refusal has nothing to do with slavery or involuntary servitude, and that if it is violative of any right of the party, his redress is to be sought under the laws of the state; or if those laws are adverse to his rights and do not protect him, his remedy will be found in the corrective legislation which Congress has adopted, or may adopt, for counteracting the effect of state laws or state action prohibited by the Fourteenth Amendment. It would be running the slavery argument into the ground to make it apply to every act of discrimination which a person may see fit to make as to the guests he will entertain, or as to the people he will take into his coach or cab or car, or admit to his concert or theater, or deal with in other matters of intercourse or business.

Innkeepers and public carriers, by the laws of all the states, so far as we are aware, are bound, to the extent of their facilities, to furnish proper accommodation to all unobjectionable persons who in good faith apply for them. If the laws themselves make any unjust discrimination, amenable to the prohibitions of the Fourteenth Amendment, Congress has full power to afford a remedy under that amendment and in accordance with it.

When a man has emerged from slavery and, by the aid of beneficent legislation, has shaken off the inseparable concomitants of that state, there must be some stage in the progress of his elevation when he takes the rank of a mere citizen and ceases to be the special favorite of the laws, and when his rights as a citizen, or a man, are to be protected in the ordinary modes by which other men's rights are protected. There were thousands of free colored people in this country before the abolition of slavery, enjoying all the essential rights of life, liberty, and property the same as white citizens; yet no one, at that time, thought that it was any invasion of his personal status as a freeman because he was not admitted to all the privileges enjoyed by white citizens, or because he was subjected to discriminations in the enjoyment of accommodations in inns, public conveyances, and places of amusement. Mere discriminations on account of race or color were not regarded as badges of slavery. If, since that time, the enjoyment of equal rights in all these respects has be-

come established by constitutional enactment, it is not by force of the Thirteenth Amendment (which merely abolishes slavery) but by force of the Thirteenth and Fifteenth amendments.

On the whole, we are of opinion that no countenance of authority for the passage of the law in question can be found in either the Thirteenth or Fourteenth Amendment of the Constitution; and no other ground of authority for its passage being suggested, it must necessarily be declared void, at least so far as its operation in the several states is concerned.

Mr. Justice Harlan: The Thirteenth Amendment, it is conceded, did something more than to prohibit slavery as an *institution*, resting upon distinctions of race and upheld by positive law. My brethren admit that it established and decreed universal *civil freedom* throughout the United States. But did the freedom thus established involve nothing more than exemption from actual slavery? Was nothing more intended than to forbid one man from owning another as property? Was it the purpose of the nation simply to destroy the institution and then remit the race, theretofore held in bondage, to the several states for such protection, in their civil rights, necessarily growing out of freedom as those states, in their discretion, might choose to provide? Were the states against whose protest the institution was destroyed to be left free, so far as national interference was concerned, to make or allow discriminations against that race, as such, in the enjoyment of those fundamental rights which by universal concession inhere in a state of freedom? . . .

That there are burdens and disabilities which constitute badges of slavery and servitude, and that the power to enforce by appropriate legislation the Thirteenth Amendment may be exerted by legislation of a direct and primary character for the eradication, not simply of the institution but of its badges and incidents, are propositions

Justice John Marshall Harlan

which ought to be deemed indisputable. They lie at the foundation of the Civil Rights Act of 1866. Whether that act was authorized by the Thirteenth Amendment alone, without the support which it subsequently received from the Fourteenth Amendment, after the adoption of which it was reenacted with some additions, my brethren do not consider it necessary to inquire. But I submit, with all respect to them, that its constitutionality is conclusively shown by their opinion. . . .

I am of the opinion that such discrimination practised by corporations and individuals in the exercise of their public or quasi-public functions is a badge of servitude the imposition of which Congress may prevent under its power, by appropriate legislation, to enforce the Thirteenth Amendment and consequently, without reference to its enlarged power under the Fourteenth Amendment, the act of March 1, 1875, is not, in my judgment, repugnant to the Constitution. . . .

In every material sense applicable to the practical enforcement of the Fourteenth Amendment, railroad corporations, keepers of inns, and managers of places of public amusement are agents or instrumentalities of the state because they are charged with duties to the public, and are amenable, in respect of their duties and functions, to governmental regulation. It seems to me that, within the principle settled in *Ex parte Virginia,* a denial by these instrumentalities of the state to the citizen because of his race, of that equality of civil rights secured to him by law, is a denial by the state within the meaning of the Fourteenth Amendment. If it be not, then that race is left, in respect of the civil rights in question, practically at the mercy of corporations and individuals wielding power under the states. . . .

I agree that if one citizen chooses not to hold social intercourse with another, he is not and cannot be made amenable to the law for his conduct in that regard; for even upon grounds of race, no legal right of a citizen is violated by the refusal of others to maintain merely social relations with him. What I affirm is that no state, nor the officers of any state, nor any corporation or individual wielding power under state authority for the public benefit or the public convenience can, consistently either with the freedom established by the fundamental law or with that equality of civil rights which now belongs to every citizen, discriminate against freemen or citizens in those rights because of their race or because they once labored under the disabilities of slavery imposed upon them as a race. The rights which Congress, by the act of 1875, endeavored to secure and protect are legal, not social, rights. The right, for instance, of a colored citizen to use the accommodations of a public highway upon the same terms as are permitted to white citizens is no more a social right than his right, under the law, to use the public streets of a city or a town, or a turnpike road, or a public market, or a post office, or his right to sit in a public building with others, of whatever race, for the purpose of hearing the political questions of the day discussed.

Scarcely a day passes without our seeing in this courtroom citizens of the white and black races sitting side by side, watching the progress of our business. It would never occur to any one that the presence of a colored citizen in a courthouse or courtroom was an invasion of the social rights of white persons who may frequent such places. And yet, such a suggestion would be quite as sound in law — I say it with all respect — as is the suggestion that the claim of a colored citizen to use, upon the same terms as is permitted to white citizens, the accommodations of public highways, or public inns, or places of public amusement, established under the license of the law, is an invasion of the social rights of the white race. . . .

My brethren say that when a man has emerged from slavery and, by the aid of beneficent legislation, has shaken off the inseparable concomitants of that state, there must be some stage in the progress of his elevation when he takes the rank of a mere citizen and ceases to be the special favorite of the laws, and when his rights as a citizen, or a man, are to be protected in the ordinary modes by which other men's rights are protected. It is, I submit, scarcely just to say that the colored race has been the special favorite of the laws. The statute of 1875, now adjudged to be unconstitutional, is for the benefit of citizens of every race and color. What the nation, through Congress, has sought to accomplish in reference to that race is — what had already been done in every state of the Union for the white race — to secure and protect rights belonging to them as freemen and citizens; nothing more. It was not deemed enough "to help the feeble up, but to support him after." The one underlying purpose of congressional legislation has been to enable the black race to take the rank of mere citizens. The

difficulty has been to compel a recognition of the legal right of the black race to take the rank of citizens, and to secure the enjoyment of privileges belonging, under the law, to them as a component part of the people for whose welfare and happiness government is ordained.

At every step in this direction, the nation has been confronted with class tyranny, which, a contemporary English historian says, is, of all tyrannies, the most intolerable, "for it is ubiquitous in its operation and weighs, perhaps, most heavily on those whose obscurity or distance would withdraw them from the notice of a single despot." Today, it is the colored race which is denied, by corporations and individuals wielding public authority, rights fundamental in their freedom and citizenship. At some future time it may be that some other race will fall under the ban of race discrimination. If the constitutional amendments be enforced according to the intent with which, as I conceive, they were adopted, there cannot be, in this republic, any class of human beings in practical subjection to another class, with power in the latter to dole out to the former just such privileges as they may choose to grant.

The supreme law of the land has decreed that no authority shall be exercised in this country upon the basis of discrimination, in respect of civil rights, against freemen and citizens because of their race, color, or previous condition of servitude. To that decree — for the due enforcement of which, by appropriate legislation, Congress has been invested with express power — everyone must bow, whatever may have been, or whatever now are, his individual views as to the wisdom or policy, either of the recent changes in the fundamental law or of the legislation which has been enacted to give them effect.

For the reasons stated I feel constrained to withhold my assent to the opinion of the Court.

119.

FREDERICK DOUGLASS: The Color Line in America

After 1887, following the withdrawal of Union troops from South Carolina, Louisiana, and Florida, Reconstruction officially ended. In theory African Americans were free, but in practice, their status was far from equal. The intent of the Fourteenth and Fifteenth Amendments with regard to African Americans was being whittled away by state legislation in the South and Supreme Court decisions. African American participation in all phases of American life was qualified by prejudice; most avenues of social and economic improvement remained closed. Frederick Douglass, the best-known and most influential African American spokesman of his time, considered these facts and offered a solution in the following speech of September 24, 1883.

Source: *Three Addresses on the Relations Subsisting Between the White and Colored People of the United States,* Washington, 1886, pp. 3-23.

IT IS OUR LOT to live among a people whose laws, traditions, and prejudices have been against us for centuries, and from these they are not yet free. To assume that they are free from these evils simply because they have changed their laws is to assume what is utterly unreasonable and contrary to facts. Large bodies move slowly. Individuals may be converted on the instant and change their whole course of life. Nations never. Time and events are required for the conversion of nations. Not even the character of a great political organization can be changed by a new platform. It will be the same old snake though in a new skin.

Though we have had war, reconstruction, and abolition as a nation, we still linger in the shadow and blight of an extinct institution. Though the colored man is no longer subject to be bought and sold, he is still surrounded by an adverse sentiment which fetters all his movements. In his downward course he meets with no resistance, but his course upward is resented and resisted at every step of his progress. If he comes in ignorance, rags, and wretchedness, he conforms to the popular belief of his character, and in that character he is welcome. But if he shall come as a gentleman, a scholar, and a statesman, he is hailed as a contradiction to the national faith concerning his race, and his coming is resented as impudence. In the one case he may provoke contempt and derision, but in the other he is an affront to pride and provokes malice. Let him do what he will, there is at present, therefore, no escape for him. The color line meets him everywhere, and in a measure shuts him out from all respectable and profitable trades and callings.

In spite of all your religion and laws, he is a rejected man. He is rejected by trade unions of every trade, and refused work while he lives and burial when he dies; and yet he is asked to forget his color and forget that which everybody else remembers. If he offers himself to a builder as a mechanic, to a client as a lawyer, to a patient as a physician, to a college as a professor, to a firm as a clerk, to a government department as an agent or an officer, he is sternly met on the color line, and his claim to consideration in some way is disputed on the ground of color.

Not even our churches, whose members profess to follow the despised Nazarene, whose home, when on earth, was among the lowly and despised, have yet conquered this feeling of color madness, and what is true of our churches is also true of our courts of law. Neither is free from this all-pervading atmosphere of color hate. The one describes the Deity as impartial, no respecter of persons, and the other the Goddess of Justice as blindfolded, with sword by her side and scales in her hand, held evenly between high and low, rich and poor, white and black; but both are the images of American imagination rather than American practices.

Taking advantage of the general disposition in this country to impute crime to color, white men *color* their faces to commit crime and wash off the hated color to escape punishment. In many places where the commission of crime is alleged against one of our color, the ordinary processes of the law are set aside as too slow for the impetuous justice of the infuriated populace. They take the law into their own bloody hands and proceed to whip, stab, shoot, hang, or burn the alleged culprit, without the intervention of courts, counsel, judges, juries, or witnesses. In such cases it is not the business of the accusers to prove guilt, but it is for the accused to prove his innocence, a thing hard for any man to do, even in a court of law, and utterly impossible for him to do in these infernal lynch courts.

A man accused, surprised, frightened, and captured by a motley crowd, dragged with a rope around his neck in midnight-darkness to the nearest tree, and told in the coarsest terms of profanity to prepare for death, would be more than human if he did not, in his terror-stricken appearance, more confirm suspicion of guilt than the contrary. Worse still, in the presence of such hell-black outrages, the pulpit is usually dumb, and the press in the neighborhood is silent or openly takes sides with the mob. There are occasional cases in which white men are lynched, but one sparrow does not make a summer. Everyone knows that what is called lynch law is peculiarly the law for colored people and for nobody else.

If there were no other grievance than this horrible and barbarous lynch-law custom, we should be justified in assembling, as we have now done, to expose and denounce it. But this is not all. Even now, after twenty years of so-called emancipation, we are subject to lawless raids of midnight riders, who, with blackened faces, invade our homes and perpetrate the foulest of crimes upon us and our families. This condition of things is too flagrant and notorious to require specifications or proof. Thus in all the relations of life and death we are met by the color line. We cannot ignore it if we would, and ought not if we could. It hunts us at midnight, it denies us accommodation in hotels and justice in the courts; excludes our children from schools, refuses our sons the chance to learn trades, and compels us to pursue only such labor as will bring the least reward.

While we recognize the color line as a hurtful force, a mountain barrier to our progress, wounding our bleeding feet with its flinty rocks at every step, we do not despair. We are a hopeful people. This convention is a proof of our faith in you, in reason, in truth, and justice; our belief that prejudice, with all its malign accompaniments, may yet be removed by peaceful means; that, assisted by time and events and the growing enlightenment of both races, the color line will ultimately become harmless. When this shall come it will then only be used, as it should be, to distinguish one variety of the human family from another. It will cease to have any civil, political, or moral significance, and colored conventions will then be dispensed with as anachronisms, wholly out of place — but not till then.

Do not marvel that we are not discouraged. The faith within us has a rational basis and is confirmed by facts. When we consider how deep-seated this feeling against us is; the long centuries it has been forming; the forces of avarice which have been marshaled to sustain it; how the language and literature of the country have been pervaded with it; how the church, the press, the playhouse, and other influences of the country have been arrayed in its support, the progress toward its extinction must be considered vast and wonderful.

If liberty, with us, is yet but a name, our citizenship is but a sham, and our suffrage thus far only a cruel mockery, we may yet congratulate ourselves upon the fact that the laws and institutions of the country are sound, just, and liberal. There is hope for a people when their laws are righteous, whether for the moment they conform to their requirements or not. But until this nation shall make its practice accord with its Constitution and its righteous laws, it will not do to reproach the colored people of this country with keeping up the color line; for that people would prove themselves scarcely worthy of even theoretical freedom, to say nothing of practical freedom, if they settled down in silent, servile, and cowardly submission to their wrongs from fear of making their color visible.

They are bound by every element of manhood to hold conventions in their own name and on their own behalf, to keep their grievances before the people and make every organized protest against the wrongs inflicted upon them within their power. They should scorn the counsels of cowards and hang their banner on the outer wall. Who would be free, themselves must strike the blow. We do not believe, as we are often told, that the Negro is the ugly child of the national family, and the more he is kept out of sight the better it will be for him. You know that liberty given is never so precious as liberty sought for and fought for. The man outraged is the man to make the outcry. Depend upon it, men will not care much for a people who do not care for themselves.

Our meeting here was opposed by some of our members because it would disturb the peace of the Republican Party. The suggestion came from coward lips and misapprehended the character of that party. If the Republican Party cannot stand a demand for justice and fair play, it ought to go down. We were men before that party was born, and our manhood is more sacred than any party can be. Parties were made for men, not men for parties.

If the 6 million colored people of this country, armed with the Constitution of the United States, with a million votes of their own to lean upon and millions of white men at their back, whose hearts are responsive to the claims of humanity, have not sufficient spirit and wisdom to organize and combine to defend themselves from outrage, discrimination, and oppression, it will be idle for them to expect that the Republican Party or any other political party will organize and combine for them or care what becomes of them. Men may combine to prevent cruelty to animals, for they are dumb and cannot speak for themselves; but we are men and must speak for ourselves, or we shall not be spoken for at all. We have conventions in America for Ireland, but we should have none if Ireland did not speak for herself. It is because she makes a noise and keeps her cause before the people that other people go to her help. It was the sword of Washington and of Lafayette that gave us independence.

In conclusion upon this color objection, we have to say that we meet here in open daylight. There is nothing sinister about us. The eyes of the nation are upon us. Ten thousand newspapers may tell if they choose of whatever is said and done here. They may commend our wisdom or condemn our folly, precisely as we shall be wise or foolish. We put ourselves before them as honest men and ask their judgment upon our work.

120.

A. J. McWhirter: An Appeal to European Immigrants to Come to the South

The South made special efforts after the Civil War to attract immigrants as craftsmen and laborers. Although some of the larger cities in the South had sizable immigrant populations, that part of the country had little to attract a newcomer who wished to start a small farm or ply a trade, compared to the industrial centers of the North and the great free lands of the West. State bureaus of immigration were established in the Carolinas, Florida, Virginia, Texas, Alabama, Georgia, and Louisiana soon after the Civil War. The Southern Immigration Association attempted to coordinate the efforts of these state agencies, as well as those of private groups. In the following address, delivered at Vicksburg, Mississippi, November 21, 1883, the president of the Southern Immigration Association encouraged all Southerners to cooperate in drawing immigrants to the South.

Source: *Proceedings of the First Annual Session of the Southern Immigration Association of America*, Nashville, 1884, pp. 341-348.

CIVILIZATION IS A GREAT EQUALIZER, whether or not the philosophies of men admit it, the conglomerate elements of the living world arrange themselves like undissolved fluids in the order of their specified gravities.

In no phase of civilization is its equalizing tendency more signally displayed than in the distribution and fixation of the population of the world.

The influences which determine the development of a country through the influx of people are manifold and varied. Time was when the shores of our own beloved country, unknown as it then was in all its boundless wealth and illimitable resources, offered an asylum and a refuge in its luxuriant wilds to those who sought only safety from persecution and "freedom to worship God." And when political oppression succeeded religious intolerance in the march of ages, the tide of immigration to the land of the free and the home of the brave received a new and grander impulse. Later on the sovereigns of western Europe came to regard America as Russia did Siberia — the cesspool for their criminals and the dumping ground for their rebellious and banished subjects.

But when the wonderful possibilities of our country, under a system of government unequaled in its encouragement of individual enterprise and unsurpassed in its support of its individual interests, rose up before the world like Aladdin's magic palace before Persia's astonished morn, new impulses were brought into play and new influences lured the crowded population of Europe and of Asia to the soil of America, where there was bread enough and to spare for men of honest toil, and boundless wealth for those whose capital and energy could find too little room in the overtaxed resources of the Old World.

Today, when religious tolerance is the order of all civilized government, when political oppression is largely tempered by governments of the world, it is clear that the great stimulus to emigration is now the search for wealth and independence in the resources of an undeveloped land. And it is this which today commands our serious attention, as it is soon to become the most important factor in the great problem of American civilization.

The Southern Immigration Association, which was organized by the Commissioners of the Southern States, in convention assembled, at Louisville, Ky., on the 11th of October last, and of which they did me the honor of electing me president, comprehends in part the work of devising the ways and means of determining immigrants and capital to our sparsely populated section.

The states embraced in our Association are, viz.: the two Virginias, the two Carolinas, Georgia, Florida, Alabama, Mississippi, Louisiana, Texas, Arkansas, Missouri, Kentucky, and Tennessee — fourteen states representing an area of 887,480 square miles and a population of only 17,425,575 — a population something less than one-half of Austria and Hungary, that enjoy an area of only 240,834 square miles, or 25,000 square miles in round numbers less than the single state of Texas; or only a little larger than one-half the population of Great Britain and Ireland, that possess an area of 121,607 square miles, which is within a fraction of the combined area of two of our states, viz.; North Carolina and Missouri.

In a word, the area embraced in the fourteen states comprehended in the system of this Association is greater than the combined area of Austria, Hungary, France, Germany, Great Britain, Ireland, Belgium, Denmark, Netherlands or Holland, Portugal, and Switzerland, which sustain a population, as per census reports of 1870, of 163,869,055, or 186 to the square mile, as compared to ours, which is something less than 20 to the square mile.

To this broad, to this grand field of ac-tion, we are here today, not alone to procure your endorsement but to invite your cooperation. We invoke the aid of every intelligent planter in our Southland to this glorious work, which has already been deferred too long. We shall, at an early day, make our appeal to those great commercial arteries of the Southern states, the railroads, and also to the steamship lines, for their endorsement and cooperation.

Heretofore the shrewd capitalists of the North and East have taken time by the forelock, and by their well-ordered systems they have turned the tide of immigration into their centers of manufacture and other industrial fields, populating their cities and their forests and their plains, and giving them a balance of power in the sway of government and the control of wealth never otherwise to be obtained. The old aristocratic tendencies of the South, while they developed a race of noblemen, have stood very much in the path of industrial progress.

Social culture has, in the South, crystallized about it all those elements which tend to materialize a country and develop its wealth. Our "peculiar institution," as it has been called, had developed in us a carelessness or apathy toward the development of other resources then apparently so little needed to fill out the complement of southern political economy. But the cataclysm of civil war, disrupting our inherent customs, overthrowing our cherished institutions, and forever destroying the policy of our people, if I may so term it, has brought us face to face with the grand necessity for the utilization of our undeveloped resources if we expect to keep pace with the march of civilization and hold our place as factors in its mighty problem.

Throughout the Old World, the idea prevails even among the educated that south of Mason and Dixon's Line there is naught but cotton-crested fields belted by dismal swamps and choked with malaria — a land that denies ingress to all but the hot-blooded Southerner and the swarthy African. Whether these ideas have been disseminated with purpose or not, it is for us to demonstrate their fallacy and make known to the world the inexhaustible treasures of our soil and the perfect congeniality of our clime with any nation, or kindred, or people, or tongue within the limits of the civilized world.

The tendency of emigration to follow isothermal lines has done much to determine the settlement of Scandinavians and other thrifty people of northern Europe into the colder regions of America, while those of the South, who emigrate in fewer numbers, have been retained in the Northern and in the Eastern states by the extraordinary facilities for earning a livelihood offered by those states to immigrants of every class.

What immigrant from the Old World thinks of reaching any point of destination except through Castle Garden? And with what avidity they are seized upon by those who would utilize their labor and fill their own coffers with the result of their thrift and industrial skill? It is the purpose of our Association to devise those measures which will place us on an equal footing with the North and the East in the interest of American immigration. Our ports of entry, New Orleans, Norfolk, etc., are to be made points of destiny for the emigrant and the wonderful resources of our own Southland are to be brought out in prominent contrast with the already crowded centers of the North and East and the less genial clime and productive soil of those sections which hitherto have laid the largest claim upon foreign immigration.

Let us look into this matter a little more closely. What are the occupations of the bourgeois, burgher, or peasantry of Europe? The laboring classes of Ireland, from which our country has ever drawn large drafts of population, seem born to the pick, the shovel, and the spade. They are accustomed to the bog and the fen; and who can imagine a wider field for their employ than in the reclamation of our swampy regions and lowlands along our Southern river courses? This is a question which is now greatly agitating the powers that be, and armies of laborers will be needed for this work — enough to place a spade in the hands of every laboring Irishman that seeks American soil as a refuge from English tyranny and Irish penury.

The German emigrants, under better advantages of social and intellectual culture, are more varied in their industrial capacities. Among them you can find intelligent farmers, skillful mechanics, practical engineers, experienced stock breeders, and artists in every department of practical and cultured life. In short, the German Empire offers to the world a people better prepared to utilize all the resources of a country than history has ever known, and the stream of German emigration to America is constant and vast.

The Scandinavian peasantry are born farmers — farmers from instinct — and for industry, sobriety, economy, and general intelligence are not surpassed by any class or nationality seeking homes in free America.

Shall we, of the South, lose all this? Look at the vast plains of Texas, the Lone Star State, with an area larger than Germany, than Austria and Hungary, or than France, which latter empire, in 1868, not only supplied her teeming 38 million of population with food and raiment but exported to the United Kingdom of Great Britain more, in dollars, of eggs and poultry than the whole of the United States did of beef and pork. Not only did she do that but she also exported to the same kingdom in the same year more beef than we did! Texas, that vast empire of domain, is thirsting for cultivation and bursting with food for man and beast. A thousand educated Germans or Scandinavians thrown into the state of Texas would do more for its development and bring it more actual wealth out of its resources than could ever be hoped for from the native Texan.

The very vastness of our resources has made us indifferent to their development. The knowledge of wealth is too often the paralysis of industry. Look at Louisiana. Its sugar plantations have been relegated, as a matter of course, to the Negro, whose Boeotian skull has been ever considered the only organism capable of resisting the heat of the Southern sun, But skilled and intelligent labor laughs at these old traditions, and even the oldest and most prejudiced among us now recognize the fact that such conclusions are the offspring of ignorance nurtured in luxurious idleness. In Alabama, Mississippi, Georgia, and South Carolina, states which before the war had come to be regarded as nothing more nor less than vast cotton fields, Northern and foreign capital is beginning to flow, and the mineral and manufacturing interests of these states are rapidly rivaling in revenue the wealth derived from their own peculiar staple. For the development of these resources we are to look to foreign capital and foreign labor. The Negro is foreordained to the cotton field. Nature has arranged all this matter by a system of economic selection, if I may borrow the term from science.

There is work enough in the cotton, rice, and sugar fields for every Negro on the continent to obtain his livelihood thereby. Beyond this, however, at least three-fourths of the possible wealth of the Southern states lies undeveloped, and to immigration alone can we look for the realization of wealth from these resources. Tennessee, my own state, has of late been vigorously alive to the importance of inviting immigration to her borders, and a new and healthful impulse in every department of industrial pursuit has been the natural result.

But we of the South are today sadly at a disadvantage. Of all the emigrants that turn their faces to America, as I have before intimated, there are but few who expect to enter America by any other channel than Castle Garden. Can we wonder, then, that the South has not received the benefit of immigration?

These isothermal lines of which our Northern brethren talk so learnedly and so persistently, that many of them actually have come to accept this chimerical fancy as the living truth — these "isothermal lines" have built up the cities of the Northwest and made its bleak, cold wilderness blossom as the rose.

The creameries of New York, Pennsylvania, Ohio, and Iowa, the great breweries of the East and the West are almost exclusively the result of foreign labor. The same may be said of their great forges, foundries, rolling mills, glassworks, and furniture factories. But does anyone who knows aught of climate and soil of the Southern states dare to say that all this could not be accomplished here? The cry has gone up against us that we breathe an atmosphere of death; that the vampire of infection hangs ever over us and sucks the lifeblood from the channels of industry and trade. Immigrants are imposed upon by corrupt agents representing the railway and other real estate corporations of the great and unfathomable Northwest, a majority of whom have been made opulent in public domain at the expense of the general government, and these agents often display maps of the United States, with the entire list of the Southern states marked in Ethiopian darkness, with here and there a skull and crossbones labeled *Yellow Fever District — Famine and Pestilence.*

The cold and icebound regions of the Northwest, Dakota for example, if their land happens to lie in that state, is portrayed in roseate hues, with deeper red lines of the ethereal railways they represent, permeating their Eden and Eldorado. They, poor fellows, are told to follow these bright lines, follow the latitude from which they are about to emigrate, and all will be well.

There is no one there to tell them that mere latitude does not determine climate, and that the same line of latitude upon the map belts a variety of climes, differing as much from one another as do the varying seasons of the year.

Even so prominent a political economist as Alexander Delmar will persist in promulgating this specious fallacy. In a learned article on American immigration, he writes as follows:

Immigration has always been encouraged by the federal and state governments of this country, and by many of the latter the inducements held out to the settlers are very attractive. The Federal Homestead Act of May 20, 1862, however, continues to remain the most substantial provision of this sort. It secures to every actual settler — the head of a family — 160 acres of public land, substantially gratis, in absolute fee simple. A fact likely to prove of considerable importance to the future history of this country is the disposition of migrators to confine themselves to isothermal lines. Our immigrants from the United Kingdom and Germany will be found settled mainly in the same latitudes they left, viz.: on the Ohio, Northern Mississippi, and Missouri rivers and their affluents, and on the shores of the Great Lakes. The Scandinavians settle in the most Northern states. The Southern states are almost destitute of foreign population, migrators from Spain and Italy going chiefly to South America. This may be due to language or religion, but is mainly attributable to climate and the similarity of agricultural productions, the staples of our Southern states — cotton and tobacco — being unfamiliar to the peasants of Southern Europe. These facts would indicate a serious diminution of immigration whenever the causes that now superinduce it from Northern Europe to this country shall cease to prevail.

And yet this is in the face of the census, which shows that the immigrants, consisting mainly of farmers and farm laborers, healthy and in the prime of life, die much faster than the native population where the isothermal theory is applied like a procrustean bed to determine the locality of settlement. I have given much thought to this subject of late years, with large opportunities for investigation, and I fail to find that even the hardy Norsemen of Scandinavia find a more healthful and congenial clime along the icy lakes of the North than by the magnolia-bordered Gulf of the Sunny South, and the same may be said of those from other lands who have sought and found healthful homes among us. Sanitary science is fast eliminating epidemic disease from all quarters of the civilized world where once it was wont to lurk, while at all other times than during localized epidemics the health of the South is remarkable, and *its death rate singularly low in comparison with that of the North.*

The unsettled political relations of the South have been urged against us in determining the settlement of emigrants, but this has come to be regarded even in the North by sensible men as merely the trick of politicians, without any foundation in fact whatever. Our people, though fierce in war, are mild in peace. Throughout the length and breadth of the civilized universe, no people can be found who would have fallen so heartily into the grand purposes of the general government when the issues which once alienated them became dead letters in their political history.

Partisans to the contrary notwithstanding, the people of the South *are* a peace-loving, law-abiding, and proverbially hospitable people, and the political freedom and civil liberty of the immigrant will be as sacredly preserved to him in any quarter of our land as beneath the great white dome of liberty itself.

Our needs and our capacities are both before you, and we are here in the initiative before this intelligent audience, representatives of, I believe, all the states embraced in our Association, to inaugurate the proper means of correlating them into practical issues.

Our first need is the establishment, at our Southern ports, of a well-ordered system of reception for foreign immigrants. We want them to come directly to our ports, to be met by our own people, and to be determined in their destination by men who know our country and can intelligently differentiate the masses and direct the individual to those environments best adapted to his previous condition of life and occupation.

From Norfolk to Galveston! What a sweep of shore! And along that ocean margin the finest harbors of the world are found. It is a burning shame that we have not waked up to this matter earlier in the history of our development. Our ports of entry present no appearance of activity or life such as give reputation to the crowded harbors of the North, and it is immigration which will give them life. Committees from every state legislature should be appointed to consider the subjects of determining and distributing emigrants throughout our lovely and healthful Sunny Southland; and if it be thought advisable, and I do so think, a representative should be appointed for the port of entry most contiguous to the state, who shall take hold of these people, bring before them the peculiar advantages of his own section, and apply to their needs whatever assistance or appropriation his state may have seen fit to offer in the interest of immigration.

Gentlemen, Mahomet must go to the mountain! Never until a thorough organization is effected can we hope to secure for ourselves the wonderful prosperity which the wellspring of emigration has poured out over the states of the North and West. We must offer proper inducements. Our legislatures must help us by positive enactments anent this great vitalizing element of political economy around which crystallize so many and such important interests. We, therefore, *emphasize* our invocation of your

aid. You, the representatives of 75 percent of the taxpayers of those sparsely settled Southern states, speak through your legislators, state and national; demand of them your rights, and that demand will not be disregarded.

There is nothing which so brings to light the resources of a country as a direct oceanic communication with the outer world. If immigration has to be filtered, let us do it for ourselves.

Through Castle Garden, the North is enabled to retain the very best immigrant elements, leaving the refuse to drift at will where bare sustenance may be a possibility. With immigration agencies at our Southern ports, the distribution of these people would be in our own hands, and under such a system our population would receive a healthful increase and the resources of our country experience a steady and fruitful development. Our plantations have always been too large; they are but half cultivated at best; we should divide them up and cultivate less land and cultivate it better; skilled labor and machinery would go a long way toward remedying this.

Granted that the experience of planting in the South has demonstrated the necessity for the Negro in the cultivation of cotton. The plantations are all much larger than necessary to produce the same amount of this staple, and it has ever been the bane of the South that she has sent her wealth out of her borders to purchase from the great Northwest food for the stock used in the raising of this cotton, and that might, with but little effort, be produced upon their own soil without the expense of transportation, and better adapted to the digestion and healthful condition of animals in the South than any grain that the North or West can produce.

If Southern planters do not want to worry with this, as being an interest too small for their consideration, let them rent, lease, or sell to a German, Swiss, or a Scandinavian a small portion of their lands, and enough of grain will be produced to supply the wants of every such plantation without the payment of one dollar for transportation.

And, then, again, with the skilled laborers from the crowded centers of England, France, and Germany, what is to prevent the manufacture of goods from cotton and from wool right upon the fields of their production? With a right system of Southern immigration, with proper inducements held out for settlement among us, the day is not far distant when the smoke of the foundry, the factory, and the cotton gin will go up together as incense to the heaven that has blessed us with such illimitable and varied resources of industrial wealth.

An erroneous impression seems to have prevailed in the South that emigrants are all outcasts, that no one would leave his home for residence in a foreign land but an exile, or one under the ban of social, political, or civil ostracism. Ah! it is difficult, indeed, for our Southern people, with their broad acres of rich and productive land, to conceive of the want, the penury, the abject poverty of the European laborer. Skilled as he generally is in the department of life to which he has been called, the overcrowded thoroughfares can give him in return for his labor but little else than his daily bread and a fire to shelter him from an ungenial clime.

It is scarcely creditable to a Southern planter, whose acres of black prairie soil is almost bursting with pregnant wealth; it is hard for him to believe that within a few square yards of old and worn-out soil a German family find its sole support, and thanks the God who gave him so much as even that. It is hard to believe in this land of liberty that whole households stand shivering at the door of the huts from which they have been evicted, hungering for bread and clamoring for labor to make it. These things are no fancy sketches, but the living, burning truth, and civilization has suffered it too.

The honest laborer of Europe is often highly cultivated and well-prepared for any station in life, and yet for want of occupation he must remain a pauper at home or find employment in other lands where labor is in demand, and the soil more productive, and the burden of life less difficult to bear.

The fact that paupers and criminals were once sent over to America by the wholesale from Europe has done much to prejudice the South against immigration. To guard against this practice, however, which really is now almost a thing of the past, most of the states have enacted severe laws. In Georgia, for example, an alien felon is punishable with banishment, and for a second offense "he shall suffer death without benefit of clergy." In Massachusetts, a town rendered liable for the expense of supporting or burying any pauper immigrant may maintain an action of debt for the same against the master of the vessel who brought him in. In Rhode Island, the importation of any person of a notoriously dissolute, infamous, and abandoned life and character "is punishable with heavy fines." In the states of New York, New Hampshire, Maine, Maryland, Louisiana, and Texas, the shipmaster must indemnify the state against the expense of maintaining any pauper immigrants he may bring in. Commutation money may, in certain cases, be substituted, and this is generally the practice in the state of New York.

As a matter of course it becomes us to protect ourselves against any abuse of this privilege of settling among us, which we throw open to the world. But this can easily be avoided by a thorough system of organization, and the needs of our country met without inconvenience or injury. This is our mission here. A great work lies before us. What we shall inaugurate here at this time is to be the *avant courier* of a more glorious destiny for our Southern land.

Under the formative hand of intelligent industry, all the plastic elements of national success will be molded into monuments of wealth and glory to which the eyes of a universe will turn as a pilgrim to his Mecca.

Exhaustless possibilities are ours. The future is pregnant with glory, and it is a well-ordered immigration that shall pronounce the "open sesame" to the treasures of our Southern soil.

A new era is dawning upon us. The prejudices of the past are vanishing before the necessities of the present. A broader, grander view of life spreads out before us:

> And I doubt not through the ages,
>   One increasing purpose runs,
> And the thoughts of men are widened
>   With the process of the suns.

121.

WILLIAM GRAHAM SUMNER: What Social Classes Do Not Owe Each Other

William Graham Sumner served for forty years as an apologist for the American industrial oligarchy and as an opponent of social reformers. He regarded the growth of giant corporations as both natural and desirable, and widespread poverty as an inevitable part of the social order. Sumner's logical criticisms of social legislation and socialism won him the approval of conservatives and recognition as the foremost American advocate of the philosophy of Herbert Spencer. The following selection includes parts of three chapters of What Social Classes Owe To Each Other.

Source: *What Social Classes Owe To Each Other*, New York, 1883, pp. 13-24, 113-121, 157-168.

IT IS COMMONLY ASSERTED that there are in the United States no classes, and any allusion to classes is resented. On the other hand, we constantly read and hear discussions of social topics in which the existence of social classes is assumed as a simple fact. "The poor," "the weak," "the laborers" are expressions which are used as if they had exact and well-understood definition. Discussions are made to bear upon the assumed rights, wrongs, and misfortunes of certain social classes; and all public speaking and writing consists, in a large measure, of the discussion of general plans for meeting the wishes of classes of people who have not been able to satisfy their own desires. These classes are sometimes discontented, and sometimes not. Sometimes they do not know that anything is amiss with them until the "friends of humanity" come to them with offers of aid.

Sometimes they are discontented and envious. They do not take their achievements as a fair measure of their rights. They do not blame themselves or their parents for their lot, as compared with that of other people. Sometimes they claim that they have a right to everything of which they feel the need for their happiness on earth. To make such a claim against God or Nature would, of course, be only to say that we claim a right to live on earth if we can. But God and Nature have ordained the chances and conditions of life on earth once for all. The case cannot be reopened. We cannot get a revision of laws of human life. We are absolutely shut up to the need and duty, if we would learn how to live happily, of investigating the laws of Nature, and deducing the rules of right living in the world as it is. These are very wearisome and commonplace tasks. They consist in labor and self-denial repeated over and over again in learning and doing.

When the people whose claims we are considering are told to apply themselves to these tasks, they become irritated and feel almost insulted. They formulate their claims as rights against society — that is, against some other men. In their view they have a right, not only to *pursue* happiness but to *get* it; and if they fail to get it, they think they have a claim to the aid of other men — that is, to the labor and self-denial of other men — to get it for them. They find orators and poets who tell them that they have grievances, so long as they have unsatisfied desires.

Now, if there are groups of people who have a claim to other people's labor and self-denial, and if there are other people whose labor and self-denial are liable to be claimed by the first groups, then there certainly are "classes," and classes of the oldest and most vicious type. For a man who can command another man's labor and self-denial for the support of his own existence is a privileged person of the highest species conceivable on earth. Princes and paupers meet on this plane, and no other men are on it at all. On the other hand, a man whose labor and self-denial may be diverted from his maintenance to that of some other man is not a free man and approaches more or less toward the position of a slave.

Therefore we shall find that, in all the notions which we are to discuss, this elementary contradiction, that there are classes and that there are not classes, will produce repeated confusion and absurdity. We shall find that in our efforts to eliminate the old vices of class government we are impeded and defeated by new products of the worst class theory. We shall find that all the schemes for producing equality and obliterating the organization of society produce a new differentiation based on the worst possible distinction — the right to claim and the duty to give one man's effort for another man's satisfaction. We shall find that every effort to realize equality necessitates a sacrifice of liberty. . . .

Certain ills belong to the hardships of human life. They are natural. They are part of the struggle with Nature for existence. We cannot blame our fellowmen for our share of these. My neighbor and I are both struggling to free ourselves from these ills. The fact that my neighbor has succeeded in this struggle better than I constitutes no grievance for me. Certain other ills are due to the malice of men and to the imperfections or errors of civil institutions. . . .

The distinction here made between the ills which belong to the struggle for existence and those which are due to the faults of human institutions is of prime importance. It will also be important, in order to clear up our ideas about the notions which are in fashion, to note the relation of the economic to the political significance of assumed duties of one class to another.

That is to say, we may discuss the question whether one class owes duties to another by reference to the economic effects which will be produced on the classes and society; or we may discuss the political expediency of formulating and enforcing rights and duties respectively between the parties. In the former case, we might assume that the givers of aid were willing to give it, and we might discuss the benefit or mischief of their activity. In the other case, we must assume that some at least of those who were forced to give aid did so unwillingly. Here, then, there would be a question of rights. The question whether voluntary charity is mischievous or not is one thing; the question whether legislation which forces one man to aid another is right and wise, as well as economically beneficial, is quite another question. Great confusion and consequent error is produced by allowing these two questions to become entangled in the discussion. Especially we shall need to notice the attempts to apply legislative methods of reform to the ills which belong to the order of Nature. . . .

Under the names of the poor and the weak, the negligent, shiftless, inefficient, silly, and imprudent are fastened upon the industrious and prudent as a responsibility and a duty. On the one side, the terms are extended to cover the idle, intemperate, and vicious, who, by the combination, gain credit which they do not deserve and which they could not get if they stood alone. On the other hand, the terms are extended to include wage receivers of the humblest rank, who are degraded by the combination. The reader who desires to guard himself against fallacies should always scrutinize the terms "poor" and "weak" as used, so as to see which or how many of these classes they are made to cover.

The humanitarians, philanthropists, and reformers, looking at the facts of life as they present themselves, find enough which is sad and unpromising in the condition of many members of society. They see wealth and poverty side by side. They note great inequality of social position and social chances. They eagerly set about the attempt to account for what they see and to devise schemes for remedying what they do not like. In their eagerness to recommend the less fortunate classes to pity and consideration, they forget all about the rights of other classes; they gloss over all the faults of the classes in question; and they exaggerate their misfortunes and their virtues. They invent new theories of property, distorting rights and perpetrating injustice, as anyone is sure to do who sets about the readjustment of social relations with the interests of one group distinctly before his mind and the interests of all other groups thrown into the background.

When I have read certain of these discussions, I have thought that it must be quite disreputable to be respectable, quite dishonest to own property, quite unjust to go one's own way and earn one's own living, and that the only really admirable person was the good-for-nothing. The man who by his own effort raises himself above poverty appears, in these discussions, to be of no account. The man who has done nothing to raise himself above poverty finds that the social doctors flock about him, bringing the capital which they have collected from the other class, and promising him the aid of the State to give him what the other had to work for. In all these schemes and projects the organized intervention of society through the State is either planned or hoped for, and the State is thus made to become the protector and guardian of certain classes.

The agents who are to direct the State action are, of course, the reformers and philanthropists. Their schemes, therefore, may always be reduced to this type — that A and B decide what C shall do for D. . . . In all the discussions, attention is concentrated on A and B, the noble social reformers, and on D, the "poor man." I call C the forgotten man, because I have never seen that any notice was taken of him in any of the discussions. When we have disposed of A, B, and D, we can better appreciate the case of C, and I think that we shall find that he deserves our attention for the worth of his character and the magnitude of his unmerited burdens. Here it may suffice to observe that, on the theories of the social philosophers to whom I have referred, we should get a new maxim of judicious living: Poverty is the best policy. If you get wealth, you will have to support other people; if you do not get wealth, it will be the duty of other people to support you.

EVERY MAN AND WOMAN in society has one big duty. That is, to take care of his or her own self. This is a social duty. For, fortunately, the matter stands so that the duty of making the best of one's self, individually, is not a separate thing from the duty of filling one's place in society, but the two are one, and the latter is accomplished when the former is done. The common notion, however, seems to be that one has a duty to society, as a special and separate thing, and that this duty consists in considering and deciding what other people ought to do.

Now, the man who can do anything for or about anybody else than himself is fit to be head of a family; and when he becomes head of a family he has duties to his wife and his children, in addition to the former big duty. Then, again, any man who can take care of himself and his family is in a very exceptional position, if he does not find in his immediate surroundings people who need his care and have some sort of a personal claim upon him. If, now, he is able to fulfill all this, and to take care of anybody outside his family and his dependents, he must have a surplus of energy, wisdom, and moral virtue beyond what he needs for his own business. No man has this; for a family is a charge which is capable of infinite development, and no man could suffice to the full measure of duty for which a family may draw upon him. Neither can a man give to society so advantageous an employment of his services, whatever they are, in any other way as by spending them on his family. Upon this, however, I will not insist. I recur to the observation that a man who proposes to take care of other people must have himself and his family taken care

of, after some sort of a fashion, and must have an as yet unexhausted store of energy.

The danger of minding other people's business is twofold. First, there is the danger that a man may leave his own business unattended to; and, second, there is the danger of an impertinent interference with another's affairs. The "friends of humanity" almost always run into both dangers. I am one of humanity, and I do not want any volunteer friends. I regard friendship as mutual, and I want to have my say about it. I suppose that other components of humanity feel in the same way about it. If so, they must regard anyone who assumes the role of a friend of humanity as impertinent. The reference of the friend of humanity back to his own business is obviously the next step.

Yet we are constantly annoyed and the legislatures are kept constantly busy by the people who have made up their minds that it is wise and conducive to happiness to live in a certain way and who want to compel everybody else to live in their way. Some people have decided to spend Sunday in a certain way, and they want laws passed to make other people spend Sunday in the same way. Some people have resolved to be teetotalers, and they want a law passed to make everybody else a teetotaler. Some people have resolved to eschew luxury, and they want taxes laid to make others eschew luxury. The taxing power is especially something after which the reformer's finger always itches. Sometimes there is an element of self-interest in the proposed reformation, as when a publisher wanted a duty imposed on books to keep Americans from reading books which would unsettle their Americanism; and when artists wanted a tax laid on pictures to save Americans from buying bad paintings. . . .

The social doctors enjoy the satisfaction of feeling themselves to be more moral or more enlightened than their fellowmen. They are able to see what other men ought to do when the other men do not see it. An examination of the work of the social doctors, however, shows that they are only more ignorant and more presumptuous than other people. We have a great many social difficulties and hardships to contend with. Poverty, pain, disease, and misfortune surround our existence. We fight against them all the time. The individual is a center of hopes, affections, desires, and sufferings. When he dies, life changes its form but does not cease. That means that the person — the center of all the hopes, affections, etc. — after struggling as long as he can, is sure to succumb at last. We would, therefore, as far as the hardships of the human lot are concerned, go on struggling to the best of our ability against them but for the social doctors, and we would endure what we could not cure.

But we have inherited a vast number of social ills which never came from Nature. They are the complicated products of all the tinkering, muddling, and blundering of social doctors in the past. These products of social quackery are now buttressed by habit, fashion, prejudice, platitudinarian thinking, and new quackery in political economy and social science. It is a fact worth noticing, just when there seems to be a revival of faith in legislative agencies, that our states are generally providing against the experienced evils of overlegislation by ordering that the legislature shall sit only every other year. During the hard times, when Congress had a real chance to make or mar the public welfare, the final adjournment of that body was hailed year after year with cries of relief from a great anxiety. The greatest reforms which could now be accomplished would consist in undoing the work of statesmen in the past, and the greatest difficulty in the way of reform is to find out how to undo their work without injury to what is natural and sound.

All this mischief has been done by men who sat down to consider the problem (as I heard an apprentice of theirs once express it): What kind of a society do we want to make? When they had settled this question a priori to their satisfaction, they set to work to make their ideal society, and today we suffer the consequences. Human society tries hard to adapt itself to any conditions in which it finds itself, and we have been warped and distorted until we have got used to it, as the foot adapts itself to an ill-made boot. Next, we have come to think that that is the right way for things to be; and it is true that a change to a sound and normal condition would for a time hurt us, as a man whose foot has been distorted would suffer if he tried to wear a well-shaped boot. Finally, we have produced a lot of economists and social philosophers who have invented sophisms for fitting our thinking to the distorted facts.

Society, therefore, does not need any care or supervision. If we can acquire a science of society, based on observation of phenomena and study of forces, we may hope to gain some ground slowly toward the elimination of old errors and the reestablishment of a sound and natural social order. Whatever we gain that way will be by growth, never in the world by any reconstruction of society on the plan of some enthusiastic social architect. The latter is only repeating the old error over again and postponing all our chances of real improvement.

Society needs first of all to be freed from these meddlers — that is, to be let alone. Here we are, then, once more back at the old doctrine — laissez-faire. Let us translate it into blunt English, and it will read — Mind your own business. It is nothing but the doctrine of liberty. Let every man be happy in his own way. If his sphere of action and interest impinges on that of any other man, there will have to be compromise and adjustment. Wait for the occasion. Do not attempt to generalize those interferences or to plan for them a priori. We have a body of laws and institutions which have grown up as occasion has occurred for adjusting rights. Let the same process go on. Practice the utmost reserve possible in your interferences even of this kind and by no means seize occasion for interfering with natural adjustments. Try first, long and patiently, whether the natural adjustment will not come about through the play of interests and the voluntary concessions of the parties. . . .

A MAN WHO HAD NO SYMPATHIES and no sentiments would be a very poor creature; but the public charities, more especially the legislative charities, nourish no man's sympathies and sentiments. Furthermore, it ought to be distinctly perceived that any charitable and benevolent effort which any man desires to make voluntarily, to see if he can do any good, lies entirely beyond the field of discussion. It would be as impertinent to prevent his effort as it is to force cooperation in an effort on someone who does not want to participate in it. What I choose to do by way of exercising my own sympathies under my own reason and conscience is one thing; what another man forces me to do of a sympathetic character, because his reason and conscience approve of it, is quite another thing.

What, now, is the reason why we should help each other? . . . We may philosophize as coolly and correctly as we choose about our duties and about the laws of right living; no one of us lives up to what he knows. The man struck by the falling tree has, perhaps, been careless. We are all careless. Environed as we are by risks and perils which befall us as misfortunes, no man of us is in a position to say, "I know all the laws, and am sure to obey them all; therefore I shall never need aid and sympathy." . . .

Men, therefore, owe to men, in the chances and perils of this life, aid and sympathy, on account of the common participation in human frailty and folly. This observation, however, puts aid and sympathy in the field of private and personal relations, under the regulation of reason and conscience, and gives no ground for mechanical and impersonal schemes.

We may, then, distinguish four things:

1. The function of science is to investigate truth. Science is colorless and impersonal. It investigates the force of gravity and finds out the laws of that force and has nothing to do with the weal or woe of men under the operation of law.

2. The moral deductions as to what one ought to do are to be drawn by the reason and conscience of the individual man who is instructed by science. Let him take note of the force of gravity and see to it that he does not walk off a precipice or get in the way of a falling body.

3. On account of the number and variety of perils of all kinds by which our lives are environed and on account of ignorance, carelessness, and folly we all neglect to obey the moral deductions which we have learned, so that, in fact, the wisest and the best of us act foolishly and suffer.

4. The law of sympathy, by which we share each others' burdens, is to do as we would be done by. It is not a scientific principle and does not admit of such generalization or interpretation that A can tell B what this law enjoins on B to do. Hence the relations of sympathy and sentiment are essentially limited to two persons only, and they cannot be made a basis for the relations of groups of persons or for discussion by any third party.

Social improvement is not to be won by direct effort. It is secondary and results from physical or economic improvements. That is the reason why schemes of direct social amelioration always have an arbitrary, sentimental, and artificial character, while true social advance must be a product and a growth. The efforts which are being put forth for every kind of progress in the arts and sciences are, therefore, contributing to true social progress. Let anyone learn what hardship was involved, even for a wealthy person, a century ago, in crossing the Atlantic, and then let him compare that hardship even with a steerage passage at the present time, considering time and money cost.

This improvement in transportation by which "the poor and weak" can be carried from the crowded centers of population to the new land is worth more to them than all the schemes of all the social reformers. . . . If the economists could satisfactorily solve the problem of the regulation of paper currency, they would do more for the wages class than could be accomplished by all the artificial doctrines about wages which they seem to feel bound to encourage. If we could get firm and good laws passed for the management of savings banks, and then refrain from the amendments by which those laws are gradually broken down, we should do more for the noncapitalist class than by volumes of laws against "corporations" and the "excessive power of capital." . . .

Now, the aid which helps a man to help himself is not in the least akin to the aid which is given in charity. If alms are given or if we "make work" for a man or "give him employment" or "protect" him, we simply take a product from one and give it to another. If we help a man to help himself by opening the chances around him, we put him in a position to add to the wealth of the community by putting new powers in operation to produce. It would seem that the difference between getting something already in existence from the one who has it and producing a new thing by applying new labor to natural materials would be so plain as never to be forgotten; but the fallacy of confusing the two is one of the commonest in all social discussions.

We have now seen that the current discussions about the claims and rights of social classes on each other are radically erroneous and fallacious, and we have seen that an analysis of the general obligations which

we all have to each other leads us to nothing but an emphatic repetition of old but well-acknowledged obligations to perfect our political institutions. We have been led to restriction, not extension, of the functions of the State, but we have also been led to see the necessity of purifying and perfecting the operation of the State in the functions which properly belong to it. If we refuse to recognize any classes as existing in society when, perhaps, a claim might be set up that the wealthy, educated, and virtuous have acquired special rights and precedence, we certainly cannot recognize any classes when it is attempted to establish such distinctions for the sake of imposing burdens and duties on one group for the benefit of others. The men who have not done their duty in this world never can be equal to those who have done their duty more or less well.

If words like wise and foolish, thrifty and extravagant, prudent and negligent have any meaning in language, then it must make some difference how people behave in this world, and the difference will appear in the position they acquire in the body of society and in relation to the chances of life. They may, then, be classified in reference to these facts. Such classes always will exist; no other social distinctions can endure. If, then, we look to the origin and definition of these classes, we shall find it impossible to deduce any obligations which one of them bears to the other. The class distinctions simply result from the different degrees of success with which men have availed themselves of the chances which were presented to them. Instead of endeavoring to redistribute the acquisitions which have been made between the existing classes, our aim should be to *increase, multiply, and extend the chances.*

Such is the work of civilization. Every old error or abuse which is removed opens new chances of development to all the new energy of society. Every improvement in education, science, art, or government expands the chances of man on earth. Such expansion is no guarantee of equality. On the contrary, if there be liberty, some will profit by the chances eagerly and some will neglect them altogether. Therefore, the greater the chances the more unequal will be the fortune of these two sets of men. So it ought to be, in all justice and right reason. The yearning after equality is the offspring of envy and covetousness, and there is no possible plan for satisfying that yearning which can do aught else than rob A to give to B; consequently all such plans nourish some of the meanest vices of human nature, waste capital, and overthrow civilization. But if we can expand the chances, we can count on a general and steady growth of civilization and advancement of society by and through its best members. In the prosecution of these chances we all owe to each other goodwill.

122.

Henry George: The Paradox of Poverty

After the publication of Progress and Poverty *in 1879, Henry George became a widely read, if not always popular, author. He continued to amplify his theories on the growing disparity between wealth and poverty in a series of articles for* Frank Leslie's Illustrated Newspaper. *In 1883 the articles were collected in a book, from which the following chapter is taken.*

Source: *Social Problems*, Chicago, 1883, Ch. 8: "That We All Might Be Rich."

The terms rich and poor are of course frequently used in a relative sense. Among Irish peasants, kept on the verge of starvation by the tribute wrung from them to maintain the luxury of absentee landlords in London or Paris, "the woman of three cows" will be looked on as rich, while in the society of millionaires a man with only $500,000 will be regarded as poor. Now, we cannot, of course, all be rich in the sense of having more than others; but when people say, as they so often do, that we cannot all be rich, or when they say that we must always have the poor with us, they do not use the words in this comparative sense. They mean by the rich those who have enough, or more than enough, wealth to gratify all reasonable wants, and by the poor, those who have not.

Now, using the words in this sense, I join issue with those who say that we cannot all be rich; with those who declare that in human society the poor must always exist. I do not, of course, mean that we all might have an array of servants; that we all might outshine each other in dress, in equipage, in the lavishness of our balls or dinners, in the magnificence of our houses. That would be a contradiction in terms. What I mean is, that we all might have leisure, comfort, and abundance, not merely of the necessaries but even of what are now esteemed the elegancies and luxuries of life. I do not mean to say that absolute equality could be had, or would be desirable. I do not mean to say that we could all have, or would want, the same quantity of all the different forms of wealth. But I do mean to say that we might all have enough wealth to satisfy reasonable desires; that we might all have so much of the material things we now struggle for that no one would want to rob or swindle his neighbor; that no one would worry all day or lie awake at nights fearing he might be brought to poverty or thinking how he might acquire wealth.

Does this seem a utopian dream? What would people of fifty years ago have thought of one who would have told them that it was possible to sew by steam power; to cross the Atlantic in six days or the continent in three; to have a message sent from London at noon delivered in Boston three hours before noon; to hear in New York the voice of a man talking in Chicago?

Did you ever see a pail of swill given to a pen of hungry hogs? That is human society as it is.

Did you ever see a company of well-bred men and women sitting down to a good dinner without scrambling or jostling or gluttony, each, knowing that his own appetite will be satisfied, deferring to and helping the others? That is human society as it might be.

"Devil catch the hindmost" is the motto of our so-called civilized society today. We learn early to "take care of No. 1," lest No. 1 should suffer; we learn early to grasp from others that we may not want ourselves. The fear of poverty makes us admire great wealth; and so habits of greed are formed, and we behold the pitiable spectacle of men who have already more than they can by any possibility use, toiling, striving, grasping to add to their store up to the very verge of the grave — that grave which, whatever else it may mean, does certainly mean the parting with all earthly possessions however great they be.

In vain, in gorgeous churches, on the appointed Sunday, is the parable of Dives and Lazarus read. What can it mean in churches where Dives would be welcomed and Lazarus shown the door? In vain may the preacher preach of the vanity of riches, while poverty engulfs the hindmost. But the mad struggle would cease when the fear of poverty had vanished. Then, and not till then, will a truly Christian civilization become possible.

And may not this be?

We are so accustomed to poverty that even in the most advanced countries we regard it as the natural lot of the great masses of the people; that we take it as a matter of course that even in our highest civilization large classes should want the necessaries of healthful life, and the vast majority should only get a poor and pinched living by the hardest toil. There are professors of political economy who teach that this condition of things is the result of social laws of which it is idle to complain! There are ministers of religion who preach that this is the condition which an all-wise, all-powerful Creator intended for His children!

If an architect were to build a theater so that not more than one-tenth of the audience could see and hear, we would call him a bungler and a botch. If a man were to give a feast and provide so little food that nine-tenths of his guests must go away hungry, we would call him a fool, or worse. Yet so accustomed are we to poverty that even the preachers of what passes for Christianity tell us that the great Architect of the universe, to whose infinite skill all nature testifies, has made such a botch job of this world that the vast majority of the human creatures whom He has called into it are condemned by the conditions He has imposed to want, suffering, and brutalizing toil that gives no opportunity for the development of mental powers — must pass their lives in a hard struggle to merely live!

Yet who can look about him without seeing that to whatever cause poverty may be due, it is not due to the niggardliness of nature; without seeing that it is blindness or blasphemy to assume that the Creator has condemned the masses of men to hard toil for a bare living?

If some men have not enough to live decently, do not others have far more than they really need? If there is not wealth sufficient to go around, giving everyone abundance, is it because we have reached the limit of the production of wealth? Is our land all in use? Is our labor all employed? Is our capital all utilized? On the contrary, in whatever direction we look we see the most stupendous waste of productive forces — of productive forces so potent that were they permitted to freely play, the production of wealth would be so enormous that there would be more than a sufficiency for all. What branch of production is there in which the limit of production has been reached? What single article of wealth is there of which we might not produce enormously more?

If the mass of the population of New York are jammed into the fever-breeding rooms of tenement houses, it is not because there are not vacant lots enough in and around New York to give each family space for a separate home. If settlers are going into Montana and Dakota and Manitoba, it is not because there are not vast areas of untilled land much nearer the centers of population. If farmers are paying one-fourth, one-third, or even one-half of their crops for the privilege of getting land to cultivate, it is not because there are not, even in our oldest states, great quantities of land which no one is cultivating.

So true is it that poverty does not come from the inability to produce more wealth that from every side we hear that the power to produce is in excess of the ability to find a market; that the constant fear seems to be not that too little, but that too much, will be produced! Do we not maintain a high tariff and keep at every port a horde of customhouse officers for fear the people of other countries will overwhelm us with their goods? Is not a great part of our ma-

Henry George

chinery constantly idle? Are there not, even in what we call good times, an immense number of unemployed men who would gladly be at work producing wealth if they could only get the opportunity? Do we not, even now, hear from every side of embarrassment from the very excess of productive power and of combinations to reduce production?

Coal operators band together to limit their output; ironworks have shut down or are running on halftime; distillers have agreed to limit their production to one-half their capacity, and sugar refiners to 60 percent; papermills are suspending for one, two, or three days a week; the gunny-cloth manufacturers, at a recent meeting, agreed to close their mills until the present overstock on the market is greatly reduced; many other manufacturers have done the same thing. The shoemaking machinery of New England can, in six months' full running, it is said, supply the whole demand of the United States for twelve months; the machinery for making rubber goods can turn out twice as much as the market will take.

This seeming glut of production, this

seeming excess of productive power runs through all branches of industry and is evident all over the civilized world. From blackberries, bananas, or apples to ocean steamships or plate-glass mirrors, there is scarcely an article of human comfort or convenience that could not be produced in very much greater quantities than now without lessening the production of anything else.

So evident is this that many people think and talk and write as though the trouble is that there is not *work* enough to go around. We are in constant fear that other nations may do for us some of the work we might do for ourselves, and, to prevent them, guard ourselves with a tariff. We laud as public benefactors those who, as we say, "furnish employment." We are constantly talking as though this "furnishing of employment," this "giving of work" were the greatest boon that could be conferred upon society. To listen to much that is talked and much that is written, one would think that the cause of poverty is that there is not work enough for so many people and that if the Creator had made the rock harder, the soil less fertile, iron as scarce as gold, and gold as diamonds; or if ships would sink and cities burn down oftener, there would be less poverty because there would be more work to do.

The lord mayor of London tells a deputation of unemployed workingmen that there is no demand for their labor and that the only resource for them is to go to the poorhouse or emigrate. The English government is shipping from Ireland able-bodied men and women to avoid maintaining them as paupers. Even in our own land there are at all times large numbers, and in hard times vast numbers, earnestly seeking work — the opportunity to give labor for the things produced by labor.

Perhaps nothing shows more clearly the enormous forces of production constantly going to waste than the fact that the most prosperous time in all branches of business that this country has known was during the Civil War, when we were maintaining great fleets and armies, and millions of our industrial population were engaged in supplying them with wealth for unproductive consumption or for reckless destruction. It is idle to talk about the fictitious prosperity of those "flush" times. The masses of the people lived better, dressed better, found it easier to get a living, and had more of luxuries and amusements than in normal times. There was more real, tangible wealth in the North at the close than at the beginning of the war.

Nor was it the great issue of paper money, nor the creation of the debt which caused this prosperity. The government presses struck off promises to pay; they could not print ships, cannon, arms, tools, food, and clothing. Nor did we borrow these things from other countries or "from posterity." Our bonds did not begin to go to Europe until the close of the war, and the people of one generation can no more borrow from the people of a subsequent generation than we who live on this planet can borrow from the inhabitants of another planet or another solar system. The wealth consumed and destroyed by our fleets and armies came from the then-existing stock of wealth. We could have carried on the war without the issue of a single bond, if, when we did not shrink from taking from wife and children their only breadwinner, we had not shrunk from taking the wealth of the rich.

Our armies and fleets were maintained, the enormous unproductive and destructive use of wealth was kept up by the labor and capital then and there engaged in production. And it was that the demand caused by the war stimulated productive forces into activity that the enormous drain of the war was not only supplied but that the North grew richer. The waste of labor in marching and countermarching, in digging trenches, throwing up earthworks, and fighting battles, the waste of wealth consumed or destroyed by our armies and fleets did not amount to as much as the waste constantly going on from unemployed labor and idle or partially used machinery.

It is evident that this enormous waste of productive power is due, not to defects in the laws of nature but to social maladjustments which deny to labor access to the natural opportunities of labor and rob the laborer of his just reward. Evidently the glut of markets does not really come from overproduction when there are so many who want the things which are said to be overproduced and would gladly exchange their labor for them did they have opportunity. Every day passed in enforced idleness by a laborer who would gladly be at work could he find opportunity means so much less in the fund which creates the effective demand for other labor; every time wages are screwed down means so much reduction in the purchasing power of the workmen whose incomes are thus reduced.

The paralysis which at all times wastes productive power, and which in times of industrial depression causes more loss than a great war, springs from the difficulty which those who would gladly satisfy their wants by their labor find in doing so. It cannot come from any natural limitation so long as human desires remain unsatisfied and nature yet offers to man the raw material of wealth. It must come from social maladjustments which permit the monopolization of these natural opportunities, and which rob labor of its fair reward. . . .

I wish . . . to call attention to the fact that productive power in such a state of civilization as ours is sufficient, did we give it play, to so enormously increase the production of wealth as to give abundance to all — to point out that the cause of poverty is not in natural limitations, which we cannot alter, but in inequalities and injustices of distribution entirely within our control.

The passenger who leaves New York on a transatlantic steamer does not fear that the provisions will give out. The men who run these steamers do not send them to sea without provisions enough for all they carry. Did He who made this whirling planet for our sojourn lack the forethought of man? Not so. In soil and sunshine, in vegetable and animal life, in veins of minerals, and in pulsing forces which we are only beginning to use are capabilities which we cannot exhaust — materials and powers from which human effort, guided by intelligence, may gratify every material want of every human creature. There is in nature no reason for poverty — not even for the poverty of the crippled or the decrepit. For man is by nature a social animal, and the family affections and the social sympathies would, where chronic poverty did not distort and embrute, amply provide for those who could not provide for themselves.

But if we will not use the intelligence with which we have been gifted to adapt social organization to natural laws — if we allow dogs in the manger to monopolize what they cannot use; if we allow strength and cunning to rob honest labor, we must have chronic poverty and all the social evils it inevitably brings. Under such conditions there would be poverty in paradise.

"The poor ye have always with you." If ever a scripture has been wrested to the devil's service, this is that scripture. How often have these words been distorted from their obvious meaning to soothe conscience into acquiescence in human misery and degradation — to bolster that blasphemy, the very negation and denial of Christ's teachings, that the All-Wise and Most Merciful, the Infinite Father, has decreed that so many of His creatures must be poor in order that others of His creatures to whom He wills the good things of life should enjoy the pleasure and virtue of doling out alms!

"The poor ye have always with you,"

said Christ; but all His teachings supply the limitation, "until the coming of the Kingdom." In that Kingdom of God *on earth,* that kingdom of justice and love for which He taught His followers to strive and pray, there will be no poor. But though the faith and the hope and the striving for this kingdom are of the very essence of Christ's teaching, the staunchest disbelievers and revilers of its possibility are found among those who call themselves Christians.

Queer ideas of the Divinity have some of these Christians who hold themselves orthodox and contribute to the conversion of the heathen. A very rich orthodox Christian said to a newspaper reporter awhile ago, on the completion of a large work out of which he is said to have made millions: "We have been peculiarly favored by Divine Providence; iron never was so cheap before, and labor has been a drug in the market."

That in spite of all our great advances we have yet with us the poor, those who, without fault of their own, cannot get healthful and wholesome conditions of life, is *our* fault and *our* shame. Who that looks about him can fail to see that it is only the injustice that denies natural opportunities to labor and robs the producer of the fruits of his toil, that prevents us all from being rich? Consider the enormous powers of production now going to waste; consider the great number of unproductive consumers maintained at the expense of producers — the rich men and dudes, the worse than useless government officials, the pickpockets, burglars, and confidence men; the highly respectable thieves who carry on their operations inside the law; the great army of lawyers; the beggars and paupers and inmates of prisons; the monopolists and cornerers and gamblers of every kind and grade.

Consider how much brains and energy and capital are devoted, not to the production of wealth but to the grabbing of wealth. Consider the waste caused by competition which does not increase wealth; by laws which restrict production and exchange. Consider how human power is lessened by insufficient food, by unwholesome lodgings, by work done under conditions that produce disease and shorten life. Consider how intemperance and unthrift follow poverty. Consider how the ignorance bred of poverty lessens production and how the vice bred of poverty causes destruction, and who can doubt that under conditions of social justice all might be rich?

The wealth-producing powers that would be evoked in a social state based on justice, where wealth went to the producers of wealth, and the banishment of poverty had banished the fear and greed and lusts that spring from it, we now can only faintly imagine. Wonderful as have been the discoveries and inventions of this century, it is evident that we have only begun to grasp that dominion which it is given to mind to obtain over matter. Discovery and invention are born of leisure, of material comfort, of freedom. These secured to all, and who shall say to what command over nature man may not attain?

It is not necessary that anyone should be condemned to monotonous toil; it is not necessary that anyone should lack the wealth and the leisure which permit the development of the faculties that raise man above the animal. Mind, not muscle, is the motor of progress, the force which compels nature and produces wealth. In turning men into machines we are wasting the highest powers. Already in our society there is a favored class who need take no thought for the morrow — what they shall eat, or what they shall drink, or wherewithal they shall be clothed. And may it not be that Christ was more than a dreamer when He told His disciples that in that kingdom of justice for which He taught them to work and pray this might be the condition of all?

Index of Authors

*The numbers in brackets
indicate selection numbers
in this volume*

ABBOT, FRANCIS ELLINGWOOD (Nov. 6, 1836-Oct. 23, 1903), religious leader. Leader (1867-94) of the Free Religious Association; edited (1869-80) *The Boston Index;* wrote *Scientific Theism* (1885). **[63]**

ADAMS, CHARLES FRANCIS, JR. (May 27, 1835-March 20, 1915), historian, civic leader, and railroad expert. Grandson of John Quincy Adams; chairman (1872-79) of the Massachusetts Board of Railroad Commissioners; president (1884-90) of the Union Pacific Railroad; president (1895-1915) of the Massachusetts Historical Society. **[38]**

ADAMS, HENRY (Feb. 16, 1838-March 27, 1918), historian. Grandson of John Quincy Adams; assistant professor of history (1870-77) at Harvard; editor (1869-76) of the *North American Review;* wrote *The Life of Albert Gallatin* (1879), *History of the United States* (9 vols., 1889-91). **[43]**

BEARD, GEORGE M. (May 8, 1839-Jan. 23, 1883), neurologist. Initiated research in the fields of mental and nervous disorder; wrote *The Medical and Surgical Uses of Electricity* (1871), *American Nervousness* (1881). **[104]**

BLAINE, JAMES G. (Jan. 31, 1830-Jan. 27, 1893), editor, legislator, and public official. Co-owner and editor (1854-60) of the *Kennebec Journal,* (Augusta, Me.); U.S. representative from Maine (1863-76) and

speaker of the House (1869-75); U.S. senator (1876-81); secretary of state (1881) under Garfield and (1889-92) under Benjamin Harrison. **[108]**

BOARDMAN, GEORGE NYE (1825-1915), clergyman. Pastor of the First Presbyterian Church, Binghamton, N.Y.; professor of systematic theology (from 1871) at Chicago Theological Seminary; wrote *A History of New England Theology* (1899). **[14]**

BRACE, CHARLES LORING (June 19, 1826-Aug. 11, 1890), social reformer and welfare worker. Founder and executive secretary (1853-90) of the New York City Children's Aid Society; wrote *The Dangerous Classes of New York, and Twenty Years' Work Among Them* (1872). **[61]** See also Author Index, Vol. 8.

BRADLEY, JOSEPH P. (March 14, 1813-Jan. 22, 1892), associate justice (1870-92) of the U.S. Supreme Court. **[118]**

BRUCE, BLANCHE K. (March 1, 1841-March 17, 1898), public official. Assessor (1871) and sheriff (1872) of Bolivar County, Miss.; U.S. senator (1875-81), the first African American to serve a full term in that body; register of the treasury, (1881-85) under Garfield and Arthur and (1895-98) under McKinley; District of Columbia recorder of deeds (1889-95). **[79]**

CAMERON, ANDREW C. (Sept. 28, 1834-May 28, 1890), editor, publisher, and labor leader. Editor (1864-80) of the *Working Man's Advocate*, (1880-88) of the *Inland Printer*, and (1888-90) of the *Artist Printer*. **[24]**

CLEMENS, SAMUEL L., "Mark Twain" (Nov. 30, 1835-April 21, 1910), author and humorist. Journeyman printer (1847-56); Mississippi River pilot (1857-61); prospector (1861) and newspaper reporter (1862) in Nevada; wrote, among others, *Innocents Abroad* (1869), *The Adventures of Tom Sawyer* (1876), *The Prince and the Pauper* (1880), *Life on the Mississippi* (1883), *The Adventures of Huckleberry Finn* (1884), *The Man That Corrupted Hadleyburg* (1900). **[41, 52, 78, 111]** See also Author Index, Vol. 13.

DAVIS, DAVID (March 9, 1815-June 26, 1886), jurist. Associate justice (1862-77) of the U.S. Supreme Court; U.S. senator from Illinois (1877-83) and president pro tempore (1881-83) of the Senate. **[8]**

DORNEY, P. S. (fl. 1871), journalist. Reported the 1871 Los Angeles riot against the Chinese. **[58]**

DOUGLASS, FREDERICK (? Feb. 1817-Feb. 20, 1895), journalist, orator, and antislavery leader. Escaped from slavery (1838); agent (1841-45) of the Massachusetts Anti-Slavery Society; founded and edited (1847-60) the Abolitionist paper *North Star*; in Civil War, recruited African American regiments and served as consultant to Lincoln; minister to Haiti (1889-91). **[119]** See also Author Index, Vol. 7.

EDDY, MARY BAKER (July 16, 1821-Dec. 3, 1910), spiritual leader. Chartered (1879) "The First Church of Christ, Scientist"; wrote *Science and Health* (1875); founded (1883) the monthly *Christian Science Journal*, (1898) the weekly *Christian Science Sentinel*, and (1908) the daily *Christian Science Monitor*. **[116]**

ELIOT, CHARLES W. (March 20, 1834-Aug. 22, 1926), educator. Assistant professor of chemistry and mathematics (1854-63) at Harvard; professor of analytical chemistry (1865-69) at Massachusetts Institute of Technology; president (1869-1909) of Harvard. **[36, 42, 73]** See also Author Index, Vols. 11, 14.

ENO, HENRY (Feb. 12, 1798-1882), lawyer, silver prospector, and land speculator.

Edited (1865) the *Alpine* (Calif.) *Chronicle*; county judge (1865-69). **[39]**

FIELD, STEPHEN J. (Nov. 4, 1816-April 9, 1899), jurist. Justice (1857-63) of the California Supreme Court; associate justice (1863-97) of the U.S. Supreme Court. **[65, 85]** See also Author Index, Vol. 9.

GEORGE, HENRY (Sept. 2, 1839-Oct. 29, 1897), economist and land reformer. Edited the *San Francisco Chronicle* and founded (1871) the *San Francisco Daily Evening Post*; developed the "single-tax" theory; wrote *Progress and Poverty* (1879). **[96, 122]**

GLADSTONE, WILLIAM (Dec. 29, 1809-May 19, 1898), British statesman. President of the Board of Trade (1843-45) and secretary of state for the colonies (1845-46) in Sir Robert Peel's cabinet; chancellor of the exchequer in the cabinets of Aberdeen, Palmerston, and Lord Russell; prime minister (1868-74, 1880-85, 1886, 1892-94). **[89]**

GODKIN, EDWIN L. (Oct. 2, 1831-May 21, 1902), editor and writer. Founder and editor (from 1865) of the *Nation*, which he merged (1881) with the *New York Evening Post*; editor in chief (1883-99) of the *Post*. **[91]**

GOMPERS, SAMUEL (Jan. 27, 1850-Dec. 13, 1924), labor leader. Founder (1886) and president (1886-94, 1896-1924) of the American Federation of Labor; member (1917) of the Council of National Defense; member of the Commission on International Labor Legislation at the 1919 Peace Conference. **[117]** See also Author Index, Vol. 11.

GRANT, ULYSSES S. (April 27, 1822-July 23, 1885), soldier and statesman. Eighteenth President of the United States (1869-77); served in U.S. Army during Mexican War; commanded Department of the Tennessee (1862-63); promoted to lieutenant general and commander of all U.S. armies (1863-65); received Lee's surrender at Appomattox Court House (April 9, 1865); promoted to general (1866); wrote *Personal Memoirs* (1885). **[48, 81]** See also Author Index, Vol. 9.

GRIMES, JAMES (Oct. 20, 1816-Feb. 7, 1872), lawyer and public official. Governor of Iowa (1854-58); U.S. senator

(1859-69); cast deciding vote for acquittal at Andrew Johnson's impeachment trial (1868). **[30]**

HARLAN, JOHN M. (June 1, 1833-Oct. 14, 1911), jurist. Attorney general of Kentucky (1863-67); associate justice (1877-1911) of the U.S. Supreme Court. **[118]** See also Author Index, Vols. 12, 13.

HARTE, BRET (Aug. 25, 1836-May 5, 1902), author and editor. Edited (1868-70) the *Overland Monthly*; U.S. consul in Germany (1878-80) and in Scotland (1880-85); wrote *The Luck of Roaring Camp and Other Sketches* (1870), *Tales of the Argonauts* (1875), **[50]** See also Author Index, Vol. 12.

HAYDEN, FERDINAND V. (Sept. 7, 1829-Dec. 22, 1887), geologist. Surgeon, Union Army; professor of geology (1865-72) at University of Pennsylvania; surveyed (1867-79) in Western territories; member (1879-86) of U.S. Geological Survey; helped establish Yellowstone National Park. **[22]**

HAYES, RUTHERFORD B. (Oct. 4, 1822-Jan. 17, 1893), lawyer, soldier, and statesman. Nineteenth President of the United States (1877-81); major general (1865), Union Army; U.S. representative from Ohio (1865-67); governor (1868-72, 1876-77). **[97]** See also Author Index, Vol. 11.

HOLLEY, ALEXANDER LYMAN (July 20, 1832-Jan. 29, 1882), metallurgist and mechanical engineer. Built (1865) the first Bessemer process steel plant in the U.S., at Troy, N.Y. **[82]**

HÜBNER, GRAF JOSEPH ALEXANDER VON (1811-1892), Austrian diplomat. Described America in his two-volume work, *A Trip Around the World* (1873). **[60]**

JACKSON, HELEN HUNT (Oct. 18, 1831-Aug. 12, 1885), author and humanitarian. U.S. special commissioner to the Mission Indians of California (1882); wrote *Verses* (1870), *A Century of Dishonor* (1881), *Ramona* (1884), and *Sonnets and Lyrics* (1886). **[107]**

JAMES, HENRY (April 15, 1843-Feb. 28, 1916), novelist. Son of Henry James and brother of William James; wrote (1865-69) for the *Nation*, the *Atlantic Monthly*,

and *Galaxy;* moved to London (1876) and became a British citizen (1915); author (among many novels) of *The American* (1876), *Daisy Miller* (1878), *The Portrait of a Lady* (1881), *The Turn of the Screw* (1898), and *The American Scene* (1907), as well as several volumes of biography and literary criticism. **[93]** See also Author Index, Vol. 11.

JOHNSON, ANDREW (Dec. 29, 1808-July 31, 1875), soldier, legislator, and statesman. Seventeenth President of the United States (1865-69); U.S. representative from Tennessee (1843-53); governor (1853-57); U.S. senator (1857-62, 1875); brigadier general, U.S. Army, and military governor of Tennessee (1862-64); Vice-President of the United States (March 4-April 15, 1865) under Lincoln; impeached and acquitted (1868) by Congress for his Reconstruction policies. **[2, 3, 4, 17, 19, 21]** See also Author Index, Vol. 9.

KING, EDWARD (Sept. 8, 1848-March 27, 1896), journalist, novelist, and poet. Reported the Paris Exposition (1867) for the *Springfield* (Mass.) *Republican*, the Franco-Prussian War (1870) for the *Boston Morning Journal,* and other European events; compiled *Cassell's Complete Pocket Guide to Europe* (1891). **[75]**

LANIER, SIDNEY (Feb. 3, 1842-Sept. 7, 1881), poet and musician. Lecturer in English literature (1879) at Johns Hopkins University; wrote "Corn" (1874), "The Symphony" (1875), *The Science of English Verse* (1880), *The English Novel* (1883). **[68, 101]**

LIVERMORE, THOMAS L. (fl. 1883), factory manager. **[117]**

MCELROY, WILLIAM (c. 1810-c. 1885), journalist. **[98]**

MCWHIRTER, A. J. (fl. 1883), president of the Southern Immigration Association. **[120]**

MEADE, EDWIN R. (July 6, 1836-Nov. 28, 1889), lawyer and legislator. U.S. representative from New York (1875-77). **[87]**

MELVILLE, HERMAN (Aug. 1, 1819-Sept. 28, 1891), novelist. Sailed on the whaling ship *Acushnet* (1841-42); jumped ship at the Marquesas Islands; sailed on the Australian whaler *Lucy Ann* but left her at

slavery. **[30, 48]** See also Author Index, Vols. 7, 8, 9.

SUMNER, WILLIAM GRAHAM (Oct. 30, 1840-April 12, 1910), Episcopal clergyman, social scientist, and economist. Professor of social and political science (1872-1909) at Yale; advocate of laissez-faire economics and personal liberty; wrote *The Forgotten Man* (1919), *The Science of Society* (1927). **[114, 121]** See also Author Index, Vols. 11, 12.

THOMAS, SAMUEL AB (fl. 1874), coal miner from Arnot, Tioga County, Pa. Born Wales. **[69]**

TILDEN, SAMUEL J. (Feb. 9, 1814-Aug. 4, 1886), lawyer and politician. Governor of New York (1874-76); Democratic candidate for President of the United States against Hayes (1876); won a plurality of 250,000 votes, but lost the election when a commission chosen by Congress rejected some disputed returns. **[29]**

TRUMBULL, LYMAN (Oct. 12, 1813-June 25, 1896), jurist and legislator. Justice (1848-54) of the Illinois Supreme Court; U.S. senator (1855-73); submitted the resolution from which the 13th Amendment to the Constitution was drawn. **[4]**

WAITE, MORRISON R. (Nov. 29, 1816-March 23 1888), jurist. U.S. counsellor at Geneva, Switzerland in the "Alabama" arbitration (1871); chief justice (1874-88) of the U.S. Supreme Court. **[85]**

WALKER, AMASA (May 4, 1799-Oct. 29, 1875), economist, educator, and legislator. Professor of political economy (1842-49) at Oberlin, (1853-60) at Harvard, and (1860-69) at Amherst; U.S. representative from Massachusetts (1862-63); wrote *The Science of Wealth* (1866). **[12]**

WALKER, FRANCIS A. (July 2, 1840-Jan. 5, 1897), educator and economist. Brigadier general (1865), U.S. Army; chief of the U.S. Bureau of Statistics (1869-71); U.S. commissioner of Indian affairs (1871-72); supervised U.S. census (1870, 1880); professor of political economy (1873-81) at Yale; president (1881-97) of Massachusetts Institute of Technology. **[62]**

WEAVER, JAMES BAIRD (June 12, 1833-Feb. 6, 1912), soldier, lawyer, and politician. Brigadier general (1864), U.S. Army;

U.S. representative from Iowa (1879-81, 1885-89); Greenback-Labor candidate for President of the United States (1880) and People's Party candidate (1892). **[99]** See also Author Index, Vol. 11.

WELLS, DAVID A. (June 17, 1828-Nov. 5, 1898), economist. Chairman of the National Revenue Commission (1865); special commissioner of U.S. revenue (1866-70) and leading advocate of free-trade policies; wrote *Our Burden and Our Strength* (1864), *The Silver Question* (1877), *Practical Economics* (1885). **[100]** See also Author Index, Vol. 11.

WESTENDORF, THOMAS P. (fl. 1876), music teacher at Plainfield, Ind. Composed "I'll Take You Home Again, Kathleen." **[77]**

WHEELER, HENRY C. (fl. 1869), farmer from DuPage County, Ill. Member of the Illinois state legislature. **[37]**

WHITMAN, WALT (May 31, 1819-March 26, 1892), poet, schoolteacher, and journalist. Edited (1846-48) the *Brooklyn Eagle* and wrote (1848) for the *New Orleans Crescent*; hospital nurse (1862-64) in Washington, D.C.; clerk in U.S. Department of the Interior (1865), but dismissed by the secretary of the interior because of the "licentiousness" of his poetry; wrote *Leaves of Grass* (1855 and nine later revisions), *Drum-Taps* (1865), *Democratic Vistas* (1871). **[11, 26, 94]** See also Author Index, Vols. 7, 8, 9, 11.

WOOD, THOMAS J. (Sept. 25, 1823-Feb. 25, 1906), Union soldier. Brigadier general (1861-65) and major general (1865) of volunteers; military administrator of Mississippi (1865-68). **[18]**

WRIGHT, CARROLL D. (July 25, 1840-Feb. 20, 1909), statistician. First commissioner (1885-1905) of U.S. Bureau of Labor; president (1897-1909) of the American Statistical Association; first president (1902-09) of Clark College, Worcester, Mass. **[115]**

YOUNG, BRIGHAM (June 1, 1801-Aug. 29, 1877), Mormon Church leader and missionary. Head of the Mormon settlement at Nauvoo, Ill. (1838); second president (from 1847) of the Church of Jesus Christ of the Latter-day Saints; leader of the Mormon migration to Utah and first governor of the Territory of Utah (1850-58). **[86]**